THE ECONOMY OF
PROSTITUTION
IN THE
ROMAN WORLD

THE ECONOMY OF PROSTITUTION IN THE ROMAN WORLD

A Study of
Social History
& the Brothel

Thomas A. J. McGinn

THE UNIVERSITY OF MICHIGAN PRESS
Ann Arbor

FOR ALL 343

Copyright © by the University of Michigan 2004
All rights reserved
Published in the United States of America by
The University of Michigan Press
Manufactured in the United States of America
⊗ Printed on acid-free paper

2007   2006   2005   4   3   2

A CIP catalog record for this book is available from the British Library.

Library of Congress Cataloging-in-Publication Data

McGinn, Thomas A.
   The economy of prostitution in the Roman world : a study of social
history and the brothel / Thomas A. J. McGinn.
      p.   cm.
   Includes bibiographical references and index.
   ISBN 0-472-11362-3 (alk. paper)
   1. Prostitution—History—To 1500.   2. Prostitution—Economic
aspects—Rome.   3. Brothels—Economic aspects—Rome.   I. Title.
HQ113.M34   2004
306.74'0937—dc22   2003021579

PREFACE

We seem to be as far from a general history of brothels as we undoubtedly are from a history of prostitution. Attempts at accomplishing such projects run a certain risk of appearing to validate the status of venal sex as "the oldest profession," an idea that has not only been repudiated but successfully refuted.[1] Nearly three decades of feminist scholarship have turned the tide, which is not turning back at any time soon, to judge from all appearances.[2] Yet, it seems obvious that the task of understanding the business of prostitution, above all the form and function of brothels in different cultures, as well as their place on the map, remains a fundamental prerequisite to understanding the place of prostitution in historical experience.[3] As an intellectual enterprise, however, this task barely seems to have begun.

For many of the cultures that have been examined by the avatars of New

---

1. For a sense of the world we have lost (and do not miss) consult Murphy, *Great Bordellos of the World* (1983), a book representative of a larger genre that might be described as "coffee-table titillation." As for Pompeian brothels, before the 1970s, and especially the 1990s, the reader found little to consult, aside from widely scattered references in various publications. An exception is found in two chapters devoted to this subject in D'Avino, *Women of Pompeii* (1964), 39–59, a work of a popular nature, at best.

2. Many would regard Walkowitz, *Prostitution in Victorian Society* (1980), as the breakthrough book in this field. There are important antecedents, among which Rubin, "The Traffic in Women" (1975), merits mention. In any case, the 1980s and 1990s have been a true golden age for feminist work on prostitution.

3. I note here that a working title of this study was *Brothels in the Roman World*. Understanding brothels in any culture requires a high degree of contextualization, which this book seeks to provide.

Prostitution Studies, information on the profession's economic aspects, including such issues as location, ownership, management, and price, is still sometimes surprisingly difficult to come by. *The Economy of Prostitution in the Roman World* has a fair claim to inaugurate a new genre in this field.[4] Too often the subject is left embedded in a broader discourse, with key questions left unasked, let alone unanswered. Other studies have proven that it is possible to write a fairly effective study of venal sex without raising the problem of venue at all. One might draw the conclusion that the problem of brothels is quite incidental to the study of prostitution. This book will, I hope, serve as a corrective to that mistaken impression. It is original in its extensive reliance on comparative evidence drawn from a variety of cultures. I defend the use of this material for reasons of method in chapter 1; at the same time, I recognize the limitations of this use. The material is of intrinsic interest all the same, and I am hopeful that students of brothels and the business of prostitution in other cultures will be able to learn from it.

It is my modest intention that *The Economy of Prostitution in the Roman World* succeeds in helping to place prostitution in its proper historical context. I seek to achieve this in large part by focusing chiefly on the single major source for our knowledge, in its material aspect, of brothels and other venues for the sale of sex in Roman antiquity, namely the city of Pompeii. Part of the book's purpose is to raise questions of method, mainly concerning the problems of identification and definition, which might be of use to historians interested in studying brothels in other historical periods. The question of "fit" between different types of evidence, here archaeological, literary, documentary, and legal, is fundamental.

To attempt such a project without the benefit of solid and significant advances in the study of Pompeian brothels would be impossible. I am privileged here to thank the leader of that welcome trend in scholarship, Andrew Wallace-Hadrill. But my debt goes well beyond what has already appeared in print. This book owes countless improvements to the great good kindness of

---

4. For works that come close in some respects to what this book is attempting to do, see Heyl, *Madam* (1979); Prus and Irini, *Hookers* (1980); Schuster, *Frauenhaus*; and Best, *Controlling Vice* (1998). The difference in emphasis between these books and mine is explained partly by the gap in the quality and sheer amount of the evidence. Thus the first two deal with modern, that is, twentieth-century brothel prostitution, the third with the brothel in medieval Germany, and the fourth with the brothel in late nineteenth century St. Paul, Minn. They are able to treat the lives of prostitutes and other brothel personnel in as much detail as the brothels themselves, which this book could never do. Reynolds, *Economics of Prostitution* (1986), and Edlund and Korn, "A Theory of Prostitution (2002)" merit mention here, despite my differences with them, as pioneers in scholarship.

Wallace-Hadrill, whose knowledge of Pompeii sustains no easy challenge.[5] I also thank Professors J. Patout Burns, John R. Clarke (whose published work is also of great importance for this study), Steven Dyson, Pedar Foss, Bruce W. Frier, Linda Jones Hall, John Humphrey, Dennis P. Kehoe, Marco Pagano, Jack Sasson, Ms. Sara Kidd, Dottoresse Doretta Mazzeschi and Gabriella Prisco, as well as Mr. Raymond Porfilio, for their varied and valued assistance. Professors John R. Clarke, Pietro Giovanni Guzzo, and Vincenzo Scarano Ussani, as well as Drs. Edward Cohen, Nicholas Horsfall, and Dr. Antonio Varone merit a particular expression of gratitude for allowing me to see their work prior to publication.

With great pleasure, I also thank the editors, readers, and assistants of the University of Michigan Press for the immense value they have contributed to this book. I should mention in particular Ellen Bauerle, Jillian Downey, Chris Collins, Mary Hashman, Sarah Mann, Erin Snoddy, and, above all, Collin Ganio.

I am once again indebted to Mr. James Toplon and his excellent staff at Vanderbilt University's interlibrary loan office for their usual heroic efforts on my behalf. In this regard I want to thank especially Rachel Adams and Marilyn Pilley. Janice Adlington, the acquisitions specialist for Classical Studies at Vanderbilt, also merits a hearty expression of gratitude. The Vanderbilt University Research Council provided much appreciated financial support.

Since much of the evidence for Roman brothels derives from the city of Pompeii, a brief caveat is in order. Those unfamiliar with the convention of Pompeian addresses need to know that this system was invented in the nineteenth century by Giuseppe Fiorelli, who divided the city into nine *Regiones*, each containing a number of blocks (*Insulae*) bordered by streets, with entryways to the buildings found in each block, numbered in a counterclockwise direction. Each address contains the number for the *Regio*, *Insula*, and entryway, in that order. (It is important to note that many locations have more than one entryway.) Revisions by various persons over time have produced slightly different addresses for a few locations. To avoid confusion, I generally give the version of the address adopted by the author in question, with the exception of the discussion of the nineteenth- and early twentieth-century literature given in the first section of chapter 7, "Eminent Victorians."

---

5. I attempt to notice as many of Wallace-Hadrill's suggestions as I can by referring to his personal communication (p.c.), though the reader should be warned that the result is not exhaustive and agreement should not be assumed, except where expressly indicated.

The reader should refer to the catalog in appendix 1 for a corrective, when necessary.

References are provided in abbreviated form in the notes; full citations are found in the bibliography. In the notes I provide references to the editions of patristic works I have used on the theory that these are not always as accessible as the texts of classical authors. The nature and scope of this work has prevented me from expanding the bibliography after the book went to press in October 2002, apart from rare exceptions.[6]

---

6. The photographs are my own. Sara Kidd drew the maps on a template that Prof. Peder Foss provided to me in electronic form, and that derives from Eschebach, *Entwicklung* (1970), foldout 1.

CONTENTS

ILLUSTRATIONS

MAPS

ABBREVIATIONS

*F*or the abbreviations of secondary literature (philological, historical, and legal), see the bibliography. The particular abbreviations, such as references to modern scholars, found in the first appendix are explained at its outset. The abbreviations of the names of ancient authors and their works generally follow those given in the major Greek and Latin dictionaries, *L & S*, *LSJ*, *OLD*: see below. For abbreviations of collections of papyri and related works, see J. F. Oates et al., *Checklist of Editions of Greek, Latin, Demotic and Coptic Papyri, Ostraca and Tablets*[5] (= *BASP* 9) Oakville, CT 2001. This list refers chiefly to standard works of reference and to editions of patristic works and also, at the end of the list, to websites.

AÉ = *L'année epigraphique* (Paris 1888–)

American Heritage Dictionary[3] = *The American Heritage College Dictionary*.[3] Boston, 1997.

Babylonian Talmud = I. Epstein, ed. *The Babylonian Talmud: Seder Mo'ed*. 4 vols. Oxford, 1938. Reprint, London, 1978.

Bidez = I. Bidez and F. Cumont, eds. *Imp. Caesaris Flavii Claudii Iuliani Epistulae Leges Poematia Fragmenta Varia*. Paris, 1922.

Blockley = R. C. Blockley, *The Fragmentary Classicising Historians of the Later Roman Empire: Eunapius, Olympiodorus, Priscus and Malchus*. 2 vols. Liverpool, 1983.

CCSL = *Corpus Christianorum: Series Latina*. Turnhout, Belg., 1953–.

Cèbe = J. -P. Cèbe, *Varron, Satires Ménippées: Édition, traduction et commentaire*. 13 vols. Rome, 1972–99.

CIL = *Corpus Inscriptionum Latinarum*. Berlin, 1863–.

CSEL = *Corpus Scriptorum Ecclesiasticorum Latinorum*, Vienna, 1866–.

CTP 2 = *Corpus Topographicum Pompeianum Pars II: Toponomy*, Rome, 1983.

CTP 3a = *Corpus Topographicum Pompeianum Pars III A: The Insulae of Regions I-V*. Rome, 1986.

Doignon = J. Doignon, *Oeuvres de Saint Augustin 4.2: Dialogues philosophiques, De Ordine-L'Ordre*. Paris, 1997.

DS = C. Daremberg and E. Saglio, eds. *Dictionnaire des antiquités grecques et romaines*. Vol. 3. Paris, 1918.

I. Portes = A. Bernand, ed. *Les Portes du désert: Recueil des inscriptions grecques d'Antinooupolis, Tentyris, Koptos, Apollonopolis Parva et Apollonopolis Magna*. Paris, 1984.

IG = *Inscriptiones Graecae*. Berlin, 1873–.

IGR = R. Cagnat et al., eds. *Inscriptiones graecae ad res romanas pertinentes*. 4 vols. Paris, 1911–27. Reprint, Chicago, 1975.

IK = *Inschriften griechischer Städte aus Kleinasien*, Bonn, 1972–.

ILS = H. Dessau ed., *Inscriptiones Latinae Selectae*, 3 vols. Berlin, 1892–1916.

Kytzler = B. Kytzler. *Minucius Felix: Octavius*. Leipzig, 1992. *Bibliotheca Teubneriana*.

L & S = C. T. Lewis and C. Short, eds. *A Latin Dictionary*. Oxford, 1879 .

LSJ = H. G. Liddell, R. Scott, H. Stuart Jones, et al., eds. *Greek-English Lexicon*.⁹ Oxford, 1940–96.

Munier = C. Munier. *Saint Justin: Apologie pour les Chrétiens: Édition et traduction (Paradosis 29)*. Fribourg, 1995.

OGIS = W. Dittenberger, ed. *Orientis Graecae Inscriptiones Selectae*, 2 vols. Leipzig, 1903–5.

OLD = P. G. W. Glare ed., *Oxford Latin Dictionary*. Oxford, 1968–82.

Oxford Dictionary = *The Oxford Dictionary and Thesaurus: American Edition*, Oxford, 1997.

PG = J.-P. Migne, ed. *Patrologia Graeca*. 161 vols. Paris, 1857–66.

PL = J.-P. Migne, ed. *Patrologia Latina*. 221 vols. Paris, 1844–64.

Preger = T. Preger. *Scriptores Originum Constantinopolitanarum*. Leipzig, 1901–7. Reprint, New York, 1975.

SC = H. De Lubac, J. Daniélou, et al., eds. *Sources chrétiennes*. Paris, 1942–.

Seeck = O. Seeck, ed. *Notitia Dignitatum accedunt Notitia Urbis Constantinopolitanae et Laterculi Provinciarum*. Berlin, 1876.

SEG = *Supplementum Epigraphicum Graecum*. Vols. 1–25 Leiden, 1923–71. Vols. 26– Amsterdam, 1979–.

Thurn = I. Thurn. *Ioannis Malalae Chronographia*. Berlin, 2000.

TLL = *Thesaurus linguae latinae*. Leipzig, 1900–.
Website/Ananova = www.ananova.com/yournews/story/sm_544717.html
Website/Georgia Powers = www.gppays.com/Bashful/THE_LAW
Website/Nevada Appeal = www.nevadaappeal.com

Chapter One

URBAN RENEWAL

DESIGN OF THE BOOK

This book is a study of the evidence for the business of female prostitution in the Roman world during the central part of Rome's history, a period extending from approximately 200 B.C. to A.D. 250. The vast bulk of the legal, literary, archaeological, and documentary evidence available for inspection falls between those dates. The main focus is on the economics of venal sex, meaning precisely the manner in which it was sold, a subject that extends to the ownership, operation, staffing, and location of brothels, as well as to various aspects of nonbrothel prostitution. Though the state of the evidence discourages any and all attempts at quantification, an attempt will be made to recover a sense of the role, the presence, and, as much as is possible, the lived experience of prostitution in the Roman city. One major obstacle especially to achieving the final goal is that the available evidence is overwhelmingly the product of male members of the elite, and so reflects their concerns, assumptions, and prejudices. Unlike in most modern societies, the Roman political and legal authorities allowed the business of venal sex to proceed virtually unregulated, with a degree of tolerance that seems strange to a modern sensibility, but with consequences that emerge as sometimes equally foreign to us.

Though I consider all types of sources in this study, I tend to privilege material evidence, particularly evidence from Pompeii for the reasons given below. The focus on archaeological evidence from Pompeii enables the development of the central argument of the book, which concerns the number and location of brothels and other venues for the sale of sex in that city. I argue in brief that there were more of these brothels, and they were more widely distributed, than most scholars have believed in recent years. Given the state of our knowledge, however, we should retain a degree of agnosticism over their precise numbers and locations.

The book focuses principally on female prostitution for two main reasons. First, the greater share of the evidence by far for the economics of venal sex concerns the prostitution of women. Second, male prostitution is an important subject nonetheless and thus is deserving of separate treatment. To be sure, I do not hesitate to adduce evidence about the latter in the course of this book when it is useful to do so, such as in the discussion of the archaeological evidence for brothels in chapter 8 or the list of possible Pompeian prostitutes in appendix 3. By the same token, I pass beyond the chronological limits of the study when necessary to shed light on the period in question. An example is my treatment of the Augustinian evidence for moral zoning in chapter 3.

I dwell longer on Augustine than I do on other Christian evidence, in part, because I share the common view that during the transition from paganism to Christianity there was a great deal of continuity in social conditions and relations as well as the ideology that surrounded them. One important change was a greater concern with the poor and the lower orders in general by members of the elite, as reflected in their writings. These writings open a window on some social practices and attitudes that we know little about from the earlier period. Still, they do not appear to represent by and large a break with the pagan past. When a change in those practices or attitudes did take place, and that which occurred with Augustine on the matter of zoning prostitution is fairly monumental, greater attention should be paid.

This book is a social history of an aspect of Roman prostitution, not an archaeological or art historical study of the same. Readers avid for lavish display of photographs of Roman erotic art must turn elsewhere. I make use of a small sample of illustrations designed to drive home the nature of art found in the brothel, other public places, and the private house. In recent years, a series of excellent studies have opened up the meaning and role of such art.[1] My contribution, such as it is, is to try to place their results in the context of other evidence, above all literary sources, in order to try to make sense of Roman indifference to brothels and prostitutes in their midst. But some of the detailed treatments already available of the art of the Surburban Baths, the Purpose-

---

1. To name just a few of the more important ones, Jacobelli, *Terme Suburbane* (1995); Clarke, *Looking at Lovemaking* (1998); Guzzo and Scarano Ussani, *Veneris figurae* (2000); and Varone, *Erotismo a Pompei* (2000).

Built Brothel, and other venues public and private are not likely to be surpassed soon, at least not by me. For that matter, definitive publication of the places listed as possible brothels in this book must await the work of archaeologists.

BROTHELS IN HISTORY

Where do we go in search of Roman brothels? Pompeii has preserved more archaeological data about brothels than anywhere else in the Roman world.[2] One obvious reason for this is the unusual way in which the site was destroyed in antiquity and preserved through the ages. Other cities that have seen more or less continuous settlement over the years, notably Rome, do not retain the kind of evidence we require to locate and to identify brothels. Unfortunately, the same is true even of abandoned sites, such as Ostia, which declined slowly and ended less violently than Pompeii did.

So it comes as no surprise that numerous brothels and so-called *cellae meretriciae* or "cribs" (one-room venues for sex lying off of a street or in the back of a bar) have been identified in Pompeii. The most interesting development in recent years, however, is the sharp decrease in the number of Pompeian brothels postulated by scholars. In short order, the numbers have fallen from "35 or more" to one certain specimen. As a result, ancient Pompeii has been in a sense "cleaned up" almost as effectively as Times Square was cleaned up by the New York authorities in the 1990s.[3] Closer examination of the problem, however, suggests that at least one of these operations has been characterized by an excess of zeal, of not a surfeit of severity.

For these reasons, Pompeii is the only city in the Roman world to receive even a remotely coherent modern treatment of its brothels. This book examines in detail the late twentieth-century scholarship on Pompeian brothels, its methods and assumptions, and, above all, the criteria used to identify these establishments in light of the ancient evidence. This evidence receives further illumination from the sources for brothels in the Roman world beyond Pompeii itself. The number and location of Pompeian brothels is shown to be more problematic than either the older school (which assumed an abundance of brothels), and more recent scholarship (which has been notably skeptical of this assumption) has postulated.

---

2. A preliminary treatment of the Pompeian material appears in McGinn, "Pompeian Brothels and Social History" (2002).

3. See Traub, "Land of the Naked Cowboy" (2002).

The uncertainty about the brothels has a useful result, I argue, because it permits a critique of the now-fashionable idea that the Romans practiced a form of moral zoning, keeping prostitution restricted to certain areas, even certain streets, and away from others. Despite some evidence that the Romans attempted to regulate the trade of venal sex, they did not have a coherent regulationist regime. Their true interest in "moral geography" turns out to be a commercially motivated one; their aim was to make as much money from the practice of prostitution as they could, both for the individual and for the state. Brothels and other venues for the sale of sex were located with an eye to maximizing profits, at least by those members of the elite who had no reservations about earning money in this way. They appear to have been fairly numerous, in fact, though we cannot be certain of their precise number. Pompeii was neither unusual nor atypical in this regard. Instead of keeping prostitution hidden away in the dark corners of their cities, the Romans preferred to have it out in the open as much as possible. The visibility of prostitutes was the ideal foil to the public persona of the respectable woman (*mater familias/matrona*).[4] It was so much easier in this way to humiliate them morally and to exploit them financially. This is the sum of the Roman policy on zoning prostitution.

In this book, I make ample use of comparative evidence in order to explain the ancient evidence. This use raises the danger of anachronism, or what might better be termed cultural inappropriateness, which it is helpful, I believe, to address in the context of arguments from social constructionism. Lack of space prohibits anything but a cursory review of the major problems. All the same, here is a welcome opportunity to defend a moderate social constructionism, which I believe in the end most authorities on Roman antiquity will be inclined to accept,[5] against some of the more extreme variants.[6]

---

4. For some of the legal and social implications of this dichotomy in sexual and social status, see McGinn, *Prostitution, Sexuality, and the Law* (1998) esp. chap. 5.

5. See the recent statements by Skinner, "Zeus and Leda" (1996) esp. 118–19; Verstraete, review of *Rethinking Sexuality and Roman Sexualities* (1998) 149. See also the reception of recent radical constructionist works by Hopkins, "Looking at Lovemaking" (1999); Frier, review of *Roman Sexuality* (1999). The flashpoint of these discussions is ancient sexuality, though the problem resonates across the interpretation of Roman history.

6. For general considerations on this theme, see Searle, *Construction of Social Reality* (1995) 2, 4, 6–7, 27, 34, 59–60, 119–20, 149, 179, 181–82, 189, 227–28; Collin, *Social Reality* (1997) x–xi, 7, 9, 134–35, 145, 217, 221–222; Hacking, *Social Construction of What?* (1999) 24, 67–68, 94. A recent essay by Karras, "Review Essay" (2000) 1252–53, distinguishes between stronger and weaker versions of social constructionism, which do not coincide with the division made here into radical and moderate, insofar as they are for the most part variants of the radical type. The more extreme of the two, advocated by Michel Foucault himself, argues that sexuality itself did not exist before the nineteenth century.

A particular problem arises here for the study of prostitution in history. Most historians these days are alert to the fact that prostitution in past times was neither static nor inert, replicating itself over time as the "oldest profession," a longstanding assumption.[7] The best way of escaping the implications of this assumption in my view is to rely on as much available data as possible, while recognizing that, given the sheer variety of ways in which prostitution configures itself in different cultural and historical contexts, some comparisons will inevitably work better than others for our purpose, or indeed anyone's purpose. Of course comparative evidence is not always and everywhere useless simply because it does not live up to its promise in every instance. That position is more appropriate for the practitioner of rhetoric than for the writer of history. To understand the role of prostitution as a component, a fundamental component I would argue, of the enduring institution of patriarchy requires a high degree of sensitivity to similarity and difference, continuity as well as change. Only judicious use of comparative evidence seems poised to make this possible.[8]

I think it important, in consequence, not to exaggerate difference, taking as proven the endless variation social anthropology has seen across cultures.[9] If the Romans were more like us or had left us better information, resort to comparative evidence might seem otiose or even an obstacle to understanding them. That is simply not the case, however. Accurately presenting the truth depends finally on a careful use of language, and when the evidence is inadequate, as in the case of Roman prostitution, the truth can only be presented in a manner that "admits of degrees."[10] To take one example of this problem as it occurs in the literary sources, the poet Martial creates a topography of Rome in his collection of epigrams as a kind of class signifier that it did not and could not function as, in quite the same way, off the page.[11] Attempts to reconcile material and literary topographies of this kind are themselves all but bound to be somewhat inexact. To put the matter another way, it is best to seek adequate explanations of Roman conduct and not perfect ones.[12]

---

7. For a useful recent review of the historiography of prostitution, see Gilfoyle, "Prostitutes in History," (1999).

8. For a useful analogy with understanding the history of the Mediterranean through a comparative approach, see Horden and Purcell, *Corrupting Sea* (2000), 465. More generally, see Macfarlane, "History and Anthropology" (1994).

9. Collin, *Social Reality* (1997) 47.

10. Searle, *Construction of Social Reality* (1995) 200.

11. See Kardos, "Épigrammes" (2001) 206, 209, 214; Kardos, "Vrbs," (2001) 389. For place as an emotional signifier in Martial, see Kardos, "Vrbs," 399.

12. See Collin, *Social Reality* (1997) 109.

One undeniable advantage of a comparative approach is that it substitutes a self-consciousness of method for naive positivism. To be sure, I should emphasize both here and elsewhere in this study, comparative evidence, though vital, only suggests a possible solution. It cannot by itself prove anything about ancient Roman brothels. Comparative evidence must be looked at in conjunction with ancient evidence. Otherwise, we can all too easily weave comparative data into a model or narrative with little probative value for antiquity.[13] Many times the most useful service comparative material can provide is to cast serious doubt on what we know, or what we think we know, about that lost and only imperfectly recoverable world. The historical evidence must in the final analysis be crucial for deciding which comparative data is most persuasive for ancient Rome.[14] Differences are not to be discarded automatically, however, since contrasting evidence serves a vitally useful purpose.[15]

The author of this study—I must emphasize—is no archaeologist, nor is the analysis based on thorough personal observation of the material remains. The only "true" archaeology practiced here is a Foucauldian exercise in the archaeology of knowledge. Unlike Foucault himself, what I am interested in unearthing is precisely the knowledge of archaeologists. There are two important questions to pose regarding Roman brothels: what did the archaeologists know and when did they know it? An attempt is made to answer these questions, at least in their broad outlines.

By the same token, no new candidates for brothelhood are advanced here, though I take seriously the possibility that not all the brothels in the Roman world have been identified. This study attempts to provoke the experts to take action, in the form of careful and critical examination of the material evidence. My task is to raise questions of the sort that I believe a social historian should pose when confronting material evidence of the kind surveyed here.

Neither social history nor archaeology is a straightforward business, a truth that is neither always very clear nor universally acknowledged.[16] We rarely know in advance how much of the former can be extracted from the latter. If I manage to advance the dialogue between social historians and archaeologists, my project will have succeeded. I hope to have made clear that those I

---

13. See the caution of Horden and Purcell, *Corrupting Sea* (2000) 301.

14. Horden and Purcell, *Corrupting Sea* (2000) 47 have a useful statement.

15. See Horden and Purcell, *Corrupting Sea* (2000) 287.

16. On the problem of the "fit" between the archaeological record and the written sources, see Horden and Purcell, *Corrupting Sea* (2000) 325. For the general lack of interest in the archaeology of the Roman sub-elite, see Funari and Zarankin, "Consideraciones" (2001) 504.

believe to be really deserving of criticism are not the scholars with whom I quibble in this book, but the social historians who still fail to grasp the importance of material remains for the understanding of Roman history.

DEFINITIONS

The problem of defining prostitution is an important and interesting one. Indeed, it is so important a serious treatment would distract us from the subject at hand.[17] The problem is directly related to the problem of defining brothel, since a broad definition of the former would almost inevitably entail a broad definition of the latter. For example, some or all of the establishments I identify in chapter 5 as "sex clubs" and attempt to distinguish from brothels would qualify as such if I were to employ a broader definition of prostitution than I do.

Often the motive for constructing a definition determines its content, so that it has little by way of broad applicability. One major challenge is to formulate a definition that avoids confusing prostitution with other instances of nonmarital sexuality, such as concubinage. A definition, borrowed from the sociological literature, that holds out the most promise features the following three criteria: promiscuity, payment, and the emotional indifference of the partners to each other.[18]

The definition provided above will not necessarily coincide with Roman attempts to define prostitution and prostitute. That is, in fact, part of its value. For example, when the jurist Ulpian defines prostitute under the Augustan marriage law, he ignores the question of emotional indifference, discounts that of payment, and raises promiscuity nearly to the status of sole valid criterion.[19] The fact that he is elucidating a rule that stipulates inappropriate marriage partners helps explain the emphasis on promiscuity and confirms the teleological premise behind many a definition of prostitution, as just set forth. In a sense, Ulpian's definition is a moral one converted into a legal one, which makes it difficult to use in other contexts.

By the same token, the Romans are of little help in defining brothel. For example, one of the terms they commonly employ to describe brothel only succeeds in conveying a sense of misogyny. *Lupanar* (or *lupanarium*) signifies in a literal sense "den of wolves," specifically she-wolves, since the word for

---

17. A fuller discussion is at McGinn, *Prostitution, Sexuality, and the Law* (1998) 17–18.
18. See, for example, Palmer and Humphrey, *Deviant Behavior* (1990) 150.
19. See McGinn, *Prostitution, Sexuality, and the Law* (1998) 126–35.

female wolf, *lupa*, is often used for prostitutes.[20] Such terminology emphasizes the rapacious, predatory, and greedy nature of the prostitute as a type, and, at the same time, denies her humanity. It tells us nothing about brothels that might help us define what one is. The same holds true for another term commonly used for brothel, the euphemism *fornix*, which literally means "archway" (and whence comes *fornicatio*, "fornication"). The term obscures the fact that the Roman brothel was not simply a location on the street or the front, or face, of a building, but an establishment, a business where venal sex was available. Examples of other terms for brothel might be multiplied, for example, *lustrum*, *stabulum*, and (at least in later Latin) *prostibulum*, to no avail. Roman words for brothel at best offer, by way of definition, the tautology that this was a place where prostitutes worked.

Using the literary and archaeological evidence to define brothel is also problematic, especially in regard to the latter. The descriptions of brothels in the literary sources are unhelpful because they are vague, stereotyped, and laden with upper-class male prejudice.[21] They do not contain anything that would enable us to be sure of the difference between a brothel and other venues where prostitution was practiced, for example. In fact, given their moralizing inclinations, we cannot know for certain if the Romans themselves routinely and consistently recognized such a difference. The clearest suggestion of such a distinction arises in the legal sources, which appear to accept a notional differentiation, for example, between *lupanarium* and *taberna cauponia* (tavern or inn), though they do not draw any consequences at law from this.[22] At least, the problem of identification is resolved for the literary and legal sources in that the texts speak of brothels, even if only to assert or assume that these are places where prostitutes work.

Using the archaeological evidence to define the brothel is even more difficult. Here the problem is inextricably tied to that of identification, itself an even thornier issue. This is because no Roman brothel has been uncovered to this day that identifies itself, in a literal sense, as a brothel. Our most certain specimen, which is for some scholars the only certain brothel in the Roman world, displays features that allow for neither easy generalization nor ready application to other contexts.

There is no eluding these difficulties. For that reason, I must return on different occasions to the problem(s) of defining and identifying brothels, above

---

20. See Adams, "Words" (1983) 333–35.
21. See the discussion in chap. 2 and in app. 1.
22. See chap. 7.

all, in the discussion of archaeological evidence in chapters 7 and 8. As with
the concept of prostitution, however, a working definition of brothel is necessary at the start for the sake of clarity. For my purposes a brothel is an establishment where two or more prostitutes can work simultaneously and whose
activity forms the main, or at least a major, part of the business as a whole. In
practical terms this means that an establishment where a prostitute must go
outside or elsewhere with a customer is not a brothel. The criterion of "main
or major" component of the business is of necessity treated loosely, so as to
include all or most taverns and inns showing evidence of prostitution, but to
exclude most baths, even if the evidence suggests that prostitutes worked
there. "Business," of course, implies that the place is open to the public at
large.

PLAN OF THE BOOK

The central problem of this book may be put in the form of a broad but blunt
question. Just how did the Roman people manage their prostitutes? In an earlier study, I looked at this problem from the standpoint of the law.[23] I con-
cluded that, while a number of legal rules could be recovered from the sources
for analysis, the Romans did not have a coherent policy, or set of laws, toward
prostitutes and pimps or toward the profession itself. There are two overriding
trends detectable in public policy on the subject, toleration and degradation,
but the legal rules themselves remain a diverse and fragmented lot.

Here we are dealing with a side of the social organization of prostitution
that seems to have been left almost entirely to the private sector. The operation of brothels was overseen loosely by junior magistrates, in Rome the
aediles, about whose precise responsibilities we are rather poorly informed.
Virtually no rules have been preserved here to guide us, though the law that
exists in regard to prostitution strongly suggests that the state recognized an
interest in the profession. The state, among other ways, profited from the sale
of sex through the imposition of a tax, and it appropriated the enormous symbolic potency of prostitution to make a series of statements about ideal social
hierarchy, above all regarding Roman women. The implications of this appropriation were more than simply symbolic. As in the case of other societies,
Rome had an interest in preserving public order on the ground, both in and
out of the brothel.

With so much at stake, it is surprising to find so little official intervention

---

23. McGinn, *Prostitution, Sexuality, and the Law* (1998).

in the business of prostitution. For that reason, and given the relentless poverty of the evidence, I shrink from characterizing those views with which I take issue, above all on the crucial matter of the number and location of brothels, in the language of subadult polemic as absurd or preposterous. The views of scholars advocating the thesis of very few brothels in very few locations merit respect, especially given the uncertainty that still surrounds much of the material evidence for prostitution. Sustained engagement with their evidence and arguments has in fact forced me to concede much to these scholars, and one major concession is worth mentioning here. They are absolutely correct about one important fact, that the Romans did have a public policy that mapped venal sex on their cityscapes. Their policy was that this aspect of the organization of prostitution should be left entirely to the private sphere, where wealthy landowners, whose interests the state was bound if not designed to serve, were free to act as their desire for profit and their sensibilities about honor dictated. It is not at all events possible to write the state out of this story entirely.

Chapter 2 contains a comprehensive discussion of the basic economic facts about prostitution that can be recovered for the Roman world. The elite showed an interest in profiting where it could from the sale of sex, a cash-rich business that required relatively little outlay beyond the cost of urban real estate, even when slaves had to be purchased, compared with the profits to be made. Partly for this reason, prostitution was widespread, implicated as it was in a series of venues and events designed to draw people in numbers, from baths to festivals. For the male consumer, sex was both widely available and relatively inexpensive. For the prostitutes themselves, the prospect of material ease from selling sex was perhaps an inducement to enter the profession when they were not compelled to do so by slave owners or aggressive pimps. Compared with the bleak alternatives the Roman economy offered women forced to find work, prostitution may have been an attractive prospect, though I argue this was illusory, given the degree to which even "free" prostitutes were exploited.

The idea that prostitution, if it is not utterly repressed, should ideally be contained in some areas and prohibited from others seems such a natural one that we have difficulty imagining a world where few people, if anyone, thought this mattered. And yet absolutely no evidence exists to suggest that this did matter for the Romans, a problem raised in chapter 3, where the arrangement of social space in the Roman cityscape is shown to be not random, but fairly promiscuous all the same. This indifference is rather striking, especially given the ample evidence that elite Romans did not at all regard brothels as wholesome places. But there is no indication that anyone proposed zoning prostitution until the Christians did. And even with them the idea was a late one and perhaps controversial. A text of Augustine's is the source for a policy that, apart from perhaps one failed experiment in late antiquity, was long left to be a weapon lying in its sheath.

Chapter 4 attempts to understand the apparent obliviousness of the Romans to the moral challenge posed by prostitutes in their midst by examining the role of erotic representation in their lived experience. There is broad consensus that erotic art was fairly ubiquitous in the public and private spaces of the Roman city, though it turns out that some places, such as brothels and certain areas of private homes, for example, were more sexualized than others. All the same, we cannot assume that Roman responses to such representations were the same as ours, if it is indeed correct to assume a monolithic modern reaction. Also surprising is the apparent indifference of the Romans, those avid and aggressive moralizers, to women's and children's exposure to erotic art.

In chapter 5, I engage what is perhaps the central problem in the Roman sexual economy, the relatively low level of state intervention. The role of the officials entrusted with oversight of brothels seems to have been limited to maintaining public order, which largely meant the preservation of status distinctions between prostitutes and respectable women, and to collecting payments for taxes and lease of public property for the state, as well as, we may imagine, bribes for themselves. They did intervene to protect the public interest in exceptional cases, such as during the great water-stealing scandal of the mid-first century B.C., which embroiled brothels and other users of the public water supply. All else was left to the discretion of the owners of private property, many of whom were no less inclined than the state to profit from the sale of sex, and some of whom felt free to install an ersatz brothel in some part of their homes, for purposes that do not appear to have been commercial in nature.

The lack of a more aggressively manifested state interest in controlling prostitution may be less surprising to readers after they finish the chapters preceding chapter 5. More importantly, the articulation and division of responsibility between the government and private investors for managing prostitution in the areas of public order and financial profit amounts to a fairly sophisticated balance of both sets of interests. It leaves scant space for primitivist concerns about the Romans' alleged inability to develop and/or implement policy of any kind.

Chapter 6 raises a set of thorny demographic questions. How many brothels and how many prostitutes might a city like Rome or Pompeii have maintained? For these cities, we have some data to generate estimates of overall population, but even so the totals largely involve guesswork. That fact in itself should encourage caution about assuming a certain number of prostitutes, whether high or low. Comparisons with other cultures and consideration of conditions in Pompeii—especially in the years between the damaging earthquake in A.D. 62 and its final destruction in A.D. 79—and in Rome as the outsized metropolis it was, suggests all the same that the number of brothels and prostitutes in such places might well have been rather high.

The next two chapters (7 and 8), supplemented by the appendices, present the archaeological evidence for Roman brothels in Rome, Pompeii, and elsewhere. Our main focus is of necessity on Pompeii, from where the vast bulk of the material evidence derives. The central challenge of course resides in defining and identifying brothels. *Cellae meretriciae* or cribs (one-room venues for sex lying off a street or in the back of a bar) are important to the economy of venal sex as well. Also important are the other places where prostitution flourished, such as baths, though it is difficult to describe many of these as brothels. That perennial favorite as a tourist attraction in the modern Pompeian *scavi,* the Purpose-Built Brothel, contains much of interest in its own right, but is of little help in identifying other brothels, even in Pompeii itself.

Chapter 9 confronts head-on some very plausible-seeming arguments for the prohibition of brothels in certain parts of the ancient city, above all in the Forum. In fact, the Roman use of space, even or especially in such high-profile and central urban areas, was designed to accommodate brothels when property values and public building programs permitted. When this was not the case, it was because a general squeeze on residential and commercial property had occurred, and not because of any campaign specifically targeted at the removal of brothels. As for prostitutes, they seem always to have been tolerated, to say the least, in the Forum. Again we see the consequences of a largely "privatized" approach to the management of selling sex.

In chapter 10 the results of the study are laid out in summary fashion. The evidence suggests the existence of three subtypes for brothels, plus two for cribs. These were scattered throughout the Roman city, though some patterns of clustering are perceptible, a fact that upon further analysis might help identify more brothels. More might be said about patterns of ownership in terms of the physical relationship of brothels to stately *domus*. The conclusion, albeit tentative, is that considerations of profit dictated the number and location of brothels in the Roman city, so that we would expect any patterns that emerge to exemplify the results of a loose and informal practice of "commercial zoning" rather than of a top-down, officially imposed "moral geography." Where prostitution is absent in the Roman cityscape this is better explained as manifesting the impact of private concerns over honor, where sheer economic calculation is not in play.

The three appendices contain a wealth of source material, both primary and secondary, on brothels, cribs, and prostitutes in Pompeii. The hope is that this evidence might be of use in pursuing a longer-term project of archaeological investigation and publication. I anticipate that at some point in the future a more satisfactory "fit" between social history and archaeology may be possible than is true at this time of writing.

No one book can do justice to as broad and complex a subject as Roman prostitution. Each type of evidence presents its own challenge, and to an extent merits discrete study. Just as my earlier book concentrated on legal sources, this one focuses mainly on material evidence. These divisions are far from airtight of course, and the best approach is to use each to illuminate the other, invoking the aid of the literary evidence where necessary. The literary evidence calls for study in its own right nevertheless, and it is my hope to devote a separate monograph more especially to this subject. This project will look back on and will integrate the results of my first two books.[24]

---

24. McGinn, *Roman Prostitution* (forthcoming).

Chapter Two

BASIC ECONOMICS

THE ENTERPRISE OF VENAL SEX

This chapter is intended to provide an overview of the economic reality of prostitution at Rome to the extent that the sources permit. The challenges presented by the ancient evidence are especially formidable here. Collecting data, evaluating their reliability, and formulating adequate conclusions about the practice of Roman prostitution are not simple or straightforward tasks. It is small comfort that modern researchers studying contemporary prostitution are faced with similar difficulties, encouraging them to abandon an econometric approach in favor of traditional social science methodology.[1] Our own difficulties with evidence prompt an assiduous cultivation of the methods of economic anthropology.[2]

To take one example, I know of no study, whether economic or sociological in focus, that attempts to determine a price structure for modern prostitution by establishing a system of prices in relation to services offered and the age, appearance, sexual and nonsexual talents, and so forth of prostitutes and then comparing this data with the cost-of-living standards of prostitutes and rates of pay from other available forms of employment. The absence of such studies has forced students of prostitution to rely on highly circumstantial and incomplete data for comparative purposes. Given the limits of this study, such

---

1. See Reynolds, *Economics of Prostitution* (1986) 8.
2. See Greene, *Archaeology* (1986), 9; Horden and Purcell, *Corrupting Sea* (2000) 365.

data must suffice, but there is no question about the benefit that a detailed analysis of the price structure of modern venal sex would bring.[3] Despite these limitations, no real choice exists. We must rely on comparative data in this field, which can, at minimum, provide a sense of the plausible.

This chapter begins by examining in detail the phenomena of the broad diffusion of brothels, of the close connection between prostitution and other forms of popular entertainment, and of prostitution's association with lower-class lodging. Next, the evidence for upper-class investment in prostitution is introduced.

The question of ownership leads in turn to a discussion of brothel management, the prices charged for sexual services and the economic implications of these prices, and the acquisition of slave prostitutes. Finally, this chapter reviews the possible motivations free women had for entering the profession. The economic motivations and expectations of masters prostituting their slaves are also taken into account. This survey does not pretend to being complete, but aims to describe those features that allow an understanding of the economic importance of the institution, as a foundation for the understanding of the place of prostitution and especially brothels both in the context of the Roman city and in Roman society as a whole.

THE MILIEU OF PROSTITUTION

Inns and Such

The broad definition of brothel adopted in chapter 1 allows us to grasp the significance of the practice of prostitution in a variety of settings. Several of the Pompeian brothels, for example, were connected with the operation of *cauponae*, that is, inns and taverns.[4] More important perhaps is the reverse relationship: generally speaking, inns, lodging houses, taverns, and restaurants of all kinds were associated with the practice of prostitution, often, though not exclusively,[5]

---

3. For some details of this problem in an historical context, see Goldman, *Gold Diggers* (1981) 91–92, and Rosen, *Sisterhood* (1982) 86–111.

4. See, for example, the tavern-brothels listed in the catalog in app. 1 and, for one example, figs. 1 and 2.

5. Pimps traveling with prostitutes stayed in public lodgings: Strabo 12.8.17. It is obvious that streetwalkers and other freelancers did in some cases take customers to lodging houses when they had no venue of their own available. See chap. 7 for additional information.

by the staff.[6] The legal sources in particular seem to reflect an implicit distinction between establishments where prostitution was practiced more or less as a sideline, and brothels, which in turn may have offered guests more than just sexual services (e.g., liquor, food, and lodging).[7] The distinction is a useful one, though obviously in many cases the line is difficult to draw with certainty, and routinely impossible, I argue, when dealing with archaeological evidence for brothels.[8] It is not clear, for example, that, insofar as they served food, brothels fell under the repressive legislation that governed the sale of food in inns and taverns.[9]

The range of establishments offering sexual services embraced *tabernae, meritoria, cauponae, stabula, deversoria, synoecia* (all terms for lodging houses that typically served food and drink),[10] as well as *popinae* and "*thermopolia*" (terms strictly for eating and drinking places).[11] It is also necessary to include such slang terms as *ganeum, ganea,* and *gurgustium,* which all mean "low dive," and are often associated with the practice of prostitution.[12] It is difficult, if not impossible, to distinguish such places from "brothels" on the basis either of archaeological or literary evidence.[13]

Familiar examples of the establishments mentioned above include Catullus's *salax taberna* ("sexually provocative tavern") and Horace's *fornix et uncta popina,* ("brothel and greasy cookhouse"), a phrase that might almost be read

---

6. See Hor. *Serm.* 1.5.82–85; Tac. *Hist.* 3.83.2; Apul. *Met.* 1.7–19 (though the client presents the sex as uncompensated); Ulp. D. 3.2.4.2; Ulp. D. 23.2.43 pr., 9; Alex. Sev. C. 4.56.3 (a. 225); Dio (in Xiph.) 62.15.3. Cf. the Mosaic regulation on marriage for priests recorded at Ios. *Ant.* 3.276 that prohibited unions with female vendors, innkeepers, and prostitutes. See also McGinn, "Definition" (1997[1998]).

7. See chap. 1.

8. See chap. 7.

9. On this issue, see Hermansen, *Ostia,* 196–203.

10. These words were often used interchangeably: see Frier, "Rental Market" (1977) 32–33, and below. On *synoecia,* see Rowell, "Satyricon" (1957) 222. For this reason, the argument of Kleberg, *Hôtels* (1957) 30–31 that *taberna* was strictly a wine shop appears unsustainable. The evidence he cites (5–6) for a change in meaning of *caupo* and *caupona* in the early Empire is not convincing. Furthermore, the terms used to designate operators of such establishments, such as *caupo* and *stabularius,* might overlap in meaning: see Földi, "Caupones" (1999). The fact that *stabulum/stabularius* might at times have a more specialized reference to facilities for travelers' animals as well as for travelers themselves (see *OLD* s.h.v.) is irrelevant to our purpose.

11. *Thermopolium* is discredited as a modernizing usage by Kleberg, *Hôtels* (1957) 24–25; Wallace-Hadrill, "Public Honour and Private Shame" (1995) 45–46.

12. Kleberg, *Hôtels* (1957) 8–11.

13. The same point appears to hold for classical Athens: Lind, "Hetärenhaus" (1988) 162–63, 166–69.

as a hendiadys.[14] Cicero describes an opponent exiting a *popina* with his head covered, a gesture associated with visiting a brothel.[15] Columella puts *popinae* and brothels on a list of urban pleasures and notes that a slave who indulges in such pleasures is unreliable.[16] In the *Copa* attributed to Vergil,[17] sex is mentioned as one of the tavern's attractions, and the pattern suggested by these sources is supported by epigraphic evidence, such as the boasts *futui coponam* and *futui hospitam*.[18] For Seneca, *fornices* and *popinae* are equally the haunts and homes of pleasure.[19] The juncture of *fornix* and *stabulum* in an invective hurled by the elder Curio at Julius Caesar, is just as telling.[20]

A caveat is in order here. Roman poets and graffiti writers were not always careful to specify whether the sex available in such places was commercial in nature, and we should not always simply assume this. Even when a price is given, we should be alert to the possible status of these claims as boasts, wishes, or insults. As with the identification of brothels, however, the precise (and admittedly difficult) evaluation of individual pieces of evidence can and should take second place to the confirmation of the overall trend. The practice of prostitution in inns and taverns was so common as to be taken for granted, as a famous graffito burlesquing the settlement of a hotel bill suggests. Among the charges, the writer lists one for (the services of) a "girl" (*puella*), which, since no separate charge is given, evidently embraces the cost of a room.[21]

The sale of liquor, in particular, helped to create a sexually charged atmosphere in inns and taverns regardless of whether sex was for sale or not.[22] It is difficult, even in light of ample comparative literature on this subject, to deter-

---

14. Catull. 37.1; Hor. *Ep.* 1.14.21.

15. Cic. *Pisonem* 13.

16. Colum. 1.8.2.

17. [Verg.] *Copa* 1–4, 33, with Rosivach, "Sociology" (1996). Cf. Iuv. 8.162: ". . . et cum venali Cyane succincta lagona" (". . . and Cyane [runs up to the client] her tunic hitched up, with a wine-jug—for sale").

18. *CIL* 4.8442, 13.10018.95 (both mean "I fucked the mistress of the tavern"); cf. 4.4884, 8258–59.

19. Sen. *Vita Beata* 7.3.

20. Suet. *Iul.* 49.1.

21. *CIL* 9.2689 (= *ILS* 7478: Aesernia). Kleberg, *Hôtels* (1957) 82–84 points out that the operators of these establishments, variously described as *caupones*, *tabernarii*, *popinarii*, and so forth are often assimilated to pimps. See also Apul. *Met.* 1.7.

22. See, for example, [Verg.] *Copa*; Apul. *Met.* 1.10 (cf. 2.17), with Moine, "Augustin" (1975) 358–59; Aur. Vict. *Caes.* 33.6, which associates pimps and wine sellers. See also Kleberg, *Hôtels* (1957) 109.

mine whether alcohol was more important for selling sex or sex for selling alcohol.[23] Certainly each tends to raise the cost of the other for the consumer, so that they both perhaps contributed much to the success of the brothel as a business. At the same time, the presence of one tends to raise the expectation of the other, making it very difficult to distinguish, say, a bar from a brothel.[24]

The fluidity of terminology and the flexibility of arrangements illustrate an important truth about the extreme variety of Roman prostitution. Of interest for this discussion is the relationship between the practice of prostitution and Roman lower-class housing.[25] There is no small significance in the fact that one of the words commonly used for lodgings, *stabulum*, could also be used specifically for a brothel[26] and, when employed in this way, might even serve as a term of abuse.[27] The double meaning of *stabulum* was so firmly established that it could be relied on for humorous effect and is found in a joke in the *Satyricon*. Encolpius cannot find his lodgings (*stabulum*) and approaches an old woman selling vegetables for information.[28] She leads him to a brothel, tacitly casting an aspersion on his moral and social status, not to speak of his intelligence. Here the words *stabulum* and *habitare* simultaneously refer to both lodgings and brothel. Less subtle is the incident where Ascyltos asks directions to the *stabulum* (lodgings/brothel) and is led to the same location as Encolpius. A prostitute demands one *as* (= one-quarter of a sesterce) as a temporary room rental, heightening the irony implicit in the contretemps.[29]

Other terms for lower-class lodgings, such as *deversorium*[30] and *meritorium*,[31] were sometimes explicitly associated with the practice of prostitution, that is, as words for brothels. Such terms were used fairly indifferently by the

---

23. See, for example, Prus and Irini, *Hookers* (1980) 6; Rosen, *Sisterhood* (1982) 83–84; Reynolds, *Economics of Prostitution* (1986) 114; Schuster, *Frauenhaus* (1992) 66, 171; Hill, *Their Sisters' Keepers* (1993) 94, 197, 244; Bernstein, *Sonia's Daughters* (1995) 151; Seigle, *Yoshiwara* (1993) 24.

24. The point is made by Trillmich, "Charitengruppe" (1983) 347–48.

25. See also the discussion of the Pompeian Purpose-Built Brothel in chap. 8.

26. Cic. *Phil.* 2.69; Val. Max. 7.7.7; Suet. *Iul.* 49.1.

27. *OLD*, s.v. "*stabulum* 2c."

28. Petron. 7. See chap. 9.

29. Petron. 8. On renting out rooms in a brothel for sex, see chap. 7.

30. See Cic. *Phil.* 2.104–5, where the former villa of Varro becomes a *libidinum deversorium*, and thus the haunt of both male and female prostitutes, as well as more respectable debauchees; Sen. *Ep.* 51.3, whose reference to Baiae as a *deversorium vitiorum* is clear enough; Apul. *Pl.* 1.13, where the physical location of the appetitive portion of the Platonic soul is associated with some unsavory places, including the "haunts of worthlessness and extravagance" ("deversoria nequitiae atque luxuriae").

31. At Schol. *ad Iuv.* 6.125, 127, *meritorium* is used for a prostitute's *cella*, if it does not refer to the brothel itself. See also Firm. Mat. *Math.* 3.6.22; Iuv. 3.234 (perhaps); HA *Tac.* 10.2.

Romans, as noted above, so that the association with prostitution might have been in a sense cumulative. Moreover, *stabulum*, in its neutral sense, was often equated with these other terms.[32] *Stabulum, hospitium, taberna, deversorium,* and so forth were used to denote places that catered to a chiefly lower-class clientele composed both of travelers and more or less permanent residents in the city and predominately the former group in the countryside.[33]

The practice of prostitution was common in all such places. Of great interest are passages that seem to equate, in moral terms, a visit to a *popina, taberna,* or even a *balneum* [bath] with a visit to a brothel in that for persons of rank such a visit incurred disgrace.[34] While, as we shall see, the Romans had differing opinions about the propriety of visiting the baths, especially when both genders were present, they consistently viewed a visit to a *popina* or *taberna* in the same light as a visit to a brothel. They felt this way, it appears, not simply because venal sex was readily available in these venues (which would make them brothels using our definition), but above all because they fostered social mixing, as a famous passage of Juvenal describing the clientele of a *popina* makes clear.[35]

Other factors helped secure the connection between brothel and tavern, and disgrace in the mind of the male elite. Apuleius makes a casual link between prostitutes and daytime drinking as constituent pleasures of the tav-

---

32. *Stabulum* is associated with *meritoria*: Ulp. D. 17.2.52.15; *CIL* 6.15640. It also is associated with *cauponae, deversoria,* and *meritoria*: PS 2.31.16. Note also the linkage of *caupones* with *stabularii* in clauses of the Praetor's Edict: Lenel, *Edictum*[3] (1927) 131, 333–34, with Földi, "Caupones" (1999).

33. This is the conclusion of Frier, "Rental Market" (1977) 34. See also Rosenfeld, "Innkeeping" (1998) 145, 147.

34. See Plaut. *Curc.* 292–94 (covering heads); Cic. *Pisonem* 13 (covering the head, see also *Phil.* 2.77), *Phil.* 2.69 (Antony turns bedrooms into *stabula* and dining rooms into *popinae*); Colum. 1.8.2; Sen. *Vita Beata* 7.3; Suet. *Nero* 26–27 (cf. *Cal.* 11, *Vit.* 7.3, 13.3, *Gramm.* 15); Tac. *Ann.* 13.25.1; Viv.-Cels.-Ulp. D. 4.8.21.11 (cf. Paul. D. 47.10.26); Dio (in Xiph.) 62.15.3; Aur. Vict. *Caes.* 33.6; HA *Verus* 4.5–6 (this emperor's alleged establishment of a *popina* in his house parallels the usage, real or imagined, of in-house brothels: see chap. 5) *Comm.* 3.7, *Trig. Tyr.* 3.4, 8.9, 9.1, 29.1. Cf. Petron. 8; Lucian. *Dial. Mort.* 10.11; *Hist. Ap. Tyr.* 34. For evidence from Josephus, see Rosenfeld, "Innkeeping" (1998) 141–43. Of course some of these authors invent or exaggerate behaviors associated with a visit to such places; it is the association itself with brothels that is important. See also chap. 3.

35. Iuv. 8.158–62, 171–82. See also Plaut. *Curc.* 288–95, *Poen.* 829–35, *Pseud.* 178, *Trin.* 1018–23; Hor. *Serm.* 1.5.4; Sen. *Prov.* 5.4; Athen. 13.566F–567A; Amm. Marc. 14.1.9, 14.6.25, 28.4.21; HA *Verus* 4.5–6. See [Quint.] *Decl. Mai.* 14.7, which makes the body of the prostitute the locus of social mixing. Social mixing in the sense of contact between Jews and non-Jews might occasion disquiet about inns in late Hellenistic Palestine: see Rosenfeld, "Innkeeping" (1998) 140.

ern (*luxuria popinalis*).[36] Drink, often available in or near brothels, spelled excess and potential disorder to members of the upper classes.[37] Like brothels, taverns could be violent[38] and physically unpleasant or, to be exact, greasy, dirty, damp, noisy, roach-infested, and smoky.[39] Other elite biases more specific to eating places fostered objections to consuming food while seated instead of reclining or simply to eating in public at all.[40] The association between these places of public resort and prostitution remained so strong that the Christian church repeatedly forbade clerics from visiting inns on journeys except in cases of dire necessity.[41]

The association of prostitution with lower-class lodging is unsurprising, and modern parallels are not lacking.[42] Nonetheless this association has important implications. Certain districts such as the Subura in Rome may have had a higher concentration of such activity, not because they functioned in any true sense as "red-light districts," but simply because these areas had a greater concentration of lower-class housing or residential buildings *tout court.*

The evidence suggests that Roman cities did not have clearly demarcated neighborhoods for the rich and poor. A pattern of limited clustering, rather than strict segregation, is what emerges from recent studies of places such as Roman Britain,[43] Egypt,[44] Pompeii,[45] Volubilis,[46] and Rome itself.[47] Here the

---

36. Apul. *Met.* 8.1.

37. Plaut. *Poen.* 661, 699–700, 834–35. See the remarks of Toner, *Leisure* (1995) esp. 77.

38. Prop. 4.8.19. On violence in brothels, see chap. 3.

39. Plaut. *Poen.* 835; Lucil. 11W; Cic. *Pisonem* 13; Hor. *Serm.* 2.4.62, *Ep.* 1.14.21, 1.17.6–8, *Ars* 229; [Verg.] *Copa* 3; Iuv. 11.78–81; Gell. 9.2.6; Sid. Apoll. *Ep.* 8.11.3.42–44; Aus. *Mos.* 124; *HA Hadr.* 16.4. See Kleberg, *Hôtels* (1957) 96–97.

40. Mart. 5.70.3; Amm. Marc. 28.4.4; cf. the animus against eating in a brothel registered at Sen. *Contr.* 1.2.11, 16.

41. See, for example, *Brev. Hipp.* 26 CCSL 149.40 (Carthage, A.D. 393) with Herter, s.v. "Dirne," 1205; Dauphin, "Bordels" (1998) 182–83.

42. Especially noteworthy is the case of Victorian England, where a large proportion of prostitutes lived in lower-class lodgings, apparently beyond the control of pimps: Walkowitz, *Prostitution* (1980) 24. For American evidence, see Goldman, *Gold Diggers* (1981) 59–63; Rosen, *Sisterhood* (1982) 78–80.

43. Clarke, "Pre-Industrial City" (1993) 56, who finds some quite disparate patterns, to be sure. See also 63 and 65.

44. Alston and Alston, "Urbanism" (1997) 211–16; Alston, *City* (2002) esp. 172, 183–84.

45. The dominant thesis of recent studies (apart evidently from the question of brothel location) is Pompeii had no social zoning: see Packer, "Middle and Lower Class Housing" (1975) 134; Raper, "Analysis of the Urban Structure" (1977) 191, 204, 207, 216, 218; Raper, "Pompeii" (1979) 137–48; Jongman, *Economy* (1988) 270–71; Perring, "Spatial Organisation" (1991) 284; Wallace-Hadrill, "Elites and Trade" (1991) 250; Dyson, *Community and Society* (1992) 176–77; Laurence, *Roman Pompeii* (1994) 121; Wallace-Hadrill, *Houses and Society* (1994) 65–90; Lau-

highest concentration of senatorial houses was in a part of the city (*Regiones* 3 and 4) where the Subura, commonly regarded by modern scholars as a brothel-district, was located.[48] I do not deny that the Subura had its brothels and its prostitutes.[49] But the brothels were just one element in the urban mix of residential (both upper- and lower-class) and commercial buildings. If any one factor made for a somewhat higher concentration of brothels in the Subura it was the relative absence of public construction, which would have meant more emphasis on residential and commercial establishments overall. Nevertheless, the presence of prostitution in the Subura was likely to have been more a matter of perception than reality. Its proximity to the Forum heightened its profile in the eyes of the male members of the elite who wrote the texts that define for us the nature of life in the capital.[50] A recent survey of the Roman urban matrix in various cities shows a broad integration of residential and commercial, public and private, rich and poor.[51]

rence, "Organization of Space" (1995) 65; Parkins, "Consumer City" (1997) 87; Robinson, "Social Texture" (1997) 142; Pirson, *Mietwohnungen* (1999) 140–41, 161–64. (Pirson argues that rental housing fostered social integration, which has obvious implications for the location of brothels); Schoonhoven, "Residences" (1999). It is not clear to me how Robinson's reliance on Fiorelli's *Regiones* vitiates his analysis, as has been argued. Any modern topographical scheme is bound to be somewhat arbitrary, and for Robinson to invent his own would have raised suspicions of a *petitio principii*. For an attempt to discern elements of the ancient organization of the city, see Van Andringa, "Autels" (2000). Zanker, *Pompeii* (1998) 41–42, lends support to Robinson's conclusions about the distribution of elite houses (though cf. Zanker, 8). *Regio* 7 did have a relatively high concentration of tradesmen and artisans: Zanker 33.

46. See Wallace-Hadrill, "Elites and Trade" (1991) 261.

47. See Ramage, "Urban Problems" (1983) 86–88; Purcell "*Plebs Urbana*" (1994) 675; Wallace-Hadrill, "Case" (2000) 204–12 (who emphasizes the numerous instances of social mixing within individual *insulae*); Kardos, "*Vrbs*" (2001) 397 (for the Esquiline; for the Subura, see note 48); Lo Cascio, "Population" (2001) 193.

48. Eck, "Cum Dignitate Otium" (1997) 177, 181, 183; cf. Guilhembet, "Densité" (1996) (esp. 15: though aristocratic houses were in all parts of the city, they clustered in certain areas). Eck, to be sure, locates these dwellings on the hills. For a clearer, and utterly convincing, presentation of the Subura as a locus of elite as well as lower-class housing, see Welch, *LTUR* (1999) s.v. "Subura" 382. (I thank Andrew Wallace-Hadrill for this reference.) For literary representations of the Subura, see also Gold, "Urban Life" (1998) 57–61. In Juvenal's work, notes Gold, the Subura is a kind of "Rome-plus," in which the most dystopian elements of life in the capital are concentrated, that is, exaggerated. According to Kardos, "*Vrbs*" (2001) 393, Martial and Juvenal suggest a decidedly mixed commercial and residential use in this area.

49. See, for example, Prop. 4.7.15; Persius 5.32–33; Mart. 2.17.1, 6.66.1–2, 9.37.1, 11.61.3–4, 11.78.11, *Priap.* 40; and the discussion in note 48.

50. "The district gained notoriety because it happened to be close to the *Forum Romanum*, the center of elite activity. It was for this reason that the S. became the proverbial demimonde of the Latin poets": Welch, *LTUR* (1999) 4:383.

51. Owens, "Residential Districts" (1996).

Because of this integration, we can expect to find brothels in many different areas. Beginning in the second century at the latest, they will have followed the *insulae*, which were scattered throughout the city.[52] Finally, this connection suggests an answer to the mystery of the apparent lack of brothels in Ostia; that is, we might conclude that they simply cannot be distinguished from the abundant lower-class housing excavated in that city.[53]

Sex and Circuses

In addition to lower-class residences and restaurants, all places of public entertainment were commonly associated with the practice of prostitution, including circuses, theaters, and amphitheaters.[54] The arcades of these buildings contained a variety of shops and strolling vendors in a venue somewhat akin to that of a modern shopping mall.[55] The setting was a convenient one for prostitutes to solicit clients, a practice that attracted the attention of Christian critics. A text attributed to Cyprian, the bishop of Carthage in the mid-third century, states that the entrance to the circus leads through the brothel.[56] Years later, Isidore of Seville notes that young men exiting the theater would cover their heads as though stepping into a brothel.[57] It is possible that space in the arcades of the amphitheater in Pompeii was leased to prostitutes or their exploiters by local officials.[58] Taken together, this evidence suggests that prostitutes were a more or less permanent feature of these public

---

52. See chaps. 7 and 8.

53. See chap. 7.

54. According to HA *Elag.* 26.3 (see also 32.9), Elagabalus knew to find prostitutes for his purposes at the circus, theater, stadium, and baths. On prostitutes at the amphitheater, see Statius *Silvae* 1.6.67; at the circus, see Lucil. 1071W; Hor. *Serm.* 1.6.113; *Priap.* 27; Iuv. 3.65–66 (this source suggests that prostitutes soliciting outside of brothels were not necessarily free of pimps: "ad circum iussas prostare puellas" (cf. *Anth. Lat.* 190.7R); Suet. *Nero* 27.2. The portico at the Theater of Pompey was such a familiar venue for the solicitation of clients that the association was elevated to a literary topos: Catull. 55.6–10; Prop. 4.8.75; Ov. *Ars* 1.67, 3.387; Mart. 11.47.3. For other porticoes cited by Propertius and Ovid as haunts of prostitutes, see Kardos, "Vrbs" (2001) 402 n. 72.

55. Astrologers, street performers, musicians, and others were found in the arcades of circuses, theaters, and amphitheaters: Hor. *Serm.* 1.6.113–14; Iuv. 6.588–91; Tac. *Ann.* 15.38.2; Suet. *Aug.* 74; CIL 6.9822 (= ILS 7496).

56. [Cypr.] *Spect.* 5 CSEL 3.3.8.

57. Isid. *Orig.* 19.26.2. Adams, "Words" (1983) 357, explains the etymology of a term for prostitute, *lodix* (which literally means "covering," "blanket"), on the basis of this passage. HA *Elag.* 32.9 may mock an earlier version of this Christian criticism.

58. See chap. 5.

buildings and did not simply appear on the days of performances, when a larger number of potential clients probably attracted more prostitutes than usual.[59]

Another type of public building where prostitutes might be found was temples. The evidence derives from authors as diverse as Plautus, Juvenal, and Dio of Prusa.[60] Juvenal, in assimilating adulteresses to prostitutes, asks ". . . quo non prostat femina templo?"[61] Temples were evidently regarded as hotbeds of adultery and prostitution.[62]

Baths

The Roman baths under the Principate developed from popular recreational venues to multipurpose entertainment centers as well as to municipal and—especially at Rome—imperial showcases.[63] The procedure of taking a bath was for the Romans a complex and varied activity; in addition to participating in the bath itself, they might engage in a number of other diversions ranging from weightlifting to philosophical discourse. Most importantly, food, drink, and sex were all for sale.[64] The baths, above all in their public, imperially funded form, were pleasure palaces dedicated to the principle of enjoyment. They celebrated beauty, luxury, love, and sexual charm.[65] Even smaller, privately owned operations might offer a taste of these attractions, however.[66]

---

59. The escapades described at Suet. *Nero* 27.2 took place, of course, on a special occasion, though they include some of the more pathological behaviors associated with the *comissatio* (drinking party): see chap. 3.

60. Plaut. *Poen.* 265–70, 339; Dio Chrys. 7.133–34; Iuv. 6.489 (Isis as a *lena*).

61. Iuv. 9.24: ". . . at what temple does a woman not prostitute herself?" See also chap. 9.

62. See Herter, "Soziologie" (1960) 86; Dyson and Prior, "Horace, Martial, and Rome," 254. The Christians, as one might expect, have plenty to say about the association of temples with adultery and prostitution. See, for example, Tert. *Apol.* 15.7 CCSL 1.114; Min. Fel. 25.11 Kytzler 24.

63. See, for example, Kleberg, *Hôtels* (1957) 106. On the design of Roman baths, see Yegül, *Baths,* (1992). Evidence from the Republic shows no explicit attestation of prostitutes at the baths, leading Bruun, "Water" (1997) 371, to argue for their absence. But this may simply be a function of the less abundant material for that period. In my view, Cicero's treatment, in his defense of M. Caelius Rufus, of the famous scene at the Senian Baths depends on a close association between prostitutes and baths in the minds of his audience, and so forms a part of his general characterization of Clodia as a *meretrix: Cael.* 62–67.

64. See Fagan, *Bathing in Public* (1999) 32–36; Kardos, "Vrbs" (2001) 411.

65. See Dunbabin, "*Baiarum grata voluptas*" (1989) 19–20 (representations of Apolausis), 23–24, 32 (representations of Aphrodite/Venus), 28 (representations of Eros).

66. Note the promises of the pimp at Plaut. *Poen.* 699–703. For further discussion of privately owned baths offering sex for sale at Pompeii, see chap. 7.

Commercial sex was only one of several sensual pleasures that were associated with the bath.[67] Prostitution is hardly unique to the baths in ancient Rome, as surviving evidence for medieval England, France, Germany, and Japan suggests, but the precise role it played in the context of the Roman baths presents some unusual features worth exploring in detail.[68]

Roman attitudes toward sex, status, and the bath are difficult to read.[69] This much seems clear, however. Male attendants were employed in baths used by females and vice versa.[70] The status of bath workers was evidently low, like that of prostitutes, with slaves and freedpersons being the majority.[71] At least some workers in some baths were prostituted by bath keepers, who thereby qualified as pimps under the Praetor's Edict.[72] Freelancers offered the employees competition and perhaps made offsite arrangements in some cases.[73] The sex sold by employees, however, seems more likely to have occurred at the baths themselves and not elsewhere. Though we cannot reasonably expect the archaeological record to preserve unambiguous evidence of this, there are some indications in the literary and epigraphic record that this was the case.[74]

We do well to avoid the trap set for us by the sources and assume that no respectable woman would attend the baths when men were present.[75] There was, to be sure, some sensitivity about this. Prostitutes, as noted in chapter 7, might visit the baths strictly as bathers, a fact that helps raise the crux of the problem of respectability. The sources transmit some very mixed signals on

---

67. See, for example, Zajac, "*Thermae*" (1999).

68. For comparative evidence, see chap. 7.

69. For a useful discussion, which does not to my mind quite resolve the problem, see Toner, *Leisure and Ancient Rome* (1995) 53–64. See also Papi "*Delenimenta*" (1999) esp. 721–24.

70. Youtie, "Records" (1949/1973) 991. Iuv. 6.422–23 has a masseur sexually servicing a female patron. Juvenal may be reverse reading a service provided to male bathers. See also Mart. 7.67.

71. Wissemann, "Personal" (1984); Nielsen, *Thermae* 1 (1990) 126–30.

72. The jurist Ulpian specifically mentions personnel hired to watch bathers' clothing who worked as prostitutes at the behest of the *balneator* ("bath keeper"): D. 3.2.4.2. Cf. *Anth. Gr.* 5.82.

73. See Mart. 3.93.14–15 (which does not to my mind imply that only prostitutes were admitted); Amm. Marc. 28.4.9; HA Elag. 26.3.

74. Lucian. *Hippias* 5 implies that facilities for sex were a standard feature of the baths according to Nielsen, *Thermae* 1 (1990):146 n. 4; Jacobelli, *Terme Suburbane* (1995) 92. See also the erotic graffiti at the Suburban Baths in Herculaneum, some of which imply the availability of venal sex, even if they cannot be taken literally: *CIL* 4.10674–78, with Della Corte, "Iscrizioni" (1958) 306–7. Again, a series of small rooms at the Sarno Baths of Pompeii that were employed for toweling, massaging, and anointing clients with oil most likely served as a venue for prostitution: see chap. 7.

75. See Ward, "Women" (1992) 134–39, 143–44; Dauphin, "Brothels" (1996).

the subject of women and men bathing together.[76] What is remarkable is not the criticism,[77] which seems to have inspired at least one attempt at legislation,[78] but the widespread popularity of mixed bathing, a popularity that seems to have increased in the early Principate.[79]

It is difficult to overemphasize the strangeness of the phenomenon, strange, that is, from what we can reconstruct of the Roman perspective itself. The paradox is that social mixing, which received vigorous disapprobation in the context of the cook shop, was widely practiced in buildings that were prized as public assets rather than shunned as low dives.[80] Aristocrats were evidently free to patronize baths but risked their reputations if they set foot in a brothel or *popina*.[81] The logic seems similar to that which despises small-scale retailing but honors large-scale wholesaling, a sheer contradiction perhaps to anyone but a Roman.[82] It finds at least a partial analogy in the popularity of luxury latrines of the imperial period, themselves municipal showcases designed to attract and cater to the needs above all of an elite clientele.[83] No

---

76. Sources and discussion in Merten, *Bäder* (1983) 79–100; Ward, "Women" (1992) 139–42; Fagan, *Bathing in Public* (1999) 26–29. See AÉ 1987.179, an epitaph in which a husband praises his deceased wife for never going to the baths (*inter alia*) without him.

77. See, for example, Plin. *NH* 29.26, 33.153; Iuv. 6.419–25. Some Romans display sensitivity even over nudity and/or bathing with members of the same sex: Ennius *apud* Cic. *Tusc.* 4.70; Cic. *De Orat.* 2.224; Cic. *Off.* 1.129; Val. Max. 2.1.7; Plut. *Cato Maior* 20.5; Ambros. *Off.* 1.79 CUF 1.134–35; *HA Gord.* 6.4. These sources suggest that Brown's assertion about the "long survival of indifference to nudity in Roman public life" needs to be modified. See "Late Antiquity" (1987) 245.

78. We can only be reasonably certain about one such attempt, by Hadrian, which is recorded at Dio (in Xiph.) 69.8.2. Scholars are rightly skeptical about the various reports of such measures preserved by the *Historia Augusta*: see Merten, *Bäder* (1983) 89–92, 97–100; Ward, "Women" (1992) 139–42. Dio's evidence, however, is difficult to ignore, as Merten acknowledges. All the same, a text by Clement of Alexandria suggests that mixed bathing was still popular in his day: *Paed.* 3.5.32 SC 158.72.

79. Fagan, *Bathing in Public* (1999) 27, suggests sensibly that Romans could choose between mixed and single-sex bathing establishments, but in my view presses this point too far. For one thing, such a choice could not feasibly be provided in every locale. Moreover Fagan's prude/pervert dichotomy strikes me as implausible for the Romans. Some, I believe, preferred to bathe in private or only with members of their own sex, while others paraded their modesty by pretending to ignore the nudity or near-nudity of the people around them. The absence of a strict polarity of virtue and vice in the baths is precisely what generated both intense interest and criticism. See Ward, "Women" (1992) 137; Jacobelli, *Terme Suburbane* (1995) 94–95, and Fagan's own comments at 51.

80. All the same, consorting with prostitutes at the baths might earn a person censure: Suet. *Dom.* 22; *HA Comm.* 5.4.

81. See chap. 3.

82. See, for example, Cic. *Off.* 1.150–51.

83. See Neudecker, *Pracht der Latrine* (1994) esp. 150–53.

one will be shocked to learn that many of these establishments were located in or near baths.[84]

Not that it renders the problem any easier to resolve, but it is worth observing that an important difference between *popina* and bath lies in the fact that in the latter case the visitors were without all or most of their clothes.[85] Lack of what were otherwise socially—in some cases legally—obligatory social markers must have made it more challenging to rank the players without the proverbial scorecard,[86] and so perhaps heightened interest in attendance at the baths.[87] Social promiscuity of this sort enhanced an atmosphere of sexual intrigue that must have been good for business, especially the business of venal sex.[88] Bathing fostered sexual attractiveness.[89] The point might seem obvious, but merits emphasis in the context of a Mediterranean calculus of honor/shame that at another point of the spectrum discourages all bathing for women precisely for this reason.[90] It is unsurprising that *balnea vina venus* served as a Roman slogan for the good life.[91]

Special Events

Prostitutes were drawn to a variety of occasions that attracted a crowd of people, including potential clients, such as markets, fairs, and public shows of every kind.[92] As a result, many prostitutes and pimps were not tied to a specific

---

84. Neudecker, *Pracht der Latrine* (1994) 83–91.

85. As Fagan, *Bathing in Public* (1999) 25, observes, the much-vexed question of whether Roman bathers were completely nude or scantily clad is of little practical import. Cf. Nielsen, *Thermae* 1 (1990) 140–42.

86. For legal rules on status-appropriate clothing, see McGinn, *Prostitution, Sexuality, and the Law* (1998) chap. 5.

87. So the parties held by Commodus at the baths, in which respectable women and prostitutes allegedly mixed, would have had added spice to the scene there: *HA Comm.* 5.4.

88. See Ov. *Ars* 3.639–40; Mart. 2.70, 3.72, 11.47.1–2, 5–6, 11.75. The baths had a reputation as a venue for illicit sex, that is, adultery: Quint. *IO* 5.9.14; Ulp. D. 48.5.10(9).1. On Ulpian's text, see McGinn, *Prostitution, Sexuality, and the Law* (1998) 242. For same-sex attraction, see Petron. 92; Mart. 1.23, 1.96.

89. Dunbabin, "*Baiarum grata voluptas*" (1989) 12.

90. See Horden and Purcell, *Corrupting Sea* (2000) 491.

91. For evidence and discussion, see Kajanto, "Balnea" (1969).

92. There is an abundance of comparative evidence to support this assertion. See, for example, Symanski, "Prostitution in Nevada" (1974) 371; Rossiaud, "Prostitution, Youth, and Society" (1978) 4; Finnegan, *Poverty* (1979) 25; Bernstein, *Sonia's Daughters* (1995) 155; Schuster, *Freien Frauen* (1995) 45. On the importance of fairs and festivals in fostering a great mobility of persons in the Mediterranean, see Horden and Purcell, *Corrupting Sea* (2000) 432–44; cf. 380–81. See also the essays in Lo Cascio, *Mercati* (2000).

location but traveled broadly in the manner of the *fahrendes Volk* of the Middle Ages.[93] We find their presence registered at festivals and the like,[94] circuit courts,[95] and military encampments, even—or especially—when the army was on campaign.[96] The evidence from Egypt merits emphasis here. It tells us that on at least three occasions prostitutes were given special permission by tax collectors to ply their trade on a particular day.[97] These were almost certainly days when festivals, fairs, or similar occasions took place. Visitors to religious events and centers might have had more than one motive. In this context pilgrimage and tourism could be viewed as two sides of the same coin.

Prostitutes also attended dinner parties.[98] The atmosphere of these functions was often sexually charged, owing not only to the presence of these women, but to the dramatic entertainment being offered, to the room decor and table service, which often featured erotic representations, and to the other guests, who might include persons of doubtful or even unknown status.[99]

The principle of circulation adumbrated here suggests an important fact about some prostitutes in the Roman world: they were mobile. Not only did clients travel to prostitutes, but prostitutes to clients. Mobility in this context must not, of course, be confused with freedom.[100] The lives of these prosti-

---

93. See the story of the traveling pimp and his prostitutes who mysteriously disappear during a nocturnal earthquake in Carura, a village on the border of Phrygia and Caria: Strabo 12.8.17. Roman comedy also has examples of some rather mobile pimps, such as Labrax in Plautus's *Rudens* and Sannio in Terence's *Adelphoi*. The entertainers in third-century Dura-Europos might also qualify: see chap. 8.

94. See Strabo 12.3.36 (Pontic Comana, already popular for a shrine and festivals dedicated to the goddess Ma, had large numbers of resident prostitutes who attracted many visitors in their own right: Strabo alleges, perhaps in error, that most of these women were sacred prostitutes); Dio Chrys. 77/78.4 (Thermopylae, the meeting place of the Delphic Amphictyony, attracted traveling pimps with their prostitutes).

95. See Dio Chrys. 35.15–16: Apamea Celaenae, every other year, with De Ligt, *Fairs* (1993) 226–27, 254–55, who places circuit courts in a broader economic context. On the "connectivity" of Apamea Celaenae, see Horden and Purcell, *Corrupting Sea* (2000) 392.

96. See Val. Max. 2.7.1; Frontinus *Strat.* 4.1.1; App. *Hisp.* 85: Scipio Aemilianus's ejection of prostitutes before Numantia suggests their presence was otherwise taken for granted, but cf. [Quint.] *Decl.* 3.12. For evidence of actresses, musicians, and dancers among the camp followers, see Petrikovits, "Lixae" (1980/1991). Many of these doubled as prostitutes to judge from the evidence from Dura-Europos examined in chap. 8. Overall, the evidence for the association between soldiers and prostitutes is surprisingly thin: see Wesch-Klein, *Soziale Aspekte* (1998) 115 n. 79.

97. For evidence and literature see McGinn, *Prostitution, Sexuality, and the Law* (1998) 279–80. Also see Montserrat, *Sex and Society* (1996) 126–29.

98. On pimps as banquet caterers, see Hor. *Serm.* 2.3.226–32.

99. See Fisher, "Associations" (1988) 1208, whose presentation, though somewhat antiquarian, is at bottom persuasive. On prostitution and the drinking party, or *comissatio*, see chap. 3.

100. See Horden and Purcell, *Corrupting Sea* (2000) 383.

tutes, therefore, did not radically differ from the lives of those confined to a brothel, a phenomenon explored above all in chapter 8.[101] Women— whether slaves or not—were a valuable commodity and exploitable as a resource that could be trafficked like any other.[102] Female performers were one part of this traffic, prostitutes another, and sometimes the two categories overlapped.[103]

Other Venues

The preceding discussion may foster the impression that prostitution was virtually universal in the Roman world. This was not, in fact, the case. Prostitution was widespread, but not universal. The elite Roman male did much to exaggerate this notion of universality because he was liable to identify almost any lower-class woman as a prostitute, especially if she worked in a trade that exposed her to indiscriminate contact with males outside of her family, that is, in any part of the Roman service economy, from selling vegetables in the marketplace to serving wine in a bar.[104] In this light, for example, Martial's insinuations about the Suburan *tonstrix* appear to reflect this simple bias rather than to serve as evidence that permits us to conclude that hairdressers typically worked as prostitutes.[105] A similar point holds for Plautus's *alicariae* ("mill-girls"), whose identification as prostitutes owes as much to modern ideas of whore-taxonomy as to ancient attempts to make sense of the text, which is far from clear.[106] What perhaps influenced ancient elite males to entertain suspicions of prostitution is paradoxically that mills were places where the sexes might routinely encounter each other without sex being the only or most

---

101. Heyl, *Madam* (1979) 95, records a high turnover rate for a modern brothel, where the average stay for a prostitute is six months.

102. See Horden and Purcell, *Corrupting Sea* (2000) 379.

103. To my mind, Horden and Purcell, *Corrupting Sea* (2000) 386, risk overrating the essentially "male" aspect of human mobility in the ancient Mediterranean (cf. 389, 391 on the Middle Ages and 447 on traveling performers, a number of whom must have been women).

104. See the evidence and discussion in McGinn, "Definition" (1997[1998]) esp. 89–97, 107–12. DeFelice, *Roman Hospitality* (2001) deserves honorable mention here for a noble, if uncontrolled, attempt to combat the misogyny of the sources.

105. Mart. 2.17; cf. Plaut. *Truc.* 405–6.

106. Plaut. *Poen.* 266. Festus 7L takes a sexual joke (*alicariae* = "women who deal in grain" becomes "women who grind" or "are ground") and turns it into a job description: see Adams, "Words" (1983) 335–37. The bakery scam reported at Socr. *HE* 5.18 *PG* 67.609–13 suggests no more in this regard than that prostitutes were associated with *popinae*, hardly a novelty.

obvious purpose.[107] This does not mean, however, that no mill-girl ever doubled as a prostitute.[108]

For this reason we have no way to be absolutely certain whether the Pompeian *(h)alicaria* Glyco, if she were a prostitute, was a part-timer or this term simply functioned as slang for "prostitute."[109] The sad truth is that the elite male misogyny of our literary texts almost certainly blurs to the vanishing point a flourishing part-time and casual economy of prostitution.[110] This leaves us ill-equipped at times even to interpret a simple epigraph in a satisfactory manner.

To put the problem another way, there is a parallel danger of hyperskepticism over the extent of prostitution in the Roman world. Its widespread nature is first suggested by a wealth of comparative evidence that shows lower-class women in a variety of trades who do supplement their incomes by resorting to prostitution.[111] In other words, it is quite possible to read the bias of the sources as a kind of backhanded acknowledgment of the existence of part-time and/or cyclical prostitution in the Roman world. What is more, not all prostitutes remained in a brothel, but went out to solicit customers or simply worked in the streets independently of a brothel.[112] Thus the presence of prostitutes in forum or marketplace is securely attested, whatever exaggerations may safely be ascribed to class and gender bias.[113]

The breadth and variety of the evidence for prostitution is suggestive. Any attempt at quantification is clearly out of the question, but it is clear that prostitution must be regarded as a major service industry in the Roman world.

---

107. See the insult leveled against Octavian's mother by Cassius of Parma recorded at Suet. *Aug.* 4.2. For a parallel example from medieval Germany, see Schuster, *Freien Frauen* (1995) 221. Cf. the medieval English attitude toward laundresses: Karras, *Common Women* (1996) 54–55.

108. For insight into the nature of this problem, see, for example, the discussion of the occupational backgrounds of nineteenth-century New York City prostitutes in Gilfoyle, *City of Eros* (1992) esp. 59–61.

109. *CIL* 4.3999, 4001. Glyco is otherwise attested as a male name: Hor. *Ep.* 1.1.30; Suet. *Aug.* 11.

110. For more discussion of the problem of part-time and casual prostitution, see below in this chap. in the section on "Recruitment."

111. See Finnegan, *Poverty* (1979) 24, 29, 73, 168, 202–5; Mahood, *Magdalenes*, 6, 58–59, 84, 116, 130–34, 150–51. I concede that no small part of this evidence may have arisen from the same sort of prejudice that colors the Roman sources on the subject, and I have tried to eliminate obvious examples of this.

112. For late antiquity, see Proc. *Aed.* 1.9.4–5; Iustinian. *Nov.* 14 (a. 535). These sources show that both prostitutes who worked in and those outside of the brothel might be subject to the control of pimps.

113. See chap. 9.

Brothels also existed in rural areas, anywhere, in fact, where clients could be found.[114] Nevertheless, prostitution was overwhelmingly an urban phenomenon, one of the distinct pleasures of life in town.[115] In cities, prostitution was fairly pervasive, at least in lower-class milieus, a fact supported by evidence that the clients of the establishments surveyed here were themselves typically of low status. Even so, considerations of commercial advantage, rather than Christianizing concerns with public morality or the aesthetics of the public sphere, determined the widespread presence of venal sex in Roman urban contexts.[116]

OWNERSHIP OF BROTHELS

Over the past quarter century, increasing attention has been paid to the investments in urban property made by members of the Roman upper classes. The evidence has shown the elite invested not only in upper-class housing such as the *domus* and the better sort of *insulae*, but also in the kinds of housing described in the preceding paragraphs.[117] Though the ancient economy was overwhelmingly agricultural,[118] comparative data suggests that as much as

---

114. Inns too were located outside of cities and might offer the services of prostitutes. Varro *RR* 1.2.23; Suet. *Claud.* 38.2 (the scene is possibly urban); *CIL* 9.2689 (= *ILS* 7478). See also Gassner, *Kaufläden* (1986) 79. For brothels outside cities in the Byzantine period, see Magoulias, "Bathhouse" (1971) 238, 241, 246; Leontsini, *Prostitution* (1989) 70–72. For other cultures, see Butler, *Daughters of Joy* (1987) 7–8 (nineteenth-century American West); Karras, *Common Women* (1996) 24–25 (medieval England).

115. See, for example, Hor. *Ep.* 1.14.18–26; Tac. *Hist.* 3.83.2; cf. Iuv. 11.81. Of course, the emphasis laid by the sources on this aspect is not simply a reflection of reality but of a moralizing bias. For a discussion about the criticism directed at entertainments in the city, see chap. 9.

116. For the complete argument, see chap. 3. Tombs perhaps functioned as improvised brothels (or at least cribs); they offered shelter and were aptly located near main gates and roads, as brothels themselves were: Catull. 59; Mart. 1.34.8, 3.93.15; Iuv. 6.O16 (prostitutes thought to practice their trade near the city's walls perhaps used tombs for sex: see Mart. 1.34.6, 3.82.2, 11.61.2, 12.32.22). For the same reasons, tombs served as a refuge for squatters and as lavatories: Scobie, "Slums" (1986) 402–3.

117. For an overview of upper-class investment in urban property, see Garnsey, "Investment" (1976). For a detailed description of Cicero's management of his urban properties, see Frier, "Management" (1978/9); for discussion of the urban rental market as a whole, see Frier, "Rental Market" (1977). Also see Frier's extensive treatment of the social, economic, and legal aspects of urban housing in *Landlords* (1980). Such investment in urban property was regarded as profitable but risky: Frier, "Rental Market" (1977) 34–35, 36 n. 51. At Pompeii, wealthy families exploited the position of their houses on commercial thoroughfares by attaching shops on the street sides: Zanker, *Pompeii* (1998) 41–42.

118. For emphasis on the importance of agriculture in the economy as a whole, see, for example, Jongman, *Economy* (1988) esp. 199, 203.

one-third of the gross domestic product was generated by commerce.[119] The superior prestige of farming made it an attractive investment, while the lure of a higher rate of return and the advantage of greater liquidity made commerce appealing, even to many aristocrats.[120]

We might suppose that, given the close connection between tenement housing and prostitution, upper-class investment in the former might at least in some cases amount to investment in the latter.[121] In fact there is explicit evidence that this was the case. The jurist Ulpian[122] lays it down that urban rents, even if they derive from a brothel, should fall within the scope of the *hereditatis petitio* (suit on an inheritance), because brothels are operated on the property of "many honorable men."[123]

Any attempt to take precise measure of the import of "many" would be misguided, but the jurist's holding is without question motivated by widespread contemporary practice, which, in turn, suggests profitability. Indirect evidence for this argument is found in a passage of Varro,[124] in which a speaker implies that the construction of inns (*tabernae deversoriae*) on opportune country estates (that is, convenient for travelers) was not only common but also profitable. Given the typical association of prostitution with *tabernae* and *deversoria*, it is likely that a good share of these profits derived from the practice of prostitution.

There is a wealth of evidence from other cultures to suggest that, despite the scorn accorded prostitutes, pimps, and procuresses, prominent, wealthy,

---

119. Frier, "Pompeii's Economy" (1991) 246.

120. See, above all, D'Arms, *Commerce* (1981). Also see Gabba, *Buon Uso* (1988); Wallace-Hadrill, "Elites and Trade" (1991); Harris, "Problems" (1993) 15, 22, 24–25; Purcell, "*Plebs Urbana*" (1994) 665; Dyck, *Commentary* (1996) 331–38 (on Cic. *Off.* 1.150–51); Mouritsen, "Mobility" (1997) 62–64; Parkins, "Consumer City" (1997); Niquet, "Senatorial Agriculturalist" (2000); D'Hautcourt, "Banquier" (2001) esp. 204–5. On the varied sources of elite income, see Mratschek-Halfmann, *Divites* (1993) 95–127. For a discussion of the modern literature, see Andreau, "Rome" (2001) 310–11. On elite problems with liquidity, see Jongman, *Economy* (1988) 223. For the monetization of the Roman economy, see the section below on "Prices."

121. I do not mean to exaggerate the economic significance of urban investment: see the cautions of Garnsey, "Investment" (1976) 131–32 and Frier, "Management," (1978/9) 1 n. 1; *Landlords* (1980) 25–26. All the same, such investment was by no means negligible. For example, the local elite of Pompeii invested in hotels: Kleberg, *Hôtels* (1957), 80. See, in general, Parkins, "Consumer City" (1997).

122. Ulp. (15 *ad edictum*) D. 5.3.27.1. For a brief discussion, see McGinn, *Prostitution, Sexuality, and the Law* (1998) 328–29.

123. Only *fructus* deriving previous to the *litis contestatio* go to the plantiff if victorious: Kaser, *Privatrecht* 1² (1971) 738, with literature. The same rule applies to rural rents: Ulp. D. 5.3.29. An example of the former occurs when Cicero is able to recover a prorated portion of the rents that had already been paid to the banker Cluvius when he inherits this man's Puteolan property (*Att.* 14.10.3): see Frier, "Management" (1978/9) 3.

124. Varro *RR* 1.2.23.

respectable members of society derive large profits from the practice of prostitution, usually in the form of rents accruing from brothels.[125] The Christian society of late antiquity was no exception.[126] The point, in fact, is fairly obvious. Who, but members of the elite, is in the best position to profit from commercial sex? While we should exercise caution when generalizing about prostitution from culture to culture, we can observe how often it is a profitable, cash-rich business, and one that is moreover conducted by highly exploitable parties. Social and legal privilege often means insulation from the obloquy directed at pimps and freedom from arrest and prosecution in societies where prostitution has been criminalized.[127] This combination of factors has proven irresistible across cultures to at least some members of the upper classes, lured in so small measure by the generous return on investment, the price—or reward—of their complaisance.[128] "Prostitutes were deviant; landlords who profited from prostitution were not."[129]

---

125. In medieval France, very prominent persons were the proprietors of baths and brothels, including municipal authorities, noble families, and high-ranking clergy: Rossiaud, *Medieval Prostitution* (1988) 6, 30, 61, 123. For medieval England, see Karras, *Common Women* (1996) 33, 43–44; Kelly, "Bishop" (2000); for medieval Florence, Trexler, "Prostitution florentine" (1981) 991; for medieval Venice, Pavan, "Police" (1980) 245–46, 249. In early modern Seville, we find city officials and religious corporations (at times employing middlemen) owning brothels: Perry, "Lost Women" (1978) 209, "Deviant Insiders" (1985) 145, 155. In 1990s China, the People's Liberation Army and the Public Security Bureau played this role: Hershatter, *Dangerous Pleasures* (1997) 336, 366. On prominent persons owning property containing brothels in nineteenth-century New York City, see Gilfoyle, *City of Eros* (1992) 42–53, 86–87, 266–67, 339–40, 366, 407; Hill, *Their Sisters' Keepers* (1993) 133; on the nineteenth-century Comstock Lode, Goldman, *Gold Diggers* (1981) 31; in nineteenth-century Glasgow, Mahood, *Magdalenes* (1990) 133–34; in nineteenth-century Paris, Harsin, *Policing Prostitution* (1985) 285–87; in nineteenth-century York, Finnegan, *Poverty* (1979) 63; in nineteenth-century England, Walkowitz, *Prostitution* (1980) 200, 208; in the early twentieth-century United States, Rosen, *Sisterhood* (1982) 70–72.

126. See Neri, *Marginali* (1998) 219.

127. Sullivan, *Politics of Sex* (1997) 111–13, on the Australian state of New South Wales in the mid-twentieth century. In some cases, publicity has acted as a discouragement to prostitution. See Walkowitz, *City* (1992) 226, on late nineteenth-century London, where notoriety forced respectable landlords out of a district associated with prostitution.

128. On the huge profits landlords made from prostitution in late nineteenth-/early twentieth-century America, see Rosen, *Sisterhood* (1982) 29, 69–77 (see, 71, for mention of the use of middlemen); Mackey, *Red Lights Out* (1987) 127, 260; Gilfoyle, *City of Eros* (1992) 34–36 (middlemen), 42–53, 124–25, 163, 166 (middlemen), 168–69; Hill, *Their Sisters' Keepers* (1993) 292; Best, *Controlling Vice* (1998) 16, 72. On the profits made in medieval France, see Rossiaud, *Medieval Prostitution* (1988) 61; for medieval England, Karras, *Common Women* (1996) 43–44 and Kelly, "Bishop" (2000); for nineteenth-century York, Finnegan, *Poverty* (1979) 65; for nineteenth-century Glasgow, Mahood, *Magdalenes* (1990) 133–34; for early twentieth-century Buenos Aires, Guy, *Sex* (1990) 123; for early twentieth-century Minsk, see Bernstein, *Sonia's Daughters* (1995) 32; for early twentieth-century Shanghai, Hershatter, *Dangerous Pleasures* (1997) 72.

129. Best, *Controlling Vice* (1998) 75.

Given the few investment options available and the imperative to avoid—or at least distribute—risk, investment in prostitution might fit either of the two important hypotheses that have attempted in recent years to explain the behavior of Roman upper-class property owners, "bounded rationality" or "rationalism."[130] In fact it falls in with a whole series of behaviors observed to be characteristic of Mediterranean producers, who for long periods tried, in the face of adverse and unpredictable conditions, to reduce risk.[131] A consistent aim of theirs was to maintain flexibility of production.[132] They achieved this, in part, by keeping in play a maximum variety of productive resources.[133] The other side of the coin in their aversion to risk was a strong appetite for profit.[134] Profit was sought wherever feasible; one did not simply choose, or feel compelled to choose, agrarian pursuits over commercial.[135] Such factors are hardly unknown outside the Mediterranean, of course, and, as seen, elites the world over in diverse eras have found the prospect of investment in prostitution irresistible. Still, they appear to have converged in this area to great effect in Roman antiquity.

All the same, the involvement of members of the Roman upper classes in the business of prostitution raises something of a paradox that in turn suggests further questions. Did this involvement have a measurable effect on attitudes, or social policy, toward prostitution? For example, did it encourage toleration? There is no direct evidence for such a trend and the ambiguity of modern evidence prompts caution.[136] Ulpian's evidence suggests that, at the very least, these interests could become factors in policy considerations, though only in a manner that benefited members of the elite.[137] The matter remains open for discussion later in this study.

---

130. For a statement in favor of "rationalism," see Rathbone, *Economic Rationalism* (1991). For the thesis of "bounded rationality" see Kehoe, "Investment" (1993); Pleket, "Agriculture" (1993); Kehoe, *Investment* (1997) esp. 16–21. The former emphasizes the sophisticated economic choices made by elite landowners and investors, the later the limits on those choices: see Kehoe, "Economic Rationalism" (1993); Rathbone, "More (or Less)?" (1994). Kehoe appears to have had the better of the debate: see Andreau and Maucourant, "Rationalité" (1999). His model is certainly better suited to economic decision making inside the world of prostitution: see chap. 3.

131. Horden and Purcell, *Corrupting Sea* (2000) 179, 221, 263, 283, 329.

132. Horden and Purcell, *Corrupting Sea* (2000) 186, 200.

133. Horden and Purcell, *Corrupting Sea* (2000) 181, 224, 263.

134. Horden and Purcell, *Corrupting Sea* (2000) 293, 366; cf. 286.

135. Horden and Purcell, *Corrupting Sea* (2000) 349, 396.

136. Often the upper classes encouraged toleration of prostitution for economic reasons; at the same time, public demands for reform could arise from similar quarters: Rosen, *Sisterhood* (1982) 72–75, 101.

137. On policy, see chap. 5.

It seems quite possible that brothels, like other kinds of property, passed into the ownership of the emperor and/or state through sale, gift, or bequest. It is even possible that they were installed on urban property already owned by either the state or emperor for the same motives that animated private individuals.[138] We have no direct evidence for this phenomenon, except for Caligula's experiment on the Palatine, which I argue elsewhere to have been of brief duration.[139] The brothels listed in the late-antique Regionary Catalogs may have been state-owned, but other explanations for their appearance are available.[140] Finally, the use of brothels as a form of punishment may reflect state ownership, but this too is speculative.[141]

Another question arises here: How closely involved were investors in the running of brothels? The role played by middlemen in various sectors of the Roman economy seems to have been crucial. For example, rich investors commonly employed middlemen to mediate between investors and the actual inhabitants of apartment houses.[142] Bruce Frier has shown that these men acted as an economic buffer, insulating building owners from a portion of the risks associated with renting urban properties.

The evidence on patterns of investment relating to prostitution suggests that middlemen provided a kind of social and legal insulation as well.[143] By leasing to an intermediary, the owner could disassociate himself from the unsavory business (if he, in fact, knew about it) that brought him a sizable rental income and be freed from the indelicacy of dealing directly with pimps and prostitutes as tenants.[144]

---

138. For the—at first separate—regimes of imperial and state property, see McGinn, *Prostitution, Sexuality and the Law* (1998) 272.

139. For a discussion of Caligula's brothel, see chap. 5.

140. See chap. 6.

141. For more on this practice, see chap. 8.

142. On middlemen, particularly their economic role, see Frier, "Management" (1978/9) 3–6, *Landlords* (1980) 30–31, 78–82, 180; Pleket, "Elites" (1984) 6, 9; Kirschenbaum, *Sons* (1987) (the legal arrangements could vary considerably); Paterson, "Trade and Traders" (1998) 1161–62; Gardner, "Women in Business Life" (1999) esp. 13–15, 18; Morley, "Markets" (2000) 217–21; D'Hautcourt, "Banquier" (2001) 206; Mouritsen, "Roman Freedmen" (2001). On social prejudice directed against middlemen, see Kudlien, "Makler" (1997).

143. For a general discussion of this role of middlemen, see Frier, "Management" (1978/9); Di Porto, *Impresa Collettiva* (1984); Reduzzi Merola, *Servo Parere* (1990); Joshel, *Work* (1992) 76; Aubert, *Business Managers* (1994) 352; Purcell, "*Plebs Urbana*" (1994) 662; Földi, "*Caupones*" (1999) 134; Morley, "Markets" (2000) 17–21; Niquet, "Senatorial Agriculturalist" (2000) 127. Recognition of their role might suggest a partial resolution to the modern debate over the extent of elite investment in on-agricultural sectors of the economy; see Andreau, "Rome" (2001) 310–11. For middlemen acting as social buffers between wealthy landowners and brothel operators in nineteenth-century St. Paul, Minn., see Best, *Controlling Vice* (1998) 75. See also Corbin, *Women for Hire* (1990) 64, 69.

144. The ultimate goal was to avoid being identified as a pimp, given the legal and social disabilities that would follow. Herter "Soziologie" (1960) 75 implies this same point. Note that

To be sure, investment in prostitution was not always so indirect as we might take the reliance on middlemen to imply.[145] The existence of innumerable slave prostitutes suggests a more direct link between owner and asset, as does, to an even greater extent, the evidence for slave pimps, above all a text by the jurist Ulpian. In this passage, Ulpian cites a holding of his predecessor Pomponius,[146] which concerns the denial of procedural rights to pimps under the Praetor's Edict. These jurists speak of a slave pimp and slave prostitutes, who are said to form part of the former's *peculium* (fund-for-use). We can only guess at the frequency of this phenomenon, but it is safe to conclude that Romans of means did occasionally set up their slaves, freedpersons, and perhaps dependent free persons as well, in the business of running brothels, just as they set them up in a variety of other businesses.[147] Given the state of the evidence, there is no point in speculating on how common this phenomenon was.[148] Freedpersons were quite able to operate independently of their former masters, and many did not even have living patrons.[149] Livy's Faecenia Hispala seems to have been very independent, at least as a freedwoman.[150]

Of course, when sources refer to slaves prostituted by their masters,[151] we rarely know whether the ultimate financial interest lay with the "owner," or

---

caupones were frequently identified as pimps (see above in n. 21). On indirect involvement of members of the elite in the slave trade, see the recent study by Bosworth, "Vespasian" (2002), who is in my view perhaps a bit too sanguine about its respectability.

145. It is worth noting that Justinian, in his campaign against pimps, punished landlords who knowingly rented property to them: Nov. 14 (a. 535).

146. Pomp.-Ulp. (6 *ad ed.*) D. 3.2.4.3. See McGinn, *Prostitution, Sexuality, and the Law* (1998) 55–58.

147. On the operation of the *peculium*, see Buckland, *Law of Slavery* (1908) 187–238; Kirschenbaum, *Sons* (1987) esp. 31–89; Watson, *Roman Slave Law* (1987) 90–114. On setting up freedmen in business, see Treggiari, *Freedmen* (1969) 87–106, 160–61; Kirschenbaum, 127–60. I can find no Roman evidence for the involvement of freedmen in managing prostitution, but I regard it as likely. For a couple of Greek parallels showing a freedwoman managing a tenement house containing a brothel and another manager who was a slave and prostitute, see Isaeus 6.19–26.

148. I argue in *Prostitution, Sexuality, and the Law* (1998) 256–64, that the elite of Tauric Chersonesus in the late second century A.D. were closely involved in the operation of brothels.

149. See Garnsey, "Independent Freedmen" (1981). Garnsey (366–67, 370) recognizes that the situation of freedmen in business showed great diversity. Even some freedmen acting as agents or managers might be very independent. For an example from Puteoli, see the activity of the freedmen moneylenders known as the Sulpicii as preserved in the Murecine archive: Rowe, "Trimalchio's World" (2001) 229–31. Their numbers may not have been as great as their social profile suggests, however: see Mouritsen, "Roman Freedmen" (2001).

150. See the discussion in McGinn, *Prostitution, Sexuality, and the Law* (1998) 86–89. Venal sexual acts did not count as *operae*, the services an ex-slave might owe an ex-owner: Call. D. 38.1.38 pr., with McGinn, 330–31.

151. Faecenia Hispala (Liv. 39.9.5) and P. Atilius Philiscus (Val. Max. 6.1.6), are two examples of slaves prostituted by their masters.

with the latter's *patronus* if he were a freedman or *dominus* if he were a slave. One or the other of the second pair of alternatives is at least a possibility in some cases, since the social and legal disabilities inflicted on pimps presumably motivated elite investors to distance themselves from the business.[152] One should be careful not to make facile assumptions either way.[153] Slave prostitutes might form part of the *peculium* of a slave pimp, who himself might be the *vicarius* (underslave) of another slave or the property of a freed or freeborn manager. Free middlemen might operate a brothel, while exploiting their own slaves as prostitutes. Or a pimp might combine in one person the roles of slave owner, brothel operator, and investor in venal sex.[154] Some pimps became quite prosperous, to judge from the example of one Elius, whom Seneca cites as a paradigm of wealth in an argument about why wealth should be despised.[155]

The general observation that the use of intermediaries in agriculture did not in the final analysis succeed in distancing the high elite from the world of production might with some qualification find application in the economy of prostitution as well.[156] What we might reasonably expect to find here is a spectrum of relationships varying in the degree of closeness between upper-class investor and working prostitute. A component of social distance worth mentioning here is physical distance. Some of the brothels identified from Pompeii (in later chapters) appear to have operated, from the perspective of elite owners, very close to home.[157]

---

152. A son or slave might be employed to put an extra layer of social insulation between *pater familias* or owner and the agent who ran the business: see Gardner, *Being* (1993) 77–78, and the literature cited for "middlemen" above in nn. 142 and 143.

153. Note the different ways in which the involvement of independent freedmen in commercial enterprises was structured. For the commercial activity of independent freedmen in Puteoli and Ostia, see D'Arms, *Commerce* (1981) 121–48.

154. One notes the imprecise terminology used to describe merchants and retailers: Joshel, *Work* (1992) 111. Cf. Kneißl, "Mercator-Negotiator" (1983) whose attempt to distinguish between the terms for merchants and retailers is a bit optimistic to my mind; see Drexhage, "Bemerkungen" (1991) for the Egyptian evidence; Colin, "Commerçants" (2000). A similar set of options existed for the economic exploitation of privately owned baths: management by owner, lease, operation by manager. See Nielsen, *Thermae* 1 (1999) 126. Fluidity of terminology implies flexibility of role.

155. Sen. *Prov.* 5.2.

156. For more on this point, see Purcell, "*Villa*" (1995) 156.

157. On the lack of physical distance between elite residences and commerce in general, see Wallace-Hadrill, "Elites and Trade" (1991) 260–61.

OPERATION OF BROTHELS

Brothel management is a broad and varied field. Important factors were the size of the establishment (the largest commonly known example is the Purpose-Built Brothel at Pompeii with its ten *cellae*),[158] its nature (whether it was run in connection with a bath, inn, etc.), and the legal status of the prostitutes (whether slave or free). Slave prostitutes seem to have been fairly tightly controlled,[159] and the sources often suggest an environment of coercion. It is clear that these prostitutes were expected to live and eat in the brothel and were perhaps permitted to leave only rarely.[160]

Larger establishments would have had a support staff, which might have included assistants to look after the prostitutes,[161] cooks,[162] water-boys,[163] hairdressers,[164] scouts for rounding up customers,[165] and others.[166] That such

---

158. For the Purpose-Built Brothel, including a glimpse of one of its *cellae*, see figs. 4–11.

159. A leaden collar from Bulla Regia in North Africa (*ILS* 9455) reads: "adultera meretrix; tene me quia fugivi de Bulla R(e)g(ia)" ("adulteress-prostitute: detain me, because I have run away from Bulla Regia"). *Meretrix* may, however, be intended as mere abuse, as *adultera* surely is. The collar is perhaps from the fourth century; earlier, tattooing (or perhaps branding) the face would have served a similar function: see Thurmond, "Slave Collars" (1994) esp. 465–66. See also chap. 8.

160. See Sen. *Contr.* 1.2, esp. 1, 11–12, 16; *Hist. Ap. Tyr.* 33–36 (the permission given Tarsia to leave the brothel is presented as extraordinary). A line of Juvenal (6.127) suggests that some prostitutes went home when the brothel closed: see n. 161.

161. At *Hist. Ap. Tyr.* 33, we encounter a *villicus puellarum* (sic), himself a slave. The title may be an invention, but the man's function surely is not: cf. the *lenonum minister* at *HA Comm.* 2.9. *Vilicus* can mean any kind of business manager working on someone else's behalf: Aubert, *Business Managers* (1994) 169–75. I do not mean to imply that such persons were not used with free prostitutes, though the evidence is spare. See, for example, evidence from the Byzantine period: Leontsini, *Prostitution* (1989) 120–21.

162. Sen. *Contr.* 1.2.11, 16 has prostitutes eating in the brothel. See also Plaut. *Poen.* 835. Lower-class lodgings of the sort routinely identified with brothels or the practice of prostitution typically maintained cooks to feed the tenants: Frier, "Rental Market" (1977) 31. On cooks et al. in modern brothels, see Rosen, *Sisterhood* (1982) 157.

163. Presumably, there were water-boys to bring water for washing after intercourse, as in Cic. *Cael.* 34. See also Festus 20M: "aquarioli dicebantur mulierum impudicarum sordidi adseculae" ("the lowly attendants of unchaste women used to be called *aquarioli*"); Apul. *Apol.* 78.1; cf. Plaut. *Poen.* 224. Tert. *Apol.* 43 CCSL 1.158 ranks *aquarioli* with pimps and procurers. See Butrica, "Using Water Unchastely 2" (1999) with references to earlier literature. For Byzantine evidence, see Magoulias, "Bathhouse" (1971) 237. For sources on the need for water after sex, see Krenkel, "Fellatio" (1980) 80.

164. See *CGL* 2.100.45: "cinerarius: doulos eteras [i.e., hetairas]" ("hairdresser: prostitute's slave").

165. Plaut. *Men.* 338–43; Petron. 7; Suet. *Cal.* 41.1, perhaps also the *perductores* ("procurers") at Tert. *Apol.* 43 CCSL 1.158, as well as the wearers of the famous "come-hither" sandals denounced by Clem. Alex. *Paed.* 2.11.116.1 SC 108.220.

166. For example, the *ovariolus*, given at *CGL* 5.636.17 as the pimp's "boy" or "slave" ("ovar-

details are not simply the stuff of literary fantasy is suggested by the evidence of other cultures. For example, a brothel in nineteenth-century St. Paul, Minnesota, might sport cooks, maids, porters, scouts, and a wine steward.[167] Food and drink were served to customers as well as to the prostitutes themselves, especially when the brothel doubled as a tavern.[168] Otherwise, such items might be brought in from a nearby establishment.

A few sources provide a glimpse of various aspects of brothel operations. In Petronius, a prostitute charges two outsiders a small fee (one *as*) for the use of a booth or small room (*cella*) for sexual purposes, which suggests that brothels catered to different types of walk-in business, much like inexpensive hotels of the present day.[169] When, in Juvenal, a pimp dismisses "his girls" ("*suas puellas*") from the brothel after a night's work, we might infer that they—or their owners—are independent contractors leasing space.[170]

A tantalizingly fragmentary text from Egypt indicates just how complex running a brothel might have been.[171] This document appears to be a denunciation made against two pimps who had leased brothels in the city to other, local pimps, referred to as *hoi epidēmountes autoi pornoboskoi*. These men, hav-

---

iolus: puer lenonis sic dicitur"), and whose precise function is unclear: see Adams, "Words" (1983) 321. Musicians are attested in comedy, though were probably rare, if they are not the projections of a Hellenizing fantasy. See, for example, Ter. *Phormio* 80–84, 109, who has a cithern player as the slave of a pimp. Comedy also suggests the possibility of an elaborate massage, complete with oil or perfume, but this seems as likely for most brothels as musical accompaniment. See Plaut. *Poen.* 220, 231, 701–3. It is easier to postulate that most massage was performed by the prostitutes themselves and was explicitly sexual in nature: see n. 70 above. Brothels had all-purpose servants as well: see Brock and Harvey, *Holy Women* (1987) 48, 55–56.

167. See Best, *Controlling Vice* (1998) 63. See also Harsin, *Policing Prostitution* (1985) 287–88; Hill, *Their Sisters' Keepers* (1993) 223; Seigle, *Yoshiwara* (1993) 176; Hershatter, *Dangerous Pleasures* (1997) 77–79, 114.

168. On liquor and food, see n. 167. For late antiquity, see *Vita Sanctae Mariae* 7 PL 73.656; Brock and Harvey, *Holy Women* (1985) 31, 33, 37, 48; Leontsini, *Prostitution* (1989) 106, 165. See Rossiaud's statement on the medieval French brothel, "[t]he managers found the kitchen nearly as profitable as the bedroom": *Medieval Prostitution* (1988) 5.

169. Petron. 8. Here Ascyltos is assaulted by the *pater familiae*, who has led him to the brothel. We cannot know for sure if the rate is for an entire night, as Frier, "Rental Market" (1977) 34, suggests, but in any case the point of the transaction is clear. This is another confirmation of the general identification of brothels with the site and function of lower-class lodgings. On the modern link between room rental and informal prostitution, see Gilfoyle, *City of Eros* (1992) 55–56.

170. Iuv. 6.127. That is, if we do not take "suas" to signify that he owns them. Nonresident status may also mean that they at least occasionally solicited customers outside the brothel: see Karras, *Common Women* (1996) 38, 46–47, for suggestive parallels from medieval England.

171. *PSI* 1055a: probably from Arsinoe, and from a period before A.D. 265, according to the editors. See Heyl, *Madam* (1979) 8, for a modern parallel.

ing paid four times the normal rent, claim to have earned little in return.[172] The dispute also centers around the unauthorized sale of a slave woman. The leasing out of a number of brothels by one group of pimps to another,[173] as well as the dispute over a productive asset, suggests a fairly sophisticated arrangement, and one that confirms the argument, made above, that investment arrangements in prostitution might be complex. It also suggests that, notwithstanding the objections of the two complainants in this case, prostitution was a profitable enterprise for those with capital to invest.

I must concede, however, that the sources are not very informative on the subject of brothel operation, in large part because their purpose was anything but a close description of this phenomenon. This is true even in the case of the most extensive treatments of brothels in the literary sources.[174] To take just one example, when Apuleius wants to depict Herennius Rufinus as his wife's pimp, he describes the man's house as a brothel, which means of course that the design elements more closely correspond to the layout of an upper-class *domus* than to a *lupanar*.

There is general agreement that the prostitute worked in a booth or small room (*cella*) within the brothel,[175] its entrance marked by a patchwork curtain (*cento*) and the booth itself closed by a door (*ostium*),[176] above or next to which a small notice advertising her price (*titulus*) was sometimes placed.[177] These arrangements did not, it seems, guarantee a great deal of privacy.[178] Nor did customers have a great expectation of privacy to judge from an epigram of

---

172. I follow the editors of *PSI*, who view the local pimps as the aggrieved party. Admittedly the text is difficult.

173. The suggestion of Johnson, *Survey* 2 (1936) 537, that the text refers to the prostitute tax is not persuasive.

174. See Sen. *Contr.* 1.2; Petron. 7–8; Iuv. 115–32; Apul. *Apol.* 75; *Hist. Ap. Tyr.* 33–36. See also [Verg.] *Copa*, which, given my definition of brothel, should be included in this group of sources.

175. Sen. *Contr.* 1.2.1, 5; Petron. 8; Iuv. 6.122, 128; *Hist. Ap. Tyr.* 33. See also the discussion of cribs in chap. 7. For a glimpse of a *cella* in the Purpose-Built Brothel, see fig. 6.

176. On the curtain, see Petron. 7; Mart. 1.34.5, 11.45.3; Iuv. 6.121. Door: Ov. *Am.* 3.14.9–10; Mart. 1.34.5, 11.45.3 (with a bolt); *Hist. Ap. Tyr.* 34. Many brothels perhaps had either a curtain or a door.

177. See Sen. *Contr.* 1.2.1, 5, 7; Petron. 7; Mart. 11.45.1; Iuv. 6.123 (with schol.); Tert. *Spect.* 17.3 CCSL 1.242 (who, evidently referring to a recital of the *titulus* at the Floralia, suggestively calls it an *elogium*); *Hist. Ap. Tyr.* 33.

178. For evidence that seems to contradict this, see the rhetorical assertion of the modesty of prostitutes: Ov. *Am.* 3.14.9–10; Val. Max. 3.5.4; Sen. *Nat. Quaest.* 1.16.6; Mart. 1.34, 11.45; Iuv. 6.014–16, 11.171–73. These assertions prove nothing about privacy in brothels in my view. We may compare the social atmosphere that prevailed in public latrines: see, for example, Barattolo and Romaldi, "Impianti igienici" (2000) 265.

Martial, in which he chides a man for seeking it.[179] Prostitutes inside the brothel were often nude (or at most scantily clad),[180] and payment was demanded up front.[181] A variety of sexual services might be offered, as discussed in the following section on prices.

The sources describe the brothel itself as a filthy place, though more in a tone of moral censure than as a literal depiction of uncleanliness. In other words, descriptions of brothels tend to reflect upper-class prejudice more than objective reality. This hardly means of course that the Roman brothel was typically a clean, well-lit place. In addition to appearing dirty, dark, and smoky, brothels were associated with violence and seem to have generated an atmosphere of criminality about them, as we shall see in chapter 3.

PRICES

Like many goods and services available to purchasers in the Roman economy, sex often came with a price and was bought with cash.[182] The availability of coins throughout the Empire, even in some rural areas, was essential to the business of prostitution.[183] The towns enjoyed a fully monetized economy, to judge from the evidence of Apuleius.[184] The evidence from country estates, where it exists in abundance, namely Egypt, suggests that much of the rural economy was monetized as well.[185]

Pimps often determined the prices prostitutes charged their customers, particularly when the prostitutes were slaves.[186] As mentioned previously,

---

179. Mart. 11.45.

180. See chap. 3.

181. Sen. *Contr.* 1.2 *thema*, 2, 7, 20; Petron. 8; Iuv. 6.125; *Hist. Ap. Tyr.* 34; cf. Labeo-Marcel.-Ulp. D. 12.5.4.3. It is difficult to find an example of prostitution in any culture where this practice does not hold true.

182. See the evidence in Temin, "Market Economy" (2001) 173.

183. On the monetization of the Roman economy—potentially of great importance for the economic profile and extent of prostitution—see Harris, "Problems" (1993) 20; Temin, "Market Economy" (2001) 174, 177. The matter is controversial. For a contrary view, see Garnsey and Saller, *Roman Empire* (1987) 46–51; Duncan-Jones, *Structure and Scale* (1990) 48–58, 187–98; Duncan-Jones, *Money and Government* (1994) 3, 20–22.

184. Millar, "World of the *Golden Ass*" (1981) 72.

185. Rathbone, *Economic Rationalism* (1990) esp. 327–30. De Ligt, "Demand, Supply, Distribution 1" (1990): 33–43, stresses the great diversity in the level of monetization among rural regions, as well as the coexistence in many places of cash and barter.

186. There is, of course, no way of knowing how many prostitutes were slaves: see below in the text.

sometimes the woman's name and her price were placed together above or adjacent to the door to her *cella* in an epigraph called a *titulus*.[187] Other types of informal advertising appear in the Pompeian inscriptions, and there is even evidence prices were sometimes negotiated.

Sources dating, with few exceptions, from the early imperial period give a range of prices for sexual services, from .25 *as* to 16 *asses* and perhaps more. I omit amounts said to be given to prostitutes (or perhaps adulteresses) that appear to be too high to be prices for a sexual act or even a short period of sexual activity, such as the HS 100,000 said by Martial to be squandered by a lover on Leda.[188] Some of the other fees cited by the epigrammatist should inspire caution as well. The details of the poet's downward spiraling negotiations with Galla are too fantastic to be reckoned as actual prices for a prostitute's services, at least until the end of the transaction. They suggest the device, familiar from both literature and law, of transforming an adulteress into a prostitute. They also indicate that negotiating prices was a reasonably common practice.[189] The 2 *aurei* (= 50 denarii) he cites as Galla's standard fee should be ranked in the same category.[190] The *amphora* of wine requested by Phyllis after a night of lovemaking is a gift, and perhaps figures in a similar transformation, or its reverse.[191] Other examples might easily be added.[192]

This does not mean that the epigraphic evidence is free from problems. I am especially suspicious of prostitute graffiti in which a prostitute purportedly praises a client's sexual prowess.[193] But while projections of male fantasy in their content, these graffiti do posit the existence of actual clients and actual prostitutes. Though only a few of the readings given in the list below are explicitly rated as unclear, we cannot assume the rest are without error.[194] Many are no longer available to be verified and those that survive are of course subject to revision. Their value as evidence of *prices* is discussed below.

---

187. For the *titulus* and its functions, see above in the text.

188. Mart. 2.63.1–2.

189. Mart. 10.75.

190. Mart. 9.4.1.

191. Mart. 12.65. The view that the relationship is one of prostitute and customer cannot be utterly excluded however. See Ramirez Sabada, "Prostitución" (1985) 228; Stumpp, *Prostitution* (1998) 220.

192. See the discussion in Ramirez Sabada, "Prostitución" (1985) 227 n. 4.

193. Cf. DeFelice, *Roman Hospitality* (2001) 98, with n. 306.

194. Though not impossible as a source for the prices of prostitutes, *CIL* 4.8565 seems more likely to record the (partial?) wages of workmen.

The known examples are weighted toward the lower end of the scale, with 38 that are 2.5 *asses* and lower, 28 that are 3 *asses* and above.

.25 *as* (not a real price?): 3 examples[195]
1 *as:* 6 examples[196]
2 *asses:* 25 examples[197]
2.5 *asses:* 4 examples[198]
3 *asses:* 5 examples[199]
4 *asses:* 7 examples[200]
5 *asses:* 4 examples[201]
7 *asses:* 1 example[202]
8 *asses:* 3 examples[203]
9 *asses:* 1 example[204]
10 *asses:* 2 examples[205]
16 *asses:* 3 examples[206]
23 *asses:* 1 example[207]
32 *asses:* 1 example[208]

---

195. All three examples allude to the same person, Clodia Metelli, as a *quadrantaria* ("quarter-*as* whore"): Cic. *Cael.* 62; Cael. *apud* Quint. *IO* 8.6.53; Plut. *Cic.* 29.4. The hostile tone of these sources, the extremely low price (compared with the other prices attested) implied for Clodia's services, and the fact that .25 *as* was the price of admission to the men's baths all prompt the conclusion that this price is not genuine, but rather is invective: see below in the text.

196. *CIL* 4.5408 (fellatio), 8248; Mart. 1.103.10 (cheap sex); Iuv. 6.125 (uncertain); *Anth. Lat.* 794.46R (insult); Firm. Mat. *Err.* 10 *CSEL* 2.91 (mythological). The *as* cited at Petron. 8 is the price for a room in a brothel, not for a sexual act. All the same it does seem to confirm the lower end of the spectrum as represented above all by Pompeian prices. On this price, see Frier, "Rental Market" (1977) 34.

197. *CIL* 4.1374 (reading uncertain), 1969 (fellatio), 2028 + p. 704 (fellatio), 3964 (reading uncertain), 3999 (cunnilingus), 4023, 4024, 4150 (bis), 4441, 4592, 5105, 5206 (reading uncertain), 5338, 5345, 5372, 7068, 8185 (bis: fellatio; reading uncertain), 8394, 8454, 8465a, 8465b (fellatio; reading uncertain), 8511; Mart. 2.53.7 (cheap sex).

198. *CIL* 4.4150, 7764 (bis), 8224.

199. *CIL* 4.3964 (bis, including a price evidently labeled "*commune*") 4259, 4439, 8160 (fellatio).

200. *CIL* 4.3964 (bis), 4259, 4277, 8939 (cunnilingus), 8940 (cunnilingus, the same person as 8939), 10078a.

201. *CIL* 4.2450 (dated to 3 B.C.), 4025, 5048 (with 10004, uncertain), 5204.

202. *CIL* 4.10033c (uncertain).

203. *CIL* 4.5203, 8187; 9.2689 (= *ILS* 7478), from Aesernia.

204. *CIL* 4.5127.

205. *CIL* 4.4259, 8357b.

206. *CIL* 4.1751, 2193 (1 denarius); Mart. 2.51 (1 denarius).

207. *CIL* 4.8034.

208. Mart. 9.32.3 (2 denarii). Possibly the sum, the equivalent of 32 *asses*, refers to a gift or to an arrangement that involves more than a single sexual act: see esp. vv. 4–6.

These prices may be compared with the sample rates of 16 *asses* (1 denarius), 8 *asses*, and 6 *asses* found in the Palmyrene tax document, a bilingual inscription (Greek and Palmyrene) dating to A.D. 137. In this document, the town council clarifies the local tax structure (including both import/export duties and a variety of local taxes, including the one imposed on prostitutes) and sets up a grievance procedure to manage disputes between taxpayers and local tax contractors.[209]

Before turning to an analysis of the prices listed above, an important objection, especially to some of the lower amounts, must be considered. Do they represent actual prices or are they intended to defame a woman's character?[210] Prices from antiquity, above all those reported in the literature, are often quite incredible, as we have seen in relation to Martial.[211] It is useful to mention the evidence for prostitutes' fees from ancient Athens, which comes mostly from Comedy. Here, prices are exaggerated upwards and downwards for various comic purposes, though 3 obols does appear to be typical.[212]

Despite these difficulties, the prices set forth above seem plausible for the most part. The references to the *quadrantaria* ("woman who charges one-quarter *as*") are perhaps sheer insults, insofar as the "price" of one-quarter *as* falls far below the attested range. In my view, it is the only one we can safely ascribe to mere defamation, although even this argument does not guarantee it could not be a price for a low (perhaps older) prostitute. Thus I include them on the list.

Some of the lower prices in inscriptions refer to fellatio, a service perhaps provided at a discount over vaginal intercourse.[213] Other prices occur in con-

---

209. *IGR* 3.1056-*OGIS* 2.629-*CIS* 2.3.3913. On the prostitute tax, see McGinn, *Prostitution, Sexuality, and the Law* (1998) chap. 7 (esp. 282–86, for this evidence from Palmgra).

210. For brief discussion of this question, see McGinn, *Prostitution, Sexuality, and the Law* (1998) 267 n. 132. Add Eichenauer, *Arbeitswelt* (1988) 121; Richlin, *Garden of Priapus* (1992) 81–83; Herrmann-Otto, *Ex Ancilla Natus* (1994) 344 n. 9 (345); Savunen, *Women* (1997) 109–10, 113; Cantarella, *Pompei* (1998) 92, 113.

211. See Scheidel, "Finances, Figures, and Fiction" (1996) who finds reason to distrust not only figures derived from fiction but from historical and antiquarian accounts as well. Of the evidence for relatively large sums he examines, he is able to reject ninety to one-hundred percent. See also Scheidel, "Progress and Problems" (2001) 49, 71.

212. See Loomis, *Wages* (1998) 166–85, who is compelled to reject nearly three-quarters of his sources as inadequate. He concludes that three obols was the fee for the average prostitute and that there is no evidence the fee changed over the classical period. This conclusion seems justified given the citation of this price by Procop. *Anec.* 17.5 in the mid-sixth century. Loomis puts it, as well as others he has collected from non-Athenian Greek literature, in a helpful list (see 334–35). Of those from the period under study, none seem, at first glance, sufficiently reliable for our purposes, though I will make an attempt below to make sense of some of them.

213. 3 *asses*: *CIL* 4.8160; 2 *asses*: 1969, 8185 (probable), 8465b (possible); 1 *as*: 5408. See also Mart. 9.4. The lower price might be explained by the advantage to the prostitute of avoiding pregnancy. For this reason, a client might also be charged less for masturbation by a prostitute,

texts that suggest advertising, not insult.[214] When the name of a prostitute does not appear, abuse seems unlikely.[215] The precision implied by the price of two and one-half *asses* seems odd as a slur. We cannot be confident, of course, that none of these prices were meant to defame, but it is difficult to determine which ones, if any, should be understood in this way, except for the insult, which even so could be construed as a realistic price for some prostitutes, delivered against Clodia Metelli.

All the same, there is some reason to regard 1 *as* as an atypically low price,[216] though even this might have been asked by older or less attractive prostitutes. Two *asses* may be accepted as a common base rate for inexpensive prostitutes, at least at Pompeii.[217] Given the nature of the evidence, these were all, or almost all, streetwalkers and brothel prostitutes. The evidence from Palmyra gives two levels below a denarius, 6 and 8 *asses*, that can be understood as typical prices for that city. It is not safe to conclude from this evidence that sex was generally cheaper in Pompeii, however, than in many other parts of the Empire.

The generally lower Pompeian prices may not be typical for all prostitutes there, but only for those prostitutes whose activity was advertised (or who in some cases were targets of abuse).[218] The upper end of the scale should be defined as 16 *asses*, whatever exceptions exist. The famous hotel account from Aesernia is obviously meant to parody the real thing.[219] But the point of the

---

though no data are available on prices charged for this service: see Catull. 58; Sen. *Contr.* 1.2.21, 23. Cunnilingus is another service in the same category: see notes 197 and 200 for evidence.

214. A price might appear with the phrase "moribus bellis," or one of its variants, which seems to be a recommendation. See, for example, *CIL* 4.4024, 4592. Cf. 2202, which does not contain a price, but only the name of the prostitute with this phrase, and 5127, where the phrase appears with a price of 9 *asses*. See also n. 215.

215. See *CIL* 4.5372, an apparent advertisement, which simply reads "sum tua ae(ris) a(ssi-bus) II ("I'm yours for two *asses*"). Two passages of Martial are apposite here. The first criticizes a man who is wealthy but miserly and contents himself with *asse Venus* (1.103.10). In the second, the joys of the simple life are said to include *plebeia Venus*, which costs two 2 *asses* (2.53.7).

216. At both Iuv. 6.125 (evidently) and *Anth. Lat.* 794.46R a woman, who is not really a prostitute but is identified as one so as to criticize her promiscuity, is accused of selling herself for 1 *as*, much as Clodia is described as a *quadrantaria*. So also Venus at Firm. Mat. *Err.* 10 CSEL 2.91. As for the other three examples, one forms part of the poet's charge of meanness against the client (Mart. 1.103.10), while another advertises fellatio (*CIL* 4.5408); the third simply has the prostitute's name and the price (Prima: *CIL* 4.8248).

217. Mart. 2.53.7 suggests that 2 *asses* was a very low price for Rome.

218. Cf. Flemming, "*Quae Corpore*" (1999) 48, for whom "2 asses is the clear mode," across the Empire.

219. *CIL* 9.2689 (= *ILS* 7478). Cf. Viti, "Insegna" (1989) who inclines to take this evidence very seriously indeed.

joke seems to depend on taking 8 *asses* as a realistic high-end price for a prostitute and a room. This seems credible for a country inn in Italy, especially
given the range of prices at Pompeii. One place where the price scale for sex
may have been somewhat higher is at Rome, for which our evidence is even
scantier. We can safely assume that prices in general were higher there than
elsewhere in the Empire.[220]

Of course, it is conceivable that prices fluctuated, as they did with other
commodities, so that a range of "spot" prices cropped up in different areas of
the empire.[221] The Romans themselves were acutely aware of this latter phenomenon:[222]

> Gaius (9 *ad edictum prov.*) D. 13.4.3.
> Ideo in arbitrium iudicis refertur haec actio, quia scimus, quam varia
> sint pretia rerum per singulas civitates regionesque, maxime vini olei
> frumenti: pecuniarum quoque licet videatur una et eadem potestas
> ubique esse, tamen aliis locis facilius et levibus usuris inveniuntur, aliis
> difficilius et gravibus usuris.

> *On that account this action (the* actio arbitraria) *is left to the discretion of
> the finder of fact, because we are aware of how varied the prices of com-
> modities are in different cities and areas, especially (the prices) of wine, oil,
> and grain. Although money too may seem to have one and the same pur-
> chasing power everywhere, nevertheless it is raised more easily and at lower
> interest in some places, with greater difficulty and at higher interest in others.*

Because of this variation in prices, we cannot use a comparison of data from
Italy, for example, to construct hypothetical prices for sex elsewhere on the
basis of the prevailing costs of goods and services. Roman Egypt, where our
documentary evidence for prices and all else is the most abundant, unfortunately does not preserve any clear data on the prices charged by prostitutes.[223]

---

220. See Hopkins, "Rome, Taxes, Rents and Trade" (1995/1996) 58–59; Prell, *Armut* (1997)
180 (cf. 152); Hopkins, "Rents, Taxes, Trade" (2000) 261.

221. See Horden and Purcell, *Corrupting Sea* (2000) 152.

222. See Andreau, "Deux études" (1997) 112–16, on the economic context for this passage.

223. We cannot, without great difficulty, derive prices from the amounts given for tax payments by prostitutes: see McGinn, *Prostitution, Sexuality, and the Law* (1998) 278–79. For information on prices from Roman Egypt, see Drexhage, *Preise* (1991); Rathbone, "Prices and Price
Formation" (1997).

A similar point holds for Roman Britain, where some price information, especially from Vindolanda ca. A.D. 100, is available.[224]

The argument could be made that the particular conditions of post-earthquake (A.D. 62–79) Pompeii encouraged a flood of prostitutes that depressed prices in that city in that period, but this seems to press the evidence very hard indeed.[225] In fact, it may be possible to use these prices to "rescue" some of the numbers given by the sources in Greek currency from suspicion of literary invention and vice versa. On the traditional exchange rate of 1 denarius to the tetradrachm, 3 obols are equal to 2 *asses*.[226] As noted above, the typical Greek price was precisely 3 obols. In this light, the figure of 2 obols or the like given in our sources, chiefly Plautus, does not seem utterly unrealistic.[227] To be plain, I am attempting to use two sets of uncertain data to shore each other up, but the result seems reasonable enough.

This evidence, taken with the ceiling of 1 denarius placed on the per diem Caligulan tax rate linked to the price of sex,[228] suggests that most prostitutes in the Roman Empire charged less than 1 denarius, and many asked significantly less. We can speculate that prices above that amount (see, e.g., the last two items on the price list) were given for more than a single sexual act, that is, for a night spent with the prostitute.[229] This practice is attested in various cultures at different periods ranging from ancient Greece to modern-day Nevada (where the management of brothels frowns upon and tends to restrict the practice because of its implicit opportunity costs).[230]

The factors that help determine the prices charged by prostitutes are for most cultures, in a word, understudied. Common sense suggests that a prosti-

---

224. See Drexhage, "Preise" (1997), who calculates the subsistence level in Roman Britain as c. 8 denarii per month.

225. For discussion of the problem of post-earthquake Pompeii, see chap. 6.

226. See McGinn, *Prostitution, Sexuality, and the Law* (1998) 278.

227. See the sources collected in Loomis, *Wages* (1998) 334–35. We might even add the title of a play by Plautus, "*Trinummus*" (= 3 obols?), to the list of sources. If the title does indeed represent a price for sex, it was probably not as high as HS 3, as proposed by Krenkel, "Prostitution" (1978) 54.

228. See McGinn, *Prostitution, Sexuality, and the Law* (1998) chap. 7.

229. So Mart. 12.65.1 in my view suggests a potential identification of Phyllis as a prostitute, in contrast perhaps with her "actual" status (i.e., a "respectable" woman is cast in the role of a prostitute). See also Plaut. *Amph.* 288; Petron. 81.5. The evidence for contracts for the hire of prostitutes in a long-term capacity is not as strong as assumed by Herter, "Soziologie" (1960) 81.

230. See Magoulias, "Bathhouse" (1971) 246; Rossiaud, "Prostitution" (1976/1978) 20; Prus and Irini, *Hookers* (1980) 57; Otis, *Prostitution* (1985) 82; Reynolds, *Economics of Prostitution* (1986) 115; Leontsini, *Prostitution* (1989) 164–65; Schuster, *Frauenhaus* (1992) 69–70, 113–14; Sturdevant and Stoltzfus, *Let the Good Times Roll* (1992) 177, 192; Schuster, *Freien Frauen* (1995) 146–47; Loomis, *Wages* (1998) 173, 182.

tute's age, appearance, and skills all play a role here, but any statement more concrete than this is in the vast majority of cases sheer speculation. The point holds, no matter whether the pimp or brothel sets the price or the prostitute is allowed to negotiate with the customer.[231] Speculation, even informed speculation, about the role of market forces, subsistence levels, and similar economic factors may, in some areas of the modern world at least, be compelled to take second place to hypotheses suggesting a link between the price of drugs and the price of sex.[232] I am not suggesting here that the "world" of prostitution is utterly irrational, but that its rationality must be qualified as different from that pertaining to other areas of social and economic life, a point to be pursued further below.

The lower prices do seem very modest. Two *asses* is, after all, the price of a loaf of bread.[233] But in order to understand better the economic position of prostitutes and derive an idea of their economic value to their exploiters, their earnings-potential must be considered in a more realistic manner. This potential is determined both by the prices charged and by the number of sexual contacts per day. There is no direct evidence from antiquity on this last point, but comparative data at least suggest possibilities. One important principle to emerge is that more expensive prostitutes tend to see fewer customers while less expensive prostitutes see more.

- In the medieval German brothel, prostitutes were required to service a minimum of 3 clients each day on the 20 days a month that they worked.[234]
- In nineteenth-century Nevada, prostitutes of the "middle rank" saw one customer per night and working-class prostitutes saw 3 or 4. No estimate is given for a category of prostitutes below that level.[235]
- In late nineteenth/early twentieth-century New York, 30 customers per evening are recorded, as well as ranges of 2–4, 1–10 (and sometimes 20), and 100 per week.[236]
- In late nineteenth/early twentieth-century Russia, streetwalkers had

---

231. Hart, *Buying and Selling* (1998) 108–9, 118, 128, 165, examines some aspects of the latter phenomenon.

232. See Høigård and Finstad, *Backstreets* (1992) 42–43, for a discussion of the principle "one fuck = one fix."

233. So remarks Duncan-Jones, *Economy²* (1982) 246. Cf. Duncan-Jones's # 1176e (at 209).

234. Schuster, *Freien Frauen* (1995) 152.

235. Goldman, *Gold Diggers* (1981) 76.

236. Gilfoyle, *City of Eros* (1992) 415, 459 n. 5; Hill, *Their Sisters' Keepers* (1993) 226–27.

difficulty finding more than two clients a night, while brothel prostitutes serviced 10–15 customers, or under certain circumstances, 30–40, 40–50, and even 60–70.[237]

- In late nineteenth/early twentieth-century America, high-priced prostitutes saw 4–5 customers a day and the lowest crib prostitutes saw as many as 13–30 customers.[238]

- In early twentieth-century Paris, a contemporary estimate yielded 7 or 8 clients each day for prostitutes working in regulated brothels, though this is now thought to be too low.[239]

- In early-twentieth-century Buenos Aires, a successful prostitute might have had 300 customers each week on average.[240]

- In 1924 Tokyo, prostitutes had on average 2.5 customers each day and that number declined to under 2 in the years that followed. Wartime "comfort women" might be compelled to service 30 men each day.[241]

- A 1948 Chinese survey of 500 prostitutes found they saw between 10 and 30 or even up to 60 customers each month, while reformers estimated they saw between 4 and 20 customers each night.[242]

- In 1970s "Middleburg," a fictional name for a U.S. city, the average number of clients was 6.2 per night for an average work week of 4.5 nights.[243]

- Twenty per night is given as a general estimate by a prostitute servicing American military personnel in Korea.[244]

- In late twentieth-century Calcutta, estimates range from 12–29 each week and 3–4 each day, not allowing for seasonal variations.[245]

---

237. Bernstein, *Sonia's Daughters* (1995) 149.

238. Rosen, *Sisterhood* (1982) 98, with references. This estimate receives rough confirmation elsewhere in Rosen's book. Included are anecdotes about the rapidity of sexual encounters for lower-priced prostitutes: Rosen, 92, 95–96 (one estimate is three minutes). There are also descriptions of the long lines outside the doors of crib prostitutes and the turnover in brothels housing Chinese and African-American prostitutes: Rosen, 94. Inhabitants of a one-dollar house (considered middle rank by Rosen, 86–87) are said to earn eighteen dollars per day: Rosen, 76.

239. Corbin, *Women for Hire* (1990) 81 (cf. 184: 2–4 for prostitutes in a *maison de rendez-vous*).

240. Guy, *Sex* (1990) 110.

241. Garon, *Molding Japanese Minds* (1996) 96, 111.

242. Hershatter, *Dangerous Pleasures* (1997) 49.

243. Decker, *Prostitution* (1979) 14, 166.

244. Sturdevant and Stoltzfus, *Let the Good Times Roll* (1992) 228.

245. Sleightholme and Sinha, *Guilty Without Trial* (1996) 85.

- In late twentieth-century Amsterdam, Birmingham (England), and New York, estimates by prostitutes range from 3 (sometimes 5–6), to 5–9 to 10–15 each day.[246]
- In 1990s "Marito," a fictional name for a Spanish city, the average is 2 clients per day.[247]

Since not all of this information is equally reliable, and the conditions of employment—especially the degree of compulsion—must vary considerably, we cannot apply these figures in any straightforward sense to the Roman context. They can only suggest ranges of possible numbers of clients. If we apply these figures to our price data in a conservative fashion, using, say, 5 sexual encounters for prostitutes who charge 8 to 10 *asses* and 15 to 20 encounters for those who charge only 2, the earnings-potential is HS 10 to 12.5 per diem for high-priced prostitutes and HS 7.5 to 10 for lower-priced prostitutes.[248] These sums are, of course, intended to serve as no more than very rough suggestions; free prostitutes may have worked less, and slave prostitutes may have been made to work more, regardless of the potential consequences for health.[249] For many prostitutes, the higher daily averages may have been unsustainable over time for medical and ultimately economic reasons. We cannot determine if even slave prostitutes worked all day every day. While some modern evidence suggests that not many prostitutes do work that much, the question of days and hours worked is usually ignored in the reporting of average numbers of clients in the evidence just given. The calculations made for Roman prostitutes serve simply to provide a very rough idea of earnings-potential. The results illustrate the economic context of the evidence that Roman prostitution was a profitable business for the wealthy and (given the choices, as we shall see) an attractive if illusorily remunerative employment option for the free poor.[250]

In order to get an idea of what these earnings might have signified in terms of living standards, the figures should be compared with the HS 3 (i.e., 3 ses-

---

246. Goodall, *Comfort of Sin* (1995) 36; Chapkis, *Live Sex Acts* (1997) 61, 90, 115.

247. Hart, *Buying and Selling* (1998) 33.

248. The conversion depends on the rate of 16 *asses* = 4 sesterces = 1 denarius. Note that the abbreviation HS = sesterces.

249. The health problems of modern prostitutes, especially those working in conditions of relatively great compulsion, are understudied. Some aspects of these problems are explored in McGinn, *Roman Prostitution* (forthcoming).

250. Cf. Clarke, *Looking at Lovemaking* (1998) 174, who bases his conclusion that prostitution was not a profitable business on the price range attested for Pompeii.

terces) that Duncan-Jones suggests was the daily wage rate for male laborers in
the city of Rome in the late Republic and with the HS 2 that was the daily rate
for an agricultural worker and (perhaps one) team of oxen in the second century B.C.[251] We have some different, at times slightly higher figures from the
early Empire, where the daily amount of 1 denarius (= HS 4) emerges, though
not always without ambiguity, from Seneca,[252] Pompeian epigraphy,[253] and
the New Testament.[254] Here we do well to consider the pay of some privileged
workers as well, who were also among the more likely clients of prostitutes, the
legionary soldiers of the early Principate, who were paid at the rate of HS 2.5
per diem, amounting to HS 900 each year, from which evidently was deducted
HS 600–700 for fodder, food, and clothing.[255]

This left soldiers with an income of less than 1 HS *per diem* to spend at
their discretion in the context of steady work, and some fixed costs covered.
They also had extraordinary, if fairly regular, opportunities for supplementing
that income, such as shaking down pimps and prostitutes while collecting the
Caligulan tax. A fair comparison with the condition of prostitutes, however,
demands that we take such "outside" sources of income into account. And the
tables could be turned in that exploitation could cut both ways between prostitute and client. While prices may vary, one aim of the prostitute in many
societies has simply been to separate as much money from the client as possible, another factor that renders precise comparison difficult.[256]

All the same, while the individual soldier lived well, his rate of pay, after
deductions were made, would not have been sufficient to support a family.[257]
Some soldiers were more privileged than others of course, with the Praetorians

---

251. The sources are Cic. *Rosc. Com.* 28–29 and Cato *Agr.* 22.3. Duncan-Jones, *Economy*[2]
(1982) 54, estimates that the rural pay rate was not more than half the urban pay. On the Cicero
passage, see also Axer, "Prezzi" (1979).

252. For the (evidently) monthly wage of five denarii plus five *modii* of grain given a slave, see
Sen. *Ep.* 80.7. The value breaks down to about one denarius per day, according to Prell, *Armut*
(1997) 173 (cf. 187), which may be a bit high as an estimate (see below in the notes). See the
other literary evidence surveyed by Prell, 174.

253. Figures of five *asses* and one denarius (plus bread) are suggested by two Pompeian
inscriptions (*CIL* 4.4000, 6877). See the other epigraphic evidence showing a daily range of HS
one to six and one-half cited by Prell, *Armut* (1997) 173.

254. The daily pay of one denarius given the vineyard workers according to Matt. 20.2 is perhaps a reflection of the cost of this kind of specialized labor, if it is not an exaggeration meant to
help convey the point of the parable.

255. See Tac. *Ann.* 1.17.4–6 with Phang, *Marriage of Roman Soldiers* (2001)182.

256. The point is made well by Butler, *Daughters of Joy* (1985) 56. See also the data examined
in the section "Operation of Brothels."

257. So Phang, *Marriage of Roman Soldiers* (2001) 182–83.

(elite soldiers stationed in Rome and responsible for the security of the Emperor's person) receiving more and the auxiliaries perhaps less.[258]

Also of relevance are data for subsistence allowances: HS 10–20/month during the late Republic for grain distributions, HS 30–40/month for an urban slave in the first century A.D., and HS 10–20/month for children in various alimentary schemes.[259] Minimal urban rent costs have been suggested of HS 360 and 500/year,[260] and thus from HS 30–48/month. More recently, Raymond Goldsmith has estimated that total national expenditures per head were around HS 380 (at least in Italy), while the average of monetary or attributed income per recipient was near HS 1000, which, when discounted for dependents, yields a total income per person of HS 380 (+/–15%, i.e., a range from HS 320–440).[261] Bruce Frier uses juristic data on subsistence annuities to show that these fall in the range of HS 376–600. Frier points out that since these annuities benefited adults, it is logical that they exceeded average annual income, while the annual values for the alimentary programs benefiting children (HS 120–240) would have been lower.[262] The annual cost of subsistence rations has been calculated by Willem Jongman—evidently for adult males—at HS 115.[263] Some anecdotal evidence might be cited in this context, such as Seneca's assumption that 2 *asses* worth of food was a feast for many poor persons and slaves.[264]

Of particular interest here is the possibility that even low-priced prostitutes earned more than two or three times the wages of unskilled male urban laborers.[265] The subsistence data are introduced in order to suggest that many prostitutes, at least independent prostitutes, may have lived far better than

258. See Phang, *Marriage of Roman Soldiers* (2001) 183–85.

259. Alimentary schemes were foundations designed to provide an allowance to feed children. The information is set forth in Duncan-Jones, *Economy*[2] (1982), 208. Note the possibility of a much higher rate of support for Pliny's freedmen: HS 70/mo. (Duncan-Jones # 1169 [at 208]). For the rate 1 *modius* = HS 2–4, see Duncan-Jones, 145–46.

260. See the discussion in Frier, "Rental Market" (1977) 34.

261. Goldsmith, "Estimate" (1984) 268–269, 272. Cf. Goldsmith, *Systems* (1989) esp. 35–36.

262. Frier, "Annuities" (1993) 229. Mrozek, *Lohnarbeit* (1989) 111–12, estimates that a comfortable level of subsistence costs was HS 2 at Pompeii, and 4 at Rome in the early Empire.

263. Jongman, *Economy* (1988) 195 n. 2.

264. Sen. *Ep.* 18.7–8. See the discussion in Prell, *Armut* (1997) 182–83, on basic living costs.

265. Of course, we have no information on wages for unskilled female laborers; given the limited opportunities for such work, wages may have been considerably lower (see in the section on "Recruitment"). Rosen, *Sisterhood* (1982) 83–84, points out that in turn-of-the-century America a woman working merely as a waitress in a milieu catering to prostitution might easily make three times the wages of a domestic worker. The standard wage for a shop girl or factory worker was under $7/week, while prostitutes are said to have made $30–$50 in various cities and sometimes much more: Rosen, 147–48.

these laborers. If a prostitute worked for a pimp, much of her earnings may have gone to him, or perhaps all of them in the case of many or most slave prostitutes.[266] In return, the prostitute received basic necessities: food, shelter, clothing.[267] But such maintenance costs pale beside the possibilities for profits, even when the cost of purchasing slaves is taken into account.

If we shift our focus from the interest of the exploiters to that of the prostitutes themselves, however, a grimmer picture begins to emerge. Common sense suggests that low-priced prostitutes, as advantaged as they appear to have been relative to many types of workers, found it difficult to conserve an adequate amount of money as a bulwark against slow periods or what seems to have been an inevitable falloff in earnings with the passage of time.[268] In many cultures, even better-situated prostitutes find themselves laboring under what might be described as "the illusion of profitability."[269] Prostitution does typically function as a cash-rich business with few—in strictly economic terms—start-up or marginal costs to the individual seller. It therefore offers the prospect of a great deal of instant income. To be sure, this income is often exaggerated for their own purposes by male observers—on whom for societies like Rome we must rely exclusively or almost so for our knowledge.[270] Even when realized, a prostitute's income is often diminished by a series of exploiters operating to the prostitute's detriment even in the best of circumstances, including exigent pimps and madams, greedy landlords, and a state that veers between complaisance and punitiveness.[271]

The means of such exploitation varies. Of course, a slave owner prostituting slaves receives in a legal, if not also practical sense, all they earn.[272] But

266. Dion. Hal. 4.24.4 suggests that at least in some cases slave prostitutes profited from their labor. See also *Priap.* 40. Both sources speak of slave prostitutes earning their freedom. Late antique evidence shows that some independent (i.e., without pimps) prostitutes might prosper. See the *Lives* of prostitute-saints translated from the Syriac by Brock and Harvey, *Holy Women* (1987) 35, 54, 55; see also Proc. *Bell. Pers.* 2.13.4.

267. For food and shelter, see the remarks on brothel-management in the section "Operation of Brothels." For clothing, see Sen. *Contr.* 1.2.7.

268. So Ramirez Sabada "Prostitución" (1985) 233 sensibly argues.

269. See, for example, Rosen, *Sisterhood* (1982) 72; Reynolds, *Economics of Prostitution* (1986) 11–23 (esp. 20); Høigård and Finstad, *Backstreets* (1992) 44–50; Schuster, *Frauenhaus* (1992) 98; Sturdevant and Stoltzfus, *Let the Good Times Roll* (1992) 223, 314–15; Bernstein, *Sonia's Daughters* (1995) 4, 138.

270. This phenomenon is well-observed by Reinsberg, *Ehe* (1989) 112, 146, 153–54.

271. On landlords, see the section "Ownership of Brothels." On the state, see Harsin, *Policing Prostitution* (1985) 216; Best, *Controlling Vice* (1998) 27.

272. Compulsion might be better conceived as falling along a spectrum rather than imagined as a question of slavery or its absence in a legal sense. For example, the economic exploitation of Chinese prostitutes in the nineteenth-century United States was so total as to suggest a kind of servitude: Tong, *Unsubmissive Women* (1994) 13, 103–4.

even in the absence of slavery, a pimp or madam may demand a sizeable share of the prostitute's income: one-third or more is common.[273] The pimp or madam may exercise an official or unofficial monopoly, charging her inflated prices for food, clothing, and personal items, sometimes even furniture, as well as exacting exorbitant amounts of rent.[274] They may also inflict fines for petty offenses.[275] Often, pimps and madams force the prostitute into debt that would make a loan shark blush, so they can increase their control over the prostitute and maximize the level of exploitation.[276] The use of debt to control the laborer is, of course, a tactic familiar to the ancient historian,[277] and one I would argue, despite a lack of evidence, that was applied to the Roman "free" prostitute.

Being a prostitute can be very expensive in other ways. Given that sexual attractiveness affects earnings, prostitutes often invest much money in expensive clothing, often sold to them at inflated prices, and seek the services of hairdressers and other beauticians.[278] The atmospherics of the bars and other locales where they ply their trade do not foster attention to long-range planning and are for various reasons costly places in which to work.[279] The behavior of many prostitutes, judged strictly in economic and not moral terms, does not appear to allow for the accumulation of savings.[280] The various drains on resources imposed by their lifestyle, their mentality, and the competitive aspects of their profession mean that pimps themselves can find it impossible to succeed financially.[281] Profit margins shrink as the cash flows to the exploiter of last resort, often a landlord.[282]

It is not surprising therefore that in many cultures prostitution can serve as a metaphor for a voracious, almost limitless mode of consumption that merges

---

273. See Prus and Irini, *Hookers* (1980) 33; Schuster, *Frauenhaus* (1992) 107, 110–11; Sleightholme and Sinha, *Guilty Without Trial* (1996) 19, 93, 95; Chapkis, *Live Sex Acts* (1997) 115, 117, 163.

274. Harsin, *Policing Prostitution* (1985) 38; Schuster, *Frauenhaus* (1992) 97; Hill, *Their Sisters' Keepers* (1993) 94.

275. Bernstein, *Sonia's Daughters* (1995) 156.

276. Bernstein, *Sonia's Daughters* (1995) 156–57; Schuster, *Freien Frauen* (1995) 139–41; Sleightholme and Sinha, *Guilty Without Trial* (1996) 95.

277. De Ste. Croix, *Class Struggle* (1981) 162–70, 238–40, has a good survey.

278. See Høigård and Finstad, *Backstreets* (1992) 49–50; Hill, *Their Sisters' Keepers* (1993) 89; Sleightholme and Sinha, *Guilty Without Trial* (1996) 95; Best, *Controlling Vice* (1998) 67.

279. Prus and Irini, *Hookers* (1980) 83, 176, 184, 251, 256.

280. See the account by Bernstein, *Sonia's Daughters* (1995) 158–60, on the futile efforts made by the late nineteenth-century sanitary commission in Minsk to shelter prostitutes from financial exploitation.

281. See Decker, *Prostitution* (1979) 258; Heyl, *Madam* (1979) 72; Prus and Irini, *Hookers* (1980) 251; Reynolds, *Economics of Prostitution* (1986) 26–28.

282. Heyl, *Madam* (1979) 99–101.

the sexual and the material.[283] The conclusion seems valid that prostitution does not profit most prostitutes, and that many women entering prostitution experience a decline in their economic status and standard of living.[284] Exceptions to this rule do not weaken it overall.[285]

My point is easier to argue in regard to late antiquity, since aside from some fourth-century evidence that may reflect the influence of the literary tradition, the sources are frank and full about the poverty of prostitutes in this period. This perhaps reflects in part the interest of Christians in poverty as a motive for resorting to prostitution in the first place.[286] Their inadequate earnings left prostitutes no way out of the profession, moreover.[287] So the (still-pagan) astrologer Firmicus Maternus can refer to their "wretched earnings" (*miserus quaestus*).[288]

To look at these prices from the perspective of potential clients, their overall low level suggests that venal sex was accessible to many low-status males. The less-expensive prostitutes charging two *asses* took one-sixth of the daily wage from late-Republican male laborers. For legionary soldiers, the percentage of pay taken was apparently a bit higher, more than one-half of daily discretionary income. But when we factor in the amounts they had to pay for fodder, food, and clothing, this begins to look like much less. If we compare the cost of a visit to a brothel in fifteenth-century Nuremberg, which Peter

---

283. See the comments of Davidson, *Courtesans and Fishcakes* (1997) 209–10.

284. For the Byzantine Empire, see Leontsini, *Prostitution* (1989) 169; for nineteenth-century Paris, see Harsin, *Policing Prostitution* (1985) 204; for the nineteenth-century United States, see Hobson, *Uneasy Virtue* (1990) 108; for twentieth-century Norway, see Høigård and Finstad, *Backstreets* (1992) 117–19; for medieval Germany, see Schuster, *Frauenhaus* (1992) 96; for medieval England, see Karras, *Common Women* (1996) 80, 97; for twentieth-century Calcutta, see Sleightholme and Sinha, *Guilty Without Trial* (1996) 93–94. Cf. Hill, *Their Sisters' Keepers* (1993) 86–91, who strains for a somewhat rosier scenario than a reasonable interpretation of the facts she cites warrants. Cf. 103, when she cites the tax assessment records of "at least" twenty-four prostitutes in nineteenth-century New York in order to argue that they might easily have acquired assets over time. This cannot be a representative sample of the city's prostitute population at that time. See also the opinion of Stansell, *City of Women* (1987) 181, 186, and Decker, *Prostitution* (1979) 179 and 301 (cf. 202 and 240), about the relative profitability of prostitution for working women, which strikes me as naive, as does the recent analysis by Edlund and Korn, "Theory of Prostitution" (2002) which seems sophisticated in theory, but uninformed as to reality.

285. See, for example, the prostitute who made a testamentary bequest to Sulla: Plut. *Sulla* 2.4.

286. See Neri, *Marginali* (1998) 202–208, 223, who is more inclined than I am to trust the late-antique evidence about well-off prostitutes. Such evidence drops off after the fourth century.

287. Neri, *Marginali* (1998) 203.

288. Firm. Mat. *Math.* 6.31.79.

Schuster estimates was equal on average to three hours of work for an apprentice, to that of a visit at Rome in the late Republic and early Empire, we see that prostitution was relatively inexpensive for the Roman male.[289]

RECRUITMENT

The task of acquiring slave prostitutes fell to the pimp—who might be acting in the guise of a *caupo* (innkeeper), for example—in other words, the person responsible for running the brothel. The means of acquisition do not seem to have differed greatly from those employed for acquiring slaves in general.[290] Women and children who were captured in war were often enslaved and prostituted[291] and persons who were already slaves might be traded across frontiers.[292] Those kidnapped by robbers and pirates are often said to have endured a similar fate: the literal truth of the sources may sometimes be doubted,[293] but they hint at a widespread trade, for which other evidence is available.[294] Clement of Alexandria appears to make a distinction between wholesalers and retailers. Wholesalers, he notes, transport prostitutes as if they were grain or wine, while retailers acquire them as if they were bread or sauce.[295] In his remarks, Clement also unites prostitution with the trade in exposed chil-

---

289. Schuster, *Frauenhaus* (1992) 113.

290. The relative importance of each of the means given here is controversial: see Horden and Purcell, *Corrupting Sea* (2000) 389. For a recent discussion, arguing for the importance of the mix of sources for slaves, see Harris, "Demography" (1999) esp. 64–72. For criticism of this view and emphasis on the importance of slave offspring for the slave supply, see Scheidel, "Quantifying the Sources" (1997).

291. For the practice in general, the clearest evidence is Dio Chrys. 7.133. Sen. *Const.* 6.5 suggests the truth of this argument. Lact. *Div. Inst.* 4.21.4 CSEL 19.1.368 cites the fate of the captives in the Jewish War. Dioclet. et Maxim. C. 8.50(51).7 (a. 291) tells of a captive woman ransomed by a third party and then prostituted (more on this text below).

292. A very profitable trade involving the importation of slave prostitutes from the Red Sea into Egypt is suggested by *I. Portes* 67 (-OGIS 2.674-IGR 1.1183: Coptos A.D. 90). See McGinn, *Prostitution, Sexuality, and the Law* (1998) 281–82.

293. The sources in general seem to derive from comedy, rhetoric, and romance: Plaut. *Curc.* 644–52; *Persa* 134–36; *Rudens* 39–41, 1105; Sen. *Contr.* 1.2; Apul. *Met.* 7.9–10; *Hist. Ap. Tyr.* 33 Though these sources might exaggerate the phenomenon of pirates procuring slaves (an argument that makes better sense of the imperial period), it still took place, especially in certain locales and time periods. See, for example, Shaw, "Bandit" (1993) 325. It does seem more based in fiction than in real life during the imperial period, though piracy was far from eradicated: Braund, "Piracy"; de Souza, *Piracy* (1999) 60–65, 214.

294. See IG 14.2000, the sarcophagus, from Rome, perhaps second or third century, belonging to one M. Sempronius Neikrokrates, a self-described "merchant of beautiful women."

295. Clem. Al. *Paed.* 3.3.22 SC 158.52.

dren.[296] A letter of Augustine indicates that kidnapping children for the purpose of enslavement was quite common in his day.[297]

At any rate, the pirate, pimp, and slave dealer were linked in the popular imagination, to judge from a text of Seneca the Elder.[298] While it is reasonable to suppose that some free immigrants to Rome practiced prostitution, most foreign prostitutes were probably slaves, or at any rate had been brought to Rome as slaves to be prostituted.[299]

The practice of raising abandoned children to be prostitutes, a favorite theme of Comedy, attracted the unsympathetic attention of Christian moralists.[300] There is also some evidence indicating parents sold (to pimps), or prostituted, their children, actions usually said to be motivated by poverty. There is no evidence that the prostitution of children by parents, especially by *patres familias*, that is, those wielding paternal power (*patria potestas*), was illegal during the classical period. In fact, legislation enacted by Christian emperors in the early fifth century allowing daughters and slave women exploited by their fathers or owners to escape from prostitution suggests that prostituting one's children, above all those in one's *patria potestas*, was every bit as legal as prostituting one's slaves.[301]

The sale of free citizen children by their parents was almost certainly illegal during the classical period.[302] This does not mean, of course, that it was not done. Quintilian,[303] who says that a common theme of the rhetorical exercises known as *controversiae* concerns a person "who has sold his child to a pimp" ("qui filium lenoni vendidit"), may provoke skepticism. Yet his assertion receives support from other sources, which also suggest that parents themselves at times prostituted their own children.

---

296. For all that the distinction Clement seems to draw may not precisely reflect reality, to judge from other evidence from Egypt: see Drexhage, "Bemerkungen" (1991). If so, the second group may be understood to be prostitutes' clients, and not retailers.

297. Augustin. *Ep.* 10* CSEL 88.46–51. On stealing—and buying—free children in late antiquity, see Nathan, *Family* (2000) 136–39.

298. Sen. *Contr.* 1.2.9.

299. See Evans, *War* (1991) 140–41; Noy, *Foreigners* (2000) 122–23.

300. See McGinn, *Roman Prostitution* (forthcoming).

301. Theod., Valent. CTh. 15.8.2 (a. 428) (= C. 1.4.12 = C. 11.41.6).

302. Here I take the view of Brunt, *Manpower* (1987) 131 n. 4, against that of Boswell, *Kindness* (1988) 65–75, 110, 171. See Mayer-Maly, "Notverkaufsrecht" (1958) 120–22; Kaser, *Privatrecht* 1² (1971): 342; Memmer, "Findelkinder" (1991) 43. There does not seem to be much evidence for the sale of children by parents, to judge from Harris, "Slave-Trade" (1980) 124. The practice of prostituting one's own children, however, does not seem to have been outlawed until late antiquity: see Theod., Valent. CTh. 15.8.2 (= C. 1.4.12 = C. 11.41.6) (a. 428) Leo C. 1.4.14 (a. 457–467) (= [?] C. 11.41.7).

303. Quint. *IO* 7.1.55.

Seneca names,[304] among the shameful bargains made to stay alive, that of "personally handing over one's children for the purpose of fornication" ("liberos ad stuprum manu sua tradere"). This may imply direct prostitution, rather than the sale of children to a pimp. Musonius knows a father who sold his handsome son "into a life of shame."[305] Justin Martyr castigates those who prostitute children and wives and who castrate children for (commercial) sexual purposes.[306] A late fourth-century papyrus from Hermopolis includes the record of a trial for the murder of a prostitute.[307] The mother of the dead woman claims financial compensation from the murderer, who has robbed her of her sole means of subsistence.[308] She explains, "it was for this reason that I gave my daughter to the pimp, so as to have a means of support." The mother wins her case and receives a tenth of the man's property.[309]

More difficult to evaluate is the practice of husbands prostituting their wives. The adultery law of Augustus renders this practice, which it identifies as criminal pimping, *lenocinium*, illegal. I argue elsewhere that the fairly plentiful sources that describe husbands prostituting their wives are grounded more in anxiety than in reality, and they were often shaped by literary convention or motivated by personal hostility.[310] This hardly means such was behavior was nonexistent, of course, especially for the lower orders about whose doings the upper-class sources tend to silence.

One might under Roman law sell oneself into slavery with attendant prostitution.[311] Although direct evidence is lacking, given the apparent readiness of pimps to acquire children and the—absolutely unquantifiable—role that breeding played in slave acquisition in general, it is likely that many slave

---

304. Sen. *Ep.* 101.14–15. Note the rhetorically charged allegations at Zos. 2.38 over the consequences of Constantine's tax program.

305. Muson. 83H. See also Augustin. *Ep.* 24* CSEL 88.126–27.

306. Iust. *Apol.* 1.27 Munier 70–72.

307. *BGU* 3.1024.6–8. On this text, see Bagnall, *Egypt* (1993) 196–98, who persuasively defends its reliability against critics; see, for example, Beaucamp, *Statut* 2 (1992): 56. Montserrat, *Sex and Society* (1996) 108, argues that the mother did not sell her daughter to the pimp given that she continued to derive an income from her daughter's earnings. Law and logic are on his side, but it seems possible that the very illegality of the transaction fostered an informal arrangement of payments over time, as though her daughter's prostitution provided a kind of annuity.

308. *BGU* 3.1024.7.

309. *BGU* 3.1024.8.

310. McGinn, *Prostitution, Sexuality, and the Law* (1998) 171–94. For a late-antique complaint, see Val. Cem. *Hom.* 20.8 *PL* 52.754.

311. Dio Chrys. 15.23 alleges that the practice of selling oneself was common. A person had to be older than twenty: Marci. D. 1.5.5.1.

prostitutes were *vernae*.[312] In other words, the sources of slave prostitutes, like those of slaves in general, were mixed.[313]

We are not well-informed about the prices charged for—as opposed to by—slave prostitutes. The evidence of Plautus is suspect, and not only because he tends to give Greek monetary units.[314] Prices given in two other sources seem too high to be judged typical if they are reliable at all. The emperor Elagabalus is alleged to have bought a *meretrix notissima et pulcherrima* ("a very prominent and beautiful prostitute") for 100,000 sesterces;[315] the episode introduces a chapter devoted to his extravagance. The same amount is the successful bid offered by a pimp for the slave Tarsia during the (fictional) auction scene in the *Historia Apollonii Regis Tyrii*.[316] Such a price was extravagant and highly unusual, but perhaps not utterly impossible.[317]

Much lower prices were the norm, in any case. Martial records a bid of 600 sesterces for a *puella* "of reputation none too exalted . . . such as sit in mid-Subura" ("famae non nimium bonae . . . /quales in media sedent Subura").[318] The bid is withdrawn after the auctioneer, in a vain attempt to up the bidding, tries to convince the crowd that she is *pura* ("chaste") by grabbing her and kissing her several times. This price is very low for a slave,[319] but hardly incredible.[320] Perhaps the most important piece of information to be derived from this poem is that a slave's status as a prostitute might exert a strong

---

312. By "*verna*" I mean slave by birth. On the difficulty of understanding this word in the context of Pompeian prostitute-graffiti, see app. 3.

313. I note in passing the consignment of women, particularly Christians, to brothels as a form of punishment. The practice is well-attested, but it is impossible to judge its economic significance: see chap. 8.

314. For a brave attempt to justify this evidence, see Delcourt, "Prix" (1948).

315. *HA Elag.* 31.1.

316. *Hist. Ap. Tyr.* 33.

317. Duncan-Jones, *Economy²* (1982) 253–54, remarks that the amount offered for Tarsia is "comparable to the sums paid at Rome under the early Principate for slaves of the highest accomplishments" (note omitted). Still, the price per trick would have to be very high to recoup such an investment.

318. Mart. 6.66.

319. We are told this at Mart. 6.66.4: "parvo cum pretio diu liceret." The joke turns in part on the understanding that this is a low bid but not outrageously so. A comparison with the other prices listed in Duncan-Jones, *Economy²* (1982) app. 10, confirms the impression that this price is at the lower end of the scale (see n. 320, however, for a similar price). Despite some extravagant exceptions, Martial tends to present female slaves as of little worth: Garrido-Hory, "Femmes" (1999) 304.

320. This price corresponds to the other lowest "price" for a slave recorded in Rome and Italy, namely, the HS 600 for which a *puella* is pledged at Herculaneum: *Tab. Herc.* 65 = Duncan-Jones, *Economy²* (1982) app. 10, # 14 (Martial's evidence is listed as # 27).

downward pressure on her price.[321] This suggests that slave prostitutes could be purchased for a relatively low amount, whether the reason was economic (i.e., there was a good supply) or social/moral (the low public regard for prostitutes), or a mixture of both.[322] One contributing factor may have been that women and children slaves seem to have been generally cheaper to purchase than adult male slaves.[323] For what it is worth, Byzantine data suggest that it was not expensive for a pimp to set up shop.[324]

When the ancient evidence registers the status of a prostitute, more often than not she is a slave.[325] The easiest explanation is that most were, in fact, slaves. Another explanation is that our sources tend to take a relatively higher interest in slaves as opposed to the free poor.[326] Or it might suggest that prostitution as practiced by the Romans was so fundamentally stamped by slavery, that the idea of this was present even where prostitutes were actually of free status, and was encouraged by the fact that so many of course were slaves.[327] These explanations do not of necessity exclude each other, and, all three are in fact more or less persuasive. The link between slavery and prostitution is confirmed further by the fact that a good many prostitutes were almost certainly freedwomen, who had been prostituted as slaves and continued to engage in the profession after being freed.[328] One cannot, to be sure, ade-

---

321. On the possible diminution of the value of a slave put to prostitution, see McGinn, *Prostitution, Sexuality, and the Law* (1998) chap. 7; see also 321.

322. See the suggestion that the sexual vulnerability attendant on being the slave of a pirate would have lowered the value of a slave woman: Sen. *Contr.* 1.2.4.

323. For children, Boswell, *Kindness* (1988), seems right to rely on the evidence of Plautus. For women, see Scheidel, "Reflections" (1996); Scheidel takes data from Diocletian's Price Edict to show that female teenagers were an exception to this rule, since their reproductive capacity (and sexual attractiveness?) was on the rise.

324. See Leontsini, *Prostitution* (1989) 79.

325. For collections of sources, see Herter, "Dirne" (1957) 1171; "Soziologie" (1960) 78. Slavery was not evenly distributed across the Empire: Bradley, *Slaves and Masters* (1984) 17. But it is difficult to relate this fact to the practice of prostitution. In ancient Athens, the evidence suggests a close association between slavery and prostitution, especially brothel-prostitution: see Schaps, "Athenian Woman" (1998) 168, 175; Cohen, "Economic Analysis" (forthcoming). On the other hand, the fact that prostitutes as well as pimps paid the Caligulan tax suggests that some, perhaps a significant number, of the former were independent: McGinn, *Prostitution, Sexuality, and the Law* (1998), chap. 7.

326. See Scheidel, "Silent Women 1" (1995); "Silent Women 2" (1996). Note in this connection the skepticism of Evans, *War* (1991) 139–40, over the idea that the vast majority of prostitutes were slaves or freedwomen.

327. See Flemming, "*Quae Corpore*" (1999) 40–41, 51, 56–61.

328. So argues Treggiari, "Ladies" (1970/1) 197, citing the case of Livy's Faecenia Hispala (39.9.5). Her assertion that prostitutes were most often slaves or freedwomen is persuasive, with the evidence stronger for the Empire. See Treggiari, *Freedmen* (1969) 142, where she cites the

quately emphasize the poor evidentiary base on which this argument, no doubt correct, about freedwomen prostitutes rests.[329] Freedom for the slave prostitute did not necessarily mean freedom from prostitution, a cold fact that makes the connection between slavery and venal sex even closer.[330] The evidence for possible prostitutes in Pompeii, given in appendix 3, suggests most were slaves, ex-slaves, or lived in social conditions that were close to slavery.[331] The same, no doubt, holds true for prostitutes living elsewhere.

It seems unlikely that one could legally compel women who were not slaves or in paternal power to prostitute themselves. But if this was the rule in practice, it was almost certainly ignored if it was not in fact unenforceable.[332] Diocletian and Maximian react forcefully when a well-born woman captured by the enemy is prostituted by the woman who redeems her and her father complains to them.[333] Not everyone could have been so lucky, even if we are correct to assume that justice triumphed here. Whether compulsion, lifestyle, or lack of realistic alternatives played a role, the original motivation to enter prostitution for freeborn women who had not been prostituted while in paternal power and freedwomen who had not been prostituted while slaves would have been different than that for slave prostitutes, only in an objective sense.

All the same, we should not exaggerate even this distinction. Roman women who were not slaves were often as vulnerable to the importunities of procurers as women in other societies without slavery. The methods of recruitment into prostitution that were uncovered by Justinian's investigative commission in the sixth century, which included promising poor women and children clothing and shoes, were not at all likely a recent development.[334] What

---

poetry of Horace, who "makes the *libertina* the mistress and harlot *par excellence.*" On the social significance of this fact, see below in the text.

329. Fabre, *Libertus* (1981) 354, in his massive study of freedpersons, can cite apart from the fictions of comedy, lyric, and other works of literature, only two "historical" freedwomen prostitutes whose names we know, Faecenia Hispala and Volumnia Cytheris; and he is tentative as to the latter's status as a prostitute.

330. See Liv. 39.9.5; *Priap.* 40.

331. See also see Treggiari, "Lower Class Women" (1976) 73 with n. 36.

332. See Treggiari, *Freedmen* (1969) 142; "Ladies" (1970/1) 197, for a similar argument. Call. D. 38.1.38 pr. prohibits acts of commercial sex from counting as *operae*. For a brief discussion of this text, see McGinn, *Prostitution, Sexuality, and the Law* (1998) 330–31.

333. Dioclet., Maxim. C. 8.50(51).7 (a. 291). The father is freed from the responsibility of reimbursing the woman for the ransom and his daughter is ordered to be returned to him. On this text, see Beaucamp, *Statut* 1(1990): 19 n. 22; Cursi, *Struttura* (1996) 207 n. 36; Neri, *Marginali* (1998) 233.

334. Iustinianus Nov. 14 (a. 535).

is new is the official concern with this phenomenon. I must regrettably leave aside here the important contemporary debate among feminists as to whether prostitution is inherently exploitative.[335] It was almost certainly so at Rome. Slave prostitutes, insofar as they counted as economic assets, might even have received better treatment in some cases than free prostitutes.[336]

Where explicit compulsion of one form or another was not in play, a primary motivation for women to enter prostitution was economic, that is, the desperation of poverty.[337] The evidence suggests that the supply of labor overall for the Romans was generous, while work conditions were unpredictable at best and unemployment was widespread.[338] Wages tended to support the worker at a subsistence level, but not the worker's family as well.[339] Modern studies of prostitution suggest that poverty, resulting from or combined with low wages, limited opportunities for work, disastrous events in the family economy, and a desire for relatively rapid and easy social mobility, has played a decisive role in influencing women's choices to enter prostitution.[340]

The steadily growing literature on lower-class women's occupations in Roman society seems to confirm the impression that their employment prospects were narrow.[341] Our focus, as ever, is on women, but it is worth invoking Epictetus's parable of the freedman who, compelled by want to pros-

---

335. For literature, see below in the section on "Prostitution and the Roman Economy."

336. This principle, however, may not have applied to slave children who were prostitutes, since slave children overall were so heavily exploited in terms of the labor they performed. See Bradley, "Social Aspects" (1986) 49–51; Bradley, *Discovering the Roman Family* (1991) 103–24.

337. The ancient evidence is abundant. See, for example, Plaut. *Asin.* 530–31, *Cist.* 40–41; Ter. *Andria* 70–79 (cf. 796–800), *Heauton* 443–47, *Phormio* 415–17; Sen. *Ep.* 101.15; Artemid. 1.56, 58; Lucian. *Dialog. Mer.* 6; Ulp. D. 23.2.43.5; Firm. Mat. *Math.* 3.6.22; BGU 3.1024.6–8; Theod., Valent. CTh. 15.8.2 (= C. 1.4.12 = C. 11.41.6) (a. 428); Proc. *Aed.* 1.9.1–10; Iustinian. Nov. 14 (a. 535). For Christian sources, which tend to be more insistent on this point, see, for example, Lact. *Inst.* 5.8.7 CSEL 19.1.422; . More evidence in Krause, *Witwen* 3 (1995):190 n. 67, 191 n. 78, 192 nn. 81–82. For discussion of the poverty motive for Byzantine prostitutes, see Leontsini, *Prostitution* (1989) 163.

338. See Mrozek, *Lohnarbeit* (1989) 94–95, 119, 161; Evans, *War* (1991) 144; Prell, *Armut* (1997) 163–69.

339. See Mrozek, *Lohnarbeit* (1989) 162.

340. See Walkowitz, *Prostitution* (1980) 15–21; Rosen, *Sisterhood* (1982) 31, 115, 137–68; Corbin, *Women for Hire* (1990) 209; Guy, *Sex* (1990) 24, 40; Gilfoyle, *City of Eros* (1992) 59; Gibson, *Prostitution and the State*[2] (1999) 104.

341. Susan Treggiari's numerous contributions to this subject supersede previous work and remain essential: "Domestic Staff" (1973); "Jobs in the Household" (1975); "Volusii" (1975); "Jobs for Women" (1976); "Lower Class Women" (1979); "Questions " (1979); "Urban Labour" (1980).

titute himself, found himself less free than he was when still a slave.[342] This story speaks volumes about the lack of real choice experienced by—I would argue—the overwhelming majority of Rome's prostitutes, male or female.

The situation regarding the domestic staffs of the great houses is instructive. Because of their size and corresponding distribution of highly specialized work assignments, these establishments offered a variety of jobs for both men and women.[343] Nevertheless, the roles allotted females were relatively few in number and narrow in scope.[344] Women were not employed in great numbers by male owners,[345] and, even among female owners, positions for women were not as many or as varied as those held by male servants.[346]

It may be supposed that many female slaves in the great *familiae* held no separate position of their own but simply functioned as the partners (*contubernales*) of male slaves or freedmen who did have a position.[347] In any case, the relative lack of women slaves found in large households has been noted.[348] The conclusion seems justified that employment opportunities for women in the great houses were extremely limited. They tended to be confined to strictly domestic tasks such as making clothes, which as we shall see, tended to define women's work experiences generally.[349] In the countryside, jobs were filled

342. Epict. 4.1.35.

343. It was considered shameful and mean to have the same slave perform more than one role: Cic. *Pisonem* 67.

344. Flory, "Family" (1978) 87–88. The gender imbalance may have been even more dramatic in the *familia Caesaris*, the imperial household, where women played no role in administration: see Herrmann-Otto, *Ex Ancilla Natus* (1994) 117–18, 346.

345. See Treggiari, "Domestic Staff" (1973) 243–50, "Volusii" (1975) 92; Bradley, *Slaves and Masters* (1984) 73–75.

346. Treggiari, "Domestic Staff" (1973) 248, "Jobs in the Household" (1975) 58. Female servants served as hairdressers, masseuses, escorts/attendants, dressers, medical orderlies (all typically, if not exclusively, for the women of the household), wet nurses, midwives, spinners, weavers (production of clothing was in fact the principal occupation), and (probably, though unattested) humble domestics. The owner's gender affected the distribution of staff by sex, as one might expect.

347. Brunt, *Manpower* (1987) 144, points out that the lack of positions for women on domestic staffs reduced the number of these relationships. On the marriage partners of female servants, see Treggiari, "Domestic Staff" (1973) 249.

348. See Treggiari, "Questions" (1979) 189–90 (cf. "Volusii" [1975] 400–401); Sigismund Nielsen, "Ditis Examen Domus?" (1991) esp. 230–32; Herrmann-Otto, *Ex Ancilla Natus* (1994) 346–47; Smadja, "Affranchissement" (1999) 360–61, noting some correction of earlier work. It is significant that female positions did not display the same complex hierarchy that male jobs did: Treggiari, "Questions," 191.

349. So Brunt, *Manpower* (1987) 143–44, esp. 144 n. 1 drawing his conclusion on the basis of an examination of M. Maxey's evidence; Treggiari, "Domestic Staff" (1973) 245, "Questions" (1979) 190. See also Günther, *Frauenarbeit* (1987) 136; Eichenauer, *Arbeitswelt* (1988) 126;

overwhelmingly by males.[350] We can assume that female job holders are to an extent underrepresented in the evidence, because they held positions that the Romans felt were not worth recording or too shameful to report.[351] But their underrepresentation might also be taken as evidence of depressed employment chances *tout court*.

Prospects seem to have been even more limited in the free labor market, or, at any rate that not tied to the great households.[352] The available evidence suggests job offerings were very meager, particularly when jobs that were obviously domestic are excluded,[353] and those jobs available to women of a higher social level or in a favored position.[354] In Le Gall's *CIL* survey,[355] there is a total of about fifteen to twenty professions, most of which are attested only once or twice in the inscriptions. Treggiari adds a dozen more items to this list,[356] and

---

Evans, *War* (1991) 115; Rodríguez Neila, "Trabajo" (1999) 13; Smadja, "Affranchissement" (1999) 362. For the definition and identification of domestic job titles, see Treggiari, "Jobs for Women" (1976) and the next note. For the ideological aspects of domestic wool-working, see Maurin "Labor" (1983); Lyapustin, "Women" (1985); Eichenauer, esp. 301 (it was shameful for elite women to work, but idleness for them was suspect); Larsson Lovén, "*Lanam Fecit*" (1998).

350. See Krause, *Witwen* 2 (1994) 127, who, citing Artemid. 1.31, declares that, unlike most households, which included both males and females, farm households only included men, just as brothels only included women (see chap. 8). See also Bradley, *Slaves and Masters* (1984) 75, and below in the text.

351. See Günther, *Frauenarbeit* (1987) 21, 42; Herrmann-Otto, *Ex Ancilla Natus* (1994) 346; Dixon *Reading Roman Women* (2001) 114–15, 120–24, 130–32.

352. Out of eighty-five types of jobs attested at Pompeii, only about a half-dozen are unambiguously female: for the total, see Hopkins, "Growth" (1972) 72. For a general survey of the limited employment opportunities available to women, see Krause, *Witwen* 2 (1994) 123–73; Krause, *Witwen* 3 (1995) 178–93.

353. Job designations for slave women and freedwomen in a household include the *ornatrix*, *obstetrix*, *lanipenda*, *quasillaria*, *nutrix*, *unctrix*, *sarcinatrix*, *cantrix*, *medica*, and others: see Treggiari, "Jobs for Women" (1976), "Questions" (1980). Cf. Le Gall, "Métiers" (1969) 124, whose list is incomplete; the evidence for *sarcinatrix*, *cantrix*, and *medica* as domestic positions is not fully taken into account. Treggiari shows that the last two positions, together with *obstetrix*, could be freelance ones. The position of *tonstrix* should perhaps be included among the domestics, as Le Gall, 125 n. 6 suggests, given the epigraphic instances from Rome. Bradley, *Slaves and Masters* (1984) 72, argues that many women of low status worked as wet nurses. See also Bradley, *Discovering the Roman Family* (1991) 13–36.

354. These would include the position of *vilica*, and the isolated attestations of *actrix*, *negotiatrix*, and *conductrix* (not a real job), and possibly *medica* as well: see Le Gall, "Métiers" (1969) 126–29.

355. Le Gall, "Métiers" (1969). In addition to the jobs excluded in the previous two notes I would omit *popa* from Le Gall's list. The word seems to refer exclusively to males: *OLD*, s.v. "*popa.*" *Popinaria* is the correct female equivalent: *CIL* 14.3709.

356. Treggiari, "Lower Class Women" (1979) 80 n. 1. See the list she provides at "Urban Labour" (1980) 61–64.

estimates the total to be about thirty-five.[357] Once again, a certain level of underreporting must be assumed.[358] But the overall comparison with the number of jobs available to men is still striking.[359]

No doubt many women and children participated in the economy as marginal producers, who were summoned when conditions permitted or demanded.[360] In many traditional societies, we can detect the phenomenon of "substitution," in which women function as a labor reserve for their husbands or male members of their families.[361] Flexibility and adaptability are essential, though most women perhaps have to work at something on a regular basis. A similar point should be made for casual or part-time prostitutes in Roman society. This was the kind of choice likely to be invisible to, or misunderstood by, the elite observer.[362] Evidence for casual and part-time prostitutes is abundant for other cultures, while all but nonexistent for Rome.[363] Part of the problem is that it is difficult to establish the status of many women, whether they appear in the sources as historical or fictional figures, as prostitutes in the first place.[364] Another problem is the difficulty of drawing a line between part-time and full-time prostitution, a problem we cannot simply attribute to the elite

---

357. Treggiari, "Lower Class Women" (1979) 78. The best attested nondomestic female professions are jewelry making, clothing production, retail sales, and various service industries (especially prostitution): Treggiari, 66–68. Eichenauer, *Arbeitswelt* (1988) 56–59, drawing upon epigraphic, literary, and legal sources, is able to raise the total to a much more comforting, though highly doubtful, 103. A few of the difficulties with her list may be canvassed briefly. Some of the job titles Eichenauer cites are not given in the sources. Others are unlikely to be real titles at all, such as *puella*. It would be useful to have a matching list of male titles for comparison. One hopes this is possible without having to list, for example, all of the ranks in the Roman army.

358. For what it is worth, 31 percent of the persons named in the index of *gentilicia* in Zimmer, *Berufsdarstellungen* (1982), are female.

359. See Eichenauer, *Arbeitswelt* (1988) 146.

360. See Horden and Purcell, *Corrupting Sea* (2000) 268–69. Here they cite Columella's advice (12.3.6) that women and children should be set to wool working when the weather made work outside impossible. See also Frasca, *Mestieri* (1994), 89.

361. See Signorelli, "Legittimazione" (1999) 8–11.

362. For this point, see Horden and Purcell, *Corrupting Sea* (2000) 266.

363. See Evans, "Prostitution" (1976) 112; Decker, *Prostitution* (1979) 4–5, 13; Harsin, *Policing Prostitution* (1985) 15; Tong, *Unsubmissive Women* (1994) 19; Bernstein, *Sonia's Daughters* (1995) 119; Karras, *Common Women* (1996) 53–54, 60, 71; Sleightholme and Sinha, *Guilty Without Trial* (1996) 11; Sullivan, *Politics of Sex* (1997) 27; Hart, *Buying and Selling* (1998) 33. I agree with Flemming, "*Quae Corpore*" (1999) 42, that the story in Sext. Emp. *Pyrrh.* 3.201, about Egyptian girls earning a dowry through prostitution, while dubious in itself, does suggest the possibility that some women sold sex for a short period of time. For more on part-time and casual prostitution, see above in this chapter in the section "The Milieu of Prostitution."

364. I examine this difficulty in *Roman Prostitution* (forthcoming).

male bias found in the sources discussed above. In modern society, many prostitutes do not work all day every day and yet would not therefore qualify as casual workers.[365] Two possible examples may be cited from Pompeii to illustrate the poverty of our evidence and the challenges this poverty presents. One is the mill-girl (if she was, in fact, a mill-girl) Glyco, the price of whose services is given as two *asses*.[366] The other is the weaver Amaryllis, who is said to offer fellatio (if this is not pure insult).[367] In neither case can we be certain that the woman was both a (part-time) prostitute and worked in another profession as well.

Evidence for women leaving the profession is very rare. There is no room here to explore the contours of the comic/elegiac procuress, who is typically presented as a former prostitute.[368] That portrait is too expressive of elite male prejudice to be of much help to us in attempting to sketch the lived experience of such women. We can be certain that some prostitutes eventually came to act as procuresses, while no doubt others married and left the profession.[369] Still others perhaps entered and left the profession from time to time.[370] It is important to know something about when and under what circumstances the majority of women left the profession. Was prostitution a short-lived part of the life cycle for many lower-class women or did they have no way out? The answer would tell us a great deal about the degree of exploitation that characterized Roman prostitution. But the sources are deeply disinterested in this problem. We can only say that the association of slavery with prostitution does not encourage optimism on this score.

To return to women workers in general, of particular interest are those cases in which a woman was married to a man in the same trade.[371] It is likely

---

365. See Prus and Irini, *Hookers* (1980) 8.

366. *CIL* 4.3999, 4001 ("grinder-girl").

367. *CIL* 4.1510; cf. 1507. For the suggestion of part-time prostitution, see Evans, *War* (1991) 144. It is quite possible Amaryllis prostituted herself, though she might simply have been the recipient of a slur. See Dixon *Reading Roman Women* (2001) 128, 151.

368. A good treatment of the *lena* from literature is in Myers, "Poet and Procuress" (1996).

369. On marriage with prostitutes, see McGinn, "Marriage Legislation and Social Practice" (2002). Artemid. 5.67 has a case of a long-term relationship that evidently did not involve marriage (and which was deemed not at all auspicious). Marriage by itself, of course, did not guarantee retirement. For a rare ancient recognition of marriage as a way out of the profession, see Iustinianus Nov. 14 pr. (a. 535).

370. For a sense of this phenomenon in nineteenth-century New York, see Gilfoyle, *City of Eros* (1992) 167–68.

371. See *CIL* 5.7023; 6.9211. See also Treggiari, "Lower Class Women" (1979) 67–72, 76, 79.

that for many lower-class women participation in a profession was conditioned by the existence of a family business, especially one conducted by a husband, and which represented in many cases an extension of "domestic" labor.[372] Social status mattered greatly here. Behavior, that is, women's participation in business on the level of society visible to us, may have reflected to a certain extent the practice of the upper classes, for whom profit-making ventures were viewed, often at least ideally, as an extension of the domestic economy.[373] A woman's status might determine whether her "work," for example, in making clothes for the household, was viewed as virtuous or degrading.[374]

While it was far from impossible for women to work outside the home in Roman antiquity, it was risky, since some of the fundamental reasons limiting women's participation in the workforce were cultural and not economic.[375] The job titles that survive often do not allow us knowledge of the scope of a woman's role. For example, we cannot be certain that a worker in gold leaf (*brattiaria*) actually worked on the gold leaf or simply sold what her husband produced.[376]

As in the case of prostitutes, most of the working women attested in the sources were slaves or freedwomen. All the same, to understand the overall position of women in the labor market, we must view practically all of them as operating in conditions of dependency.[377] This cultural ideology was not just dominant but overwhelmingly so. Yet to judge from comparative evidence, it was perhaps flexible enough to permit accommodation when circumstances,

---

372. Evans, *War* (1991) 119–20, 121, 124–25, 136, has a useful survey of a series of fields, including the crafts industry, retail, and medicine. See also Treggiari, "Urban Labour" (1980) 55–56; Eichenauer, *Arbeitswelt* (1988) 21, 126, 295, 297; Bradley, *Discovering the Roman Family* (1991) 108–9, 115 (with an interesting evocation of honor/shame); Bradley, *Slavery and Society* (1994) 59; Frasca, *Mestieri* (1994) 89–91; Rodríguez Neila, "Trabajo" (1999) 112–13 (treating evidence from Roman Spain); Günther, "Matrona" (2000) 354; Traina, "Mestieri" (2000) 118; Dixon, *Reading Roman Women* (2001) 115, 122, 132. A useful comparative perspective is afforded by Mitterauer, *Familienforschung* (1990) 305–7. See also Hobson, *Uneasy Virtue* (1990) 57, 65.

373. See Treggiari, *Roman Marriage* (1991) 378.

374. Günther, "Matrona" (2000) 354–55.

375. See van Minnen, "Trade" (1998) who adduces exactly three examples of apprenticeship contracts for freeborn females from Egypt (but three more than previously known). In all cases, there was provision for supervision by a woman, reaffirming the general principle asserted here.

376. Eichenauer, *Arbeitswelt* (1988) 296. See also Savunen, *Women* (1997) 117; Gourevitch and Raepsaet-Charlier, *Femme* (2001) 186.

377. So Eichenauer, *Arbeitswelt* (1988) 298–99. The point extends in some measure to the labor market overall, which is marked both ideologically and in practical terms by notions of dependency: Prell, *Armut* (1997) 147–50, 161, 168.

above all the necessity of making a living, dictated a change.[378] Thus some of the women attested, for example, in the commercial sector of Pompeii seem to have worked relatively independently.[379] The ancient sources in general tend to advertise virtue rather than acknowledge necessity, except when it came to prostitution.

For those women without a husband or, at any rate, a husband engaged in a suitable trade, opportunities were more limited,[380] though there is some tantalizing evidence of small-scale female production and/or distribution networks.[381] Moralizing views that supported a gender-based division of labor, approved moral behavior, and a proper lifestyle for women accentuated the job squeeze.[382] One great exception to the general trend appears to have been acting, where stars at least were richly rewarded and, as slaves, cost a great deal.[383]

Objections may be raised to my use of the evidence. The list of jobs developed by modern scholars is obviously incomplete. We can hardly assume that the epigraphic and literary record adequately represents even the middling to upper-middling social stratum, let alone what lay beneath.[384] Such criticism is valid and yields a useful caution. Yet Treggiari's totals of "some 160" different male job titles for Rome itself and 225 just in the Latin inscriptions for the Roman West provide a valuable perspective.[385] Viewed in this light, Treggiari's estimate of about 35 women's professions suggests employment opportunities for lower-class women were meager indeed. Nevertheless many were compelled to find some way of making a living.[386]

---

378. The fascinating study by Giovannini, "Dialectics" (1985) shows how the ideal that women should work exclusively in the home counterintuitively allowed for their extensive participation as workers in a clothing factory opened in Garre, Sicily, in 1966. Further contextualization and generalization are found in Giovannini, "Female Chastity Codes" (1987); Horden and Purcell, *Corrupting Sea* (2000) 500.

379. See the cautious optimism on this score in Savunen, *Women* (1997) 117.

380. Some of those involved in luxury-oriented occupations, such as making gold leaf or spinning gold (see *CIL* 6.9211; 9213), may have been exceptional: they may have owned property and perhaps possessed a marketable skill. For more on the argument made in the text, see Honoré, *Sex Law* (1978) 114.

381. Clark, *Women* (1993) 94, 104. All the same, the economic profile of these women was lowered by both social and legal factors: see Gardner, "Women in Business Life" (1999).

382. See the comments of Scheidel, "Silent Women 1" (1995): 206.

383. Leppin, *Histrionen* (1992) 84–90.

384. Social stratification existed even among peasants: see De Ligt, "Demand, Supply, Distribution 1" (1990) 49.

385. Treggiari, "Urban Labour" (1980) 56. I count 162 examples in her appendix.

386. For a caution against simply assuming a difference in attitudes about women's work dependent on class, see Scheidel, "Silent Women 1" (1995) 206–7.

A final objection is that the small number of possible jobs conceals large numbers of women working in them. There is no doubt that women are underrepresented in the epigraphic evidence, above all in such positions as vendors, because of animus and/or the subsumption of female activity into that of male family members. To put it another way, women's role as wife trumped their role as worker.[387] It is difficult to believe, for example, that the four examples of female food sellers or the twelve of female retailers overall from the city of Rome cited by Rosmarie Günther exhaust these categories.[388] The evidence, whether literary, epigraphic, legal, or artistic, tends to idealize women workers, denigrate them, or omit them altogether.[389]

A partial response to this objection is that, as noted, many of the professions attributed to women are only occasionally attested. The majority of female laborers perhaps worked in agriculture, and their labor went almost as unrecorded as that of their male counterparts.[390] Beyond agriculture, there is no evidence that large numbers of women were employed outside the household. That women, slave or free, were valued economically less than men is suggested by the gender-differentiated valuation of slaves under Diocletian's Price Edict.[391]

The story is a familiar one then, though perhaps more extreme than in some other cultures.[392] Women had access to fewer jobs, and these were less prestigious and (we may perhaps assume) less well-paid.[393] So it is no surprise to find the ancient sources citing economic need as a motive for resort to prostitution. Lack of employment opportunities for women, however, is not a sufficient explanation for the decision to become a prostitute, since many poor

---

387. See the comments of Joshel, *Work* (1992) 142; Günther, "Matrona" (2000) 354; Dixon, *Reading Roman Women* (2001) 115, 122, 132.

388. Günther, *Frauenarbeit* (1987) 129–30. See also Eichenauer, *Arbeitswelt* (1988) 83–89.

389. See the comments of Scheidel, "Silent Women 1" (1995) 206.

390. See Sigismund Nielsen, "Ditis Examen Domus?" (1991) 224. Sigismund Nielsen, relying on the evidence of Columella, suggests that female workers were vastly outnumbered by males in the countryside; more comprehensive is Scheidel, "Silent Women 1" (1995) esp. 208, and "Silent Women 2" (1996) with references to his earlier work on this subject. On seasonal and structural underemployment in Roman agriculture overall, see Erdkamp, "Agriculture" (1999).

391. Scheidel, "Reflections" (1996): only at or just before puberty did the valuations achieve parity, explained by the fact that women were in, or about to enter, their childbearing years.

392. See, for example, Gilfoyle, *City of Eros* (1992) 344–45 nn. 9–14.

393. On prestige see the comparison drawn between *medicus* and *medica* by Günther, *Frauenarbeit* (1987) 118. More generally, see Maurin, "*Labor Matronalis*" (1983) 147; Eichenauer, *Arbeitswelt* (1988) 301. For cross-cultural comparisons, essential reading is Mitterauer, *Familienforschung* (1990) 303, 310–12. The point may be derived simply from the failure to record women's jobs on tombstones: see Flory, "Family" (1978) 80.

women did not become prostitutes. Poverty, in other words, did not "cause" prostitution.

"Immorality" is adduced, both by ancient and modern commentators,[394] in order to explain a woman's decision to become a prostitute.[395] Often the language used to explain this decision includes words like "lust" or "nymphomania." Recent research encourages great skepticism about the value of this kind of explanation.[396] Indeed, other factors emerge as more important. We do not know anything about the wages paid to women workers at Rome, but even if they resembled those paid to men (a generous assumption, in my view),[397] the earnings-potential of a prostitute was greater, or at least would have seemed greater for low-status women in straightened circumstances.[398] Prostitution is not caused by poverty in any simple sense but is part of a culture that is shaped by poverty.[399]

Charity, public or private, was unlikely to provide a respite for many. Under any definition, the numbers of poor in Roman society were likely to have been vast.[400] Their ranks would have swelled from time to time through

---

394. For the ancients (especially patristic authors), see Herter, "Soziologie" (1960) 78; Montserrat, *Sex and Society* (1997) 109; Flemming, "*Quae Corpore*" (1999) 41, cites evidence of Firmicus Maternus describing women driven by lust to prostitute themselves: *Math.* 3.6.22, 6.31.91, 7.25.9; cf. 8.4.10. This differs from Christianizing explanations in that the "lust" is generated by a birth constellation, compelling such women to act and implicitly relieving them of fault. (Firmicus does explicitly recognize necessity as a motivation at 3.6.22.) See Augustine's denunciation of this belief at *Enarr. in Ps.* 140.9 CCSL 40.2032. The first Firmican text also speaks of *necessitas vitae* as a motive for prostitution. For the moderns, see below in nn. 396–99.

395. Personal and political enemies were accused of being prostitutes, as were their wives and children, and of prostituting their wives and children. Examples are too numerous to relate; see, for example, the gossip about Verres's son: Plut. *Cic.* 7.5.

396. Rosen, *Sisterhood* (1982) 137–68 (especially 166–68). "Depravity" is useless as an analytic category: see above. In fact, early sexual initiation and exposure to incest played an important role: Walkowitz, *Prostitution* (1980) 17–21; Rosen, 144–45, 161–65.

397. See n. 337 for ancient sources that recognized that economic pressures forced some women into prostitution. The important role played by low wages (for women's professions besides prostitution) in motivating women to enter prostitution is demonstrated in a modern context by Rosen, *Sisterhood* (1982) 147–61. (See literature above in n. 340.)

398. Prostitution may also have seemed easier to some women in comparison to other obvious possibilities for earning money. For ancient evidence of dislike of the hard work of spinning, weaving, and so forth, as a motivating factor in entering prostitution, see Herter, "Soziologie" (1960) 78; for a modern parallel, see Rosen, *Sisterhood* (1982) 156–61. This is not to say that Roman prostitutes escaped textile work, though the evidence is not decisive (see, e.g., Petron. 132). For spinning prostitutes in other cultures, see Schuster, *Frauenhaus* (1992) 11; Davidson, *Courtesans and Fishcakes* (1998) 87–88.

399. Rosen, *Sisterhood* (1982) 147. See also Gibson, *Prostitution and the State²* (1999) 101, 104–9.

400. Bruhns, "Armut" (1981) 31; Prell, *Armut* (1996) 66.

seasonal work stoppages, crop failures, and sudden spikes in prices.[401] Even a well-organized and well-funded system of social welfare might have found such challenges daunting. As it was, however, the Romans did not even conceive of the poor as a special social category.[402] Benefits from both public and private sources did not accrue on the basis of need but rather in pursuit of political aims and/or out of an existing social relationship, such as patron and client.[403] Public largesse in particular was structured along status lines, so that privileged recipients were typically adult citizen males.[404] What this means is that during the classical period the poor did not receive charity because they were poor, but rather because they were members of a privileged group of "poor." This only changed with the spread of the Christian ethic of relief for the poor and the structural changes in society that accompanied the advent of late antiquity.[405] In the classical period there was nothing resembling a "social safety net" in the modern sense for the vast numbers of poor.[406]

Another important factor in becoming a prostitute, when compulsion was not explicit, was a major disruption of the family economy, whether this was provoked by the death of one or both parents or the loss of a husband through death, desertion, or divorce.[407] Comparative data suggest that women without men, above all, unmarried girls and widows, were especially vulnerable.[408] Direct evidence from antiquity is lacking, but it is likely that the loss of husbands and fathers in foreign and civil wars, or simply their prolonged absence from home, reduced many women to prostitution.[409] The most important point is perhaps that most women, with or without the support of an adult male, simply had to work to eke out a living.[410] Many children found them-

---

401. Prell, *Armut* (1996) 65.

402. Bruhns, "Armut" (1981) 37, 42; Prell, *Armut* (1996) 64; Brown, *Poverty* (2002) 3–5.

403. Bruhns, "Armut" (1981) 34–38, 42; Brown, *Poverty* (2002) 3–5.

404. See Bruhns, "Armut" (1981) 35; Purcell, "Rome and Italy" (2000) 434.

405. Bruhns, "Armut" (1981) 43–49; Brown, *Poverty* (2002) 6, 74.

406. See Prell, *Armut* (1997) 144.

407. Modern studies emphasize the relatively high number of prostitutes who are half or full orphans, or who have lost their husbands and may have children to support: Walkowitz, *Prostitution* (1980) 20; Rosen, *Sisterhood* (1982) 143, 149. See, for example, Lucian. *Dialog. Mer.* 6; Lib. *Or.* 45.9; and Krause, *Witwen* 3 (1995) esp. 190–93.

408. See, for example, on thirteenth-century Paris, Farmer, "Down and Out and Female" (1998) 353–55.

409. The economic changes and dislocations in Italy following upon the Hannibalic War and the subsequent rise of a free and poor urban populace perhaps contributed to a widespread growth of prostitution in Rome and in other cities in Italy: see Evans, *War* (1991) esp. 101–65. Generally, demographic probabilities made a high number of widows and orphans very likely: Krause, *Witwen* 1 (1994) esp. 7–85.

410. See Scheidel, "Silent Women 1" (1995) 207–8.

selves in a similar position, which rendered them likewise vulnerable to sexual exploitation.[411] Dependency does not always take obvious forms.[412] All of these elements contributed to an economy that encouraged freeborn women and freedwomen to enter prostitution.

PROSTITUTION AND THE ROMAN ECONOMY

The economic importance of prostitution at Rome seems guaranteed by a number of factors. Its widespread diffusion, as well as its complex and varied structure, suggest a brisk, prosperous trade, and one that might well attract, as we have seen, upper-class investors. Such investment took place despite the social opprobrium associated with it, which the investors seem largely, if not entirely, to have escaped. It, in turn, assured a good supply of slave prostitutes, supplemented by lower-class free women who were propelled most of all by economic and familial considerations and attracted by the prospect of a relatively generous remuneration, a prospect that I argue was largely illusory.

I do not mean to imply here that upper-class investors were the only ones to profit from prostitution. Despite the generally exploitative character of the business, individual pimps and even some prostitutes were able to improve their economic positions dramatically. In fact, some rare exceptions appeared at the fringes of the upper classes.[413] The consistent refusal of the Romans to allow these individuals to gain admittance to the upper rungs of the social scale, despite their new economic status, does not diminish its significance.

At the same time, the overall economic importance of prostitution and the apparent success enjoyed by some of its practitioners should not blind us to the fact that its location on the Roman socioeconomic scale was very low. The trappings and atmosphere of Roman brothels,[414] which were inextricably associated with lower-class housing, the low prices charged by many prosti-

---

411. Petermandl, "Kinderarbeit" (1997) esp. 124–26, 128. The emphasis in the ancient sources is decisively on the exploitation of male children, at least in classical antiquity. (I find Petermandl's conclusion a tad optimistic.) For the Byzantines, see Leontsini, *Prostitution* (1989) 85–86; Dauphin, "Bordels" (1998) 188–89.

412. Horden and Purcell, *Corrupting Sea* (2000) 275. See also Prell, *Armut* (1996) 147–50; Günther, "Matrona" (2000) 366.

413. This is indicated not only by the large economic potential that prostitution had for some of its practitioners but by many of the legislative enactments concerning prostitutes and pimps: see McGinn, *Prostitution, Sexuality, and the Law* (1998) chap. 2. For example, both were denied a role in municipal government. The lives of such women as Volumnia Cytheris and Chelidon suggest that it was possible for some prostitutes to exist at the fringes of upper-class society.

414. This is so despite the fact that an attempt was sometimes made to mimic an upper-class ambience: see chaps. 4, 7, 8, and 10.

tutes, and, above all, the information we have about the clients of brothels, who were usually of lower-class if not servile status, speak to this point.[415] All of this helps explain the odium attached to visiting brothels for members of the upper classes.[416]

The somewhat surprising lack of evidence for upper-class brothels is partly explained by the elite's negative attitude toward venues for prostitution and partly by the sexual availability of slaves in *familiae* (slave households) owned by the upper classes.[417] Even more fundamental was the elite Roman male's low estimate of prostitutes themselves. Despite some slight indications to the contrary, prostitution was by and large a lower-class phenomenon at Rome. This seems to have been chiefly because the Romans preferred it that way.

As with most other aspects of the Roman economy, it is impossible to quantify the presence of prostitution.[418] Comparative evidence drawn from societies where prostitution is also common may help illuminate the order of magnitude of venal sex in ancient Rome, but only in a very approximate sense.[419] One is limited to making the following generalizations, which must by and large remain impressionistic.

Prostitution was, on any estimate, widespread.[420] Its popularity as an elite investment vehicle seems to have been in part a function of the fact that relatively little investment, beyond the cost of urban real estate, even given the

---

415. Most of the evidence consists of epigraphic data from Pompeii: See Della Corte, *Case*[3] (1965) 170; Franklin, "Games and a *Lupanar*" (1986); Clarke, *Looking at Lovemaking* (1998) 196–99. For prostitutes, see the list of names in app. 3. Treggiari, "Volusii" (1975) 401 n. 37, suggests that the slave clients of brothels "lived in households with an unnatural balance of the sexes."

416. See chap. 3.

417. On the sexual exploitation of slaves, see the evidence given in McGinn, *Prostitution, Sexuality and the Law* (1998) chap. 8. Slave ownership was not confined to the elite (see Bradley, *Slavery and Society* [1994] 10–12), though it was hardly universal. While we can imagine that members of the sub-elite sexually exploited slaves as well, the practice would not have been as widespread—or possible—as it was among the upper classes.

418. For a discussion of the difficulties in understanding the Roman economy, see Garnsey and Saller, *Roman Empire* (1987) 43–103.

419. Even in modern societies, the data do not allow us to do more than make guesses: see, for example, Sleightholme and Sinha, *Guilty Without Trial* (1996) 10, 146; Hershatter, *Dangerous Pleasures* (1997) 264. Prostitution is estimated to comprise between 0.25 and 1.5 percent of the GDP in contemporary Indonesia, Malaysia, the Philippines, and Thailand: Edlund and Korn, "Theory of Prostitution" (2002) 182.

420. For a sense of the broad extent of prostitution in a modern setting with little regulation, see Sturdevant and Stoltzfus, *Let the Good Times Roll* (1992) 173: "[I]n Seoul women were available on almost every block—in a bathhouse, massage room, restaurant, or in the ubiquitous tea houses all over the city." Compare this statement with the following about nineteenth-century New York City, "prostitutes were readily found in saloons, theaters, dance halls, tenements, and even restaurants": Gilfoyle, *City of Eros* (1992) 164 (see also 197–223, 224, 394 n. 2, 399 n. 41).

need to purchase slaves, might lead to sizeable profits.[421] Partly for these reasons, it was commonplace and accessible to customers and did not show any obvious signs of being tucked away in remote areas of the Roman city. Its association with various venues and forms of public entertainment guaranteed this accessibility. A Roman might encounter prostitutes in bars, hotels, outside circuses and amphitheaters, and at festivals and fairs.

For the male customer, venal sex was both widely available and relatively inexpensive. This fact, taken with the evident profitability of prostitution, presents something of a paradox that might be explained in the following way. The two factors of availability and low cost perhaps interacted with each other; for example, vigorous competition depressed prices to an extent. At the same time, the heightened exploitation of individual prostitutes generated more opportunities for clients and, ultimately, more cash for upper-class investors. The truth of this paradox seems borne out by the experience of the Nevada brothels, where prostitutes who are free to set their own prices and retain a goodly share of their earnings find it easier to maximize profits by charging less and attracting more customers.[422]

In Roman society, this win-win scenario for the two main types of exploiter, the Roman brothel owner and the client, did not spell prosperity for most prostitutes. Slave owners and aggressive pimps probably compelled the vast majority of slave and free prostitutes to work and to work a great deal for little reward. For those few women who were not otherwise coerced into entering the profession, economic constraints, above all the depressed job market for women, might have made prostitution seem more remunerative than was actually the case. The supply of women must have been at all times full.

Female prostitution at Rome involved relationships characterized by sheer dependency. Slave owners prostituted their slaves, fathers their daughters, and husbands their wives. In a sense, prostitution functioned as a just another form of exploitation of women's labor, one of a series of unprestigious jobs in which slaves worked for their masters, daughters their fathers, and wives their husbands. In this way, prostitution reflected women's participation in the economy as a whole, with selling sex only one in a series of quasi-domestic responsibilities that were foisted upon women.[423]

---

421. This fact undermines the assertion that, if only repressive laws were repealed, profiteering from prostitution by landowners would abate or even cease altogether: for this argument, see Ericsson, "Charges against Prostitution" (1980) 352.

422. See Symanski, "Prostitution in Nevada" (1974) 361.

423. See the comparison of the lifestyles of respectable women and prostitutes from the municipal brothel in medieval Germany drawn by Schuster, (*Freien Frauen* [1995] 14).

One sign that this is not the whole story is the criminalization of hus-bandly *lenocinium* (pimping) under Augustus. Another is the animus directed at pimps in general. Prostituting one's slaves or daughters was not, in fact, the moral equivalent of making them work wool or run a shop. It is precisely this moral calculus that distinguishes the prostitution of women from other forms of economic exploitation of women's labor. All are embedded nonetheless in the relations of dependency just described. These factors of morality and gen-der hierarchy are what distinguished "women's work" in Roman culture. This means that professions in which women played a role were not "economic" in the modern ideal of rational, profit-maximizing enterprises, but were deeply influenced by considerations of status and social as well as moral constraint. Prostitution, in that it was oriented toward maximum exploitation and there-fore maximum profits, does appear more "economic" in the modern sense at first glance, but only if one absolutely refuses to view it from the perspective of the woman herself, whose choice of a profession was very likely to have been forced upon her. For the Romans, the prostitute was a "good" rather than a "worker."[424] For this reason alone, it is not accurate to speak of Roman prosti-tutes as "sex workers."

The link between Roman slavery and prostitution is so central and so peculiar that it raises the question of whether the Roman experience has much to teach students of venal sex in other cultures and at other times. The first point to make is slavery was simply the most obvious of a series of institu-tions involving power and dependency in which ideally masters ruled over slaves, fathers over daughters, and husbands over wives. The balance of power was far from equivalent in each case, and few would argue, in the wake of important work by Richard Saller and Susan Treggiari, that sons and wives were treated like slaves, certainly on the social level of the upper classes from which the vast bulk of our sources derive.[425] In the sub-elite world in which prostitution flourished, however, these differences may have diminished con-siderably.

When thinking about the economics of venal sex at Rome, it is important to consider gender, which leads to my second point. What slavery, paternal power, and husbandly authority do is to take a given, the inequality in Roman society between men and women, and allow for its articulation in a number of rather nuanced ways. So it is agreed that the status of slave women, daughters-

---

424. This strengthens the statement on exploitation made by Flemming *"Quae Corpore"* (1999) 57.

425. Treggiari, *Roman Marriage* (1991); Saller, *Patriarchy* (1994).

in-power, and wives is not at all the same, unless of course they are prostituted by their owners, *patres familias,* or husbands. In other words, in Roman society slavery facilitated patriarchy but was not an essential, indispensable component of patriarchy. As for the link between prostitution and slavery, this seems to be especially apt, as an element of patriarchy, for female slaves. When authors such as Martial and Juvenal develop the themes of sexual exploitation (Martial) and sexual degeneracy (Juvenal) they rely on this connection as a datum, so that, to generalize the distinction, Martial assumes female slaves are eminently exploitable as slaves and/or prostitutes while Juvenal criticizes the behavior of high-status women precisely as servile and/or whorish.[426] It is well to raise the caution that male prostitution may well have a different relationship to slavery than female. This is one reason why it merits separate and further study.

The last point to make is that the experience of the antebellum American South suggests that we cannot automatically link slavery and a flourishing economy of prostitution.[427] Even where slave owners could have profited from prostituting slaves, such as in the brothels of Nashville, they refrained from doing so. Their motives remain obscure, and race, as well as economics, may well have played a role in this decision.[428] It is beyond doubt that these slave owners found other means of exploiting their slaves both sexually and economically. What is of central importance for us is that slavery as a legal institution is not inevitably tied to prostitution across cultures.

Paradoxically, this fact allows us both to recognize the Roman experience as particular and, at the same time, to draw lessons for other societies crucial to the sociological, historiographical, and ultimately moral debate between liberal and radical feminists over the nature of prostitution.[429] The central issue at stake is this: is prostitution inherently degrading to prostitutes—the radical position—or does it deserve recognition as a legitimate means of making a living, as liberals argue?

The debate will continue regardless of what we conclude about Rome. It is

---

426. See the analysis of Garrido-Hory, "Femmes" (1999).

427. So the classic econometric study of American slavery, Fogel and Engerman, *Time on the Cross* (1989) 131–35. This point is conceded by Flemming, "*Quae Corpore*" (1999) 58–60, with whom I am otherwise at variance. In my view, she relies too heavily on the deeply flawed study of prostitution in colonial Nairobi by White, *Comforts of Home* (1991).

428. Fogel and Engerman, *Time on the Cross* (1989) 135, characteristically prefer an economic explanation.

429. The literature is vast, so that only a small sample can be given here. For the liberal position, see, for example, Chapkis, *Live Sex Acts* (1997); Delacoste and Alexander, *Sex Work²* (1998). For the radical position, see Barry, *Prostitution of Sexuality²* (1995); Jeffreys, *Idea of Prostitution* (1997).

risky to attempt a definitive response to this question even for Roman culture given the lack of evidence provided by the voices of prostitutes themselves. But I would maintain that the evidence we do possess offers cold comfort for those who wish to argue that prostitution is not inherently degrading to women. The Romans represent an extreme when it comes to the sexual and economic exploitation of women, no doubt, and they were also perhaps simply more blatant about this. I believe, however, that when we compare this evidence to evidence from other cultures without legalized slavery, we find these cultures have equivalents or substitutes for this exploitation, rather than a really kinder, gentler version of prostitution than that found at Rome.

A final factor to consider here is the role of the state. It too could not resist the vast profits to be made from the sale of sex. Beginning with the emperor Caligula, a tax was collected that appears to have more than fulfilled expectations of revenue levels. The tax on prostitution turned out to be so indispensable that many Christian emperors in late antiquity could not do without it.[430] The tax, of course, gave the Roman state a financial interest in the profitability of prostitution, an interest it shared with many upper-class Romans. But it was not the extent of that financial interest. As we shall see in subsequent chapters, it is likely that municipalities leased public space to prostitutes or their exploiters and not impossible that the state owned brothels at least by the fourth century.[431]

We must not assume that because prostitution was "legal," it required no legitimization to function as it did or was not in fact legitimized by the creation of the Caligulan tax.[432] Prostitution had been, and remained afterwards, a sordid business operated by a class of persons the Romans regarded as the proverbial scum of the earth, *lenones* and *lenae*.[433] What Caligula accomplished, in part, was to legitimize the interest of private landowners in profiting from prostitution at a polite remove. He did not escape criticism for this initiative, though it is impossible to say whether he would have escaped caricature as a pimp if he had not gone as far as setting up a brothel on the Palatine.[434] Recognition that the tax legitimized prostitution is the reason why Christian emperors fought so long and so hard to eliminate it.

---

430. See McGinn, *Prostitution, Sexuality and the Law* (1998) chap. 7.

431. See chaps. 5 and 6.

432. For another view, see Flemming, "*Quae Corpore*" (1999) 54.

433. See McGinn, *Prostitution, Sexuality, and the Law* (1998) 68–69, on how this prejudice was articulated into a core set of civic and legal disabilities.

434. This may be doubted. See McGinn, "Caligula's Brothel" (1998) esp. 96; *Prostitution, Sexuality, and the Law* (1998) chap. 7.

Prostitution permeated many aspects of the Roman service sector and leisure economy. Its association with various businesses and special occasions increased profitability, a fact that renders attempts to isolate the precise role it played in the economy problematic. While there is no reason to assume prostitution was ubiquitous, it was very common.[435] Like other economic aspects of slavery, it tended toward the maximum exploitation of its workers, no matter what their actual legal status in this case. For all of these reasons, there is something close to paradigmatic about the Roman economy of prostitution in that a series of factors converged here to assert the primacy of male privilege in almost every way conceivable.

---

435. For further discussion of this theme, see chap. 9.

ℰ Chapter Three ℒ

ZONING SHAME

tonsor, copo, cocus, lanius sua limina servant.
nunc Roma est, nuper magna taberna fuit.
—Mart. 7.61.9–10

WHERE THE BOYS ARE

*I*n the first appendix to this book I set out a list of some forty-one possible brothels, about half of which I regard as more likely to have been brothels than the rest. My purpose in doing this is chiefly to provoke further discussion on the subject. Even if my "more likely" list meets with skepticism, I trust even the skeptics will agree that a great deal of uncertainty surrounds the identification of brothels at Pompeii.

This uncertainty paradoxically makes it difficult to agree with the argument of Ray Laurence and Andrew Wallace-Hadrill that the Romans practiced a kind of moral zoning, keeping brothels in certain areas and out of others.[1] Laurence, who depends on Wallace-Hadrill's restrictive identification of

---

1. A similar view is more assumed than argued by Chauvin, *Chrétiens* (1983) 17–18. Hoskins Walbank, review of *Urban Society* (1996); Schoonhoven, "Residences" (1999) 229; Patterson, "On the Margins" (2000) 95, agree with Laurence and Wallace-Hadrill. A prescient objection is raised by Kellum, "Spectacle" (1999) 291. DeFelice, *Roman Hospitality* (2001) 129–49, also expresses skepticism, though not without self-contradiction and lack of clarity. For what it is worth, my views first appeared in McGinn, *Prostitution* (1986) 13–15.

brothels,[2] holds that the concern was to render the sale of sex isolated from, and invisible to, elite women and children. Wallace-Hadrill posits a more general purpose, arguing that the aim was to purify one area of the town center by displacing and concentrating "impure activities in another inconspicuous and hidden, but nevertheless central area."[3] He supports this contention by referring to the location of "the definite brothels," by which he means the Purpose-Built Brothel and the *cellae meretriciae*.[4]

What is striking about the topography of Roman prostitution, however, is the complete absence of any evidence for such moral zoning. First, to turn the argument about "definite brothels" on its head, we cannot be certain that any of the possible brothels listed in the first appendix was *not*, in fact a brothel. In other words, the Roman list of "definite brothels" would almost certainly be longer than any we can construct, if it is correct to assume that they recognized the concept of "definite brothel" at all.[5] At a certain point in the analysis the problem of identifying individual brothels is less important than the conclusion that Pompeii was home to a number of brothels scattered throughout the city.[6] This means that what we should focus on are the probable, or even possible, venues for the sale of sex in Pompeii, that is, if we want to argue for the segregation of prostitution in that city.

In the matter of zoning, moreover, it is a bit misleading to concentrate on brothels and ignore prostitutes.[7] Public buildings and elite town houses may have squeezed the former, but not the latter, out of some areas to judge from the fairly abundant evidence,[8] which shows a wide pattern both of public

---

2. Laurence, *Roman Pompeii* (1994) 73, expresses some confusion over the precise number of brothel sites identified by Wallace-Hadrill and, like him, lumps the Purpose-Built Brothel with the cribs.

3. Wallace-Hadrill, "Public Honour and Private Shame" (1995) 51. He contrasts the irregular plan of *Regio* 7, immediately to the east of the Forum (where the Purpose-Built Brothel and most of the known cribs are located), approached by through "narrow, dark, winding streets," to the "conspicuous, regular, symmetrical, open spaces of the Forum or the upper Via dell'Abbondanza." His point seems to apply Della Corte's design criterion for brothel-identification to the city as a whole: see chap. 7.

4. Wallace-Hadrill, "Public Honour and Private Shame" (1995) 54.

5. There survives, for example, no Roman legal definition of brothel, which would have been essential, one would think, for any serious attempt at zoning. The jurists even seem to have gone out of their way to avoid constructing such a definition, to judge from Ulp. D. 3.2.4.2; Ulp. D. 23.2.43 pr., 9. See app. 1.

6. Cf. Jongman, *Economy* (1988) 252, for a similar argument regarding onomastics, where (un)certainty over individual cases yields to a possible statistical application overall.

7. Cf. DeFelice, *Roman Hospitality* (2001) 101. Much more might be said about Pompeian prostitutes than is possible here: see the list in app. 3.

8. See chaps. 2 and 9.

solicitation and nonbrothel prostitution in places of public entertainment such as circuses, temples, and baths as seen in chapter 2.

The Vicus Sobrius at Rome may be relevant to the argument. According to the grammarian Festus,[9] the Romans called one street "Sober," because it had no *tabernae* or *cauponae*. We may doubt it was the only street of its kind, but even if it were not, the notion suggests that it is wrong to assume that the Romans practiced moral zoning. Brothels, including what would be termed, on a narrower definition than the one I have adopted, strictly nonbrothel venues such as *cauponae* and *popinae* where sex was sold, tended to blend in with a city's lower-class housing stock in a manner that rendered them invisible to many elite Romans and, unfortunately, to us as well.[10] While most scholars would not assume that every *caupona, popina,* and *deversorium* offered sex for sale, it is far from certain which ones did and which ones did not, a point made in chapter 7 in regard to baths. For this reason, the well-explored Roman port city of Ostia, for example, has not one certain example of a brothel and not many good candidates at that.[11]

A further point to make is that brothels were often not located at any great distance from upper-class dwellings.[12] The houses of the Roman elite were not distributed evenly throughout their cities, but neither were they packed together in a manner isolated from the rest of urban society.[13] As we have seen in chapter 2, a pattern of modest clustering, as opposed to rigid segregation, has been found in a number of Roman cities, including Rome itself, where a large number of aristocratic dwellings were located in and near the Subura, supposedly the city's main red-light district. If Roman cities were relatively

---

9. Festus 382–83L. See Kleberg, *Hôtels* (1957) 60. Mart. 7.61 also suggests retailers were ubiquitous in Rome, not only before imperial intervention, but afterwards as well: Domitian seems only to have aimed at clearing the streets; see also 1.41; Spano, "Illuminazione" (1920) 62–64; Purcell, "*Plebs Urbana*" (1994) 659–73; Purcell, "Rome and Italy" (2000) 419.

10. All kinds of shops were integrated into the context of urban housing, Gassner, *Kaufläden* (1986) 84, 88. For cross-cultural parallels on the integration of brothels and lower-class urban housing, see the notes to chap. 8.

11. See the discussion in chap. 8.

12. See Stansell, *City of Women* (1987) 174–75; Corbin, *Women for Hire* (1990) 141; Gilfoyle, *City of Eros* (1992) 47; Hill, *Their Sisters' Keepers* (1993) 178, 195, 378, for evidence from nineteenth-century Paris and New York. In fourteenth-century London, the phenomenon generated complaints: Hanawalt, *Repute* (1998) 116. Cf. the mix of respectable and nonrespectable commerce in 1880s London: Walkowitz, *City* (1992) 129. For a pattern of mixed residence in Renaissance Rome, see Cohen, "Courtesans and Whores" (1991) 205.

13. Martial's suggestion that the houses of his patrons were scattered throughout the city may well have involved some degree of exaggeration. It should not be taken, however, as sheer invention: see Kardos, "Quartiers" (2002) 120.

socially homogeneous,[14] as the evidence suggests, there is simply no rationale supporting the theory of moral zoning. Given the absence of officially segregated prostitution-districts, we can assume brothels were distributed throughout the city, with some clustering in areas that presented the right mix of residential and commercial elements, especially a good share of lower-class housing, in what we might describe as the "Subura-effect."[15]

Even where Roman authors appear to suggest a different pattern, that is, the existence of a clear distinction between wealthy and poor districts, an alternative reading is often possible and perhaps preferable. For example, when Ovid writes of the heavenly Palatine, almost certainly in reference to the Rome of his own day, that "the common people live elsewhere" ("plebs habitat diversa locis"), the obvious meaning is that the rich had made that hill exclusively their own, but a covert reference to imperial usurpation of prime urban real estate seems an even more plausible explanation, at least to me.[16] In any event, the point is that literary topography—topography on the page— is not always coterminous with material topography—topography on the ground, though scholars will inevitably disagree on how precisely to reconcile these different maps of the ancient Roman city.[17] Even when they appear to coincide, there is perhaps at times more than a literal interpretation of the evidence at stake.[18]

In an important sense, the point I have just made should end the discussion on moral zoning. If there is no evidence for any rules, legal or administrative,[19] enforcing the geographic segregation of brothels, and if the location of such establishments is uncertain and quite possibly widespread, the argument for moral zoning fails. The difficulty is, however, that the thesis advanced by

---

14. For a general statement in support of this thesis, see Storey, "Population" (1997) 969.

15. See chap. 9. For an important parallel from nineteenth-century New York City, see Hill, *Their Sisters' Keepers* (1993) 95.

16. Ov. *Met.* 1.173. For the first interpretation, see Wallace-Hadrill, "Emperors and Houses" (2001) 134. For sensitivity over the issue of imperial appropriation of property, especially in the first century, see McGinn, "Caligula's Brothel" (1998).

17. For a similar point regarding the poet Martial's use of topography, see Kardos, "*Épigrammes*" (2001) 206, 209, 214; Kardos, "*Vrbs*" (2001) 389. Essential reading on the *urbs scripta* is Edwards, *Writing Rome* (1996). See also the collection of sources in Kardos, *Topographie de Rome* (2000).

18. There is evidence to suggest that the Romans themselves were mindful of the distinction drawn here. On Augustus's use of a text, the *Res Gestae*, to construct an ideology of space in Rome, see Elsner, "Inventing Imperium" (1996). For the competing efforts of Horace and Ovid in this vein, see Edwards, *Writing Rome* (1996) 7 and 24. See also Dyson and Prior, "Horace, Martial, and Rome" (1995).

19. The aedilician regulations cited by Laurence, *Roman Pompeii* (1994) 80–81; Wallace-Hadrill, "Public Honour and Private Shame" (1995) 45, 50–51 are irrelevant: see chap. 5.

Laurence and Wallace-Hadrill, even in the absence of evidence to support it, remains somewhat compelling, at least from a modern perspective.

Just how compelling this modern perspective can be is well illustrated by the dire problems facing Nevada's legalized brothels at the time of writing. Nevada is famously the only state in the Union to permit these establishments, a situation that has prevailed in ten of its seventeen counties since 1971, though the tradition of prostitution in the state dates back to the days of the Gold Rush in the nineteenth century.[20] While legal, these brothels are nevertheless heavily regulated. They are for the most part permitted only in a few rural areas, in contrast to the much more common urban setting that is characteristic of illegal and unregulated prostitution. Advertising is not permitted, nor is public solicitation in any form.[21]

The prostitutes who work in such places are not strictly employees of the brothels but independent contractors who are required to pay for weekly examinations for sexually transmitted diseases. The brothels themselves pay hefty registration and licensing fees to their local communities. They prefer to call themselves "ranches" and most retain the same 1970s decor that they had when they opened three decades ago. In fact, when a brothel owner in Pahrump, about sixty miles west of Las Vegas, announced a plan to convert his "ranch" into a major resort facility with a golf course, casino, and steak house, the proposal rocked the entire state's prostitution industry, since publicity of any kind is something akin to poison.[22]

The paradoxical situation of Nevada's brothel business shows how deeply rooted assumptions in our culture are about how prostitution should be, and often actually is, hidden away from public view. The barriers to thinking outside of this box are uncomfortably high. Nevada also serves as an example of the false promise held out by some of the comparative evidence available on the subject of prostitution.

Given the lack of ancient evidence for zoning, however, it is difficult, if not impossible, to raise the issue without resort to comparison with other cultures. A useful example lies in attempting to see a link between official approaches toward brothels on the one hand and sewers on the other. Wallace-Hadrill draws a connection between keeping the streets and sewers clean and controlling prostitution that is reminiscent of much nineteenth-century

---

20. On prostitution in nineteenth-century Nevada, see Goldman, *Gold Diggers* (1981).

21. For the information provided in this paragraph, see Nieves, "Anxious Days" (2001).

22. For these details, see again Nieves, "Anxious Days" (2001). Note also the hostile reaction of brothel owners to the appearance of the website Georgia Powers (see the list of abbreviations): Albert, *Brothel* (2001) 240.

discourse on venal sex, above all that of the famous Alexandre Parent-Duchâtelet.[23] The key question, of course, is whether such a connection existed regarding Roman policy on prostitution.[24] This is not a simple matter of anachronism, but, given the variety of experience with prostitution in past cultures, an issue of just what kind of comparative evidence is most likely to shed light on ancient Rome.[25]

We might try to evade the problem of the "brothel next door" posed by Roman comedy, where in such plays as Plautus's *Menaechmi*, *Mostellaria*, and *Pseudolus*, brothels are shown on stage next to respectable dwellings, by citing dramatic convention, Greek influence, and so forth. But the truth is the Romans had no difficulty with this juxtaposition. Much is made in the *Menaechmi* of the Epidamnian brother's affair with a prostitute *ex proxumo*, but the heft of this criticism has to do with the nature of the relationship, that is, with its material and moral consequences for his marriage, as well as its blatantly high profile.[26] Plautus never suggests that the prostitute's dwelling should be relocated. For a young, that is, unmarried man involved with a prostitute, the very proximity of that prostitute might help absolve him of responsibility, as we see was the case for Livy's Aebutius and Hispala.[27]

A policy aimed at the segregation of venal sex from respectable elements of the population has every appearance of having emerged following the rise of Christianity. It may be relevant that, despite a longstanding association between brothels and filth and a "special relationship" between the sewer and the kind of moral criticism found in satire (a genre quite familiar with the brothel),[28] the first ancient to identify brothel with sewer appears to have been Cyprian, Bishop of Carthage. He writes of a putative follower of his opponent Novatian ". . . having entered a brothel, the location of the sewer

23. Wallace-Hadrill, "Public Honour and Private Shame" (1995) 50–51; cf. Harsin, *Policing Prostitution* (1985) 96–130; Bernheimer, *Figures of Ill Repute* (1989) esp. 6–33; Corbin, *Women for Hire* (1990) 3–8. For an anticipation of the theory of "moral geography," see the argument of the sociologist Robert Park in 1915 that it was in the very nature of urbanization for a city to develop "moral regions": Connelly, *Response* (1980) 11.

24. On what is meant by policy here, see chap. 5.

25. The problem is put with striking clarity by a reviewer who writes of Wallace-Hadrill's arguments concerning Pompeii, "Should we be entirely surprised at these arrangements? Zoning into public, residential and commercial areas is commonly found in modern North American cities; brothels or their equivalent are often located centrally near places of entertainment": Hoskins Walbank, review *Urban Society* (1996).

26. See Plaut. *Men.* 790: the wife complains of her husband's behavior. The Senex praises this behavior at 790–91.

27. Liv. 39.9.6, with McGinn, *Prostitution, Sexuality, and the Law* (1998) 88–89.

28. On this special relationship, see Gowers, "The Anatomy of Rome" (1995) 30–32.

and the slimy black hole of the rabble, he has befouled his own sanctified body, God's temple, with hateful filth. . . ."[29]

By itself, however, this account cannot explain an inclination to zone brothels away from respectable establishments. The sewer itself presents a complex metaphor at least in pre-Christian discourse. Though possessing its dark side like the city itself (chapter 9), the sewer might also form the object, along with aqueducts, of fulsome praise from pagan moralists.[30] Cyprian's concern with squalor and the horrors of class mixing are very old hat from a Roman elite perspective and, importantly, do not necessarily range beyond the walls of the brothel in their consequences. From what he writes, it does not appear that he believes a person would be implicated in the evils of the brothel without actually setting foot in one.

BAD COMPANY

The evils of the brothel are worth a closer look. It is easy to find evidence that they were filthy and poorly lit, but the evidence we should remember has the odor of an upper-class sensibility about it that must be discounted at least to some degree.[31] This is also true for the issue of class mixing, obviously, though curiously the Romans, as already seen, did not display a particular sensitivity to this phenomenon in the matter of urban planning.[32] Nevertheless, their negative attitude toward class mixing and brothels meant that some Romans found it dishonorable even to set foot in a brothel or *popina*.[33]

---

29. Cypr. *Ep.* 55.26 *CCSL* 3.1.289: ". . . lupanar ingressus ad cloacam et caenosam voraginem vulgi sanctificatum corpus et dei templum detestabili conluvione violaverit. . . ." See Gowers, "The Anatomy of Rome" (1995) 27 with n. 42.

30. See Gowers, "The Anatomy of Rome" (1993); Edwards, *Writing Rome* (1996) 105–9.

31. See Plaut. *Poen.* 834–35; Hor. *Serm.* 1.2.30; Sen. *Contr.* 1.2.21; Petron. 7 (*locus deformis*); *Priap.* 14.10; Mart. 12.61.8; Iuv. 6.131–32, 11.172–73; Dio Chrys. 7.133; Apul. *Met.* 7.10, *Plat.* 1.13. It is difficult to believe lamps in brothels were as a rule smokier than those elsewhere; all the same, the lamp, when placed outside the door, may have served an iconographic function for the Roman brothel akin to the "red light" in other cultures: see chap. 7.

32. See chap. 2. On prejudice against class mixing in general, see Joshel, *Work* (1992) 68. On class mixing in Athenian inns, bars, and brothels, see Davidson, *Courtesans and Fishcakes* (1998) 55–59, 223, 225; in medieval German brothels, see Schuster, *Freien Frauen* (1995) 249.

33. Viv.-Cels.-Ulp. D. 4.8.21.11; Paul. D. 47.10.26, with McGinn, *Prostitution, Sexuality, and the Law* (1998) 329–30. See also Sen. *Ep.* 51.4; Gell. 9.2.6; *HA Pesc.* 3.10. The insults of Apuleius are instructive here: *Apol.* 57.3, 59.2. More evidence of criticism of those who visited taverns and the like is found in Kleberg, *Hôtels* (1957) 93; cf. 103–5. On tales of emperors visiting brothels, see McGinn, "Caligula's Brothel" (1998). The point appears contradicted by Cato's salute to the young man exiting the brothel at Hor. *Serm.* 1.2.31–32, but I argue that this gesture is not well understood: see Chap. 8.

When an elite Roman entered or exited a brothel, or any establishment that was taken for a brothel, he might have covered his head to disguise his identity.[34] As Isidore of Seville later explains, prescriptively if not descriptively, "he who sets foot in a brothel usually blushes."[35] Cicero describes how embarrassed honest men were when they had to debase themselves by visiting the house of Verres's mistress—which he equates with a brothel (*domus meretricis*)—in order to conduct business.[36]

Brothels were extremely inauspicious. The dream-specialist Artemidorus warns that dreaming of a brothel is generally harmful and even fatal in some circumstances, comparing the brothel to a cemetery. He concedes that actually having sex with a prostitute in a brothel entails a bit of disgrace and some minor expense.[37] Prostitutes in dreams, on the other hand, are always a good sign, according to Artemidorus.[38]

According to a rhetor whose opinion is recorded by Seneca the Elder,[39] if a magistrate entered a brothel in his official capacity preceded by lictors, this action threatened to breach the criminal statute that safeguarded the interest and dignity of the state, the *lex maiestatis*. This text mentions the office of praetor, a magistrate who—we may presume—had no official business in the brothel, and so could not without disgrace set foot in one. The fuss made about lictors can be explained by the fact that it was even considered inappropriate for these attendants to enter the brothel because they were associated with an official whose high rank and range of duties kept him out as well.[40] Otherwise, we would have to conclude that the aediles themselves could not enter, without risk of social censure, some of the places they oversaw as part of their duties, an idea that seems extreme and implausible, given an incident involv-

---

34. See the sources in chap. 2. To be clear, it is not true that upper-class Romans never visited inns or other places of low repute, but they are criticized for such behavior by the sources or shown coming to a bad end: see Kleberg, *Hôtels* (1957) 91.

35. Isid. *Orig.* 19.26.2: ". . . solet erubescere qui lupanar intraverit."

36. Cic. *Verr.* 2.1.120, 137.

37. The qualifications suggest that Artemidorus is writing with a broad audience (or at least a broad social spectrum of past and possible clients) in mind that reached below the level of the elite. For discussion of this somewhat controversial point, see Winkler, *Constraints of Desire* (1990) 17–44 (drawing on the work of Michel Foucault); Bowersock, *Fiction as History* (1994) 77–98; Walde, *Antike Traumdeutung* (2001) 144–99. On social values reflected in Artemidorus's dream-interpretations, see also Annequin, "Entre signifiant et signifié" (1999) esp. 260.

38. Artemid. 1.78, 4.9.

39. Pompeius Silo *apud* Sen. *Contr.* 9.2.17.

40. Another speaker suggests the proper use of a lictor is to remove prostitutes from the path of the praetor: Sen. *Contr.* 9.2.2; cf. 21, also 1.2.7.

ing the aedile A. Hostilius Mancinus, which I discuss below. Aediles would have had to rely on their attendants to enforce their will in any case.[41]

Sensitivity over visiting a brothel extended even to images. At the death of King Agrippa of Judaea in A.D. 44, the people of Caesarea and Sebaste insulted his memory by carrying statues of his daughters into brothels.[42] According to Suetonius, carrying a ring or a coin with the emperor's likeness into a latrine or brothel might ground an accusation of *maiestas* under Tiberius.[43] In the highly charged political atmosphere of Tiberius's last years it is not inconceivable that such a prosecution was brought or even that it was successfully brought.[44] But it is obvious that routine enforcement of such a rule would have brought the brothel business to a standstill or at least seriously compromised it. Interfering with the revenues generated by brothels was in nobody's interest.

For obvious reasons, the social mix in a brothel was very close, closer even than in a *popina*. The atmosphere in both places was sexualized to a degree, but more so where prostitutes worked, since they often walked about nude or at any rate scantily clad.[45] Brothels, like prostitution itself, were supposed to assert the social hierarchy, but could, through implicating upper-class visitors in their "evils," threaten to overturn it. What really distinguished the brothel as "bad" however, was the combination of social mixing and atmosphere of criminality that pervaded it, first and foremost in the elite imaginary, but not only there.

Comparative evidence suggests that brothels, as well as the prostitutes working inside and outside of them, have only rarely *not* been exposed to criminal activity, in the form of beatings, rape, murder, robbery, theft, and destruction of property.[46] "Fighting, drunkenness, and mayhem filled the air of the

---

41. According to Mommsen, *Staatsrecht* 1³ (1887/1969) 386 n. 4, 2.1³484, aediles had no lictors to attend them, though that is hardly the issue here.

42. Ios. *Ant.* 19.357.

43. Suet. *Tib.* 58. Dio 58 fr. 2C (4B) has the latrine version, with more detail. For a recent attempt to explain this latter version, see Ryan, "Majestätsverbrechen" (2002).

44. Cf. Bauman, *Impietas* (1974) 80. A similar charge was brought against an equestrian who carried a coin with Caracalla's image into a brothel; sentenced to death, he was saved by the emperor's own death: Dio (in *Exc. Val.*, Xiph.) 77.16.5. No evidence supports the modern theory that so-called *spintriae*, small bronze or brass tokens with erotic scenes, were used in lieu of coins to pay for sex in brothels, precisely to avoid a criminal charge of insulting the emperor: see chap. 4, n. 15.

45. See Petron. 7; Iuv. 6.121–24, 11.172; Tac. *Ann.* 15.37.3; Dio (in *Exc. Val.*, Xiph.) 79.13.3; [Cyprian.] *Spect.* 5 CSEL 3.8. Cf. Sen. *Contr.* 1.2.7.

46. Barry, *Slavery* (1979) 8; Finnegan, *Poverty* (1979) 27; Heyl, *Madam* (1979) 149–59, 159, 162; Pavan, "Police" (1980) 246, 253, 261; Prus and Irini, *Hookers* (1980) 2, 12, 22,

brothel."[47] The behavior of prostitutes themselves might contribute to the negative atmospherics. Dio of Prusa cites prostitutes trading obscenities from their respective booths as a *malum exemplum* of civic behavior, the sort of thing that persons with a pretense to respectability should avoid.[48] But the main threat to order came from elsewhere. The idea that there is a connection between space and violence is supported by the fact the same close confines that encouraged the mixing of ranks and genders also bred disorder.[49] Rome itself has been persuasively described as a culture of violence,[50] a judgment thoroughly supported by evidence about the climate prevailing in and near brothels. Two questions emerge from this discussion[51]: Were brothels more violent than other places in the Roman city? Were they perceived as more violent than they actually were?

Definite answers are impossible, but one is inclined to respond, in turn, "yes" and "perhaps not." A combination of factors, such as the consumption of alcohol, social mixing, and the presence of young men prone to impulsive behavior, might produce explosive results. One manifestation was the high level of noise generated, for example, by drunken, often obscene singing, and violent, often bloody confrontations.[52] The practices of male boasting, performing, and competing lent an edge to an already volatile atmosphere.[53] The

---

64–65, 76, 80, 162–67, 180, 200; Goldman, *Gold Diggers* (1981) 1, 33, 88, 113–16, 132–33; Rosen, *Sisterhood* (1982) 98, 131, 172; Harsin, *Policing Prostitution* (1985) 121, 138–48, 166–204, 299; Otis, *Prostitution* (1985) 68, 83–85, 91; Reynolds, *Economics of Prostitution* (1986) 114, 125–26, 141; Butler, *Daughters of Joy* (1987) 27, 33, 42–43, 61, 110–11; Sutton, "Pornography" (1992) 32; Guy, *Sex* (1991) 110–11; Gilfoyle, *City of Eros* (1992) 76–92, 98, 321–29; Høigård and Finstad, *Backstreets* (1992) 57–63, 142–43, 146–49, 154; Schuster, *Frauenhaus* (1992) 72–77, 125; Hill, *Their Sisters' Keepers* (1993) 40, 166–70, 202, 211, 224–29, 247, 255, 270, 295, 305, 315; Tong, *Unsubmissive Women* (1994) 126–58; Bernstein, *Sonia's Daughters* (1995) 68–69, 154–55, 178–83; Schuster, *Freien Frauen* (1995) 79, 117–18, 137, 199–202, 249–50, 313; Karras, *Common Women* (1996) 58, 61, 71, 95, 100; Sleightholme and Sinha, *Guilty Without Trial* (1996) 85–91; Hershatter, *Dangerous Pleasures* (1997) 82, 87, 157, 292–94; Davidson, *Courtesans and Fishcakes* (1998) 82, 329.

47. Butler, *Daughters of Joy* (1985) 61.

48. Dio Chrys. 40.29. I take *oikēma* here to be the equivalent of *cella*, though the word could mean "brothel."

49. See the comments of Hanawalt, *Repute* (1998) 111.

50. See Brown, "Death" (1992). See also Eyben, *Youth* (1993) 107–12; Nippel, *Public Order* (1995); Purcell, "Rome and Italy" (2000) 418–19 on urban violence.

51. Similar questions are asked in Schuster, *Frauenhaus* (1992) 72, in regard to the brothel in medieval Germany.

52. See, for example, Plaut. *Merc.* 408–9, *Persa* 568—69; Prop. 2.5.21–26, 2.19.5–6, 4.8.19; Tib. 1.1.73–75; Sen. *Contr.* 1.2.10; [Quint.] 15.2, 6, 7; Suet. *Nero* 26–27, *Otho* 2.1; Tac. *Ann.* 13.25.1–4; Apul. *Apol.* 75; Dio (in *Exc. Val.*, Xiph.) 61.8.1–2; *Vita Sanctae Thaisis* 1 PL 73.661; Eyben, *Youth* (1993) 91, 94, 96, 107–12.

53. See Cantarella, *Bisexuality* (1992) 147, for a good evocation of this atmosphere.

competition might take the form of gambling, which, despite its being for the most part illegal, was rife throughout taverns and brothels.[54] The basic premise of the brothel was to celebrate all forms of transgression, not just the sexual.[55]

Violence was such a familiar part of the experience of visiting a brothel or bar, it came to be represented in the wall decorations of some establishments.[56] The potential sources of violence included not only pimps, clients, and public officials, but prostitutes themselves, who were at a minimum acting in self-defense.[57] Since the dynamics of power inevitably meant the prostitute was on the receiving end of the larger share of this violence, it is fair to regard it as "violence against women rather than as violence per se."[58] Indeed, the comparative evidence cited above suggests that one important use of violence in the brothel is to keep women working there.

A well-known incident concerning an attack on a brothel by the aedile A. Hostilius Mancinus, datable to the mid-second century B.C.,[59] illustrates various aspects of the problem of violence in Roman brothels. Mancinus approached the lodging of a prostitute named Manilia one night in the course of a drinking party. Repulsed by a shower of stones, he brought a suit against her, claiming assault. Manilia appealed to the tribunes, asserting that Mancinus had approached her building in the garb of a reveler, that it was not in her best interest to admit him, and that he attempted a forced entry.

The remark about Manilia's "best interest" is evidently a polite reference to her fear that Mancinus would destroy her property, subject her to rape or another form of physical assault, and/or murder her.[60] The tribunes accepted

---

54. Cic. *Cat.* 2.10; [Verg.] *Copa* 37; Mart. 5.84; Paul. D. 47.10.26; C. Titius *apud* Macrob. 3.16.15–17. Depictions of a game of dice erupting into a violent confrontation and ending in expulsion by the *caupo* is found on the wall of one Pompeian tavern (6.14.35–36) and a more placid version of a game of dice is found in one of two possible brothels (6.10.1, 19 = Cat. no. 12). See Kleberg, *Hôtels* (1957) 118. The legal regime on Roman gambling has been the focus of a series of studies by Marek Kurylowicz; see, for example, "Glücksspiel" (1985).

55. On the latter point, see chap. 7.

56. Kleberg, *Hôtels* (1957) 118; DeFelice, *Roman Hospitality* (2001) 112.

57. I do not want to suggest here that nonbrothel prostitutes, namely streetwalkers and crib prostitutes, were less exposed to violence than those who worked in brothels: see Gilfoyle, *City of Eros* (1992) 84, 89; Tong, *Unsubmissive Women* (1992) 144–45.

58. See Sleightholme and Sinha, *Guilty Without Trial* (1996) 91. See also Harsin, *Policing Prostitution* (1985) 167; Walkowitz, *City* (1992) 225; Hill, *Their Sisters' Keepers* (1993) 181; Tong, *Unsubmissive Women* (1994) 40.

59. Gell. 4.14; literature at McGinn, *Prostitution, Sexuality and the Law* (1998) 60 n. 324. For the identification of the brothel with prostitutes' lodgings, see chap. 8.

60. Gell. 4.14.5: "eum sibi recipere non fuisse e re sua." Flemming, "*Quae Corpore*" (1999) 46, suggests that Manilia refused a "paying customer," but there is no evidence to suggest that Mancinus had anything but rape and other forms of violence on his mind.

her plea, holding that Mancinus had been with justice barred entry, since it was inappropriate for him to approach her residence wearing a garland, a finding that would hardly deter violence from being visited upon prostitutes in the normal course of a magistrate's duties.[61] The judgment also implies that Mancinus could enter a brothel while performing his duties as aedile, a rare exception to the usual animus against members of the elite visiting brothels.

Rape was a very real prospect for a brothel-prostitute, who might otherwise be thought to enjoy a modicum of protection, in comparison to a street-walker, for example.[62] Her vulnerability is illustrated by the sarcastic comments of the speakers in the rhetorical exercise recorded by the Elder Seneca about the brothel-inmate who kills her rapist.[63] They question the woman's ability to avoid rape by the pirates who captured and sold her, the pimp who acquired and installed her in a brothel, and the various customers who confronted her, including drunks, gladiators, and hot-blooded young men bearing arms.[64] The visitors she could expect to receive amounted to "a low and hurtful mob" ("sordida iniuriosaque turba").[65] In other words, rape was the fate of a woman in a brothel: the place raped her, if no man did.[66]

Forced entry, or its attempt, into a brothel is a theme with a long history in Roman literature and, it seems, life as well.[67] Perhaps most interesting is a *Digest* text in which Ulpian holds that a man who has broken down a prostitute's doors because of lust ("libidinis causa") is not liable if thieves enter independently and take her property.[68] The assumptions embedded in the text sug-

---

61. In other words, the magistrates responsible for maintaining order in brothels were apt to provoke disorder themselves. On the escalation of violence as a consequence of rule-enforcement, see Marx, "Ironies of Social Control" (1981) esp. 223–26. One should not, at all events, overestimate the magistrates' effectiveness or even interest in preventing commonplace violence in public areas: for the latter point, see the suggestive observation of Suet. *Aug.* 45.2, with Scobie, "Slums" (1986) 433.

62. The legal position on the liability for raping a prostitute is not clear: McGinn, *Prostitution, Sexuality, and the Law* (1998) 326–27.

63. Sen. *Contr.* 1.2.

64. Sen. *Contr.* 1.2.2–4, 6–8, 10, 12, 18.

65. Sen. *Contr.* 1.2.8.

66. Sen. *Contr.* 1.2.7; see also Ter. *Eun.* 923–33, where it is assumed that in a brothel rape was part of the atmospherics.

67. See Plaut. *Persa* 569; Ter. *Ad.* 88–92, 100–103, 120–21; Lucil. 793–803W, 937–48W; Cic. *Cael.* 38; Hor. *C.* 1.25.1–3, 3.26.6–8; Prop. 1.16.5–6, 2.5.21–26; Tib. 1.1.73–74; Ov. *Am.* 1.6.57–60, 1.9.19–20, *Ars* 3.71–72, 567–70; *Rem.* 31–32; Apul. *Apol.* 75. Given its status as a literary topos, it is perhaps worth citing evidence for this theme from other cultures. Prus and Irini, *Hookers* (1980) 163; Gilfoyle, *City of Eros* (1992) 79–80; Schuster, *Frauenhaus* (1992) 73; Hill, *Their Sisters' Keepers* (1993) 169–70.

68. Ulp. *D.* 47.2.39, with McGinn, *Prostitution, Sexuality, and the Law* (1998) 325–28.

gest that such behaviors were both common and usually deemed beneath the attention of the law. A prostitute who denied a client entry to a brothel—in many cases no doubt apprehending violence from the start—had good reason to fear an assault on her property and person. Manilia's successful defense should not lead us to conclude that all or most such encounters ended so happily.

Ulpian's focus on theft in this passage raises another point about the disorderly and criminal atmosphere associated with the brothel. Violence did not tend to occur in the absence of other behaviors associated with delinquency, such as theft and drunkenness, a point supported by the comparative evidence.[69] Theft and the consumption of alcohol have often formed part of the dynamic of the brothel as the drunken state of clients makes it easier for prostitutes to steal from them and vice versa.[70] In any case, pimps, madams, and prostitutes have commonly resorted to theft as a way of supplementing their incomes, sometimes by stealing from each other.[71] Brothels have witnessed numerous deceptions designed to relieve customers of their money, the most popular one perhaps being the "adultery" scam, wherein a client in bed with a prostitute is discovered by an irate "husband" and forced to pay a premium. Examples come from ancient Greece, Rome, as well as more recent periods.[72] Balzac's symbolic coupling of prostitution and theft, located in his critique of contemporary Parisian society, has deep roots in the lived experience of the brothel.[73]

In medieval England, the line between a brothel and a den of thieves appears to have been very thin, if it existed at all.[74] This was in part because brothels have traditionally acted as a magnet and a haven for criminals of all

---

69. See Best, *Controlling Vice* (1998) 19, 28–29, 53, 71, 101–2.

70. See Prus and Irini, *Hookers* (1980) 59; Hill, *Their Sisters' Keepers* (1993) 37, 157, Tong, *Unsubmissive Women* (1994) 145; Best, *Controlling Vice* (1998) 70–71.

71. See Decker, *Prostitution* (1979) 207, 331; Finnegan, *Poverty* (1979) 104–6, 112; Butler, *Daughters of Joy* (1985) 43, 56–58, 105; Harsin, *Policing Prostitution* (1985) 37 n. 62, 50, 134, 148–51, 155, 183, 385, 391; Mahood, *Magdalenes* (1990) 143–48; Gilfoyle, *City of Eros* (1992) 217, 360 n. 14; Hill, *Their Sisters' Keepers* (1993) 57, 122, 145, 155, 165, 278–79, 256, 307, 315; Bernstein, *Sonia's Daughters* (1995) 170; Hershatter, *Dangerous Pleasures* (1997) 47, 222–23.

72. [Dem.] 59; Plaut. *Miles*; Prus and Irini, *Hookers* (1980) 151–57; Gilfoyle, *City of Eros* (1992) 173, 285; Hershatter, *Dangerous Pleasures* (1997) 14, 137.

73. See Bernheimer, *Figures of Ill Repute* (1989) 58–59.

74. Karras, *Common Women* (1996) 100. See also Harsin, *Policing Prostitution* (1985) 150, on nineteenth-century Paris.

stripes, not simply thieves to steal from the prostitutes.[75] Evidence from a number of cultures shows how easily stolen property makes its way to the brothel and there is divided up among thieves or fenced to third parties.[76] So at Rome, an experiment of Nero's provides the most secure parallel to Caligula's foundation of a brothel on the Palatine:[77]

Suet. *Nero* 26.1:
quintana domi constituta, ubi partae et ad licitationem dividendae praedae pretium absumeretur.

A market was set up in his [i.e., Nero's] house, where the booty he had acquired was split up, auctioned off, and the proceeds squandered.

As for the consumption of alcohol, the details offered by the Roman legal and literary evidence make clear that a violent visit to a brothel was a common feature of the male drinking party, the *comissatio*, a topic that deserves more extensive treatment than is possible here.[78] Often associated with the aristocratic banquet, the *comissatio* was a sort of after-dinner entertainment for young men in their late teens and early twenties.[79] It might have entailed the heavy consumption of alcohol, gambling, casual acts of violence against persons and property, and resort to prostitutes.[80] The atmosphere of the *comissa-*

---

75. See Prus and Irini, *Hookers* (1980) 91; Hershatter, *Dangerous Pleasures* (1997) 82, 137, 215, 225.

76. See Prus and Irini, *Hookers* (1980) 184–85, 222, 225; Schuster, *Frauenhaus* (1992) 66; Karras, *Common Women* (1996) 100. For late-antique evidence, see Socr. HE 5.18 PG 67.609–12.

77. See the discussion in McGinn, "Caligula's Brothel" (1998) 99.

78. See also chap. 2.

79. See, for example, Sen. *Contr.* 2.6.7. Mau, RE comissatio (1901) 612 (cf. 618) appears to assume the *comissatio* was closely tied to the dinner party; cf. Marquardt, *Privatleben* 1 (1886) 331; Eyben, *Youth* (1993) 103–4. This was not always the case, especially if the *comissatio* was held off-site: see, for example, Cic. *Verr.* 2.3.31; Eugraph. *ad Ter. Ad.* 783 (which can be taken to imply any of the three alternatives mentioned below) and below in the text. By the same token, eroticized entertainment after dinner was not necessarily a *comissatio*: see Gell. 19.9. On the conventions of elite dinners, see, for example, Landolfi, *Banchetto* (1990) esp. 68–70, 95; Treggiari, *Roman Marriage* (1991) 422–23; D'Arms, "Performing Culture" (1999) with literature.

80. For example, Plaut. *Capt.* 72–73, *Curc.* 354–61, *Men.* 124, *Miles* 652, *Most.* 959–61; Ter. *Ad.* 101–2, *Eun.* 934–36, *Heauton* 206–10; C. Titius *apud* Macrob. 3.16.15–16; Cic. *Verr.* 2.1.33, 2.5.28, 81, *Mur.* 13, *Pisonem* 22, *Phil.* 2.6, 42, 63, 67, 105 (Antony is accused of eliding the distinction between respectable *cena* and debauched *comissatio*); Liv. 3.13.2; Philo *Vita Contempl.* 40–56; Plin. *NH* 14.142 (who complains of the potential for adulterous liaisons at 141); [Quint.] *Decl.* 9.10; Tac. *Ann.* 13.25.1; Suet. *Nero* 26–27; Plut. *Ant.* 9.3–6, *Sulla* 36.1–2; Lucian. *Conviv.* 43–46 (mythological); Galen. *Meth. Med.* 1.1 Kühn 10.3; Dio (in Xiph.) 62.15.6; HA *Verus* 4.6.

tio, with its sex, drink, and potential for violence, is notably exploited in different ways by the sources in order to condemn the heinous behavior of L. Quinctius Flamininus, who is said to have executed a man at such an affair at the behest of a prostitute.[81]

The heavy consumption of alcohol with attendant disorder might occur in a private venue, such as the site of the preceding *cena*, if there was one, in a brothel or tavern, or in an even more public place such as the Forum.[82] After drinking with friends, individuals were free to seek out prostitutes on their own, a practice perhaps reflected in the literary tradition of the *exclusus amator*, the elegiac lover shut out of his mistress's house.[83] There is a strong affinity in all this with the Greek practice of the male drinking party known as the *kōmos*.[84]

The evidence discussed above allows me to state with confidence that an atmosphere of disorder and criminality was associated with the operation of Roman brothels. It is impossible, however, to determine the extent to which this evidence reflects upper-class prejudice or social reality. The casual nature of some of the references suggests that they do not simply reflect elite bias. On the other hand, the problems of the brothel did not loom so large as to prompt a shift in official approaches to the brothel. The aediles in Rome and, we may suppose, their equivalents in other cities were, as we shall see, entrusted with the oversight of brothels, but this meant above all the preservation of public order without resort to an elaborate system of regulation or repression.[85] This

---

81. See Landolfi, *Banchetto* (1990) 62; Suerbaum, "Sex und Crime" (1993).

82. For the first option, see Plaut. *Miles* 652; Ter. *Eun.* 422–25; Cic. *Cat.* 2.10; Liv. 39.6.8 (female musicians at dinner); Val. Max. 9.1.8 (the house-brothel mentioned here was perhaps an elaboration of the custom of inviting prostitutes for the *comissatio*; for the evidence, see chap. 5); Sen. *Ep.* 95.24; Iuv. 11.171–79; Plut. *Ant.* 9.5. For the second option, see Gell. 4.14; *Hist. Ap. Tyr.* 34; *HA Verus* 4.6 (in Pompeii, at least one of the now-destroyed sexual scenes on the south wall of Room b of the *caupona*/brothel at 6.10.1, 19 [cat. no. 12] appears to have depicted sexual violence against a prostitute: Clarke, *Looking at Lovemaking* [1998] 211). For the third option, see Sen. *Ben.* 6.32.1; though the details given about Julia's behavior are incredible, the point was to make her out to be a prostitute, assisting in a revel: see McGinn, *Prostitution, Sexuality, and the Law* (1998) 168–70. On prostitutes in the Forum, see chap. 9. At times, entertainers, including actresses, dancers, and musicians, provided sexual services on-site or elsewhere: Mau, *RE* comissatio (1901) 617–19.

83. Lucr. 4.1177–84; Hor. *Serm.* 1.4.48–52, Prop. 1.16.5–8; Ov. *Rem.* 31–32; [Quint.] 15.2, 7, with McKeown, "Elegy" (1979) 82 n. 27.

84. See Landolfi, *Banchetto* (1990) 48; Henry, "Edible Woman" (1992) 256–58 (very good on the "sexualization of food" in the descriptions by Athenaeus); Davidson, *Courtesans and Fishcakes* (1998) 81–82.

85. See chaps. 3 and 5.

may mean that the social pathologies the Romans associated most intimately with the brothel may well have been contained there for the most part.[86]

CHRISTIAN TOPOGRAPHY

In regard to segregation itself, the first well-attested example is a text that attributes to Constantine the establishment, in his new city of Constantinople, of a large brothel in the Zeugma district, complete with a statue of Aphrodite outside on a stone pillar (a nice touch), which was supposed to be the only brothel, indeed the only place where prostitutes worked, in the entire city.[87] I am inclined to distrust this report as representing yet another effort in the long campaign to make Constantine appear more Christian than he ever was in actual fact.[88] This example perhaps represents a case of wholesale invention or, more probably, the recounting of a popular legend.[89] At any rate, the notion that this pragmatist emperor attempted to limit prostitution in his new capital to a single venue defies belief. Nevertheless, it must stand as an example of what some Christians thought a Christian emperor ought to do. This is where its true value as evidence lies.

I hasten to point out that even a Christian might shrink from such an attribution. By establishing a brothel as an act of public policy, Constantine would seem to join the distinguished, if at the same time dubious, company of ruler-pimps such as Solon and Caligula.[90] A fundamentalist of this kind might

---

86. Violent activity itself by *iuvenes* (groups of young men) was hardly linked exclusively to the brothel. See, for example, Apul. *Met.* 2.18; Call. D. 48.19.28.3. On this last text, see Randazzo, "Collegia Iuvenum" (2000) esp. 208; Legras, "Droit et violence" (2001). More generally, Kleijwegt, "*Iuvenes*" (1994).

87. *Patria Const.* 2.65 185–87 Preger. On this work of c. 995, see Kazhdan, "Patria of Constantinople" (1991) 1598.

88. For some—other—examples of Christian spin on Constantine's actions, see McGinn, "The Social Policy of Emperor Constantine" (1999) esp. 70–71.

89. This example seems unlikely to be derived from Constantine's measure repressing some or all aspects of male prostitution (below), especially since the text of the *Patria* mentions female prostitutes. A better candidate is the shelter established for poor prostitutes by Theodosius I (below), but even this would require considerable elaboration.

90. We owe knowledge of Solon's brothel to the evidence of fourth-century comic poets. See Rosivach, "Solon's Brothels" (1995); Kurke, *Coins* (1999) 196–97; Frost, "Solon" (2002) all of whom are rightly skeptical about the historicity of the anecdote. McGinn, "Caligula's Brothel" (1998) is inclined to credit Caligula with actual pimping, though this may be a case of the exception that proves the rule regarding the truth of the tradition. According to one tale, which is no doubt apocryphal, Cato the Elder recommends recourse to the brothel and in so doing, falls more or less into the category of ruler-pimps: see the evidence and discussion in chap. 8.

not view as a saving grace the attempted "paganification" of the brothel-site through the alleged installation of the statue of Aphrodite. At any event, let us not saddle emperor Constantine with more credit, or blame, than the sources allow. For example, as one scholar writes, "[i]t is characteristic of his pragmatic approach to prostitution that Constantine designated a section of his new capital city, Constantinople, as an official red-light district and required all of the city's harlots to remain within its confines".[91] The legend lives on.

A more likely candidate for the first Christian intervention in the business of zoning brothels is perhaps seen, albeit indirectly, in the *Historia Augusta,* which reports that the emperor Tacitus "outlawed brothels in the capital, a measure which, to be sure, could not hold for long."[92] The author is almost certainly making fun of Christian antiprostitution legislation, rather than reporting an action that we can reliably attribute to the third-century emperor. We might guess the measure was an initiative of the Theodosian dynasty, which has been lost to us at least in part because of its swift and manifest failure.[93] Even if one believes the report about Constantine's Zeugma brothel, a similar conclusion is inevitable, namely that the policy of zoning failed. Brothels in Constantinople, as in other Byzantine cities, were located where the customers were found— at the harbors, near the holy shrines, and, where we might expect the administrative heirs of the classical aediles to be most attentive, in the heart of the city center.[94]

Where did the Christian ideas about zoning prostitution arise? Before attempting an answer to this question, I must first confront a difficulty in my argument. If it is indeed possible to show, or simply to suggest strongly, that the impetus to segregate venal sex within cities originated with Christianity, this does not render the arguments of the proponents of zoning at Pompeii

---

91. So Brundage, *Law, Sex, and Christian Society* (1987)105, argues, though without citing a source.

92. *HA Tac.* 10.2: "meritoria intra urbem stare vetuit, quod quidem diu tenere non potuit."

93. See McGinn, *Prostitution, Sexuality, and the Law* (1998) 269–74, for a discussion of the anti-Christian disposition of the author of the *HA*. Christian sensitivity to the problem at this time is suggested by the evidence of *Mac. Aeg./Alex. Acta* 1 PG 34.221A, if this is correctly dated to the late fourth century. Though the *HA* text does not specify male brothels, it does perhaps refer to the suppression of such brothels in 390: see below in the section on "Augustinian Policy." For another view, see Neri, *Marginali* (1998) 205 (206) n. 29, who sees in the text a possible historical reference to the reign of Tacitus.

94. *Mac. Aeg./Alex. Acta* 1 PG 34.221A; Iustinianus Nov. 14 (a. 535); Proc. *Aed.* 1.9.2–4; with Leontsini, *Prostitution* (1989) 63–65, who accepts the report about Constantine's brothel, arguing for its utter failure.

somehow automatically anachronistic. Such an argument in fact opens the door to the suggestion that the Christians, as with a number of aspects of their teaching on sexual matters or morality in general, took some elements of the various moral traditions that predated them in the Mediterranean world and made them their own.[95]

What makes the difficulty particularly acute in the matter of segregating prostitution is that there is nothing about Christian moral teaching in antiquity that in any sense predestines it to favor this policy over others. A peculiar fact about Christian doctrine is that over the centuries it has shown itself remarkably supple in accommodating itself to any number of policies regarding the sale of sex, ranging from repression, to regulation, to tolerance, to various combinations of these approaches.[96]

AUGUSTINIAN POLICY

A useful demonstration of the point I have just made is provided by a text of St. Augustine, which has been of monumental importance in the formation of public policy on prostitution in the Christian West and beyond and in the historical understanding of this policy:

> Augustinus *Ordine* 2.12 CCSL 29.114; Doignon 198:
> Aufer meretrices de rebus humanis, turbaveris omnia libidinibus.
>
> *Remove prostitutes from human societies and you will throw everything into confusion through lusts.*

By itself, this text is polyvalent. By itself, all it really amounts to is an argument against the repression of prostitution, rather than one for the regulation, or tolerance, of the profession. Because of its ambiguous nature, the text has been interpreted in various ways, as justifying tolerance, or regulation, or some combination of the two. The historical—and historiographical—record in fact is full of such varied interpretations.[97] This fact does not render the search for Augustine's meaning any easier.

---

95. For an elegant presentation of this question regarding the particular aspect of sexual renunciation, see Brown, *Body and Society* (1988).

96. See McGinn, *ESH* (1994) s.v. "Prostitution." Cf. Chauvin, *Chrétiens* (1983) 27, 52, 68–71, 85, 93, 96, who cannot be followed on many points of detail.

97. See Chauvin, *Chrétiens* (1983) 60 (for this general point); Harsin, *Policing Prostitution* (1985) 110 (for the point that Alexandre Parent-Duchâtelet used Augustine to justify his work, which laid the foundation for French nineteenth-century regulationism); Otis, *Prostitution* (1985)

Of course, the approach Augustine is implicitly criticizing in the *De Ordine* was not characteristic of pre-Christian Roman policies on prostitution, at least, not in the drastic form he presupposes, that is, complete removal from human society. In other words, this too was a Christianizing policy. We do not have to go far to find Christian hostility toward prostitution in the sources.[98] The Roman practice of punishing Christian women, mentioned by Tertullian, among others, by interning them in brothels may have helped sour them on the profession.[99] But the disfavor is much older than that, based in no small measure on a text by Paul that appears to exclude both prostitute and client from the Christian Church.[100]

We may reasonably question whether all of this evidence is inevitably linked to the repression of prostitution, since disapproval of the practice can notably coexist with other official approaches, though admittedly is unlikely to be found alongside sheer tolerance. In any event, we do find various repressive measures launched by Christian emperors, albeit partial in nature. In most cases, these measures were directed at pimping, rather than at prostitutes or prostitution itself.[101] We may contrast these measures with the official line taken toward male prostitution in late antiquity, which began with a pagan emperor, Philip the Arab, and which was significantly harsher, as well as an anomalous campaign directed against male and female prostitution under Julian.[102] It is worth reviewing briefly the late-antique measures adopted against prostitution in the years before Augustine wrote.

12, and Rossiaud, *Medieval Prostitution* (1988) 80–81 (for the idea that Augustine was critical for the medieval intellectual position on fornication); Brundage, *Law, Sex, and Christian Society* (1987) 106 (for the argument that Augustine advocated the toleration of prostitution); Perry, *Gender and Disorder* (1990) 46–47 (for the point that authorities in sixteenth-century Spain used Augustine to prove prostitution was a necessary evil); Guy, *Sex* (1991) 13, 50, 181, 200, 202 (for the fact that both Catholics and anti-clerics cited Augustine to justify regulating prostitution instead of repressing it in late nineteenth- and early twentieth-century Buenos Aires and discussion of at least one important objection to this position); Karras, *Common Women* (1996) 6 (for the point that Augustine was critical for the development of the medieval version of the hydraulic thesis of male sexuality).

98. See, for example, Iustin. Martyr. *Apol.* 1.27 Munier 70–72; Tert. *Apol.* 15.7 CCSL 1.114, 50.12 CCSL 1.171, *Cultu Fem.* 2.12.1 CCSL 1.367, *Pallio* 4.9 CCSL 2.745; Min. Fel. 25.11 Kytzler 24.

99. Tert. *Apol.* 50.12 CCSL 1.171. See chap. 8.

100. Paul. 1 *Cor.* 6.15–16: below in the text.

101. Valent., Theod., Arcad. *Coll.* 5.3 (a. 390); Nov. Theod. 18 (a. 439): one can certainly more accurately describe the latter as a measure repressing pimps. See also Constantius CTh. 15.8.1 (a. 343); Theod., Valent. CTh. 15.8.2 (a. 428) (= C. 1.4.12 = C. 11.41.6); Leo C. 1.4.14 (a. 457—-67) (= [?] C. 11.41.7); Iustinianus Nov. 14 (a. 535).

102. On the alleged Christianity of Philip, see the recent negative assessment of Körner, *Philippus Arabs* (2002) 273.

Aurelius Victor tells us that Philip the Arab during his short reign (A.D. 244–49) decided to outlaw male prostitution when, following an unsuccessful sacrifice, he caught sight of a young male prostitute soliciting outside of a brothel who resembled his own son.[103] Victor asserts that the measure failed, while also implying that male prostitution remained illegal in his own day just over a century later. Jerome reports that Constantine prohibited male prostitution, at a minimum from the arches of places of public entertainment such as theaters and amphitheaters, though a broader ban might be implied as well.[104] Jerome, of course, wants to claim this measure as a victory of Christian ideology, though it is hardly necessary to assume that this was a motive of Constantine, given the precedent set decades before by Philip.

All the same, Christian emperors continued to repress male prostitution. Constantine's sons instituted yet another ban in A.D. 342, which is laid down in a law that seems to embrace nonvenal same-sex relations as well as prostitution.[105] Worth mentioning, though it occurred just after Augustine's time of writing the *De Ordine*, is the violent attack on male brothels that was launched in Rome in 390.[106] We may compare the official attitude toward male prostitution with that toward female prostitution. To our knowledge, one repressive measure (apart from a very partial exception noted below) was taken by a fourth-century Christian emperor against female prostitution, a law by Constantius that placed limits on, if it did not prohibit outright, the prostitution of Christian slave women against their will.[107]

The measures mentioned by the emperor Julian in a speech delivered at Constantinople in 362 were nothing new for male prostitution; but for female prostitution they were quite extraordinary. Julian, in the midst of a denunciation of his bitter enemies the Cynics, describes an unnamed city filled with temples and secret rites as well as many holy priests who dwelled in its sacred precincts. These priests, notes Julian approvingly, had driven out everything unnecessary, low, and base from the city, such as baths, brothels, and taverns, in order to preserve its purity.[108]

Baths, brothels, and taverns were three of the leading centers of prostitu-

---

103. Aur. Vict. *Caes.* 28.6–7. With this move, Philip placed himself in the conservative Roman moral tradition, according to Körner, *Philippus Arabs* (2002) 180–81.

104. Hier. *Comm. in Esaiam* 1.2.5–6 CCSL 73.32.

105. Constantius, Constans, CTh. 9.7.3 (= C. 9.9.30[31]) (a. 342). The literature is vast. Among the more reliable guides are Dalla, *Ubi Venus Mutatur* (1987) esp. 167–70 and Cantarella, *Bisexuality* (2002) 175—76.

106. Valent., Theod., Arcad. Coll. 5.3 (a. 390).

107. Constantius CTh. 15.8.1 (a. 343). The language of the statute suggests a very limited protection at best was made available: see Evans-Grubbs, "Virgins and Widows" (2001) 235.

108. Iulian. *Or.* 6.7.

tion in the Roman city, as we saw in chapter 2. Thus, Julian's campaign may be regarded as fundamentally directed against the presence of prostitution, though of course it went even further than that.[109] Despite the misgivings of some moralists, as noted, baths were an important aspect of city life for the Romans. Thus it seems as if Julian's intent here was as much about reforming the basic experience of urban culture.[110] One may compare this initiative with his implacable hostility toward the theater.[111] Julian mentions just one city, evidently a religious center where pagan priests enjoyed great political influence, but may be taken to imply that more than one was involved. All the same, it is difficult to imagine that many urban centers participated in this project of repression, not only for reasons of ideology, culture, and pragmatic policy (not to speak of self-interest), but also given the fact of Julian's very brief reign.

Julian does not claim credit for this project of urban purification, though there can be little doubt he was behind it. He took a great interest in reforming the pagan priesthood in order for it to serve as the spearhead of his religious reform of all of Roman society.[112] So he forbade priests from visiting the theater, drinking in taverns, or engaging in any occupation that was shameful or degrading.[113] Thus, it is not surprising to find pagan priests tasked with enacting an ambitious moral reform. As with other aspects of Christian social reform, such as poor relief, Julian perhaps wanted to beat them at their own game.[114] While the attempt to repress completely male prostitution had pre-Christian roots, extending this attack to venal sex *tout court* was a novelty. Even so, there is some reason to think that Dio of Prusa's hostility toward prostitution influenced Julian, insofar as Julian depended on him for certain other aspects of his attack on the "uneducated Cynics."[115] If so, this is another sign

---

109. We cannot describe this policy as zoning, since the point was to drive brothels, and prostitution in general, outside the physical limits over which the local authorities enjoyed power, i.e., the city itself. Worth noting is that Julian uses the metaphor of the body in his speech, not to accommodate venal sex in the Roman city as Augustine does (below), but to describe the hierarchical structure of philosophy itself: see *Or.* 6.10, with Prato and Micalella, *Giuliano* (1988) 74–75, on the tradition.

110. So Bouffartigue, *Julien* (1992) 668–69.

111. See, for example, Iulianus *Misopogon* 21.351C–D.

112. See Bowersock, *Julian the Apostate* (1978) 87–88; Renucci, *Idées politiques* (2000) 324–59; van Nuffeln, "Deux fausses lettres" (2001) 137–38, 141–43.

113. Iulianus *Ep.* 84.430B Bidez, 89.304B Bidez. Van Nuffeln, "Deux fausses lettres" (2001) 136–48, argues that the first letter (84) is spurious, though his argument seems undercut by the radical measures taken against taverns, brothels, and baths.

114. See, for example, Raeder, "Kaiser Julian" (1944/1978) 210–15; Bowersock, *Julian the Apostate* (1978) 87–88.

115. Dio Chrys. 7.133. See Athanassiadi-Fowden, *Julian and Hellenism* (1981) 128–29; Prato and Micalella, *Giuliano* (1988) xxv–xxvi, for Dio's influence on this speech.

of just how extraordinary his position was on prostitution, given Dio's radical stance.

The evidence about attempts to repress prostitution does encourage an inference to be drawn about the significance of the *De Ordine* regarding the politics of prostitution. A number of different measures had been taken against prostitution in late antiquity, none of which seem to have enjoyed success beyond a limited period of time at best. The initiative taken under Julian, despite its evident failure, might still have been regarded by some Christians as a challenge to their own position, especially regarding the tolerance of female prostitution. As suggested, it may very well have been intended as a challenge. The matter was therefore still open for debate. Disagreement among Christians was perhaps rendered sharper by the repressive measures taken against brothels, at least some brothels, in Rome by Theodosius I in 385, the year before the composition of the *De Ordine*.[116] What we seem to have in this passage by Augustine is the outline, bare as it is, of a debate among Christians about the optimal public policy on prostitution.

Can we be any more precise about Augustine's own position? It is perhaps possible if we look at the context of the sentence quoted above in the text. The future bishop is grappling with the problem of the place of Evil in God's creation.[117] Does it show the limits of His power or, worse, suggest that God endorses Evil?[118] Centuries later Thomas Aquinas, who was likewise grappling with the problem of Evil, adapted Augustine's words regarding the repression of prostitutes in order to justify the toleration of the religious practices of nonbelievers.[119] With that context in mind, it is not surprising to find that, immediately before introducing the problem of prostitution in this passage, Augustine cites the need to abide the existence of the marginal and socially despised figure of the executioner in a well-ordered society (*bene moderata civitas*).

Augustinus *Ordine* 2.12 CCSL 29.114; Doignon 198–200:
Quid sordidius, quid inanius decoris et turpitudinis plenius meretri-

---

116. A tavern-brothel attached to a bakery had a practice of abducting patrons to work in a mill; other brothels had adulteresses work as prostitutes. Theodosius not only ended these practices but ordered the brothels in question destroyed: Socr. *HE* 5.18 PG 67.609–13; Theoph. *Chron.* PG 108.208–9.

117. The dialogue *De Ordine* is one of Augustine's earliest surviving works, dated to December of 386 by Brown, *Augustine of Hippo* (2000) 64. On the problem in Augustine's works overall, see Cancelo, "Anotaciones" (1994).

118. The dilemma is laid out at Augustin. *Ordine* 1.1 CCSL 29.89; Doignon 69–71.

119. Aquinas, *Summa* 2a2ae.10.11. I rely on the text and translation furnished by the monument of scholarship produced by the English Dominicans: "Blackfriars." *St Thomas Aquinas, Summa Theologiae* 32 (1975) 72–75.

cibus, lenonibus ceterisque hoc genus pestibus dici potest? aufer meretrices de rebus humanis, turbaveris omnia libidinibus; constitue
matronarum loco, labe ac dedecore dehonestaveris. sic igitur hoc genus
hominum per suos mores impurissimum vita, per ordinis leges condi-
cione vilissimum. nonne in corporibus animantium quaedam membra,
si sola adtendas, non possis adtendere? tamen ea naturae ordo nec, quia
necessaria sunt, deese voluit nec, quia indecora, eminere permisit.
quae tamen deformia suos locos tenendo meliorem locum concessere
melioribus. quid nobis suavius, quod agro villaeque spectaculum con-
gruentius fuit pugna illa conflictuque gallinaciorum gallorum, cuius
superiore libro fecimus mentionem? quid abiectius tamen deformitate
subiecti vidimus? Et per ipsam tamen eiusdem certaminis perfectior
pulchritudo provenerat.

*What can be said to be baser, more devoid of honor, more laden with disgrace
than prostitutes, pimps, and the other vermin of this type? Remove prostitutes
from human society and you will throw everything into confusion through
lusts. Confer on them the status of respectable women, and you will only disgrace the latter through blot and humiliation. So instead this kind of person is
rendered most foul in terms of lifestyle by their conduct, and lowest in social
status by the laws of the universal order (ordo). Aren't there, in the bodies of
living creatures, certain parts, which if you should pay attention only to them,
you wouldn't be able to pay attention? Nevertheless, the natural, universal
order (naturae ordo) did not wish them to be lacking, since they are necessary, nor did it allow them to stand out, because they are ugly. These mis-
shapen elements, all the same, by retaining their own contexts, yield a better
place to the better parts. What has been more pleasant to us, what entertainment more appropriate for field and farm, than that combat and contestation
of barnyard-bred cocks, of which we spoke in the preceding book? All the
same, what have we seen that is more cast down than the defacement of the
one who is defeated? And yet it is through that very defacement that the
beauty of this same competition had emerged as more perfect.*

First, we must note that much of this passage is woven simply from the more
or less whole cloth of traditional Roman male upper-class attitudes about prostitutes and prostitution. The characterization of prostitutes in the language of
social disgrace and sexual shame (e.g., *dedecus, turpitudo*) is very familiar,[120] as

---

120. Such language also plays an important role in moral discourse about *decorum*, particularly in relation to the body: see Doignon, *Ordre* (1997) 347 citing Cic. *Off.* 1.126 (see also 127),
3.85, and below in the text.

is the contrast between the status of respectable women (*matronae*) and that of prostitutes, which had been, after all, a fundamental premise of the Augustan law on adultery.[121] The same statute assumed that prostitutes ideally served to distract male lust away from respectable women and so exempted both prostitutes and the men who had sexual relations with them from its penalties.[122] We can easily see that the idea, which we would locate in a kind of biological determinism, that prostitutes functioned—or should function—as a safety valve for male sexual desire is central to Augustine's thinking in the passage quoted above. His use of the map of the human body to help chart the coordinates of the body politic also has an excellent classical pedigree, traceable, for example, to Livy's Menenius Agrippa.[123]

A closer examination of the passage, however, suggests that Augustine's stress on the precise *location* of the parts in his version of the fable of the body finds only very limited precedent in the tradition. The degree of emphasis he places on this one aspect is far, far greater, suggesting an intent to marginalize the prostitute not only socially but topographically as well. The difference is essential then for understanding the nature of his own particular contribution to this discourse on the body. Livy, in his account of Menenius's fable, mentions merely in passing that the stomach is found *in medio*.[124] Most of the other authors who trade in the tale of the parts of the body, such as Xenophon, Aesop, Cicero, Dionysius of Halicarnassus, Seneca, and Polyaenus, are silent on the point of location.[125]

There are two significant exceptions to this rule, however. In one of the many passages where he adopts the body metaphor, Dio of Prusa implicitly rejects zoning vice, when he states that publicly displayed flaws in the body politic are preferable to hidden vice, just as physical illness that is visible is preferable to illness that it is internal, since the former is easier to treat.[126] In one of his speeches, Aelius Aristides, who also favors this metaphor, compares internal diseases, which are the most severe for the body and require the most

---

121. See McGinn, *Prostitution, Sexuality, and the Law* (1998) 147–71.

122. See McGinn, *Prostitution, Sexuality, and the Law* (1998) 194–202.

123. Liv. 2.32.9–12. For discussion of this passage and its parallels, see Ogilvie, *Commentary on Livy* (1970) 312–13; Martin, *Spirit* (1984) 22–23; Collins, *First Corinthians* (1999) 458–61. Dionysius of Halicarnassus, at 6.86, also has Menenius use the fable of the body, which the historian says was based on Aesop: 6.83.2.

124. Liv. 2.32.9. For a brief discussion of the evidence—not as rich as we would like—for the literary transformation of Rome into "a kind of bodily map," see Gowers, *Loaded Table* (1993) 14–15.

125. Xen. *Mem.* 2.3.18; Aesop. 159; Cic. *Off.* 1.85, 3.22–23, 26–27, 32; Dion. Hal. 6.86; Sen. *Ep.* 95.52, *Ira* 2.31.7; Polyaen. 3.9.22. For the emperor as *caput imperii*, see Ando, *Ideology* (2000) 392–93 with literature.

126. Dio Chrys. 9.2.

attention, to domestic problems and conflict, which are the worst mischance for a city.[127] Far from testifying to the practice of zoning, such evidence suggests that for the pre-Christian ancients an entirely different calculus prevailed regarding the screening of vice from public view.[128]

An evident third exception is even more telling. Notably, it involves a passage by St. Paul in which the Body of Christ is analogized to the human body. Paul offers the closest precedent to Augustine's thought in the *De Ordine*, though perhaps not in any straightforward sense. He argues that the different parts of the body ideally exist in accord with one another, and he asserts that Christians should bestow greater honor on those parts they deem less honorable, just as they should bestow greater honor on those less seemly among them, since the more seemly have no need of this.[129] Paul seems less concerned with the location of body parts than with matters of social, moral, and even aesthetic hierarchy, but we are getting close to the heart of the matter of zoning, as we shall soon see.

These issues are obviously of central concern to Augustine as well, though he presents them in a very different manner. For one thing, Paul appears to question or even subvert the social hierarchy in the passage in First Corinthians, while Augustine is evidently concerned about shoring up and defending that hierarchy.[130] He is surely more "Roman" in this sense than is Paul.

Where, then, is the line that leads from the earlier text to the later? Very possibly, it runs through Cyprian's text, which I discussed above. Its content is very conservative, aside, as we have seen, from the identification made of sewer and brothel. Perhaps it was this citation of a public facility, ideally covered over and hidden from view, that suggested to Augustine a model for the

---

127. Aristid. 24.18.

128. On the Roman moralists' concern with hidden vice in particular, see chap. 9. The idea of removing diseased body parts seems too extreme for zoning prostitution: cic. *Phil.* 8.15–16.

129. Paul 1 *Cor.* 12.12–31. The crucial lines are at 12.23–24.

130. On Paul as a questioner or subverter of hierarchy, at minimum that of the Christian Church at Corinth, see Martin, *Spirit* (1984) 28–29; Watson, *First Epistle* (1992) 135–36; Martin, *Corinthian Body* (1995) 94–95; Witherington, *Conflict and Community* (1995) 258–61; Hays, *First Corinthians* (1997) 215–16; Horsley, *1 Corinthians* (1998) 172–73; Collins, *First Corinthians* (1999) 464–65; Schrage, *Evangelisch-Katholischer Kommentar* (1999) 226–28, 242. It is obvious enough that Augustine is asserting the importance of social hierarchy, and one that even in its most immediate implications of a Christian society reaches far beyond the conception of Paul. I note that the (extensive) literature on Augustine's debt to Paul tends to privilege Augustine's later works and to conceive of this debt as highly changeable, informed by Augustine's inner spiritual development, itself a product in part of contemporary events, but placing no emphasis, as far as I can tell, on the radically different worlds each man inhabited. See, for example, the contributions by R. A. Markus, P. Fredriksen, and W. S. Babcock, in Babock, *Paul* (1990). Bammel, "Pauline Exegesis" (1993/1995) (a very partial exception). On Paul and the body see also Sandnes, *Belly* (2002).

geographic disposition of brothels. About this crucial element Cyprian says nothing, so the connection remains speculative. The same holds for the role of the sewer as a body metaphor in pre-Christian discourse, figuring as "the bowels of the city."[131] Augustine was perhaps aware of this tradition and made the connection upon reading Cyprian. We cannot know for certain.

It would require an exegete far braver than I am to exclude categorically the possibility that Paul refers to prostitutes in some way or other in the passage from First Corinthians. I am content to point out simply that Paul's comments earlier in that same Letter appear to exclude any possibility that the bodies of prostitutes—and those of their clients, who may fairly be described as the author's true concern—can belong to the Body of Christ.[132] The difference between Augustine's and Paul's perspective might be explained by the fact that Christian Church was Paul's frame of reference and for him ideally did not include practicing prostitutes or their customers and a Christian society was Augustine's frame of reference and for him embraced both groups.[133] For this reason perhaps, Paul's challenge to male sexual autonomy is far more radical than what Augustine seems prepared to accept.[134]

At the same time, there is no doubt that Augustine shares Paul's low estimate of male sexual behavior and may even be more pessimistic on this score. Many commentators, pointing to the language of honor and shame that Paul deploys in the passage from First Corinthians, are almost certainly right to insist that he refers to the sexual organs and their veiling,[135] a suggestion that at the very least approaches the idea of zoning on a metaphorical plane. This helps clarify, to an extent, Augustine's possible reliance on a line of thought

---

131. See Gowers, "The Anatomy of Rome" (1993) 14–15: the evidence for the tradition is itself tenuous.

132. Paul. 1 *Cor.* 6.15–16. See Watson, *First Epistle* (1992) 60–61; Kirchhoff, *Sünde* (1994) (whose argument at 34–37 that Paul means here a broader group of women than prostitutes is undercut by her concession at 37 that Paul writes primarily of prostitutes); Martin, *Corinthian Body* (1995) 176–79; Witherington, *Conflict and Community* (1995) 168–69; Hays, *First Corinthians* (1997) 101–9; Horsley, *1 Corinthians* (1998) 92; Collins, *First Corinthians* (1999) 245–46.

133. See, on a general level, Brown, *Poverty* (2002) 6, 24–25, 74. This does not mean, however, that in other contexts Augustine hesitated to adopt Paul's position on the prostitute's body and the Body of Christ: see, for example, *Sermo* 161.1 PL 38.878; *Sermo* 162.1–2 PL 38.885–87; *Moribus Eccl. Cathol. et Manich.* 78 CSEL 90.84; *Retractationes* 1.19 CCSL 57.58; *Speculum* 31 CSEL 12.211. Furthermore, the perspective of the *De Ordine* was hardly inevitable, even in Augustine's day. See, for example, Hier. *Ep.* 77.3 CSEL 55.2.39; Ioh. Chrys. *In Ep. 1 ad Cor. Hom.* 30 PG 61.249–58.

134. For Paul's approach to male sexual autonomy, see Hays, *First Corinthians* (1997) 109. If anything, Augustine's views seem more the product of gender than class bias, despite Brundage, *Law, Sex and Christian Society* (1987) 106.

135. See Martin, *Spirit* (1984) 28; Carson, *Showing the Spirit* (1987) 48–49 (though Carson goes too far, I believe, in denying the passage's sociological import); Ellington and Hatton, *Trans-*

that in other respects seems very different from his own. What does seem reasonably clear at a minimum is Augustine has taken up the tradition of the human body as a metaphor for human society as found in Cicero, Livy, Paul, and the rest and utterly transformed it.

One influence on Augustine in this matter that cannot be discounted is that of Plotinus. In his *Enneads,* the neo-Platonist philosopher argues that the organizing principle of the universe assigns, on the basis of justice, a place (*topos*) to each person according to his moral character and in this way sustains the harmony of the whole.[136] According to Plotinus, there are diverse areas of the universe, both better and worse, and each area suits some souls more than others, a fact that contributes to, rather than detracts from, the general harmony. Plotinus, in order to explain the accommodation of Evil in the universe, even includes the example of the public executioner, who holds his own place in the well-governed city. He does not, however, mention prostitutes or brothels nor employ the metaphor of the body and its parts.[137]

Augustine also seems to have made use of a passage by Cicero, which deals not so much with the body as metaphor as with the body as body.[138] Nature, he asserts, shows a great plan (*ratio*) in the arrangement of the body's parts in that she places the honorable/attractive (*honesta*) parts in plain view, while she covers over and conceals those that are ugly, unsightly, and given over to necessity, a reference to the organs of reproduction and excretion. Human modesty is modeled on that of nature, so that all right-minded persons keep from view the ugly parts of the body and perform the functions associated with them in private.[139] The emphasis on the proper aesthetic of the ideal order of

---

*lator's Handbook*² (1994) 286; Martin, *Corinthian Body* (1995) 92–96 (good on the subject of social status); Witherington, *Conflict and Community* (1995) 258–61 (also helpful on social status); Collins, *First Corinthians* (1999) 464–65 (usefully invokes Mikhail Bakhtin's concept of "heteroglossia" or polyvalent vocabulary); Schrage, *Evangelisch-Katholischer Kommentar* (1999) 226–27; Soards, *Biblical Commentary* (1999) 265.

136. Plotin. *Enn.* 3.2.17, with Doignon, *Ordre* (1997) 197 n. 44, commenting on the Augustinian passage that immediately precedes ours (2.11).

137. For some of the differences between Plotinus's and Augustine's treatment of the problem of Evil, see Pacioni, *Unità* (1996) 232–34.

138. Cic. *Off.* 1.126–27. On Cicero's engagement in general with Cicero's work in this dialogue, see Foley, "Cicero" (1999) esp. 71–75. I note in passing that the assertion of Dyroff, "Form" (1930) 51 n. 77, that Augustine owes a debt to Varro is not persuasive.

139. See the useful discussion of this passage in Dyck, *Commentary on Cicero, De Officiis* (1996) 300–303.

things must have had some import for the question of zoning in Augustine's mind.[140]

It is obvious that what Augustine did was take disparate elements of the different traditions on the universe, including the social order, and on the body, such as its construction, its decorum, and, above all, its use as a metaphor for the universal hierarchy of things and transform these elements into something new.[141] His purpose was to explain what for him was only apparently a paradox in God's providential design. Evil, he believed, was not simply an inconvenience, but a part of the deep structure of the universe, the DNA or source code of the universal order.

What the passage from *De Ordine* offers us, in a nutshell, is the Christian rationale for zoning prostitution. Just as the human body segregates certain elements, so too does a well-ordered society isolate and render as inconspicuous as possible the sale of sex.[142] By displacing and concentrating this "impurity" in a hidden, though nevertheless central area, society concedes and guarantees a purity to the rest. The social order is confirmed, with respectable women (*matronae*) at the top; the natural order is ratified, with prostitutes at the bottom. Unlike Paul apparently, Augustine does concede prostitutes a place, however humble, in society, even Christian society. He felt prostitutes are necessary for a desirable social order, in the same paradoxical way that for Augustine and his audience the splendor of a cock fight was dependent on the harm wrought upon its vanquished participant.

Because he wanted to regulate prostitution does not necessarily mean Augustine approved of it, or even avoided criticizing it. He wrote in subsequent works many times and at some length on the subject of venal sex, in a spirit of manifest hostility toward its practice.[143] There is no obvious caesura

---

140. On this aesthetic and its connection with Cicero, see the comments of Gunermann, "Tradition" (1974) 205–8.

141. That the body itself in this discourse enjoys the status of a construction should be reasonably clear. For a discussion of various aspects of historical experience in this field, see Turner, *Body and Society*[2] (1996).

142. Augustine prepares us for this discussion in the passage immediately preceding at *Ordine* 2.11 CCSL 29.113; Doignon, 196, where he says, regarding the way of life of the imprudent (*vita stultorum*), which is embraced in the order of things (*rerum ordo*) by Divine Providence, ". . . and, just as certain places are arranged by that ineffable and eternal law, it is in no way allowed to be where it ought not to be" (". . . et quasi quibusdam locis illa ineffabili et sempiterna lege dispositis nullo modo esse sinitur, ubi esse non debet").

143. On Augustine's hostility to prostitution, see the texts cited in n. 133 above regarding his use of the Pauline contrast between the prostitute's body and Body of Christ. Add, for example, the condemnation of the practice under the *divina atque aeterna lex* at *Faustum* 22.61 CSEL

between the prebaptismal *De Ordine* and what follows, as has been suggested.[144] This is not to deny Augustine's position on prostitution was complex or even inconsistent. But there is no good evidence of a conversion on his
part from the policy of "tolerance" to something else, whether regulation or
repression.

This much may be clear, but later evidence from the writings of the Bishop
of Hippo makes it far less certain whether he himself actually ever intended to
advocate the segregation of brothels by the civil authorities. In book 14 of the
City of God, composed in the years 418–20, he observes that while in the
earthly city no law regulates prostitution, sex that is permitted and goes
unpunished still shuns the public gaze, and brothels themselves, as though
they possessed a sense of shame (*verecundia naturalis*), provide for privacy.[145]

> Augustin. *Civ. Dei* 14.18 CCSL 48.440–41:
> Opus vero ipsum, quod libidine tali peragitur, non solum in quibusque
> stupris, ubi latebrae ad subterfugienda humana iudicia requiruntur,
> verum etiam in usu scortorum, quam terrena civitas licitam turpi-
> tudinem fecit, quamvis id agatur, quod eius civitatis nulla lex vindicat,
> devitat tamen publicum etiam permissa atque inpunita libido conspec-
> tum, et verecundia naturali habent provisum lupanaria ipsa secretum
> faciliusque potuit inpudicitia non habere vincla prohibitionis, quam
> inpudentia removere latibula illius foeditatis. sed hanc etiam ipsi
> turpes turpitudinem vocant, cuius licet sint amatores, ostentatores esse
> non audent.

> *Of course the very act which is accomplished by such lust (is characteristic)*
> *not only of all manner of illicit sex, where hiding places are sought in order to*
> *escape the criminal courts established by humankind, but also of recourse to*
> *prostitutes, which base conduct the earthly city has rendered lawful.*
> *Although no ordinance of this city punishes the latter practice, this sort of lust*
> *which is tolerated and goes unpunished all the same avoids the public gaze.*

25.656, as well as *Civ. Dei* 14.18 CCSL 48.440–41, where he implicitly criticizes the earthly city
for tolerating prostitution: see below in the text for this passage. A similar line of thought is found
in *Sermo* 153.5 *PL* 38.828. The assertion that adultery is worse than prostitution at *Bono Coniug.*
8 CSEL 41.198 hardly compromises this perspective.

144. Chauvin, *Chrétiens* (1983) 57, suggests there was a caesura in order to reconcile perceived differences between the statement in *De Ordine* and Augustine's later work.

145. For the date of the book, see Brown, *Augustine of Hippo* (2000) 282.

So brothels themselves, from an inborn sense of shame, have made provision for a place set apart, and unchastity has been able more easily to do without the chains of repression than shamelessness has been able to take away the seclusion of that disgraceful behavior. But this sort of thing even base persons describe as base behavior. And although they may be its patrons, they dare not act as such in public view.

This would indeed be a wonderful world if I could cite this passage as evidence that between the time of writing the *De Ordine* and the *City of God*, Augustine's ideas on brothel-location had been read as prescriptive by an imperial legislator and turned into law, the first certain experiment in zoning brothels.[146] Unfortunately, if this did in fact happen, the statute was already a dead letter, since the author is very clear that no law governed the operation of brothels at this time. It is even more tempting to take Augustine's words as an assertion of the tendency of brothels to self-segregate. The idea would still be attractive, even if it were modified, as indeed it must be, by the reflection that the alleged *verecundia naturalis* of brothels is in no small part a misreading of motive by Augustine. Perhaps then he misunderstands the tendency of brothels to avoid major thoroughfares because the rents are prohibitive.[147] This suggestion, however, also melts away on closer inspection, as does the idea that privacy prevailed in the brothel.

All Augustine appears to be saying in the passage above is that venal sex takes place within the confines of a brothel and that this is a good thing as far as it goes. As with other forms of human sexuality, whether adulterous or marital, people prefer privacy, even relative privacy. Even so, there is more than a hint here of the traditional rhetorical *topos* on the modesty of prostitutes.[148] Thus we cannot use this passage to argue that prostitution was practiced any less openly in Augustine's day than in the classical period. What matters most for us is that this text from the *City of God* raises the possibility that a policy

---

146. Regrettably, I cannot follow Neri, *Marginali* (1998) 212 with n. 58, who sees in the references to *casae in vicis* at Augustinus *Enarr. in Ps.* 80.2 CCSL 39.1121, 80.17 CCSL 39.1130 an indication that brothels were removed to suburban areas. If true, this would represent a regime of repression akin to that pursued under Julian, as opposed to the kind of zoning outlined in *De Ordine*, but the evidence does not support even the latter.

147. For similar instances of upper-class male misreading of behavior related to prostitution, see McGinn, *Prostitution, Sexuality, and the Law* (1998) 137–38, 297 n. 43. The idea that (private) considerations of honor and shame might have in some way influenced the location of brothels does retain a measure of plausibility, however: see chap. 10.

148. See chap. 2.

of mere tolerance might for Augustine achieve the ideal result represented in the body imagery of the *De Ordine*.

This possibility seems highly unlikely, however, given Augustine's hostility to prostitution, which is visible in the context of his remarks in the *De Ordine* itself. Prostitution was an evil, and some Christians evidently thought that it should be prohibited. Few if any would have advocated a policy of tolerance. Augustine argues that it should be allowed only under conditions that permit the social order to be preserved. The most obvious, and most important, condition to emerge in this passage is that the practice of prostitution should be limited only to certain inconspicuous places. We might at most concede an element of ambivalence, or indifference, over the precise role of the State in overseeing this result, parallel to Augustine's notorious unconcern even with the basic form that a government should take.[149] At any rate, in political matters he was no utopian.[150]

As suggested above, few of Augustine's readers have viewed the passage from *De Ordine* as ambiguous, even—or especially—when they seem to have misread it. We can easily see how a late fourth or even very early fifth-century emperor might have been tempted to translate what could appear to be no more than Christian common sense into action. Segregating brothels might have seemed both more practical and palatable than the alternative of repression, which we know was tried at this time.[151] It may have been the attempted (I write this because it cannot have been any more successful than most campaigns aimed at repressing prostitution) suppression of male brothels at Rome in 390 that inspired the author of the *Historia Augusta* to attribute, satirically, the prohibition of brothels in the city to the third-century emperor Tacitus.[152] Augustine himself may have been moved, in part by the evident failure of Julian's policy of repressing venues of prostitution, both male and female, to develop a Christian regulationist response.

Zoning was certainly more acceptable to Christians than tolerance, which would have led to more (and louder) of the sort of complaints about the urban distribution of brothels from this period registered above. It may be that, if the story of Constantine's Zeugma brothel has any small kernel of truth to it, that

---

149. On the latter, see Fortin, "Introduction" (1994) esp. vii, xiv–xv, xxii–xxvi; Taylor, "St. Augustine" (1998) esp. 293–94, 300–302. For Augustine, "the Empire is theologically neutral": Markus, "Early Christian Historiography" (1963) 347. On his attitude toward law, see Fortin, "Augustine's City" (1979) 337.

150. Taylor, "St. Augustine" (1998) 290.

151. Cf. the later experience of Justinian, as traced by Chauvin, *Chrétiens* (1983) 29–30.

152. On the date of the *Historia Augusta*, which is often given as c. 395, but which might have been a bit later, see the discussion with bibliography in McGinn, *Prostitution, Sexuality, and the Law* (1998) 270–73.

experiment dates to this period, that is, the late fourth or very early fifth centuries and did not last very long.[153]

A possible candidate for a policy of Christian zoning occurs with Theodosius I, who reigned from 379 to 395. According to John Malalas, this emperor converted a temple of Aphrodite in Constantinople into a garage for vehicles for the praetorian prefecture and installed lodgings on the site to which he invited "the very poor prostitutes."[154] The details as reported are very different from those associated with the story of the brothel attributed to Constantine recorded above. Theodosius's gesture may simply have been intended as a social welfare measure or even as a means to allow at least some prostitutes to escape the oppression of pimps.[155] There is a third alternative. It perhaps represented an attempt to limit the geographic distribution of prostitution within the city; we cannot be certain of this, however.[156]

I admit that the evidence for the Christianizing segregation of brothels in late antiquity is not as strong as I would like it to be.[157] It lies beyond proof, to say the least. The important point, however, is simply that the evidence is so much stronger than anything we have for the classical period. In any case, the real impact of Augustine's thought on prostitution policy was not felt until centuries later. One decisive step was its reception by Thomas Aquinas in the thirteenth century. Aquinas falls in with an effort made by some canon lawyers and other authorities to create a legal and moral space, albeit a tenuous one, for prostitutes in medieval society.[158] Another manifestation of this tendency is the interlinear gloss on Augustine, nearly contemporaneous with Aquinas, that introduced the famous metaphor of palace and sewer to describe the ideal place of the prostitute in human society.[159] This metaphor was to mesmerize and confuse later ages and authorities, ranging from sixteenth-cen-

---

153. It seems unlikely to have been in force in A.D. 418–20, when Augustine asserts that there was no law regulating brothels: *Civ. Dei* 14.18 CCSL 48.440–41. See also *Civ. Dei* 2.20 CCSL 47.52, which indicates a widespread presence of prostitution in the late Roman city.

154. Ioh. Mal. *Chron.* 13.38 Thurn 267.

155. Neri, *Marginali* (1998) 204, speculates that the second alternative was true.

156. Malalas places the measure in the context of the suppression of pagan temples at Constantinople, making it tempting to date the measure to the early 390s (and thus after the *De Ordine* was written) and to name Ambrose as a conduit for Augustine's ideas on zoning: see, on Theodosius's anti-pagan campaign and relationship with Ambrose, Williams and Friell, *Theodosius* (1994) 119–33. But all of these ideas are a matter for speculation.

157. One other possible reference to such a policy is at Iustinianus *Nov.* 14 (a. 535): see Neri, *Marginali* (1998) 205, 223.

158. See Brundage, "Prostitution" (1975/6); Kelly, "Bishop" (2000) 343–49.

159. See Chauvin, *Chrétiens* (1983) 21; Rossiaud, *Medieval Prostitution* (1988) 80–81 with n. 17.

tury Spanish clerics to the great Alexandre Parent-Duchâtelet, down until our own time.[160]

The basic elements of the Augustinian model are clear enough. Prostitution is assumed to be inevitable and therefore attempts at repressing it are futile. Even worse, to whatever extent that they are successful, male lust will be diverted to prey upon respectable women. Meanwhile prostitution, if unsupervised and therefore uncontrolled, poses even more of a danger to the social order.[161] But if venal sex is not to be repressed, where and under what conditions should it be permitted?

Christianizing and post-Christianizing policies to "zone" prostitution within cities, as well as those designed to expel prostitutes, emerged from the concern that the presence of prostitution could lead to moral if not also medical contagion, as well as public disorder. These policies were a hallmark of the medieval and early modern periods. Though they managed to survive a new campaign of repression in the latter, they were generally toughened considerably.[162]

An institution of central importance in the Middle Ages was the municipal brothel, a structure owned or leased by a town and subject to stringent regulation, while at the same time granted an at least theoretical monopoly on the local practice of venal sex. The first beginnings of this institution can be traced to the early thirteenth-century regulations of prostitutes' public behavior by Occitan towns like Arles, a softening of the rigorously exclusionary policy adopted by neighbors such as Toulouse and Carcassonne.[163] Aquinas's restatement of the Augustinian doctrine paved the way for the first permanent establishments of officially recognized zones of prostitution, beginning in Montpellier in 1285.[164]

A few decades later the municipal brothel, or *Frauenhaus*, began its long arc as an increasingly common feature of the life of the towns in the German-

---

160. On Parent-Duchâtelet and Augustine, see, for example, Corbin, *Women for Hire* (1990) 62.

161. See, for example, Best, *Controlling Vice* (1998) 5.

162. The generalization made in the text should not obscure the fact that these concerns gave rise to some quite varied policies. See Pavan, "Police" (1980) 242–45, 250–51; Trexler, "Prostitution florentine" (1981) 990; Chauvin, *Chrétiens* (1983) 22, 64–65; Otis, *Prostitution in Medieval Society* (1985) 17–18, 25–26, 31–32, 35, 41, 56, 77–78, 95–97, 104; Perry, "Deviant Insiders" (1985) 142, 148, 156–57; Brundage, *Law, Sex, and Society* (1987) 524–25; Rossiaud, *Medieval Prostitution* (1988) 4–5, 9; Schuster, *Frauenhaus* (1992); Schuster, *Freien Frauen* (1995) 26, 45, 52, 56, 67, 71–79, 88–102, 131, 181–82, 215–23, 262, 305–15, 342–50, 352, 358–95, 399–404, 411–19; Karras, *Common Women* (1996) 15, 18–20, 32–33.

163. Otis, *Prostitution in Medieval Society* (1985) 17–19.

164. Otis, *Prostitution in Medieval Society* (1985) 25.

speaking areas of Europe, a development that also occurred in southern France and northern Italy.[165] The authority of Augustine and Aquinas was so total and, one may say, consistent with the cultural matrix of the time that there is typically little or no justification for these developments found on record until long after the fact. A rare exception took place in Krakow, where the citizens sought an opinion from a Dominican professor in 1398 before establishing a municipal brothel.[166] We have to wait as late as 1433 for an exposition of motive from the city authorities in Munich.[167] It was simply taken for granted that municipally regulated prostitution was the lesser of two evils, the greater one being the overthrow of chastity and public order dreaded by Augustine.

For all of their importance in this period, policies zoning prostitution reached their zenith in the nineteenth and early twentieth centuries, when concern with moral pollution and social instability was—if only partially—subsumed into a fear of sexually transmitted disease.[168] The Romans themselves appear to have been utter strangers to this apprehension of contagion both medical and moral. Evident lack of concern over the spread of disease might be explained by reference to the existence among them of less-virulent forms of sexually transmitted diseases and/or inadequate medical knowledge. But what is the reason for their apparent indifference to what any of us might regard, with justice, as the moral challenge of brothels and prostitutes?

---

165. Schuster, *Frauenhaus* (1992) 36, dates the first foundation to Lucerne in 1318, with a wave cresting in and around 1400. For foundations in France and Italy, see Schuster, 39–40.

166. Schuster, *Freien Frauen* (1995) 184.

167. Schuster, *Frauenhaus* (1992) 40–41, 199, 209.

168. Here, too, there was no uniform approach to zoning. See Evans, "Prostitution" (1976) 111, 117–18; Walkowitz, *Prostitution* (1980) 34, 41, 58, 78, 103, 130, 179, 183, 229; Goldman, *Gold Diggers* (1981) 59–63, 147–48; Rosen, *Sisterhood* (1982) 78–80; Mackey, *Red Lights Out* (1987) 188–92, 199 (which discusses problems in legally evaluating damages arising from the "moral taint" of prostitution), 208 n. 56 (which notes a house did not actually have to be disorderly to qualify as a "disorderly house" under the law); Corbin, *Women for Hire* (1990) 54–60, 84–86, 205, 317, 322–25, 333; Mahood, *Magdalenes* (1990) 18, 116; Clayson, *Painted Love* (1991) 15; Gilfoyle, *City of Eros* (1992) 313–14; Best, *Controlling Vice* (1998) 5; Gibson, *Prostitution and the State*[2] (1999), 136–37, 240 n. 93 (which describes an informal clustering of brothels, much like the Roman model). For a late twentieth-century perspective, see Gorjanicyn, "Sexuality and Work" (1998) 181–84.

℘ Chapter Four ℘

HONOR AND EROTIC ART

Saepe supercilii nudas matrona severi
et veneris stantis ad genus omne videt.
—Ov. Tr. 2.309–310

PORNOGRAPHY AS REPRESENTATION

To understand the Roman elite's sufferance for brothels in their midst, it is useful to consider the Romans' "tolerance" of erotic art in many venues even our secular culture might find problematic.[1] Explicit sexual scenes were on view in a number of settings and thus were easily accessible to upper-class women and children. They could be found in aristocrats' bedrooms, dining rooms, the reception areas known as *tablina*, peristyles, gardens, and so forth, as well as on household objects used by both sexes (and all social ranks), such as terra-cotta lamps, Arretine bowls, and (for the rich) silver cups, and objects thought primarily, or even exclusively, favored by women, such as mirrors.[2]

---

1. Brendel, "Erotic Art" (1970) 3–69, figs. 1–48 (at 6 [cf. 8]) lists Greece and Rome as one of only five ". . . places and periods in which, for a time at least, erotic situations were depicted directly and factually as well as with a degree of frequency, originality of variation, and on a level of quality sufficient to command attention . . . ." See also Myerowitz, "Domestication of Desire" (1992) 133, 135, 138, 146; Jacobelli, *Terme Suburbane* (1995) 83, 86, 89, 90, 92, 98; Clarke, *Looking at Lovemaking* (1998) 12–13, 61–82, 91–118; Zanker, *Pompeii* (1998) 17; De Caro, *Gabinetto segreto* (2000) esp. 12, 30–34; Varone, *Erotismo a Pompei* (2000) 40–53; Jacobelli, "Pompeii" (2001).

2. See Brendel, "Erotic Art" (1970) 45, 47; Zevi, "Arte" (1991) 270; Myerowitz, "Domestication of Desire" (1992) 139, 142, 156 n. 9; Riggsby, *"Cubiculum"* (1997) 39; Cantarella, *Pompeii* (1998) 95; Clarke, *Looking at Lovemaking* (1998) 61–82, 91–118; Kellum, "Spectacle" (1999) 291; Varone, *Erotismo a Pompei* (2000) 54–87; Jacobelli, "Pompeii" (2001).

Some matrons were not averse to having themselves represented as nude exemplars of Venus, a practice that seems to have resonated differently for the Romans than it might for us.[3]

The preceding paragraph reflects what has been the common opinion about Roman erotic art. Very recently, Pietro Guzzo and Vincenzo Scarano Ussani have raised an important qualification to this view, arguing that a dis-tinction should be drawn between the location of paintings of actual persons (i.e., nonmythological) engaged in explicit lovemaking and that of allusive and/or mythological depictions of sex. The first type of representation, they assert, could be found in the brothel, or other public establishments where sex was sold, and the slave quarters of private houses, or at least at some remove from the master's quarters, while the second could be found almost anywhere else, including the master's living and reception rooms in private houses.[4]

There are, of course, exceptions found for example in bedrooms of the master's family, as the authors acknowledge.[5] A quibble also arises over whether the distinctions drawn among these rather complex categories are always as clear in fact as they are in theory.[6] A similar point holds for the classification of room types. Not all *cubicula*, for example, were created equal; one belonging to an emperor might be a fairly public place. So much is I think taken for granted by Suetonius when he writes of Tiberius's enthusiasm for a painting by Parrhasius depicting Atalanta fellating Meleager: ". . . not only did he display it, but he even enshrined it in his *cubiculum*" (". . . non modo prae-tulit, sed et in cubiculo dedicavit").[7]

Particular difficulties arise when Guzzo and Scarano Ussani draw a direct connection between the erotic art found in the *apodyterium* of the Suburban

---

3. D'Ambra, "Calculus of Venus" (1996) 222, 225, 229, who (at 219–20) points out, citing Larissa Bonfante, that in these instances ". . . Venus's nudity is worn as a costume . . . that replaces rather than reveals the body of the deceased."

4. Guzzo and Scarano Ussani, *Veneris figurae* (2000) 25–35. A summary of their argument is found at Guzzo, "Quadretti erotici" (2000) 42–47.

5. Guzzo and Scarano Ussani, *Veneris figurae* (2000) 29. See also app. 2 of their book, in which Antonio Varone discusses the decorative program of a house recently excavated in *Insula* 9.12, where a single *cubiculum* shows three types of erotic painting—allegorical, mythographic, and explicit/nonmythological: see esp. 64–65.

6. The authors appear to recognize this difficulty: Guzzo and Scarano Ussani, *Veneris figurae* (2000) 48. Note Varone's division of erotic art into three types in n. 5. Cf. Clarke, *Looking at Love-making* (1998) who distinguishes between scenes of explicit lovemaking on one side and depic-tions of phalluses, mythological encounters, and dinner parties on the other (12–13), but does not omit from consideration, for example, representations of Priapus and Hermaphroditus (48–55; cf. 174–77).

7. Suet. *Tib.* 44.2. On this passage, see Riggsby, "*Cubiculum*" (1997) 39–40.

Baths at Pompeii and the sale of sex there.[8] It is highly debatable whether prostitution was practiced *in situ,* that is, in the changing room itself.[9] Another difficulty with their argument is the erotic art in question may have been intended to inspire mirth in its viewers, rather than serve a primarily pornographic function.[10] It has even been argued that the function of the various sexual acts depicted in these paintings, which we know were positioned above the rows of wooden boxes that held the bathers' clothing, boxes which were themselves represented on the wall, was mnemonic, that is, the paintings served to help the bather remember where to look after bathing.[11]

Another difficulty with the general argument of Guzzo and Scarano Ussani is with the explicit sexual representations found on objects, and not walls. It is very unlikely these were solely used outside the master's quarters in private houses and thus undermine to some extent arguments about wall decoration. Finally, there is a scene of the type the authors identify as allusive on the wall of the Purpose-Built Brothel (see fig. 10), which suggests, of course, that this type of representation—as well as the more explicit kind—was considered appropriate for the brothel.[12]

In fact, the paintings from the Purpose-Built Brothel nicely illustrate some of the problems and possibilities raised by the location and presumed purposes of Roman erotic art (for a sample of these, see figs. 7–11). The graffiti reveal that the clientele were lower-status males.[13] Aside from a representation of Priapus, there were seven erotic *tabellae* on the inside walls of the main passageway downstairs, six of which are still legible. Of these, four depict various

8. Guzzo and Scarano Ussani, *Veneris figurae* (2000) 17–25. See photographs 13–17.

9. See my discussion of this difficulty in app.1. To be sure, there is a "more likely" candidate for a brothel among the upstairs apartments: see no. 32 in the catalog.

10. See the discussion in Clarke, *Looking at Lovemaking* (1998) 212–40; also now Clarke, "Laughing" (2002).

11. Jacobelli, *Terme Suburbane* (1995) 99. The fact that the painted versions of the clothing boxes were themselves numbered is no argument against this view. In many modern multilevel parking garages, the levels are not only numbered but color-coded as well. A variety of erotic representations presumably would serve at least as well as different colors as a mnemonic device.

12. As the authors acknowledge, the presumably erotic content of the panel at which the lovers gaze does not remove the anomaly of a non-explicit representation of lovers on the wall of a brothel. Guzzo and Scarano Ussani, *Veneris figurae* (2000) 43. According to Helbig, *Wandgemälde* (1868) 371, the panel, now no longer visible, showed an erotic coupling ("Symplegma"). One is tempted to adapt the authors' own explanation for the appearance in the brothel of a wall painting that is purely decorative or mythographic and nonsexual in nature, namely that it was aimed at encouraging clients to imagine the ambience as upper-class: 50–51. See also chaps. 7, 8, and 10.

13. See Clarke, *Looking at Lovemaking* (1998) 199.

explicit acts of lovemaking in action, another a moment immediately preceding penetration, and the sixth a couple reclining on a bed, gazing at a *tabella*
that was presumably erotic but is now illegible (fig. 10). Though much detail
is lost, we can see that the beds in the paintings are richly furnished and at
times accompanied by other elegant pieces of furniture, such as lampstands,
that contrast dramatically with the austere trappings of the brothel itself.
What was marketed to the lower-class clients of this establishment then was
not simply sex, but a fantasy of sex that included companionship, comfort, and
culture, an image of elite sexuality that might embrace an affair with a *hetaira*,
an adulterous liaison, or at any rate the seduction of a higher-status woman.[14]
In this way, the art of the brothel established a frame of reference that reached
beyond the brothel and venal sex, which is an important reason why we
should not be surprised to find such art in nonbrothel settings.

Similar considerations may have been at work with the so-called *spintriae*,
the small bronze or brass tokens produced in the latter part of the reign of
Tiberius (i.e., in the years A.D. 22–37) that depict explicit sexual scenes.[15] The
erotic activity portrayed on these objects takes place within the context of
lavish interior decorations that include expensive-looking furniture and generous amounts of drapery. The point is evidently to suggest a high degree of
luxury and sexual pleasure.[16] Do these tokens depict a brothel? A fantasy of a
brothel? An upper-class *domus*? Part of an upper-class *domus* converted into a
private "sex club?"[17] The very indeterminacy of the locale supports the argument made here, namely that the erotic associations of the brothel were a
moveable feast.

That may not exhaust the implications of brothel-art, however. It is likely
that not all of the brothel's clients reacted to these paintings in exactly the
same way on every visit. Would it make a difference whether the customer was
there for the first or the fiftieth time? Whether he was drunk or sober?
Whether he was there on his own or in the company of his pals? It is obvious

---

14. This idea is developed from the cogent analysis of Clarke, *Looking at Lovemaking* (1998)
202.

15. Buttrey, "*Spintriae*" (1973) 52, points out that the term is modern. See Buttrey, 57, for the
dates. The date and purpose of these tokens are controversial, but the better opinion is that they
are Tiberian and were used as gaming pieces (rather than to pay for sex in a brothel: chap. 3); for
different points of view see, besides Buttrey, Simonetta and Riva, *Tessere* (1981); Bateson, "*Spintriae*" (1991); Jacobelli, *Terme Suburbane* (1995) 70–74; Clarke, *Looking at Lovemaking* (1998)
244–47; Jacobelli, *Spintriae* (2000).

16. See Buttrey, "*Spintriae*" (1973) 58.

17. See chap. 5.

that we lack the evidence to answer these questions directly. All the same, a caution against assuming a unique, unequivocal response to this art comes from an unlikely source, the same Purpose-Built Brothel in the *modern* setting of ancient Pompeii.

The site of the excavations at Pompeii is without doubt one of the most visited archaeological venues in Italy, Europe, and the planet. And it is no exaggeration to cite the Purpose-Built Brothel, the good old *"Lupanare,"* as one of its most popular attractions. Almost every day of the year, hundreds of tourists of diverse nationalities troop in after their guides to gape slack jawed at the *cellae,* the paintings and, if they are especially observant, the remains of the graffiti, perhaps adding one or two specimens of their own before departing. Few will doubt that the place sees a lot more traffic as a museum of a brothel than it ever did in the days before Vesuvius, when it was still an actual brothel. If Pompeii were Disney World, the Purpose-Built Brothel would be its Space Mountain.

The modern tourist's typical reaction to the erotic art of the brothel is laughter and lots of it. This holds true, in my experience, across lines of gender, age (among adults), and nationality. This laughter stands in direct contrast to the solemn, or mock-solemn, intonations of the guides, who are often busy trying to convince the visitors that the paintings were used to overcome a language barrier between the local prostitutes and their clients from overseas, as if prostitutes confronting this difficulty ever are or have been compelled to rely upon such visual aids. The explanation invariably delights the tourists, many of whom have been struggling with a language barrier all day long. No one thinks to ask how the painting of the couple gazing at a *tabella* figures into the Specialties of the House.

My survey is hardly scientific, of course. Other possible responses, ranging from sexual excitement to tacit condemnation, cannot be ruled out simply because they go unnoticed. Some visitors may laugh to mask their discomfort. Most importantly, like all other evidence of a comparative nature, modern reactions cannot be probative, only suggestive, for ancient Rome. But they do suggest that sexually explicit art, when viewed in public by groups of people, can seem ridiculous. We do not have to resort to absurd theories of biological determinism to admit the possibility that some Roman visitors to the Purpose-Built Brothel may have reacted in much the same way. If this was the case, the most interesting result would be that the art of the Suburban Baths, for all its over-the-top quality, differs in degree rather than in kind from the art of the Purpose-Built Brothel, making a connection between the two places more likely, though still, I very much regret to say, elusive in terms of hard proof.

Two important points emerge from this discussion. The first is there are enough exceptions and qualifications to the thesis offered by Guzzo and Scarano Ussani to show that both "explicit" and "allusive" examples of erotic art may be found in a variety of locations. Thus the arguments both for the near-universality and broad definition of erotic art in a Roman context still retain their validity. All the same, Guzzo and Scarano Ussani have certainly succeeded in showing a tendency or preference for explicit sexual representation in the context of the brothel. They usefully encourage us to take seriously the pornographic content of erotic art or at least some of it. The distinction they make between art on the walls of the master's own living and reception areas and art on the walls of slave quarters and the like has, despite the qualifications offered here, its attraction, because it builds on a foundation for an improved understanding of the articulation of space within the aristocratic house already laid down in the scholarship.[18] The validity of their conclusion that here too, within aristocratic houses, brothels operated is evaluated in chapter 5. For now, we might observe that the lower-class idea of elite sex on view in the Purpose-Built Brothel meets its mirror image in upper-class fantasies of the brothel that appeared in some of the grander Pompeian *domus*. What mediated between these class-differentiated settings were explicit, and even sometimes allusive, depictions of lovemaking.

Roman erotic art seems then to have been almost universal both in its placement and in its appeal. Public venues where respectable persons of both sexes might congregate, such as baths, offer some of the most lurid, or interesting, examples, depending on one's point of view. Phallic lamps, made of terra-cotta and bronze, hung from the facades of shops, lighting the public streets. This practice seems practically to have been universal at Pompeii.[19] There was no difference in content, only, at times, quality, between representations in public places (including brothels) and in private houses, which seem to have derived their erotic material from the same sources.[20] The Romans evidently had no concern about keeping sex out of the home and recreational centers and in the brothels or art museums where we might think it belongs. I might also mention here the evidence for penis-shaped drinking vessels, as well as baked goods shaped like male and female genitalia, though I doubt that these particular items, especially given the literary context in

---

18. Essential here is Wallace-Hadrill, *Houses and Society* (1994).
19. See Spano, "Illuminazione" (1920) 17–18, 25–27.
20. See above all Jacobelli, *Terme Suburbane* (1995) 83.

which they are mentioned, were as commonly distributed in homes as the other erotica discussed here.[21]

What did these representations mean to the Romans? The best answer is that more than one response was possible, not only for different persons, but also for the same viewer.[22] Romans found erotic art stimulating in more than just the obvious sense. This art possibly functioned as an aphrodisiac; a didactic paradigm; an expression of humor, above all sexual satire; a display of wealth and/or culture, especially Greek culture, which was highly prized by the elite; or merely as decoration.[23] So it is reductionist, for example, to view wall paintings in a brothel as a sort of pictorial menu of the specialties of the house.[24] It is equally simplistic to assume that erotic art in the changing room of a public bath solely functioned as a mnemonic device, an assumption that excludes other possible reactions.[25] Of course any reaction, not just one of a sexual nature, might well be attenuated by the length of time a painting remained on the wall.

This last point inspires a note of caution regarding the erotic wall paintings in the *apodyterium* of the Suburban Baths in Pompeii (figs. 13–17). We know that toward the end of the city's life these were painted over with nonerotic representations.[26] It is tempting to attribute this change to the arrival of a new owner with different tastes, an owner who was perhaps a bit of a prude or highly sensitive to the moralizing politics of the Flavian dynasty.[27] But perhaps the art was painted over because it had been visible long enough to lose its power to inspire mirth, to arouse, or to help an addled bather recover clothing left in the changing room. For this reason, we cannot assume the disappearance of the paintings meant the Suburban Baths no longer functioned as a brothel.

---

21. For penis-shaped drinking vessels, see Iuv. 2.95; *HA Pertinax* 8.5. For baked goods in the form of genitalia, see Petron. 60.4; Mart. 9.2.3, 14.70(69).

22. Jacobelli, *Terme Suburbane* (1995) 100. Clarke, *Looking at Lovemaking* (1998) esp. 212–40, is admirably sensitive to the possibility that the gender of the viewer affected the response to the art. See now Clarke, "Laughing" (2002).

23. See Myerowitz, "Domestication of Desire" (1992) 135, 137, 138, 148, 149, 151; Jacobelli, *Terme Suburbane* (1995) 88–90, 99; Cantarella, *Pompei* (1998) 95; Zanker, *Pompeii* (1998) 20, 23, 32, 35, 37, 139–40; De Caro, *Gabinetto segreto* (2000) 25–26, 34; cf. Brendel, "Erotic Art" (1970) 58, 64.

24. So Jacobelli, *Terme Suburbane* (1995) 100 n. 8, rightly emphasizes. For the view I criticize, see Dierichs, *Erotik* (1997) 74.

25. So Scarano Ussani, "Lenocinium" (2000) 260–61, rightly argues.

26. Jacobelli, *Terme Suburbane* (1995) 78–80. See, in particular, fig. 15.

27. See Jacobelli, *Terme Suburbane* (1995) 80–82; Scarano Ussani, "Lenocinium" (2000) 262; Clarke, "Laughing" (2002) 154.

Pornography is just one element, then, of erotic art. Given the multiple purposes we can trace for Roman art of this kind, we might more profitably view its role in terms of a spectrum, with its presence stronger or weaker in various contexts rather than always simply present or absent. We must keep in mind, however, that perceptions of this role may well be conditioned by the gender and status of the viewer, as well as by other factors. We cannot, by the same token, be certain of distinguishing pornography from art and literature overall.[28] Crucial for our purpose is the point that, where pornography is most in evidence, so is prostitution, or the idea of it.

THINGS SEEN AND HEARD

One might object that what I am talking about here is a matter of art and not of life.[29] We cannot simply assume that our notion of erotic art is identical to that of the Romans or that the impact of erotic representations was not informed, or even diminished, by packaging in a Greek cultural format.[30] But this is precisely my argument. Roman ideas about what is objectionable may differ radically from our own. There is a famous anecdote wherein Livia dismisses any possible injury to her sense of shame through an inadvertent glimpse of some naked men, who were evidently prisoners of war, because she regarded them as though they were statues.[31] The incident makes for a good point.[32] Prostitutes soliciting in the streets were not typically nude and/or engaged in sex.[33] In other words, the erotic art of the Romans tended to be

28. See Sullivan, *Politics of Sex* (1997) 76, 79.

29. It is worth noting that live sex shows, often performed in private houses, may have helped bridge whatever gap existed between "art" and "life": see Jacobelli, *Terme Suburbane* (1995) 100–101. Cf. Tiberius's multimedia approach at Capri: Suet. *Tib.* 43.2. Kondoleon, "Timing Spectacles" (1999) usefully describes the importation of "public" themes into domestic contexts. More discussion of the erotic element in this regard would be welcome.

30. See the remarks of Jacobelli, *Terme Suburbane* (1995) 98–99; Clarke, *Looking at Lovemaking* (1998) 12–13, 19, 55; Varone, *Erotismo* (2000) 14–27.

31. Dio (in Xiph.) 58.2.4.

32. The Livia anecdote also implies the possibility of the opposite attitude. A respectable woman might be expected to display outrage at such a sight. Significantly, however, Livia does not react in this way. Livia, to be sure, was a model, ethical and otherwise, for Roman women: see Purcell, "Livia" (1986); Barrett *Livia* (2002) esp. 123–27, 143, 159. In this passage, she is praised for setting a standard others were meant to follow.

33. The nudity of prostitutes seems more characteristic of the brothel itself: see chap. 2. In a passage discussed in the text below, Ovid describes matrons as "often" (*saepe*) gazing upon "naked" (*nudas*) prostitutes in public: Tr. 2.309–10. *Nudus*, of course, can mean "scantily clad": Fagan, *Bathing in Public* (1999) 25. The latter would seem to be the preferred translation, though my argument would be strengthened if the prostitutes were, in fact, nude.

much more explicit than their public sexual behavior.[34] More importantly, Livia's reaction suggests that the respectable Roman woman chose to see what she wished to see and no doubt taught her children to do the same.[35]

In an apologetic strain, Ovid relates how the Vestal's gaze was untrammelled by the appearance of prostitutes:

Ov. *Tr.* 2.309–12:
saepe supercilii nudas matrona severi
    et veneris stantis ad genus omne videt.
corpora Vestales oculi meretricia cernunt,
     nec domino poenae res ea causa fuit.

Many a time a matron of stern brow catches sight of women clad scantily, prepared for every sort of lust. The eyes of a Vestal behold the bodies of prostitutes, nor has that fact been a reason to punish their owner.

It is important to recognize that the poet is concerned here with defending himself against a charge of encouraging adultery in his *Ars Amatoria*, arguing first that the work was explicitly intended only for prostitutes, next (in implicit admission of the weakness of the prior argument?) that it is after all no offense (*facinus*) to read erotic verse, only to act on it.[36] Ovid clearly suggests here that the Vestal, as a model of probity, sets the standard with her demure reaction to the sight of prostitutes for everyone else with pretensions to respectability, including, Ovid hopes regarding his own case, the emperor Augustus himself.

We can certainly discern a tension here between the ideal of shielding Vestals from the sight of prostitutes and the practical impossibility of doing so.[37] Indeed, Ovid at the very least might be thought to allude to a failed policy of moral zoning in this passage. The ideal of shielding Vestals is well supported by evidence from Seneca the Elder regarding physical contact between priestesses and prostitutes though it does not mention Vestals explicitly.[38] In

---

34. For another sign of Roman sensitivity about public sexual behavior, see the rule attributed to Romulus that men should not be seen naked by women: Plut. *Rom.* 20.3. See also Seneca's complaint about *matronae* in see-through clothing: *Ben.* 7.9.5. This evidence helps explain the controversy over mixed-gender bathing: see below in the text and chap. 2.

35. Argued from the Roman mother's role in the moral education of her children, see Dixon, *The Roman Mother* (1988) 109–11, 117, 121.

36. Ov. *Tr.* 2.303–8.

37. I owe this point to Wallace-Hadrill, p.c.

38. Sen. *Contr.* 1.2.1, 3–5.

my view, Ovid resolves the tension by showing that the moral contrast between pure Vestal and impure prostitute is actually enhanced by their (inevitable) physical proximity. It is worth noting that the matron precedes the Vestal in the comparison and that the matron, with her greater freedom of movement as well as her lesser, if still exalted, status, cannot have been held to the same ideal. There is thus no evidence of a policy in the passage, even of a failed one.[39] The Romans were of course fond of drawing the general moral contrast between respectable women and prostitutes, and this passage certainly belongs to that tradition.[40]

The point holds that prostitutes and brothels were invisible, at least ideally so, to members of the Roman elite, including women and children. What was not seen was also evidently not heard: we do not have evidence of complaints about the noise and violent behavior that must have been a feature of life in close proximity to brothels and even cribs, as we know a few stately Pompeian townhouses were. Even if we can correctly assume that brothels as a rule were sturdily constructed, that is, fairly soundproof, a great deal of the noise generated by clients who were singing, fighting, and so forth would have spilled out onto the street.[41] Complaints about noise, violence, and criminal behavior in and near brothels across historical periods are not at all rare.[42] Elite Romans did complain loudly and at length about the racket and disorder arising from other sources such as baths, which were much more respectable than brothels and therefore worthier of notice.[43]

Here is a sign that we are in a world foreign in important respects to our

---

39. For more on this theme, see chap. 5.

40. See McGinn, *Prostitution, Sexuality, and the Law* (1998) esp. 147–71.

41. See the evidence discussed in chap. 3.

42. See, for example, Bernstein, *Sonia's Daughters* (1995) 32, 151, 178–80; Karras, *Common Women* (1996) 15; Hershatter, *Dangerous Pleasures* (1997) 200, 211, 292–93, 298. For an interesting analysis of why neighbors of brothels find them so annoying, see Decker, *Prostitution* (1979) 348–49, 463. In light of this evidence, the absence of Roman evidence might seem remarkable and even incredible, but we should keep in mind that objections to noise from brothels were not universal in past times: see Hill, *Their Sisters' Keepers* (1993) 173. See also Mackey, *Red Lights Out* (1987) 258.

43. See the complaints registered at Ramage, "Urban Problems" (1983) 81–83, 86; André, "Sénèque" (1994); Kardos, "*Épigrammes*" (2001) 210–11. For a catalog of urban noises, see Mart. 12.57 (cf. 9.68). On the racket generated at the baths, the lament by Sen. *Ep.* 56.1–2 is classic. See the remarks of Fagan, "Interpreting the Evidence" (1999) 29. The closest we get to an objection about noise from brothels is Juvenal's complaint about sleepless nights in *meritoria* (which may not refer to brothels at all): 3.234, unless this is meant as a double entendre suggesting that sleeplessness in a brothel had nothing to do with noise (so also perhaps Juvenal's *pervigiles popinae* at 8.158 and Propertius's reference to the "wakeful Subura" at 4.7.15). For the lack of nuisance-abatement rules, see chap. 5.

own. The kinds of concerns that modern societies have with the location of brothels are familiar enough. These include falling property values, possible damage to the tax base of a locality, loss of business from tourists and conventions, and a perception that a town or neighborhood has become a haven for criminality of various kinds.[44] None of these concerns had much resonance for the Romans.[45]

Baths are also relevant to the issue of public sexual behavior.[46] Some Romans objected to the practice of men and women bathing together, encouraging some scholars to argue that mixed bathing occurred only in low establishments, that the only women who participated were prostitutes, that mixed bathing went in and out of fashion, and so forth. According to a recent study, attendance at such baths was, both at Rome and many other places, simply a matter of personal choice for women and for men.[47] A decision not to attend mixed baths was not necessarily a sign of prudishness.[48] Slaves attending their masters and mistresses at the baths did not have a choice of course, but their presence raises the question of whether attendants of the opposite gender violated prescriptions against mixed bathing where they existed, were barred for this reason (or were supposed to be barred), were simply deemed invisible, or at any rate unseeing.[49] This evidence seems too complex and discontinuous to argue for a policy of moral zoning.

To return to Ovid, we would not, naturally, expect such apologetics from the poet in his pre-exile career. Elegy in particular seems an ill-suited genre for raising this sort of issue. It is all the more suprising therefore to find that another elegist, Propertius, expresses a concern with the threat to morality posed by *obscenae tabulae*:

----

44. See Reynolds, *Economics of Prostitution* (1986) 52 (cf. 44).

45. Cf. the objections posed by neighbors to medieval German brothels, some of which resemble, some of which differ from, modern complaints: Schuster, *Freien Frauen* (1995) 305–7.

46. This paragraph is entirely indebted to Fagan, *Bathing in Public* (1999) 24–29. For more extensive discussion of this topic, see chap. 2.

47. Fagan, *Bathing in Public* (1999) 27, 29.

48. I understand Martial's coy warning about poetry full of naked men at the baths to be a joke meant to tease respectable women about their true proclivities: 3.68.1–4. The joke seems to apply equally to women who attended mixed baths and those who did not. For Martial and his female readers see the section below "Women and Children First."

49. On slaves at the baths, see the evidence collected by Fagan, "Interpreting the Evidence" (1999); Fagan, *Bathing in Public* (1999) 199–206.

Prop. 2.6.27–36:

Quae manus obscenas depinxit prima tabellas
　　　et posuit casta turpia visa domo,
illa puellarum ingenuos corrupit ocellos
　　　nequitiaeque suae noluit esse rudis.
ah gemat in tenebris, ista qui protulit arte
　　　orgia sub tacita condita laetitia!
non istis olim variabant tecta figuris:
　　　tum paries nullo crimine pictus erat.
sed nunc immeritum velavit aranea fanum
　　　et mala desertos occupat herba deos.

*The artist who first painted erotic panels and placed obscene pictures in
chaste homes was the one to corrupt the eyes of innocent/well-born girls and
insist on acquainting them with his own depravity. Let him suffer in blind-
ness, who with that skill of his rendered public sexual couplings that were hidden behind silent pleasure! The houses of our ancestors were not made elegant by those sorts of designs—in those days the walls were not painted with
matter for moral criticism. But now spiderwebs veil the undeserving temple
and weeds overgrow the abandoned statues of our gods.*

The text provides confirmation, if needed, that some Romans found erotic art
sexually stimulating.[50] The poet may well be referring strictly to representations of adultery and not to erotic art in general as discussed here.[51] In any
case, the fundamental difficulty in accepting this criticism at face value lies in
taking the protestations of the self-professed expert seducer seriously—is he
concerned about competition, for example? We might reasonably conclude
that when we must rely upon an elegist to assert old-fashioned morality, the
game is up.

Whatever the value of Propertius's evidence, we should focus our attention less on general moral sensitivities about erotic art and more on concerns
about the art's impact on women and children.[52] We might begin by asking
the following questions: Was there a moral code of any kind in regard to these
groups, and how well was this code enforced?

---

50. See also Ter. *Eun.* 583–90.

51. So Goold, *Propertius* (1999) 121 n. 17.

52. By *puellae*, Propertius is almost certainly referring to the love object(s) he constructs in
his poems and not to children: see for example Wyke, *Roman Mistress* (2002) 46–77.

WOMEN AND CHILDREN FIRST

When we examine evidence suggesting that women and children should be shielded from obscene language, an interesting ambiguity arises. For children, some of our best evidence comes from Martial, a fact that should inspire caution, given that author's proclivity for flouting convention or at least for appearing to do so.[53] In one epigram the poet defends his verses against the charge that they are *parum severi*, unfit for a schoolmaster to recite to a class.[54] At most this suggests a certain decorum ideally prevailed in the schoolroom. He also cites, as an absurdity parallel to that of cleaning up his poetry, the project of dressing prostitutes at the Floralia, where they danced in the nude, or otherwise assigning them the *stola*, the garb of the respectable Roman matron.[55] We might argue that this shows he viewed prostitutes as "obscene." If so, the epigram helps establish the Romans' casual acceptance of "obscenity" in public venues.[56]

The reference to the Floralia hearkens back to the dedication in Martial's first book, where the epigrammatist rejects as a reader the person who is "ostentatiously prudish" ("ambitiose tristis").[57] His ideal readership, Martial states, are the spectators at the Floralia, which would include everyone, except the "ostentatiously prudish" Cato. "Let Cato stay out of my theater or, if he does come, let him watch."[58] In the event that Cato was converted, there would be no one left to object or to exclude.

In another poem Martial praises Cosconius for writing epigrams suitable for good boys and girls (*pueri virginesque*), and remarks that his own ideal audience consists of bad boys and girls (*nequam iuvenes facilesque puellae*), plus the occasional older man (*senior*) who is tormented by an *amica*.

---

53. See Richlin, *Garden of Priapus* (1992) esp. 57–80; O'Connor, "Martial the Moral Jester" (1998).

54. Mart. 1.35.

55. Mart. 1.35.8–9.

56. Though I put the word *obscenity* in quotation marks, it is clear that the Romans did have a concept of obscenity, however subject to disagreement and change (in different directions) over time. See, for example, Cic. *Fam.* 9.22, *Off.* 1.126–28; and Meyer-Zwiffelhoffer, *Phallus* (1995) 24–48..

57. Mart. 1 *praef.* 14.

58. Mart. 1 *praef.* 16–18; see also the questions put to Cato at the very end: "Why did you come to the theater, harsh Cato? Did you only come in order to leave?" For a more sympathetic account of Cato's exit from the Floralia, which also makes clear that the Cato here was Cato the Younger, see Val. Max. 2.10.8.

Mart. 3.69.5–8:

Haec igitur nequam iuvenes facilesque puellae,
	haec senior, sed quem torquet amica, legat.
at tua, Cosconi, venerandaque sanctaque verba
	a pueris debent virginibusque legi.

*So let the boys gone bad and chicks who are easy read this stuff, plus the
occasional older guy, if he's got a girlfriend doing him wrong . . . whereas
your words, Cosconius, holy and to be hallowed as they are, ought to be read
by the good boys, and the good girls.*

The terminology (*pueri*, etc.) denotes not strictly age, but moral character,
though its reference to age is admittedly elastic.[59] The sarcasm is evident—
Cosconius, ergo, does not really write Epigram at all—as is the debt to Ovid.

Martial dedicates his fifth book, after Domitian himself, to *matronae
puerique virginesque*.[60] Here, in contrast to the first four books, is material the
emperor can read without blushing. The compliment to Domitian's modesty
should not mislead us.[61] If there was in fact a rule that children should not be
exposed to obscenity, it most often, at least in the period from which derive
our literary sources, was observed in the breach. In his Menippeans, Varro evidently has a speaker claim that the ancestors (*maiores*) removed *virgines* from
wedding banquets to shield them from obscenity (*veneria vocabula*).[62] Whatever the truth of the claim about the usage of the *maiores*, the clear implication is that in Varro's day children were not so shielded. This helps explain
the premise behind Seneca's argument that children cannot be guilty of *con-
tumelia* ("insult," "outrage"), even when they use rather obscene language
(*verba obsceniora*).[63] They were hardly capable of speaking what they had
never heard spoken. Confirmation comes from Quintilian, who complains of
the impact on children of the obscene sights and sounds at dinner parties.[64]

---

59. On the chronological imprecision of Roman age-terminology and its moral aspect, see
Eyben, *Restless Youth* (1993) esp. 5–41. On the sociology of Martial's postulated audience, see
Cavallo, "Segni e voci" (2000) 264, with literature.

60. Mart. 5.2.

61. It is worth mentioning here Dio of Prusa's idealistic and unusual recommendation that
the good emperor ban from Rome indecent dancing and singing as well as corrupting forms of
music and even obscene language: Or. 2.55–56.

62. Varro Men. 9 Cèbe, with Cèbe, *Varron* 1 (1972) 56–57.

63. Sen. *Const.* 11.2.

64. Quint. *IO* 1.2.8.

Finally, there is the hilarious confusion of the grammarian Festus over the meaning of *sermo praetextatus*. Some of his authorities believe that the term refers to the idea that obscene speech (*obscenum verbum*) is inappropriate for the young (*praetextati*), while others connect it to the practice wherein boys (*pueri*), after laying aside their *togae praetextae*, launched obscenities (*obscena*) at wedding parties.[65] The evidence suggests that the second alternative is correct, and thus *praetextatus* can mean "obscene."[66] The ritual role played by boys at weddings was matched by that of girls, who chanted obscenities at the festival of Anna Perenna on 15 March.[67] This nexus of ritual, youth, and obscenity was peculiarly Roman.[68] What emerges from the evidence is that, if the ideal was that Roman children should be spared obscene language, this ideal was not shared by everyone and was rarely if ever respected in actual fact.

With adult women, the sense is even stronger that the ideal, if it existed at all, was often breached or even held up to ridicule.[69] Again, Martial is a chief witness. In his third book, we encounter two poems, the first of which warns the *matrona* against reading further in the book, and then undercuts the seriousness of the warning by predicting that the warning itself will provoke her to read with greater attention. The second poem goes on to scold the *matrona* for having acted in accordance with this prediction.[70] Between these two poems he berates Saufeia for being a willing sexual partner but refusing to bathe with him while she is nude or at any rate scantily clad.[71] Of course he is constructing here not—or not only—his ideal bed and bath partner, but his ideal reader.

---

65. Festus 282–84L.

66. See Catull. 61, 62; Varro *Men.* 10 Cèbe, Iuv. 2.170; Suet. *Vesp.* 22; Gell. 9.10.4, with OLD s.h.v 3.

67. Ov. *Fasti* 3.675–76. For both boys and girls, see Adams, *Latin Sexual Vocabulary* (1982) 4–6.

68. See the remarks of Kleijwegt, "Iuvenes" (1994) 88–90. He cites Serv. *ad Georg.* 2.387 on the necessity for the role of the playful and obscene in the performance of the sacred.

69. For a statement of this convention, see the rule attributed to Romulus that nothing "shameful" ("aischron") be uttered in the presence of Roman women: Plut. *Rom.* 20.3. For what is possibly the earliest example preserved of the puncturing of this convention, see the fragment of Plautus's *Dyscolus* (fr. 68), which reads "Virgo sum: nondum didici nupta verba dicere": "I'm an unmarried girl: I haven't yet learned the discourse of a married woman [i.e., to talk dirty]." This interpretation must remain insecure because we lack the context of the remark, but the adjective *nuptus* does appear to correspond to *praetextatus* in the meaning of "obscene." If so, it implies that married women, like boys, were at home with obscene speech.

70. Mart. 3.68, 86, with Adams, *Latin Sexual Vocabulary* (1982) 217. For another view of the first poem, see Kardos, "Vrbs" (2001) 411. It is important not to be too earnest in reading Martial.

71. Mart. 3.72. On the problem of nude bathing, see above in the text and chap. 2.

Elsewhere Martial claims that upright readers of either gender will find his work sexually stimulating. Lucretia blushes at his poems in the presence of Brutus and puts them aside, but reads them in Brutus's absence.[72] "[Martial] writes with the attitude of one deliberately flouting conventional attitudes."[73] He does this in order to define his poetry and its audience as sophisticated, or even edgy. Of course the readership Martial constructs for his work need not have coincided with its actual one, though Ovid's experience with the vogue his poetry enjoyed among women of respectable status discourages great pessimism on this score.

It is difficult to find a text that convincingly demonstrates respect for the convention that women should be shielded from obscenity, however. In a satire extolling modest dinner arrangements, Juvenal seems to attack the staging of erotic dances in front of wives reclining with their husbands, a spectacle, he suggests, that a person would be ashamed even to narrate in their presence.[74] Unfortunately, the crucial lines are "certainly spurious."[75]

Augustine's criticism of the pagans for using obscene rituals to worship Cybele relies on the assumption that the actors would be ashamed to rehearse at home in the presence of their mothers what they recited publicly in the presence of a multitude of both sexes.[76] Though the notion is somewhat at odds with the author's purpose, we are not far from Martial's intimation of ideal schoolroom decorum here. More importantly, the *public* manifestation of obscenity is guaranteed in the text. In a similar way, Augustine's choice of Scipio Nasica as a model of filial piety reaches far back into the past, as does Mar-

---

72. Mart. 11.16. See also 5.2 (above), 10.64 (Polla is asked to discount the sexual content of Martial's poems and read them anyway), 11.15 (is nicely ambiguous about whether Martial's poetry—or some of it at any rate—would be to the taste of Cato's wife and the *horribiles Sabinae*).

73. Adams, *Latin Sexual Vocabulary* (1982) 217, though I disagree with his point that Martial is a special case. See Meyer-Zwiffelhoffer, *Phallus* (1995) 60–61.

74. Iuv. 11.162–68.

75. Courtney, *Commentary on Juvenal* (1980) 510, on Iuv. 11.165–66. Ovid complains that respectable adults and children of both sexes attend the mimes, whose content is sexual and whose language is obscene: Ov. *Tr.* 2.497–516, with Adams, *Latin Sexual Vocabulary* (1982) 219. Ovid is at bottom concerned with his perception of Augustus's unfair treatment of him, however, and not with the corruption of morals. Cf. *Anth. Lat.* 683.19–20R, which assumes the attendance of women at mime performances.

76. Augustin. *Civ. Dei* 2.4–5 CCSL 47.37–38. Respectable women were also present at the Floralia's erotic stage show: Tert. *Spect.* 17 CCSL 1.242–43 (cf. Iuv. 6.249–50, which to my mind does not prove the point). As Tertullian describes it, the prostitutes on stage not only performed sexually but also solicited customers from the audience. On the festival, see Wiseman, "Games of Flora" (1999) whose informed speculation about the contents of the stage shows does not exclude the possibility of more explicit fare. Wiseman's description (at 196) of the "erotically charged flagellation spectacle" of the *Lupercalia* supports the general point made here.

tial's choice of Cato's wife and the Sabine women.[77] Both authors imply through their selections of exemplary behavior that popular usage has not lived up to this standard for some time. A *Priapeum* has a warning to *matronae* to stay away, a warning that is ignored in much the same spirit as is Martial's warning reported above.[78] The reluctance of Terence's Chremes to utter the word *scortum* in the presence of a woman must also be a joke, since the word is frequently used in Comedy and prostitutes are often both seen and heard in this very public genre.[79] Despite Ovid's self-interested and rather desperate-sounding protestations concerning his own work,[80] it should surprise no one to learn that Roman women, and not just prostitutes, were avid consumers of pornography.[81]

The idea of shielding women and children from erotic representation is difficult to find even in works where we might expect to encounter it. The work of Pliny the Elder is an excellent example. He was an enthusiastic moralist who wrote extensively on Roman art.[82] One of the most charming and—for the social historian at least—useful aspects of his *Natural History* is his moralizing tirades. These tirades are launched against everything and everyone from the size of contemporary slave households to the first person to cut marble and are evidently designed to look like spontaneous rants. When it comes

---

77. Mart. 11.15.

78. *Priap.* 8, with Mart. 11.15, 16. For other poems in the collection that advertise their transgression regarding obscenity, see *Priap.* 2, 29, 49.

79. Ter. *Heauton* 1041–42. The popularity of representations of prostitutes in Comedy might itself help refute the theory of zoning, unless one wishes to insist on a tidy distinction between art and life. Comedy is also not at all shy in alluding to bodily functions: see the list given by Krenkel, "Skopophilie" (1977) 623. Afranius's plays were supposed to be particularly explicit: Auson. *Epigr.* 79.4; cf. Cic. *Fam.* 9.22.1.

80. See Ov. *Tr.* 2.303–8, which I have discussed above in the text. It will be obvious that I do not mean to imply here that Ovid's work qualifies as pornography in any strict sense, though the difference ideally postulated, as well as the practical difficulty in distinguishing, between porn and serious literature may explain in large part its controversial nature. The *Ars Amatoria* presents itself, and was certainly regarded, as an erotic manual: see Cestius *apud* Sen. *Contr.* 3.7. As with viewers of erotic art, some readers of Ovid perhaps saw pornography where others saw a parody of porn.

81. On this subject, see the comments of De Martino, "Storia" (1996) 306–7, 311, 316–18. Illustrations were included in at least some manuals: De Martino, 318, 322. On the general availability of pornography and obscenity in Roman culture, see Horsfall, *Culture* (2003) 79–80.

82. Pliny devoted five books to art in his *Naturalis Historia:* 33 (metalwork: gold and silver), 34 (metalwork: copper and bronze), 35 (painting and pottery), 36 (marble), 37 (gems). On his moralism, see Wallace-Hadrill, "Pliny the Elder" (1990); Citroni Marchetti, *Plinio* (1991); Isager, *Pliny* (1991).

to condemnations of erotic art, however, the naturalist is a severe disappointment.

Pliny passes over most nude, or scantily clad, representations of males or females, especially depictions of Venus, without comment.[83] In a couple of cases, he even lavishly praises a statue of this goddess shown without clothing.[84] One of his very rare attacks on erotic art occurs in the context of a denunciation of greed and gold:

> Plin. *NH* 33.4–5:
> Accessit ars picturae, et aurum argentumque caelando carius fecimus. didicit homo naturam provocare. auxere et artem vitiorum inritamenta; in poculis libidines caelare iuvit ac per obscenitates bibere. abiecta deinde sunt haec ac sordere coepere, ut auri argentique nimium fuit.

> *Added to this was the art of painting, and we raised the value of gold and silver through engraving. Mankind learned to challenge nature. Stimulants to misbehavior also enhanced the art. It has been popular to engrave erotic subjects on drinking-cups and drink right through scenes of explicit sex. Afterwards these were tossed away and considered to be of little value, when there was a surplus of gold and silver.*

Sexually explicit scenes on drinking cups raised their value, already high because of the materials, gold and silver, used in their manufacture.[85] Pliny assumes that at least some people found the art on these cups to be sexually stimulating ("vitiorum inritamenta"), but not, evidently, indefinitely so. When the value of the materials dropped through oversupply, the value added by the erotic decoration vanished entirely. Pliny seems to imply here that familiarity with such artistic representation bred tedium.

---

83. Plin. *NH* 34.60, 35.58, 35.64, 35.91, 36.16.

84. Pliny praises, for instance, the famous Cnidian Aphrodite by Praxiteles: Plin. *NH* 36.20–21. He notes (at 21) "it is equally praiseworthy from every viewpoint" ("nec minor ex quacumque parte admiratio est"). But later he asserts that the statue of this goddess by Scopas is superior: 36.26.

85. Perhaps the most famous example of the kind of drinking cup Pliny talks about is the Warren Cup. For a discussion, with other pertinent examples, see Clarke, *Looking at Lovemaking* (1998) 61–72. Elagabalus is said to have extended the principle broadly: *HA Elag.* 19.3. Compare the penis-shaped drinking vessels mentioned previously in this chapter, which are not precisely relevant here because they are made of glass.

Pliny does offer much better evidence than Propertius for genuine moral sensitivity over the impact of erotic art on the viewer. In any case, there is not a word here about women and children and whether their morals in particular might be affected by art of this kind. In fact, it is rather curious how the emphasis of his criticism falls on the use to which the object is put. One wonders whether the cups would have elicited any comment at all if they had been simply admired for their subject matter and not used for consuming (we may assume) wine. A similar point holds for another passage where Pliny criticizes representations of adultery on drinking cups in the context of a denunciation of the ill-effects of inebriation.[86] Beyond this, Pliny stresses the irony in the fact that the erotica enhanced the value of the cups when the price of gold and silver was high but could not do so when the price fell. This observation is clearly tied to the author's discourse on the proper use of nature's resources versus waste and extravagance. The two passages I have just mentioned each provided an opening for a rhetorical rant on the ill-effects of sexual subject matter on consumers of art, but Pliny chose not to proceed in that direction.[87]

Pliny records Nero's devotion to a small statuette of an Amazon,[88] and Tiberius's passion for the Apoxyomenos of Lysippus, which was so great that he moved it from its post in front of the Baths of Agrippa to his bedroom, causing a public outcry that compelled him to return it.[89] He also mentions Caligula's unsuccessful attempt, motivated by lust, to remove nude paintings of Atalanta and Helen from the wall of a collapsed temple at Lanuvium.[90] These examples further show Pliny was aware that some examples of erotic art could prove sexually stimulating to some viewers, an observation that mostly passes without comment, aside from a couple of very mild indications that for Pliny having sex with a statue was *not* an appropriate aesthetic response to fine art.[91]

---

86. Plin. *NH* 14.140: ". . . quae vasa adulteriis caelata, tamquam per se parum doceat libidines temulentia!" (". . . the vessels engraved with representations of adultery, as though drunkenness by itself were not enough to teach lustful behavior!"). Again, Pliny focuses on the connection between erotica and the consumption of alcohol. Adultery was a form of sexual behavior many Romans found objectionable and was illegal in Pliny's day (unless the word "adulteriis" is meant more generally in this passage). Here, too, there is no mention of women and children as objects of particular concern.

87. At *NH* 33.150 Pliny criticizes Gaius Marius for drinking out of Dionysiac tankards, but the point here is to contrast the general's humble beginnings with his divine, or quasi divine, aspirations.

88. Plin. *NH* 34.82.

89. Plin. *NH* 34.62.

90. Plin. *NH* 35.18.

91. See Plin. *NH* 36.21 (on the Aphrodite of Cnidos by Praxiteles), 36.22 (on a naked Cupid at Parium, again by Praxiteles).

Beyond this, there are instances where Pliny seems to criticize the creators of erotic art. After recording the achievements of the great Greek painter Parrhasius, he notes that "he also painted erotic subjects on miniature panels, finding recreation in this sort of immodest amusement."[92] The sense here is that Parrhasius's interest in this genre was incommensurate with his talents. "Immodest" (*petulans*) is a moral reproof, though it is not any stronger, nor any more relevant to our concerns, than Pliny's criticism of erotic art on drinking cups. Here the writing is so breezy it almost amounts to mere description, as opposed to severe moral condemnation.[93]

Finally there is the case of the well-known, late-Republican painter Arellius, who was notorious for having prejudiced his work by repeatedly representing his mistress of the moment in it.[94] Ostensibly he was rendering the images of goddesses, but in actual fact he was painting the portraits of his girlfriends. Therefore his painting contains a number of, as Pliny puts it, "sluts" (*scorta*).[95] Pliny's criticism of Arellius is severe in that he strongly implies Arellius prostituted his art by acting as a mediator for his girlfriends precisely in the way a pimp does for his prostitutes ("*lenocinans*" has a marvelous double sense here)[96]—but also by representing them in a way that was at odds with their moral status. Erotic art is not even in question here, and one has the sense that Pliny uses a relatively high standard to judge Arellius, given that he lightly criticizes Greek artists who relied on mistresses and/or actual prostitutes as models for their work, if he criticizes them at all.[97]

Pliny seems to have taken erotic art by and large for granted. He may be drawing a distinction between nude representations of the human form, which might rise to the level of great art, and scenes of explicit lovemaking, which were unworthy of great artists, or portraits of promiscuous women, which were unworthy of great *Roman* artists. He also objects to sexual content on objects like drinking cups. But we should not view that distinction as too significant, since Pliny accepted that both types of erotic art might summon forth a sexual response in the viewer. In regard to the impact of this subject matter on women and children, Pliny utters not a word.

---

92. Plin. *NH* 35.72: "Pinxit et minoribus tabellis libidines, eo genere petulantis ioci se reficiens."

93. See also Plin. *NH* 35.110, where he describes a painting by Nicomachus of three Sileni engaged in a *comissatio* as *lascivia*.

94. Plin. *NH* 35.119.

95. "*Scorta*" need not refer to professional prostitutes, but simply to women deemed promiscuous: Adams, "Words" (1983) 321–24.

96. *Lenocinor* is more commonly used in its transferred sense of "serve the interests of" vel *sim.*: see *L & S, OLD* s.h.v.

97. See Plin. *NH* 34.70, 72, 35.86; cf. 35.64.

Pliny's concerns seem to lie elsewhere. When he has occasion to complain of painting in Roman bedrooms, he speaks of representations of mountains supplemented by paint applied to marble.[98] His silence on the subject of sexual representation is most striking in light of the copious numbers of erotic paintings brought to light at Pompeii. Pliny the Elder would have been writing his *Natural History* just as all but the very last of the last erotic paintings were going up on the walls of Pompeii.[99]

The practice of flouting conventional attitudes implies that such attitudes exist, but it is very difficult in light of the evidence to grasp exactly what these were, how strongly they were held, and by whom. We are left to speculate that some Romans felt that exposing children and even adult women to obscene and/or pornographic language and other forms of representation was a breach of decorum—without the graver implications even this much might perhaps have in a Christianized society permeated by the concept of sin—and complained that this convention was rarely if ever observed in their own day. They might have gone on to contrast the usage of the *maiores* with conditions perceived to prevail in their own day, as any Roman moralist—or someone lampooning a Roman moralist—would do almost reflexively. Other Romans were presumably indifferent at best to such appeals, and yet others, we may imagine, were utter hypocrites about such matters.

If persuasive, such speculation may help reveal what a complex society Rome was in the early Principate; it hardly reflected the monolithic, linear-evolutionary model that many historians—encouraged in no small measure by the Romans themselves—have favored. As we shall see in chapter 5, there were no laws that repressed offenses against public decency per se. Hence, it is difficult to see how the impetus to zone prostitution might have developed out of such a set of social values and practices as discussed in this chapter.

Finally, there is an important theoretical distinction to draw between the location of erotic art in the Roman city and that of prostitution. The motivation behind the latter was, as I argue, largely economic, while the former was presumably dictated overall by moral and aesthetic considerations. The current state of the question regarding erotic art, however, suggests the truth of this last point in the positive sense that there are few perceptible limits on its location. This does not mean that the placement of erotic art was random, any

---

98. Plin. *NH* 35.2–3.

99. The dedication of the work to Titus the son of Vespasian dates to A.D. 77: see Plin. *NH Praef.* 3.

more than the placement of brothels was. The location of some erotic art, to be sure, was economically motivated, in the sense that it was meant to attract and please the patrons of baths, bars, and brothels. For the same reason, prostitutes worked in many of these same venues. This fact makes the connection recently established by Guzzo and Scarano Ussani between explicit representation of sex and places where it was sold all the more attractive.

Chapter Five

THE FORCES OF
LAW AND ORDER

Corpora Vestales oculi meretricia cernunt,
nec domino poenae res ea causa fuit.
—Ov. *Tr.* 2.311–312

VICE VERSUS SQUAD

*I*f a policy of moral zoning was in fact established in the Roman Empire, its
implementation almost certainly would have been the responsibility of the
aediles in the capital and their equivalents in towns outside Rome. Such a role
in designing and enforcing a policy of this kind logically raises the question of
comparison with other cultures, where the police or other officials enjoyed
similar responsibilities. Unfortunately, if there is a case to be made that the
aediles and their like resembled something like the modern vice squad, the
comparison will not stand—unless one looks not at the goal of regulating or
repressing prostitution but, if anything, at the results that have been achieved.
Rome's lack of zoning regulations may thus be compared with the failure of
such regulations in more recent periods.

Before we assess the state of affairs for Rome, let us grasp the essence of the
modern regulationist trend, which began in early nineteenth-century Paris
and was widely imitated, or at least found parallels, elsewhere.[1] In the United

---

1. The fundamental study of nineteenth-century French regulationism is by Corbin, *Women
for Hire* (1990). See also Harsin, *Policing Prostitution* (1985); Bernheimer, *Figures of Ill Repute*
(1989); Clayson, *Painted Love* (1991).

States, for example, a series of municipal campaigns sought to push prostitution to the edges of the urban landscape, both in the absolute sense and in relation to legitimate businesses and respectable neighborhoods. In a way the idea was to render the visible invisible.[2]

The thesis of moral zoning assumes a model for Rome of the formation and implementation of rules with which I find myself in broad sympathy.[3] It must be admitted, however, that this model is difficult to reconcile with some broader historical assumptions often made about the nature of law finding and administration in the Roman Empire.[4] According to the latter, it might seem anachronistic to argue for a regulationist regime at Rome that embraced such zoning. To put the matter in the form of a double question: Were the Romans capable of designing an effective system of moral zoning? And on a deeper level, were they capable of developing anything we might recognize as public policy regarding prostitution?[5]

CONSTRUCTIVE POLICY

A negative response to the second question would, of course, make the first unnecessary. For this reason, the second question will be the focus of my discussion. What is needed is a definition of public policy with which most historians will agree and that is reasonably clear without being culturally specific, either to ancient Rome or to the modern West, for example.[6] Our best resort

---

2. See Hobson, *Uneasy Virtue* (1990) 25.

3. See, for example, Laurence, *Roman Pompeii* (1994) 80, who states, while drawing a link between the law's treatment of *popina* and brothel, "There was a distinction between the morally good elite and the rest of the population. This is important, because the elite controlled, managed and enforced the law and imposed their will upon the population of the city." These premises seem fairly unassailable to me. I also emphatically agree with Wallace-Hadrill, "Public Honour and Private Shame" (1995) 56, when he writes that ". . . ideologies could indeed shape the life of a Roman city." Elsewhere, Wallace-Hadrill, "Emperors and Houses" (2001) 132, sketches a link between policy and political form that in my view cries out for further study.

4. For a primitivist perspective on public-health legislation, see Cilliers, "Public Health" (1993).

5. The second question is put, albeit in even broader form, by Bradley, "Prostitution" (2000) esp. 473–75. Space limitations allow me to do but scant justice here to his query.

6. In the case of the latter, the point is to avoid anachronism. I therefore prefer to conceive of "policy" in the simplest, most lowbrow way possible. For a deployment of the word "idea" in this way on roughly similar grounds, see Hacking, *Social Construction of What?* (1999) 228 n. 12. Those who assume that public policy on prostitution is the property of modern liberal democracies might contemplate the disturbing alacrity that totalitarian regimes have shown at times in formulating and executing policy on prostitution: Paul, *Zwangsprostitution* (1994); Hicks, *The Comfort Women* (1997); Falck, *VEB Bordell* (1998). Nor is policy merely a feature of the modern age. For some pre-

is the dictionary, which provides the following definition: "a course or principle of action adopted or proposed by a government, party, business, or individual, etc.,"[7] with the rather obvious qualification that what renders a policy "public" is its adoption or proposal by the state or its representatives.[8] By adopting such a definition, we avoid prejudging the kind of policy the Romans developed in regard to the location of brothels, meaning in effect the aims, level of sophistication, and effectiveness of this policy.[9]

As in the case of using comparative evidence, a subject discussed in chapter 1, a difficulty arises here with arguments from social constructionism. In essence a radical constructionist might oppose my method on two scores. First, if there is no Roman word or concept for public policy, how can we justify introducing this term into our analysis? Should we not attempt to understand the Romans on their own terms, without danger of the distortion posed by a modernizing conceptual apparatus? Second, even if we accept this point, given that sexuality is a social construction, meaning that each and every culture will show in this area its own forms of meaning, often manifested in a matrix of rules, regulations, laws, and policies, what possible good can come from such comparisons?

In the face of evidence that is weak at best, it is desirable and even necessary to rely on analogy.[10] Where it is a matter of attempting to establish a link between action and motives, which is to describe the very heart of policymaking on the definition of policy presented above, the explanation should be comprehensible to us either on a rational or at least an empathetic level.[11] The logical alternative is resort to a crude determinism.[12] If we fail to exploit comparable data, specifically from societies that have various policies in regard to prostitution, we are guilty of a cultural relativity that bodes ill for the illumination of past experience, since this experience is rendered more remote

---

modern approaches regarding prostitution see, for example, McGinn, *Prostitution, Sexuality, and the Law* (1998) 207–15; more generally, McGinn, *ESH* (1994) s.v. "Prostitution."

7. *Oxford Dictionary* (1997) s.v. "policy[1]."

8. See, for example, *American Heritage Dictionary*[3] s.v. "public policy," which has the following definition: "The policy or set of policies forming the foundation of public laws, esp. when not yet formally enunciated." The idea of political choice is key: see Hacking, *Social Construction of What?* (1999) 184.

9. Given my definition, policy might refer to any political choice, even to the refusal to act: see Hacking, *Social Construction of What?* (1999) 184.

10. Hacking, *Social Construction of What?* (1999) 199–200.

11. Collin, *Social Reality* (1997) 109.

12. See Horden and Purcell, *Corrupting Sea* (2000) 48–49.

and inaccessible by the very untenable premise of such relativity.[13] Rejection of a comparative approach begs a very big question. In other words, it proves only what it is trying to assume.

We might even question whether it is really worth looking for a Roman concept of public policy.[14] After all, most ancient historians seem comfortable with deploying a series of modern conceptual frameworks to describe aspects of Roman experience for which they lack a precise equivalent, such as "family," "economy," "society," "ideology," "law," and, yes, "concept."[15] We permit ourselves to use these terms without inverted commas more often than not.[16] We might as well add "policy" in all of its flavors, among them public, social, and legal, to the list.[17] In so doing, we recognize that both ancient and modern perceptions belong equally to the history of ideas and that there is no valid a priori reason to prefer Roman constructions to our own.[18] This does not mean rejecting Roman perceptions out of hand, but using them judiciously. The construction of a polarity between modernism and primitivism will lead neither to accuracy nor to clarity.[19]

One caveat is therefore in order. It is crucial to guard against the assump-

---

13. See Collin, *Social Reality* (1997) 32, 47–48, 52–54, 59, 84–85. For a brief catalog of primitivist errors, see Horden and Purcell, *Corrupting Sea* (2000) 337 (cf. 338).

14. See the considerations offered at Collin, *Social Reality* (1997) 213.

15. See the comments of Morel, "Artisanat" (2001) 259. Students of Roman urban planning have well noted that there is no word in Latin that communicates what we mean by "city" in either its demographic or economic sense: Vismara, "*Civitas*" (1994) 49. There is much value here in relying on the Foucauldian premise that different forms of knowledge can exist for different cultures: Hacking, *Social Construction of What?* (1999) 170, 209. Different forms can also coexist within the same culture: Collin, *Social Reality* (1997) 215. This stands as a useful example of the fact that the moderate constructionist has much to learn from the radical constructionist.

16. "Quotation marks" are catnip to the radical constructionist: see the discussion in Collin, *Social Reality* (1997) 66–69, 121. A similar purpose is achieved by the negating qualifier, such as the adjective "ancient" in the phrase "the ancient economy." For an appraisal, see Horden and Purcell, *Corrupting Sea* (2000) 146, 301. Yet another example is "the ancient city." For the moderate constructionist, it is a matter of determining where to draw a line, as opposed to rejecting the use of quotation marks entirely.

17. See Collin, *Social Reality* (1997) 213. Not all terms can be accommodated under the rainbow of Foucauldian forms, to be sure. For example, as noted in chap. 1, Foucault himself and some of his followers deny that sexuality existed before the nineteenth century: see Karras, "Review Essay" (2000).

18. See Horden and Purcell, *Corrupting Sea* (2000) 13, 93; Veyne, "Plèbe" (2000) 1169–70; Morel, "Artisanat" (2001) 244.

19. Horden and Purcell, *Corrupting Sea* (2000) 181. For a forceful presentation of this perspective in the context of the Roman economy, which condemns the view I criticize as "sociological manichaeism," see Carandini, "Columella's Vineyard" (1983) esp. 178–81, 186, 201–2; see also the remarks of Lo Cascio, "Introduzione" (2000) 10.

tion that in the matter of policy the modern world shows a higher level of sophistication than the facts sustain.[20] The difficulty lies not only in the idea that modern policymaking is inevitably very highly sophisticated in the rationality of its aims and process—though even here any current appraisal will have to be revised downward in the wake of the Florida presidential election debacle of 2000—but above all in the effectiveness of its results.[21] For example, even in a modern market economy, not all transactions consist of market exchanges; that is far from the case.[22]

This problem of assuming the sophistication of policy in more recent periods is a particularly delicate matter for policy on prostitution, where the historical record is, in a word, bleak.[23] For this precise reason resort to an abundance of comparative evidence is useful for provoking a spirit of skepticism. Excessive piety toward the ancient sources leaves us vulnerable to their capacity for self-delusion and self-interest.[24] At bottom, there is nothing really "primitive" about primitivism. It is yet another form of modern constructionism, though more often than not it is advanced without self-recognition as such.[25]

The advocates of a moral zoning theory find themselves in an awkward position because they must reason back from their perception of the success of a policy to its existence in the first place.[26] This difficulty makes the moral zoning hypothesis per se neither anachronistic nor impossible, however, a

---

20. It seems easier for the ancient historian to admit the limits of Roman power than those operating for modern states. More generally, see the cogent remarks of Searle, *Construction of Social Reality* (1995) 90–92, 117. For some choice examples from the history of the Mediterranean that serve to illuminate the point, see Horden and Purcell, *Corrupting Sea* (2000) 149, 290, 294, 359. The discussion in Carandini, "Columella's Vineyard" (1983) is also useful.

21. We do well to keep in mind that there are often vast differences in policy, sometimes amounting to the simple matter of its presence or absence, among modern polities that are in many respects very similar, including Western democracies in Canada, the United States, and Western Europe: see Nivola, *Laws of the Landscape* (1999) 5, 22–23, 27, 32, 100 n. 40; Rybczynski, "City Lights" (2001) 69–70. These nations sometimes show important regional differences as well: see Nivola, 28, on the significant differences, in terms of stringency, of urban land-use plans among the German *Länder*.

22. Temin, "Market Economy" (2001) 180. See also, Horden and Purcell, *The Corrupting Sea* (2000) 567 in criticism of F. Braudel.

23. This is unfortunately as true for modern, even contemporary, approaches to prostitution as it was for the ancient. Thus, the vagaries of Roman policy on prostitution are at best cold comfort for the primitivist: see McGinn, *Prostitution, Sexuality, and the Law* (1998) chap. 10, with the bibliography given in McGinn, *ESH* (1994) s.v. "Prostitution."

24. See Horden and Purcell, *Corrupting Sea* (2000) 147.

25. See Horden and Purcell, *Corrupting Sea* (2000) 342.

26. Awkward though it may be, this position is all too familiar to the Roman historian. For a good discussion, see Peachin, review of *Rome and the Enemy* (2000).

point that will be developed further below. A brief defense must suffice for now. "More damaging . . . than the deficiencies of the evidence is a mistaken conclusion from those deficiencies: the conclusion that the processes of the reception and diffusion of ideas were as meagre as are the literary accounts of them."[27] There are many facts about their physical and social world(s) that the Romans did not recognize or articulate, at least in a way that has come down to us.[28] It is especially easy to take for granted the (non)existence of a policy where there is a gap between intention and result.[29] In this context, the notion of "accidental policy" has potentially great significance.[30] The "law of unintended consequences" has been little studied in this field.[31] Policies can fail, suffer from lax, partial, or puritanical enforcement, conflict with each other, resist change, or be conspicuous by their absence.[32]

The success of almost any policy can be affected by economic constraints.[33] The very notion of "success" must itself be measured by a realistic appraisal of what is possible and what is intended. Few, for example, would insist that a policy on criminal law that failed to eliminate all crime was a failure.[34] A good example of the enormous influence the lack of a policy can enjoy, taken from an area of study relevant to the general theme of zoning, is shown by the development of urban sprawl, which is encouraged in part by the nonexistence of a national land-use statute in the United States.[35]

In other words, bad, ineffective, or even nonexistent policy still matters.[36] Sometimes of course the act of judging the success of a policy depends on developing a precise idea of what the policy really is, not always as easy a task as it might seem.[37] At the same time, the fact that few policies are implemented with complete success should discourage pure speculation about their

---

27. Horden and Purcell, *Corrupting Sea* (2000) 288.

28. See Hacking, *Social Construction of What?* (1999) 80–84, for a useful treatment of nominalism versus inherent-structuralism (a.k.a essentialism). It is always easier, of course, to attack one or the other than to deploy either in the service of historical explanation. For example, Hacking, 220, has a good discussion of problems that arise in reconciling a sense of universalism with a careful survey of relevant ethnographic data. For striking examples of Roman silence on things that matter to us, see Horden and Purcell, *Corrupting Sea* (2000) 259 (the water mill), 288 (more generally on the history of technology).

29. See Searle, *Construction of Social Reality* (1995) 4, on taking social reality for granted.

30. See Nivola, *Laws of the Landscape* (1999) 3, 12, 89.

31. For an important exception, see Marx, "Ironies of Social Control" (1981).

32. See Nivola, *Laws of the Landscape* (1999) 28, 52–53, 58, 71, 74, 78, 90–91.

33. Reynolds, *Economics of Prostitution* (1986) 61; Best, *Controlling Vice* (1998) 8.

34. See Best, *Controlling Vice* (1998) 10.

35. Nivola, *Laws of the Landscape* (1999) 27.

36. See Searle, *Construction of Social Reality* (1995) 19.

37. Best, *Controlling Vice* (1998) 32–34.

"true" purpose. So, for example, we can reasonably suppose that the exorbitant rate imposed on prostitutes by the Coptos Tariff from Egypt (108 drachmas) was not fully enforceable, since its mere existence would have encouraged attempts at evasion.[38] That does not mean the purpose of this high rate was anything but making money for the state.[39] The mere fact of exacting a fee might serve another purpose, that of social control, to which end evidently a flat rate of four drachmas was demanded of all women.

Perhaps most importantly, to ignore questions of policy on prostitution is to turn a blind eye to an important way in which patriarchal societies imagine, express, and indulge the male interest.[40] Tolerance of prostitution, so easy to construe as the absence of policy, should not be taken for that which it is not.[41] It is moreover impossible to understand the phenomenon of deviance without coming to grips with social control.[42] It is crucial here to avoid casual assumptions and false distinctions between state and nonstate activity.[43] The line between them shrinks almost to the disappearing point in the Roman economy of prostitution.

The view I have outlined is I believe consistent with the broad definition of public policy adopted above. A modern conceptual framework, accompanied by the introduction of relevant comparative evidence, is no luxury but a necessity in light of the gaps and silences on the subject of women in the historical record, examination of which depends on careful inference for anything like a coherent understanding.[44]

This brings us, in reverse order, to the first of our two questions. On the surface, it seems perfectly possible that the Romans could have enacted some form of zoning. The Romans were experts in counting and measuring the peoples and places they had conquered and were equally accomplished in the art of town planning. Though moderns have exaggerated their achievements in the latter field, their skill at developing street plans and placing public build-

---

38. *I. Portes* 67 =*OGIS* 2.674 = *IGR* 1.1183 (Coptos A.D. 90), with discussion in McGinn, *Prostitution, Sexuality, and the Law* (1998) 281–82. Add Young, *Rome's Eastern Trade* (2001) 47–51.

39. Montserrat, *Sex and Society* (1996) 131, argues that the point of the high rate for prostitutes was to create a "symbolic demarcation."

40. See Paul, *Zwangsprostitution* (1994) 135.

41. On tolerance as an important strain in public policy on prostitution in past time, see McGinn, *ESH* (1994) s.v. "Prostitution."

42. Best, *Controlling Vice* (1998) 6.

43. See Horden and Purcell, *Corrupting Sea* (2000) 376.

44. See Skinner, "Rescuing Creusa" (1986) 3; Joshel, *Work* (1992) esp. 3–24; Scheidel, "Silent Women 1" (1995) 202.

ings in the urban mix suggests they might, in fact, have attempted to zone brothels.[45] The placement of the temple of Venus Erycina, with its explicit identification with venal sex, outside the Porta Collina, is suggestive.[46] Denial of burial, at least informally, to prostitutes and pimps is itself an exclusion for which we have vague evidence.[47] Rules for the placement of cemeteries are themselves an example of ancient zoning practice.[48] In fact the city of Rome was characterized by a series of boundaries—physical, ritual, economic, and legal.[49] Why not moral or sexual ones as well?

The Roman boundary par excellence was of course that of the city itself, the *pomerium*, which straddled all of the four categories just named.[50] A clear demarcation of this kind allowed for the practice of what we might describe as "zoning out" or, more precisely, repression. It facilitated the expulsion from the city of certain groups at different times, among them adherents or members of certain religions, ethnic groups, or professions.[51] The last category is of particular interest for us. For example, the censors forced actors out of Rome in 115 B.C.[52] A whole series of persons, activities, and things considered (ob)noxious were routinely placed outside the city, including undertakers,

---

45. For the first point, see Nicolet, *Space, Geography, and Politics* (1991); for the second, see Perring, "Spatial Organisation" (1991) (whose distinction between intentional, i.e., official and unconscious, i.e., social and economic, spatial organization might be drawn more firmly); Laurence, "Modern Ideology" (1994); Owens, "Residential Districts" (1996) 12–14 (who discusses the adaption of Greek usage in urban design to Roman needs). Roman city planning is notable for its almost inexhaustible variety. For some examples, see Di Vita, "Urbanistica" (1994); Trousset, "Organisation" (1994) esp. 608; Vismara, "Civitas" (1994). For a more general survey, see Gros and Torelli, *Storia dell'urbanistica*[3] (1994); and now Parrish, "Introduction" (2001).

46. On the temple, see McGinn, *Prostitution, Sexuality, and the Law* (1998) 25. Add Wiseman, "Stroll on the Rampart" (1995) 22; Orlin, "Second Temple" (2000). There is no need to assume the presence of sacred prostitution.

47. CIL 1[2] 2123 = 11.6528 = ILS 7846, with McGinn, *Prostitution, Sexuality, and the Law* (1998) 65. The *Tabula Larinas*, containing an SC from A.D. 19, may indicate that those who were engaged in dishonorable professions were denied an official burial, though this is far from certain: *Tab. Lar.* 14–15. On the subject of the denial of burial, see Hope, "Contempt and Respect" (2000) 116–20.

48. See Lindsay, "Death-Pollution" (2000) 170–71. These rules appear to have had a special force regarding the offical demarcation of space for the Roman city: see Horden and Purcell, *Corrupting Sea* (2000) 434–35.

49. I owe this series to Patterson, "On the Margins" (2000) 86. See also Champlin, "*Suburbium*" (1982) 97.

50. The literature is extensive. See, for example, Hinard, "Rome dans Rome" (1991) who also discusses how certain religious festivals served to define space in the capital.

51. For the exclusion of Egyptian cults, see Patterson, "On the Margins" (2000) 92. For the expulsions of Jews, see Smallwood, *Jews under Roman Rule*[2] (2001) index s.v. "Rome."

52. Cassiod. *Chron.* (under consuls for 115 B.C.), with McGinn, *Prostitution, Sexuality, and the Law* (1998) 41–42.

brick production, and wild animals destined for the city's games.[53] We might also regard the prohibitions against dumping bodies and other refuse in or near the city as a type of zoning regulation.[54]

These regulations were presumably inspired by considerations of pollution, public safety, or both. Other displacements occurred for economic reasons. As John Patterson has shown, the institution of a customs-boundary helped put a number of businesses on the urban margin, as did the requirements of a massive distribution system designed chiefly for agricultural products coming into the city.[55]

Of course, the expulsion of actors from the city was not permanent. The sources contain no mention of the exclusion, even of a temporary nature, of pimps and prostitutes. Their status was arguably as low as that of performers, if not lower. This suggests that in the case of pimps and prostitutes policy considerations were different from those that operated for actors. The same must have been true for undertakers. We might argue that they were relegated to working outside the city boundary because of their lower status, but in fact we have no evidence to suggest they were inflicted with the core set of civic disabilities accruing to prostitutes, pimps, actors, and gladiators. Fear of pollution might be advanced as a reason for the policy on undertakers, but a more important reason might be perhaps concerns with public health.[56]

The existence of such concerns, however, does not necessarily mean they were translated into public policy. It is noteworthy, for example, that medical expertise on questions of public health was directed at the individual's welfare and not the formation of public policy that might have advantaged an entire city.[57]

Roman policy toward prostitution contained elements of what we would call regulationism, but only in a limited way.[58] Roman officials were not, in

---

53. Morel, "Topographie" (1987) 131; Bodel, "Dealing with the Dead" (2000) esp. 135–44; Patterson, "On the Margin" (2000) 92–93; Morel, "Artisanat" (2001) 248. See *lex Ursonensis* ch. 76 for a ban on large tile works within the town boundaries.

54. See Bodel, "Dealing with the Dead" (2000) 134; Hope, "Contempt and Respect" (2000) 111.

55. Patterson, "On the Margins" (2000) 94–95.

56. See the views of Bodel, "Dealing with the Dead" (2000); Lindsay, "Death-Pollution" (2000). For the core set of civic disabilities inflicted on prostitutes and the other three types named in the text, see McGinn, *Prostitution, Sexuality, and the Law* (1998) chap. 2.

57. Nutton, "Medical Thoughts" (2000) 71–72.

58. The aedilician regulations listed by Laurence, *Roman Pompeii* (1994) 80–81; Wallace-Hadrill, "Public Honour and Private Shame" (1995) 45, 50–51, which deal with the consumption of certain edibles in *popinae*, the wearing of togas in the Roman Forum by male citizens, the registration of prostitutes, and even the supervision of the practice of prostitution, prove nothing about zoning brothels.

terms of their training, methods, and responsibilities, the ancient version of the modern *police des mœurs*.[59] As previously suggested, we have no evidence of any regulation of prostitution regarding zoning, which means we have to contemplate a sort of regulationism without regulations.[60] Fair enough. Construing policy in the absence of discourse is a familiar task for the historian.[61] As suggested in the previous chapter, however, the Romans did not perceive a need for the physical or symbolic separation of brothels from respectable society.

The failure of the comparison drawn here between ancient and modern official approaches to prostitution, however, lies in more than just a matter of identifying or classifying a type of official policy. Wallace-Hadrill and Laurence not only argue for a regulationist regime for the Romans that embraced zoning, but assume this regime was successful, at least in Pompeii. Their perspective is unusual to say the least, given the recent historiography on prostitution. The consensus among scholars is that the highly sophisticated regulationist regime at modern Paris, for example, was a miserable failure.[62]

The nineteenth-century Parisian system did not, in fact, include a general system of zoning as postulated for Pompeii. Instead, efforts were limited to managing the moral geography of prostitution through regulations on public solicitation or at most through minor prohibitions on brothel-location.[63] This is one reason why Balzac can refer to the entire city of Paris as a brothel.[64] In regard to segregating venues for prostitution, Alexandre Parent-Duchâtelet,

---

59. Laurence, *Roman Pompeii* (1994) 143, seems to assume something like the opposite when he cites Alain Corbin, the greatest authority on the nineteenth-century Parisian vice squad, as support for his theory that the aediles' registration of prostitutes was meant to enforce a moral geography.

60. Wallace-Hadrill, "Public Honour and Private Shame" (1995) 51, draws a connection between traffic regulations and the symbolic cleanliness of the city.

61. See the cogent observations of Best, *Controlling Vice* (1998) 139.

62. See Corbin, *Women for Hire* (1990) 115–85 (a chapter entitled "The Failure of Regulationism"); Gilfoyle, "Prostitutes in History" (1999) 121–22.

63. See the zoning rules from the 1878 Paris regulations, as translated by Flexner, *Prostitution in Europe* (1914) 405: "[Public prostitutes] are not permitted to be in the vicinity of churches (Catholic or Protestant), schools and lycées, covered arcades, boulevards, the Champs-Élysées, the railway stations and their approaches, and the public parks. They are not permitted to live in houses in which there are boarding-schools or day-schools." The last sentence, as well as the general context, might well suggest that the rules regarding the vicinity of churches and so on pertain to public solicitation. Otherwise, this is a very mild form of zoning for brothels, which does not amount to segregation. See Flexner, *Prostitution*, 175–79; Corbin, *Women for Hire* (1990) 55–56, 84–86, 205 (other French towns were more aggressive, at least on paper); Clayson, *Painted Love* (1991) 15.

64. Bernheimer, *Figures of Ill Repute* (1989) 38; see also 159, 165; Harsin, *Policing Prostitution* (1985) 316.

that great connoisseur of sewer and brothel, argued that policymakers could not prevent prostitution from locating itself in whatever areas it found congenial (much like water seeking its own level, it seems), so that attempts to contain it in designated areas were bound to fail.[65] Even where they existed, zoning regulations that aimed at segregating brothels from respectable society have tended to be more ideological than practical in their implications.[66]

The evidence does not in any reasonable sense support the theory that Rome had a full-scale nineteenth-century regime, whether successful or not. In other words, my difficulty with the argument made by the advocates of the moral zoning theory does not have to do with the problem of anachronism or with the plausibility of their model in general terms, but lies instead with some of the inferences they draw from the comparative evidence.[67] To accept even a modified version of the zoning thesis, it would be helpful to address the following sorts of questions, albeit necessarily, given the lack of evidence, in speculative form. How did the aediles in the capital communicate such regulations to the authorities elsewhere?[68] Who was the authority ultimately responsible for making sure these regulations were enforced? Did this take place at the instigation of central authority by imperial decree, *senatus consultum*, comitial law, or through a more capillary process, as some scholars posit for the municipal rules contained on the *Tabula Heracleensis*? Did this originate during the Republic or Principate?[69] Before we can accept the idea that zoning regulations were the norm, we must resolve, even if in the abstract, the issue of how such regulations were communicated and enforced.

If we focus on Pompeii, and resist the temptation to view zoning as an

---

65. Bernheimer, *Figures of Ill Repute* (1989) 20.

66. Corbin, *Women for Hire* (1990) 85–86, 205, 317; Bernstein, *Sonia's Daughters* (1995) 176; Hershatter, *Dangerous Pleasures* (1997) 9, 213–14, 274. Some laws designed to segregate prostitution never got off the ground: Hill, *Their Sisters' Keepers* (1993) 134–36.

67. On the invocation, unpersuasive in my view, of the nineteenth-century ideology of the sewer for Roman prostitution, see chap. 3. Laurence, *Roman Pompeii* (1994) esp. 70, 73, 87, argues for the physical isolation (above all from members of the elite) of prostitution at Pompeii. He relies on comparisons that show the topography of urban deviance as, in part, the result of policy, to be sure, but a result that is unanticipated and undesired, and on comparisons that represent solutions to urban problems, which are largely, indeed almost exclusively, utopian in nature: see B. Cohen, *Deviant Street Networks* (1980) 1–7; S. Cohen, *Visions of Social Control* (1985) 206–7.

68. Most scholars believe that the duties of aediles in the capital and those of their equivalents elsewhere were very similar; for a recent challenge to this view, see Andrés Santos, "Función jurisdiccional" (1998).

69. It is awkward that the duties spelt out for aediles (evidently at Rome) in the *Tabula Heracleensis* (20–82) and for their equivalents (in the Latin municipalities of Spain) in the Flavian Municipal Law (chap. 19) do not mention brothel-zoning. We might argue that one or both—especially the first—is incomplete, but there is no other evidence of this kind.

empire-wide phenomenon, the case is at first glance plausible. Local regulations did notably zone members of certain professions out of certain cities. For example, embalmers were excluded from Egyptian Thebes—but not Oxyrhyncus—and gladiators from Rhodes, on the analogy of executioners who were also forbidden to enter the city.[70]

There have been, at different times, successful local attempts to clean up prostitution, like the one that occurred in late twentieth-century New York City's Times Square.[71] Other examples range from the experiment in the famous Storeyville quarter of early twentieth-century New Orleans, to the less well-known experiments with vice districts in cities such as Houston in the same period.[72] Such policies have required a significant investment of money, manpower, and political will, but they often have succeeded for a time at least in keeping much of the rest of those cities, to borrow a phrase from Garrison Keillor, "almost pure."

This rosy scenario must be qualified, however. The success enjoyed by such campaigns has typically been limited in its scope so that its effects have been narrow and imperfect and its time-frame temporary at best. Furthermore, they have operated, paradoxically enough, in the context of an official policy of repression of prostitution, something foreign to the Romans.[73] Given the nature of this evidence, we might expect that such regulationism for the Romans was nothing but a sporadic, local phenomenon and perhaps enjoyed some limited measure of success in the event that adequate resources were devoted to it. There is not, however, attestation even of this much.

Finally, we might look to a premodern model for zoning prostitution, such as that found in medieval Germany. This tradition shows not only that a variety of approaches were taken but also that some significant changes were introduced over time. We see, for example, an emphasis on zoning as a form of regulation, or even toleration, metamorphose over time into an emphasis on

---

70. For evidence and discussion, see Bodel, "Dealing with the Dead" (2000) 142–43, 148. Bodel observes that funerary workers were commonly pushed to the margins of towns.

71. On this, see now Traub, "Land of the Naked Cowboy" (2002).

72. For these two examples, see Mackey, *Red Lights Out* (1987) 290–387. For mid-nineteenth-century San Francisco, see Tong, *Unsubmissive Women* (1994) 112–13.

73. Pre-Giuliani street-sweeping campaigns generated little but cynicism in the end: see Decker, *Prostitution* (1979) 109–10. See also, on the limits of, and problems with, police intervention, Decker, 176, 198, 271, 339; Mackey, *Red Lights Out* (1987) 200 (who notes civil suits enjoyed greater success than criminal sanctions in the late nineteenth- and early twentieth-century United States), 265, 299, 397; Best, *Controlling Vice* (1998) 87–97 (who shows that the failure of a modest and informal policy of regulation in nineteenth-century St. Paul sparked a series of futile attempts at repression).

zoning as a first step toward repression.[74] In most towns the municipal brothel, or *Frauenhaus*, was itself located centrally, as we might expect of a public institution, or at least in a place deemed easily accessible to clients.[75] Nonofficial brothels were illegal but were often tolerated within certain bounds.[76] The municipal brothels were rather heavily regulated, with rules governing hours and days of operation, and prostitutes' clothing, as well as prostitutes' freedom of movement generally.[77] Prostitutes were allowed, and even encouraged, to attend church, though even there they were zoned; they had to remain apart from the respectable congregation, at least in the later period.[78]

The period from the middle of the fifteenth century onwards saw a renewal and a sharpening of existing regulatory norms, as well as tougher enforcement of these rules. The reasons for this greater intensity were various—the perception that the existing policy was a failure, increased hostility toward prostitutes and their trade, a heightened sensitivity to, and sense of stronger purpose regarding, the forms of political organization and administration.[79] Obviously, the change in policy was informed by the same complex of factors that led to the Reformation and the Counter-Reformation.

One aspect of this change was the more uniform repression of unofficial brothels. These brothels were closed and their prostitutes were expelled from the city, or at minimum a greater effort was made to control them. A good example of the latter approach occurred in the city of Strasbourg. In 1469 an attempt was made systematically to list all the brothels in the city. Additional limits were placed on the mobility of "official" prostitutes, that is, those from the municipal brothel. The idea was to segregate venal sex and its practitioners within the confines of the municipal brothel. This policy reached its culmination in the latter part of the fifteenth century, while in the next, municipal brothels were closed throughout Germany and the rest of Europe.[80]

This example should be sufficient to show that there is nothing necessarily "modern," and thus anachronistic, about the idea of zoning brothels as

---

74. See P. Schuster, *Frauenhaus* (1992) 42. See also B. Schuster, *Freien Frauen* (1995) 44, 50, 73–75.

75. Schuster, *Frauenhaus* (1992) 27, 34, 42–45, 54–55.

76. See Schuster, *Frauenhaus* (1992) 125.

77. P. Schuster, *Frauenhaus* (1992) 61–64, 145–53; B. Schuster, *Freien Frauen* (1995) 56–57, 99, 131–33, 179.

78. Schuster, *Frauenhaus* (1992) 172–73.

79. P. Schuster, *Frauenhaus* (1992) 157–58. See also B. Schuster, *Freien Frauen* (1995) 97, 219, 397.

80. See Schuster, *Frauenhaus* (1992) 159–74.

advanced by Laurence and Wallace-Hadrill. There are some elements of the German picture in fact that may well have been present for Rome, such as aedilician oversight of clothing regulations and hours of operation for brothels. What is lacking is evidence for the officially regulated location of brothels, centrally or elsewhere, as well as an Augustinian ethic (chapter 3) that would have motivated this regulation.

We might, however, refuse to postulate the existence of such norms, either for the empire as a whole, or locally, for Pompeii, and still credit the existence of a pattern of segregation of brothels that was generated by an "accidental policy," as described above. There is, in fact, one very good candidate for an official policy that might have produced this unintended consequence. This is the tax on prostitutes instituted by emperor Caligula in A.D. 40, which was set at a high rate and enforced with great vigor, and which in many places— though probably not at Pompeii—was collected by the military.[81] It is very reasonable to ask whether the operators of brothels, eager to escape the expense exacted by the tax and the depredations often inflicted by its collectors, moved their venues to hidden and inconspicuous locales. The brothels of Pompeii, however, though some are more noticeable than others, are simply not that inconspicuous overall. It is difficult, at the same time, to imagine another example of a policy that might have had a similar, wholly unintended, effect.

Beyond accidental policy, one further candidate remains and that is an informal policy that limited the locations of brothels and perhaps also checked the movements of prostitutes themselves. Examples are found in late nineteenth-century St. Paul, Minnesota, where police enforced a policy of regulation against the grain of a policy of outright prohibition at law, as well as in late twentieth-century Nevada, where the rules segregating prostitutes from the communities in which they worked were not always enacted into law.[82] This kind of policy almost inevitably requires the cooperation of police and brothel operators for implementation. Yet it is one of the most difficult to trace because, at least in the examples known to me, the policy, intended to control deviants, is itself somewhat deviant. There is no evidence the Romans practiced such a policy.

---

81. See McGinn, *Prostitution, Sexuality, and the Law* (1998) chap. 7.

82. For St. Paul, see Best, *Controlling Vice* (1998); for Nevada, see Albert, *Brothel* (2001) 48 (whose grasp of the precise meaning of the term "unofficial" does not seem firm).

OFFICIAL BUSINESS

Certainly policies often fail, and the historical record suggests that policies on prostitution fail more often than most. Sometimes the failure is due not so much to a poorly designed policy, but to a compromise solution among various ideologies and/or strategies. Therefore it is unreasonable to the point of misleading to expect a coherence to a policy that may be somewhat contradictory or simply unsatisfactory in consequence of the different forces at work upon it. At Pompeii, for example, it is easy to posit a policy promoting the segregation of brothels running counter to the desire of property owners who wanted to make the most profitable use of their urban real estate.[83] On the ground, the results might look very mixed, not to say confusing, with zoning functioning better in some parts of the city than in others, or not at all.

If regulationism of this sort failed at Rome itself and in other Roman cities like Pompeii, however, the preferable view is that this occurred because it never was attempted in the first place. The aediles were not able to keep burial places outside the city of Rome free from prostitutes,[84] though of course there is no evidence that they even tried. The aediles were responsible for keeping the streets clean and clear, a task at which they did not always succeed to judge from the need for imperial intervention signaled by Martial.[85] Caligula's punishment of Vespasian for his ineffectiveness as an aedile is also relevant.[86] In short, the aediles sometimes failed at their responsibilities by Roman standards, which are very different from our own.[87]

I do not intend to deny here that the aediles were concerned with public morals.[88] These magistrates were certainly no strangers to prostitution. They were entrusted with the oversight of brothels, just as they were with other businesses and places of popular entertainment.[89] What exactly were their responsibilities in this regard? The sources are generally vague and unhelpful,

---

83. I owe this point to Professor Dennis Kehoe.

84. This is to judge from Mart. 3.93.15.

85. Mart. 7.61.

86. See Suet. *Vesp.* 5.3.

87. For a sense of this difference, see Scobie, "Slums" (1986) esp. 407–22, with the qualifications of Laurence, "Writing the Roman Metropolis" (1997). Further elucidation may be sought now among the essays collected in Dupré Raventós and Remolà, *Sordes Urbis* (2000).

88. We might go as far as to claim that the aediles functioned in a sense as "petty censors": McGinn, "SC from Larinum" (1992) 283; see also McGinn, *Prostitution, Sexuality, and the Law* (1998) 201–2. I argue that the *regimen morum* routinely embraced (male) prostitutes and pimps: *Prostitution, Sexuality, and the Law*, esp. 40–44. We are still very far from a regime for moral zoning, however.

89. For the evidence and a more detailed statement, see McGinn, *Prostitution, Sexuality, and the Law* (1998) 201–2; cf. 60. To the literature on aediles' duties, add Frayn, *Markets and Fairs in Roman Italy* (1993) 117–32; Andrés Santos, "Función jurisdiccional" (1998).

but allow a few useful conclusions to be drawn. The aediles' main role regarding prostitution was to preserve public order, as can be inferred by a remark of Seneca's in which he directly or indirectly names brothels, taverns, and baths as "places fearing the aedile" ("loca aedilem metuentia").[90] The importance of this main role may be judged from the potentially or actually violent and criminal atmosphere that reigned in many brothels (chapter 3).

The evidence often makes it difficult, however, clearly to distinguish the aediles' main responsibility from some of their other tasks. Aediles may have entered brothels and taverns to repress illegal gambling.[91] They also may have enforced the rules forbidding the sale of certain foods in brothels where food was sold.[92] Couples resorting to brothels as assignation houses, in order to evade the strictures of the Augustan law on adultery, may have fallen under the aediles' purview.[93]

Did the aediles enforce hours of operation for venues of prostitution? A rather opaque line of the satirist Persius might refer to such a practice: ". . . if a *nonaria* should teasingly pluck the beard of a Cynic philosopher" (". . . si Cynico barbam petulans nonaria vellat").[94] If *nonaria* signifies "nine-o'clock girl" in reference to the legal opening time for brothels, this would mean on our reckoning that brothels remained closed until 1:30 to 2:30 P.M. depending on the season.[95]

This theory is based on the explanation of an ancient commentator, who writes about the passage, "The woman called a *nonaria* is a prostitute, because in the good old days (*apud veteres*) they used to solicit from the ninth hour, so that young men would not visit them in the morning, having neglected their military training" ("nonaria dicta est meretrix, quia apud veteres a nona hora prostabant, ne mane omissa exercitatione militari illo irent adulescentes").[96]

There are a number of problems with the commentator's interpretation, to be sure.[97] First, as modern scholars emphasize, there is no certainty that Per-

---

90. Seneca *Vita Beata* 7.3. See chap. 9 for a fuller discussion of this passage. For the aediles' maintenance of public order in brothels, see McGinn, *Prostitution, Sexuality and the Law* (1998) 201 with n. 489.

91. See, for example, Mart. 5.84.3–5, which concerns aedilician intervention in a tavern; cf. 14.1.3. For gambling in brothels and taverns, see chap. 3.

92. See chap. 2.

93. See chap. 7.

94. Persius 1.133.

95. See Bickerman, *Chronology of the Ancient World*[2] (1980) 15.

96. Schol. *ad Pers.* 1.133. No suitable modern edition of this ancient scholiast exists; the text must be consulted, for example, in Jahn, *Saturae*[4] (1910) 17.

97. This interpretation is not compromised, however, by the assertion of Nonius Marcellus that prostitutes (the ones he terms "prostibula") would solicit night and day: Non. Marc. 684L. So also the reference to the unfortunate client playing the slave in a brothel both night and day: [Quint.] *Decl.* 15.2.

sius is referring to prostitutes here, and not slave girls associated with the festival of the Nones, as a passage of Plutarch's suggests.[98] The fact that the scholiast places the practice in the past does not encourage confidence either. The reference to the usage of the *veteres* has a whiff of *Sittenverfall*-theory about it, while the postulated concern with the neglect of military training seems too just-so to be true. It is, in fact, contradicted by another scholium, this one to Juvenal, that explains Messalina's alleged nocturnal expedition to the brothel in the following way: "Because beforehand prostitutes on account of the celebration of sacred rites used to solicit customers the whole night long beginning at the ninth hour, they were also called "*nonariae*" ("Quoniam antea meretrices propter sacrorum celebrationem ab hora nona totam noctem prostabant, inde etiam 'nonariae' dictae sunt").[99]

Unfortunately, this explanation is no more credible than the first—just what sacred rites occurring most of the day, every day are in question here? Finally, we would expect a concern with public order to be manifested in the regulation of closing hours rather than that of opening hours, as we find with the rules for the medieval German brothel.[100] The scholiasts communicate one important matter to us, however, namely that the *idea* of regulating a brothel's operating hours was not foreign to antiquity. The notion of opening hours hardly excludes the possibility that closing hours were enforced as well.

If we turn from the text of the scholiast to that of the satirist, the picture is not quite so bleak. A reference to a prostitute seems more at home in a satire than one to the "slave-girls of the Nones" (or whatever), especially in the context of a challenge to the authority of a Cynic philosopher, given, for example, the ancient tradition on Diogenes and Lais.[101] We have a reference to the aedile smashing fraudulent weights and measures in Arretium just three lines above. And in the very next line, the last one of the poem, we find "I grant them [the *nonaria* and the Cynic] the Edict in the morning, Callirhoe after lunch" ("his mane Edictum, post prandia Callirhoen do").[102] Commentators ancient and modern take this as a reference to the Praetor's Edict, but it seems

---

98. Plut. *Camil.* 33 with Jenkinson, *Persius* (1980) 76; Harvey, *Commentary* (1981) 54; Lee, *Satires of Persius* (1987) 87. See, however, Kißel, *Satiren* (1990) 284.

99. Schol. *ad Iuv.* 6.116.

100. Schuster, *Frauenhaus* (1992) 63–64.

101. See, for example, Davidson, *Courtesans and Fishcakes* (1998) 114. On Satire's challenge to authority, see McGinn, "Satire and the Law" (2001). Horace has the beard of a Stoic plucked at *Serm.* 1.3.133–34.

102. Pers. 1.134.

just possible that the aedilician is meant.[103] So Persius closes his first satire with the assertion and negation of authority, not so much of the aediles' in the matter of brothel-regulation, but of his own as a moral teacher. In this way, he urges his reader to respect the operating hours of the brothel in a twofold sense.

I conclude that Persius's satire perhaps refers to the regulation of brothels by the aediles, but we cannot know for sure. If the argument is correct that the aediles stipulated operating hours for brothels, they did so with an eye to maintaining public order. It would be imprudent to try to draw too many conclusions from this however. We are skating on very thin ice here, but the evidence is still more conclusive than that for zoning brothels.

Aside from overseeing brothels and other haunts of prostitutes and their clients, aediles were assigned another task of possible relevance to the regulation of prostitution, namely, that of maintaining status distinctions. They accomplished this, in part, through the famous aedilician register of prostitutes, which was established, I have argued, pursuant to the *lex Iulia de adulteriis coercendis* and which was abandoned after it was brought into disrepute in A.D. 19, when a woman of senatorial rank named Vistilia attempted to shield herself from being prosecuted for adultery by registering as, and so claiming exemption under the law for being, a prostitute.[104] The point of the registry was not simply to establish eligibility for the statutory exemption but to place a symbolic boundary between respectable and nonrespectable women.[105]

The aediles also helped preserve status distinctions by enforcing the use of appropriate clothing. According to Suetonius, this responsibility was assigned to the aediles by Augustus, who was moved to quote Vergil's tag about the *gens togata* when he saw a crowd of men in dark-colored clothing at a public meeting.[106] Regulation soon followed:

Suet. *Aug.* 40.5:
Negotium aedilibus dedit, ne quem posthac paterentur in Foro circave nisi positis lacernis togatum consistere.

---

103. I take the reference to Callirhoe to be at minimum sexual and think it likely is connected with prostitution, though disagreement reigns on its precise meaning: Jenkinson, *Persius* (1980) 76; Harvey, *Commentary* (1981) 54–55; Lee, *Satires of Persius* (1987) 87; Kißel, *Satiren* (1990) 286–87.

104. McGinn, *Prostitution, Sexuality and the Law* (1998) 197–201, 216–19.

105. McGinn, *Prostitution, Sexuality and the Law* (1998) 207–15.

106. Verg. *Aen.* 1.282.

He (Augustus) assigned to the aediles responsibility for enforcing the rule that no one in future was to appear in the Forum and its environs except without a cloak and wearing a toga.

I suggest that the same Augustan adultery law that enjoined the registration of prostitutes also called for the aediles to enforce proper dress for prostitutes (the toga) and respectable women (the *stola*), at least in the center of Rome.[107] This aspect of aedilician responsibilities stands out from the others, even those regarding prostitution, in its reliance on a statute for authorization.

The aediles were also responsible for intervening in special situations of crisis that threatened public order. As we have seen in chapter 2, brothels were in such constant need of water that particular personnel—called in the sources *aquarioli*—were sometimes appointed to the task of acquiring it. In 50 B.C. a scandal erupted over the illegal diversion of public water to private enterprises, including brothels. The practice was denounced by M. Caelius Rufus in a speech at a public meeting.[108] This speech is mentioned in a work on aqueducts by Frontinus, which was composed some one hundred and fifty years later when the capital evidently faced a similar set of difficulties:[109]

Front. *Aqu.* 76.1–2:
Ac de vitiis eiusmodi nec plura nec melius dici possunt, quam a Caelio Rufo dicta sunt in ea contione, cui titulus est "De Aquis." quae nunc nos omnia simili licentia usurpata utinam non per offensas probaremus: inriguos agros, tabernas, cenacula etiam, corruptelas denique omnes perpetuis salientibus instructas invenimus.

And concerning abusive practices of this sort [the illegal channeling of public water for private use] no more can be said—and it cannot be said any bet-

---

107. See McGinn, *Prostitution, Sexuality, and the Law* (1998) 154–61.

108. See also Caelius's reference in a letter to Cicero of 50 B.C. to his battle with *tabernarii* (shopkeepers) and *aquarii* (water-supply specialists): Cic. *Fam.* 8.6.4

109. For details such as the date of Caelius's speech, the parts of Frontinus's work that might directly quote this speech, and the relationship of the speech to a comment made by Cicero in 56 B.C. that refers to the use of water in brothels, see Rodgers, "Frontinus" (1982); Bruun, "Water for Roman Brothels" (1997); Butrica, "Using Water 1" (1999); Butrica, "Using Water 2" (1999). I accept that "inriguos . . . invenimus" is a quotation from Caelius Rufus that Frontinus deploys to characterize the problems of his own day, but am less certain that this holds for what immediately precedes in the text and do not believe that six years earlier at *Cael.* 34 Cicero refers to the *illegal* diversion of water by brothels. For a possible example of Frontinus altering a quotation to suit his grammar, see Crawford, *Roman Statutes* 2 (1996) 729–30.

ter—than by Caelius Rufus in the speech he gave at that public meeting enti-
tled "On the Waters." Now that all of these usages are appropriated with a
similar lack of respect for the law, would that we not bestow an illegal
approval upon them! For we find irrigated fields, taverns, even private apart-
ments, in short, every brothel in town equipped with a permanent set of (ille-
gal) water-runoffs.

For Frontinus, the true scandal was evidently that no one in his day was scandalized by such practices.[110] One wonders what motivated the aediles to look the other way when confronted with such obvious illegality. The answer to this puzzlement is given below. Unfortunately, however, the chief focus of Caelius Rufus's concern was precisely responsibility for the water supply, which the aediles shared with the censors during the Republic, not the oversight of brothels in their own right.[111] So the incident adds little to our understanding of the official regulation of prostitution.

The aedilician oversight of brothels seems largely to have been embedded in the oversight of commerce and the maintenance of public order overall. This is why the result is similar for the epitomator Justin's report of Dionysius's squabbling with pimps before the "aediles" of Corinth.[112] We might suppose Justin is reading the competence of the Roman aediles to adjudicate disputes with pimps into the non-Roman historical record. If we can correctly assume that this account reflects a Roman practice, it may well fall within, or at least have grown out of, the aediles' general oversight of commercial activity and not just that of brothels.[113]

Like civilian officials in other areas with no military presence, the aediles in some Roman cities may have been charged with collecting the tax on prostitutes that was launched by Caligula.[114] The role aediles played—at Pompeii certainly—in overseeing street vendors[115] may have embraced streetwalking prostitutes as well, that is, prostitutes who did not work in brothels. We know also from Pompeii that the aediles leased space to merchants in such public areas as the arches of the amphitheater.[116] Given the abundant literary evi-

---

110. The last person we know (before Frontinus) to have been scandalized by misappropriation of public water resources was Pliny the Elder (*NH* 31.42), whose account together with the other evidence suggests that this was a constantly recurring problem.

111. Mommsen, *Staatsrecht* 2.1³ (1887/1969) 436, 508; De Kleijn, *Water Supply* (2001) 93–98.

112. Iustinus 21.5.7.

113. On this, see Mommsen, *Staatsrecht* 2.1³ (1887/1969) 499–504.

114. See McGinn, *Prostitution, Sexuality, and the Law* (1998) chap. 7.

115. Gassner, *Kaufläden* (1986) 15.

116. *CIL* 4.1096–97b, 1115, 2485.

dence suggesting prostitution was practiced in these venues, it is possible that the aediles were thus indirectly involved in the business of venal sex.[117] We may safely conclude that the aediles' chief interest in regard to prostitution, like that of the Roman state itself, was to make as much money as possible out of it.

A glimpse of the cozy relationship between brothels and aediles may be obtained from the proximity of electoral inscriptions, supporting candidates for the position of aedile, to the walls of brothels (such as the Purpose-Built Brothel)[118] and other establishments, such as taverns and inns, which were presumably overseen by these officials.[119] I concede that these inscriptions are of dubious value for identifying the individual occupants, yet the overall pattern seems suggestive of a relationship somewhat similar to that between brothels and the authorities in nineteenth-century New York City, where in one case, a brothel was located next door to a police station, an arrangement both parties found mutually convenient in a variety of ways.[120] This stands in contrast to say, Reformation Augsburg,[121] or even late twentieth-century New York City, where no "Sex Workers for Giuliani" posters have been reported. In this one regard alone, we can reasonably argue the aediles resemble the modern vice squad, though it is perhaps accurate to stress that they were more vice than squad.

The economic exploitation of venal sex by the Roman state and its representatives might take the form of taxes, lease payments, or (it is safe to speculate) bribes. Why bribes, given that prostitution was decidedly legal in the Roman world? Those who have never worked in an establishment where the definition of illegal behavior (including police behavior) is almost entirely a matter of police discretion may be surprised to learn that even the highly regulated and—to all appearances—eminently law-abiding brothels of contemporary Nevada must factor in payments to the police as a cost of doing busi-

---

117. See chap. 2 for this evidence. Given the shallowness of the arcades at Pompeii, the crib rather than the brothel may serve as the model for a venue of prostitution here.

118. CIL 4.817–18, with Franklin, "Games and a *Lupanar*" (1985/6) 323.

119. DeFelice, *Roman Hospitality* (2001) 132.

120. Hall, *Their Sisters' Keepers* (1993) 150; see also 125, 146–48, 152–54, 158, 292 (police officers living in brothels); Gilfoyle, *City of Eros* (1992) 86–87, 251–56. Brothels and streetwalkers were perceived as universal in this period: Hill, 197–99, 212. We might compare the arrangements in Pompeii with those in a Nevada county in 1967, where the sheriff owned the two local brothels: Symanski, "Prostitution in Nevada" (1974) 376.

121. In 1532 the city council abolished the municipal brothel at the instigation of Lutheran clergy: see Roper, "Discipline and Respectability" (1985) 3; Roper, *Holy Household* (1989) 89.

ness.[122] In the Roman city, for example, bribery might help eliminate the need for tedious negotiation over the meaning of "legal water supply."

Public order, naturally, was another concern, but this could have been secured without resort to zoning. The evidence for specific details of zoning is, as we have seen, thin; the arguments rather speculative. The profit motive, at any event, appears to have been paramount.

We might still argue that the evidence given above does not absolutely preclude the possibility of a local, that is, municipal, segregation of brothels, and I would agree with this premise, at least in the abstract. Let us suppose for a moment that there did exist a policy at Rome favoring the relegation of prostitution to the back streets. How would this be implemented in a town like Pompeii? More importantly, just what moral code was our Roman vice squad supposed to enforce? Here are, in summary, some of the more plausible reactions upper-class Romans may have had to prostitutes and brothels in their midst. One is not to see them at all or to see them only in a light that asserted the viewer's dignity in contrast to what he or she deemed pathetic and ridiculous. Another is to view brothels as manifestations of Hellenistic luxury, whether for good or ill, but with the edge removed; in other words, to view them through a romanticizing or fantasizing lens. The third possibility is that Romans reacted to brothels with outright disapproval, resentment, and indignation. All three reactions are possible, and no one reaction precludes the possibility of the others. Only the third could have led to a campaign of moral zoning, and this one is the least well attested and, in my opinion, the most unlikely for the ancient Romans.[123]

For what it is worth, the dream-interpreter Artemidorus holds that encountering prostitutes in a dream is utterly and unreservedly auspicious, while brothels themselves are almost always a bad sign.[124] There is no guaran-

---

122. Reynolds, *Economics of Prostitution* (1986) 120. On police discretion and its implications in the implementation of policy, see Marx, "Ironies of Social Control" (1981). On the law-abiding tendencies of Nevada brothels and the reasons for these, see Symanski, "Prostitution in Nevada" (1974) 375.

123. Compare the ideal function of the police force in nineteenth-century Britain: "[t]he constables' [sic] role was to act as a 'domestic missionary, ' translating and mediating bourgeois values in working-class communities, which historians describe as a radical effort to remake working-class culture and to root out the traditional social and sexual habits of the poor" (Mahood, *Magdalenes* [1990] 120).

124. Artemid. 1.78, 4.9, with the minor qualification (which rather proves the rule) that dreaming of being able to leave a brothel is a good sign. If someone dreams his wife is a prostitute in a brothel (and is wearing purple clothing!), this simply signifies the husband's profession, especially if the profession is something shameful, like collecting taxes: 4.42.

tee that what is valid in a dream also holds in actual experience, though this is certainly true for the inauspiciousness of brothels in real life, as we saw in chapter 3.[125] At a minimum, the evidence of Artemidorus makes it difficult to argue for the third option.

Private law and public regulations placed limits on the ability of property owners to dispose of their urban real estate as they pleased, but these limits were small in number and narrow in scope.[126] These rules dealt not only with threats to the safety of persons and property, such as the threat of fire, but also with what we might describe as aesthetic or quality-of-life concerns, such as the proper height of buildings, the regular flow of water, the integrity of joint structures, access to light, and even the preservation of the view. Public regulations, where they existed, were exclusively oriented toward issues of safety, especially the threat of fire, whereas for all other issues it was left to neighbors to enforce or even to create in the first place liability for infringements. No evidence exists, for example, of an urban servitude designed to prevent or allow operation of a business that might have been deemed simply undesirable, such as a brothel or *popina*, but the important point is that at most this was an area of the law governed by private arrangement, not by the intervention of the state, which tended to give property owners fairly free discretion.

Indeed, scholars have noticed that the Romans lacked law that repressed what we consider to be offenses against public decency.[127] The delict of outrage (*iniuria*), though it might under certain circumstances be used to punish the expression of *turpia verba* (obscene language), was framed as an offense against individual victims, not the community as a whole, which did, of course, maintain an interest in its enforcement.[128] Partly for this reason, we cannot be absolutely certain about how the Romans conceived of such offenses, apart from what they regarded as breaches of upper-class decorum.[129]

---

125. The heft of Artemid. 1.78 (4.9 refers back to this passage) seems to concern a visit to the brothel, and not simply the brothel itself.

126. See for the material in this paragraph especially Rainer, *Bestimmungen* (1987); also Saliou, *Lois des bâtiments* (1994), with the comments of Scarano Ussani review of *Lois des bâtiments* (1998).

127. Cipriani and Milano, "Atti osceni" (1996) 106.

128. On *iniuria*, see Kaser, *Privatrecht* 1² (1971) 623–25. For repression of *turpia verba*, see Ulp. D. 47.10.15.21. That this delict was used against prostitutes soliciting clients seems implausible to me.

129. See, for example, Cic. *Fam.* 9.22 (which suggests that great differences of opinion existed on this subject), *Off.* 1.126–28, with Meyer-Zwiffelhoffer, *Phallus* (1995) 24–48; Dyck, *Commentary on Cicero, De Officiis* (1996) 300–309. See also Cipriani and Milano, "Atti osceni" (1996) esp. 123. I would amend their analysis of Tac. *Ann.* 15.37.3, so that the *gestus motusque obsceni* of the women at Nero's party are made not just by the prostitutes but by their notional

Indecent behavior on the part of members of the lower orders was to be expected.[130] However deplorable, this behavior was not punishable per se under the law.[131] One way of putting the point, at the risk of oversimplification, is that for the Romans, above all for Roman women, what mattered was not where you were, but who you were.

Also puzzling is the lack of a coherent legal position on nuisance-abatement. In general, modern doctrine on the subject allows for relatively easy recourse against those whose actions are a source of discomfort to their neighbors. This has even proved, within limits, effective against brothels, as noted above. Rome had no such doctrine. There the operation of a brothel would have had to produce actual physical damage to a neighbor's property in order to ground an action under the *lex Aquilia*, a theoretical possibility rendered even more remote by the evident exclusion from liability of loss resulting from the normal use of property.[132] A famous juristic text shows that, for members of the Roman elite, brothels operating on their urban properties was quintessentially a matter of business as usual.[133] As we saw in chapter 2, no one was in a better position to profit from the sale of sex than they were.

"SEX CLUBS"

As I have shown so far, the evidence makes it difficult to argue for a policy of zoning brothels. This conclusion is supported, in my view, by the recent linkage demonstrated by Guzzo and Scarano Ussani between explicit representations of actual, that is nonmythological, persons engaged in sexual acts and

---

opposites and, in this context, mirror images, namely, the respectable women stationed on the other side of the pool of water. In the eyes of the historian, it is the conjuncture of the two types of women that gives real offense

130. See the comments of Edwards, *Politics of Immorality* (1993) 190–91, who points out that the upper classes largely discounted bad behavior from their inferiors. What really caused them concern was similar behavior on the part of members of the elite. See also Meyer-Zwiffelhoffer, *Phallus* (1995) 46.

131. So Ovid can write that the owner of the prostitutes seen by the Vestals goes unpunished: *Tr.* 2.311–12. Whatever the man's status, I think it fair to assume that the prostitutes went unpunished as well.

132. See Johnston, *Roman Law in Context* (1999) 71–72. Johnston, 75, cites a text suggesting that, by analogy to water, smoke from a smelly cheese factory might be regulated by servitude: Alf.-Aristo-Ulp. D. 8.5.8.5. In other words, in the absence of private agreement to the contrary, damages might be sought. There is no evidence that noise—whether from baths, brothels, or other establishments—ever received such treatment at law: Johnston, 76. To be sure, some businesses deemed (ob)noxious tended to be located on the periphery of Rome: see n. 53 above.

133. Ulp. D. 5.3.27.1 with McGinn, *Prostitution, Sexuality and the Law* (1998) 328–29.

the practice of prostitution in brothels and other venues of public resort.[134] When such representations do appear in private dwellings, they more often than not are found in slave quarters or areas of the house separate from the master's own living and recreational/hospitality areas. The authors, with some justification, suggest that these facilities, which were decorated like brothels and which were often equipped with a separate side entrance, functioned precisely as brothels.[135] This is an attractive hypothesis, especially when the crib or brothel had not only separate access from, but no direct physical access to, the *domus* itself.[136]

In cases, however, where there was access to the *domus* and especially no independent entry, such as the House of the Vettii, the hypothesis of on-site sale of sex seems more doubtful. High-status Pompeians might well find a way to tolerate a brothel on their property, even one that was right next door, but not one in their own *domus*, even if it was located in the slave quarters. Given the social animus and legal disabilities directed against pimps, operating a brothel in the *domus* might be a little risky for anyone with even a pretension to social respectability. If entry was possible through the servants' entrance, the risk might be mitigated, though perhaps not in cases where there was direct access to the *domus* itself.

To be clear, there are three possible configurations and two possible uses. Where the erotic art in question was in a part of the house accessible only from the street, this was quite possibly a brothel. Where there were both internal and external means of access, a brothel seems less likely. Where there was only internal access, a brothel is very unlikely. But then to what use were such rooms put?

What we have in some or all of the houses in question is not a brothel in the commercial sense, but rather a private "sex club."[137] These were designed to reproduce the atmospherics of actual brothels, down to the details of artistic decoration. The phenomenon represents another instance of the importation of public elements into private dwellings.[138] It is not, of course, the case that these houses were real (i.e., commercial) brothels, or that they attest to a

---

134. Guzzo and Scarano Ussani, *Veneris figurae* (2000) 9–35. The linkage, as argued in chap. 4, is not airtight, but it is sufficient to demonstrate a tendency or preference.

135. Guzzo and Scarano Ussani, *Veneris figurae* (2000) 31–33.

136. The examples given are the cribs at 7.13.15 and 16 and the brothels at 1.10.5 (no. 5), 7.3.26–28 (no. 19), 7.4.44 (no. 21: doubtful), 7.9.32 (no. 25), 9.5.19 (no. 36): Guzzo and Scarano Ussani, *Veneris figurae* (2000) 31 with n. 130.

137. I employ this term for lack of a better alternative, having canvassed "private brothel," "rumpus room," and others. Its modernizing flavor dictates the use of quotation marks.

138. This phenomenon is well demonstrated by Wallace-Hadrill, *Houses and Society* (1994) 17–37.

kind of "private" prostitution that existed alongside the commercial. Admittedly, this idea seems difficult to accept, particularly if we postulate that on certain occasions the services of actual prostitutes were sought for these places, as seems likely. But I believe that it holds true, since a requirement for status as a true brothel was the indiscriminate admission of the public, a fact Caligula seems to have understood very well, when he installed a brothel on the Palatine in Rome.[139]

I do not mean to imply here that a Roman could not strive—more or less successfully—to reproduce the ambience of a brothel in his private home. This was achieved by a man named Gemellus, who hosted a dinner party with some rather high-profile guests in 52 B.C., which may have helped set the precedent for the Pompeian "sex clubs":

Val. Max. 9.1.8:
Aeque flagitiosum illud convivium, quod Gemellus, tribunicius viator, ingenui sanguinis sed officii intra servilem habitum deformis, Metello Scipioni consuli ac tribunis plebis magno cum rubore civitatis comparavit: lupanari enim domi suae instituto, Muciam et Fulviam, cum a patre tum a viro utramque inclitam, et nobilem puerum Saturninum in eo prostituit. probrosae patientiae corpora, ludibrio temulentae libidini futura! epulas consuli et tribunis non celebrandas sed vindicandas!

Just as scandalous[140] was that dinner-party which Gemellus, a messenger for the tribunes who was of free birth but disgraceful, below the bearing of a slave, in his behavior toward his superiors,[141] staged for the Consul Metellus Scipio and the Board of Tribunes of the Plebs, to the great embarrassment of the community. What he did was to set up a brothel in his house, in which he prostituted Mucia and Fulvia,[142] both women distinguished not only by their fathers but by their husbands, as well as a well-born boy named Saturninus.

---

139. See McGinn, "Caligula's Brothel" (1998) and chap. 1.

140. The previous anecdote, at Val. Max. 9.1.7, deals with Clodius's misconduct in regard to the Bona Dea episode. For the significance of this sequence of anecdotes for the passage under discussion, see below in the text.

141. Cf. the translation of Shackleton Bailey, *Valerius Maximus* 2 (2000) 301, who understands Maximus's objection here as connected to Gemellus's position as a *tribunicius viator*: ". . . but by employment base below servile condition. . . ."

142. Shackleton Bailey, *Valerius Maximus* (2000) 300 n. 8 prefers, with others, to read the names of Mucia, the daughter of Scaevola Augur and ex-wife of Pompey, and Fulvia, of undistinguished parentage but married in turn to Clodius, Curio, and Mark Antony, in place of those of Munia and Flavia, as transmitted by the manuscripts. For a defense of the latter, see Bauman, *Women and Politics in Ancient Rome* (1992) 239 n. 8.

Bodies shamefully compliant, destined to be the sport of drunken lust! Ban-
quet not fit for enjoyment by a Consul and Tribunes but for punishment!

We can infer from this passage that it was acceptable, at least for some members of the apparitorial *curiae,* to attempt to curry favor with the magistrates
they served by entertaining them, just not with the kind of party described
here. That is the point of Maximus's criticism of Gemellus's sense of
officium,[143] and not that Gemellus's position as *tribunicius viator* was below
slavish, which even as hyperbolic moral criticism or mere snobbery goes too
far. Though about three-quarters of the *viatores* known to us were freedmen,
some were equestrians or municipal officials. They were on the whole an
upwardly mobile group, a number of whom became quite wealthy,[144] and it is
worth noting that Gemellus himself, about whom nothing else is known, is
credited by the author with having some version of an upper-class house
(*domus*). Impugning such men as a gratuitous piece of upper-class snobbery
might make a certain amount of sense,[145] but it is hard to see why they should
be ranked below slaves for this purpose. Maximus is instead interested in what
this incident shows about the corruption of relationships between social superiors and inferiors in the late Republic. In his view, Gemellus had a very per-
verse view of his responsibilities toward the tribunes he served as a messenger.

Pimping for the tribunes was, in short, considered inappropriate. This is
where Gemellus's slavishness comes in. What exercises Maximus the most,
however, is not the pimping, or even the installation of a brothel in the private home, but the alleged prostitution of persons of high status. For this reason, the excellent editorial emendations of the women's names from the
obscure Munia and Flavia of the manuscript tradition to the better-known
Mucia and Fulvia, already plausible on other grounds, acquire some further
justification. The higher the status, the greater the outrage at the allegation.

The substitutions also make sense in light of Mucia's and Fulvia's connec-

---

143. *Officium* in the sense of duty/favor performed by a socially subordinate person to a superior hardly exhausts the meaning of this word in the context of Roman patronage: see Saller, *Personal Patronage* (1982) 15–21.

144. See Purcell, "*Apparitores*" (1983) 152–54, with the case histories of the *tribunicii viatores*
Geganius Clesippus and Julius Salvius at 140–41 and 163, respectively.

145. It is perhaps less gratuitous if we accept the argument that Maximus was himself a down-
on-his-luck aristocrat, even a patrician: see Skidmore, *Practical Ethics* (1996) 113–17. Such a person might well be expected to resent the ambition of a social climber like Gemellus, but unfortunately the precise social status of our author remains a matter for speculation.

tions by marriage to prominent *Populares*.[146] Maximus seems to be mining in this section of his work a vein of anti-Popularist tradition, attributing various kinds of sexual depravity to *Populares*. He begins with the notorious outrage ("famosa iniuria") inflicted on well-born youths attributed to Scribonius Curio,[147] continues with Clodius's embroilment in the Bona Dea scandal, which evidently necessitated the bribing of jurors at Clodius's trial for *incestum* ("impurity")[148] through the prostitution of women and young men of respectable status at a high price, and then the passage under discussion, and finally culminates with the worst of the lot, Catiline, whose "especially criminal lust" for Aurelia Orestilla led him to poison his own son.[149] What concerned Maximus was not the cause of the *Optimates* versus the *Populares*, a struggle which he must have viewed as a dead letter, but the theme of sexual corruption in high places and the political overtones of that corruption.[150] The status of the alleged "prostitutes" actually makes it less, rather than more, likely that they participated in Gemellus's brothel party, given the conventions of Roman moral discourse. The Romans were all too ready to level the charge of "prostitution" against women and men of high rank in the event of sexual impropriety, real or imagined.[151]

Skepticism about the identity of the participants does not, however, enjoin skepticism about the event itself, which seems too rich in incidental detail (e.g., the name and professional position of the host are given even though neither Maximus nor his source can have cared very much about

---

146. For their husbands, see n. 142. As for the *nobilis puer* Saturninus, some have connected him with the family of the Appuleii Saturnini, which suggests a fine *Popularis* pedigree in the person of the erstwhile ally of Marius and tribune of 100 B.C., L. Appuleius Saturninus. Shackleton Bailey, *Valerius Maximus* 2 (2000) 301 n. 9, argues him however to be a Sentius Saturninus, grandson of the praetor of 94 B.C., or his brother, that is, from a family that was much less politically prominent, but which reached the consulate under Augustus, and one which evidently had connections to *Popularis* politicians like Curio and Antony. See Shackleton Bailey ibid. and the references to his own work he provides.

147. Val. Max. 9.1.6.

148. Val. Max. 9.1.7: "the services of women and young men of high status were bought at a large sum and paid out to members of the jury in place of a bribe" (". . . noctes matronarum et adulescentium nobilium magna summa emptae mercedis loco iudicibus erogatae sunt").

149. Val. Max. 9.1.9: ". . . praecipue Catilinae libido scelesta. . . ."

150. See the discussion of political figures from the late Republic, especially Marius, Cinna, and Sulla, by Bloomer, *Valerius Maximus* (1992) 147–84.

151. On such allegations made regarding women of high status, such as Julia the daughter of Augustus and Messalina the wife of Claudius, see McGinn, *Prostitution, Sexuality, and the Law* (1998) 168–70. For men, see the invective launched by Cicero against Antony and Scribonius Curio at *Phil.* 2.44–45, with McGinn, 159.

either in their own right) to be pure invention. If Gemellus did, in fact, set up a *lupanar* in his house, it is worth asking the following questions: Just how did he go about this? Did he install masonry beds? Commission erotic paintings? Scratch a few "hic bene futui" ("I had a good fuck here") and/or price-graffiti on the wall?

Suetonius, when he describes Caligula's establishment of a brothel on the Palatine, provides a clue as to what decorative choices Gemellus might have made. He writes that the imperial *lupanar* consisted of a series of small rooms (*cellae*) that were furnished in a manner appropriate to the high-class setting.[152] The latter detail suggests masonry beds were not present, but rather something much more luxurious. Of course, we cannot say for sure that Gemellus's house was decorated in a similar fashion, since it could not, it seems fair to say, aspire to the standard of luxury attained by Caligula's palace. We can, however, tell from Suetonius's description that what mattered in designing a *lupanar* (chapter 7) was not the inclusion of the masonry bed, which was characteristic of some Purpose-Built Brothels, but the division of space into small rooms or cubicles. As a consequence, we cannot doubt that Gemellus resorted to this arrangement, and we might further speculate that erotic art was another feature of his brothel-in-a-house. We cannot, however, ascertain whether it included erotic graffiti, smoking lamps, patchwork curtains, and the rest. Instead, we can only remind ourselves of the extreme difficulties inherent in the evidence and criteria available to us for the purpose of identifying Roman brothels.

One way out of the present dilemma is to postulate that Gemellus's establishment, whoever actually staffed it, was a pretend brothel and not a real one. The same is true of the Pompeian "sex clubs," which were, I argue, intended to reproduce the ambience of the brothel without necessarily duplicating its features in exact detail. Juvenal implies that a person might accomplish this without trying very hard, let alone deliberately attempting to establish something resembling an actual *lupanar* in the home. The satirist criticizes some forms of after-dinner entertainment popular among the elite, such as the lyrics of songs performed by troupes of dancers from Cadiz, as too obscene for the brothel-prostitute, as if that were really possible.[153]

In the opinion of some Romans, simply inviting actual pimps and prostitutes to mix with respectable guests was enough to raise the prospect of a

---

152. Suet. *Cal.* 41.1, with McGinn, "Caligula's Brothel" (1998) esp. 95.
153. Iuv. 11.162–78 (165–66 are spurious: see chap. 4).

brothel-in-a-*domus*.[154] We find, for example, Cicero castigating several of his enemies, such as Verres, Piso, and Antony, for this practice.[155] The evidence suggests that the link between the brothel and the upper-class *domus* was never far from the imagination either of Roman moralists or of those who chose to ignore their precepts. Though indirect, the evidence is valuable in regard to how the Romans themselves might have viewed the "sex clubs," as found at Pompeii. In fact it is difficult to see how the moralizing directed against the brothel-in-a-*domus* could not apply to "sex clubs" with equal force. It is just that the former involved members of the elite in some way, thus winding up in the literary record. All the same, visiting one might have been viewed as less dishonorable than visiting an actual brothel, something which upper-class Romans did only at risk to their reputation.

It is worth remarking that these private "sex clubs" were, as far as we know from Pompeii, not very numerous. Once the possible examples of true brothels included in appendix 1 are excluded, the following examples are left as possibilities (see figs. 18 and 19, as well as maps 4 and 5):[156]

- 1.9.1–2. *Casa del Bell'Impluvio*.[157] In *cubiculum* 11, just off the atrium, the only one of three paintings to survive (now itself badly damaged) shows a man and woman in bed evidently preparing to make love. Though the painting does not show actual lovemaking, it seems more explicit than allusive in nature.
- 1.13.16.[158] In summer *triclinium* (dining room) 3, a poorly preserved painting shows a man and woman making love on a bed.

---

154. For negative attitudes on the socializing of upper-class Romans with prostitutes, see Suerbaum, "Sex und Crime" (1993) esp. 98.

155. Cic. *Verr.* 2.3.6, 2.4.83, (cf. 2.5.81–82, 137), *Red. Sen.* 11, 14, *Phil.* 2.15, 62–63, 69. In the last passage, Cicero accuses Antony of converting his bedrooms into *stabula* and his dining rooms into *popinae*. We may interpret this passage as suggesting the rooms were physically made over, but I think the point remains that bad company makes a home a brothel. At any rate, it is interesting to note that Cicero, like Maximus and Suetonius, does not bother to throw erotic art in anyone's face in order to make this argument. See Treggiari, "Upper-Class House" (1999) 49–50. For what I take to be an echo of *Phil.* 2.69, see *HA Pesc.* 3.10.

156. For the moment I look past the distinction drawn by Guzzo and Scarano Ussani, *Veneris figurae* (2000) 33, between "allusive" and explicit depictions of sex. The former occur (at most) in two of the examples given, the *Casa del Bell'Impluvio* and the House of Iucundus.

157. See Clarke, *Looking at Lovemaking* (1998) 148–53; Guzzo and Scarano Ussani, *Veneris figurae* (2000) 33.

158. See Clarke, *Looking at Lovemaking* (1998) 187–94; Guzzo and Scarano Ussani, *Veneris figurae* (2000) 25–26, 29–31.

- 5.1.10, 23, 25–27. House of L. Caecilius Iucundus.[159] A painting on the wall of the peristyle shows a man and a woman on a bed either just before or after lovemaking. To the right of the painting is a bedroom with double alcoves that has paintings of Mars and Venus, Bacchus, and Erato. These evidently were intended to continue the theme of amorous pleasure.
- 6.14.41–42. *Casa dell'Imperatrice di Russia.* See below in the text.
- 6.15.1, 27. House of the Vettii.[160] The secluded Room x', reached through a servants' *atrium* (off the main *atrium*) and then through the kitchen has three wall paintings of heterosexual couples making love in bed. Two of these are still quite legible. (For a glimpse of one of these, and the room itself, see figs. 18 and 19.)
- 9.8.3, 6, a. *Casa del Centenario.*[161] Room 43, with its two erotic wall paintings, was very secluded indeed. To reach it, one had to pass through an *atrium*, down a corridor, through a *triclinium* (Room 41), and then an antechamber (Room 42). The paintings each show a heterosexual couple making love in bed.
- 9.12.9.[162] This recently, only partially excavated house has a *cubiculum* x preceded by a small antechamber. *Cubiculum* x has three paintings of varying erotic content, including a badly preserved depiction of a man and woman making love on a bed.

As we saw in chapter 4, sexual stimulation might not serve as the only, or in some cases even the primary, purpose behind erotic art, even for some explicit examples. As in the case of other kinds of art, erotic art could function at least in one sense as a social marker—it asserted a house-owner's aspirations to participation in a widespread and easily recognizable aspect of elite culture. Partly for this reason, and not simply for its "allusive" quality, we may question whether the presence of the erotic painting in the House of Iucundus is enough to warrant the argument that the bedroom next to the painting was a "sex club." By the same token, the *triclinium* in the small house at 1.13.16 seems a relatively weak case, though here the erotic representation is explicit.

---

159. See Clarke, *Looking at Lovemaking* (1998) 153–61; Guzzo and Scarano Ussani, *Veneris figurae* (2000) 33.

160. See Clarke, *Looking at Lovemaking* (1998) 169–77; Guzzo and Scarano Ussani, *Veneris figurae* (2000) 26, 31–35.

161. See Clarke, *Looking at Lovemaking* (1998) 161–69; Guzzo and Scarano, *Veneris figurae* (2000) 26–27, 33.

162. See Guzzo and Scarano Ussani, *Veneris figurae* (2000) 33; Varone, "Programma" (2000).

The rooms from the *Casa del Bell'Impluvio* and the last partially excavated house at 9.12.9 are more likely examples of private "sex clubs," while the most probable examples of all are the rooms from the *Casa del Centenario* and the House of the Vettii. The relative seclusion within each house of the last two instances was perhaps grounded less in a desire for privacy than in a desire to advertise one's wealth and status. The possibility of placing such a room in a relatively remote location meant the owner had a great deal of space of which to dispose. A friend allowed access to such an intimate part of the house would be made aware of his own close relationship to the owner.

An interesting distinction emerges all the same between our two most prominent examples. The architectural and decorative context of the *Casa del Centenario* exudes an aura of luxury and refinement, while that of the Vettii does quite the reverse. The latter, in a sort of "slumming" manner, appears more faithfully to reproduce the atmospherics of the brothel. The former provides a salutary reminder that it is reductive to assume that these facilities and others like them were used only for sex. In fact the rooms in Roman houses could be quite flexible in their uses, and these "sex clubs" were presumably no exception. The principle of multiple use is more difficult, though not impossible, to argue for Room x^1 in the House of the Vettii, which stands forth as our firmest example of a "sex club." For this reason, I have included two photographs of this establishment (see figs. 18 and 19). The popular theory that this room was a retreat allotted to a favored cook does no real harm to its standing as a "sex club," though we should be prepared to concede that he must have been a very good cook.

These six examples, even if all can be credited, probably did not exhaust the number of private "sex clubs" in Pompeii. Guzzo and Scarano Ussani list eight examples of explicit erotic paintings now in the Naples Museum whose provenance is unknown. One of these evidently came from the *triclinium* 7 facing the *atrium* in the *Casa dell'Imperatrice di Russia* (6.14.41–42), which might therefore count as a seventh possible example.[163] At most, the evidence would allow us to posit fourteen such clubs. This is, of course, if we assume that all of the detached paintings in the Naples Museum derived from different locations. Other paintings may have been lost, destroyed before they were recorded, or never found. It would be rash to assume that there were very many of these, however.

Whether we agree with Guzzo and Scarano Ussani that brothels operated in the context of private homes or adopt my view that these establishments were private "sex clubs," the principle of moral zoning seems fatally compromised. Whether members of the local elite exploited persons they owned and property they inhabited in the service of prostitution, or whether they utilized their resources to mimic this practice in pursuit of pleasure for themselves and their guests, or even for members of their domestic staffs, the result is very much the same. Certain elements of the Pompeian upper classes were deeply implicated in prostitution, at a minimum through their attempt to reproduce its ambience in their private dwellings. Where they refused to draw a clear and unambiguous line between the public *lupanar* and aristocratic *domus*, we should hesitate to do so ourselves.

❦ *Chapter Six* ❧

THE LOCAL DEMOGRAPHICS
OF VENAL SEX

BROTHELS PER CAPITA

A major concern of scholars arguing for a small number of brothels at Pompeii might be styled economic or demographic rather than moral or aesthetic.[1] How might Pompeii, with a population of 10,000 (or 12,000) support as many as 34 (or 35) brothels, when the city of Rome with a population of 1,000,000 (or 500,000) supported only 45 (or 46) in the fourth century?

The question is based on a number of dubious premises, as is already plain enough. The population of Pompeii is unknown and unknowable. Estimates range from as low as ca. 7,000 to as high as ca. 20,000, though the range of figures given in the preceding paragraph is now more in vogue.[2] We are no better informed for classical Rome, where the longstanding preference for the figure of 1,000,000 has recently been challenged with a controversial proposal

---

1. See Jacobelli, *Terme Suburbane* (1995) 65 n. 119; Clarke, *Looking at Lovemaking* (1998) 195 (using a population estimate of 10,000 and the figure of 35 brothels, he comes up with a ratio of one brothel for every 71 [adult] males). DeFelice, *Roman Hospitality* (2001) 11, takes Clarke's analysis one step further, estimating a "*minimum* [his emphasis] of one 'waitress-prostitute' for every seven men in Pompeii." These estimates appear to assume gender-parity in the adult population of Pompeii, which is just one problem with them.

2. See Wallace-Hadrill, *Houses and Society* (1994) 74–75, 95–103, for a useful discussion. See also Jongman, *Economy* (1988) 267–68, which includes a breakdown by age, sex, and so on, as well as the recent summary in Scheidel, "Progress and Problems" (2001) 59–61.

that cuts that figure in half.[3] Half a million might at first glance seem more plausible for the fourth century, the era of the Regionary Catalogs, with their 45/46 brothels.[4] But there has been great controversy over the size of the late-antique population.[5] The current consensus is, to say the least, cautious about assuming a decline in the capital's population in that period, at least as early as the fourth century.[6]

The late-antique figures for Roman brothels are misleading and perhaps refer only to large purpose-built brothels, if they mean anything at all.[7] Other theories explaining the low numbers of brothels recorded are difficult to rule out, however. Perhaps only those brothels large and conspicuous enough to qualify as tourist attractions are given, most or all of which would be purpose-built. Or, just as the numbers of some buildings, especially in the city center, are inflated to add luster to the late-antique capital city, so the number of brothels may be downplayed for the same motive.

The fifth-century *Notitia Urbis Constantinopolitanae* notably omits mention of brothels altogether, even the one allegedly founded by Constantine himself.[8] It is tempting to attribute this reticence to Christian ideology, but we might reasonably conclude that it is not the absence of brothels from the Constantinopolitan *Notitia* that is odd, but rather their inclusion in the Roman Regionaries. None of the literary accounts of the marvels of Rome that have

---

3. Storey, "Population" (1997). Cf. Coarelli, "Consistenza" (1997) 107; Coarelli, "Roma" (2000) 292–96, which resurrects Guido Calza's estimate of 1,200,000; Tantillo, "Uomini" (2000) 91, which gives an estimate of between 700,000 and 1,000,000 at a minimum; Bustany and Géroudet, *Rome* (2001) 64–69, who give 800,000 to 1,000,000 under Augustus. See also Lo Cascio, "Population" (2001) 185–86; Scheidel, "Progress and Problems" (2001) 51–52, 63, in criticism of Storey.

4. For these, see Nordh, *Libellus* (1949) 105.10.

5. See Hermansen, "Population" (1978) esp. 146–48; Purcell, "Populace of Rome" (1999) esp. 138–40.

6. See Tantillo, "Uomini" (2000) 92; Guidobaldi, "Abitazioni" (2000)153; Lo Cascio, "Population" (2001) 185–87; Scheidel, "Progress and Problems" (2001) 37–44, 69. See also Lo Cascio, "Crisi" (1999).

7. Hermansen, "Population" (1978) shows that many of the figures given in the fourth-century Regionary Catalogs are unreliable. Purcell, "City of Rome" (1992) 425, argues that they form a part of the city's marvel-literature, a long tradition enumerating and often exaggerating Rome's wonders. See also Arce, "Inventario" (1999).

8. *Notitia Urbis Constantinopolitanae* Seeck. On this document, see Unger, *Quellen* (1878/1970) 102–9. For what it is worth, the *Notitia Urbis Alexandrinae*, a Syriac document presumably based on a Greek original that dates perhaps to the early to mid-fourth century, also mentions no brothels: see Fraser, "*Notitia*" (1951). A late sixth-century Syriac *Notitia* for Rome has 45 brothels: Nordh, *Libellus* (1949) 43.

come down to us sees fit to mention the city's brothels.[9] For example, in the relatively lengthy exposition of Rome's wonders that we owe to Pliny the Elder, not one word is spoken on this subject, though the author has a lot to say in praise of the city's sewers, which he regards as its most noteworthy feature.[10] A comparison with the experience of cities in the mid-nineteenth-century United States may be relevant here. The decennial national census taken in that period invited local police departments to register the numbers of brothels in their districts. Some reported none at all or certainly seem to have underreported them; this appears to have occurred even in cities like St. Paul, Minnesota, where brothels were subject to informal regulation and so enjoyed a measure of legitimacy.[11]

There may well be an administrative interest reflected in the numerations of brothels given in the Regionaries, but it is difficult to know exactly how this interest might have affected the tallies.[12] One possibility, not utterly at odds with the Purpose-Built thesis just advanced, is that these brothels had come into the patrimony of the state by the usual means of acquisition, purchase, gift, bequest, and so forth.[13] As such they would have operated not as state or municipal brothels on the model that we see in a number of cultures, such as medieval France, Germany, and Italy, but as privately-owned brothels did in the city of Rome. Nor need we imagine any more experiments in the style of Caligula, which despite the evidence for them, remain doubtful.[14] The phe-

---

9. For some of these passages, see the brief mention in André and Baslez, *Voyager* (1993) 156–59.

10. Plin. *NH* 36.101–25, which includes the remarks about the sewer-system at 104. It is worth noting that both the Roman Regionaries, which mention brothels, and the Alexandrian *Notitia*, which does not, appear to derive from a pagan cultural context: see Arce, "Inventario" (1999) for the first and Fraser, "*Notitia*" (1951) 106–7 for the second. The Syriac *Notitia* for Rome (A.D. 596), which mentions brothels, may depend on both pagan and Christian traditions: see Nordh, *Libellus* (1949) 42–46.

11. In 1880 in St. Paul, Minn., fourteen brothels were reported for a population of 41,473: see Best, *Controlling Vice* (1998) 26.

12. Wallace-Hadrill, "Emperors and Houses" (2001) 138–39, reasonably suggests that a state interest in taxing and registering prostitutes was a possible motive behind the listing of brothels. If so, we might expect a more aggressive attempt at defining "brothel" and a much longer list of places. More generally, on the question of the state's interest, as it is reflected in the Regionaries, see Nicolet, *Space, Geography, and Politics* (1991) 196–97; Wallace-Hadrill, "Case" (2000) 199. Arce, "Inventario" (1999) denies this interest and argues that the numbers of buildings given in the Catalogs are drawn from fantasy. For criticism of Arce, see Storey, "Insulae 1" (2001); Storey, "Insulae 2" (2002).

13. On the increasing state ownership of economic assets and enterprises over the first two centuries A.D., see Lo Cascio, "Introduzione" (2000) 8.

14. See McGinn, "Caligula's Brothel" (1998).

nomenon would seem to be a logical outgrowth of the lease of public space to prostitutes or their exploiters by municipal officials, which was postulated in chapter 5. Unfortunately, we cannot be certain of this.

To draw another comparison with Pompeii, the Regionaries (*Notitia* and *Curiosum*), when corrected, show a total of 1,790 *domus* for Rome,[15] while a rough count of the listings in Eschebach's index yields 504 examples.[16] Some of these may be dismissed as duplicate entries or misidentifications, but will anyone believe that there were, say, one-fourth as many *domus* at Pompeii as at Rome?[17] We may object that building styles, and therefore the definition of *domus*, changed between the first and fourth centuries, but that is precisely the problem. The concept not only changed over time, but so too did the physical plant of many *domus*.[18] We may compare this with the much-vexed question of how to understand *insula* in the Regionaries.[19]

We can be no more sure of what *domus* meant to the compilers of the Catalogues than we can be certain of their concept of *lupanar*. Was "*domus*" as given the Regionary Catalogs built in the classic Pompeian style, or was it of the fourth-century type, an intermediate type, or a combination of two or more of these?[20] Or did it function in the usage of the Regionaries as a social marker rather than as an architectural type, used to designate the dwellings of persons of rank, whatever their form? Even here, size may have mattered, to judge from the evidence of Pompeii and perhaps Rome as well.[21]

Another difficulty in the matter of linking numbers of brothels with

---

15. Eck, "Cum Dignitate Otium" (1997) 165; Guidobaldi, "*Domus*" (1999) 55; Purcell, "Populace of Rome" (1999) 150.

16. Eschebach, *Entwicklung* (1970) 166–72. I have attempted to eliminate the more obvious duplicate entries. Cf. Jongman, *Economy* (1988) 274, who estimates the number of Pompeian *domus* as not many more than six hundred.

17. Olympiodorus famously implies that there were 10,000 *domus* in fifth-century Rome, meaning simply "a lot": fr. 41 Blockley, with Guidobaldi, "*Domus*" (1999) 55. Compare the listing of 4388 *domus* in the fifth-century *Notitia Urbis Constantinopolitanae* (243 Seeck).

18. See Guidobaldi, "Abitazioni" (2000) 150, 155.

19. See Lo Cascio, "Recensus" (1997) 58–63; Guidobaldi, "*Domus*" (1999) 58 with n. 36; Coarelli, "Roma" (2000) 296; Tantillo "Uomini" (2000) 88–89; De Kleijn, *Water Supply* (2001) 253–55; Wallace-Hadrill, "Case" (2000) 199; Wallace-Hadrill, "Emperors and Houses" (2001) 139–40; Lo Cascio, "Population" (2001) 184; Storey, "Insulae 1" (2001); Storey, "Insulae 2" (2002).

20. See Meiggs, *Roman Ostia*[2] (1973) 252–62, for a sense of the possibilities.

21. See Frier, "Pompeii's Economy" (1991) 246, on the notably larger dimensions of houses known to have belonged to municipal magistrates at Pompeii. Cf. Hermansen, "Population" (1978) 156, who identifies *domus* in the Catalogues precisely as the late-antique variety in an unpersuasive attempt to explain the apparent *domus*-gap in that period between Rome and Constantinople; Guilhembet, "Densité" (1996) 8–9 with n. 5, who recognizes that size may have varied significantly at Rome.

demography lies in the attempt to reason from the population of Pompeii. The problem is not just that we really have no idea how many people lived in Pompeii and that these figures are just educated guesses, but that the number, even if known, would be by and large irrelevant.[22] The clients of Pompeian brothels all but certainly hailed not only from the town but from the surrounding territory, other towns in the area, and the entire Mediterranean world. With respect to the economy of venal sex, as well as in other matters, the city of Pompeii, like other Roman towns, was "epiphenomenal."[23]

In other words, "Pompeii," far from being an island in a rural sea, is really just an expression for a microregion lying adjacent to it (that is, its "immediate hinterland") as well as a dispersed hinterland that ranged as far as the distant shores across the Mediterranean Sea.[24] The town, like other Roman towns, would drive, and be driven by, a broader economy.[25] And similar to other urban centers, it had services to provide—including, of course, the sexual ones that are our concern—and might support itself reasonably well by attracting visitors from various points of departure with money to spend.[26] "Pompeii" was a convenient place to install a brothel, and more generally a convenient place for prostitutes and clients to meet, but the town itself does not exhaust the geographical implications of its own sexual economy.

Pompeii was a recognized commercial center from an early period. Cato the Elder names it as an important source of oil presses; Strabo describes it as the port city of a local trading network embracing Nola, Nuceria, and Acher-

---

22. Horden and Purcell, *Corrupting Sea* (2000) 382, argue forcefully that it is theoretically impossible to talk about the population of a city. For ancient Pompeii's population, all we really have to rely on is theory. Partly for this reason, cross-cultural comparisons are highly suspect in *this* regard (see below), but we may note all the same that mid-nineteenth-century New York City had over 600 brothels with a population of over 500,000: Gilfoyle, *City of Eros* (1992) 163. The now-fashionable figure of 10,000 for Pompeii is the number used as a crude demographic criterion defining the minimum for an urban system to justify study as such: Horden and Purcell, 93.

23. For a discussion of this idea, see Horden and Purcell, *Corrupting Sea* (2000) 90–91.

24. See Horden and Purcell, *Corrupting Sea* (2000) 95 (see also 102, 363, 436); Erdkamp, "Beyond the Limits" (2001) 342–45. On the immediate hinterland of Pompeii, see now Mastroroberto, "Pompeii" (2000). On the connections between the Roman city and its microregion, see, in particular, Hopkins, "Models, Ships and Staples" (1983) esp. 94–96; Garnsey, *Famine and Food Supply* (1988) 56–58; De Ligt, "Demand, Supply, Distribution 2" (1991) 42–58; Wallace-Hadrill, "Elites and Trade" (1991); Purcell, "*Villa*" (1995). For connections between cities and different regions in the Roman world, see Hopkins, esp. 88–93, 96–105; Fulford, "Economic Interdependence" (1987); several of the essays in Parkins and Smith, *Trade, Traders and the Ancient City* (1998); Hopkins, "Rents, Taxes, Trade" (2000) esp. 260–62. For medieval evidence on the mobility of traders and craftsmen, see Jacoby, "Migration" (1994/1997).

25. Horden and Purcell, *Corrupting Sea* (2000) 107.

26. See Horden and Purcell, *Corrupting Sea* (2000) 108, 114–15; Erdkamp, "Beyond the Limits" (2001) 340.

rae.[27] Imports and exports—the latter including especially wine and *garum*—ranged across the Mediterranean.[28] A further and more significant sign of the city's economic vitality and connectivity is the fact that a wine-producing region as rich as the Vesuvian also imported wine from as far away as Crete.[29]

The city had its own economic microregion, whose population, inclusive of the urban center, has been estimated to be as high as 36,000.[30] This is once again only a guess,[31] but I should point out here that most of the rural surplus probably consisted of unmarried male agricultural workers, even if they did not number as many as 26,000.[32] These men, unless they were slaves in chains, were prime candidates as clients of Pompeian prostitutes. We cannot be certain, as a matter of fact, that the city of Pompeii supplied either the majority, or the overwhelming majority at any rate, of its prostitutes or their customers.[33] This is not necessarily true only of Pompeii. Whether Las Vegas or Atlantic City, Pompeii or Baiae, Nuceria or Puteoli have more prostitutes is—other things being equal—less likely to be function of how many people live there than of how many visitors each city receives. Pompeii was a node in a complex network of people and goods moving throughout the Roman Mediterranean, a network that linked city with city and region with region.[34] This connectivity, scholars have argued well, was more a function of human mobility than of physical geography.[35]

It is worth asking whether Pompeii enjoyed a privileged status in this network in that it was linked to a number of other areas and thus served as a "gateway settlement." The question is an important one since if Pompeii was a gateway settlement, the number of prostitutes working there would conceiv-

---

27. Cato *Agr.* 22.3–4, 135.2; Strabo 5.4.8. See Morley, "Cities in Context" (1997) 51–53.

28. See Kleberg, *Hôtels* (1957) 108; Gassner, *Kaufläden* (1986) 20; Frier, "Pompeii's Economy" (1991) 244; Morley, "Cities in Context" (1997) 48.

29. See Andreau, "Economia" (2001) 109.

30. Jongman, *Economy* (1988) 112, 135.

31. Jongman's notion of Pompeii's "economic territory" has been strongly criticized by Frier, "Pompeii's Economy" (1991) 244. On a town's economic relationship with its surrounding territory, see also Morley, "Cities in Context" (1997) 51–53.

32. Even some urban crafts may have had an imbalance in favor of male workers: Jongman, *Economy* (1988) 162.

33. Cf. the study by Finnegan, *Poverty* (1979) 133, of prostitution in York between 1837 and 1887: 43 percent of all recorded prostitutes' clients were visitors to the city.

34. See Horden and Purcell, *Corrupting Sea* (2000) 295, 354, 358.

35. See Horden and Purcell, *Corrupting Sea* (2000) 395, 407. On the importance of the transient population of the city of Rome in particular, see Purcell, "*Plebs Urbana*" (1994) 649–50, with a dissent by Lo Cascio, "Population" (2001) 192–94.

ably have been well above any number we might postulate as typical (it is impossible to speak of "average") for a Roman city of its size and location. This question is taken up below. For now, I hope to have weakened the assumption that Pompeii or other Roman towns, including the capital itself, had a "carrying capacity" for prostitutes that was directly linked to the populations of those towns, whatever their numbers might have been.[36]

PROSTITUTES PER CAPITA

For demographic purposes, to be sure, the real source of our interest is not the number of brothels Pompeii might have supported, but the number of prostitutes. If, for example, we eliminate roughly half of the brothels cataloged in the first appendix, and then assume a generous average of four prostitutes per brothel,[37] plus a dozen more or so in the *cellae meretriciae* and just as many "independent" streetwalkers, we arrive at just over one hundred prostitutes for Pompeii.[38] This estimate does not attempt to account for part-time or seasonal prostitutes and so is intended to be conservative in nature.

For what it is worth, comparative evidence tends to show relatively modest-sized brothels:[39]

---

36. For a more general attack on the idea of "carrying capacity" as a putative measure of maximum population, see Horden and Purcell, *Corrupting Sea* (2000) 388. The population of a town or region, of course, is not static: see Wallace-Hadrill, *Houses and Society* (1994) 97–98, on Pompeii and, more broadly, Horden and Purcell, 95.

37. One of the largest, if not the largest, establishments, the Purpose-Built Brothel, yields the names of more than a dozen women identifiable as prostitutes: *CIL* 4.2166–2306. Not all of these women necessarily worked contemporaneously. They probably worked more or less in the same period, however, given that the owner had the walls of the brothel repainted not long before the city was destroyed: Clarke, *Looking at Lovemaking* (1998) 199, who cites the imprint of a coin from A.D. 72 that was found on one wall. Comparative evidence shows high physical mobility for prostitutes and much turnover in brothels: Symanski, "Prostitution in Nevada" (1974) 368–70; Best, *Controlling Vice* (1998) 48–51. This would be mitigated in the Roman context by the presence of slavery. In any case, given the presence of ten *cellae*, the figure is not implausible and might even be viewed as a bit low, especially if some or all of the women working there lived off-site. Most Pompeian brothels, however, were small, like Pompeian hotels. On the size of the latter, see Casson, *Travel* (1994) 208.

38. The list of names offered in the third appendix provides, given the uncertainties, an unreliable guide to the total number of prostitutes working in Pompeii at any one time.

39. An important exception is the medieval municipal brothel, which often sought to monopolize the prostitutes working in a town and so sometimes tended to be on the large side: see Otis, *Prostitution* (1985) 64.

- 2–3 prostitutes in small, private medieval French brothels.[40]
- an average of 5–7 prostitutes in early 1970s Nevada[41]
- 2–3 prostitutes in a mid-twentieth-century United States brothel[42]
- 4–6 prostitutes in late nineteenth-century St. Paul, Minnesota, brothels informally tolerated by the local authorities[43]
- ca. 5 prostitutes in "unofficial" brothels in medieval Germany[44]

In any event, it is unclear to me why scholars might think the number of one hundred prostitutes, which amounts to just over 1 percent of the (postulated) population, was too high for a city of 10,000, unless they are relying on assumptions left unexamined or at any rate unstated. This is to say that at least some of those protesting against what they regard as a large number of brothels at Pompeii have overlooked the fact that prostitution, like many other aspects of human sexuality, though it is found in a wide number of cultures, configures itself differently in different societies.[45] In other words, they appear to assume that there is something fixed about the need for prostitution and adjust the numbers of brothels and/or prostitutes downward in response to this assumption. The historical experience of prostitution, however, suggests this procedure is problematic. Let us consider some figures reported from early twentieth-century Shanghai. A 1921 study showed that one in 137 residents was a licensed prostitute.[46] The qualification "licensed" deserves emphasis, since on the common estimate there were many more unlicensed prostitutes working in the city at that time.[47] An estimate dating from the mid-1930s suggests that at this time approximately one out of every thirteen women in Shanghai was a prostitute. This ratio increases if children and older women are excluded from consideration.[48]

Contemporary Japan shows a similar picture. In 1925 one out of every

---

40. Rossiaud, "Prostitution, Youth, and Society" (1978) 4.

41. Symanski, "Prostitution in Nevada" (1974) 365, gives the figure of five as the average for town brothels and seven for rural brothels, with the now-defunct Mustang Ranch as the great exception. The ranch boasted over fifty prostitutes.

42. Heyl, *Madam* (1979) 91–94.

43. Best, *Controlling Vice* (1998) 41.

44. Schuster, *Frauenhaus* (1992) 123.

45. For example, Clarke, *Looking at Lovemaking* (1998) professes to adopt a strict cultural-constructionist approach but unguardedly allows what appear to be biologically based assumptions about the demand for prostitution creep into his analysis.

46. Hershatter, *Dangerous Pleasures* (1997) 421 n. 31: in contemporary Beijing, one in every 258 residents was a prostitute.

47. Hershatter, *Dangerous Pleasures* (1997) 39 (see also 40).

48. Hershatter, *Dangerous Pleasures* (1997) 422 n. 39 (see also nn. 40 and 42).

thirty-one young women, that is, women between the ages of eighteen and twenty-nine, were prostitutes, a ratio that included licensed prostitutes, registered barmaids, and geisha.[49] Similarly in Calcutta in 1911 nearly 25 percent of working women were prostitutes, and the total number in that year was second only to that recorded for domestic servants.[50]

The experience of many cities in nineteenth-century Europe and the United States suggests that the numbers of working prostitutes were vast in comparison with recent experience. Mid-nineteenth-century New York City had an estimated (by William Sanger) 6,000 prostitutes for just over 500,000 inhabitants.[51] This estimate, amounting to "5 percent of all young females" or a ratio of approximately 1 to 83 for the entire population, is probably too low.[52] The experience of Chinese immigrants to the United States in this period, a population with a strong gender-imbalance in favor of males, offers an even more striking picture. Census figures reveal, for example, that in 1860 San Francisco the nearly 600 women engaged in prostitution constituted 85.6 percent of the Chinese female population and 96 percent of Chinese women employed in a money-earning capacity.[53]

The demography of prostitution in more recent times shows a dramatic contrast, at least in the developed world. For example, a 1970s survey of a small Midwestern city found a ratio of 1.39 prostitutes per 1,000 inhabitants, a minimum estimate to be sure, but much lower than one would expect to find a half-century or so before.[54] The situation in less-developed countries is far different, a phenomenon in part influenced by the development of sex tourism. In such places as Indonesia, Malaysia, the Philippines, and Thailand, it is estimated that between .25 percent and 1.5 percent of the female population are prostitutes and that selling sex amounts to somewhere between 2 percent and 14 percent of the gross domestic product.[55]

Some of the factors that played a role in this phenomenon of high proportions of female prostitutes in Europe and the United States from the mid- to

---

49. Garon, *Molding Japanese Minds* (1997) 94.

50. Sleightholme and Sinha, *Guilty Without Trial* (1996) 9. For the observation that unlicensed prostitutes outnumbered registered ones, see 66–67.

51. See Gilfoyle, *City of Eros* (1992) 184.

52. Gilfoyle, *City of Eros* (1992) 344 n. 7. See also Hill, *Their Sisters' Keepers* (1993) 26–33 (an 1831 estimate that prostitutes comprised 10 percent of females of all ages was criticized by Sanger, who was perhaps too conservative), 345 n. 51 (in the year 1897 a higher estimate was given of the percent of females engaged in prostitution).

53. See Tong, *Unsubmissive Women* (1994) 94.

54. See Decker, *Prostitution* (1979) 12 (see also 18).

55. See Edlund and Korn, "Theory" (2002) 182.

late nineteenth and early twentieth centuries, such as industrialization, rapid urbanization, and mass immigration, were foreign to the Roman experience, but other factors, such as poor opportunities for female employment and dim prospects for marriage for many lower-status males, were not and may have been worse for Rome. Indeed, we might very well expect to find a similar ratio of female prostitutes for the medieval and early modern periods as well.[56] The available statistics from cities in southern France and Germany, when viewed in light of the strong possibility that they underreport (by a factor that cannot be recovered) suggests the ratio of prostitutes to inhabitants corresponds closely to that offered here for Pompeii, closer than the nineteenth-century ratios in fact.[57]

One peculiarity of the Roman situation, that is, slavery, may have led to both an increased demand for, and supply of, prostitutes. I do not argue here that this was necessarily true, and the comparative data can, of course, only offer a range of possibilities and not proof.[58] Nevertheless, I invite my colleagues to consider such factors before they decide how many brothels, or how many prostitutes, were too many for Pompeii.

We are now in a position to try to estimate the economic value of prostitution for Pompeii. To take the most common price charged for sex (chapter 2), two *asses*, and to multiply this first by the number of prostitutes, which I estimate to be about one hundred, and then by the average number of clients per prostitute per day, which I postulate to be five, gives us a gross total of at least 1,000 *asses* or HS 250 (i.e., 250 sesterces) each day. Although this estimate is rough at best, it seems on the low end, especially when the costs of purchasing slave prostitutes, of maintaining these prostitutes, of renting or purchasing the brothels, and other miscellaneous expenses are factored in, and these amounts are deducted from that total. Given the level of exploitation we saw was characteristic of Roman prostitution in chapter 2, we might prefer to postulate an average of ten customers per day, which would raise the gross income to a minimum of HS 500 each day, or over HS 180,000 each year for Pompeii. The estimate of ten customers per day, for each prostitute means an

56. Though counting every laundress in the sixteenth-century Parisian census is almost certainly a flawed approach, the result, that one in five women were prostitutes, is not as absurd as asserted by DeFelice, *Roman Hospitality* (2001) 9, in criticism of Jean Delumeau.

57. Otis, *Prostitution* (1985) 210 n. 2; cf. Schuster, *Frauenhaus* (1992) 122–23. Schuster in criticizing Otis overlooks his own concession that the estimates he reports from four German cities almost certainly underrepresent the actual numbers of prostitutes.

58. We should not in any case simply assume that prostitution in Pompeii was more or less diffuse than in a modern city of the same population; for the former assumption, see Cantilena, "Vizi" (1998) 53.

average of 1,000 tricks per day for Pompeii, which seems like a high number in itself, though perhaps not impossible.

The state's profit is easier to calculate. At the Caligulan rate of the price of one sexual act per day, the revenue generated by the tax on prostitutes in Pompeii should have been a minimum of HS 50 each day, or over HS 18,250 each year.[59] This estimate is based on the price of two *asses*, though as seen in chapter 2, some Pompeian prostitutes charged more than this for their services (and a very few less) and would have been taxed accordingly.

If the numbers given above seem too low, we might use for our calculations the number of fifteen to twenty clients per day, which we postulated for low-priced prostitutes in chapter 2. That would increase the overall level of revenue for private exploiters, but not for the state, since the Caligulan tax was based on the price of one sexual encounter per day, without respect to the number of clients. It may well be, however, that the rough estimates employed here of twenty brothels and one hundred prostitutes are simply too low for ancient Pompeii. The uncertainties over the total population of Pompeii and the numbers of visitors discourage further attempts at speculation, however.

SYBARIS ON THE SARNO

Before concluding first that brothels were widely diffused in Pompeii and next that this evidence is significant for Rome and elsewhere, we must confront one other difficulty. This concerns a peculiar set, or rather sets, of conditions prevailing in Pompeii, which may discourage drawing generalizations from evidence coming from that city. Even if we accept the idea of the broad diffusion of brothels at Pompeii, it is of little value to us if circumstances there were so particular that the result cannot be generalized. The problem of the "typicality" of Pompeii is a traditional one in the scholarship, with particular resonance for the economy.[60] No attempt is made here to address that question in general terms, though the hope is that an examination of the particular

---

59. On the rate of the tax, see McGinn, *Prostitution, Sexuality, and the Law in Ancient Rome* (1998) chap. 7.

60. See the recent remarks of Andreau, "Economia" (2001). On the question of generalizing from cultural developments at Pompeii, especially in regard to house design, see Grahame, "Material Culture" (1998) 157. Allison, "Placing Individuals" (2001) argues that Pompeii's ethnic makeup, in particular the alleged presence of a longstanding Greek community, renders it different from other Roman towns. While reasonable on the face of it, this point is far from proven. And if it were, I suspect this cultural diversity might make Pompeii more like other nodes of Mediterranean connectivity, rather than less like them.

aspects relating to prostitution might help facilitate a more nuanced treatment of it.

First, the sheer bulk of evidence for erotic life in general that has been recovered from Pompeii, especially when contrasted with the leaner yield from Herculaneum, prompts the suggestion that the situation there was unusual, more conducive to the experience of *amor* than elsewhere in the Roman world. This seems unlikely, however.[61] Pompeii was no Baiae, if it is indeed correct to assume that Baiae actually lived up to its reputation. Pompeii was known as a port city, a good place to purchase an oil press, not as a hotbed for *la dolce vita*. We established above that Pompeii enjoyed a fairly high degree of "connectivity" with its own microregion and dispersed hinterland, the latter extending across the Mediterranean. The city moreover appears to have been a highly permeable place to judge from the concentration of doorways and graffiti along through routes leading to and from the city's gates.[62] Of course, information of this kind is not preserved elsewhere, so comparisons are out of the question. It seems possible that Pompeii functioned as a minor gateway settlement and so attracted more visitors perhaps than such places as Nola, Nuceria, and Acherrae.[63] Admittedly, certainty in this matter is impossible. The different levels of urbanization shown by Roman towns are many, complex, and often difficult to read.[64] The differences among Roman towns in terms of the numbers of brothels, prostitutes, and clients may not have been all that large in many cases. Pompeii was not only no Baiae, it was no Puteoli, a true gateway settlement, material knowledge of whose prostitutes and brothels is unfortunately forever lost to us. For this reason, it seems reasonably safe to generalize from the evidence of Pompeii in erotic matters, including venal sex.[65]

The second set of conditions discouraging generalization is more intractable. It has been argued[66] that in the period following the devastating

---

61. For another view, see Della Valle, "Amore" (1937).

62. Laurence, "Organization of Space" (1995) 72.

63. On the concept of gateway settlements, see Horden and Purcell, *Corrupting Sea* (2000) 133, 399.

64. See Garnsey and Saller, *Roman Empire* (1987) 26–34.

65. See the comments of Gallo, "Eros" (1994) 209–10. There is no point here in discussing the argument that discourages generalization from almost any archaeological find: see Greene, *Archaeology* (1986) 10.

66. By La Torre, "Impianti" (1988) 78, building on a suggestion made by Andreau, "Histoire des séismes" (1973/1997) 280; Andreau, "Terremoto" (1984) 43, as well as Maiuri's theory that a new business class replaced the old aristocracy to exploit fresh opportunities of commerce at this time: Maiuri, *Ultima fase* (1942). On this last point, see n. 70 below. On possible, though inconclusive, evidence for a housing squeeze, see Gassner, *Kaufläden* (1986) 57.

earthquake of 62 the need for housing at Pompeii was acute, because many res-idences were damaged and because a massive rebuilding campaign attracted a large transient population of workers from the countryside, most of whom would have been male. Aside from hotels, these workers patronized other ser-vice outlets, including *tabernae* and *lupanaria*. Pompeians were not, it would seem, slow to exploit their urban properties and so transformed many resi-dences into hotels, taverns, and so forth in order to accommodate this increased need.[67]

The problem is complicated by the strong possibility that seismic activity continued at Pompeii in the period A.D. 62–79.[68] Presumably such activity would have aggravated, and extended in time, the impact of the earthquake of 62 on the service sector of the Pompeian economy, including prostitution.

If we can correctly assume that a mass of transient workers was present in the period 62–79, then we should not be surprised to find the service sector responding, through an abrupt expansion, to the growth in demand for lodg-ing, food, and sex.[69] It is not necessarily true, however, that the attested post-62 repairs, structural reinforcements, and remodellings prove by themselves that the service sector expanded dramatically in this period, unless it can be shown that the hotels, inns, taverns, and the like did not exist in the period before the earthquake (or existed only in a significantly smaller form).[70] A recent study has shown that there was much more rental property at Pompeii than previously thought, and much of this property appears to date from the period before 62.[71] There is another difficulty as well. Presumably, such estab-lishments were, like much else in Pompeii, in great need of repair after the dis-

---

67. See, for example, Meneghini, "Trasformazione" (1999) 17.

68. For consideration of the implications, see the collection of essays in *Archäologie und Seis-mologie* (1995).

69. This is not the place to address the question of the alleged biological basis for male sex-ual need, often advanced as an explanation, if not a pretext, for prostitution. We can simply pos-tulate for the present that more men meant greater demand for the services of prostitutes, a demand that was in part at least possibly stimulated by cultural factors and social expectations. For an overall useful discussion of the issues, see McIntosh, "Who Needs Prostitutes?" (1978), who in an attempt to escape *aporia* settles in the end for a modified Freudian line of analysis that leaves much to be desired.

70. See Zanker, *Pompeii* (1998) 124. Wallace-Hadrill, *Houses and Society* (1994) 118–31, convincingly refutes Maiuri's theory that upstarts replaced the older elite, showing that it was the latter who profited from commercial ventures in the city's final period. See also the skepticism of Gassner, *Kaufläden* (1986) 24–26; Mouritsen, "Order and Disorder" (1996) 140–41; Pirson, *Miet-wohnungen* (1999) 159. It seems far from certain, however, that upper-class resort to commerce was limited to this period: see below in the text.

71. Pirson, *Mietwohnungen* (1999) esp. 174–75.

aster, so that new construction may have aimed at filling in gaps rather than at exploiting fresh opportunities.[72]

The hypothesis that the local service sector expanded dramatically in this period rests in part on the observed contrast between the great numbers of *popinae* at Pompeii and the small numbers at Ostia. This is puzzling, just as the apparent lack of brothels in Ostia is puzzling. But these disparities hardly describe an overall difference in the total service sector relative to each of these two cities. Ostia had its share of *deversoria*, like the *Casa di Diana*, and we know that Ostian *cenacula* could be split up in the fashion of Pompeian houses to provide accommodation for transients.[73] To be sure, both the port city of Ostia and the capital itself must at all times have had a significant transient population served by such lodgings. It is also true that we cannot be certain about how the needs of this population for food, drink, and sex were met.

To return to Pompeii, if we make the counterfactual assumption that no earthquake occurred in 62, it is difficult to conclude that most or many of the brothels and other venues where sex was sold would not exist. Care must be taken when making assumptions about conditions in the last period of the city's life, which is, of course, the best known. To invoke the earthquake as an explanation for these conditions is to risk arguing *post hoc ergo propter hoc*. And given the revolution now in progress over the criteria for dating the material remains of the city, caution is necessary over what really represents post-earthquake Pompeii.[74]

By 79, seventeen years after the event, had Pompeii more or less recovered from the effects of the earthquake? This is a question archaeologists might one day be able to answer. Noteworthy in this connection are the indications of economic recovery in the area (they are much longer in coming, we may stipulate) that eventually followed the destruction of 79.[75] The earthquake itself may not have been quite the unmitigated disaster it has at times been portrayed as in the scholarship, but instead may be thought of as a challenge to

---

72. Even before A.D. 62, elements of the service sector appear to have been displaced by new public building on the east side of the Forum: see Gassner, *Kaufläden* (1986) 40, 60; Zanker, *Pompeii* (1998) 57. See also Guzzo and Scarano Ussani, *Veneris figurae* (2000) 68–69, for a caution against assuming too great a need for food service in the post-62 period.

73. For literary, legal, and archaeological evidence on dividing up Ostian *cenacula*, see Frier, "Rental Market" (1977). For Pompeian houses, see Wallace-Hadrill, *Houses and Society* (1994) 103–16, 131–34. On a more general level, see Scobie, "Slums" (1986) 428. On the challenges in identifying specific buildings in Ostia as brothels, see chap. 8.

74. For the general point, see Fulford and Wallace-Hadrill, "Unpeeling Pompeii" (1998) 128–30; for skepticism about post-62 dating, see Grahame, "Recent Developments" (1999) 570, in part anticipated by Gassner, *Kaufläden* (1986) 25, 47–48.

75. See Jashemski, "Pompeii and Mount Vesuvius" (1979) 612–17.

the city that matured over time into an opportunity.[76] This raises one more question for archaeologists. Is it possible that Pompeii in A.D. 79 was a more populous and prosperous place than in 61?

In sum, while the "earthquake hypothesis" may well explain, in part, the evident diffusion of brothels in Pompeii, proof for this argument is not adequate at this point. Closer examination of these establishments at Pompeii may shed light on the extent to which the earthquake encouraged, indirectly, the practice of prostitution.[77] At present, we may cautiously conclude that it had some impact, however limited. In drawing this conclusion, we would also have to conclude there was a gender-imbalance, with more men, perhaps many more, than women. A higher percentage of the female population were perhaps prostitutes than in other Roman cities that did not experience Pompeii's difficulties in this period.[78] Another result is that the Pompeian evidence suggests that brothels were a widespread feature of Roman urban life. To this extent, it does seem safe to generalize from the evidence of Pompeii. Most importantly, the precise number and location of Roman brothels were a function of economics and not of morality, or the result of a public policy directed at relegating prostitution to the back streets of Pompeii or other Roman cities.

---

76. See Horden and Purcell, *Corrupting Sea* (2000) 308 (cf. 311) on the baneful consequences of catastrophe-theory in the historiography of Mediterranean earthquakes.

77. See, for example, Meneghini, "Trasformazione" (1999) who traces the transformation of a residence into a *caupona* at 1.11.1–2.

78. In the early 1930s, the Chinese-governed sector of Shanghai showed a gender-ratio of 135 men to 100 women: Hershatter, *Dangerous Pleasures* (1997) 40.

Chapter Seven

THE GREAT POMPEIAN
BROTHEL-GAP

EMINENT VICTORIANS

The story of brothel-identification is an interesting one, worth at least a modest amount of attention. Unfortunately, the critical waters have been muddied by charges of "Victorianism," which allegedly amounts to an overeagerness to identify a location as a brothel on the basis of its erotic art.[1] This strain of criticism, most prominent in a recent book by John DeFelice Jr., amounts to a crudely reductive version of Michel Foucault's famous "repressive hypothesis," which revealed the nineteenth century to be paradoxically a fertile source of discourse about sexuality.[2] Indeed, given the trend in revisionist history on the Victorian period that has been dominant since 1970, DeFelice and the others are in danger of paying the Victorians a compliment that they do not deserve.[3]

---

1. Cf. the accusation of "nineteenth-century racial theory" raised recently in regard to the issue of Pompeii's ethnic composition: Allison, "Placing Individuals" (2001) 70.

2. DeFelice, *Roman Hospitality* (2001) 7, in a published version of a doctoral dissertation that makes a similar point: *Women of Pompeian Inns* (1998). The other examples of this strain of criticism devote far less space to it: see Jacobelli, *Terme Suburbane* (1995) 65 n. 119; Clarke, *Looking at Lovemaking* (1998) 179, with the comments of Anderson, review of *Looking at Lovemaking* (1998). For the repressive hypothesis, see Foucault, *History of Sexuality* 1 (1978) esp. 15–49. Supporting evidence for Foucault's thesis is found, for example, in the enthusiasm of the popular press for the subject of brothels in nineteenth-century St. Paul, Minn.: Best, *Controlling Vice* (1998) 3, 11.

3. For a sense of this historiographical trend, see, for example, Walkowitz, *Prostitution* (1980) vii–viii. Of great importance is Marcus, *Other Victorians* (1966). See also the choice comments of

In evaluating this criticism, it is important to make two points. First, the modern history of scholarly and popular reaction to the discovery of erotic art at Pompeii is far more complex and interesting than such vague and value-laden terminology can suggest.[4] Second, I would argue that great care should be taken in attributing motives to those writing on Roman brothels, for reasons not only of fairness, but also of method.[5] It has long been customary, at any rate, to belabor, however gently, the naiveté of one's predecessors regarding sexual matters at Pompeii.[6] This is a tradition with which I hope to break, if possible. The sheer difficulty of doing so, however, might well form one of the themes of this book. As the reader will note, the fault is far easier to criticize in others' work than to avoid in one's own.

It must be conceded that the charge of "Victorianism," whatever one thinks of it, does raise the interesting question of just what constituted the nineteenth-century discourse on brothels at Pompeii. As noted in chapter 1, this book focuses particularly on late twentieth-century scholarship devoted to Pompeian brothels. While it is possible, even salutary, to spare a backward glance at the previous century, I must make a necessary caveat here to the effect that the coverage cannot be as complete as it is elsewhere for the twentieth century. One difficulty is that works from the nineteenth century are far less accessible as a rule than those from the twentieth.[7] There is also the problem of method. The nineteenth-century discourse on Pompeian brothels is so spare, as it turns out, that we are often left accounting for lacunae. Finally, there is the question of breadth of coverage. It would be interesting to place this discussion in the context of an "archaeology" of nineteenth-century tourism, with particular attention to women's role in that tourism. But that would take me far beyond the scope of my present purpose.

Foucault, *History of Sexuality* 1 (1978) 3–13. For the purpose of this discussion, "Victorian" refers to the nineteenth century and somewhat beyond, and includes other European cultures, not just the British.

4. For a good sense of the various and mutable quality of these reactions, see Cantilena, "Vizi" (1992).

5. Excessive concern with motive has been identified as a flaw of the radical constructionist approach: see Boghossian, "Social Construction" (2001).

6. See Spano, "Illuminazione" (1920) 25, on the interpretation of the use of lamps in brothels (more on this subject in the text below).

7. This is not only true for published works but even more so for unpublished work of all periods, which in some cases can be found only in the archives of the Soprintendenza di Pompei. See Berry, "Domestic Life" (1997) 105, on this problem for 1.9.11–12 (= cat. no. 4), first excavated in the 1950s. For a similar challenge regarding an excavation from the nineteenth century, see Koloski Ostrow, *Sarno Bath Complex* (1990) 1–13. For an historical overview of problems with publication of finds from Pompeii, see Zevi, "Storia" (1981).

All the same, it is worth trying to locate information on brothels in the more general literature from this period. I freely concede that more brothel-identifications may be found lurking in the nineteenth-century excavation reports and specialist literature, the examination of which should properly form a separate object of study. The challenge I put to those who postulate the identification of a large number of brothels in the nineteenth century, or at any time before Hans Eschebach published a comprehensive attempt at listing all Pompeian brothels in 1970,[8] is to document their assertions as thoroughly as possible. The fact that only thirty (or, discounting doublets, twenty-seven) of the forty-one possible brothels listed in the catalog were first excavated in the nineteenth century might appear to impose that number as an upper limit, but this need not be the case at all.[9] If the Victorians were as active in this field as has been claimed, many more, albeit highly improbable, identifications must have been made.

My goal is not to attempt a complete inventory of brothel-identifications, but the more modest task of first locating the scholarly consensus on brothel-identification in the nineteenth century and then evaluating what became of this in the years that followed. What brothels were routinely and unambiguously identified as such and why? The results are interesting to the point of cautionary for the purpose of this study.

I must raise another caution in regard to periodization. Many persons would regard 1914 as the terminus of nineteenth-century culture. This is sensible enough, though it is remarkable all the same how long a shadow that culture went on to cast. Many of its classic works of scholarship continued to reappear in new editions (though often with few substantial changes or none at all) for many years to come. These editions routinely seem to have eclipsed their predecessors. This cultural drag (and what a drag it was) manifests itself here in the fact that I am able to cite several works from the early years of the twentieth century that are directly rooted in the previous one. Toward the conclusion of this section, I cite works from a bit later in the twentieth century, which help show that, while in some respects nothing essential changed in the attitude and approach of scholars in regard to brothel-identification, a new direction can be perceived in the work of Matteo Della Corte.

A good reason for preferring late- or even strictly post-Victorian products

---

8. Eschebach, *Entwicklung* (1970) 175.

9. The years of first excavation are given for each entry in the catalog in appendix 1. The possible brothels first excavated in the twentieth century are cat. nos. 3, 4, 5, 6, 7, 8, 9, 15, 32, 40, 41.

is that the nineteenth century witnessed a great deal of excavation at Pompeii. Later works, or at least later editions of works published at that time, seem at least notionally to stand a better chance of rounding up more brothels. We might reasonably object that the "nineteenth century" may seem to prove almost as elastic a concept as "Victorian." Nevertheless, it is essential to try to be as clear as possible about the method adopted here.

Despite the difficulties mentioned above, the chief threads of the nineteenth-century discourse on the subject of brothels are fairly easy to discern. The Victorians turn out to be surprisingly reticent on this subject at Pompeii. Whether this relegates them to some new subcategory (e.g., the Other, Other Victorians) or unmasks them as no true Victorians at all, readers are left to decide for themselves.

We begin with guidebooks, or at any rate those with a scholarly bent. An early version is the guidebook by Ludwig Goro von Agyagfalva, which was published in 1825. It discusses one of the catalog entries (7.2.32–33, cat. no. 18), without identifying this establishment or any other as a brothel.[10] A later best-seller of this genre by August Mau was first published in 1893, then went through five editions in less than two decades and culminated in a sixth and final version in 1928. The last two editions, the first of which was edited by Walther Barthel, the second by Albert Ippel, appeared after Mau's death in 1909.[11] The index to the fifth edition contains a reference to precisely one brothel. This is the relatively large installation familiar to most modern visitors to Pompeii and located not far from the Forum, which in this book I refer to as the Purpose-Built Brothel.[12] The description is one paragraph in length and spare at that and includes a bare allusion to "obscene paintings."[13]

The sixth edition duplicates word for word the description of the Purpose-Built Brothel offered by the fifth, but adds a photograph showing the *outside* of the brothel (for an early twenty-first-century version, see fig. 4). The index offers, aside from this specimen, what appears at first glance to be a reference to another brothel. This is the so-called "*gran Lupanare*," also known, among other names, as the "*Scavi degli Scienzati*" at 6.14.43. The odds this establishment was actually a brothel are so unlikely I have excluded it from my catalog

---

10. Goro von Agyagfalva, *Wanderungen durch Pompeii* (1825) 110; cf. his index.

11. Mau/Barthel, *Führer durch Pompeji*⁵ (1910); Mau/Ippel, *Führer durch Pompeji*⁶ (1928).

12. So also in the second edition: Mau, *Führer durch Pompeji*² (1896) 54 (one-paragraph description of Purpose-Built Brothel), 112 (index reference to single *lupanar*).

13. Mau/Barthel, *Führer durch Pompeji*⁵ (1910) 62 (description), 141 (index). The brothel in question is nos. 26 and 27 in the catalog in appendix 1.

of possible brothels. For that matter, it is unclear whether Mau, or rather Ippel, regarded it as one or was simply repeating a conventional designation.[14]

Such reticence on the part of the putatively sexually loquacious Victorians is rather surprising.[15] The brevity of the descriptions offered by these books of the Purpose-Built Brothel may be explained by the fact that in their day, as both editions acknowledge, this establishment was closed ("verschlossen") to visitors. There might have seemed little point in extensively describing to visitors something they could not see for themselves. On the other hand, the descriptions are not really shorter than those provided in these guides for buildings that were open to the public. And this explanation does not account for why these guidebooks offer only one, or at the most two, examples of brothels. Here again we confront the difficulty, which I raised above, of speculating about motive. Nineteenth-century scholars knew of other venues for prostitution; hence why not allude to these?[16]

William Gell published a third version of his guide to the antiquities of Pompeii, not a guidebook in the sense Mau's was, but which was wildly popular nonetheless, in 1832 after his first two editions were sold out.[17] The date was late enough for Gell to take notice of the brothel now known as 6.10.1, 19 (= cat. no. 12), which had been excavated just five years before, in 1827.[18] Gell does this almost grudgingly, however.[19] This establishment does appear to have been identified as a brothel very early on.[20] But not every nineteenth-century writer who discusses it mentions this fact, and as we shall see, some

---

14. See Mau/Ippel, *Führer durch Pompeji*[6] (1928) 73 (description of the *Scavi degli Scienzati/gran Lupanare*), 174 (description of the Purpose-Built Brothel), 261 (index).

15. For what it is worth, the later guidebook by Warscher, *Pompeji: Ein Führer durch die Ruinen* (1925) 144, describes the Purpose-Built Brothel in a brief paragraph. It justifies the identification of this establishment as a brothel by referring to "the obscene scenes on the walls." Warscher does not canvass the possibility that sex was sold at the two *cauponae* located at 6.10.1, 19 and 6.10.2 (= cat. nos. 12 and 13), which she takes as one establishment, analogous to the modern *rosticceria* (71–72). We might conclude from the coy language she uses to describe 9.11.2–3 (= cat. no. 40), however, that she regards this as a brothel.

16. It is interesting to note that in a specialized work Mau identifies a brothel, which he was the first to characterize as such, but does not refer to this venue as a brothel in either of the guidebooks discussed here. Compare Mau, "Scavi" (1879) 209–10, with Mau/Barthel, *Führer durch Pompeji*[5] (1910) 69, and Mau/Ippel, *Führer durch Pompeji*[6] (1928) 42. The brothel in question is 9.5.14–16, no. 35 in the catalog. Mau and his epigones did not therefore attempt to enumerate in their guidebooks all of the brothels known to them.

17. Gell, *Pompeiana*, 1[3] (1832) i–ii. On the professional and popular success of this book, see Wallace-Hadrill, "Case" (2001) 114.

18. For the date of excavation, see Overbeck, *Pompeji* (1856) 437.

19. Gell, *Pompeiana* 2[3] (1832) 10–13, 135; the micromap in the first volume faces 182.

20. See, for example, the passing references in Bonucci, "Scavi" (1829) 146; Fiorelli, *PAH* 2 (1862) 204 (entry for January 1, 1828); 223 (entry for June 14, 1829).

later scholars back away from the identification, referring to the establishment as the "so-called brothel."

As the century progressed, and more information on brothels became available, this development was not always received with enthusiasm by the writers of guides to Pompeii. Thomas Dyer, in his revised 1875 edition of a book that first appeared in 1867, is almost strident in his refusal to discuss the Purpose-Built Brothel:

> A little beyond the house of Siricus, a small street, running down at right angles from the direction of the Forum, enters the Via del Lupanare. Just at their junction, and having an entrance into both, stands the Lupanar, from which the latter street derives its name. We cannot venture upon a description of this resort of Pagan [sic] immorality. It is kept locked up, but the guide will procure the key for those who may wish to see it.[21]

This is still more information than the reader receives from the later guide by Rolfe, who discusses the tavern at 6.10.1, 19 (= cat. no. 12) without mentioning the possibility that sex was sold there and who on one of his walking tours ("itineraries") takes the reader right past the Purpose-Built Brothel without acknowledging its existence (though it does appear as "Lupanare" on the Italian-language map at the end of the book).[22] This trend toward reticence is developed further by Forbes in his 1893 guide to Naples and its surroundings, when the Pompeian brothel all but completely disappears from sight.[23] On the map of Pompeii provided in the book the wedge-shaped form of the Purpose-Built Brothel is discernible, although it is not labeled.

I am inclined to attribute this silence to the exigencies of the genre, though it is clear that differences of approach do exist. Even the guidebooks that do mention brothels, however, may be thought to fix on one or two for reasons of economy of presentation.[24] This is pure speculation, but when we

---

21. Dyer, *Pompeii* (1875) 471.

22. Rolfe, *Pompeii* (1888) 250, 272.

23. Forbes, *Rambles in Naples* (1893) 43–87 (tour of Pompeii).

24. As late as 1982, a guidebook to Pompeii offers only three entries in the index under *lupanar*, 1.10.5 (= cat. no. 5), 7.9.33 (= cat. no. 25: 7.9.29–34), 7.12.18–20 (= cat. no. 26/27): A. De Vos and M. De Vos, *Pompei* (1982) 378. A later publication gives only one entry in the index, 7.12.18–20 (= cat. nos. 26/27), though several others are mentioned in the text: La Rocca, A. De Vos, and M. De Vos, *Pompei* (1994). A 1998 publication treats only that brothel, while alluding to "25 or so places of prostitution": Guzzo and D'Ambrosio, *Pompeii* (1998) 71–73, 160; cf. Nappo, *Pompeii* (1998) 74 ("[o]ver 30"); Amery and Curran, *Pompeii* (2002) 90 ("an abundance"), 91 ("twenty-five organized brothels"), both of which focus on the Purpose-Built Brothel.

move on to other types of publication from the nineteenth century, the overall picture changes but little.

Francophone guidebooks from the nineteenth century appear to strike a balance between the scholarly and the popular, a fact that suggests that these were not so much mutually exclusive categories as types that fell along a broad spectrum. In André De Jorio's contribution from 1828 there is a brief description of the establishment I catalog as no. 25, without any hint that sex might have been sold there.[25] We at last emerge from this desert into the oasis, albeit a very small one, of Stanislas D'Aloe's 1861 guidebook. D'Aloe identifies two establishments as brothels, one a likely candidate, the other less so, and he misses two or more possibilities.[26] What is interesting is that he uses the criteria of erotic art and graffiti for this purpose, though he does so rather tentatively, and in both cases in the context of (that is in or near) a tavern, rather than, for example, a private house.

Ernest Breton seems to have had an interest in identifying brothels to judge from the second edition of his survey of Pompeii, an interesting combination of scholarly treatise and guide for tourists, published in 1855. His index contains only two "brothels."[27] The first is the tavern at 6.10.1, 19, identified as no. 12 in the catalog. Though Breton does not present criteria for this identification, he does mention the "obscene" wall paintings, suggesting that erotic art almost certainly played a role in this identification.[28] The other is the false identification of 6.14.43 as a brothel, which Breton is the first to make.[29] The criteria are of interest. First is the location of the establishment near the "*Vico Storto.*" I am tempted to speculate that Breton depends here on the ancient cliché that had brothels on winding, secluded streets and that has had such a long life.[30] Next are the numerous epigraphs, which the author deems too obscene for a respectable establishment. Unfortunately the epigraphs were illegible only a decade after excavation, and Breton permits himself to cite only a few of the "more decent" examples, which do not prove much of anything about the presence of a brothel.

In the third edition of this book, dating to 1870, Breton displays an even

---

25. De Jorio, *Plan de Pompi* (1829) 114.

26. See D'Aloe, *Ruines de Pompéi* (1861) 66 (= cat. no. 12), 113 (= cat. nos. 29 and 30: not canvassed as brothels), 116 (= cat. no. 7), 133–34 (= cat. no. 34: not canvassed as a brothel).

27. Breton, *Pompeia²* (1855) 368.

28. See Breton, *Pompeia²* (1955) 288–90. Cf. Schulz, "Scavi" (1838) 186–88, who is content only to mention nonerotic paintings from this location, which he refers to as the "Lupernale."

29. Breton, *Pompeia²* (1855) 305–6. Breton discusses at least one other possible brothel, 9.2.7–8 (= cat. no. 34), without identifying it as such: 315–16.

30. See chap. 9.

greater interest in the subject. In addition to the two brothels mentioned in the second edition,[31] there is the Purpose-Built Brothel at 7.12.18–20, discovered in 1862 (= cat. nos. 26 and 27), which receives a rather full description.[32] Erotic paintings and graffiti are mentioned without giving details, while Breton also acknowledges the presence of the masonry beds in the downstairs *cellae*. The author does not explicitly present any of these items as probative criteria for the existence of a brothel, but we might reasonably infer that they played such a role for him. Breton also cites a total of four cribs, one (evidently) at 7.12.33, plus 7.13.15, 16, and 19, the last three of which are said to explain the presence of a representation of a phallus, the name Daphne, and an obscene inscription.[33] Beyond this he expresses the belief that prostitutes, especially young ones, lived in houses on the *Vico Storto* on the ground that erotic art and objects were found there.[34]

Johannes Overbeck's monumental work on Pompeian antiquities contains, in its first edition, published in 1856, two references to brothels in its index, both of which are located on the map he provides. One of these is known now by the address of 6.14.43, the so-called *gran Lupanare* or *Scavi degli Scienzati*. In the text, Overbeck cites the authority of Ernest Breton for this identification, which as already noted is now regarded as almost certainly an error.[35] The other is a tavern with back rooms now identified as 6.10.1, 19 (= cat. no. 12), which quite likely was indeed a brothel.[36] These two brothels, plus the Purpose-Built Brothel, discovered subsequently, in 1862, are the only ones mentioned in the fourth edition to the work, published in 1884.[37] In the text of this edition, the existence of brothels at Pompeii is alluded to very sparingly indeed.[38]

As the nineteenth century wore on, excavators unearthed more and more of the ancient city. A progress report for a period lasting just over a decade, from 1861 to 1872, is offered by Giuseppe Fiorelli in *Scavi di Pompei*. Fiorelli,

---

31. Breton, *Pompeia*³ (1870) 359–60 (= cat. no. 12); 379–81 (the false brothel at 6.14.43).

32. Breton, *Pompeia*³ (1870) 434–36.

33. Breton, *Pompeia*³ (1870) 441–42, 452.

34. Breton, *Pompeia*³ (1870) 411.

35. Overbeck, *Pompeji*⁷ (1856) 338–39 (which provides a brief discussion of the rationale for identifying 6.14.43 as a brothel), 437 (index for the map). The criterion employed was evidently the presence of erotic graffiti, which makes identification of this establishment as a brothel, though almost certainly erroneous, hardly absurd.

36. The already mentioned guidebooks identify this establishment simply as a tavern: Mau/Barthel, *Führer durch Pompeji*⁵ (1910) 105–6; Mau/Ippel, *Führer durch Pompeji*⁶ (1928) 230–32.

37. Overbeck/Mau, *Pompeji*⁴ (1884) 673, 675.

38. Overbeck/Mau, *Pompeji*⁴ (1884) 380.

inter alia, gives what by the standards of the day are fairly close descriptions of seventeen *Insulae*, or street blocks, on the plan he himself devised for Pompeii.[39] Ten of these contain establishments that are listed as possible brothels in appendix 1. Not all of these *Insulae* were completely excavated at the time of publication, but Fiorelli has references to nine of these entries, encompassing what are a minimum of seven possible brothels: catalog nos. 17, 18, 19, 20 (19 and 20 may be one brothel or two), 26, 27 (26 and 27 may also be one brothel or two), 31, 33, 34. Of these, he identifies only two explicitly as brothels, the downstairs and upstairs of the Purpose-Built Brothel (26 and 27), and at most implies that one other location served as such (here to take 19/20 as one establishment).[40] Again, this is a report on recent progress in excavation, not a survey of the entire city, but the low number of brothels reported is striking all the same.

The language Fiorelli uses to identify these brothels is of interest. He describes the downstairs of the Purpose-Built Brothel with a common Latin word for brothel, *fornix*. Was he being euphemistic here? It does not seem so, given that Fiorelli uses *lupanare* to describe the upstairs. But there is no question that his overall description is laconic, to say the least: he mentions neither erotic paintings nor graffiti.[41] Of course we know that these items were present, and that they almost certainly figured into Fiorelli's own identification of these establishments as brothels. All the same, as they do not appear in his discourse, it is difficult to know exactly how much weight Fiorelli gave them. Aside from describing the layout of the *cellae*, with their masonry beds and pillows, he chiefly mentions that the brothel is recognizable as such "by the dark and narrow space in which it was contained" ("dal tetro ed angusto spazio ov'era confinato"), drawing on a brothel cliché traceable all the way back to antiquity, as we shall see in chapter 9.

In regard to the brothel he perhaps identifies through implication, Fiorelli writes the following: "Stairway to an upstairs dwelling, where various women were accustomed to congregate, among whom at one point there was Euplia, *cum hominibus bellis.*"[42] Here the Latin reference to male partners, to say noth-

---

39. A list is provided at Fiorelli, *Scavi di Pompei* (1873) vi–vii. For a brief description of Fiorelli's system of Pompeian addresses, see my preface.

40. Fiorelli, *Scavi di Pompei* (1873) 20, 42–43. Fiorelli in this publication does seem to regard the Purpose-Built Brothel as two separate establishments: see chap. 8 for a discussion of this problem.

41. Fiorelli, *Scavi di Pompei* (1873) 20.

42. Fiorelli, *Scavi di Pompei* (1873) 42: "Scala di un'abitazione superiore, ove solevano convenir varie donne, tra le quali fuvvi una volta Euplia, *cum hominibus bellis.*" For more on this site, see below in the text.

ing of the description of the women as "various," seems an unmistakable euphemism. It is not entirely clear, however, whether he understands this place to be an assignation house, rather than a brothel. I argue below in this chapter that the Romans did not distinguish between assignation houses and brothels, though Fiorelli may well have done so. Or, perhaps, for reasons given below, he employed a different definition of brothel than we do.

Matters do not improve in a lavishly produced survey of a later group of nineteenth-century excavations, covering the period 1874 to 1881, by Emil Presuhn. The author simply does not canvass one candidate for brothelhood at 9.5.19 (= cat. no. 36) as such, while for another, a tavern at 9.5.14–16 (= cat. no. 35), the author at most alludes to the possibility that sex was sold there, when he cites Bacchus and Venus as patrons of the clientele.[43]

When we come to August Mau's great work on life and art in Pompeii, the second edition of which appeared in 1908, brothels seem to have disappeared entirely. There is no mention of them in the index, nor in the text, as far as I can see.[44] This silence is consistent with Mau's treatment of Pompeian paint-ing in this book, which ignores the presence of erotic subjects. The same holds for his discussion of graffiti.[45] The result is a brighter, cleaner, and nicer Pom-peii than we believe it actually was. It is almost as if Mau had found the City of Venus and transformed it into a Victorian version of Chicago. Whether his motive was sheer hypocrisy or a sense of propriety difficult to contemplate in an age ruled by a radically different sense of honor and shame I leave to the reader to decide. A third alternative, mere lack of interest, is an even more unintelligible motive to us. But even this motive cannot be ruled out as a rea-son for Mau's omitting this information in this work.

If lack of interest was indeed the motive behind such reticence, it may have been shared by others with an interest in the life and art of the ancient city of Pompeii. Wolfgang Helbig's encyclopedic treatment of Campanian wall painting, published in 1868, virtually ignores erotic subjects. Although Helbig occasionally mentions prostitutes and brothels, he describes them in a manner that suggests their status as the proverbial exceptions that prove the rule. The apparent backing away from recognition of 6.10.1, 19 as a brothel

---

43. Presuhn, *Pompeji²* (1882) Abt. 7.6, Abt. 8.5–6.

44. The lone exception appears in the appendix Mau published independently of the second edition, where he repeats Helbig's skeptical identification of 6.10.1, 19 (= cat. no. 12) as a "so-called brothel": Mau, *Pompeji: Anhang* (1913) 56. On Helbig, see below in the text.

45. Mau, *Pompeji in Leben und Kunst²* (1908) 419–24 (inns and wine shops), 472–89 (paint-ings), 509–15 (graffiti). See also the English translation of the first edition: Mau, *Pompeii: Its Life and Art* (1899) 392–96 (inns and wine shops), 461–74 (paintings), 481–88 (graffiti).

stands as the most striking instance, at least from my perspective.[46] Henry Thédenat's 1910 volume on Pompeian *vie publique* shows scant interest in venal sex. The chapter on taverns, hotels, shops, professions, and streets does not raise the subject, though at least one catalog item comes in for discussion, 6.10.1, 19 (= cat. no. 12).[47] The detailed map at the rear of the book shows two more such items, one of which, the Purpose-Built Brothel, is identified as a *lupanar*; the other, 6.16.32–33 (= cat. no. 15), is not.

Aside from Ernest Breton, Giuseppe Fiorelli cites the largest number of "brothels," for a grand total of four, in the index to his *Descrizione*. Only one of these, the Purpose-Built Brothel, is explicitly identified as a brothel in the text.[48] The four "brothels" are:

1. 6.10.1, 19
2. 6.14.a (scil. 6.14.43)
3. 7.4.42 (a misprint gives the *Regio* as 6)
4. 7.12.18–20

The first is a tavern that doubled as a brothel (= cat. no. 12), the second is now recognized as a likely misidentification (the *Scavi degli Scienzati*), the third is a crib, or *cella meretricia*, and the fourth is the Purpose-Built Brothel (= cat. nos. 26/27). At least four cribs not included in the index are found in the text. One is at 7.11.12, while the others are found in a cluster located at 7.13.13, 15, 19.[49]

Furthermore, there are three additional establishments that Fiorelli might also have considered to be brothels. For 6.11.5, 15–16 (= cat. no. 14), he declares that "facili donne" ("loose women") lived there on the basis of erotic graffiti.[50] According to Fiorelli, who again cites epigraphic evidence, at the tavern known as 7.3.26–28 (= cat. no. 19) "giocondamente passavano le ore

---

46. Helbig, *Wandgemälde* (1868) has a very brief section on "obscene paintings" (370–71, which refers to some published examples; see also 369), another on women, possibly *hetairai*, at banquets, plus a short survey of *Liebescenen* (342–45), and *hetairai* in scenes from Comedy (352–56). The identification of 6.10.1, 19 (= cat. no. 12) as a brothel is doubted (471: "Sog. Lupanar"), while the identification of 6.14.43 as such, now discarded, is accepted as secondary and evidently unreliable to judge from his description of its nomenclature (472: "Scavi degli scienziati, auch Gran lupanar genannt").

47. Thédenat, *Pompéi*² (1910) 118.

48. Fiorelli, *Descrizione* (1875) 461; cf. 286–87, where the Purpose-Built Brothel is identified as a *lupanare*. Fiorelli discusses at least two other possible brothels without identifying them as such: 7.7.18 (= cat. no. 24) and 9.2.7–8 (= cat. no. 34) at 248 and 379–80, respectively.

49. Fiorelli, *Descrizione* (1875) 279, 298.

50. Fiorelli, *Descrizione* (1875) 151, has this as 6.11.15.

uomini e donne" ("men and women were accustomed to pass time pleas-antly").[51] Elsewhere for 7.9.29–34 (= cat. no. 25) he refers to apartments that "non erano frequentati da donne pudiche" ("that were not used by chaste women").[52] It is odd that Fiorelli, who does not hesitate to include four brothel-identifications in his index, should resort to euphemism elsewhere, and it may be that he did not in fact regard all of the three establishments in question as brothels. An explanation for this strange result might be that Fiorelli had a different, more restrictive, definition of brothel than our work-ing one, which defines brothel as a public place where two or more prostitutes can service clients at the same time. A nineteenth-century European accus-tomed to a Parisian-style system of regulationism might have had a more ele-vated set of expectations for a brothel from the institutional perspective. In other words, he might more easily locate a brothel in the physical plant of the Purpose-Built Brothel, for example, than in most of the other places we would accept as Pompeian brothels using my definition.[53] Or, as already suggested, perhaps Fiorelli regarded these simply as assignation houses and not as broth-els. Both solutions are far from certain, but might help explain why Fiorelli and some other nineteenth-century scholars identified far fewer brothels than we might have expected.

Even so, this last piece of information, together with the cribs missing from Fiorelli's index, raises an obvious caution. The publication of brothels and cribs in the nineteenth century was far from systematic, so that it is easy to miss them in the literature. More are perhaps found elsewhere in Fiorelli's published work or, as I have already pointed out, in the nineteenth-century specialist literature overall.[54] All the same, I do not believe the total of cribs identified, rightly or wrongly, in that period is going to exceed by more than a half dozen or so that which I have already unearthed. In regard to brothels, I would be surprised to find that their number exceeded the numbers identified as such in the course of the twentieth century by Matteo Della Corte, let alone by Hans Eschebach. It is interesting to note that in the second edition of

51. Fiorelli, *Descrizione* (1875) 206, has this as 7.3.27. See also the discussion above.

52. Fiorelli, *Descrizione* (1875) 267, has this as 7.9.32, the more usual listing.

53. On the experience of nineteenth-century regulationism in Italy, see Gibson, *Prostitution and the State in Italy*[2] (1999).

54. The collection of excavation records edited by Fiorelli that is known as the *PAH* (*Pompeianarum Antiquitatum Historia*) does not promise well in this regard. *PAH* 2.204 identifies what is evidently 6.10.1, 19 (= cat. n. 12) as a brothel on the basis of erotic art and graffiti; cf. *PAH* 2.223, 250, 3.84. Otherwise reticence appears to rule on the subject of brothels to judge from the sampling I have done. *PAH* 2.369–70, 446–47, 449–50 do not identify 6.14.43 as a brothel. Cf. *PAH* 2.64–65 (cat. no. 25), 2.381–82, 384, 400 (cat. no. 29), 2.496–99, 506–7 (cat. no. 34).

Pierre Gusman's book on Pompeii, published in 1906, in a chapter promisingly entitled "Les lupanars et les cellae meretriciae," a few specifics are included: the Purpose-Built Brothel, the (probably misidentified) *Scavi degli Scienzati*, and one crib, at 7.11.12.[55] Gusman's knowledge of Pompeian brothels and cribs appears to be derivative at best, but the results may serve as an indication of what was by then commonly known or accepted on the subject. Thus when the article on prostitutes in the great *Dictionnaire des antiquités grecques et romaines*, edited by C. Daremberg and E. Saglio, appears in 1918, the author, citing Gusman, confidently asserts that at Pompeii "at least two brothels" ("au moins deux lupanars") had been excavated.[56]

The brothels routinely and unambiguously cited as such by nineteenth-century scholars amount to a total of three, two of which are quite likely to be brothels (= cat. nos. 12 and 26/27), while the third is not likely to be one at all (6.14.43).[57] We may add to this tally the six cribs given by Breton and Fiorelli (three of which overlap).

This is a disappointing harvest, particularly in regard to the brothels. Given the sheer amount of excavation in the nineteenth century, a Foucauldian, or anyone for that matter, might reasonably have expected more. A passing remark of Ludwig Friedländer's in his classic encyclopedia on Roman life and manners, which originated back in 1861 and, like August Mau's work, continued to be published in new editions after the author's death (by sheer coincidence, in the same year as Mau's), suggests as much. Friedländer remarks that moral conditions in the capital could hardly be worse than in Pompeii, "where among so many hundreds of wall paintings obscene subjects were hardly found elsewhere than in brothels."[58] He makes as straightforward a connection between the location of erotic art and brothels as we would like, and so it is not surprising to find this text cited as a kind of "smoking gun" in the modern Victorian-*jagd*.[59] But Friedländer disappointingly fails to connect the dots. In other words, he does not employ the criterion of erotic art to identify any brothels, either real or imaginary.

Far from a smoking gun, then, this passage is a dead end. Nineteenth-cen-

---

55. Gusman, *Pompéi²* (1906) 271–73: there are also vague references to taverns and houses, the latter in the *Vico Storto*, an idea perhaps derived from Ernest Breton.

56. Navarre, *DS* s.v. "meretrices" (1918) 1836.

57. Compare Mau's index to *CIL* 4, published in 1909, which has (at 787–90), in addition to these three listings and the six *cellae meretriciae* of Breton and Fiorelli, the "*Casa del lupanare*" at 6.10.2 (= cat. no. 13).

58. Friedländer/Wissowa, *Sittengeschichte Roms* I¹⁰ (1922) 288: ". . . wo [sc. in Pompeji] unter so vielen Hunderten von Wandgemälden obszöne Bilder schwerlich anderswo als in Bordellen gefunden worden sind."

59. By DeFelice, *Roman Hospitality* (2001) 7.

tury scholars may have enjoyed the most lurid—or prosaic—fantasies about the large number of Pompeian brothels. If so, these fantasies found scant expression in the literature surveyed here. Their legacy regarding the identification of brothels in post-Victorian Pompeian studies is therefore somewhat negligible. It is significant that, as late as 1920, in his extensive study of street lighting in Pompeii, Giuseppe Spano cites only one "true brothel" in the city, the one characterized in this book as the Purpose-Built Brothel.[60] Though he does acknowledge that "alcuni termopolii" functioned as brothels, he gives only one example, the tavern-brothel known to us as 6.10.1, 19. For serious and sustained efforts at brothel-identification, at least as reflected in print, readers had to wait until the twentieth century was well underway.

Why this silence? A clue to Victorian reticence on the subject of brothels may be found in the Victorians' bizarre approaches to ancient latrines. In terms of "hardware," these latrines were more difficult to ignore than were the brothels. Perhaps for this reason, resort to fanciful explanations was a necessity; worth mentioning in this regard is the theory that the characteristic stone benches with perforations served as "amphora-holders."[61] As with scatology, so perhaps with sex.[62] If feelings of embarrassment prevented nineteenth-century archaeologists from saying more about Pompeian brothels, this can easily be reconciled with Foucault's repressive hypothesis. This is especially true if we assume that they were quite prepared to talk about sex in the present tense, just not in the past, as though uncovering certain aspects of Roman sexuality might undermine public confidence in the entire enterprise of ancient archaeology.

Another possible explanation—which is not inconsistent with the one just given—is simply that the tentative suggestions that were periodically made for the identifications of brothels in the specialist literature were tacitly rejected by mainstream scholars because they were deemed unconvincing.[63] We should not assume that these earlier scholars were, on the whole, less skep-

---

60. Spano, "Illuminazione" (1920) 35.

61. See Neudecker, *Pracht der Latrine* (1994) 7–9, for this and alternative versions.

62. For a good discussion of the "prudish reticence about sex . . . in Anglo-American scholarship of the Victorian and post-Victorian era," see Nussbaum and Sihvola, "Introduction" (2002) 2–7 (quotation at 3). On material culture in particular, see Johns, *Sex or Symbol* (1982) 15–35.

63. This point is impossible to prove. See perhaps the tentative identification of some shops at 6.6.14–16 as brothels by Mazois, *Ruines* 2 (1824/38) 24. The suggestion evidently awaits Pirson, *Mietwohnungen* (1999) 33 n. 127, for explicit refutation. It is passed over in silence, for example, by Niccolini, *Case* 2 (1862): 9. Another sign is the evident backing away from identification of 6.10.1, 19 (= cat. no. 12) as a brothel by scholars such as Helbig (see n. 46 above).

tical than some of us are, regardless of whether that skepticism is in the end justified. It is also possible that at least some of them, as noted above, defined brothel differently from the way we do and/or made tacit distinctions between assignation-houses and brothels.

Once we move past the limits of what may be reasonably described as "Victorian," let alone nineteenth-century scholarship, a change occurs, which appears very dramatic in comparison to what precedes it, though much less so in comparison to what follows. In 1926 Matteo Della Corte published the first edition of his study of the houses and inhabitants of Pompeii. The work is in fact a collation of a series of articles that appeared from 1914 to 1925 in such journals as *Neapolis* and the *Rivista Indo-greco-italica*. In the text, Della Corte gives a total of seven brothels, a modest number by today's standards but one which more than doubles the total of the consensus I have been able to unearth for the previous period.[64] In a postscript to the book, Della Corte adds one more example.[65] This did not, to be sure, exhaust the number of venues for venal sex in Pompeii known to Della Corte at that time,[66] but the question of why he did not add to the list of brothels in 1926 must remain a matter for speculation.

The original number of seven brothels given by Della Corte was taken up by the Pauly-Wissowa encyclopedia in an article on Roman prostitution published just five years later.[67] Thus it came to stand as, in a sense, canonical for much of the twentieth century. Indeed, it was cited as late as 1963 by J. P. V. D. Balsdon in his book on Roman women.[68] Guidebooks to Pompeii published in this period, however, including one written by Della Corte himself, mention the Purpose-Built Brothel and very little else.[69]

In the second edition of his book, published in 1954, Della Corte increases the number of brothels he lists to ten.[70] He also includes two cribs in his index,

---

64. Della Corte, *Case*[1] (1926) nos. 58 (= my cat. no. 14), 207 (= cat. no. 36), 220 (= cat. no. 22), 285 (= cat. nos. 26/27), 348 (= cat. no. 33), 399 (= cat. no. 1), 401 (= cat. no. 2).

65. Della Corte, *Case*[1] (1926) no. 208 (= my cat. no. 37). The change is reflected in the book's index s.v. "*Lupanar*" (at 111), which therefore gives a total of eight brothels.

66. Cf. Della Corte, *Case*[1] (1926) index s.v. "*Leno, Meretrices*" (at 109).

67. Schneider, *RE* s.v. "meretrix" (1931) 1023.

68. Balsdon, *Roman Women* (1963) 225 ("at least seven" brothels for Pompeii, citing the Pauly article). See also Della Valle, "Amore" (1937) 149.

69. Della Corte, *Piccola Guida di Pompei* (1939) 40–41 (cf. 42 for the crib at 7.11.12); Ciprotti, *Conoscere Pompei* (1959) 93 (has two brothels, the Purpose-Built and cat. nos. 22/23).

70. The additions are found at Della Corte, *Case*[2] (1954) 122–23 (= my cat. no. 19), 378 (= cat. no. 12); see 429 s.v. "*Lupanaria*."

but just two cribs, less than the number cited by nineteenth-century scholars such as Breton and Fiorelli.[71]

It is interesting to note that one of the two "new" brothels included in the second edition of *Case,* and only in a postscript, is my catalog number 12, which, for well over a century, some thought had functioned as a brothel. This fact, taken with Della Corte's underreporting of cribs, suggests a significant break with the tradition of scholarship that preceded his publication. To put the matter another way, of the three "usual suspects" I have been able to unearth for the nineteenth century, Della Corte cites one (the Purpose-Built) consistently, names one (= cat. no. 12) belatedly, and completely ignores the third, which is probably a false attribution, as it turns out (6.14.43). The changes made between the first two editions are modest in nature, as are those between the second and third edition of *Case,* posthumously published in 1965, which contains two more brothels and one less crib, as we shall see.[72]

What all of this might suggest is that instead of simply relying on the reports of others, Della Corte relied on personal observation and knowledge of the physical remains and in so doing, generated a higher number of possible brothels for the ancient city of Pompeii. For now this explanation of Della Corte's departure from precedent must remain an hypothesis. The same holds for the evident absence of a great legacy of Pompeian brothels identified, rightly or not, by generations of scholars in the nineteenth century. What does seem reasonably certain is that Della Corte and his twentieth-century successors moved well beyond the limits of the mainstream discourse on brothels recoverable from the Victorian period, and that it is at minimum an exaggeration to characterize these later developments as inevitably "Victorian" in nature. The systematic identification, collation, and above all counting of Pompeian brothels is a distinctly twentieth-century phenomenon and, apart from the contributions of Della Corte himself, a late one at that.

---

71. Della Corte, *Case*[2] (1954) 72–76 (if anything this is likely to be a brothel and not a *cella meretricia*), 170 (the crib at 7.11.12); cf. 429, index s.v. "*Meretriciae cellae.*"

72. I am unable to verify the assertion of Berry, "Domestic Life" (1997) 104, that in an article published in 1958 Della Corte identified the then recently excavated 1.9.11 as a brothel, the "Lupanar di Amarantus" (sic). She gives no page reference, while Della Corte, "Pompei" (1958) twice refers to this establishment, once as the *Caupona Amaranti* (79) and again as an "osteria" (105). See also Della Corte, *Case*[3] (1965) 340, 504; *CIL* 4.9829a (editorial note), 10017 (editorial note). For what it is worth, Della Corte, *Amori e amanti* (1958) does not explicitly identify any brothels not given in the various editions of *Case,* though his coy description (72–73) of the establishment at 2.1.6 (scil. = 1.11.6–7) is of interest.

COUNTING BROTHELS

The figure of "thirty-five or more" for the total number of Pompeian brothels introduced in chapter 1 is of late vintage, dating in published form to the 1994 harvest of books on Pompeii by Ray Laurence and Antonio Varone.[73] Before this date, counting the number of brothels in Pompeii seems to have held little interest for scholars.[74] These authors arrived at the number thirty-five by taking the largest number of brothels compiled up to that point, namely Gioacchino La Torre's twenty-five,[75] adding the nine *cellae meretriciae* (cribs) identified at that time, and throwing in the recently excavated Suburban Baths for good measure.[76]

The result is vulnerable to criticism. Lumping the *cellae meretriciae* together with the brothels in this manner is a mistake, in my view.[77] Worth noting is that La Torre appears to be the first scholar to have done this, while Laurence and Varone are the first ones, as far as I know, to count the total number of brothels in more than a casual manner and publish a total for the entire city.[78] Beyond the error of including the *cellae meretriciae*, there is some double counting, as we shall see, and as for Laurence's phrase "or more," this may simply be a case of erring on the side of caution.

These criticisms may appear to be quibbles, and in a very real sense they are, but they are nonetheless important given the impact that the total num-

---

73. Laurence, *Roman Pompeii* (1994) 73; Varone, *Erotica Pompeiana* (1994) 135 n. 228.

74. For a pre-90s tally, see Alföldy, *Social History of Rome* (1988) 135, who gives the number of twenty-eight, though this is evidently a casual estimate. Eschebach himself gives the number of twenty-three in *Pompeji* (1978) 18: "Bisher wurden ungefähr 23 Freudenhäuser (Lupanare) identifiziert" ("Up to this point approximately 23 brothels have been identified"). Cf. the desultory list given at Hermann-Otto, *Ex Ancilla Natus* (1994) 345 n. 10.

75. La Torre, "Impianti" (1988) 93 n. 29: "[a] Pompei sono attestati ben 18 lupanari e 9 *cellae meretriciae* . . . [v]i sono poi anche 7 lupanari connessi a case private. . . ." ("at Pompeii a good 18 brothels and 9 *cellae meretriciae* are in evidence . . . there are also 7 brothels attached to private houses") Cf. 71, where he presents a bar graph giving the number of "lupanari" by *Regio:* (I:4, VI:4, VII:15, VIII:1, IX:10), once again without giving the total for the entire city. While La Torre distinguishes the *cellae* from the "lupanari" in the footnote, he does not do so in the graph.

76. So Varone, *Erotica Pompeiana* (1994) 135 n. 229. Laurence, *Roman Pompeii* (1994) 73, is silent about the basis of his calculation, though Wallace-Hadrill assures me that it derives ultimately from La Torre as well: Wallace-Hadrill, p.c.

77. Wallace-Hadrill, "Public Honour and Private Shame" (1995) 54, refers to the *cellae* as brothels, though at 53 he appears to distinguish *cellae* from *lupanar*.

78. I note that Wallace-Hadrill gave the original oral presentation of his paper, in which he added up the number of La Torre's brothels for Pompeii, in July 1991: see Cornell and Lomas, *Urban Society* (1995) vii. Thirty-four is his top estimate for previously identified brothels: "Public Honour and Private Shame" (1995) 51 and 53.

ber of "thirty-five or more" brothels has had on the scholarly mind. This number has struck more than one researcher as wholly inappropriate, if not simply absurd, for a city of Pompeii's size. In turn, it has helped inspire a search for a radical solution to the problem that I hope to show is not convincing.

Eliminating the *cellae* and the Suburban Baths from the total of thirty-five leaves us with twenty-five brothels,[79] which is still a large number and one that Andrew Wallace-Hadrill, the first scholar to employ criteria for identifying brothels in a manner that is both rigorous and clear, reduces to one certain example, the famous Purpose-Built Brothel.[80] Wallace-Hadrill's three criteria for identification are: (1) "the structural evidence of a masonry bed set in a small cell of ready access to the public," which the author regards as the most reliable measure; (2) "the presence of paintings of explicit sexual scenes"; and (3) "the cluster of graffiti of the 'hic bene futui' type" (they display male boasting: "I had a good fuck here").[81] Appearing too late for Wallace-Hadrill to take it into account is the "revised Eschebach,"[82] which in raw form presents a very long list of brothels, forty-six, by my count. This number excludes the *cellae meretriciae*, which for the "revised Eschebach" numbered eleven. Before assessing the value of Wallace-Hadrill's criteria, I want briefly to trace the genesis of the figure of twenty-five and then explore why this figure has ballooned to thirty-five, or as many as forty-six, of late.

Before Wallace-Hadrill's intervention, there existed four important sources of information on the subject of Pompeian brothels. They are the descriptions of Pompeian buildings offered by Matteo Della Corte and the lists of brothel-locations provided first by Hans Eschebach, then by Gioacchino La Torre, and, most recently, by Liselotte Eschebach. Unlike the others, Della Corte gives explicit criteria for identifying a site as a brothel.[83] His approach

---

79. La Torre, "Impianti" (1988) 93 n. 29.

80. Wallace-Hadrill, "Public Honour and Private Shame" (1995) 51–54, followed by Hoskins Walbank, review *Urban Society* (1996); Savunen, *Women* (1997) 105—6, 111; Cantarella, *Pompei* (1998) 87; Clarke, *Looking at Lovemaking* (1998) 195; Flemming, "*Quae Corpore*" (1999) 45; Pirson, *Mietwohnungen* (1999) 55 with n. 233, 154; Guzzo and Scarano Ussani, *Veneris figurae* (2000) 12. For an echo, albeit critical, of the older view, see Dierichs, *Erotik* (1997) 73–78. This brothel—renamed the Purpose-Built Brothel for this study—is discussed in detail in chap. 8.

81. Wallace-Hadrill, "Public Honour and Private Shame" (1995) 52.

82. Eschebach and Müller-Trollius, *Gebäudeverzeichnis* (1993) 491–92.

83. See Della Corte, *Case*[3] (1965) 55, for the criteria (not expressed as clearly as one would like); on brothels and such: 55–56 (*caupona-lupanar*: 6.10.1), 60–61 (6.11.16), 149–50 (7.3.26–28), 162–63 (9.5.19), 163 (9.6.8), 169–72 (7.6.34–35), 203 (7.12.18–20), 204–5 (*cella meretricia*: 7.11.12), 237–38 (*ganeum-lupanar*: 8.4.12), 272 (*caupona-lupanar*: 1.2.18–19), 273–74 (1.2.20–21), 299 (1.10.5–6), 440–43 (7 Occ. in front of the Porta Marina N).

is unsystematic and therefore somewhat arbitrary[84] and perhaps partly for this reason he does not name as many brothels as the Eschebachs and La Torre do. By my count, he comes up with nine, or at most twelve, brothels and one *cella meretricia*.[85] His most consistent criteria are, however, broadly similar to those employed by Wallace-Hadrill: (1) a particular design, with the difference that Della Corte is more concerned with the layout of the rooms than with the presence of a masonry bed; (2) the presence of erotic art; and (3) the presence of erotic graffiti. Della Corte also construes the latter two criteria more broadly than does Wallace-Hadrill, in that he considers art beyond painting and graffiti beyond the "hic bene futui" type. These differences in defining criteria are not by themselves sufficient, however, to explain the brothel-gap that has emerged in 1990s Pompeii.

Hans Eschebach lists twenty-two brothels, which represents a significant increase over the dozen given in Della Corte's third and last edition.[86] La Torre offers twenty-five, eighteen of which are identified as "public" (ten of these are associated with *cauponae* and eight are independent) and seven of which are connected with private houses.[87] The discrepancy in their overall totals is explained by the fact that for three locations Eschebach lists one brothel and La Torre two.[88] In addition, each author gives two brothels not listed by the other author.[89] Finally, one more brothel is listed in the "Indirizzario" ("Address-Book") of the publication in which La Torre's article is found, than he himself offers in the article.[90] As noted above, the new list by Liselotte Eschebach shows forty-six items, though when duplicates, double counts, and other errors are discounted, the number is reduced to thirty-five.[91] To complicate matters even further, a late entry into the brothel fray, a doc-

---

84. In recent years, scholars have been increasingly critical of Della Corte's work: see, for example, the severe treatment by Mouritsen, *Elections* (1988) 13–27. What follows should in no way be interpreted as a defense of his methods. At the same time, his contribution to Pompeian studies can scarcely be denied.

85. The higher total includes two items Della Corte places under the rubric of *caupona-lupanar* and one under that of *ganeum-lupanar*. This may well distort the author's intent, it must be conceded.

86. Eschebach, *Entwicklung* (1970) 174–75.

87. La Torre, "Impianti" (1988) 93 n. 29.

88. The locations are 7.3.26–28 (E.), 7.3.27.28 (L.); 7.6.34–36 (E.), 7.6.34.35 (L.); 7.12.18–20 (E.), 7.12.18–19.20 (L.).

89. These are 6.14.43, 7 Occ. in front of the *Porta Marina* N, 6.14.4 (a mistake for 6.14.43?), 7.7.18.

90. This is 1.9.11–12 (= cat. no. 4): De Simone et al., *Pompei* (1988) 110.

91. Eschebach and Müller-Trollius, *Gebäudeverzeichnis* (1993) 491–92. Among others, I eliminate 7.12.34–35, which is given the wrong address in the list (491) and is not identified as a brothel in the text (332).

toral dissertation, now published as a book, by John DeFelice Jr., while accepting Wallace-Hadrill's criticism of the apparently high number of Pompeian brothels, goes on to suggest a handful of new candidates.[92]

As noted, neither the Eschebachs nor La Torre offer explicit criteria for identifying brothels. A skeptic might object that this omission is of little consequence, since the criteria available for this purpose are patently inadequate. To take that of design first, Della Corte's reliance on room layout seems too porous in that it provides no effective way of distinguishing a brothel, say, from an inn.[93] On the other hand, Wallace-Hadrill's insistence on the presence of masonry beds seems overlimited, in that it will only reveal the existence of a purpose-built brothel and no other kind.

It is impossible to believe that no Pompeian prostitute ever used a wooden bed (or no bed at all). Like other wooden objects from Pompeii, such beds are unlikely to have survived.[94] In a study surveying possible brothels at Rome, Giuseppe Lugli names two establishments where a form of wooden bed was used and another showing a lighter form of masonry than the one used at Pompeii.[95] Comparative evidence shows that low-budget brothels sometimes lack beds.[96] This evidence suggests that prostitutes may offer sexual services that do not require a bed, if indeed any of them do.

The other two criteria promise no better. As I discussed in chapter 4, erotic art appears to have been a near-universal feature of Roman social life,[97] a fact that has encouraged brothel-spotting in some controversial places.[98] Moreover, even where an identification is plausibly made, the kind and qual-

---

92. DeFelice, *Women of Pompeian Inns* (1998) now published as *Roman Hospitality* (2001) (at 6–7, 11). The new brothels are given in the catalog in the first appendix.

93. Now-vanished wooden partitions may have divided space in brothels as they did in both shops and houses: see Gassner, *Kaufläden* (1986) 64, for shops; Wallace-Hadrill, "Houses and Households" (1991) 213, for houses.

94. Gassner, *Kaufläden* (1986) 38, estimates that only 5 percent of Pompeian shops had a stone or masonry table. Though wooden ones have not survived, they are amply attested in paintings and reliefs. On the problem of using beds to identify *cubicula* in private houses, see Riggsby, "*Cubiculum*" (1997) 42, with literature.

95. Lugli, *Monumenti* (1947) 143, 150, 158.

96. For an example of a brothel in nineteenth-century New York City that had no beds, but "a field bed of straw spread over the whole floor," see Hill, *Their Sisters' Keepers* (1993) 221.

97. On the broad construction and dispersal of erotic art, see chap. 4.

98. A good example is the House of the Vettii brothers (6.15.1, 27), which sports an apparent advertisement for a prostitute at its entrance (*CIL* 4.4592) and erotic paintings in a back room off the kitchen (Room x¹) of a style and quality similar to those on the ground floor of the Purpose-Built Brothel. Varone, *Erotica Pompeiana* (1994) 133–34, connects the dots and argues for the presence of a brothel, an idea refuted by Clarke, *Looking at Lovemaking* (1998) 169–77.

ity of erotic art in public establishments cannot serve as a straightforward index of the socioeconomic level of the clientele.[99]

As for the third criterion, graffiti, we do not have to be radical skeptics to note that they are as liable to communicate jokes, insults, and/or idle (male) boasting as the facts of commercial sex.[100] Some of the surviving examples almost certainly were meant as jokes, insults, or empty boasts, though it is difficult to determine which ones.

In regard to identifying the *cellae meretriciae*, Wallace-Hadrill seems to use the presence of masonry beds as the sole criterion, since he cites neither painting nor graffiti here. As far as erotic art and graffiti are concerned, 7.11.12 has a phallus made of tufa, 7.13.15 a phallic amulet, 7.4.42 an erotic painting, 7.13.15, 16, and 19 show a price nearby,[101] while 9.6.2 has sexual graffiti nearby, and 9.7.15 and 17 have several prices in the vicinity.[102] Evidence of this kind is not, of course, available for all cribs. The absence in some instances of such features raises the question of whether or not we should insist on the same criteria for both the brothels and the *cellae*. Perhaps not all of the latter were in fact venues for prostitution. Is it impossible that not one of these had a different use, for example, as storage or by a watchman?

All the same, it is possible to turn all of these objections inside-out, insofar as not one of the three criteria is essential to the operation of a brothel, ancient or modern. In fact, not one of these three criteria is employed to identify brothels in any other culture known to me.[103] The proper reply to the

---

99. Guzzo and Scarano Ussani, *Veneris figurae* (2000) 12, 47. For attempts to mimic an upper-class ambience in a classical Athenian brothel, see Davidson, *Courtesans and Fishcakes* (1998) 94. See further my comments in chaps. 8 and 10.

100. On some difficulties of using Pompeian graffiti as a source, see Mouritsen, *Elections* (1988) 17. Those concerning sexual matters appear most vulnerable to misapprehension. For a discussion of the reliability of Pompeian prostitute graffiti, see chap. 2.

101. When the crib at 7.13.19 was excavated on February 25, 1863, the following objects were found: a gold ring with an engraving of Cupid holding a crown, a silver handle for a mirror, a fragment of a mirror, and a silver ladle. See Eschebach, "Casa di Ganimede" (1982) 248.

102. Savunen, *Women* (1997) 113–14. The erotic significance of the phallus is open to dispute: Spano, "Illuminazione" (1920) 25–27; Clarke, *Looking at Lovemaking* (1998) 13; Varone, *Erotismo* (2000) 15–27. Whatever view we take, insofar as such representations appear in venues like the Purpose-Built Brothel, they are treated in this article as "erotic art" for the purposes of brothel identification. This avoids having to create a cumbersome fourth category for evaluation. Representations of Priapus do have a role to play, however limited, in the identification of brothels: see chap. 9.

103. Cf. the criteria used to identify a building in the Athenian Ceramicus (Building Z) as a brothel, none of which correspond precisely with those used at Pompeii: Davidson, *Courtesans and Fishcakes* (1998) 85. The ancient historian can only envy the resources at times available to those who study more recent periods. The archaeologists who excavated a nineteenth-century brothel in Washington, D.C., could rely on public records detailing the precise location, proprietor's

skeptic is that the three criteria, while far from definitive, are all—aside perhaps from a few modest suggestions given in chapter 10—that we have and are likely to have for the purpose of identifying brothels in ancient Pompeii.[104]

To take just one example of what we lack in terms of evidence for identifying brothels, let us look at the question of lamps. Lamps, when placed outside the door, may have served an iconographic purpose for the Romans akin to that of our "red light," to judge from several passages from Tertullian.[105] The author inveighs in three separate places against the practice of decorating the doors and facades of houses by hanging both laurel branches and lamps (even in daytime, we are told in one text), particularly by Christians. He denounces this practice by asserting that it characterizes the adorning not just of a brothel, but a new brothel at that.

It is not precisely clear whether Tertullian is thinking of the equivalent of a "Grand Opening" etiquette for venues of prostitution, as has reasonably been proposed,[106] or is simply cautioning against presenting to the outside world any suggestion of a house-to-brothel makeover. In any case, lamps (and, if this is relevant, laurel branches) do not turn up in the archaeological record in a manner that permits us to exploit them for the purpose of identifying brothels, just as we cannot use the "red light" to identify most brothels today.[107] Tertullian's information might be dismissed as mere cliché, but it seems entirely possible that brothels were equipped with more lamps than were other establishments and/or that, unlike elsewhere, the brothel lamps were lit both day and night.[108] All the same, no one has ever succeeded in identifying a brothel using this criterion and the outlook remains bleak.

It is not always the case that students of more recent cultures are blessed with better evidence for identifying brothels. Here is a description of a room

---

name, and the number of prostitutes: Himmelfarb, "Capitol Sex" (1999) 18; Seifert et al., "House" (2000). See also Gilfoyle, *City of Eros* (1992) 331–36 (a particularly useful treatment); Hill, *Their Sisters' Keepers* (1993) 175–216; Costello, "Voices" (2000), and below in the text.

104. McDonald, "Villa or Pandokeion?" (1951) 368 with n. 13, hesitates to identify an establishment at Olynthus he views as an inn (*pandokeion*) as a brothel as well, because although it contains a mosaic inscription mentioning Aphrodite, ". . . there is no open indication of this aspect here, as there is in the seductive paintings and inscriptions in certain rooms of the *cauponae* at Pompeii."

105. So Courtney, *Commentary on Juvenal* (1980) 277, citing Tert. *Apol.* 35.4 CCSL 1.145 and *Uxorem* 2.6.1 CCSL 1.390. See also Tert. *Idololatria* 15 CCSL 2.1115–17.

106. By Spano, "Illuminazione" (1920) 36; Casson, *Travel* (1994) 211.

107. This result emerges from the extensive study by Spano, "Illuminazione" (1920) who finds copious evidence of bronze and terracotta lamps adorning the facades of all manner of shops: see esp. 10, 17–23, 25–29 (for a discussion of Tertullian's evidence, see also 33–36, 57–60).

108. See Spano, "Illuminazione" (1920) 33–36.

in a French brothel from the early twentieth century: "An iron bed with a flea-infested mattress, a wooden table, and a straw-stuffed chair were usually the only furniture in the rooms available to the inmates."[109] What is an archaeologist, if she has no other information, to conclude from this description? It seems inevitable that archaeologists will underreport the presence of brothels and not just because of the "Victorian" constraints reviewed earlier in this chapter.

DEFINING BROTHEL

I propose to address the dilemma of brothel-identification by beginning, for the sake of clarity, with what everyone will agree are the *most* certain venues for the sale of sex at Pompeii, the *cellae meretriciae* and the Purpose-Built Brothel (see figs. 3 [a crib] and 4–11 [the Purpose-Built Brothel], as well as map 2 [cribs]).[110] First, however, there is the problem, knottier than it might at first appear, of setting forth a definition of brothel.[111] A brothel for our purposes is a location open to the public where sex is the principal business or, at any rate, is a major component of the business of the place, and where two or more prostitutes can work simultaneously.[112] Such a definition is hardly to be taken for granted, however. This is clear when we consider contemporary efforts to define the brothel in counties from the state of Nevada where prostitution is legal, though heavily regulated. The statute from Storey County, for example, has the following definition for "houses of ill-fame": "any house, building, trailer (with or without wheels), vehicle, or other structure or property wherein or whereon acts of prostitution are committed, or offered to be committed."[113]

Such a definition is left deliberately vague and open-ended, because the

---

109. Corbin, *Women for Hire* (1990) 81. Cf. the inventory of furniture drawn up for a brothel in Nîmes in 1505: Otis, *Prostitution* (1985) 53.

110. I deliberately contrast my point of departure with the conclusion of Wallace-Hadrill, "Public Honour and Private Shame" (1995) 51–54, who argues that these are the *only* certain venues. Once again, his definition of brothel differs from mine, in that he would count the *cellae* as brothels: "Public Honour," 54.

111. See chap. 1.

112. For a similar definition, see Sleightholme and Sinha, *Guilty without Trial* (1996) 56.

113. Chapter 5.16.010, citing Ord. 39 Section 1, 1971. The definition of "House of Prostitution" in the Nye County ordinance is almost identical, though it does include tents: Chapter 9.20.020 subsection 11; cf. subsection 4 "Brothel." Lyon County curiously appears to avoid defining brothel entirely, preferring for the most part the euphemism "licensed operations" or the like in its statutory language. For these rules, see the Georgia Powers website (see list of abbreviations).

county's policy is to repress any sale of sex *not* under its regulatory purview. So the authorities, for the purposes of administrative (and ultimately judicial) flexibility, are both able and willing to rely on a means of identifying brothels that is simply beyond the reach of the ancient historian. A similar motive explains why the same Storey County statute establishes the following: ". . . evidence of general reputation shall be deemed competent evidence as to the question of the ill-fame."[114] Legal definitions of brothel, like those of prostitution itself, are often baldly teleological in nature.

Disagreement on how to define—and in turn identify—brothels can reign even within a culture. To illustrate this crucial point, I present the answers offered by various state courts in the nineteenth-century United States to the following question: "Does one woman resorting to a room in a building for prostitution render that house 'disorderly,' that is, a brothel in the eyes of the criminal law?"[115]

North Carolina trial court: yes
North Carolina supreme court: no
Massachusetts trial court: yes
Massachusetts supreme court: no
Michigan trial court: yes
Michigan supreme court: no

There is an evident conflict here between the trial courts, which perhaps display a more "popular" conception of what makes a brothel, and the appeals courts, which seem more concerned with the role of logic in the law.

It is also worth noting that the definition of prostitution that we choose plays at least an indirect role in the number of brothels that we identify. The broader the definition of prostitution, the more numerous the possible venues we fill find. Nevertheless, I believe the Roman evidence supports the definition of brothel that I have offered here.[116] I therefore exclude the *cellae* (cribs) from my list of possible brothels, as well as one or two other places where sex was very likely to have been for sale, out of the conviction that an analytical approach allows for a better understanding of the scale of prostitution at Pompeii. Counting a venue where one prostitute worked in the same

---

114. Chapter 5.16.040, citing Ord. 39C 1986, Ord. 39 Section 9 1970.

115. See Mackey, *Red Lights Out* (1987) 173–75 (see also 210 n. 35). Cf. Decker, *Prostitution* (1979) 129. For the classical Athenian moralist, just one "whore" might transform a home into a "house": Davidson, *Courtesans and Fishcakes* (1998) 112–13.

116. On defining prostitution, see chap. 1.

total as one where five or ten worked does not aid the cause of clarity and merely inflates the number of brothels. At the same time, most of the Pompeian brothels seem to have been relatively small, containing no more than a half-dozen prostitutes at most, so that distortion generated by a contrast in the size of brothels from large to small is minimized.[117]

Our literary and legal sources make it reasonably clear that multiple prostitutes worked in brothels, so that my definition conforms in this sense to the Roman notion of "brothel."[118] It is not, however, absolutely bound by this notion. One example of a possible contradiction comes from Ulpian's definition of pimp under the Praetor's Edict.[119] The jurist draws a distinction between a pimp who prostitutes slaves in his *peculium* (fund-for-use) as a main component of his business and one who does this as a sideline to another type of business, such as managing a tavern, inn, or bath (*caupo, stabularius, balneator*). The legal consequences are the same in all of these cases, and Ulpian is of course defining pimp and not brothel. All the same, we could argue that he is operating from a core concept of brothel and extending this concept to other establishments, at least as far as the legal implications of defining pimp under the Edict are concerned.

Ulpian's method is similar to the one he employs in another passage in which he defines prostitute under the *lex Iulia et Papia* to include not only the woman who sells herself in a *lupanarium* but also the one who does so, for example, in a *taberna cauponia*: both are liable under the law's marriage prohibitions.[120] The aim here is to define prostitute, and not brothel, though the jurist does appear to depart from a notional distinction between brothel and tavern. He makes the relatively rare suggestion that the paradigmatic *lupanar/lupanarium* did not embrace the tavern. Ulpian, who is chiefly interested in the prostitute, does not draw any consequences at law from this, however, and it might even be said that he broadens the concept of brothel through the

---

117. Cf. chap. 6, where a generous notional average of four prostitutes per brothel is adopted.

118. For the sources, see chaps. 1 and 3 and the discussion in the first appendix. On the importance of a culturally specific concept of "brothel," see P. Schuster, *Frauenhaus* (1992) 31–35; B. Schuster, *Freien Frauen* (1995) 12. An example may be taken from the complex scheme for classification of brothels in the licensed district of Yoshiwara in seventeenth- and eighteenth-century Japan, which depended on the type of courtesan, the size of the establishment, as well as the style of construction of an internal partition: see Seigle, *Yoshiwara* (1993) 233–35.

119. Ulp. D. 3.2.4.2.

120. Ulp. D. 23.2.43 pr.; see also 9 for a similar implication regarding the definition of procuress. Even the woman who operates a *caupona* with prostitutes qualifies as a *lena* under the marriage law. Cf. Viv.-Cels.-Ulp. D. 4.8.21.11; Alex. Sev. C. 4.56.3 (a. 225).

inclusion of one or more new types of establishments, at least for the purpose of the Augustan marriage legislation.

All the same, even if we accept Ulpian's reasoning in a fairly broad sense, the postulated extension of the concept of "brothel" to baths in his fragment from the commentary on the Edict goes too far for us in most cases, for reasons explored below. As for the evidence from literature, this is so riddled with cliché that, used incautiously, it would place undue limits on its application to the archaeological evidence.[121] For that reason, a somewhat broader definition than the one that is implied by the literary sources is desirable here.

My definition is an expansive one in that it does not attempt to distinguish between primary and secondary venues of prostitution.[122] There are two reasons for this. First, the Pompeian evidence does not as a rule allow us to distinguish a "brothel" from, say, a *caupona* when the brothel is in the back and/or upstairs. These represent at most subtypes of brothel. Second, such a distinction is unnecessary for the argument that the Romans did not know moral zoning, which is the main thesis of this book: for this latter purpose, to underline the point, cribs count as well. It would make no sense to zone one subtype of brothel and ignore others, as well as the cribs.

I confess to inconsistency in that I do not, in principle, include public buildings (e.g., baths), where prostitution was commonly practiced in my definition of brothel. I do this because prostitution rarely qualifies as the main or a major business of the bath and so fails to meet my definition of brothel.[123] Such edifices are unlikely to preserve archaeological evidence of the practice of prostitution, making it impossible to measure the extent, or even mark the presence, of prostitution at most sites. Even if we do not consider them—for the most part—to be brothels, however, the literary evidence for the practice of prostitution in baths is strong enough to cast doubt on any theory of zoning. They functioned in this sense in a manner analogous to that of cribs, which were not brothels and yet are highly relevant to the question of segregating prostitution. This is so in spite of the fact that we can rarely be certain as to

---

121. See chap. 9 and the first appendix.

122. See Hill, *Their Sisters' Keepers* (1993) 196, for the distinction—in nineteenth-century New York City—between, on the one hand, establishments such as the brothel, the prostitution-boarding house, and the assignation-house, all devoted to the express purpose of selling sex, and, on the other hand, other places of public entertainment, such as saloons, theaters, concert halls, and dance halls, which ostensibly served other commercial functions.

123. Prostitution is found in baths in a variety of cultures, such as ancient Greece, and medieval England, France, Germany, and Japan: Otis, *Prostitution* (1985) 98–99; Geremek, *Margins* (1987) 220; Seigle, *Yoshiwara* (1993) 45; Karras, *Common Women* (1996) index s.v. "Stews"; Kurke, *Coins* (1999) 199. On medieval Germany, see below in the text.

precisely which baths had prostitutes working in them and which did not.[124]

The problem with identifying baths as brothels also holds for the *cauponae, popinae,* and *deversoria.* For all of these types of establishment, the possibility that sex was sold on site should not be completely dismissed in some doubtful instances. That does not necessarily make them brothels under my definition, which requires sale of sex as a major component of the business. A specific example of the sale of sex as a possible sideline to a larger business occurs with the Sarno Baths at Pompeii, discussed below.

Like baths, *popinae* and *cauponae* would, we can reasonably assume, often have had a sexually charged atmosphere, like their modern counterparts, bars.[125] A factor to consider is the presence of waitresses assumed by their male customers to be sexually available and, if the modern parallel holds true, dependent on them for a share of their income, perhaps in the form of tips.[126] The physical proximity of waitresses to their customers when dispensing alcohol meant that they would have had to manage a balance between distance and intimacy that at times tipped toward prostitution.[127] In *popinae* and *cauponae,* the role of liquor would have functioned like that of nudity (or near-nudity) at the baths in fostering this kind of atmospheric.[128] The modern phenomenon of stripper bars perhaps conveys this idea most acutely, though it must always be kept in mind, as we saw in chapter 2, that baths alone of this group were respectable places for members of the elite. In most cases involving *popinae, cauponae, deversoria,* and baths, we are strictly uncertain about the presence of prostitution.[129] I deal with this uncertainty by placing all Pompeian baths in operation near the time of the city's demise on the maps I

---

124. See the evidence collected by Fagan, *Bathing in Public* (1999) esp. 34–36. The issue is complicated by the fact that prostitutes at times attended the baths not to work but to bathe (see, e.g., Plaut. *Truc.* 324–25; Mart. 2.52, with Fagan, 45) and that at least some of the ambiguous evidence for their presence there might be explained by this factor. For more discussion of baths as venues for prostitution, see chap. 2.

125. See Prus and Irini, *Hookers* (1980) 116–17, 178–79, 202, 204, on the erotic atmospherics of twentieth-century bars. The authors find little or no substantive difference in the behavior of staff across different types of bars, meaning those with a reputation as havens for prostitution and notionally more respectable places: 189 with n. 40, 191.

126. On this assumption in antiquity, see McGinn, "Definition" (1997 [1998]). I know of no evidence for tips from antiquity, but believe that the crucial point in the next sentence in the text still holds.

127. See Prus and Irini, *Hookers* (1980) 148, 157–59, 168–74.

128. See Prus and Irini, *Hookers* (1980) 175.

129. Cf. the medieval English tavern, where every female role might be suspected of involving prostitution: Hanawalt, *Repute* (1998) 108–9.

fig. 1. Entrance to Tavern-Brothel cat. No. 12, with counter and oven

fig. 2. Paintings of eating, drinking, and gambling on the south wall of Room b in Tavern-Brothel cat. no. 12

fig. 3: Crib at 7.11.12, with masonry bed

fig. 4: The Purpose-Built Brothel cat. nos. 26/27: Exterior view with modern scaffolding

fig. 5: The Purpose-Built Brothel cat.
nos. 26/27: Downstairs corridor showing
erotic panels and *cellae*

fig. 6: The Purpose-Built Brothel cat.
nos. 26/27: Downstairs *cella* with
masonry bed

fig. 7: The Purpose-Built Brothel cat. nos. 26/27: Downstairs panel with male-female couple making love on bed

fig. 8: The Purpose-Built Brothel cat. nos. 26/27: Downstairs panel with male-female couple making love on bed

fig. 9: The Purpose-Built Brothel cat. nos. 26/27: Downstairs panel with male-female couple making love on bed

fig. 10: The Purpose-Built Brothel cat. nos. 26/27: Downstairs panel with male-female couple reclining on bed, gazing at erotic (?) panel

fig. 11: The Purpose-Built Brothel cat. nos. 26/27: Downstairs panel of Priapus

fig. 12: The Suburban Baths cat. no. 32: Exterior view

fig.13: The Suburban Baths cat. no. 32: General view of *Apodyterium*

fig. 14: The Suburban Baths cat. no. 32: *Apodyterium* panel of two males and a female making love on bed

fig. 15: The Suburban Baths cat. no. 32: *Apodyterium* panel of male-female couple making love on bed (with evidence of more recent overpainting on the right)

fig. 16: The Suburban Baths cat. no. 32: *Apodyterium* erotic panels above paintings of numbered clothes-boxes (left side)

fig. 17: The Suburban Baths cat. no. 32: *Apodyterium* erotic panels above paintings of numbered clothes-boxes (right side)

fig. 18: House of the Vettii, Room x^I, west wall: Panel of male-female couple making love on bed (possible "sex club")

fig. 19: House of the Vettii, Room x^I, general view (possible "sex club")

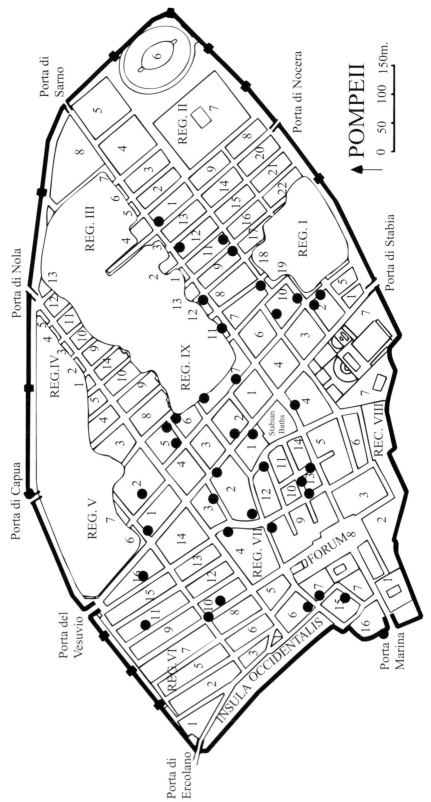

Map 1: Possible brothels

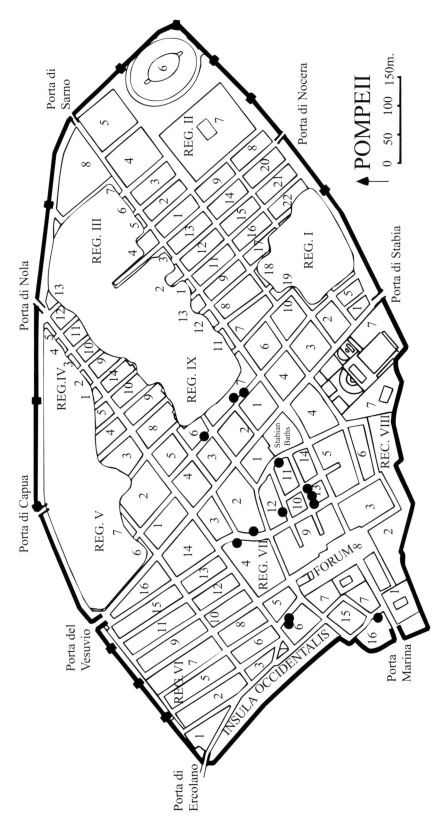

POMPEII

0　50　100　150m.

Porta di Sarno

Porta di Nocera

Porta di Stabia

Porta di Nola

Porta di Capua

Porta del Vesuvio

Porta di Ercolano

Porta Marina

REG. II

REG. III

REG. I

REG. IX

REG.IV

REG. V

REG. VI

REG. VII

REG. VIII

FORUM

Stabian Baths

INSULA OCCIDENTALIS

Map 2: Possible cribs

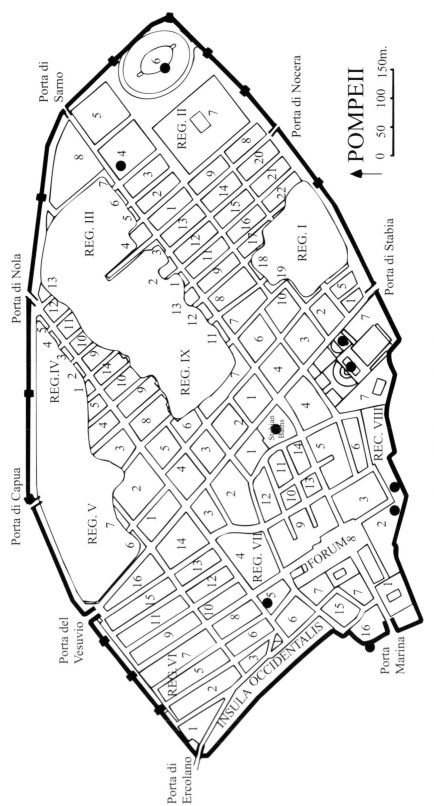

Map 3: Baths, theaters, and amphitheater

POMPEII

0 50 100 150m.

Porta di Sarno

Porta di Nocera

Porta di Stabia

Porta di Nola

Porta di Capua

Porta del Vesuvio

Porta di Ercolano

Porta Marina

REG. II

REG. III

REG. I

REG. IX

REG.IV

REG. V

REG. VI

REG. VII

REG. VIII

Stabian Baths

FORUM

INSULA OCCIDENTALIS

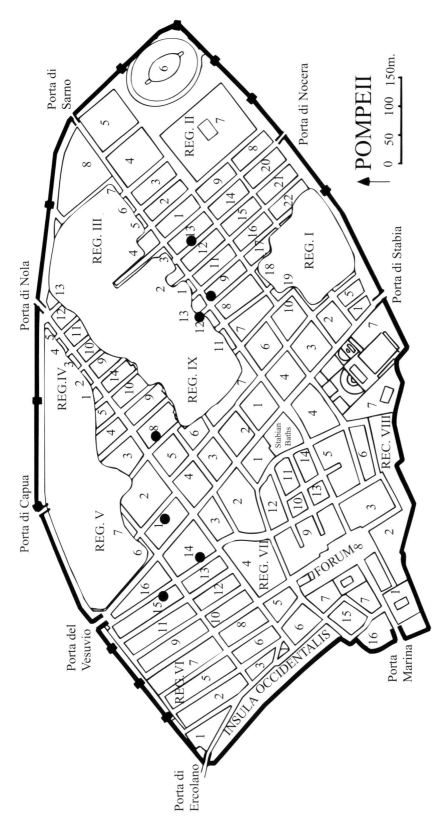

Map 4: Possible "sex clubs"

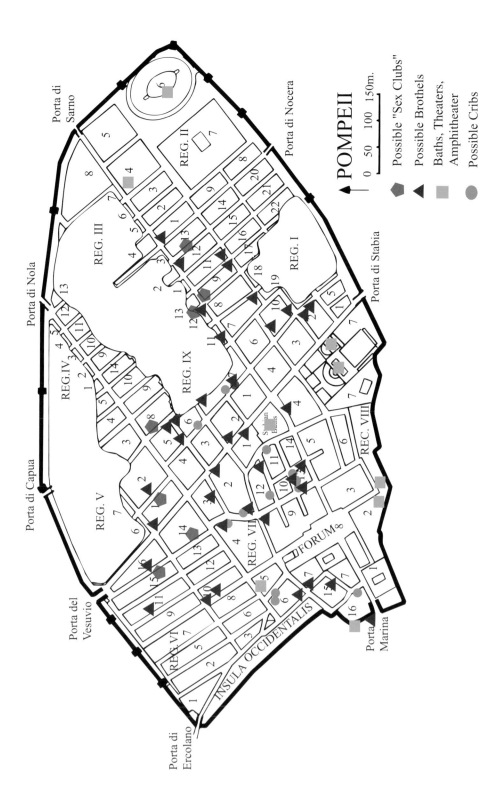

POMPEII

0   50   100 150m.

◆ Possible "Sex Clubs"

▲ Possible Brothels

■ Baths, Theaters, Amphitheater

● Possible Cribs

Map 5: Composite map of possible venues for prostitution

include in this book, but indicating only those taverns that might actually be brothels (see maps 1, 3, and 5).

When we attempt to link baths with brothels, we experience a few near misses, which are worth citing in order to drive home the difficulty inherent in making such connections. First, at Roman Ephesus an inscription that appears to mention a brothel has been found, while the brothel itself remains impossible to locate.[130] At Ostia, a mosaic inscription in the Trinacrian Baths commemorating the "meeting place of cunt-lickers" ("statio cunnulingiorum") is better understood as a joking reference to the clubhouses of merchants and members of the *collegia* than as evidence of venal sex on the premises.[131] At most the epigraph helps confirm the idea that baths were highly sexualized places.

An even less likely example comes from late-antique Ascalon (Ashkelon) in Palestine, where archaeologists have raised the possibility that a fourth-century bath might have also functioned as a brothel.[132] Aside from a fragmentary Greek inscription found on a plastered panel of a bathtub that read "*eiselthe apolauson kai* [. . . .]" ("Enter, enjoy, and [. . . .]") which, as the principal author of this theory acknowledges, might have been found in almost any bath in the eastern half of the Empire, the excavators found the remains of nearly one hundred newborns in a sewer under the bathhouse.

Unfortunately, there are more plausible explanations for this burial than that prostitutes working in the bathhouse placed their newborn babies there. More likely, the local community buried in this place babies who were stillborn, cut down by an epidemic (older children were presumably buried elsewhere), and/or victims of infanticide. At the site in Ascalon we have no satisfactory epigraphic evidence, no erotic art, and no remains of rooms or beds that might have been used for sex to suggest the presence of prostitution. We are not even certain whether the bathhouse was public or private. To admit this bath as a brothel, we would almost have to identify all baths in the Roman world as brothels, including a recent example asserted for Thessalonica. Here too there is no evidence to justify identifying the bath as a brothel, apart from the presence of a bath.[133] On the other hand, I hasten to add, we cannot prove

---

130. See the discussion of this site in chap. 8.

131. See Pavolini, *Ostia*³ (1989) 130; Jacobelli, *Terme Suburbane* (1995) 46–47; Scarano Ussani, "*Lenocinium*" (2000) 262 n. 93; Clarke, "Laughing" (2002) 180 n. 32.

132. Stager, "Eroticism and Infanticide at Ashkelon" (1991) 45–46. In this article, the author, to be sure, suggests the presence of a brothel and then backs away from the brothel-identification. It is accepted, however, by Dauphin, "Bordels" (1998) 189–90.

133. See Stavrakakis, "Brothel" (1998).

that prostitution was *not* practiced here, or at any other bath catering to male clients.

To make a point that is explored at greater length in chapter 2, baths were, apart from the issue of prostitution, highly sexualized places, and they might easily acquire a reputation as centers of prostitution, especially if both sexes were present. Peter Schuster makes an interesting argument along these lines for the baths of medieval Germany, which have been regarded by contemporary moralists and modern scholars as havens for venal sex. Schuster holds that this was in fact a fantasy—unlike in the case of baths in southern France of the same period, which did in fact function as brothels—promoted if not created by critics agog at the eroticism inherent in the enterprise.[134] The argument, despite its difficulties, makes for a good point.[135] We encounter more or less the same problem as the medievalist in our evaluation of Roman baths as havens of prostitution or loci of male fantasy about sexually available women. But in our case, the evidence is much, much more meager.

At Pompeii, the case of the Suburban Baths perhaps illustrates the problem of identifying baths as brothels most clearly. All three criteria for brothel-identification are found scattered throughout the complex, and so do not line up as neatly as we would like. Still, the possible presence of semiseparate facilities on-site makes, not precisely the Baths themselves, but an upstairs residential area a strong candidate for inclusion on the list of Pompeian brothels.[136]

The quality of the evidence, poor as it is, makes it worthwhile for us to focus on this one example. The changing room of the Baths (*apodyterium*) contains some notably erotic paintings, which are explicit to the point of being over the top (see figs. 13–17).[137] The jurist Ulpian, when defining "pimp" in the context of the Praetor's Edict, mentions ". . . the bath-manager who, as is the practice in certain provinces, keeps in his baths slaves hired to watch over clothing and they ply this sort of trade in the workplace. . . ."[138] There is in fact a great deal of literary evidence for sex, and specifically prostitution, in the Roman baths, as seen in chapter 2. As noted in appendix 1, the location shows a few sexual graffiti, including a prostitute's price. Finally, the upper-level complex of apartments, connected to the *apodyterium*, but also

---

134. Schuster, *Frauenhaus* (1992) 129–33.

135. For evidence that prostitution was in fact practiced in medieval German baths, see B. Schuster, *Freien Frauen* (1995) 217–21.

136. See cat. no. 32 in appendix 1.

137. See the discussion in chap. 4.

138. Ulp. (6 *ad edictum*) D. 3.2.4.2: ". . . sive balneator fuerit, velut in quibusdam provinciis fit, in balineis ad custodienda vestimenta conducta habens mancipia hoc genus observantia in officina. . . .", with McGinn, *Prostitution, Sexuality, and the Law* (1998) 53–58.

equipped with an independent street entrance, seems a very likely venue for the sale of sex.

The conclusion is easy to criticize. The evidence relevant to the three criteria—graffiti, art, and design—is scattered throughout the complex, instead of cohering in one part of it. The evidence for the design-criterion is weak, insofar as there are no masonry beds and no obvious *cellae*, as in the Purpose-Built Brothel. The graffiti are hardly numerous, and, for the most part, they are not very clear. The art is perhaps a bit *too* erotic, if we agree with the point, advanced in earlier chapters, that over-the-top presentations were intended to provoke mirth, rather than sexual arousal, in many or even most viewers. There is also the problem that sex seems unlikely to have been sold in the *apodyterium* itself, which must reduce the probative value of the paintings, even if we concede that their content is suitable for a brothel. As for Ulpian's locker-room prostitutes, we can perhaps ignore his implication that this is provincial, as opposed to Roman or Italian, usage. Pompeii no longer existed in his day, anyway. But it seems highly unlikely that every bath complex sponsored prostitution, and he in no way implies that every changing room contained prostitutes. How can we be certain then that prostitutes plied their trade in this location?

Perhaps in this case we are being far too skeptical. Though the evidence is uncertain enough to deny the Suburban Bath complex status as a "definite" brothel, it is adequate to characterize it as "more likely" than not a brothel. The archaeological evidence may be as good as we can ever reasonably expect to get from such an establishment. In fact, it is better than any other bath complex excavated thus far at Pompeii, Herculaneum, or elsewhere in the Roman world. What distinguishes this location as a brothel, and not merely as baths with prostitutes operating in or near them, is precisely the feature of a quasi-independent residential quarters, quasi-independent in the sense that it is accessible both from the baths and from the street. The same person or persons, however, would have owned both baths and brothel.[139]

A more difficult example, again from Pompeii, is the series of seven (or more) small rooms at the privately owned Sarno Baths, which possibly were intended to serve as venues for venal sex.[140] If so, the fact that these cubicles,

---

139. See the discussion of the Purpose-Built Brothel in chap. 8 for the legal principle. For the evidence of private ownership of the Suburban Baths, see Jacobelli, *Terme Suburbane* (1995) 20. On the basis of a comparison with the Purpose-Built Brothel, Clarke, "Laughing" (2002) 151–55 argues that there is no brothel here. In my view, it is unsafe to generalize from that example in attempting to identify other brothels: chap. 8.

140. In regard to the Sarno Baths, I prefer the cautious acceptance by Koloski Ostrow, *Sarno Bath Complex* (1990) 94–95 and by Fagan, *Bathing in Public* (1999) 67, against what I regard as the

though secluded, were not as isolated from the baths proper as the residential quarters were atop the Suburban Baths, suggests the practice of prostitution was merely a sideline in the context of the baths themselves. These small rooms very likely had other uses, such as massage, besides prostitution. All of this makes it difficult for us to characterize the Sarno Baths as a brothel. Complicating matters still further is the fact that these baths were under construction at the time of Vesuvius' eruption.[141] Expert opinion, however, does hold it possible that visitors enjoyed access to the cubicles and the surrounding area by then.[142]

There are other examples where the possibility of prostitution has been detected at baths open to the public but caution militates against identification of the baths as brothels. These include two small rows of rooms flanking the *apodyterium* of the Baths of Faustina at Miletus.[143] Another is the Suburban Baths of Herculaneum, where epigraphs seem to testify to the availability of on-site sex.[144]

One more example exists at Pompeii of a privately owned bath complex that, like the Sarno Baths, may have accommodated prostitution as a sideline, though the evidence is even more tenuous. This is the complex located near the amphitheater known as the *Praedia Iuliae Felicis* (2.4.4, 6), which advertises a *balneum* described (in part) as *venerium*.[145] This adjective does not necessarily stand as a specific or exclusive reference to prostitution, but may communicate broadly a sense of the availability of sexual pleasure.[146] The matter is far from clear.[147]

Unlikely as a brothel, but still worth mentioning as a possible venue for

---

hyperskepticism of Ioppolo, *Terme del Sarno* (1992) 70–75 (who would raise the number of rooms in question from seven to nine); Savunen, *Women* (1997) 114 n. 174.

141. See Fagan, *Bathing in Public* (1999) 66–67, who emphasizes that the connection between the Sarno Baths and the nearby Palaestra Baths, which were in operation in 79, remains unclear (see below).

142. Koloski Ostrow, *Sarno Bath Complex* (1990) 53.

143. See Guzzo and Scarano Ussani, *Veneris Figurae* (2001) 70 n. 87. For similar structures in baths at Tarracina and Magnesia-on-the-Meander, see Fagan, *Bathing in Public* (1999) 67 n. 92.

144. Jacobelli, *Terme Suburbane* (1995) 97; Guzzo and Scarano Ussani, *Veneris figurae* (2000) 21.

145. *CIL* 4.1136.

146. Thus I agree with Pirson, *Mietwohnungen* (1999) 19, that the adjective need not refer to prostitution, at least not exclusively so. Perhaps the word has a double meaning here, referring both to the luxurious accommodation and to sexual pleasure. This would explain why the adjective was used instead of a substantive (i.e., *Veneris*), which we might otherwise expect on the basis of the comparative evidence cited by Pirson.

147. For attempts to elucidate the meaning of the adjectives *venerium* and *nongentum* (the latter is even murkier than the former) in describing this *balneum,* see Fagan, *Bathing in Public* (1999) 318–19.

prostitution, are the Stabian Baths, also of Pompeii. It appears that some erotic art was found in a *nymphaeum* in the complex, though the art has long since disappeared without being properly documented.[148] It is uncertain whether facilities for venal sex, like those postulated for the Sarno Baths, were available on-site.[149] What is really striking about these baths is their location, not simply in the center of the city, but in the midst of an area thickly populated by brothels, cribs, taverns, and hotels.[150] This hardly makes the Stabian Baths a brothel, but does put the complex on the map of prostitution at Pompeii.

The discussion of the uses and limits of the archaeological evidence in defining and identifying baths as brothels suggests the possible utility of setting forth the status of baths as possible venues for prostitution from our single richest source for such evidence, the city of Pompeii. It is necessary, however, to omit examples that had long since ceased operating at the time of the eruption, such as evidently the Republican Baths, as well as those that were incomplete at that time, namely the Central Baths, and those whose location is not known, such as the Baths of M. Crassus Frugi (thought to have been outside the city).[151] This leaves us with six sites for baths that were accessible to the public in Pompeii in the mid-first century A.D., though not all of these sites may have been operating precisely in 79 owing to seismic damage caused in or after 62 (see maps 3 and 5):[152]

- The Forum Baths (7.5.2, 7–8, 10, 12, 24)
- The Baths of Julia Felix (2.4.4, 6)
- The Palaestra Baths (8.2.22–24)
- The Sarno Baths (8.2.17–20)
- The Stabian Baths (7.1.8, 14–15, 17, 48, 50–51)
- The Suburban Baths (7.16.A)

The evidence for prostitution differs from place to place. There is no direct evidence for the Forum Baths, and that for the privately owned Baths of Julia Felix is very thin indeed.

For the privately owned Palaestra Baths, we depend on an inference that

---

148. See Jacobelli, *Terme Suburbane* (1995) 10.
149. The Stabian Baths did have a row of secluded cubicles, which evidently included tubs for individual bathers, according to Fagan, *Bathing in Public* (1999) 67.
150. See chap. 8.
151. See Fagan, *Bathing in Public* (1999) 59–67.
152. See Fagan, *Bathing in Public* (1999) 64–65.

can be drawn from the seven (or nine) cubicles in the nearby Sarno Baths, which were also privately owned. As seen in the notes above, the relationship between these two baths remains to be clarified. I think it fair to suppose, however, that whether or not they were meant to be part of the same complex, merely had the same owner, or were in fact business rivals, the result for us is the same, in that the possible presence of prostitutes at the one spells the same possibility for the other. The cubicles in the Sarno complex may have been intended to supplement, or to surpass, whatever facilities for paid sex, if any, were available at the Palaestra Baths. This is not to deny that the evidence is thin and that it is hardly any better for the Stabian Baths. In fact, the privately owned Suburban Baths are among the baths the only example of a possible brothel, in my view.

How do we reconcile this poor showing with the thrust of the literary evidence for prostitution in baths, which I set forth in chapter 2? It seems that most baths fall into a different category than brothels, regardless of whether they contained on-site facilities for prostitution or did not. They were likely places for prostitutes to meet clients, even if the operators of the baths did not themselves sponsor prostitution. So it seems right that they take their place on the map of possible venues for the sale of sex, provided that they are distinguished from brothels in most cases.

As we have seen above in this section, the relationship between baths and prostitution is not exactly unique. A similar argument might be made regarding taverns, for example, which also might have been havens for prostitutes even if not they did not qualify as brothels. In this case, however, the Pompeian evidence does allow us to draw a more satisfactory distinction between tavern-brothels and other kinds of taverns. Though we can never be absolutely sure that the latter were in each and every case free of prostitutes, the archaeological evidence for prostitution in taverns does a better, by which I simply mean more adequate, job of accounting for what the texts tell us, so that we can more confidently set them aside where explicit evidence is lacking. That approach does not seem prudent in the case of baths.

Baths join some other places of public resort that, again on the basis of the literary evidence, we may reasonably suppose functioned in a similar fashion in regard to prostitution, at least on the occasion of a public performance. These are the two theaters (8.7.20–21, 27, 30; 8.7.17–20) and the amphitheater (2.6.1–11). All may be found on map 3 and again on the composite map 5.

So much can be said for the definition of brothel. Beyond this, I make no claims. Unfortunately, this definition, like any reasonable alternative one might propose, will not get us very far, as we shall see in chapter 8, where the problem of defining and identifying brothels is put to the test.

CRIBS

The *cella meretricia*, or crib, is an important nonbrothel venue for prostitution (see fig. 3 and maps 2 and 5). The crib was a single room used by a lone pros-titute (or perhaps more than one working in shifts) to entertain customers, and it often opened directly onto the street. Since Hans Eschebach compiled a list of them in 1970, there has been general agreement on the number and location of the *cellae meretriciae*,[153] with only two new candidates proposed by Liselotte Eschebach in 1993.[154] What makes the identification convincing is not so much the presence of a masonry bed,[155] but the presence of a single small room with direct access to the street. This corresponds closely with what in another culture is termed a "crib," signifying a small, crude building or room which is used by a prostitute who does not work in a brothel and which is often clustered with other cribs in an alley or along a roadway.[156]

I introduce this term because it is convenient to do so and for the same reason continue to use the phrase *cella meretricia*, though I have not been able to find attestation of the latter in the ancient evidence.[157] It seems doubtful in any case that we would find this phrase used in a technical sense for the facil-ity described here. When used to refer to a facility for prostitution, *cella* refers invariably to a booth in a brothel.[158] *Calyba*, featured in the *Copa* attributed to Vergil, appears to be a literary version of this.[159] This also seems true of *mer-itorium* as it appears in the scholia to Juvenal, if it does not simply mean "brothel."[160] *Pergula* in Plautus may also refer to a crib, perhaps at the back of a shop or tavern.[161]

---

153. The 1970 list of *cellae meretriciae* consists of 7.4.42, 7.11.12, 7.12.33, 7.13.15, and 16 and 19, 9.6.2, 9.7.15, and 17.

154. Eschebach and Müller-Trollius, *Gebäudeverzeichnis* (1993) 492: 7.2.28 and 7.16.8. The former, which may have been associated with the brothel at 7.2.32–33, is identified as a public latrine at Pugliese Carratelli, *Pompei 6* (1996) 718.

155. Only 7.16.8 seems to lack this feature, at least among the group of those *cellae* already identified: see Eschebach and Müller-Trollius, *Gebäudeverzeichnis* (1993) 347. The point is that a masonry bed is a sine qua non either for brothel or crib.

156. For the crib, a common feature in American frontier towns of the nineteenth century, and elsewhere as well, see Symanski, "Prostitution in Nevada" (1974) 357; Goldman, *Gold Dig-gers* (1981) 74, 93, 147; Butler, *Daughters of Joy* (1985) xviii, 60, 86; Otis, *Prostitution* (1985) 53 (described here as "huts"); Mackey, *Red Lights Out* (1987) 192, 195–96; Hill, *Their Sisters' Keepers* (1993) 223, 226; Bernstein, *Sonia's Daughters* (1995) 153; Davidson, *Courtesans and Fishcakes* (1998) 90–91; Cohen, "Economic Analysis" (forthcoming).

157. See, for example, *TLL* s.v. "cella, meretricius."

158. See, for example, Petron. 8; Iuv. 6.122, 128.

159. [Verg.] *Copa* 7 (cf. *calybita* at 25). See Goodyear, "Copa" (1977) 125; Franzoi, *Copa* (1988) 68, 86; Rosivach, "Sociology" (1996) 609–10.

160. Schol. *ad Iuv. 125, 127*. Cf. *HA Tac.* 10.2, where *meritoria* must mean "brothels."

161. Plaut. *Pseud.* 214, 229.

Of the eleven Pompeian cribs known up to this date, five are clustered together in two groups of three and two respectively,[162] while two others are in close proximity to the Purpose-Built Brothel.[163] Their location suggests they were used by prostitutes rather than by watchmen, for example.[164] My knowledge of Pompeian topography is not adequate to inspire confidence that these eleven examples exhaust the range of possibilities for Pompeian cribs. The (re)excavation of various sites might turn up more examples. A more expedient procedure would be to survey these eleven sites and then to look for other candidates whose dimensions and layout correspond closely. The presence of a masonry bed should not be an absolute requirement. All known examples appear to be located on the ground floor of a building; owing to the destruction pattern in Pompeii, where even second stories are rare to find, we will never know how many upstairs cribs we are missing.

The possibility of another subtype of crib, not directly accessible to the street, but located in the back room of a bar, is offered by two examples found adjacent to each other at 7.6.14–15. These have together been identified as a brothel on the basis of their decoration with erotic art.[165] The two taverns are joined together, and each has a back room in which sex might have been sold. Therefore, they may be identified as a brothel only if we use the most technical of definitions. It seems better to classify them as cribs, since explicit recognition might facilitate the discovery of new specimens.[166] Thus the number of cribs now rises to a minimum of thirteen.

What sorts of prostitutes used cribs in Pompeii? Direct evidence is lacking, but it seems unlikely that most of them were affiliated with brothels. Streetwalkers and waitresses working in bars and restaurants without on-site facilities for the sale of sex are leading candidates.[167] Such prostitutes may also have

---

162. 7.13.15 and 16 and 19; 9.7.15 and 17.

163. 7.11.12; 7.12.33. 7.2.28 is not that far removed; 7.16.8 is located near a town gate.

164. Byzantine prostitution knew the *kellion* (derived from the Latin *cella*), also called the *tamieion*, which has been identified as a room for sex in a prostitute's house, but which in some cases at least might have been a crib in the sense described here: evidence and discussion in Leontsini, *Prostitution* (1989) 59–60, 104. We cannot exclude the notion that at times these cribs were used for storage rather than for sex, as Wallace-Hadrill, p.c., suggests to me.

165. By A. De Vos and M. De Vos, *Pompei* (1982) 52; Jacobelli, *Terme Suburbane* (1995) 96.

166. It is almost possible to identify the crib at 7.13.19 as an intermediate subtype between these two; though it opens on to the street, it is part of the same building plot as the possible tavern-brothel at 7.13.20–21 (see cat. no. 30): see the reconstruction by Pirson, *Mietwohnungen* (1999) 154.

167. Waitresses in nineteenth-century Parisian brasseries are thought to have worked mainly as prostitutes, though they often went off-site to service their clients: Clayson, *Painted Love* (1991) 138–42. For a contemporary parallel from New York City, see Hill, *Their Sisters' Keepers* (1993) 206. And from York in that period, see Finnegan, *Poverty* (1979) 61, 93, 102.

taken their clients to brothels or hotels.[168] In other words, the client would be
expected to pay for the room as well as sex with a woman who worked independently, or quasi-independently, of the brothel itself. Another conclusion
to draw is that there is little to distinguish, even if we accept Tönnes Kleberg's
characterization of the first as offering food, drink, and lodging and the second
only food and drink, between *cauponae* and *popinae* as centers for prostitution,
if members of the staff did indeed sell sex.[169] What makes examples of either
type brothels or cribs is the presence of on-site facilities for this purpose.

ADULTERY AND BROTHELS

The idea that some prostitutes more or less freelanced in brothels is suggested
by Juvenal's tale of the empress Messalina setting up shop in one, though most
historians now would not accept this story as literal truth.[170] Some brothel-
prostitutes may have solicited on the street as well. We also know that brothels functioned in part as assignation-houses. This is securely attested, I believe,
by the incident recounted by Petronius, where a prostitute charges the com-
panion of Ascyltos for the use of a room (*cella*).[171]

Occasional use of brothels for such purposes perhaps helped fuel the recur-
rent fantasy (realized by Caligula, at any rate) that respectable women worked
in them as prostitutes.[172] This fantasy is reflected in the idea, popular with the
writers of Comedy but above all with the declaimers, that adultery committed
in a brothel was not in fact adultery.[173] This notion is consistent of course with
the exemptions for prostitutes and their partners from the criminal penalties
that came to be enacted in the Augustan law on adultery.[174] The idea that
paid sex in a brothel could not qualify as adultery was a popular one in
medieval Germany, though there it was the status of the *male* partner (as a
married man) to the act that determined the issue of liability, an interesting
departure from the Roman model.[175]

---

168. An obvious point, but the reader might still with profit consult Prus and Irini, *Hookers*
(1980) 15.

169. For Kleberg's distinction between *cauponae* and *popinae* see *Hôtels* (1957) 17. On the
validity of such distinctions, see chap. 2. For the point about sale of sex, see Scarano Ussani,
"*Lenocinium*" (2000) 256 (257) n. 9.

170. Iuv. 6.115–32.

171. Petron. 8.

172. For evidence and discussion, see McGinn, "Caligula's Brothel" (1998).

173. This idea does provide a kind of popular pretext for the exemption of prostitutes from
penalty under the adultery law of Augustus: evidence and discussion at McGinn, *Prostitution, Sexuality, and the Law* (1998) 198.

174. McGinn, *Prostitution, Sexuality, and the Law* (1998) 194–202.

175. Schuster, *Frauenhaus* (1992) 61, 116–17, 216.

In the *Story of Apollonius of Tyre*, the idea that Tarsia's recounting of her noble lineage and cruel fate deterred, rather than encouraged, the men who approached her in a brothel, including the pimp's henchman, the brothel-manager (*villicus puellarum*), may safely be reckoned among the more miraculous aspects of that tale.[176] The cynicism displayed by Seneca's declaimers at the would-be priestess' allegation that she similarly fended off clients is telling in this regard.[177] It presents itself as a convincing reflection of the psychology of the vast majority of patrons of Roman brothels. The chance—however remote—of enjoying or humiliating a woman of higher status is very likely to have attracted many Roman men to the brothel in the first place.[178]

The line between brothels and assignation-houses is a thin one in many cultures.[179] What is more, in a Roman context, it makes sense that the latter would have operated discreetly, that is, as brothels, in light of the harsh punishment stipulated for persons who furnished venues to violators of the Augustan law on adultery.[180] The fact that brothels might have accommodated non-commercial sexual trysts means of course that we cannot strictly calculate numbers of prostitutes by counting cubicles and cribs. This does not, however, mean that the facilities outnumbered the personnel, since it is quite possible that some prostitutes worked in shifts.[181] And, surely, resort to brothels by adulterous couples did not have to be all that commonplace, in the sense of statistically significant, to ensure the notoriety of this practice.[182] Its role in the fantasy life surrounding the brothel was without doubt the most important aspect, as images and imaginings of sex with upper-class women came to be

---

176. *Hist. Ap. Tyr.* 34–36.

177. Sen. *Contr.* 1.2.

178. See Roper, "Discipline and Respectability" (1985) 20, on the similar attraction of the brothel in late medieval Germany. Schuster, *Freien Frauen* (1995) 239, tells of a procuress in fourteenth-century Nuremberg who pretended to set her out-of-town clients up with the wives and daughters of the elite, whereas in fact these women were only spruced-up prostitutes. When these men returned home to their own cities to brag about their "conquests," word eventually got back to the town council of Nuremberg, brewing trouble quickly.

179. On assignation-houses (and brothels that have functioned as such), see Harsin, *Policing Prostitution* (1985) 246; Schuster, *Frauenhaus* (1992) 124; Hill, *Their Sisters' Keepers* (1993) 93–94, 198; Karras, *Common Women* (1996) 67.

180. On the offense of *domum praebere* under the *lex Iulia* on adultery, interpreted extensively by the jurists, see McGinn, *Prostitution, Sexuality, and the Law* (1998) index of subjects s.h.v.

181. See Hill, *Their Sisters' Keepers* (1993) 223.

182. On the assignation-house as a locus for male fantasy and fear in nineteenth-century New York City, see Hill, *Their Sisters' Keepers* (1993) 382.

reflected in brothel decoration.[183] What drew men to the brothel aside from sexual pleasure was the pleasure of transgression, real or imagined, seasoned with the spice of possible danger.[184]

183. See chaps. 4 and 8. See Hershatter, *Dangerous Pleasures* (1997) 45, on the attraction of the trysting house in early twentieth-century Shanghai: ". . . within its walls a man could sleep with another man's concubine or the daughter of a respectable family."

184. See Hershatter, *Dangerous Pleasures* (1997) esp. 50–51.

Chapter Eight

THE BEST OF ALL
POSSIBLE BROTHELS

OUT OF POMPEII

The uniqueness, not to say the utility, of the Purpose-Built Brothel at Pompeii can be appreciated best through comparison not just with other brothels in Pompeii, but with evidence from elsewhere in the Roman world. We can safely conclude that the practice of prostitution was widespread in that world, though its extent was doubtless exaggerated by moralists.[1] Sex, a point that cannot adequately be emphasized, does not require a brothel to be sold. And yet it is greatly disappointing how little good evidence we have for brothels beyond the false archetype from Pompeii. If I have missed any identifications launched by enterprising archaeologists on the Internet, in the media, or even in the scholarship, I beg pardon, but doubt that much of consequence has been omitted all the same.[2]

Given the state of the evidence, it must seem ungrateful to reject any

---

1. Herter, "Soziologie" (1960) 71–75, provides a useful overview of the wide extent of venal sex in classical antiquity, including a list of cities and regions where it is attested. For an example of moralizing exaggeration, see Clem. Al. *Paed.* 3.3.22.2 SC 158.52, who declares that the whole world is full of *porneia* and *anomia* (*porneia* here can refer to all forms of illicit sex, not just prostitution; *anomia* has the sense of "iniquity"). Clement must be thinking mainly of cities, though even there it would be unwise to take his remark as gospel.

2. For an example of an "Internet Brothel," see the one allegedly uncovered at a temple of Aphrodite fifteen kilometers southeast of central Athens in connection with preparations for the 2004 Olympics: Website/Ananova (see list of abbreviations). I am skeptical of the identifcation as a brothel of the House of the Trifolium at Dougga (Thugga), despite its popularity on the Internet.

brothel nominations out of hand. And yet, some of these are not at all well-supported except by the sort of bare conjecture or wishful thinking that can find no place in a post-Wallace-Hadrill world of brothel-identification. So I exclude the recently reported first-century B.C. "brothel" in Thessalonica, an identification that appears to depend on a functionalist confusion between bath and brothel.[3] The same holds for the proposed late-antique bath/brothel complex in Ascalon, which seems based more on mere assertion than on actual evidence and falls well beyond our time frame.[4] Even later is a sixth-century complex identified as a brothel in Palestinian Bet She'an-Scythopolis.[5]

The natural focus of curiosity is the capital, so we begin with Rome and then proceed alphabetically, starting with Catania.

Rome

For all of the information we possess about the practice of venal sex in the capital city, that regarding the number and location of brothels must rank among the aspects most weakly attested. Statistics naturally are lacking, aside from those of a very rudimentary kind. For fourth-century Rome, the Regionary Catalogs give a total of 45/46 brothels, a figure which is not very telling in itself.[6] They suggest for only one of the city's sections, the Caelian hill area (*Regio* 4),[7] how brothels were distributed in the city. Otherwise we must depend on literary evidence for this sort of information.[8]

Of course we cannot know what the criteria were for selection and identification in the Catalogs. For example, were brothels associated with commercial establishments included? In other words, would a *caupona* with a small brothel upstairs show up on this list? Nor can we be certain that the compilers of the list did not lower the numbers out of a sense of discretion. In any case, the number is not likely to be accurate, given most estimates of the size of Rome in this period. These numbers perhaps reflect the presence of large, purpose-built brothels on the order of the Purpose-Built Brothel at Pompeii and ignore much else besides. If these Roman brothels were on average

---

3. See Stavrakakis, "Brothel" (1998).

4. See chap. 7.

5. See Dauphin, "Brothels" (1996); Dauphin, "Bordels" (1998) 183–84.

6. The *Curiosum* gives forty-six, the *Notitia*, forty-five: Nordh, *Libellus* (1949) 105.10.

7. Nordh, *Libellus* (1949) 75.4. The brothels were in proximity to the *macellum magnum* (large food-market), the *castra peregrina* (camp for soldiers from the provincial armies on detached duty at Rome), and the station of the fifth cohort of *vigiles* (the police/fire service). The presence of such installations is sufficient to explain the location of these brothels.

8. On prostitution in the Subura, see chap. 2.

the same size as our Purpose-Built Brothel, they would include a total of 450 (or 460) *cellae*. At a postulated two professionals each, this yields fewer than 1,000 brothel prostitutes for Rome, which must represent only a fraction of the number of prostitutes working in the city.[9]

Of course, the brothels listed in the Regionary Catalogs are only brothels on paper and so are of very limited use to us. For brick-and-mortar examples, we know of precisely three possibilities, all of which were identified as such by Giuseppe Lugli in the middle of the twentieth century and since then have been fairly well ignored, aside from a few instances when his identifications have been rejected out of hand.[10] Lugli identified one brothel in the Roman Forum, another just outside of it, and a third in the area of the Forum Boarium. All three would qualify as purpose-built brothels, though not a single one of them is absolutely certain to be a brothel, as we shall see below in this chapter. The same lack of certainty holds for the upper floors of the *Casa di Via Giulio Romano* on the lower reaches of the Capitoline Hill, which at minimum might qualify as a *deversorium*.[11]

Catania

A rectangular room (m. 3.27 x 2.80) decorated with stucco decorations, wall paintings, and graffiti has been dated to the first century A.D. Paolo Orsi envisioned this as a sort of "love-among-the-ruins" venue, an underground chamber turned into a trysting place in a later period after it was partly destroyed by earthquakes.[12] More recently, Giacomo Manganaro has suggested that the room functioned aboveground in the first century as the dining hall of a *hospitium* or *caupona* or, as he puts it, ". . . one of those places that used to operate as a hotel and restaurant and at the same time as a brothel, and particularly close by to bathing establishments."[13] Manganaro justifies the aspect of this identification regarding the brothel by referring to wall paintings of Eros and Mercury, as well as to graffiti that may be described as amorous in nature, though not explicitly erotic.

---

9. The problems and possibilities presented by the lists of brothels included in the Regionary Catalogs are discussed further in chap. 6.

10. Lugli, *Monumenti* (1947) 139–64. For further discussion of this point, see chap. 9.

11. See Packer, "Casa" (1968/1969) esp. 136–48.

12. Orsi, "Catania" (1918) 61.

13. Manganaro, "Graffiti e iscrizioni funerarie" (1962) 487.

Dura-Europos

The remains of a private house show that part of it in the period A.D. 250–56 was converted into the headquarters of a troupe of performers, some of whom may have been prostitutes.[14] For what it is worth, this establishment apparently meets all three criteria developed at Pompeii for the identification of brothels: design, erotic art, and graffiti.[15] To take them in order of usefulness, the art consists of a small, painted plaster relief of Aphrodite that was evidently affixed to an interior wall. The graffiti are not of the casual, client-generated kind, but are rather an official register painted within a relatively brief span of time that identifies the members of the group not exactly as prostitutes, but as performers, many of whom were slaves.[16] Finally, we come to the design of the building: there is perhaps only one room that might have served as a venue for sex, which means we would identify it as a crib.[17] So if the criteria are met, they are met in a weak manner, which has encouraged scholars to be cautious about identifying this structure as a brothel.[18]

Without doubt, the ancients would have regarded females in the group of performers as prostitutes, and there is some reason in this case for moderns to concur.[19] The justification lies in their legal status, their professional role, and the nature of the clientele they served. Because many if not most members of the group were slaves, they were completely at the disposition of their masters.[20] Some of the men have specific job designations (e.g., *skēnikos* [actor])

---

14. G5 House C: see Brown, "Houses" (1944) 116–17; Immerwahr, "Dipinti" (1944) 204–5, 210, 246.

15. See Brown, "Houses" (1944) 116–17; Brown, "Sculpture" (1944) 166–67; Immerwahr, "Dipinti" (1944) 205, 224–25.

16. One woman is called *hē paleopor<nē>*, "the old prostitute": Immerwahr, "Dipinti" (1944) 213, 225. This is a joke and/or an insult, as opposed to a job description. On the relative chronology of the graffiti, see Immerwahr, 209–10.

17. Room C3. See chap. 7 for the criteria for defining cribs. Room C4 was blocked off at this time, while C1 and C2 appear unsuitable as venues for sexual relations: see Brown, "Houses" (1944) 116–17.

18. Brown, "Houses" (1944) 116 ("headquarters of a guild of entertainers and prostitutes"); Immerwahr, "Dipinti" (1944) 261 ("it is not an organized brothel of the kind known from Greece and Italy"); Pollard, "Army" (1996) 225 ("brothel or guild centre for prostitutes and entertainers").

19. So Brown, "Houses" (1944) 116–17; Immerwahr, "Dipinti" (1944) 242, 257–62 (with great sensitivity to the difficulty in simply assuming such an identification); Pollard, "Army" (1996) 225. Immerwahr makes a valid connection (258) with Horace's *ambubaiae* (*Serm.* 1.2.1; see also Suet. *Nero* 27.2) and further draws a useful comparison (264) with the *fahrendes Volk* of the Middle Ages.

20. Immerwahr, "Dipinti" (1944) 238, 250, 255; Pollard, "Army" (1996) 225.

but not the women, who tend to be described in terms of physical appearance, for better or for worse.[21] The performers seem to have formed two subgroups, one of which was based in Dura-Europos, the other in Zeugma.[22] Both of these frontier towns sported major military installations.[23] Mention of an army official (*optio*) in the painted register appears to signify that the performers were under military supervision,[24] and it has been plausibly suggested that they were owned by the army.[25] If so, it must be stressed that this establishment ill corresponds to the modern concept of the military brothel.[26] It may, moreover, have been a far from universal phenomenon even in antiquity. Such arrangements, operating under the supervision of very junior officers, seem especially appropriate for relatively isolated frontier areas. High-ranking officers, of course, would have wanted to avoid the opprobrium of identification as pimps.[27] But surely the ambitious, upwardly mobile soldiers among the lower ranks would also have had this concern, leading one to surmise that their role in organizing prostitution for the troops may have been hampered by social constraints. When the opportunity presented itself and willing impresarios could be found, as at Dura-Europos, perhaps adopting as the thinnest of veils the theory that they were simply making arrangements for a troupe of "entertainers," commanders doubtless tended to turn a blind eye.

The number of performers—as many as sixty-three names are listed—suggests that they must have been broken up into smaller groups that lived in other dwellings.[28] They presumably gave performances mainly in private houses and were hired out for short periods.[29] The army base was only a couple of blocks away from their "headquarters."[30] These details suggest that most of the prostitution taking place must have occurred off-site as well. If true, this

---

21. Immerwahr, "Dipinti" (1944) 224–25, 230, 255; Pollard, "Army" (1996) 225. I note in passing that no one has suggested that any of the male members of the troupe acted as prostitutes.

22. Immerwahr, "Dipinti" (1944) 250–60. There is no evidence that they served other towns, as Immerwahr speculates (258).

23. As Pollard, "Army" (1996) 225, points out.

24. Immerwahr, "Dipinti" (1944) 245, 252, 261 (also a *stathmouchos*).

25. Pollard, "Army" (1996) 225. Immerwahr's notion that the performers were bad for morale seems to reflect his own mentality rather than that of the Roman soldier: "Dipinti" (1944) 264.

26. Phang, *Marriage of Soldiers* (2001) 249.

27. Phang, *Marriage of Soldiers* (2001) 251.

28. Immerwahr, "Dipinti" (1944) 254, 259, who suggests (261) their quarters were provided by the military.

29. Immerwahr, "Dipinti" (1944) 257, 259.

30. Immerwahr, "Dipinti" (1944) 260.

does not inevitably mean that the headquarters was not in some sense a brothel. Rather, it suggests that our efforts to identify brothels are liable to constant challenge not only from the inadequacy of physical evidence but also its apparently wide variety.[31]

Ephesus

Anyone wanting a sense of the absurd difficulties confronting the search for brothels in the ancient world would do well to contemplate the situation at Roman Ephesus, where an inscription that appears to mention a brothel has been found, while the brothel itself remains impossible to locate. The fragmentary inscription, carved on an architrave,[32] mentions a latrine, in connection with *paidiskēia* (scil. "brothel facilities"). The inscription was in fact found in a latrine adjacent to an important bath complex called after two of its benefactors, the Varius or Scholasticia Baths.

No certain brothel can be identified here, however. The structure located behind the latrine, which was once thought to be a brothel, is almost certainly a Roman peristyle house and not the purpose-built brothel that the inscription seems to imply. In fact, the inscription may have been taken from another, unknown location for reuse in its findspot.[33] The formal commemoration of a brothel or the like in an elaborate inscription of this kind is a singular, not to say strange, phenomenon, and it may well be that we simply do not understand this reference.[34] At Pompeii, for example, we would not expect to find an ancient inscription identifying a building as a *lupanar*. In fact, such a find might seem automatically to disqualify such an identification, falling as it does under the rubric "too good to be true."

---

31. See Pollard, "Army" (1996) 225, who rightly emphasizes that the distinction between guild headquarters and place of employment is far from clear.

32. *SEG* 16 (1959) 719 = *IK* 12 (Ephesos 2) 455. The text and a photograph are in Jobst, "Freudenhaus" (1976/7) 63–64, who dates the inscription (65) to the period following the reign of Domitian. The inscription is ambitiously reconstructed by Fagan, *Bathing in Public* (1999) 335–36, who risks making a functionalist confusion of bath with brothel.

33. So argues Jobst, "Freudenhaus" (1976/7) 65, 69. The plural *paidiskēia* may suggest an informal arrangement, not something identifiable as a "brothel," though it is difficult to see why such an establishment should receive epigraphic commemoration: see the text below.

34. In the end, sadly, the agnosticism of *LSJ* Suppl. s.v. "*paidiskeios*" ("with uncertain significance") may have to be preferred.

Ostia

It is worth observing that no certain brothels are known among the extensive remains of the main port for the city of Rome at its height.[35] We have only to do with possibilities. Perhaps the likeliest candidate for brothel-status at Ostia is the House of Jupiter and Ganymede (1.4.2, Casa 3). Guido Calza some time ago identified this establishment as a hotel for homosexuals and was followed in this opinion, at least for a time, by John Clarke after he conducted a detailed study.[36]

These scholars employ the very criteria adopted first by Matteo Della Corte and later by Andrew Wallace-Hadrill for identifying brothels at Pompeii. First, there is design, effected by a remodeling accomplished between A.D. 184–92 that articulates a series of rooms. Next is erotic graffiti, which here exclusively relates to sex between males. Third is erotic art, here in the form of paintings of Flora, Bacchus, and Jupiter with Ganymede.[37]

Despite seeing all three criteria fulfilled, both Calza and Clarke prefer to identify the establishment as a hotel rather than as a brothel, persuaded as they are that the size of the rooms is too large and the quality both of the construction and of the wall paintings is too high for a brothel.[38] Such caution seems too extreme, however. Calza and Clarke imply that there must be a fundamental difference between the design and appointments of a hotel and those of a brothel, which is unlikely to be true for the Romans.

Worth noting is the fact that there are some examples of hotels in Pompeii that are indeed relatively well-appointed. It is established in fact that both inns and restaurants at Pompeii commonly featured elements associated with the high-end *domus*, such as *atria* with *impluvia* (water-basins embedded in the floor), or were simply converted from such dwellings.[39] Given the elite prejudice against patronizing such places, it is difficult to conclude that their client

---

35. Meiggs, *Ostia*² (1973) 229, has a nice statement of the problem. See also Dierichs, *Erotik* (1997) 72. Kleberg, *Hôtels* (1957) 45–48, notes an apparent scarcity of other service establishments such as hotels and eating places; his explanations for this phenomenon do not convince, however: 55–56. The precise significance of the reference with regard to prostitution to the *statio cunnulingiorum* ("meeting place of the cunt-lickers") in the mosaic inscription from the Baths of Trinacria is difficult to establish: see chap. 7.

36. Calza, "Scavi" (1920) 334–75, 384–410; Clarke, "Decor" (1991). On the painting of Jupiter, Ganymede, and Leda, see also Clarke, "New Light" (1991).

37. Clarke, "Decor" (1991) 91, summarizes the criteria. See Clarke, 92, for the date; 94, for the graffiti.

38. Calza, "Scavi" (1920) 373–75; Clarke, "Decor" (1991) 94–95, 101.

39. See Packer, "Inns at Pompeii" (1978) 12, 18, 24, 26, 44, 46–47; Jashemski, *Gardens of Pompeii* I (1979) esp. 167–68.

base was exclusively or even mainly upper-class. They may have been designed instead to appeal to members of the sub-elite who had the cash to enjoy a faux elite atmosphere, on a short-term basis at any rate. The same point holds for brothels as for hotels, in that any attempt to create a elite ambience, whether successful or not, might bring in more profit.[40] The crux is that the distinction between hotels and brothels is functionally and formally impossible to maintain for the Romans.[41]

If this reasoning is correct, it suggests that not all Roman brothels were decorated in the same fashion. The contrast is stark, for example, between the luxurious atmospherics of the Ostian example and the austerity of the Pur-pose-Built Brothel at Pompeii, where the only glimpse of high living was afforded by the erotic *tabellae* on the walls (chapter 4). Luxury, or the appear-ance of it, is for similar reasons a component of some modern brothels. The following description of the parlor of a Nevada brothel is worth quoting in full, to try to get a sense of what the owners and operators of the establishment in the House of Jupiter and Ganymede were setting out to accomplish with their decorative scheme:[42]

> During the line-up, the customer lounges in one of several plump leather chairs in the enormous red-carpeted parlor. The sumptuous room bulges with sizzling crimson sofas, enhanced by a scattering of virginal-white love seats, glass-and-brass tables, lush floral arrange-ments, and marble statuary. Luxuriant scarlet-velvet draperies fall into folds over windows and in corners, adding a sense of voluptuousness. The thick noise-absorbing carpet dulls sounds, while the sparkle of marble and glass creates a visual spectacle. The soft chairs in which customers sit, anticipating pleasure to come, face a raised alcove lighted by an enormous crystal chandelier. And beneath it, in solitary splendor, gleams the pièce de résistance—a highly polished, snow-white, baby grand piano.

The alert reader will note that the language is deliberately designed to sexual-ize the space being described; in fact, it is no accident that descriptions of extravagant appointments have been an important part of popularizing works

---

40. For a classical Athenian example, see Davidson, *Courtesans and Fishcakes* (1998) 94.

41. Clarke, "Decor" (1991) 95, points out that the location of the House of Jupiter and Ganymede near the Forum and its baths and across the street from a tavern serving food and drink is conducive to the operation of a hotel. The same holds for a brothel, of course.

42. From Shaner, *Madam* (2001) 44.

on brothels. There is, for example, an entire subgenre of literature devoted to mythologizing the Victorian brothel.[43]

The aim of this discourse obviously is to titillate.[44] The author of this passage takes the theme one step further when she writes in the next paragraph, "In short, the parlor at Sheri's is a very sexy room, vulval in the billowing of its smooth scarlet cushions and the soft folds of its 'stroke-me' velvet draperies."[45]

It is worth noting that the room described at Sheri's Ranch is found in a building haphazardly constructed around the original nucleus of a double-wide trailer. Despite that fact, as well as the self-consciously literary aspects of the presentation, the description of the parlor does seem to capture the actual ambience of the establishment, itself so self-consciously a brothel as to sport an actual red light, said to be visible for miles around.[46] A Victorian brothel that burned down in nineteenth-century St. Paul, Minnesota makes the same odd connection between life and literature in the items it featured. A list of these items was made for the purposes of an insurance claim and published in the local newspapers; it included a piano valued at one thousand dollars. Evidently pianos were standard equipment even in relatively humble St. Paul brothels of that time.[47]

Such luxury, or the appearance of it, is not of course an inevitable feature of brothels in every culture. An example is the municipal brothel of medieval Germany, a visit to which might in some places almost itself be construed as an act of penance. Though local authorities in some places realized that for many visitors the municipal brothel was the public face of the town and thus sought to impress them with the installation of glass windows and ovens, in many other places they furnished the brothels in a spare manner and allowed only limited sexual options.[48] The familiar comparison of brothel with sewer perhaps makes more sense here than in many other settings. The institution was no luxury for the town in which it was located, in that there was little or no interest in turning a profit on the part of local authorities.[49] For all that, the

---

43. See Best, *Controlling Vice* (1998) 2, 14.

44. On conventions in brothel literature (a much understudied topic), see Best, *Controlling Vice* (1998) 2.

45. For a more "realistic," but still unsatisfactory, description of the quondam Mustang Ranch, see Albert, *Brothel* (2001) 11–13, 42, 53, 98–99.

46. Shaner, *Madam* (2001) 140–41.

47. Best, *Controlling Vice* (1998) 68–89.

48. P. Schuster, *Frauenhaus* (1992) 58–59, 64. On the lack of sexual freedom in the German medieval brothel, see also B. Schuster, *Freien Frauen* (1995) 26, 130–31.

49. P. Schuster, *Frauenhaus* (1992) 47; B. Schuster, *Freien Frauen* (1995) 95. Of course the authorities did at times succeed in raising revenue, which they might divert to a special use, for example, maintenance of the poor: see Schuster, *Freien Frauen* 261, 364. The interests of the brothel-manager were of course quite different: B. Schuster, *Freien Frauen,* 112–13.

atmosphere, aided in part by the availability of alcohol, might still be described as erotically charged, at least given the cultural context of the day.[50] Of course it was so in the eyes of the Reformers.[51]

More recently, John Clarke has rejected his cautious argument regarding the House of Jupiter and Ganymede, and withdrawn his identification of the establishment as a hotel for homosexuals, evidently out of concerns grounded in orthodox social constructionism.[52] It may be, however, that it is easier simply to accept the presence of a brothel, rather than a hotel catering to persons of a given "sexuality." On the basis of the evidence that is available to us, we can be certain neither of the gender of all of the prostitutes nor of the sexuality of the clients. In other words, the fact that the graffiti refer exclusively to same-sex relations does not inevitably mean women did not sell sex there as well, any more than the presence of all-heterosexual graffiti at a brothel means that male prostitutes did not work there.

The evidence from Pompeii tends to support this argument. There are at least a couple of brothels where we know both male and female prostitutes worked.[53] There were surely others, though it is perhaps safe to conclude that most of the Pompeian brothels had only female prostitutes. Was this single-sex configuration a local phenomenon? A text by the dream-specialist Artemidorus suggests that all-female brothels were the norm elsewhere as well.[54] Dreams about the mouth represent the household, he writes, with the teeth signifying the inhabitants. Those on the right stand for the men, those on the left for the women, except for some rare cases where, for example, all the teeth represent women (a brothel-keeper with only women) or men (a farmer with only men). Artemidorus here contrasts the typical or ideal configuration of the *oikos* containing both male and female members with examples that violate this norm. Here he seems to be implying that brothels, for example, were typically unisex rather than that such arrangements were rare for brothels. Even if we accept the latter interpretation, however, we cannot cite this passage as evidence for male brothels.

Of course such brothels did exist in antiquity. An imperial constitution of A.D. 390, for example, orders the repression at Rome of all male brothels (*virorum lupanaria*).[55] The possibility of such brothels in Pompeii merits further

---

50. See Schuster, *Frauenhaus* (1992) 67.
51. See Schuster, *Freien Frauen* (1995) 236–37.
52. Clarke, *Looking at Lovemaking* (1998) 88 with n. 79.
53. See cat. nos. 10 and 14.
54. Artemid. 1.31.
55. Valent., Theod., Arcad. *Coll.* 5.3 (a. 390). See chap. 3.

study, in my view. But even if we could be certain that all the prostitutes in the House of Jupiter and Ganymede at Ostia were male, few scholars, given that we are mostly social constructionists of one stripe or another, would accept that this means the clients were exclusively homosexual or, to give the radical constructionist view its full weight, "homosexual" at all. In other words, we can reasonably try to separate the problem of sexuality from that of brothel-identification. This is not to say that characterization of the establishment as one that catered to same-sex preferences is unfounded or impossible, but that it cannot be strictly proven. This idea pays tribute to the careful considera-tions of Calza and Clarke, but is perhaps a bit more optimistic. Identification of the House of Jupiter and Ganymede as a brothel remains merely possible and far from certain. The same holds for the theory that, as a brothel, it spe-cialized in selling sex between males.

As for other possible brothels in Ostia, the first of the difficulties raised by Calza and Clarke seems the more intractable. The lack of a fine line between brothels on the one hand and hotels and, as we shall see below, lower-class housing in general on the other means that almost any of the structures in Ostia identified by modern scholars as *deversoria* might have been used as brothels. The lack of certainty here is too great to name more than a couple of the more likely examples. The House of Diana (1.3.3–4) shows evidence of partitioning on its upper level into small, perhaps makeshift spaces, ideal for the Roman hotel/residence/brothel.[56] An even better candidate, given its third-century erotic wall paintings, two of which adorn a single room, is the *Casa delle Volte Dipinte* (3.5.1), which has been identified both as a hotel and a brothel, owing also to a ground-floor layout featuring two rows of simple rooms divided by a corridor and evidently sharing a kitchen and latrine.[57]

---

56. The House of Diana, at least on the upper stories, is commonly understood to be a *dever-sorium*: Hermansen, *Ostia* (1981) 127. For a recent study of the ground floor, see Marinucci, "Mai-son" (2001). On housing in Ostia, see also Gering, "Habiter" (2001); Heres, "Cherche" (2001). On the evidently widespread use of partitions in lower-class housing in Ostia, see Frier, *Landlords* (1980) 4–5; Scobie, "Slums" (1986) 428. Note the room divisions of the *Casa di Via Giulio Romano* at Rome: Packer, "Casa" (1968–1969) esp. 136–48.

57. See Kleberg, *Hôtels* (1957) 46; Calza and Nash, *Ostia* (1959) 29–30, 80; Pavolini, *Vita* (1986) 233–37; Scarano Ussani, "*Lenocinium*" (2000) 257; Guzzo and Scarano Ussani, *Veneris fig-urae* (2001) 74 n. 216; Heres, "Cherche" (2001) 225; both identifications are tepidly accepted by Packer, "Inns at Pompeii" (1978) 12, 170, who lists other Ostian buildings with a similar plan. The northwest corner shows a bar connecting with the house: Girri, *Taberna* (1956) 26; Hermansen, *Ostia* (1981) 151–52. Hermansen (at 193) argues against identification as a brothel on the basis of the kitchen. Clarke, *Looking at Lovemaking* (1998) 265–74, as ever must be recommended for repro-ductions and discussion of the wall paintings (in this case poorly preserved). He is skeptical (at 271) of the brothel-identification here too because of the high quality of the art. On the paintings and the building, see also Felletti Maj, "Ostia" (1960); Felletti Maj, *Ostia* (1961).

Other possible candidates worth mentioning are the large bars/restaurants that show multiple rooms in back and/or upstairs suitable for lodging as well as for the sale of sex.[58]

Finally, we note that as bleak as the situation is in regard to Ostian brothels, that concerning Ostian prostitutes is not one bit better. The graffiti preserved in the House of Jupiter and Ganymede do not allow us to distinguish with certainty the customer from the prostitute, if we can indeed correctly assume that this was a brothel. Despite the evidence for the status and role of women in ancient Ostia at various social levels, not a single name has come down to us of a female who might with any reason be conjectured to be a prostitute.[59]

Sayala (Lower Nubia)

A tavern district dating to the end of the third century A.D. was located very near the southern edge of Egypt, in close proximity to the Roman border garrison at Hiera Sycaminos.[60] A number of these taverns, whose remains, including ovens, show that food as well as drink was for sale, are equipped with a small side room that appears to have functioned as a *cella* or crib, that is, a venue for private parties that may have featured the sale of sex.[61] One building, connected through a stone walkway with one of the taverns, seems to have functioned precisely as a kind of—relatively well-appointed—crib.[62] These are perhaps not brothels in a strict technical sense, since it is far from clear either that two or more prostitutes worked in them at the same time or that the sale of sex was the chief or even a major component of business. All the same, they demonstrate once more the futility of insisting that the "classic" profile of the Purpose-Built Brothel at Pompeii serve as the model for brothels elsewhere.

---

58. See Girri, *Taberna* (1956) 9, 14–15, 32; Rowell, "Satyricon" (1957) 223; Hermansen, *Ostia* (1981) 147–50, 152, 167–68, 175, 193–94; Scarano Ussani, "Lenocinium" (2000) 257.

59. On Ostian women, see Kampen, *Image and Status* (1981); Herzig, "Frauen in Ostia" (1983).

60. Kromer, *Weinstuben* (1967) dates (at 128) the complex to A.D. 274–98.

61. Lamps, animal bones, drinking cups, and a hearth were all found in these rooms, suggesting at minimum that food and drink were consumed there: see Kromer, *Weinstuben* (1967) 21–22, 30–31, 50, 54, 59–60, 62, 65, 67, 72–76. Kromer (72) appears to believe these spaces were used for storage, which would not obviate other uses.

62. Objekt 4: Kromer, *Weinstuben* (1967) 41–47, 76, who cites as criteria for identification design and graffiti (the latter consisting of obscene doodling on potsherds).

THE NAME OF THE ROSE

The Purpose-Built Brothel is almost too good to be true. One element that adds to its cachet is its elusive name. The various names proposed for this brothel include *Lupanare nuovo*, *Lupanare grande*, and *Lupanar* of Africanus (and Victor). None of these seem suitable. The brothel was "new" only at the time of its discovery in 1862. It is indeed large, if only by the standards of other Pompeian brothels, but, confusingly, *Lupanare grande* or a variant of it is attached to another building that is almost certainly not a brothel, the *gran lupanare* or *lupanare grande* (6.14.43).[63] It may not in fact stand as the largest brothel in Pompeii,[64] nor can we ascribe it with confidence to proprietors named Africanus and Victor.[65]

Some authors refer to this brothel simply as (the) *lupanar*, a piece of Pompeianist slang that would be accurate if it were indeed the only brothel in town. "Forum Brothel" is not strictly accurate either, since the brothel is not in the Forum, but two or three blocks away. I thus propose to rename it the Purpose-Built Brothel, which I will be the first to admit is not the most elegant of attributions, in the hope that my argument that it was the only one of its kind at Pompeii gains favor.

LOVE SHACK

Located on a narrow, winding street not far from the town Forum, the Purpose-Built Brothel conforms nicely to the Roman literary cliché that brothels were located on winding, secluded back streets (figs. 4–11).[66] It contains five simple small rooms on the ground floor, each of which features a masonry bed which almost certainly would have sported some sort of mattress or cushions in antiquity. On the upper walls of the passageway that connects the rooms are a series of erotic paintings. Five more rooms are upstairs, accessible by a separate entrance stairway and a balcony.[67] The whole is complemented by a painting of Priapus located downstairs (fig. 11), which sports two phalluses no less (as though to confirm the brothel-hunter's good fortune);[68] a latrine under

---

63. See the first appendix.

64. See no. 6 in the catalog (appendix 1).

65. The attribution of various properties to "proprietors" whose names are included in the graffiti is highly dubious: see the notes to appendix 1.

66. See chap. 9.

67. For a description of the Purpose-Built Brothel, see Clarke, *Looking at Lovemaking* (1998) 196–206. We lack a really satisfactory account of the upstairs.

68. On the significance of the representation of Priapus in the context of the brothel, see appendix 1.

the stairway; and more than one hundred graffiti, many of them erotic, in and around the building.[69] It is worth emphasizing that this establishment stands as our most certain example of a brothel, not only in Pompeii, but in the entire Roman world.[70] This might suggest a lack of good evidence, or flaws in the application of our criteria for identifying brothels, or both.

The certainty of this identification, as well as its uniqueness, clearly rests on the status of this brothel as a structure made for the purpose of selling sex, which makes it precisely a purpose-built brothel.[71] Such enterprises are rare not only in the Roman world.[72] It is difficult to trace examples even in other societies, which, like the Roman, tolerate prostitution reasonably well. We might argue that it is even more difficult than in less tolerant cultures because in these societies, as in the Roman world, brothels are often not located in any one area (and can be very mobile at that).[73] An exception might be found in the institution of the municipal brothel in medieval Germany, though the evidence is ambiguous. In some cities, preexisting structures were leased or purchased by the authorities, while in others the town brothel was built from scratch.[74] In general, however, the acquisition and construction of these brothels is not directly documented.[75] A pattern of a series of small rooms arranged around larger "hospitality rooms" emerges from the descriptions of brothels in Wurzburg and Munich, but even if typical, it is difficult to see how precisely this arrangement would differ from that of an inn, for example.[76]

Remodeling, even extensive remodeling, of a structure to accommodate a brothel through partitioning and furnishing is unlikely to leave much of use for identification in the archaeological record.[77] Furthermore, a building is not

---

69. Barattolo and Romaldi, "Impianti igienici" (2000) 268 n. 36, record the presence of two latrines in this brothel.

70. See the comments of Guzzo, "Quadretti erotici di Pompei" (2000) 41.

71. The brothel's uniqueness may also depend in part on its irregular shape. According to DeFelice, *Roman Hospitality* (2001) 103, there are only three other building lots similar to that of the Purpose-Built Brothel in all of Pompeii.

72. I should note the three examples identified at Rome by Lugli, *Monumenti* (1947) and discussed in the text above. There are differences among these examples. One was built from scratch, while the others are significant makeovers; they have differently constructed beds; and they apparently vary in regard to the presence or absence of an on-site *caupona*. Nevertheless, if their identification as brothels is accepted, we can argue in all three cases that they qualify as purpose-built brothels.

73. See Hill, *Their Sisters' Keepers* (1993) 175–87. For examples of purpose-built brothels in other cultures, see Decker, *Prostitution* (1979) 138; Bernstein, *Sonia's Daughters* (1995) 181; Hershatter, *Dangerous Pleasures* (1997) 291.

74. Schuster, *Frauenhaus* (1992) 51, 54, 165.

75. See Schuster, *Freien Frauen* (1995) 92.

76. Schuster, *Frauenhaus* (1992) 58–60.

77. See Hill, *Their Sisters' Keepers* (1993) 199, 221; Tong, *Unsubmissive Women* (1994) 75 (fabric partitions).

strictly required for the sale of sex.[78] All of this raises further difficulties in the matter of defining what a brothel is.

Defining, and in turn identifying, brothels has been as acute a problem for those living in past societies as it has been for historians.[79] An aspect of this is a tendency toward "brothel-bias," that is, an overemphasis on obvious venues, which in recent years has been extreme for Pompeii.[80] Brothels tend to blend in indiscriminately with the urban housing stock and/or are found in businesses that pursue some other more visible purpose such as the sale of food and drink.[81] Hence, no brothel "type" can be distinguished apart from a hotel or motel "type."[82]

As for possible parallels in other cultures, one looks in vain to the classic study of building types by Nikolaus Pevsner.[83] Pevsner develops three rationales for the development of building-types in history: diversification of function, discovery of new materials or new uses of existing materials, and the emergence of new styles.[84] It is persuasive to view building types and their

---

78. See Mackey, *Red Lights Out* (1987) 204 n. 21, on nineteenth-century U.S. attempts to define tents and wagons as brothels.

79. See Decker, *Prostitution* (1979) 373 (defining brothels makes for bad law; cf. 404: problems with defining massage parlors as brothels), 345 n. 49, 361 n. 82; Harsin, *Policing Prostitution* (1985) 307–13 (problems in classifying brothels by type); Mackey, *Red Lights Out* (1987) 93–123 (problems with defining under the nuisance-abatement law), 152–57 (for some courts, the defendant's character was crucial for identifying a brothel), 162 (no clear standard for a legal definition), 162–69 (formidable problems of evidence), 173–79 (much dissension and obscurity in defining brothels at law), 199 (a lack of confidence on the part of nineteenth-century U.S. legal authorities in defining and identifying brothels); Hill, *Their Sister's Keepers* (1993) 132 (a mid-nineteenth-century New York City judge finds that prostitutes in residence do not a brothel make, since they must dwell somewhere after all). See also chap. 7.

80. On brothel-bias, see Hill, *Their Sisters' Keepers* (1993) 184. For the lack of a Roman concept of "definite brothel," see in the text below.

81. See Finnegan, *Poverty* (1979) 35, 39–45, 53, 55, 58, 66–69, 91–92, 97, 100–104, 107, 112, 134–35, 150; Pavan, "Police" (1980) 253; Walkowitz, *Prostitution* (1980) 24; Rosen, *Sisterhood* (1982) 70, 78; Harsin, *Policing Prostitution* (1985) 32–49; Stansell, *City of Women* (1987) 174; Corbin, *Women for Hire* (1990) 36–42, 116–18, 139–54; Mahood, *Magdalenes* (1990) 43, 121, 135; Gilfoyle, *City of Eros* (1992) 34, 39, 47, 52, 52, 120, 166–73, 177, 197–250, 265–69, 295, 394; Hill, *Their Sisters' Keepers* (1993) 175–216; Bernstein, *Sonia's Daughters* (1995) 153; Schuster, *Freien Frauen* (1995) 14, 72, 88–102, 120, 215–23; Karras, *Common Women* (1996) 71–72; Gibson, *Prostitution and the State*[2] (1999) 87. For the Roman evidence, see chap. 2.

82. See Ginouvès, *Dictionnaire méthodique* 3 (1998) 121–22. The ramshackle and improvisational structure of a Nevada brothel provides a useful modern parallel: see Shaner, *Madam* (2001) 140–41. See also Symanski, "Prostitution in Nevada" (1974) 365; Schuster, *Freien Frauen* (1995) 95–96.

83. Pevsner, *Building Types* (1976).

84. Pevsner, *Building Types* (1976) 289–90.

development as specific to a given culture, so that lack of evidence for purpose-built brothels by itself proves nothing for Rome.[85]

Even so, the evidence, or the lack of it, leads me to make the following
sweeping statement. None of Pevsner's criteria suit the Roman brothel, or
brothels in most other cultures, as far as I can see. For that matter, I am not at
all certain that the Romans knew a hotel or motel "type." The *deversorium* (by
any other name) seems to have been a fairly elastic concept in terms of both
form and function, though great labors have been expended by moderns in an
effort to pin it down, distinguishing the *caupona* from the *hospitium* and so
forth.[86] One word for lodgings in particular, *stabulum*, was often used to mean
"brothel," a usage that indicates a high rate of interchangeability between the
two concepts.[87] Mark Grahame's recent analysis of houses in Pompeii's *Regio*
6 appears to bear this argument out. He finds that the specimens of the lowest-
status type, that is, noncourtyard houses, show little regularity in their layouts,
leading him to conclude that there existed no standard design for them. In
fact, he describes their design pattern as "almost random" in nature.[88]

These considerations suggest that for the purpose of defining and identifying brothels we cannot safely generalize from the example of the Purpose-Built
Brothel.[89] We may compare this situation with medieval Germany, where the
most commonly drawn distinction between the town brothel and the other

---

85. Purcell, "Town in Country" (1987) 197–98, usefully points out that the ambiguity
between elements of the public and private in Roman villa design helped discourage the development of purpose-built government buildings in antiquity.

86. See Kleberg, *Hôtels* (1957) 12–14, 17, 19, 27; Packer, "Inns at Pompeii" (1978) 5, 12,
44–53; Hermansen, *Ostia* (1981) 192–93; DeFelice, *Roman Hospitality* (2001) 16–23. Cf. Frier,
"Rental Market" (1977) 30–34. The older analysis in Rowell, "*Satyricon* 95–96" (1957) of a key
piece of literary evidence for inns is still worth consulting. Finally, McDonald, "Villa or Pandokeion?" (1951) 366–67, observed long ago in regard to ancient Greek inns and so forth that
"[p]robably there was little in location, general outward appearance, or even in ground plan to distinguish them from private houses, and the equipment and furnishings which would assist in the
identification were doubtless almost all of a perishable nature" (note omitted). Further discussion
in chap. 2.

87. See chap. 2.

88. Grahame, "Material Culture" (1998) esp. 171.

89. Wallace-Hadrill, "Public Honour and Private Shame" (1995) does this implicitly, in my
view. DeFelice, *Roman Hospitality* (2001) 13, adopts the Purpose-Built Brothel "as a working
model to delineate what features could be expected in suspected brothels throughout the city." Cf.
102, where he apparently contradicts himself by seeming to accuse Wallace-Hadrill of a *petitio
principii*, stressing the brothel's "unique features." Clarke, "Laughing" (2002) 151–55 dismisses the
possibility of a brothel at the Suburban Baths on the basis of a comparison with the Purpose-Built
Brothel.

houses of the municipality turned on the status of the women who lived in each.[90] It would be just as rash, I believe, to posit any establishment in the late twentieth or early twenty-first century United States as a typical brothel. Worth emphasizing as a deterrent to facile generalization is the example of the brothel found in Barbara Heyl's classic study of the madam. This brothel was a modest-sized apartment of two and one-half bedrooms allowing two to three prostitutes to work at the same time.[91]

The only true difficulty we have in regard to identifying the Purpose-Built Brothel involves determining the relationship of the upstairs to the downstairs. The upstairs does not seem to have contained masonry beds or erotic art or graffiti.[92] This would of course disqualify it as a brothel according to the severe criteria of the 1990s. It is, in fact, quite possible that the upstairs was the sleeping quarters of the women who worked downstairs. In a heavily stereotyped description of a brothel, Juvenal has a pimp send the prostitutes who work for him home at the end of the day.[93] The detail is necessary, in that Messalina in this fiction must be allowed a way back to the imperial palace, while at the same time her reluctance to stop working, in contrast to her colleagues, who evidently depart quite readily at the pimp's behest, allows the satirist to show her outwhoring the whores. This is very much a central concern of the passage. And yet the detail seems unlikely to be sheer invention. In other words, while the empress' participation in the life of the brothel should be regarded as utter fiction, the details of the establishment's structure and operation are supposed to be "realistic," at least in the sense that they conform to the literary conventions for representing brothels.

The bulk of the evidence, however, points in another direction, in favor of very limited freedom of movement for women who worked in brothels or none at all.[94] For example, both the would-be priestess denounced by Seneca the

---

90. See Schuster, *Freien Frauen* (1995) 88–89.

91. Heyl, *Madam* (1979) 91–94.

92. Della Corte, *Case*[3] (1965) 203, states that the walls upstairs are also painted "though less unworthily" ("epperò meno ignobili"), whatever that means; cf. Guzzo, "Quadretti erotici" (2000) 40. Wallace-Hadrill, p.c., assures me there is no erotic art upstairs. DeFelice, *Roman Hospitality* (2001) 103, asserts that there are no masonry beds upstairs. See Nappo, *Pompeii* (1998) 74: no erotic art and "probably" wooden beds. For the inscriptions, see the editorial notation introducing *CIL* 4.2173. Varone, "Lupanare" (2002) 194 attributes the absence of erotic art and graffiti to the excavation techniques that prevailed in 1862, when the brothel was discovered.

93. Iuv. 6.127.

94. For Rome, see Flemming, "*Quae Corpore*" (1999) 43. Brothels in many cultures tend to confine prostitutes, even those who are in fact rather mobile. On the justification of the term "inmate" to describe prostitutes in Nevada brothels, see Symanski, "Prostitution in Nevada" (1974) 359.

Elder's declaimers and the unfortunate Tarsia in the *Story of Apollonius of Tyre* seem fairly well immured in their workplaces.[95] Eventually, consignment to the brothel served as a form of punishment, inflicted notably by the pagan authorities on Christian women, a practice that suggests working conditions were generally constraining even before this development took place.[96] The medieval German practice of interning in brothels women deemed unchaste reads almost as an ironic comment on the Roman practice with Christian women, and the latter was not tolerated, at least by the Christian emperor Theodosius I.[97]

The mere fact that brothels blend in indiscriminately with the residential housing stock of a city suggests that prostitutes lived as well as worked in the same place. In a famous anecdote, Cato the Censor praises a young man for resorting to a brothel, as an alternative, or antidote, to adultery. When he sees the same person exiting the same brothel rather often ("frequentius") he is moved to criticism: "Young man, I praised you on the basis that you paid an occasional visit here, not that you lived here."[98] Near the beginning of the *Satyricon* as preserved, Encolpius loses his way and asks directions to his lodgings from an old woman selling vegetables. She leads him to a brothel and declares, "Here . . . is where you ought to live."[99] This evidence suggests one or two conclusions. One is that brothels might have functioned as lodging houses (or vice versa), a point I have already made. The other is that prostitutes routinely lived in the same place where they worked. This much is strongly implied by both speakers, that is, Cato and the old woman; they are in effect saying that the addressee is a whore. The two conclusions do not contradict each other. In fact, the first almost assumes the second in the sense that if any persons at all lived in the brothel these were very likely to be the prostitutes who worked there.

---

95. Sen. *Contr.* 1.2; *Hist. Ap. Tyr.* 33–36

96. There is no firm evidence for this practice on the part of the state before the reign of Septimius Severus: see Tert. *Apol.* 50.12 CCSL 1.171. The practice seems to have had a history before this as a private punishment, to judge for example from Apul. *Met.* 7.9. See literature and discussion in McGinn, "SC" (1992) 277 with n. 20; McGinn, *Prostitution, Sexuality, and the Law* (1998) 305–12. Cf. the Nye County, Nevada, rule that prostitutes must remain at the brothel except for closely supervised excursions outside: Shaner, *Madam* (2001) 279; more generally for Nevada, Albert, *Brothel* (2001) 5, 48.

97. See Schuster, *Frauenhaus* (1992) 145, 166, 168. For Theodosius, see chap. 3.

98. [Acro.] *ad Hor. Serm.* 1.2.31–32: ". . . adulescens, ego te laudavi, tamquam huc intervenires, non tamquam hic habitares." Neither Horace at *Serm.* 1.2.31–32 nor Porphyrio *ad loc.* preserves this part of the anecdote.

99. Petron. 6–7 (at 7): "'Hic . . . debes habitare.'"

The allocation of a separate space designated for sleeping quarters on-site, or more or less on-site, seems difficult to accept. Such an arrangement would represent a gross diseconomy in a business that tended to exploit its workers to the greatest extent possible. In other words, I believe that Roman brothel-prostitutes, unless they lived absolutely off-site (an arrangement that would allow them to work in shifts), typically slept in the beds in which they worked, if they slept in beds at all.[100] What is more, the design, as reported, of the second story of the Purpose-Built Brothel added to the everlasting principle that in matters of real estate location (times three) is everything seems to guarantee its usage as a venue for the sale of sex. It does not, however, clarify the relationship between the two levels, namely whether the building consists of one brothel, as most scholars appear to assume, or two, as Giuseppe Fiorelli and Gioacchino La Torre appear to believe.[101]

Roman law stipulates that the owner of the ground floor also owns what lies above,[102] and yet this fact does not resolve the issue as neatly as we would like. An owner of any status would presumably resort to a middleman to operate a brothel, and the idea of two separate operations run by two individual middlemen therefore remains possible, especially if we credit the modern tendency to attribute separate street entrances to different tenants/occupants,[103] keeping in mind that the building was evidently designed, as a brothel, precisely in this way. At the same time, we might argue that the separate entrance for the second story was intended to allow it to remain closed except as needed, for example, in times of expected high usage, such as festivals or games, so that the appearance of a separate operation on the upper level is illusory. Given the uncertainty, I allow separate entries in the catalog provided in the first appendix, but otherwise treat the "two" brothels as one.

Whatever the case, we can safely conclude that not only the Purpose-Built Brothel itself but the immediate neighborhood around it was an *unofficial* center of sexual activity. The presence of one crib virtually across the street,[104]

---

100. For a parallel from a Nevada brothel, see Albert, *Brothel* (2001) 13, 98–99. For a similar argument about prostitutes in ancient Athenian brothels, see Cohen, "Economic Analysis" (forthcoming). For another view about sleeping arrangements in Roman brothels, see DeFelice, *Roman Hospitality* (2001) 101; in this brothel, Varone, "Lupanare" (2002) 194.

101. Fiorelli, *Scavi di Pompei* (1873) 20; La Torre, "Impianti" (1988) 93 n. 29.

102. On the principle *superficies solo cedit*: Gaius 2.73 with Kaser, *Privatrecht* 1² (1971) 375, 429.

103. See, for example, Wallace-Hadrill, *Houses and Society* (1994) 108.

104. 7.11.12.

another down the block,[105] the largest hotel in town across the way,[106] a size-able tavern facing one entrance,[107] and an important bath complex a few steps away[108] are all evidence of this. Sex might have been for sale in any or all of these places, and they might have helped generate business for the brothel. The tavern just across the street was potentially a source not only of customers but of food and drink as well. In the following chapter, we will examine the question of whether this situation was extraordinary or not.

---

105. 7.12.33.

106. 7.11.11, 14, so described by Jashemski, "Copa" (1963/4) 344.

107. 7.1.44–45a, which is sometimes identified by the man thought to be its owner, Sittius, or the painting of an elephant that graces its facade: Jashemski, "Copa" (1963/4) 346; Franklin, "Games and a *Lupanar*" (1985/6) 321.

108. The Stabian Baths, located at 7.1.8, 14–17, 48, 50–51.

❡ Chapter Nine ❡

THE CITY OF VENUS

SEX AND THE CITY

Both brothels and cribs are spread throughout the city of Pompeii instead of being confined to one area (see maps, 1, 2, and 5). This distribution is neither even nor random, however.[1] In fact the motive for the location of these establishments seems purely economic (convenient access to clients) rather than moral or social.[2] The proximity of the town Forum, a public bath, a hotel, or a town gate are all characteristic features. For example, all of the relatively high number of brothels and cribs alleged for *Regio* 7 are, as we might expect, quite accessible from the Forum. The brothel thought to lie at 7.16.B is just outside the *Porta Marina*, atop the Suburban Baths. The area east of the Forum sporting the Purpose-Built Brothel seems to have benefitted from a kind of commercial-erotic synergy. Another such area appears to have been the section in *Regio* 1 near the *Porta Stabiana* and extending back toward, and inclusive of, the *Insula del Menandro*. Still another might be seen in *Insula* 13 of

---

1. Brothels are not reported for areas of the city that remain largely unexcavated and/or where there is a high concentration of public building: to use Fiorelli's *Regiones* as a rough guide, 3 and 4 have no brothels alleged, 2 and 8 only one. On the other hand, *Regiones* 1 and 9 are well represented, though significant areas in both remain unexcavated. *Regio* 7 is the best attested, with as many as seventeen possible brothels and ten *cellae meretriciae*.

2. Compare the distribution of hotels and eating/drinking places that Kleberg, *Hôtels* (1957) 49–53, claims for Pompeii: a clustering near the town gates, main streets, and places of public entertainment (in my view, however, eating/drinking establishments are scattered more widely than he allows). Consider also the *taberna* at Plaut. *Pseud.* 658–64, which is located just outside the town gate and which offers at minimum food and lodging.

Regio 7, an area with its several brothels and cribs. The pattern of distribution for brothels corresponds fairly well to that for inns, restaurants, and hotels.[3]

A similarly uneven, but nonrandom pattern is reflected in the distribution of upper-class townhouses, which were located in many, though not all, parts of the city, with some clustering perceptible. This pattern is not the inverse of the one for brothels, though the elite's preference for showy locations on the main roads might have made it economically difficult at minimum for brothels to locate there, a fact that does not mean all of them were found in out-of-the-way places, as has been suggested.[4]

Here the question of the "fit" between archaeological and other kinds of evidence, especially literary sources, arises with particular insistence. Two texts, one from Petronius and the other from Seneca, have been used to argue the existence both of an ideology and practice of moral zoning. If correct, the argument would threaten to overturn the conclusions just drawn from the material evidence for Pompeii, or at minimum help to establish that city as a special case. The claim evaporates on close inspection, however, allowing for a more focused examination of various types of evidence in the context of specific locations in the Roman city where such zoning has been alleged.

In an important passage, Petronius emphasizes the backstreet location of a brothel in order to illustrate the gross stupidity of both Encolpius and Ascyltos, rather than to communicate a fixed rule about brothel-topography:[5]

> Petron. 6: . . . Sed nec viam diligenter tenebam [quia] nec quod stabulum esset sciebam . . . 7: . . . 'Rogo,' inquam 'mater, numquid scis ubi ego habitem?' . . . Subinde ut in locum secretiorem venimus, centonem anus urbana reiecit et 'hic' inquit, 'debes habitare'. Cum ego negarem me agnoscere domum, video quosdam inter titulos nudas meretrices furtim spatiantes. Tarde, immo iam sero intellexi me in fornicem esse deductum . . . 8: Per anfractus deinde obscurissimos egressus in hunc locum me perduxit prolatoque peculio coepit rogare stuprum. Iam pro cella meretrix assem exegerat. . . .

---

3. As described by Jashemski, *Gardens* I (1979) 167–81, 352–53.

4. For a different view, see Laurence, *Roman Pompeii* (1994) 70, 72, 75 (brothels were relegated to the backstreets to screen them from upper-class housing [a relatively mild form of zoning], though they were often in close proximity to this housing) and Wallace-Hadrill, "Public Honour and Private Shame" (1995) 51, 54–55 (who names the Forum and part of the *Via dell'Abbondanza* as areas with zoning prohibitions on prostitution: see below in the text). Cf. Clarke, *Looking at Lovemaking* (1998) 311 n. 10.

5. Even so, the stereotype on which he relies may have greater resonance for Rome than for other towns: see Ramage, "Urban Problems" (1983) 66, 82.

6–7. (Encolpius). But neither was I paying careful attention to the street nor was I conscious of where our lodgings were . . . I asked (the little old woman selling vegetables) "If you please, good woman, do you have any idea where I live/am staying?" . . . Then when we came to a place set pretty far back, the charming old lady threw open a patchwork curtain and said "Here is where you ought to live." When I started to say that I didn't recognize the house, I noticed naked prostitutes tiptoeing around some notices with prices written on them. Slowly, or rather much too late, I realized that I'd been led into a brothel . . . 8. (Ascyltos). Next, passing through some very dark twists and turns he led me to this place, whipped out his wallet, and asked for sex. A prostitute had already charged an as for a room. . . .

Encolpius misses a series of clues as to where he is headed. First, there is his vegetable-peddling Sibyl, the old woman herself, who in the mindset of male members of the upper-classes must be selling more than vegetables.[6] The patchwork curtain is, or rather should be, another giveaway.[7] Ascyltos is so oblivious that he misses the significance of the room-payment. There is also the fact that the word *stabulum* can either mean lodgings or brothel or—not at all to be ruled out—both at once. The word *habitare* also can have more than one meaning; it can refer to temporary quarters or to permanent lodgings and again has the sense that the same establishment might cater to both arrangements at the same time for different sorts of guest. The passage is valuable evidence for confirming the association of brothels with lower-class housing.[8] Both of our (anti-) heroes fail to pick up on the ambiguity of the terminology and its implications until it is too late. Their respectability as would-be members of the elite is sadly compromised by a foray, however unintentional, into the brothel.

The most significant clue that both men overlook, however, is the cliché that brothels are set back along winding streets removed from a main thoroughfare and far out of the way. The cliché means of course that neither all or most nor—conversely—that no brothels were thus secluded in actual fact.[9] If

---

6. On female retailers as prostitutes, see McGinn, "Definition" (1997 [1998]) esp. 107–12. What marks the woman as a procuress rather than as prostitute is her age (i.e., an "old woman" [*anus*]).

7. This detail appears at Iuv. 6.121 as part of a stereotypical description of a brothel. Some (literary) brothels have *cellae* with doors: see chap. 2.

8. See chaps. 2 and 8.

9. Propertius as well picks up on the cliché of the "arcana . . . taberna": 4.8.19. See also Mart. 5.84.4: "arcana . . . popina."

Homer Simpson were led past a sign of golden arches to discover—to his utter amazement!—that he was in a fast food restaurant we could not safely conclude that all such places displayed golden arches. By the same token, I expect that few persons nowadays would visit a red-light district expecting to find a red light, though there are of course places that cater to some customers' expectations through reliance on this symbol. Amsterdam has some good examples. This is why the cliché about brothel-location does not mean that no brothels were actually set in out-of-the-way places, as we saw with the Purpose-Built Brothel in chapter 8.

It is also possible that the cliché is treated in an exaggerated way here because Petronius wants the reader to associate a visit to this brothel with a passage to the Underworld. If true, this interpretation would explain why this locale is set further back and more out of the way than others of its kind. It is hardly necessary to insist on this point, however.

Next, in a comparison sometimes thought to reflect a notion of moral geography, Seneca provides an idealized moral distinction between good places and bad, which is valid in my view neither as prescriptive nor descriptive topography:[10]

Sen. *Vita Beata* 7.3: Quid dissimilia, immo diversa componitis? Altum quiddam est virtus, excelsum et regale, invictum, infatigabile; voluptas humile, servile, imbecillum, caducum, cuius statio et domicilium fornices et popinae sunt. virtutem in templo convenies, in foro, in curia, pro muris stantem, pulverulentam, coloratam, callosas habentem manus; voluptatem latitantem saepius ac tenebras captantem circa balinea ac sudatoria ac loca aedilem metuentia, mollem, enervem, mero atque unguento madentem, pallidam aut fucatam et medicamentis pollinctam.

Why do you unite things that are unlike, or, rather, completely different? Virtue is something lofty, exalted and king-like, undefeated and untiring.

---

10. See Wallace-Hadrill, "Public Honour and Private Shame" (1995) 39 with n. 1, who is criticized by Kellum "Spectacle" (1999) 291, who points out that some upper-class Romans such as Catullus, Augustus, and Seneca himself seem to have been well-acquainted with the seedier locales described in this text. For what is in my view a more persuasive treatment of the passage, see Edwards, *Politics of Immorality* (1993) 173–75, who omits considerations of zoning entirely. The observation of DeFelice, *Roman Hospitality* (2001) 133, regarding this evidence that upper-class attitudes were not monolithically Stoic is important. I note in passing Seneca's wish (*Ep.* 51.4) not to live "inter popinas": the context suggests this means he does not want to live "in," rather than "near," these fast-food restaurants—Baiae in fact emerges as one great *popina*!

Pleasure is something low, slavish, weak, perishable, whose hangout and home are brothels and taverns. You will find virtue in the temple, in the Forum, in the Senate-House, standing in front of the city walls, sunburned, with calloused hands. Pleasure you'll find more often hiding out, lurking in the shadows, around the baths, the sweating-rooms, the places afraid of the aedile. It is delicate, languid, soaked in unmixed wine and perfume, either pale or painted with cosmetics and laid out like a corpse.

It is interesting that in the end *Virtus* has to be moved to the edge or outside of the city entirely, evidently represented as an idealized soldier or agricultural worker. Seneca's discourse stands as a variant of the city:bad/country:good theme so popular in Roman moralistic writing.[11] His choice of a soldier as symbol, if this interpretation is correct, is interesting in light of the fact that soldiers were among the leading clients of prostitutes. No matter how we interpret this passage we can safely conclude that Seneca writes in a highly moralizing way and not as a topographer, at least as we conceive of this role today.[12] One of the types of "bad places" he cites are baths, which no one has argued to be the object of moral zoning.

In the end I argue that there is indeed a fit between literary evidence and archaeological evidence in the matter of moral zoning. But there is little cause for celebration here. We may be dealing more with coincidence than with an actual fit. There is a deeper problem with literary evidence in its relation to the physical geography of a city, which should not be overlooked. This difficulty we saw arise in chapter 3 in the always immanent contrast between topography on the page and topography on the ground. A similar difficulty comes to us from nineteenth-century New York City, where middle-class residents and visitors were inclined to make sense of their city by dividing it into honorable and dishonorable zones. "They envisioned a city with regions of

---

11. See, for example, Wallace-Hadrill, "Elites and Trade" (1991) 244–49, where he shows that the city, the whole city, and nothing but the city was associated in this discourse with brothels, taverns, and lowlife, in contrast to the rustic virtues of country living. See also Braund, "City and Country" (1989); André, "Espace urbain" (1991); Edwards, *Politics of Immorality* (1993) 190–91; Edwards, *Writing Rome* (1996) esp. 125–29; Gold, "Urban Life" (1998); Dalby, *Empire* (2000) 208–42; Bond, "*Urbs*" (2001). The theme is taken up by medical writers who gloss the moral contrast of city and country with health concerns: Nutton, "Medical Thoughts" (2000) 66. DeFelice, *Roman Hospitality* (2001) 139, argues that the point of the passage is that pleasure is found everywhere in the city, and it is up to the good Stoic to rein in his passions.

12. See the cautions of Braund, "City and Country" (1989); Laurence, "Writing the Roman Metropolis" (1997) against taking the elements of such evidence as facts and not as attitudes.

virtue and vice, of safety and danger, of sunshine and shadow."[13] In so doing, they misread the areas they were attempting to describe, constructing a cityscape that was tidier in the popular imagination than it was in actual fact. There is no reason to suspect the Romans were incapable of a similar sort of error, imagining Rome as better, or worse, than it really was. To be certain that we understand the Roman city correctly, we must approach the literary and archaeological evidence concurrently, the cultural constructions as well as the physical.

Seneca mentions the Forum as one of the "good places," which leads me to my final point about the argument for moral zoning. Andrew Wallace-Hadrill makes a strong argument that undesirable activities, which in concrete terms occurred in brothels and *popinae*, were zoned away from certain highly marked and highly charged public spaces.[14] He identifies these spaces as the Forum at Rome and the Forum and a stretch of the *Via dell'Abbondanza* between the Forum and the Stabian Baths at Pompeii. I will argue that, despite its manifest strengths, the argument cannot hold in the end. In the end, to be sure, the Roman city is not quite as "bad" a place as the moralists would have us believe.

MORAL GEOGRAPHY

First, let us look at the *Via dell'Abbondanza*. Wallace-Hadrill emphasizes that the pavement here shows at the western end faint wheel ruts and at the eastern end, where the street opens into a small piazza, no rutting at all, which leads him to conclude that there was a restriction on wheeled traffic for this area.[15] He speculates that this section of the street formed "a processional route in public festivals, religious and civic ceremonies passing between forum

---

13. Gilfoyle, *City of Eros* (1992) 223.

14. Wallace-Hadrill, "Public Honour and Private Shame" (1995) 46–51. The rationale behind privileging the Roman Forum is not entirely clear, given that public building took place in various parts of the city: see Frézouls, "Rome" (1987) 388.

15. Wallace-Hadrill, "Public Honour and Private Shame" (1995) 47–49. The map he reproduces at 49 shows that the middle part of this stretch of the *Via dell'Abbondanza* is in fact heavily rutted. This suggests that his inference of a "restriction" here may not be well-founded. The drop in road level at the eastern end of the piazza in front of the Stabian Baths may have been part of an effort to monumentalize the setting. The consequent obstruction to wheeled traffic may therefore have been a side effect of this monumentalization and not its purpose. Worth noting is that the study of wheel ruts on which Wallace-Hadrill relies does not offer moral zoning as an explanation for blocked-off streets, but rather a concern with drainage, though it does leave open the possibility of other explanations: Tsujimura, "Ruts in Pompeii" (1990) 65–66, 85–86; cf. 58. See also the criticism of DeFelice, *Roman Hospitality* (2001) 131 n. 386.

and theatre, or from temple to temple."[16] But his most telling piece of evidence is the relative scarcity of *cauponae/popinae* along this route, since there is only one certain example at 7.1.1, 62, compared to other stretches of the *Via dell'Abbondanza* itself.

Unfortunately, that lone example is enough to refute the zoning hypothesis, in my view.[17] It makes no sense that the notional processional route was almost, but not completely, pure. In fact, if the participants in the hypothetical processions passed through the piazza in front of the Stabian Baths, they would have encountered another such establishment (with a number of rooms in back) at the corner of the *Via Stabiana* (8.4.17–18).[18] Upon making a right turn on this street, on the way to the temple or theater, they would have had to negotiate at least two or three additional examples of *cauponae/popinae* (see 1.4.1–3, 1.4.4, 1.4.11, 8.4.19, 8.4.25). If they tried to avoid the piazza, and the *Via Stabiana*, by making the right turn a block earlier they would have encountered both *cauponae/popinae* (see 8.4.45, 8.4.47) and a latrine (8.4.41).[19] None of these facts, however, need in the final analysis detract from the hypothesis of a processional route. Roman religion, in fact, tended to attract, rather than repel, the practice of commerce.[20] Or we may prefer the reverse statement that the religious import of space imposes itself on already existing relationships of production and (re)distribution.[21] There is simply no evidence to support this hypothesis, however.

Next, we take up the question of the Forum both in Rome and in Pompeii. Here we confront a different scenario. Bars and brothels were not simply scarce, but nonexistent, or virtually so. Is this evidence for a Roman regulationist regime and a successful one at that?

Wallace-Hadrill has shown well how the Republican Roman Forum was gradually transformed, above all in the second century B.C., from a commercial

---

16. Wallace-Hadrill, "Public Honour and Private Shame" (1995) 49.

17. This is not to deny other possibilities might exist, for example, at 8.5.17, 20; 8.5.21; 8.5.22–23.

18. DeFelice, *Roman Hospitality* (2001) 138, points out that an old entrance to the Baths opened on the alleged processional route.

19. Both streets in question are labeled as deviant on Laurence's map of deviant streets in Pompeii: Laurence, *Roman Pompeii* (1994) 85. The point is noted by DeFelice, *Roman Hospitality* (2001) 138.

20. See Morel, "Topographie" (1987) 144–45; Morel, "Artisanat" (2001) 253; Morel, "Rome capitale" (2001) 150.

21. See Horden and Purcell, *Corrupting Sea* (2000) 457.

and residential district into a monumental public center.[22] At Pompeii, the process appears to have been even more gradual, and it was not completed until the middle of the first century A.D., when a series of public buildings dedicated to the cult of the emperor replaced the remaining shops and houses on the long eastern side of the Forum.[23] In both venues, his explanation is that the Romans "cleaned up" the Forum by pushing away undesirable activities.

There are difficulties with this view, however. First, it contains something of a paradox. Either there were bars and brothels in these places before zoning—in which case we must explain why they were at one time tolerated and then not at another—or there were not—in which case zoning was unnecessary and therefore unlikely.[24] In fact, the evidence for brothels near and even in the Roman Forum is not to be despised. In recent years scholars have tended to discount Giuseppe Lugli's theory that a brothel was located along the Sacra Via near the Arch of Titus (and therefore in a strict sense just outside the Forum).[25] All the same, the case for a purpose-built brothel with *caupona* or, as recently argued, a *caupona* with attendant prostitution,[26] remains strong. Examination of the remains suggests a *terminus ante quem* of A.D. 64,[27] at which time the establishment was presumably either destroyed by the Neronian fire or removed soon afterwards in connection with the construction of the *Domus Aurea*. It is highly unlikely that its destruction/removal resulted from a campaign of moral zoning, since Nero stands as an unlikely avatar of such a campaign. We may compare the other two Roman purpose-

---

22. Wallace-Hadrill, *Houses and Society* (1994) 129–31; see also Morel, "Topographie" (1987) who inclines toward the speculative; see, for example, 153, on the motivation for the *Horrea Agrippiana*. In Morel's analysis, as well as in Wallace-Hadrill's, a nineteenth-century Parisian model emerges explicitly (139): "[p]ar ces opérations à la Hausmann, le centre de Rome . . . se trouve débarrassé des activités artisanales et commerciales. . . ." See also Morel, "Métiers" (1994) 150–59; Bustany and Géroudet, *Rome* (2001) 204–5.

23. See Zanker, *Pompeii* (1998) 53–55, 81–102.

24. The pre-79 levels of the Pompeian Forum await the necessary investigation; at Rome there is good evidence for a tavern in the Republican Forum: see App. *BC* 1.54 and the other possibilities at Kleberg, *Hôtels* (1957) 59, 135 n. 75; Morel, "Topographie" (1987) 134 (not the least of which is Catullus's *salax taberna*: 37.1–2). Among the lowlife throng of the Vicus Tuscus (adjacent to the Forum) is a pimp, ca. 30 B.C.: Hor. *Serm.* 2.3.226–31. See also Plaut. *Curc.* 482 (male—and perhaps female as well—prostitutes in the Vicus Tuscus), 485 (a brothel in the Velabrum); Porphyrio *ad* Hor. *Serm.* 2.3.228 (pimps still in the Vicus Tuscus).

25. Lugli, *Monumenti* (1947); see also Morel, "Topographie" (1987) 146 n. 108; Carandini, *Schiavi in Italia* (1988) 361; Papi, *LTUR* (1995) s.v. "Domus: M. Aemilius Scaurus," 26, 392; Wallace-Hadrill, "Case" (2000) 186, who argue against this theory.

26. See Tomei, *"Domus* oppure *Lupanar?"* (1995).

27. See Tomei, *"Domus* oppure *Lupanar?"* (1995) 610–12.

built brothels identified by Lugli, one of which was located in the Forum itself near the so-called Temple of Romulus and the other, in the Forum Boarium.[28]

At Rome before Augustus and at Pompeii even later the program of public building proceeded gradually and at private initiative. What the new buildings displaced were not simply unsavory businesses but all or nearly all commercial activities that required permanent facilities such as shops. One fate carried off pimp, brothel-prostitute, and tavern operator, as well as the proverbial butcher, baker, and candlestick maker. Martial celebrates Domitian's freeing of the Roman streets from all manner of retailers, including barbers, tavern keepers, cooks, and butchers.[29] The poem participates, to be sure, in a long tradition of anti-urban moralizing.[30] The removal of butchers from the mid-Republican Roman Forum appears to have been gradual and partial.[31] The shops of bankers appear to have been an honorable exception, at least for a time.[32] The evidence suggests that the displacement of commerce from the Forum did not proceed in a straight line nor was it permanent in nature.[33]

The same trend also resulted in the removal of private residential housing for Romans of all social levels.[34] It is difficult to find in this development the display of any official sensitivity toward the location of bars and brothels. Varro, for example, hails the transition from the butcher's shop to the banker's office as an enhancement of the *forensis dignitas*.[35] We should not conclude

---

28. Lugli, *Monumenti* (1947). On the concept of the "purpose-built brothel," and the identification of these establishments as brothels, see chaps. 7 and 8.

29. Mart. 7.61. On the widespread distribution of all manner of shops (which were also often dwellings) throughout the city, see Purcell, "*Plebs Urbana*" (1994) 659–73.

30. As shown by Joshel, *Work* (1992) 68.

31. See Wallace-Hadrill, *Houses and Society* (1994) 130.

32. Varro *apud* Non. Marc. 853L (see below in the text).

33. See Platner and Ashby, s.v. "Tabernae circa Forum" (1929) 504–5; Wagner, "Tabernen" (1982) 394; Morel, "Topographie" (1987) 139 n. 60, 154 (on the *Horrea Piperataria*); Purcell, "*Plebs Urbana*" (1994) 647. For the possible return of shops just outside the Forum after they were removed by Nero, see Lugli, *Monumenti* (1947) 160–61. The evidence of Martial suggests the continuity, or at least the return, of shops in and near the Forum: Kardos, "Quartiers" (2002) 123–24, 127. Wallace-Hadrill, "Emperors and Houses" (2001) 135, now appears to concede the point that the displacement neither proceeded in a straight line nor was permanent. See now also Morel, "Artisanat" (2001) 252–53; Morel, "Rome capitale" (2001) 148–49. Cf. the design of the imperial Fora, which shows some interesting divergences over time. The Julian had shops, the Augustan did not, and the Trajanic did: Wagner, 394–95. On commercial establishments in and near the Forum Romanum, see now the survey by Papi, "Artigiani" (2002).

34. This is well described by Guidobaldi, "Abitazioni" (2000) 143–61. For the phenomenon of the residences of the wealthy being pushed out of the center, see also Patterson, "On the Margins" (2000) 96. It is at bottom difficult to separate the removal of residential buildings from that of commercial premises: see Kunst, "Dach" (2000) esp. 300–301.

35. Varro *apud* Non. Marc. 853L. The phrase *forensis dignitas* signifies the social and moral stature of the Forum, especially as reflected in its appearance: see *OLD* s.v. *dignitas*.

that this was the reason for the change, as some historians appear to assume, or that the government was involved in zoning change, or that butchers' shops were equated with brothels. Aside from celebrating the emperor's glory, the monumentalization of public space in the urban center might have also have been designed to free up space in a very crowded area.[36] For the same reason, public building pushed out private residences. To the extent that this involved lower-class housing, brothels may well have been affected.[37] But this does not mean that they were in any sense targeted for removal.

It is instructive here to compare the absence of brothels from the monumentalized city centers with the absence of the luxury latrines that were popular in Roman cities during the imperial period. The more crowded with public buildings a forum became, the less likely it was to sport a fancy facility of this kind.[38] The rationale for not installing one there was evidently based on a perception of pedestrian traffic reduced by the spread of monumental buildings, not on the idea that such establishments were somehow aesthetically or morally inappropriate for that setting. The whole point of the imperial luxury latrine was evidently to guarantee a certain nobility to defecation, above all defecation by (male) members of the elite, in part by making it so public (which a Forum location might be thought to assist).[39] So the reasons behind the lack of showcase latrines in the Forum are vastly different from those that hold for brothels, which were incidentally displaced by the spread of public buildings. Both explanations, however, are related to the increasing monumentalization of this space, and both might seem rather foreign in different ways to modern experience and expectations.

There is no evidence here of what might be called "reverse zoning," that is, the encroachment of respectable society on a traditional vice district, resulting in calls for the latter's removal.[40] And, of course, removal of shops

---

36. For this argument, see Frézouls, "Rome" (1987) 384.

37. The *insulae* were not distributed evenly throughout the city: see Hermansen, "Population" (1978) and chap. 2. This fact in itself militates against the idea of a random distribution of brothels. Relevant here is the entry *lupanarii* in the late-antique Regionary Catalogs for Rome. Once thought to denote a concentration or even a complex of brothels in *Regio 2*, this has been interpreted to signify government offices responsible for record-keeping on, and taxation of, brothels: Richardson, *Topographical Dictionary* (1992) 238; Palombi, *LTUR* (1996) s.v. "Lupanarii" 198; Ginouvès, *Dictionnaire méthodique* (1998) 3, 84.

38. See Neudecker, *Pracht der Latrine* (1994) 76.

39. See Neudecker, *Pracht der Latrine* (1994) 153. In some cases latrines may have been provided for women: Neudecker, 63–65.

40. See Best, *Controlling Vice* (1998) 30.

does not necessarily imply banishment of ambulatory vendors or those who set up their wares under porticoes, for example.[41] Finally, the effect of a policy targeting undesirables for removal might have resulted in their displacement to the city's edge, but Rome's margin shows a decidedly mixed use at various periods of the city's history.[42]

When Wallace-Hadrill makes, in another context, the excellent point about the change in terminology for honorific arch, from *fornix*, which can mean brothel, to *arcus*, he certainly seems correct that the motivation here was sensitivity over the appearance of the ambiguous word *fornix* in official documents.[43] He notes in this context that, ". . . the rhetoric of the Principate is not the same as that of the Republic."[44] The key to the change in terminology, as he demonstrates, has to do with the change from the Republican practice of erecting an honorary arch through private initiative to that of the Principate, when the Senate authorized this. "The *fornix* was a symbol of the seamy side of city life."[45] So it was, but what remains to be demonstrated with regard to zoning is the precise connection between this rhetoric and the reality of prostitution.[46]

Two factors above all militate against the case for moral zoning in the Forum, both at Rome and elsewhere, in my view. One is that prostitutes worked in the Forum. The other is that the authorities wanted them there. The first point is attested for Pompeii, Rome, and elsewhere.[47] For example, in

---

41. Mart. 7.61 certainly seems to suggest that special measures were required to this end. See also Spano, "Illuminazione" (1920) 62–64; Sperber, *City in Roman Palestine* (1998) 12; Kardos, "Vrbs" (2001) 404; Morel, "Artisanat" (2001) 254.

42. See Wiseman, "A Stroll on the Rampart" (1998) 15; Hope, "Contempt and Respect" (2000) 112, 123; Patterson, "On the Margins" (2000) 96–97, 102–3. On prostitutes frequenting the tombs and walls on the city's edge, see also chap. 2.

43. Wallace-Hadrill, "Roman Arches" (1990) esp. 145–47.

44. Wallace-Hadrill, "Roman Arches" (1990) 147.

45. Wallace-Hadrill, "Roman Arches" (1990) 145, citing Sen. *Vita Beata* 7.3, discussed in the text above. I agree that the Seneca passage is hugely symbolic, deploying however not topography per se, but items in the Roman cityscape as metaphors for vice and virtue.

46. It is beyond doubt that with the advent of the Principate, a significant change occurred in the Roman management of public space: see, for example, Wallace-Hadrill, "Roman Arches" (1990); Zanker, "Veränderungen" (1994). But to argue that this involved the express, permanent removal of prostitution from areas like the Forum is to rely on a modernizing assumption not justified by the ancient evidence.

47. For graffiti at Pompeii alluding to the practice of prostitution in the area of the Forum, see *CIL* 4.1860, 1948 (both from the Basilica). For the Forum Romanum, see Plaut. *Curc.* 470–73, *Truc.* 66–73 (pimps and prostitutes near the shops of bankers); Prop. 2.23.15 (on the Sacra Via); Sen. *Ben.* 6.32.1 (inferred from Julia's alleged behavior); Mart. 2.63.1–2 (Sacra Via); [Quint.] *Decl.* 385.1 (though this might be any forum, not just the Forum Romanum); C. Titius *apud* Macrob. 3.16.15–16; see Papi, "Artigiani" (2002) 61–62. For cities in Roman Palestine, see *Babylonian Talmud Shabbath* 33b; further, Sperber, *City in Roman Palestine* (1998) 12–17. For late antiquity, see Proc. *Anec.* 17.5.

an important passage, Dio of Prusa attacks pimps for installing prostitutes in brothels (and/or cribs) that are in full view of every part of the city—in front of the houses of magistrates, in the marketplaces, near public buildings and temples, and in the midst of all that is holy.[48] Dio's assault on pimps is a very thinly veiled indictment of Roman society and its approach to prostitution. This speech, which was almost certainly delivered at Rome, criticizes conditions prevailing not just in the Greek cities of the East, but throughout the Empire and above all in the capital itself.[49] It is significant that Dio attacks the widespread diffusion of prostitutes and brothels in the Roman city, and equally important that he is the only Greek or Roman to do so.[50] His critique is extreme, and for all that there is not a hint here that he is exposing a failed policy of moral zoning.

In fact, on a more general level we have plenty of evidence identifying women who worked in the marketplace as prostitutes.[51] No doubt much of this evidence is grounded in elite, male bias against lower-class working women. But it would be hyperskeptical to use this conclusion to reject the idea that prostitutes were a common feature of the monumental center of many Roman towns. Of course evidence of prostitutes in the Forum proves nothing about the presence or absence of brothels there. Commercial sex does not always require a building, for one thing. Moreover, residential housing that could harbor brothels, as in the Subura, was not far away.

Why would the authorities want prostitutes in the Forum? From a modern perspective, one of the creepier aspects of Roman public policy on prostitution was the way in which it tried to make the activity as visible as possible. Hidden deviance is what tended to exercise the Roman moralist.[52] Horace exploits this theme to argue for the advantages of sex with prostitutes over sex with *matronae*: what you see is what you get.[53] Statute law gives stark expression to this concern. The *lex Iulia* on adultery insisted on the public registration of prostitutes and the wearing of the toga associated with prostitutes by

---

48. Dio Chrys. 7.133–34. The point is supported by the evidence presented in chap. 2.

49. Evidence, argument, and literature at McGinn, *Roman Prostitution* (forthcoming). In his speech to the Alexandrians, Dio appears to assume that prostitution is rife throughout their city: Dio Chrys. 32 (esp. 90–94) with Montserrat, *Sex and Society* (1996) 121.

50. For criticism from Roman Palestine over prostitutes in the marketplace (i.e., the forum), see *Babylonian Talmud Shabbath* 33b.

51. See McGinn, "Definition" (1997 [1998]) esp. 89–97, 107–12.

52. McGinn, *Prostitution, Sexuality, and the Law* (1998) 125 n. 124. Add Meyer-Zwiffelhoffer, *Phallus* (1995) 133, 150–51, 165–66. See also the discussion of body language in chap. 3. Again, I think it more appropriate to regard such evidence as Sen. *Vita Beata* 7.3 as part of this moralizing discourse, rather than as a realistic indication of where brothels were located.

53. Hor. *Serm.* 1.2.83–110; cf. Athen. 13.569A–F.

convicted adulteresses (and perhaps use of the toga by prostitutes themselves, converting what had been custom into a legal regulation). This suggests that the ideal official treatment of the prostitute was openly to humiliate her.[54] Hence, there was no advantage to driving prostitutes and prostitution underground. The prostitute would only be more difficult to tax and to blame and therefore less apt to serve the public interest.[55] For the Romans there was something honest and almost honorable about open vice, especially as compared with the hidden variety, which they thought *must* be bad.[56]

"Prostitutes were a very visible part of the cityscape."[57] Repugnant as this is to modern sensibilities, the respectable matron's honor was constructed in no small measure from the dishonor of the whore. For the Romans, as for Simone Weil, purity was the power to contemplate defilement. The prostitute had her place in the Forum, after all, just as she had her place in the moral economy. She served the purpose of maintaining not public honor and private shame, as Wallace-Hadrill would have it, but rather public honor and *public* shame.

Serving this purpose was not just a matter of prostitutes and their trade. The public humiliation and execution of criminals, in the arena located in the very center of the city, had precisely the same aim.[58] What is more, the mangled bodies of criminals might be dragged through the streets in front of a crowd to make the same point.[59] These examples might suggest that Romans had no interest in socially constructed urban space. More likely is the possibility that their practices proceeded from such a radically different set of premises and values than our own as to render our attempts to comprehend them very rough going indeed.[60] From our point of view, their conception of "honorable space," like their conception of "religious space," seems enormously mutable and flexible.[61] Discussions of the sacralization of space in the Forum and elsewhere might with profit take up this point.[62]

---

54. Only after a set period of relegation (its length is unknown) could convicted adulteresses be seen in the Forum wearing a toga. See McGinn, *Prostitution, Sexuality, and the Law* (1998) 156–71, 216–19.

55. For the role of the prostitute in Roman moral pedagogy, see McGinn, *Prostitution, Sexuality, and the Law* (1998) chap. 5, esp. 207–15. For the tax on prostitutes, see McGinn, chap. 7.

56. See the discussion about privacy in the brothel in chap. 2.

57. Kellum, "Spectacle" (1999) 295 n. 27.

58. As Laurence, "Emperors" (1993) 84, argues.

59. See Bodel, "Dealing with the Dead" (2000) 147.

60. See the comments of Horden and Purcell, *Corrupting Sea* (2000) 555. For a recent, interesting effort to tackle the problem of Roman domestic space, see Grahame, *Reading Space* (2000).

61. On the latter, see Horden and Purcell, *Corrupting Sea* (2000) 444, who point out that the geography of religion in Mediterranean cultures is neither independent of other geographies, nor particularly modern.

62. See, for example, Hinard, "Rome dans Rome" (1991) esp. 46.

From a modern perspective, it might seem highly inappropriate to allow the two brothels identified in and near the Roman Forum to stand so close, for example, to the Atrium Vestae. Ovid's Vestal did not have to look very far after all to catch a glimpse of bodies for sale. The Vestals were in fact so heavily invested in urban real estate—their activity in this field is thought to have helped legitimize private interests–we cannot exclude the possibility that they owned a brothel or two.[63] As a fundamental premise of economics and morals, the prostitute had to be as accessible as possible.[64]

The literary evidence for the diffusion of prostitution in the ancient Roman city encourages the view that it was practically ubiquitous. Catullus has Lesbia, reconfigured as a whore after their breakup, servicing her clients at the crossroads, and in the alleys, of the city.[65] Prostitutes were not only at the city's center but at its edge, among the tombs that lined the great consular roads, or near the city walls, according to Martial.[66] Dio of Prusa is not the only author to place them near temples.[67] It is Juvenal in fact who poses the famous question: "at what temple does a woman not prostitute herself?"[68] Though in this context he assimilates adulteresses to prostitutes, the most likely interpretation is that prostitutes at least might be found in and around some temples.

As for Pompeii, an examination of the next-door neighbors of establishments identified as brothels, carried out with the assistance of the two "Address-Books" compiled in recent years for that city,[69] suggests that these establishments were fully integrated into the fabric of city life.[70] The neighboring residences were of various sizes and quality, including a few *atrium*-style houses (such as the famous House of the Menander). Other neighbors were a number of commercial establishments, including a dyer's, a wool worker's, and a weaver's shop, and one or two fuller's shops, and representatives of the service sector, including a barbershop, a hotel, several inns and taverns, and, of course, other brothels.

We appear with the preceding paragraphs to have reached the much

---

63. On the Vestals' urban real estate interests, see Horden and Purcell, *Corrupting Sea* (2000) 429.

64. See Flemming, "*Quae Corpore*" (1999) 46, on this point.

65. Catull. 58. Cf. Hor. C. 1.25.10 for the alley and Prop. 4.7.19 for the crossroads.

66. See n. 47 for Martial's evidence on prostitutes in the Forum and chap. 2 for the rest.

67. See chap. 2.

68. Iuv. 9.24: ". . . quo non prostat femina templo?"

69. See De Simone, *Pompei* (1988) 103–84; Eschebach and Müller-Trollius, *Gebäudeverzeichnis* (1993).

70. For the argument that prostitution was pervasive in ancient Attica, see Cohen, "Economic Analysis" (forthcoming), citing Xen. *Mem.* 2.2.4.

desired fit between archaeological and literary evidence. Once again, however, the result is somewhat illusory. We have something of a tale of two cities here, with, minor exceptions aside, the archaeological evidence deriving from Pompeii and the literary evidence concerning Rome. Rome's exceptional status as the capital informs this literary evidence, as it functioned as the city many Romans affected to hate. To take one notable example, Tacitus, describing the spread of Christianity, has this phenomenon bursting forth ". . . not only throughout Judaea, the source of this evil, but also throughout the capital, where all things terrible or shameful from everywhere flow together and become fashionable."[71] Examples might be multiplied to no purpose.[72] This tradition, allied to, or even embedded in, the country:good/city:bad dichotomy explored above, raises the suspicion that Roman writing on the sale of sex in the city presents a darker picture than the facts can sustain.[73] In other words, just as nineteenth-century New Yorkers conceived of their city as nicer than it was in actual fact, the Romans tended to favor pessimism over realism.

This conclusion complicates our reliance on the literary evidence as a guide to the presence of sex in the city. We cannot simply cite a text such as the *Curculio* of Plautus as self-evident proof that sex was extremely widespread or mobile.[74] Such evidence emanates from a long tradition that draws the map of Roman "vice" essentially by overlaying it on the Roman city and above all on the capital itself, making that city more difficult to read.[75]

The result, we can almost say with certainty, is that the presence of prostitution is exaggerated for moralizing purposes or possibly, in the case of satirists, for making fun of moralizing purposes. Can Juvenal literally mean that at least one prostitute stands before *every* temple? It is risky to take this evidence as strictly factual. Of course this conclusion hardly means we are entitled to assume the opposite was true—that no temples had prostitutes in

---

71. Tac. *Ann.* 15.44.3: ". . . non modo per Iudaeam, originem eius mali, sed per urbem etiam, quo cuncta undique atrocia aut pudenda confluunt celebranturque."

72. It is difficult all the same to avoid mentioning such texts as Hor. *Serm.* 2.6; Iuv. 2 and 3; Amm. Marc. 14.6.

73. The positive tradition extolling to the point of exaggeration the grandeur of the capital finds its counterpoint—there is an ancient as well as a modern branch of each—in a negative one that (over)emphasizes the dark side of city life, which is often, though not always, contrasted with life in the country, the past, or both. See Purcell, "City of Rome" (1992) 424; Eyben, *Youth* (1993) 265 n. 92; Edwards, *Writing Rome* (1996) esp. 3, 7, 42–43, 102–5, 112; Laurence, "Writing the Roman Metropolis" (1997) and the country-city literature cited above in notes 11 and 12.

74. Plaut. *Curc.* 461–85.

75. See the comments of André, "Espace urbain" (1991) 94.

front of them. We would simply then fall into the trap of imagining ancient Rome as nicer than it was, in fact.

Roman practice regarding the landscape of venal sex may not seem utterly outlandish when compared with some modern official approaches to prostitution. They suggest the truth of a point made elsewhere in this study, namely that "modern" does not automatically signify rational or successful. The nineteenth-century Parisian regime advocated by Alexandre Parent-Duchâtelet sought to guarantee both the accessibility and the invisibility of prostitutes, but it devoutly feared clandestine ones.[76] It was not only successful in helping to generate that which it feared most, but allowed or encouraged clandestine prostitutes to be be bold about their activity. This led to an even more undesirable situation, the oxymoron of open clandestinity. "The clandestine prostitute of the late nineteenth century made no attempt to hide her status or to conduct her trade in secret."[77] A similar experience of policy leading to unintended and most unwanted consequences can be seen with other systems modeled on the Parisian, such as in late-imperial Russia.[78]

The Roman approach is itself easy to criticize, even easier to dislike. A full understanding of its implications, however, demands comparison with other cultures whose hostility to prostitutes is no less patent. What emerges is that the Roman policy, for all of its paradox and repulsiveness, may have done a fairly satisfactory job of managing the challenge of prostitution as perceived by the Romans themselves. The implications of this fact for the economy of Roman prostitution remain to be drawn out in the next chapter.

76. Bernheimer, *Figures of Ill Repute* (1989) 16–17, 25.
77. Harsin, *Policing Prostitution* (1985) 246.
78. Bernstein, *Sonia's Daughters* (1995) 28, 46–56, 79, 83.

Chapter Ten

LEAVING LAS VEGAS

In speaking of the locality of the houses of ill-
repute in the great city, it would be more difficult
to state where they are not, than where they are.
—George Ellington, *apud* Gilfoyle
City of Eros (1992) 53.

The result of this study, which has venues for commercial sex scattered throughout the Roman city and located in a variety of social and commercial contexts, suggests some directions that future enquiry into the problem of Roman brothels might take. The first step should almost certainly be to make a detailed examination of the physical remains in what remains our one best source for archaeological information, Pompeii. That procedure might help eliminate some of the more doubtful candidates or at least isolate the possible operation of a brothel both in spatial and chronological terms, the latter standing as a further refinement of the post-62 problem treated in chapter 6.

What might be expected to result from such a project is a more nuanced treatment of the central subject of this book. One possible direction to take is to look more closely at the three subtypes for brothels identified in this study, purpose-built, tavern (*caupona/popina*) with rooms in back and/or upstairs, and the catch-all type associated with lower-class lodgings, as well as the two subtypes for cribs, namely, a single room off the street and single room in back of a bar.[1] It is worth noting here that while these types do find equivalents in

---

1. For the crib subtypes, see chap. 7; for the brothel subtypes, see appendix 1.

other cultures they are far from universal, let alone inevitable. In medieval Germany, for example, the fundamental distinction scholars draw between brothel types is that between the municipal institution of the *Frauenhaus* and illegal (but often informally tolerated) venues.[2]

I am not very optimistic that we will be able to elaborate a typology of brothels beyond the tripartite scheme I have described above. We can imagine in theory a list of known or suspected brothels that could be analyzed to generate a set of necessary and sufficient conditions to identify brothels. There would have to be some core characteristics that function as the sine qua non of a Roman brothel, ideally based on a combination of written and material evidence. That this exercise in empirical method cannot without difficulty lead to a typology that is superior to the one we have is suggested first by the disjuncture between literary and archaeological evidence. It is more accurate perhaps to say that these two types of evidence are not so much discordant as mutually inadequate. It is naive to place too much faith in the ability of archaeologists to furnish definitive answers to all of our questions.[3] They are in no position to deliver more evidence than the sites preserve. What can we reasonably expect to turn up from establishments that have been more or less fully excavated? Graffiti, art, or masonry beds are hardly going to be found in sufficient numbers (indeed, one may question if any are going to be found at all) to allay our doubts about most possible brothel venues. More hope accrues to sites that have not been fully excavated, such as the one identified as no. 40 in the catalog (9.11.2–3). There are not many of these sites among the places already known to us, however.

Nevertheless, it must said that if social historians want to know much of value about Roman brothels they would be better advised to invest more time in investigating the material remains than in parsing the likes of Petronius and Juvenal, where the harvest is bound to be very lean indeed. Further obstacles to developing a satisfactory typology are the flaws indicated earlier in the criteria for identification, and the fact that Roman brothels, like those in other cultures, are often difficult to distinguish from lower-class housing stock in general. In this sense the present study confirms a point of central importance raised at the outset that the fit between social history and archaeology should be assumed to be neither easy nor straightforward.

One way perhaps to allay somewhat this pessimism about the further elab-

---

2. See Schuster, *Frauenhaus* (1992) 31–32.

3. On difficulties with the archaeological typology of Roman houses as viewed in light of the legal evidence, see Kunst, "Dach" (2000) 294.

oration of a typology of brothels is to examine what I would describe as "the problem of luxury." Decades ago James Packer's studies of what he termed "middle and lower class housing" in Pompeii and Herculaneum and Pompeian inns yielded the important result that some of these places sported relatively luxurious features such as "*oeci, tablina, triclinia, alae, viridaria* or light-well courts" as well as wall paintings, at times of very high quality.[4] Rosanne Gulino found that over one-half of the taverns in her study-sample from *Regio* 1 had wall paintings.[5] In other words, the taverns shared certain decorative aspects with the aristocratic *domus*. Andrew Wallace-Hadrill, building on the work of Packer and Paul Zanker, advanced our knowledge by showing how Romans living in some relatively modest houses at Pompeii attempted to emulate the material lifestyle of the upper classes.[6] More recently, Mark Grahame has examined the houses in *Regio* 6 from the perspective of the courtyard, concluding that this was an elite architectural form, its size and numbers suggestive of power and status.[7]

These results help confirm the argument made in chapter 8 that the presence of high-quality painting and similar "luxurious" appointments in an establishment do not mean that it was not a hotel or brothel. To be clear, the evidence suggests that while the social prejudice against members of the elite setting foot in brothels was not adequate to prevent this from ever occurring, it seems unlikely that this happened often enough to influence the choice of decor.[8] Even a very modest locale such as the Purpose-Built Brothel might feature touches of luxury, there seen in the erotic wall paintings, as a means of appealing to a lower-status clientele. It seems possible then to look for the presence of such criteria, including the content and quality of the wall paintings, as a means of ranking brothels, not in the vain and self-contradictory search for an upper-class brothel, but as a means of advancing our understanding of what appealed to the sub-elite, particularly

---

4. The first four items on the list can be described as various kinds of reception areas (*triclinia* have a particular function as dining rooms), while *viridaria* are interior gardens: Packer, "Middle and Lower Class Housing" (1975) 141–42; Packer, "Inns at Pompeii" (1978) 44–49.

5. Gulino, *Implications* (1987) 95.

6. Wallace-Hadrill, *Houses and Society* (1994) esp. 169–74, a book that draws upon Wallace-Hadrill's own published work in the form of articles.

7. Grahame, "Material Culture" (1998) esp. 171.

8. The same point holds for *popinae* and, in a certain sense, for hotels as well. Baths are perhaps a different case; suffice it to say that whatever the numbers of elite visitors, commercial success must have depended on the decor's appeal to a broader public: see Scarano Ussani, "*Lenocinium*" (2000) 259 n. 40, 260 (261) n. 75.

as travelers.[9] *Luxuria popinalis* was an oxymoron for members of the upper classes, but part of the lived experience of many of those lower down on the social scale.[10]

One criterion to advance toward this end of enhancing our typology of brothels is the garden. Wilhelmina Jashemski documents the presence of gardens, often found with courtyards, in a number of places identified as possible brothels in the catalog provided in appendix 1. These gardens differ from each other of course in their size, number, and appointments. I include this information in the hope that it might prove useful, along with other evidence of "luxury," in elaborating a typology of brothels.[11] Worth noting is that in the *Copa* attributed to Vergil, the tavern, which evidently is also a brothel, sports a garden along with other refinements the pretensions of which are mocked from the perspective of the (we may assume) upper-class author.[12]

Another kind of evidence concerns not just the typology of brothels, but the question of identification itself. If, as seems likely, brothels and related businesses tend to cluster together,[13] it might be possible to elevate location to the status of a criterion for identifying brothels. Location would not have to be a necessary or sufficient condition of brothel-identification, but simply a leading indicator.[14] In a pioneering and sadly neglected study of taverns in *Regio* 1, Rosanne Gulino found that a primary factor in their location was "nearness to a major thoroughfare": the majority of those found on side streets were at street corners.[15] Like brothels (which some of them might have been in fact), they tended to cluster together but were also located next door to a variety of public and private buildings.[16] Not surprisingly, from an economic perspec-

---

9. The essays in Adams and Laurence, *Travel and Geography* (2001) suggest members of this broad sector of society did a great deal more traveling than was previously thought.

10. See Apul. *Met.* 8.1.

11. Painting may help differentiate some establishments, especially those that lack gardens, though in most cases we would expect the criteria to coincide with each other. Grahame, "Material Culture" (1998) 171, finds that the noncourtyard houses in *Regio* 6 show a layout that is "almost random." The same is true of many brothels.

12. See Goodyear, "*Copa*" (1977) 119–20, 124, 125, 127 (brothel); Franzoi, *Copa* (1988) 64, 67, 71, 72, 90; Rosivach, "Sociology" (1996) 608–12.

13. In the same way shops are concentrated in certain areas: Gassner, *Kaufläden* (1986) 84, 88.

14. For informal clustering of brothels in modern Nevada, see Symanski, "Prostitution in Nevada" (1974) 365.

15. Gulino, *Implications* (1987) 89–90, 147 (a doctoral dissertation, which accounts presumably for its neglect). See also the rationale offered by Gassner, *Kaufläden* (1986) 52, for the location of different types of shops on side and main streets.

16. Gulino, *Implications* (1987) 90–93, 147.

tive, larger restaurants (over four rooms each) were more likely to be on side streets and smaller ones, on the main streets.[17] It might be feasible to employ information of this kind to locate, again in Pompeii, miniversions of the "Eros Center" surrounding the Purpose-Built Brothel in *Regio* 7 and its evident rivals in *Regio* 1 stretching from the *Porta Stabiana* to the *Insula del Menandro*,[18] and in *Regio* 7 at *Insula* 13. These were districts capable of catering to a variety of needs and desires associated with the sale of sex.

A further welcome step would be the refinement of knowledge about the way in which brothels were linked to private houses. We already know that many *domus* in Pompeii were surrounded by businesses that appear to have been owned by the proprietors of these houses.[19] No evidence exists that these proprietors were concerned that the presence of brothels would lower property values, a familiar refrain from modern contexts.[20] If anything, the reverse was true. A brothel might add value to an aristocratic *domus*, at least for some members of the elite.

How many of the businesses flanking the *domus* were brothels? Were commercial interests in the urban context typically geographically contiguous, or were they in important ways dispersed, as was the case for agricultural properties in the countryside?[21] What can we say about the status of the proprietor, even if his or her identity remains unknown? Was a brothel owner likely to be a big fish or small fry among the elite?[22]

---

17. Gulino, *Implications* (1987) 135, 142. See also the distribution of the space between doorways as illustrated by Laurence, *Roman Pompeii* (1994) 92–93. Gulino finds in her sample that erotic graffiti, as well as other graffiti of a personal nature, are more likely to appear in the larger establishments on side streets (138, 140), a fact that may, unfortunately, be ascribed to less careful excavation along the main streets (141).

18. For a similar suggestion regarding the latter, see Evans, *War* (1991) 135. "Eros Center" is not meant here in the precise sense of the present-day model found in Germany, whose like is difficult in fact to locate in historical contexts: Schuster, *Frauenhaus* (1992) 71. We might attempt to determine whether such pockets of prostitution were simply a feature of impoverished neighborhoods or stood apart as elements of a district or districts devoted to the leisure economy and entertainment. For these two models, see Gilfoyle, *City of Eros* (1992) 119–20. Both might have been present in Pompeii, perhaps in different areas of the city.

19. Kleberg, *Hôtels* (1957) 78–80; Raper, "Analysis of the Urban Structure" (1977) 193, 196, 202, 204, 207 (a sign of urban pathology!); Gassner, *Kaufläden* (1986) 12–13, 51, 61, 73, 74, 84, 96; Jongman, *Economy* (1988) 178–79, 214, 271; Parkins, "Consumer City" (1997) 102–7. On the economic role of the Roman house, see now Kunst, "Dach" (2000).

20. See Best, *Controlling Vice* (1998) 93.

21. On the latter, see the discussion of Mediterranean "latifundism" in Horden and Purcell, *Corrupting Sea* (2000) 282–83.

22. In the course of the Bacchanalia scandal in 186 b.c., the prostitute and star witness Faecenia Hispala was given refuge in a *cenaculum* located above the house of the mother-in-law of the consul Sp. Postumius. This only occurred, however, after the separate street entrance was blocked and a new one created that went through the house itself: Liv. 39.14.2–3. Security concerns

Whatever the final answers to these questions, a few tentative conclusions may be offered here. Considerations of profit dictated the number and location of brothels in Pompeii and in other Roman cities, so that we would expect any patterns that emerge to exemplify the results of a loose and informal practice of "commercial zoning" rather than of a top-down, officially imposed "moral geography."[23] The loose and informal aspect of this zoning must be stressed. Before the McDonald's corporation and others raised the practice of business-location to a demographic science, the selection of retail venues in the twentieth-century United States tended to be more passive than active in nature.[24] This is not, however, to exaggerate the usefulness of geography in defining communities of deviance.[25]

In light of the broad definition of public policy adopted in chapter 5, it is clear that this commercial zoning qualifies as an example of a public policy, though there is no evidence that it was ever formally enacted as such.[26] The truth of a basic premise held by those who have advocated a theory of zoning has been vindicated, namely that "markets for prostitution in any political jurisdiction are shaped by the super-structure of laws and enforcement."[27] From a constructionist perspective, I point out that such a policy was hardly inevitable. What is disturbing to a feminist is the reflection that this policy is likely to have been on its own terms successful.

Here the "fit" between elite perceptions and official policy was chillingly close from a modern perspective. For the Romans, prostitution, like marriage, but unlike adultery, was a form of licit sexuality. The prospects for outright repression, or even stringent regulation, of commercial sex are therefore not very good for Rome. Though no unitary policy existed on the subject, we can identify at least two important trends in play, tolerance and degradation.[28] The absence of a program of moral zoning served both ends by helping to ensure the ready accessibility and the open humiliation of prostitutes. Ideology is at the root of both trends in policy in the sense that they reconcile a

---

appear paramount in this context, but might there have been a sensitivity over propriety as well? I thank Anise Strong for calling this evidence to my attention. The questions raised in this paragraph are important for more than just the business of venal sex: see Mouritsen, "Roman Freedmen" (2001) 11.

23. Cf. the conclusions of Pirson, *Mietwohnungen* (1999) 164, over the distribution of *tabernae* in Pompeii.

24. See Heyl, *Madam* (1979) 91.

25. See Prus and Irini, *Hookers* (1980) 259.

26. We may compare this with the vote by the Tombstone (Ariz. Territory) city council in 1882 to abolish all restrictions on the location of brothels in that town, a measure motivated by a desire to promote economic development: Butler, *Daughters of Joy* (1985) 78.

27. Reynolds, *Economics of Prostitution* (1986) 7.

28. See McGinn, *Prostitution, Sexuality, and the Law* (1998) chap. 10.

strongly entrenched sense of social and moral hierarchy with the implications of the fact, that on a very basic level, for the Romans the business of prostitution was indeed business. In order to accomplish these twin goals, the Romans did not shrink from eroticizing—actually or at least potentially—the atmospherics of the Roman city.[29]

Roman ideas about articulating and enforcing a public morality must seem strange to us, though they need not be unintelligible or conceived of as a straightforward reflection of our own concerns. Social policy allowed, if it did not outright encourage, prostitutes to participate in the popular cultural tradition of public exhibitionism.[30] The sum of their weird marginality was to stand as outcasts openly for all to see in the urban center. In a similar way, the various legal rules designed for them, especially the civic and legal disabilities inflicted upon free prostitutes, had the paradoxical effect of binding them to the category of the most debased Romans while integrating them into the deep structure of the polity.

The point just made about public policy is of great importance, because it reveals something fundamental about the Roman practice of prostitution, and that is precisely its deeply exploitative nature. It is not that prostitution cannot, or should not, be regarded as inherently exploitative, but that the variant of it practiced by the Romans was extremely so,[31] a fact which helps establish its significance in historical and cultural terms. The connection recently established between explicit representations of lovemaking and venues of prostitution helps underscore this point. It suggests that the radical feminists are right, after all, in equating pornography with prostitution, and that this equation has a long history in fact if not also in theory.[32] The popularity of such representations among the Romans stands as an index of how comfortable they were with such a high level of exploitation. Prostitution, or at any rate the idea of it, was never far to seek in the ancient Roman city.

---

29. See the valuable observations of Kellum, "Spectacle" (1999) 292.

30. See Kellum, "Spectacle" (1999) 287.

31. No author to my mind brings out this aspect of Roman prostitution as effectively as Flemming, "*Quae Corpore*" (1999). See also Scarano Ussani, "Alle terme" (2001/2002).

32. See Jeffreys, *Idea of Prostitution* (1997) 231–36, esp. (at 232): "Pornography and prostitution are indivisible too, because pornography is the representation of prostitution"; Sullivan, *Politics of Sex* (1997) 4, 133. For a valuable sociological perspective, see Prus and Irini, *Hookers* (1980) 94. Still essential is Kappeler, *Pornography of Representation* (1986) esp. 153–58. Classicists will be as sensitive as Kappeler is to the etymology of "pornography" in this context above all. It is worth asking to what extent the identification of the representation of commercial sex with its practice encouraged in the popular mind an identification of actresses with prostitutes: cf. Edwards, "Unspeakable Professions" (1997).

The conclusion is not of course that venal sex was universal at Pompeii or in any other Roman city. A closer look at ownership patterns may help refine the picture, showing how, for example, a certain moral delicacy, or its absence, on the part of real-estate holders may have motivated them to choose to make money from prostitution or to refrain from doing so. I can only speculate that such reluctance, such *verecundia*, if it existed, was anything, to steal a phrase from Augustine, but *naturalis*.[33]

In the end, any choice made in the analysis of ancient motives between the economic and the moral must ring false. Each can only be studied and understood in the context of the other.[34] The balance will shift from time to time, from culture to culture, from individual to individual, as will often the very definition of "economics" and of "morality."[35]

What especially characterizes Roman prostitution, as a system of exploitation, is the degree of autonomy left to the exploiters. As with profiting from slaves, then, so with the use of urban property.[36] The decision to prostitute a slave or to establish a brothel was left to the individual property owner. By the same token no one, including the authorities, was in a position to prevent such exploitation. If anything, the discretion allowed to owners in profiting from the "prostitution" of real estate was greater than that permitted in the prostitution of slaves.[37] The moral geography of the Roman city is no more than the sum of these individual choices.

---

33. See the discussion of the evidence of Augustine in chap. 3.

34. See Best, *Controlling Vice* (1998) 139.

35. We may usefully compare the factors said to help determine where a legal brothel should be located within a Nevada county: Reynolds, *Economics of Prostitution* (1986) 103.

36. See Best, *Controlling Vice* (1998) 139.

37. It is interesting to note that in the case of real estate there is no trace of the type of restrictive covenant on sale that was intended to discourage subsequent owners from prostituting slaves: see McGinn, *Prostitution, Sexuality, and the Law* (1998) chap. 8.

APPENDICES

A CATALOG OF POSSIBLE
BROTHELS AT POMPEII

The evidence for cribs, taverns, hotels, and baths in the immediate vicinity of the Purpose-Built Brothel, which I surveyed at the close of chapter
8, suggests that insofar as our interest extends beyond purpose-built brothels to
include any venue where sex was sold, a review of the sites postulated for other
brothels might be useful. Two questions arise in light of the expansive
definition of brothel offered above. What other structures were used as brothels? In particular, are we able to locate other businesses where sex was sold as
an important sideline, such as taverns?

It seems best to pursue the answers to these questions by listing the potential brothels in Pompeii, together with the evidence that supports such
identifications, as well as references to modern discussions.[1] I include even a
couple of doubtful cases, though not implausible ones. The latter category
includes the House of the Vettii brothers.[2] Another omission is 6.14.4,
identified as a brothel connected with a private house by La Torre.[3] This site
is mentioned by no other author cited here and appears as a shop on the plan
for *Regio* 6. I believe "6.14.4" may be a mistake for 6.14.43 (the "gran
lupanare" or "lupanare grande"), which Andrew Wallace-Hadrill convinces

---

1. A number of these references are found in a convenient tabular form in Guzzo and Scarano
Ussani, *Veneris figurae* (2000) 66–67.
2. See chap. 7. n. 98; see also chap. 5, for the argument that the House of the Vettii contained
not a brothel but a "sex club."
3. La Torre, "Impianti" (1988) 93 n. 29; cf. *Pompei* (1988) 138.

me is unlikely to be a brothel, despite the presence of erotic graffiti (here evidently idle boasting/ribaldry) and (mythological) art: it is more likely to be a private house.[4]

The site 7.2.42, identified by Eschebach and Müller-Trollius as a brothel, also appears to be an error, judging from the fact that they fail to include it in their catalog.[5] I believe 7.6.14–15 are better classified as two adjacent cribs than as a brothel.[6] Three shops (?) (6.6.14–16), tentatively identified by Mazois in the early nineteenth century as a brothel on the basis of a nearby representation of a phallus, are rightly rejected as such by Pirson.[7]

Finally, recent excavations at Moregine (also known as Murecine), an area just to the south of the ancient city of Pompeii and well within any reasonable conception of its immediate hinterland or microregion, have turned up material of great interest.[8] In November 2000 the skeletal remains of two adult women and three children were found in the context of an ancient *caupona*. One of the two women, aged about thirty, was discovered wearing several items of jewelry, including a gold and silver bracelet shaped into the form of a serpent with the remarkable inscription "dom<i>nus ancillae suae" ("the master to his slave"). Pier Giovanni Guzzo and Vincenzo Scarano Ussani offer a series of possible explanations for this evidence, namely that the jewelry (which also includes a gold chain the authors show probably served to adorn the woman's nude torso) suggests that the slave woman played the role of sexual partner for her master, which seems very likely, or that of a sexual toy to be shared with his friends, which seems possible, or that of the tavern's mistress, who acted also as a procuress and perhaps a prostitute as well. If this last hypothesis were true, the *caupona* might be listed as a brothel. But there is no real evidence of prostitution here. The first, most likely hypothesis renders the other two, especially the last, less likely. We cannot moreover exclude the possibility that the woman and her companions found themselves in this locale in the midst of an attempt to flee the eruption of Vesuvius and so neither lived nor worked there.

This last example, however, offers a salutary reminder of the fact that our

---

4. Wallace-Hadrill, p.c. See also Savunen, *Women* (1997) 112. This site has been studied in recent years by teams from the University of Nijmegen: see Mols and De Waele, "Rapporto" (1998); Peterse, "Secondo rapporto" (2000).

5. Eschebach and Müller-Trollius, *Gebäudeverzeichnis* (1993) 491; cf. 258, 262.

6. See chap. 7.

7. Mazois, *Ruines* 2 (1824/38) 84; Pirson, *Mietwohnungen* (1999) 33 with n. 127.

8. Guzzo and Scarano Ussani, "Schiava" (2001) is my source for the information in this paragraph. Moregine is about 600 meters to the south of the *Porta Stabiana*. For the archaeological context, see Mastroroberto, "Quartiere" (2001); on the jewelry, see D'Ambrosio, "Monili" (2001). See also the essays in De Simone and Nappo, *Mitis Sarni Opes* (2000).

knowledge of Roman brothels is susceptible to change. Investigation of the physical remains of brothels, which for Pompeii is in its infancy,[9] may well result in a shorter or longer list of brothels. Again, the list includes only brothels that have already been identified. As with the *cellae meretriciae*, it is possible that (re)excavation, or at minimum adequate surveying, will yield some useful information about brothels. A project of this kind would be a valuable step toward the difficult goal of developing a more satisfactory typology of these establishments Without close attention to the physical remains, the enterprise of brothel-identification at Pompeii cannot proceed very far. Even so, wild optimism about discovering unknown brothels or even confirming suspected ones, is not justified.[10] Though I remain steadfast in my purpose, set forth at the beginning of this book, not to catalog "new" brothels, that is, brothels not previously identified in the scholarship, simply in order to suggest to the reader that such establishments can indeed be tracked down and identified, I offer an example of a possible brothel at 1.8.1, a *caupona* that sports an upstairs as well as graffiti referring to a woman offering fellatio and to another charging two *asses* for sex.[11]

I refer to the works of the brothel-writers by their last names or, in a few cases, by the title of their publications, in the text of this catalog.[12] Here is an alphabetical list of abbreviated forms: Cantarella, *Pompei* (1998); *Corpus Topographicum Pompeianum* (CTP) 2 (1983), 3a (1986),[13] Della Corte, *Case*[3] (1965)[14]; DeFelice, *Roman Hospitality* (2001); Dierichs, *Erotik* (1997); Eschebach, *Entwicklung* (1970); Eschebach and Müller-Trollius, *Gebäude-verzeichnis* (1993); La Torre, "Impianti" (1988)[15]; *Pompei* (1988)[16]; *Pompei:*

---

9. The treatment of the Purpose-Built Brothel by Clarke, *Looking at Lovemaking* (1998) 196–206, virtually stands alone as an intelligent discussion of an ancient brothel. To be sure, Clarke's focus is on the erotic art downstairs and one could wish for more description, especially of the upstairs.

10. See below in the text and chap. 10.

11. *CIL* 4.8185. Della Corte, *Case*[3] (1965) 323–24, identifies this establishment as a tavern that sold fruit; Eschebach and Müller-Trollius, *Gebäudeverzeichnis* (1993) 42–43, as a "*thermopolium*" (on this word, see n. 24). Other places to look for "new" brothels are 6.1.1, 6.1.2–4, 6.2.3–5, 30–31, and 6.14.28.

12. Other works are given in abbreviated form in the notes.

13. The *CTP*, esp. volume 2, restates earlier identifications, whether as brothels or not. Nevertheless, it is a resource of great value and so I have included reference to it here.

14. In what follows, I attempt to render Della Corte's vague and, I fear, inconsistent descriptive terminology in the following way: "ammezzato" = small room; "annessi" = side or back rooms; "cenacoli" = suites.

15. La Torre describes some brothels with the vague "connessi ad edifici di ristoro," which I render as "associated with food/drink service."

16. I refer to the "Indirizzario" ("Address-Book") in this work.

Pitture e Mosaici (PPM)[17]; Savunen, *Women* (1997); Wallace-Hadrill, "Public Honour and Private Shame" (1995). Full citations of all of these works are either in the bibliography or the list of abbreviations.

1. 1.2.17–19.[18] YFE: 1869.[19] "Proprietors": Demetrius and Helpis Afra.[20] Tavern. Layout includes small rooms upstairs; a sculpture [?] of an erect phallus found on an exterior wall. Della Corte 272 ("*caupona-lupanar*": 1.2.18–19); Eschebach, 117, 174 (same address as Della Corte)[21]; *CTP* 2.225 (same address as Della Corte); *CTP* 3a.4 (= 1.2.18); La Torre, 93 n. 29 (= 1.2.19, associated with food/drink service); *Pompei* 105; Eschebach and Müller-Trollius 17–18 (statue of Venus); Wallace-Hadrill, 61 n. 71 (= 1.2.18), plausible, on the basis of a cluster of "hic futui" graffiti: see *CIL* 4.3926–43, esp. 3935 and 3942 ("hic futui" type); Dierichs 77–78; DeFelice 106 ("no evidence"), 184–85 (= 1.2.18–19). *PPM* 1.37–46 (= 1.2.17, 18–19). Two gardens: a small one in back entered from the *tablinum* and a peristyle garden to the E of the atrium contained statuary, including a marble statuette of Venus found in a "shrine-like structure."[22] This establishment appears to fit the subtype of the *caupona* with a brothel upstairs and/or in back: see below.

Context.[23] Next door: 1.2.16 (private house); 1.2.20 (possible brothel [cat. no. 2]). Across: 1.3.29 (private house).

---

17. *PPM* is the great multivolume encyclopedia of Pompeian physical remains: Pugliese Carratelli, *Pompei: Pitture e Mosaici* (1990–1999).

18. In this place I give the address supplied by Eschebach and Müller-Trollius, *Gebäudeverzeichnis* (1993) noting differences registered by others after citing their respective works. They usually do not provide justifications for such changes, so that in some cases at least simple error cannot be ruled out. Exceptions to this practice occur with the possible doublet brothels: see nos. 20, 23, 27. On the general problem with addresses in Pompeii, see now Franklin, *Pompeis Difficile Est* (2001) 4–6.

19. The "YFE" is the year of first excavation, as given by Eschebach and Müller-Trollius in *Gebäudeverzeichnis*. In some cases, of course, this is the only year of excavation. For a small number of cases where no date is given, I use the date from a building next door, which is perhaps not always reliable.

20. Proprietors are often identified as such on the basis of electoral inscriptions, that is, inscriptions that communicate recommendations for candidates for public office. Unfortunately, they are of little use in identifying the occupants of any given location: Mouritsen, *Elections* (1988) 18–19, 21; Mouritsen, "Campaigning" (1999) esp. 518.

21. Eschebach's brothel-identification is cautiously accepted by Gulino, *Implications* (1987) 32–34.

22. Jashemski, *Gardens* 2 (1993) 23–24 (= 1.2.17).

23. This information derives from the entries in Eschebach and Müller-Trollius, *Gebäudeverzeichnis* (1993). I give the entries for next-door neighbors as well as for those that are located more or less directly across the street.

2. 1.2.20–21. YFE: 1869. "Proprietors": Innulus and Papilio (or Pollius or Minius). Tavern. Layout includes masonry benches for visitors, small rooms upstairs, *biclinium* in garden; *"thermopolium"* at 1.2.21.[24] Wall paintings of Bacchus and Fortuna; erotic graffiti. Della Corte 273–74; Eschebach 117, 175 (= 1.2.20)[25]; CTP 2.225 (*"caupona-lupanar"*); La Torre 93 n. 29 (= 1.2.20, associated with food/drink service); *Pompei* 105; Eschebach and Müller-Trollius 18, 491; Wallace-Hadrill 61 n. 71 (= 1.2.20), plausible, on the basis of a cluster of "hic futui" inscriptions: see *CIL* 4.3926–43, esp. 3935 and 3942 ("hic futui" type); Dierichs 77; DeFelice 106–7: hotel occasionally used for venal sex, but not a brothel, 185–86. Note that the same epigraphs are used to identify the possible brothel next door, cat. no. 1. *PPM* 1.47–48. Garden at the rear with a masonry *biclinium*.[26]

Context. Next door: 1.2.19 (possible brothel [cat. no. 1]); 1.2.22 (shop). Across: (unexcavated).

3. 1.7.13–14. YFE: 1927. "Proprietor": Masculus. Tavern. Side/back rooms upstairs and downstairs. Painting of Priapus. Della Corte identifies as *caupona*, not brothel. Della Corte 319–20; Eschebach 119, 175[27]; CTP 2.229 (*caupona*); CTP 3a.12; La Torre (= 1.7.14; connected with food/drink service); *Pompei* 109; Eschebach and Müller-Trollius 41; Wallace-Hadrill 53, with 61 n. 72: no grounds for identification as a brothel; Dierichs 77; DeFelice 108–11: no evidence for a brothel, 195. *PPM* 1.728–29 (= 1.7.13).

Context. Next door: 1.7.12 (private house); 1.7.15 (shop [sign painters' shop]). Across: 1.8.15–16 (*caupona* and private house).

4. 1.9.11–12. YFE: 1953. "Proprietor": Sex. Pompeius Amarantus and/or Q. Mestrius Maximus.[28] CTP 2.231 distinguishes brothel at 1.9.12 from *caupona* next door, as does CTP 3a.16 (but see note on 11). Not in La Torre. *Pompei* 110; Eschebach and Müller-Trollius 50: *caupona* at 1.9.11; DeFelice

---

24. *"Thermopolium"*: The reader will note that this usage was discredited by Kleberg, *Hôtels* (1957) 24–25, though it remains popular. See also the more recent criticism of the term by Wallace-Hadrill, "Public Honour and Private Shame" (1995) 45–46.

25. Gulino, *Implications* (1987) 34–36, accepts Eschebach's identification, thinking this is "likely" to be a brothel.

26. Jashemski, *Gardens* 2 (1993) 24 (= 1.2.20).

27. Gulino, *Implications* (1987) 49–51, accepts this identification by Eschebach.

28. Because address labels on *amphorae* found on-site, and not just epigraphic evidence from walls, contain the name Sex. Pompeius Amarantus, it is actually rather likely that he was the operator of the *caupona* in its final years: Fulford and Wallace-Hadrill, "House of *Amarantus*" (1995–96) 101.

199–200. The brothel and *caupona* were operated together at least in the final years of the city, and there is reason to think that both "houses" were connected from a very early stage. Recent reexamination of the remains, which has been careful and extensive, has shown the construction of a series of upper-level rooms over the peristyle of 11 in a late phase of the development of this complex, the use of room 12.4 as a stable, and employment of the *atrium* that this room opens upon (12.2) as a storage facility mostly for *amphorae* that were full. Empties were stashed in the garden next door at 11.5, which also contained benches that were evidently used in connection with some form of entertainment, possibly cockfights. The wine in question was served at the bar facing the street in 11. Archaeologists have discovered on-site the remains of thrushes (considered delicacies by the Romans), blackbirds, sheep, and domestic fowl, as well as some shellfish, complemented by a series of charred food waste that includes various fruits, nuts, and grains.[29]

The excavators believe that in the final stages of the complex the southern part of 12 functioned as a service annex to the commercial usage of the southern part of 11, while parts of both "houses" had gone to seed. The evidence for occupation at the time of the eruption in 79 is mixed to the point of contradictory, a situation which may be explained by continuing seismic activity between 62 and 79. The authors do not directly raise the question of whether some of the space in the northern parts of both houses was used for the purpose of lodging in connection with the tavern itself (which appears to have been nonfunctional in 79), let alone examine the issue of brothel-identification, but these are preliminary reports.[30] *PPM* 2.150–71 (= 1.9.12). Each part had a garden; the one for 11 was used for storage of empty *amphorae* and so forth (see above), while 12 had a peristyle garden in the rear.[31]

Context. Next door: 1.9.10: private house; 1.9.13: private house. Across: 1.17.2–3: hotel (?).

5. 1.10.5. YFE: 1932. No proprietor. Upstairs suites; erotic graffiti: *CIL* 4.8357–61, esp. 8357b (a price of 10 *asses*) and 8361 (a reference to fellatio).[32]

---

29. For these details, see the preliminary summary of excavation finds by Fulford and Wallace-Hadrill, "House of *Amarantus*" (1995–96); also the important follow-up in Fulford and Wallace-Hadrill, "Unpeeling Pompeii" (1998). Also of great value, especially for some of the details that follow, is Berry, "Domestic Life" (1997). For an examination of the pre-Roman levels on the site, see the excellent treatment in Fulford and Wallace-Hadrill, "Pre-Roman Pompeii" (1999).

30. See also Gulino, *Implications* (1987) 56–58; Berry, "Unpeeling Pompeii" (1998) 62–68.

31. Jashemski, *Gardens* 2 (1993) 45 (separate listings for each part).

32. In his forthcoming publication of the inscriptions from the *Insula del Menandro* (1.10), Dr. Antonio Varone offers new readings for *CIL* 4.8359 and 8361. The new version of the former

Della Corte 299 (= 1.10.5–6); *Pompei* 110; Eschebach 120, 175; La Torre 93 n. 29 (connected with private house); Eschebach and Müller-Trollius, 54; not in Wallace-Hadrill; part of the *Insula of the Menander*.[33] No entry in *PPM*.

Context. Next door: 1.10.4 (private house); 1.10.6 (workshop [marble workers' ?]). Across: 1.6.15 (private house).

6. 1.10.10–11. YFE: 1933. "Proprietor": Ti. Claudius Eulogos. *CTP* 2.232, 3a.18 (= 1.10.11): private residence. Eschebach and Müller-Trollius 56. Erotic graffiti: *CIL* 4.8393 (a price of 5 *asses*?), 8394 (Naereia or Nereia: 2 *asses*), 8400, 8404, 8408a–c; part of the Insula of the Menander.[34] The erotic graffiti appear to refer to client(s), plus one or two prices. *PPM* 2.433–99. Four-sided peristyle garden behind the *atrium*.[35] The house is then of the familiar *atrium*/peristyle type, with a number of small *cellae* lining both rooms.[36] If it was indeed converted to a brothel,[37] this establishment would be the largest known at Pompeii, larger even than the Purpose-Built Brothel, especially given the presence of a second floor, now reconstructed around the peristyle.

Context. Next door: 1.10.9 (workshop); 1.10.12 (workshop or public latrine [?]). Across: 1.3.28 ("*thermopolium*"); 1.3.29 (private house).

7. 1.11.10–12. YFE: 1953. "Proprietors": Euxinus and Iustus, or Euxinus and Phoenix. Tavern. Jashemski identified this as a brothel.[38] *CTP* 2.232, 3a.20 (= 1.11.10–11): *caupona*. Eschebach and Müller-Trollius 59–60

does not affect the argument here; in the latter case, his suggestion that the numerical indicators, which had been ignored by Della Corte, amount to a scorecard for acts of fellatio might actually support the case for a brothel. My thanks to Dr. Varone for sharing this information with me.

33. A brothel also according to A. De Vos and M. De Vos, *Pompei* (1982) 89, who throw in the *caupona* at 1.10.2–3 for good measure, as do La Rocca and De Vos, *Pompei*² (1994) 180. See also Ling, *Insula of the Menander* 1 (1997) 41–42, who is cautious about the status of 1.10.5 as a brothel (148). Kunst, "Dach" (2000) 301 n. 95, accepts this as a brothel. Pirson, *Mietwohnungen* (1999) 55 (see also 212) identifies this as a *cenaculum*; he rejects its characterization as a brothel because it fails to meet all three of Wallace-Hadrill's criteria. On the *Insula of the Menander*, see also Berry, *Unpeeling Pompeii* (1998) 22–25.

34. The alternative names Naereia and Nereia are proposed by Dr. Antonio Varone in his forthcoming edition of the inscriptions from the *Insula del Menandro*. The older reading was Nebris; for Nebris, see *CIL* 4.5118, 5145, 5146. On the *insula*, see also Berry, *Unpeeling Pompeii* (1998) 22–25.

35. Jashemski, *Gardens* 2 (1993) 50.

36. Many inns and restaurants at Pompeii have features usually associated with high-end *domus*; the same may have been true of Ostia as well. See chaps. 8 and 10.

37. In his exemplary publication of the building, Ling, *Insula of the Menander* 1 (1997) 197–211, does not canvass this possibility.

38. Jashemski, *Gardens* 1 (1979) 175. The idea is cautiously accepted by Gulino, *Implications* (1987) 63–65.

(*caupona*); DeFelice 124, 203–4 (painting of Priapus; two erotic graffiti: *CIL* 4.9847–48). *PPM* 2.570–92 (= 1.11.10–11 [*caupona*], 1.11.12 [house of the *caupo*]. Large garden, directly accessible from street, that contained "a colorfully painted little room," stairs leading evidently to upstairs accommodations, altars and apparatus for sacrifice, trees, vines, and a couple of semi-embedded *dolia* used to ferment the must, while behind 12 there was a large open area informally planted as a vineyard, containing statuary, including a marble statuette of Venus.[39]

Context. Next door: 1.11.9 (back door to private house); 1.11.13 (private house). Across: 1.16.4 (private house); 1.16.5 (private house).

8. 1.12.5. YFE: 1914. "Proprietor": Lutatius. Tavern. *CTP* 2.233; 3a.22 (*caupona*). Eschebach and Müller-Trollius 63–64 (*caupona*); DeFelice, 124–25, 206–7 (*caupona* with prostitutes working in it; graffito with a price: *CIL* 4.8454—Firma, 2 *asses*; at *CIL* 4.4259, a woman of that name is listed for 3 *asses*: see cat. no. 11 below); cf. *CIL* 4.8449: fellatio. *PPM* 2.735–46. Small open area at the rear of the lodgings.[40]

Context. Next door: 1.12.4 (shop/workshop); 1.12.6 (private house). Across: 3.2.2 (shop); 3.2.3 (workshop/dwelling) (neither are completely excavated).

9. 2.1.1, 13. YFE: 1915. "Proprietor": Hermes. Tavern. Della Corte 366 (*caupona*). *CTP* 2.234; 3a.40 (*caupona*). Eschebach and Müller-Trollius 85 ("*thermopolium*"-*caupona*); DeFelice 125, 213–14: possible brothel because of design (multiple rooms), presence of graffiti (*CIL* 4.8473, 8475). *PPM* 3.1–4. Small garden at the rear of the lodgings area behind the tavern.[41]

Context. Next door: 2.1.2 (private house); 2.1.12 (cult complex). Across: 3.4.1a (tavern); 1.13.4–6 (dwelling/workshop).

10. 5.1.13. YFE: 1875. "Proprietor": Salvius. Tavern. *CTP* 3a.70 ("*thermopolium*"); Eschebach and Müller-Trollius 124 (*popina*); DeFelice 126, 227–28 (*taberna/popina* with prostitutes working in it, multiple rooms, graffiti with prices). *CIL* 4.4023: Felic(u)la, 2 *asses*, 4024: Menander, 2 *asses* ("bellis

---

39. Jashemski, *Gardens* 2 (1993) 51–52, with separate entries for 1.11.10–11 and 12.

40. Jashemski, *Gardens* 2 (1993) 54. See also the description in Gulino, *Implications* (1987) 69–70.

41. Jashemski, *Gardens* 2 (1993) 75.

moribus"), 4025: Successa ("bellis moribus"). A woman named Felic(u)la is implied to be a prostitute at *CIL* 4.2199, 2200, 8917. No entry in *PPM*.

Context. Next door: 5.1.12 (back door to private house); 5.1.14 (private house and bakery). Across: 6.14.28–32 (private house, *popina*, and bakery).

11. 5.2.B–C, D. YFE: 1880?/1882? "Proprietors": N. Fufidius Successus and/or N. Herennius Castus. Tavern. *CTP* 2.243 appears to regard as three separate private dwellings; cf. *CTP* 3a.72 (= 5.2.C–D), whose plan suggests the address(es) should be given as B, C–D. Eschebach and Müller-Trollius 134–35 (B–C, "*thermopolium*" with lodgings; D, row house); DeFelice 126, 229 (= 5.2.C–D): *taberna/popina* with erotic graffiti, multiple rooms; possibly functioned as a brothel. One of the graffiti shows prices: *CIL* 4.4259: Acria, 4 *asses*, Firma, 3 *asses*, Epafra, 10 *asses* (cf. 4.4264: cunnilingus with Rustica); one is of the "hic futui" type: *CIL* 4.4260. *PPM* 3.628–35 (= 5.2.D, i.e., no entry for B–C).

Context. Next door: 5.2.A (private house); 5.2.E (*caupona*). Across: 5.1.9 (back door to private house); 5.1.10 (back door to private house).

12. 6.10.1, 19. YFE: 1827. See figures 1–2. No proprietor. Tavern. Layout has a bar on street and small rooms in back. Erotic art.[42] Della Corte identifies as a *caupona-lupanar*. Della Corte 55–56 (= 6.10.1); Eschebach 132, 175; *CTP* 2.258; La Torre 93 n. 29 (= 6.10.19; connected with food/drink service); *Pompei* 133–34; Eschebach and Müller-Trollius 192; Wallace-Hadrill 53, with 61 n. 72: no grounds; DeFelice 111–14: not a brothel.[43] *PPM* 4.1005–28 (= 6.10.1).

Context. Next door: 6.10.2 (possible brothel [cat. no. 13]); 6.10.18 ("*thermopolium*" with dwelling). Across: 6.8.23–24 (private house); 6.9.6–9 (private house).

13. 6.10.2. YFE: 1827. "Proprietor": Obellius (?) or Avellius (?) Firmus. Not in Della Corte (cf. 56: a *caupona* at 6.10.3–4); Eschebach 132, 175; *CTP*

---

42. On this see Clarke, *Looking at Lovemaking* (1998) 206–12; Clarke, *Art in the Lives of Ordinary Romans* (forthcoming), chap. 6.

43. See also Packer, "Inns at Pompeii" (1978) 46, 49; Clarke, *Looking at Lovemaking* (1998) 211–12; Guzzo and Scarano Ussani, *Veneris figurae* (2000) 14. Clarke sees prostitution occurring only in one room (d). If he is right, 6.10.1, 19 would be a crib, according to my definition, and not a brothel.

2.258; La Torre 93 n. 29 (connected with private house); *Pompei* 133–34; Eschebach and Müller-Trollius 192–93; Wallace-Hadrill, 61 n. 73: dubious. *PPM* 4.1029–43. Small garden with a partial portico and a dining room in back.[44] Ranks as one of the weakest identifications: see cat. no. 21 as well.

Context. Next door: 6.10.1, 19 (possible brothel [cat. no. 12]); 6.10.3 ("*thermopolium*" with dwelling). Across: 6.8.23–24 (private house).

14. 6.11.5, 15–16. YFE: 1842. "Proprietor": Restituta. Tavern? Layout has suites upstairs; downstairs is a central room with four "cubicoli," as well as a few side/back rooms; Della Corte compares to the Purpose-Built Brothel. Erotic graffiti, some of which list prices: *CIL* 4.1375–91, 4434–44 (see 4439: Pitane, 3 *asses*; 4441: Isidorus, 2 *asses*. Della Corte, 60–61 (= 6.11.16, the more usual listing); Eschebach 132 (= 6.11.4, 15–17), 175 (= 6.11.16); *CTP* 2.260 (= 6.11.16)[45]; La Torre 93 n. 29 (associated with food/drink service); *Pompei* 135; Eschebach and Müller-Trollius 198; Wallace-Hadrill 61 n. 73 (dubious: "the graffiti . . . are inconclusive"); Cantarella 91; Dierichs 135 n. 42; DeFelice 114–15, 249–50: not a brothel. No entry in *PPM*. Large cultivated area in W part with remains of a masonry *triclinium* from an earlier period.[46]

Context. Next door: 6.11.4 (workshop/dwelling); 6.11.6 (workshop/dwelling); 6.11.14 (small private house with workshop [?]); 6.11.17 (workshop/dwelling). Across: 6.9.2, 13 (private house); 6.15.23 (hotel [?]).

15. 6.16.32–33. YFE: 1904. "Proprietor": L. Aurunculeius Secundio. Tavern. Della Corte 94–95 (*domus* and *caupona*); *CTP* 2.266; Eschebach and Müller-Trollius 231: *popina* with "*thermopolium*," brothel, and home of Secundio (erotic art, representation of phallus, and table with Bacchant herm); Dierichs 77; DeFelice 257. *PPM* 5.960–73.

Context. Next door: 6.16.31 (private house/workshop [?]); 6.16.34 (shop). Across: 6.15.4 (stair to upstairs evidently part of private house at 6.15.5, 24–25).

---

44. Jashemski, *Gardens* 2 (1993):141.
45. *CTP* 2.260 n. 4, alerts us to an error made by Pietro Soprano in compiling the indices to the third edition of Della Corte in which this brothel is identified as that of Africanus and Victor: Della Corte, *Case*[3] (1965) 507.
46. Jashemski, *Gardens* 2 (1993) 143 (= 6.11.5).

16. 7.1.20. YFE: 1853. No proprietor. Tavern? Eschebach and Müller-Trollius 246: shop (wine shop?) with back room; brothel upstairs? No entry in *PPM*.

Context. Next door: 7.1.19 (shop); 7.1.21 (private house). Across: 9.2.11, 12 (shops).

17. 7.2.12. YFE: 1843. No proprietor. Tavern. Eschebach and Müller-Trollius 256: *caupona* with brothel; erotic art. *PPM* 6.496–509 (= 7.2.11–12 ["Tintoria"]; see 509).

Context. Next door: 7.2.11 (clothes dyers/cleaners); 7.2.13 (shop/dwelling). Across: 9.3.1–2 (clothes dyers/cleaners); 9.4.9 (shop).

18. 7.2.32–33. YFE: 1822. "Proprietor": Philippus (or Aprasius Felix). Tavern. Della Corte 177–78 (*caupona*); *CTP* 2.275; Eschebach and Müller-Trollius 261: wine shop and *caupona* (relief of phallus sculpted in tufa); Dierichs 76–77 (= 7.2.28–29, 32–33, taking the crib at 28—a suggestion of Eschebach and Müller-Trollius—and "*officina*" at 29 as part of the brothel), DeFelice 264. Brothel upstairs? *PPM* 6.720–21 (*caupona*).

Context. Next door: 7.2.31 (private house with shops); 7.2.34 (shop). Across: 7.9.29–34 (possible brothel [cat. no. 25]); 7.4.31–33, 50–51 (private house); 7.12.1–2, 36 (bakery).

19. 7.3.26–28. YFE: 1868. "Proprietors": Euplia and Phoebus. Tavern. Upstairs suites and erotic graffiti (*CIL* 4.2310b, 3103). Della Corte 149–50; Eschebach 138, 174–75; *CTP* 2.277; La Torre 93 n. 29 (= 7.3.27 [cf. cat. no. 20, which La Torre identifies as a separate brothel]; associated with food/drink service); *Pompei* 147; Eschebach and Müller-Trollius 270 (*caupona*-"thermopolium"-*lupanar*); Wallace-Hadrill 53 with 61 n. 71 (= 7.3.28): plausible, though only one erotic graffito [cf. cat. no. 37], discounting or ignoring *CIL* 4.3103).[47] Dierichs 135 n. 41; DeFelice 115–16, 267–68: doubtful. No entry in *PPM*.

Context. Next door: 7.3.25 (private house); 7.3.29 (private house). Across: 7.2.17 (shop); 7.2.18–19, 42 (private house).

---

47. Pirson, *Mietwohnungen* (1999) 55 (see also 226) (= 7.3.27) identifies this as a *cenaculum*; he rejects identifying this as a brothel because it fails to meet all three of Wallace-Hadrill's criteria.

20. 7.3.28. YFE: 1868. "Proprietors": Euplia and Phoebus (?). Tavern. For Della Corte Eschebach, and Eschebach and Müller-Trollius, see cat. no. 19. La Torre, 93 n. 29, regards as separate brothel (associated with food/drink service); *Pompei* 147 and Wallace-Hadrill also appear to regard as separate, but are unclear: see cat. no. 19. No entry in *PPM*.

Context. See cat. no. 19.

21. 7.4.44. YFE: 1833. No proprietor. Della Corte identifies as a private house, not a brothel. Della Corte 124–26 (= 7.4.44, 48); Eschebach 139, 175 (= 7.4.43, 48); La Torre 93 n. 29 (connected with private house); *Pompei* 148; Wallace-Hadrill 61 n. 73 (= 7.4.44): dubious; "was not suspected even by Della Corte . . . and is presumably confused with the *cella* [i.e., crib] at VII.4.42." One of the weakest identifications: see cat. no. 13 also.[48] *PPM* 7.4–5 (= 7.4.44–47).

Context. Next door: 7.4.43 (back door to private house); 7.4.45 (business/commercial establishment). Across: 7.3.38–40 (private house with *caupona*, etc.).

22. 7.6.34–36. YFE: 1822. "Proprietor": Venus. Two taverns with upstairs *cellae* or booths. Graffiti mentioning clients. *Caupona* across the street. Della Corte 169–72 (= 7.6.34–35); Eschebach 140, 175 (same address as Della Corte); *CTP* 2.283; La Torre 93 n. 29 (= 7.6.34 [cf. cat. no. 23, which he gives as a separate brothel]; "independent"); *Pompei* 152; Eschebach and Müller-Trollius 297–98; Wallace-Hadrill 53 with 61 n. 71 (= 9.6.34): plausible, with various graffiti (*CIL* 4.1626–49b), though "none pointing conclusively to sexual activity"; Savunen, 111–12 (allows Della Corte might be right in brothel-identification); Cantarella 90 (whether or not a brothel, prostitutes worked here). See *CIL* 4.1631 (fellatio), 1645b ("hic futui" type). *PPM* 7.207–9 (= 7.6.34–35).

Context. Next door: 7.6.33 (shop); 7.6.37 (back door to private house). Across: 7.7.18 (possible brothel [cat. no. 24]); 7.15.11–11a (private house); 7.16.19 (workshop).

23. 7.6.35. YFE: 1822. "Proprietor": Venus (?). For Della Corte, Eschebach, Eschebach and Müller-Trollius, see cat. no. 22. La Torre 93 n. 29,

---

48. Rejected as a brothel also by Pirson, *Mietwohnungen* (1999) 55 (see also 227) (= *cenaculum*).

regards as separate brothel ("independent"), as does Wallace-Hadrill (= 7.6.35–36). *PPM:* see cat. no. 22.

Context. See cat. no. 22.

24. 7.7.18. YFE: 1859. "Proprietor": L. Numisius. Tavern. Not in Della Corte. Eschebach 165 regards as a *caupona,* not a brothel, as does *CTP* 2.283; but see the assertion at Eschebach 140 that this is a branch of the brothel lying across the street (cat. nos. 22/23). La Torre 93 n. 29 (connected with food/drink service); *Pompei* 152; Eschebach and Müller-Trollius 302 (*caupona* with brothel; obscene relief); Wallace-Hadrill 53 with 61 n. 72: no grounds; Dierichs 76: *caupona;* DeFelice 275: erotic graffiti (*CIL* 4.549 a–b). As many as three back rooms, erotic art.[49] *PPM* 7.277–81.

Context. Next door: 7.7.17 (back door to private house); 7.7.19 (private house). Across: 7.6.33 (shop); 7.6.34–36 (possible brothel [cat. nos. 22/23]).

25. 7.9.29–34. YFE: 1822. "Proprietors": Donatus and Verpus. Tavern. Not in Della Corte. Eschebach 141, 175 (= 7.9.32, the more usual listing); *CTP* 2.289 (= 7.9.33); La Torre 93 n. 29 (associated with food/drink service); *Pompei* 154; Eschebach and Müller-Trollius, 314–15 (listed with 7.9.29–34, as the "*thermopolium*"-*caupona* of Donatus and Verpus); Wallace-Hadrill 53 with 61 n. 73: dubious; DeFelice 116–17 focuses on the two *popinae* at 7.9.30–31 and 33: the latter has three rooms (one with erotic painting) and an upstairs.[50] A *caupona/popina* type of brothel with more than one backroom and/or an upstairs seems very possible here.[51] No entry in *PPM* aside from 7.9.33 (= *Casa del Re di Prussia*): 7.353–57. At the rear of 33 was a *lararium* painting of Mars and Venus on the wall above a fountain set in what was evidently a small garden.[52]

Context. Next door: 7.9.28 (shop); 7.9.35 (business/commercial establishment). Across: 7.2.32–33 (possible brothel [cat. no. 18]); 7.4.31–33, 50–51 (private house); 7.12.1–2, 36 (bakery).

---

49. On this, see Guzzo and Scarano Ussani, *Veneris figurae* (2000) 14–17.

50. See Clarke, *Looking at Lovemaking* (1998) 259–60; Guzzo and Scarano Ussani, *Veneris figurae* (2000) 14, 17. There is also an erotic inscription, "lente impelle" (*CIL* 4.794), on the significance of which see De Martino, "Storia" (1996) 326.

51. Rejected as a brothel by Pirson, *Mietwohnungen* (2000) 55 (see also 229) (= *cenaculum*), because all three of Wallace-Hadrill's criteria are not met.

52. Jashemski, *Gardens* 2 (1993) 189 (= 7.9.33).

26. 7.12.18–20. YFE: 1862. The Purpose-Built Brothel. See figures 4–11. "Proprietors": Africanus, or Africanus and Victor.[53] Its ground floor has a hall-way connecting five small rooms (each with a masonry bed) and featuring erotic paintings on the upper walls above the doorways. There is a painting of Priapus in the hall and a latrine under the stairs. A stair off a separate street entrance leads to a balcony connecting five small rooms upstairs: see cat. no. 27. One hundred and twenty-three graffiti according to Della Corte, many of them erotic: see *CIL* 4.817–18, 2173–2301. Della Corte 203; Eschebach 142, 174–75; *CTP* 2.291; La Torre 93 n. 29 (= 7.12.18–19, because he regards the upstairs as a separate brothel; identifies it as "independent"); *Pompei* 157–58; Eschebach and Müller-Trollius 330; Wallace-Hadrill 51–53 (the only certain *lupanar*); Dierichs 76; Savunen 111; Cantarella 87; DeFelice 102–3. Extensive description in chap. 8.[54] *PPM* 7.520–39.

Context. Next door: 7.12.17 (wool works); 7.12.21 (private house). Across: 7.1.40–43 (private house with workshop); 7.1.44–45a (hotel with *caupona*); 7.11.11–12, 14 (hotel with *caupona* and crib).

27. 7.12.20. YFE: 1862. Upstairs of Purpose-Built Brothel (cat. no. 26). "Proprietors": Africanus, or Africanus and Victor (?). See references under cat. no. 26. La Torre 93 n. 29, regards as separate brothel. Wallace-Hadrill, p.c., suggests these are the sleeping quarters of the women who worked down-stairs. A better description of this site is urgently needed. *PPM*: see cat. no. 26.

Context: see cat. no. 26.

28. 7.13.13. YFE: 1847 (?). No proprietor. Eschebach and Müller-Trollius 335: upstairs brothel? Price graffito: *CIL* 4.2028 (with p. 704). No entry in *PPM*.

Context. Next door: 7.13.12 (business/commercial establishment); 7.13.14 (back door to private house). Across: 7.14.5, 17–19 (private house).

29. 7.13.18. YFE: 1839 (?). No proprietor. Eschebach and Müller-Trollius 336 ("*Casa di Ganimede*"): upstairs brothel? This upstairs complex was located

---

53. In this case, Africanus also appears in nonelectoral graffiti in and around the brothel. Franklin, "Games and a *Lupanar*" (1985/6) 323, identifies Victor as a *scriptor* who assisted Africanus in lettering electoral graffiti and also as a client of the brothel. On the unreliability of identifications of proprietors, see n. 20 above.

54. See also La Rocca and De Vos, *Pompei²* (1994) 313–16.

over the service sector of the *Casa di Ganimede* and so was the property of the owner of that house. There are two cribs at 7.13.15 and 16. These appear, however, to have been constructed after the earthquake, that is, in post-62 Pompeii, at a time when the access to the upstairs at 18 seems to have been cut off, presumably as a consequence of earthquake damage, while the upstairs itself dates to the years immediately preceding 62.[55] PPM 7.616–35 (= 7.13.4, 17–18). It seems clear that the owner or owners of the *Casa di Ganimede* had an appreciable interest in exploiting their property for the sale of sex, at least from the middle of the first century onwards. See cat. no. 30 as well. It is not necessary to suppose that the entire house was given over to prostitution at any time to make this point.[56]

Context. Next door: 7.13.17 (private house); 7.13.19 (possible brothel [cat. no. 30]). Across: 7.10.1–2, 15 (business/commercial establishment).

30. 7.13.19–21. YFE: 1820. No proprietor. Tavern. Eschebach and Müller-Trollius, 336: *popina* and brothel (19 is a *cella meretricia*)[57]; Dierichs 135 n. 41 (= 7.13.19); DeFelice 282 (= 7.13.20–21). PPM 7.655–57 (= 7.13.20–22). This establishment was evidently a property of the owner of the *Casa di Ganimede* in the final years of the city's existence.

Context. Next door: 7.13.18 (possible brothel [cat. no. 29]); 7.13.22 (shop). Across: 7.9.1, 43, 66–68 (Eumachia building [rear]); 7.10.1–2, 15 (business/commercial establishment).

31. 7.15.4–5. YFE: 1872. No proprietor. Tavern. Della Corte 199–200 (= 7.15.4–6): a *taberna lusoria*, not a brothel, similarly Eschebach 143, CTP 2.294 (same address as Della Corte); Eschebach and Müller-Trollius 343 (business with "*thermopolium*"-*caupona*); DeFelice 126–27, 283–84: possible brothel. Erotic graffiti of the "hic futui" type: CIL 4.4815–16, 4818. PPM 7.781–90. A small garden in the back of 5 is visible through a large window installed in a diningroom.[58]

55. Eschebach, "Casa di Ganimede" (1982) 240–41, 274–75, 311–12.

56. Eschebach, "Casa di Ganimede" (1982) 277, suggests, if I understand him correctly, that the entire *Casa di Ganimede* may at some point have functioned as a brothel, partly on the basis of two representations of the phallus at different points of the facade.

57. Eschebach, *Entwicklung* (1970) 143, 175, also identifies 7.13.19 as a crib. Eschebach, "Casa di Ganimede" (1982) 248–49, 312, proposes that this tavern, which shows the remains of a staircase to an upper floor, offered prostitution there. The crib at 7.13.19, though it faces the street (see Eschebach, 245), very likely operated in conjunction with the tavern as well.

58. Jashemski, *Gardens* 2 (1993) 199.

Context. Next door: 7.15.3 (private house); 7.15.6 (business/commercial establishment). Across: 7.7.2, 5, 14–15 (private house).

32. 7.16.B. YFE: 1955. See figures 23–27. "Proprietor": Faustius. The Suburban Bath complex. Della Corte knew only some erotic graffiti, only one of which is really secure: CIL 4.1751 features the relatively expensive—for Pompeian graffiti—price of 16 *asses*) and a masonry bench. See also *CIL* 4.1740–41, 1746, 1748, and 1750 (as restored by Della Corte, NB), 9146a–b, 9147b–d (names of clients?), 9146f (a reference to a client/prostitutes?), 9146h (a greeting to a *caupo*?). Della Corte 440–43 (= 7 Occ. [in front of the *Porta Marina* N.]); Eschebach 144, 174 (same address as Della Corte); not in La Torre nor in Wallace-Hadrill. Eschebach and Müller-Trollius 240, 491.[59] Explicit erotic art is found in the changing room (*apodyterium*) of the Baths themselves. The post-Della Corte excavations of the Suburban Baths show a group of three apartments on the top floor. Though connected with the *apodyterium* of the Baths by a service ramp/stairs, this level also has an entrance independent of the Baths.[60] One or more of these apartments might well have been used as a brothel at some point.[61] No entry in *PPM*.

Context. The entrance to the *Porta Marina* and the city wall.

33. 8.4.12. YFE: 1861. No proprietor. Tavern. Layout has a vestibule leading to peristyle and upstairs rooms. Seven *dolia* were found embedded in the soil in back, as well as a metal chest. Della Corte has a barbershop in the entranceway: see *CIL* 4.743. Della Corte and Eschebach identify as a *ganeum-lupanar*; Eschebach and Müller-Trollius as a *ganeum-lupanar* behind a *caupona* and barbershop. Della Corte 237–38; Eschebach 145, 175 (= 8.4.12–13); La Torre 93 n. 29 (associated with food/drink service); *Pompei* 164; Eschebach and Müller-Trollius 372; Wallace-Hadrill 53 with 61 n. 72 (= 8.4.12–13): no

---

59. The address is taken from the catalog at Eschebach and Müller-Trollius, *Gebäudeverzeichnis* (1993) 491. The brief discussion of the Suburban Baths at 240, viewed in the context of the city map, suggests an address of 7.A.1.

60. Conticello, "Lavori" (1988) 62, accepts the presence of a brothel on this level on the basis of the now-famous erotic paintings in the Baths themselves. The logic is suspect (see chaps. 4 and 7), and yet in this case a faulty premise does not necessarily preclude a correct conclusion; see also La Rocca and De Vos, *Pompei*² (1994) 96; Guzzo and Scarano Ussani, *Veneris figurae* (2000) 21–24 Scarano Ussani, "Alle terme" (2001/2002).

61. Jacobelli, *Terme Suburbane* (1995) 65, 97; Clarke, "Laughing" (2002) 151–55 are skeptical. For other examples of apartments built into baths, see Soricelli, "Piano Superiore" (1995) 112; for comparison with other rental property in Pompeii, see Soricelli, 116–17. Not all of the decoration, to be sure, seems consistent with a brothel.

grounds for identification as a brothel; Dierichs 77; DeFelice 118, 288 (= 8.4.12–13): not a brothel. No entry in *PPM*. The garden in back, in addition to the *dolia* mentioned above, had a four-sided portico and a masonry pool with a fountain.[62]

Context. Next door: 8.4.11 (workshop); 8.4.13 (barbershop). Across: 7.1.8, 14–17, 48, 50–51 (Stabian Baths); 7.1.9 (shop).

34. 9.2.7–8. YFE: 1851. "Proprietor": Hilario. Layout includes access to living quarters on ground floor and suites upstairs. Della Corte identifies as a tavern, not a brothel. Della Corte 208–9 (= 9.2.6 or 7); *CTP* 2.315 (lists 9.2.6 or 7 separately from 9.2.7–8); Eschebach 148, 175 ("*Casa della Fontana d'Amore*"); La Torre 93 n. 29 (= 9.2.8); *Pompei* 171; Eschebach and Müller-Trollius 406 (relief in tufa of a phallus); Wallace-Hadrill 61 n. 73 (= 9.2.8): dubious, Dierichs 77. *PPM* 8.1068–87 (= 9.2.6–7). The garden at the rear of 7, surrounded on three sides by garden paintings, flanked a pool with a fountain, a marble statuette of an *amorino*, and a wall painting of a nymph.[63]

Context. Next door: 9.2.6 (shop/dwelling); 9.2.9 (shop). Across: 7.1.23 (public latrine); 7.1.24 (shop); 7.1.25, 46–47 (private house).

35. 9.5.14–16. YFE: 1878. No proprietor. Tavern. Not in Della Corte.[64] *CTP* 2.320 (= 9.5.16); Eschebach 149, 175; La Torre 93 n. 29 (= 9.5.14; connected with private house); *Pompei* 174; Eschebach and Müller-Trollius 425 (*popina* in 16); Wallace-Hadrill 53 with 61 n. 73 (= 9.5.14): dubious. The layout is irregular; some erotic art found. DeFelice 118–19, 295 (= 9.5.16): not a brothel.[65] *PPM* 9.600–69 (also skeptical of its identification as a brothel). A garden with portico lay at the back of 14, while the *atrium* of 16 had an *impluvium* enclosed by a low wall with a planting bed in the top.[66]

---

62. Jashemski, *Gardens* 2 (1993) 213 (= 8.4.12–13).

63. Jashemski, *Gardens* 2 (1993) 228 (= 9.2.7).

64. Evidently first identified as a combination *caupona*-brothel by Mau, "Scavi" (1879) 209–10.

65. See Clarke, *Looking at Lovemaking* (1998) 178–87, who appears concerned to split the difference on the brothel-identification (at 186–87): ". . . [this is] simply a house-to-tavern makeover, with one of the attractions being a room [?] that could be used—among other things—for the occasional tryst by willing (and sometimes paid) partners." The effort to limit the experience of prostitution both spatially and temporally is characteristic of much 1990s writing on Pompeian brothels.

66. Jashemski, *Gardens* 2 (1993) 237.

Context. Next door: 9.5.13 (private house); 9.5.17 (back door to private house). Across: 9.8.A (private house); 9.8.B (hotel); 9.6.8 (possible brothel [cat. no. 37]).

36. 9.5.18–21 (at 19). YFE: 1878. "Proprietor": Somene. Upstairs room(s). Erotic graffiti (*CIL* 4.5099–5157, esp. 5105, 5123, 5127), mentioning clients, prostitutes, prices. Della Corte 162–63 (= 9.5.19, the more usual listing); Eschebach, 149–50, 175; *CTP* 2.320 (= 9.5.19); La Torre 93 n. 29 (connected with private house); *Pompei* 174; Eschebach and Müller-Trollius 425; Wallace-Hadrill 53 with 61 n. 73, identifies as a private house, not a brothel, Savunen 112, agrees; Cantarella 91.[67] *PPM* 9.670–719 (= 9.5.18, "*Casa di Giasone*"): the entry at 19, with its staircase leading to the brothel, is a post-earthquake arrangement.[68] An *atrium* enclosed by a four-sided portico served as a garden with a pool and fountain in the middle and surrounded on three sides by a *viridarium*.[69]

Context. Next door: 9.5.17 (back door to private house); 9.5.22 (private house). Across: 9.4.13–14 (Central Baths); 9.6.4–7 (private house).

37. 9.6.8. YFE: 1880. "Proprietor": Amandus. Its design has eight rooms around a small *atrium*. Erotic graffito of a kind: *CIL* 4.5187. Della Corte 163; Eschebach 150, 174; *CTP* 2.321; La Torre, 93 n. 29 (for whom this brothel is connected with a private house); *Pompei* 175; Eschebach and Müller-Trollius 427–28; Wallace-Hadrill 53 with 61 n. 73 thinks dubious, because only one erotic graffito; Savunen 112 agrees; Cantarella 91. *PPM* 9.765–67. A small garden lies behind the *atrium* in the SW portion of the "house."[70]

Context. Next door: 9.6.7 (private house), (unexcavated). Across: 9.5.14–16 (possible brothel [cat. no. 35]); 9.8.B (hotel); 9.8.C (private house [partially excavated]).

38. 9.7.14. YFE: 1880 (?). No proprietor. Not in Della Corte. Eschebach 150, 175; La Torre 93 n. 29 ("independent"); *Pompei* 175; Eschebach and

---

67. Rejected as a brothel by Pirson, *Mietwohnungen* (1999) 55 (see also 225–26) (= *cenaculum*) because not all of Wallace-Hadrill's criteria are met.

68. The presence of a brothel here would make a nice counterpoint to the moralizing program of wall paintings in this house, above all those found in *cubiculum* e: Pugliese Carratelli, *Pompei* 9 (1999) 671.

69. Jashemski, *Gardens* 2 (1993) 237.

70. Jashemski, *Gardens* 2 (1993) 238–39.

Müller-Trollius 433: *posticum?* Not in Wallace-Hadrill. Appears to be a double crib. Cribs are also at 9.7.15 and 17. Associated with the tavern at 9.7.13? No entry in *PPM*.

Context. Next door: 9.7.13 ("*thermopolium*"); 9.7.15 (crib). Across: 9.1.22, 29 (private house); 9.1.28 (*stabulum* [lodgings for persons and draft animals]).

39. 9.7.26. YFE: 1880. "Proprietors": Fabius Memor and Fabius Celer. Tavern. Della Corte, 197: tavern with side rooms, similarly Eschebach, 150; *CTP* 2.322 (= 9.25–26); Eschebach and Müller-Trollius 436: *caupona*-brothel. Evidently associated with the "*thermopolium*"-*popina*-*hospitium* attributed to Fabius Memor and Celer at 9.7.24–25: Eschebach and Müller-Trollius 435–36; DeFelice 301. No entry in *PPM*. A small garden in the rear of 25 has a mosaic fountain with depictions of Venus and *amorini*, while at the rear of 26 there is a small open courtyard paved with *opus signinum*.[71]

Context. 9.7.25 ("*thermopolium*"-*popina*-hotel); (unexcavated). Across: 9.6.F (shop); 9.6.G (private house).

40. 9.11.2–3. YFE: 1911. "Proprietor": Asellina. Tavern. Della Corte identifies this as a "*thermopolium*," not a brothel. Ithyphallic-lamp found, plus graffiti argued to show that prostitutes were interested in local elections. Della Corte 307–9 (= 9.11.2); Eschebach 151, 174 (= 9.11.2–4, rooms upstairs); *CTP* 2.324 (= 9.11.2); La Torre 93 n. 29 (= 9.11.3; "independent"); *Pompei* 177; Eschebach and Müller-Trollius 445–46 (depiction of Mercury with phallus and two women: "*thermopolium*"-*caupona* with brothel); Wallace-Hadrill 53, with 61 n. 71 (= 9.11.3), deems plausible on the basis of "suggestive graffiti," but points out, however, that the site has not been excavated; Dierichs 77 (= 9.11.3); Cantarella 75 (= 9.11.2: doubtful); DeFelice 35, 119–20, 304–5 (= 9.11.2–4): *CIL* 4.7221, 7862–76, 9096–99, 9351.[72] No entry in *PPM*.

Context. Next door: 9.11.1 (private house [unexcavated]); 9.11.4 (shop). Across: 1.7.1, 20 (private house); 1.7.2–3 (private house with workshop).

---

71. Jashemski, *Gardens* 2 (1993) 242, with separate entries for each.
72. There is a regrettable scholarly tradition of coyness in evaluating the nature of this site. For more or less indirect identification as a brothel, see Della Corte, *Pompeii: The New Excavations* (1927) 25 ("... the establishment in which, according to custom, not only foods and drinks were sold"); Maiuri, "Scavi" (1950) 25; La Rocca and De Vos, *Pompei²* (1994) 213–14.

41. 9.12.6–8. YFE: 1912. "Proprietor": Crescens or C. Iulius Polybius or Porphyrio/Purpurio. Tavern? Layout suggests the existence of an upstairs level; side/back rooms still unexcavated per Della Corte, who identifies this as a tavern, not a brothel. Della Corte 322 (= 9.12.6); Eschebach 151, 175 (same address as Della Corte); CTP 2.325 (same address as Della Corte, but has a separate listing for 9.12.7); La Torre 93 n. 29 ("independent"); *Pompei* 177 (= 9.12.6–7?); Eschebach and Müller-Trollius 448 (ithyphallic Mercury with purse). Not in Wallace-Hadrill. Dierichs 77 (= 9.12.6); Savunen 110: recent excavations show a bakery on the ground floor, which in her view excludes identification as a brothel.[73] DeFelice 305 (= 9.12.7). No entry in *PPM*.

Context. Next door: 9.12.5 (shop); (unexcavated). Across: 1.8.7 (shop); 1.8.8–9 ("*thermopolium*"); 9.13.1 (private house).

The gaps and inconsistencies in this list merit no great comment. For the reasons given in chapter 7, none of the three criteria of layout, art, and graffiti are really probative in themselves. A skeptic might object that even in the case of the Purpose-Built Brothel the evidence is not inherently better, just more abundant, than elsewhere. Just how easy it is to slide from reasonable doubt to hyperskepticism is well illustrated by the case of the Suburban Baths, which is no. 32 in the catalog. This complex also serves as an excellent example of the challenge in showing that a brothel operated in connection with a bath, a point discussed in chapter 7.

The descriptions of brothels in the literary evidence are of little help in identifying the material remains of such establishments,[74] since the salient details they provide do not survive in the archaeological record, with the possible exception in some cases of the *titulus*.[75] Beyond that they are impossibly

---

73. See Varone, "Terremoti" (1995) 29–35, with literature, above all his own work, with more extensive description of the finds. Besides the bakery, there is a dining facility, a retail outlet, and bedrooms both upstairs and downstairs, as well as erotic art. Definite exclusion as a brothel hardly seems justified.

74. The most important ones are in Sen. *Contr.* 1.2; [Verg.] *Copa* (at least using our definition); Petron. 7–8; Iuv. 6.115–32; Apul. *Apol.* 75; *Hist. Ap. Tyr.* 33–36.

75. The *titulus* was an inscription giving the price charged by a prostitute, which was found near the door to her room in a brothel, to judge from *Hist. Ap. Tyr.* 33–34. From among the over two dozen graffiti that give the prices of prostitutes at Pompeii, there is not a single unambiguous example of such a *titulus*, though some of those found in doorways might be thought to qualify: see, for example, CIL 4.4439, 4441. Of course the sources mention *cellae*, for example, but do not describe them in any detail.

vague—they are not really intended as full or accurate descriptions of broth-els—and laden with clichés. They betray an upper-class sensibility about how dirty, smoky, and smelly brothels were, in other words, how low-class, rather than impart much information that is useful to us.[76] This does not mean, of course, that Roman brothels were clean, well-lit places, only that the literary evidence is inadequate to prove that they were not.

One index of the poverty of this literary evidence is that it does not allow us to conclude with absolute certainty that the concept of *lupanar* could embrace either *caupona* or *popina*, though it hardly excludes the possibility either.[77] The best evidence comes from the least likely source, Apuleius's accusation that his enemy Herennius Rufinus turned his house into a brothel in order to prostitute his wife and daughter.[78] In this case we have an upper-class *domus* that is made to seem like a *lupanar*, but is not the real thing. In any case, we might take the alleged occupation of the *triclinium* by partyers (*comissatores*) to suggest that the on-site vending of drink might facilitate the holding of a *comissatio* in a brothel, though it hardly proves it.[79]

One instance where the literary and archaeological evidence actually aligns will give a fair idea of the absurd difficulties involved in identifying the remains of Roman brothels. In the *Story of Apollonius of Tyre*, the innocent Tarsia, immediately after her acquisition at auction by the pimp, is brought to a brothel, where she spies a golden statue of Priapus, adorned with jewels and gold trim.[80] When instructed by the pimp to pay homage to his patron deity, she asks him whether he hails from Lampsacus, Priapus's hometown. The question is obviously meant to betray her naiveté and her innocence. The pimp's reply drives this point home: "are you ignorant of the fact, wretched girl, that you have entered the house of a greedy pimp?"[81]

If we compare this incident with the adventures of Encolpius and Ascyltos, which are discussed in chapter 9, we see that knowledge about brothels was ideally differentiated by gender. The obliviousness that Petronius's heroes display in regard to their surroundings makes them look ridiculous, while Tarsia's ignorance guarantees her respectability and heightens the pathos of her

---

76. The same holds, of course, for *popinae, cauponae,* and so forth: see evidence in Chevallier, *Voyages* (1988) 75.

77. The presence of drunken clients proves nothing either way: Sen. *Contr.* 1.2.10. Nor does evidence for consuming food in a brothel: see chap. 2.

78. Apul. *Apol.* 75.

79. See the legal evidence discussed below in the text.

80. *Hist. Ap. Tyr.* 33.

81. *Hist. Ap. Tyr.* 33: "'ignoras, misera, quia in domum avari lenonis incurristi?'"

situation. Her failure to recognize the statue of Priapus as a sign that she had been brought to work in a brothel suggests that this was an icon of such establishments, a premise that receives support from the double-barreled painted exemplar found on an interior wall of the Purpose-Built Brothel.[82] We would not of course expect to find a gold and jewel-encrusted specimen outside of a literary text.

Unfortunately, this cliché, even if it is echoed from time to time in the archaeological record, is of no more service in identifying the material remains of brothels than those which pepper the accounts of Petronius and the other literary sources. The reason should be obvious. Representations of Priapus and, more generally, the phallus, were found in a number of contexts, most of them having nothing to do with brothels.[83] At the same time, it would be unreasonable to expect to see Priapus or the phallus in every brothel. We might conclude that while their presence is not irrelevant to identifying a building as a brothel, it is hardly probative, and their absence proves nothing. The two types of evidence, literary and archaeological, seem to pass each other like the proverbial two ships in the night.

Neither the archaeological nor the literary evidence in fact will allow us to distinguish with conviction a tavern, inn, or another form of lower-class dwelling from a brothel, unless the latter is purpose-built.[84] The scarce legal evidence is of a piece with this. In one passage, for example, the jurist Ulpian appears to distinguish *lupanaria* from other establishments in which prostitutes worked, but draws no legal consequences from this contrast, and we may even argue extends the concept of brothel, at least for specific ends at law.[85]

We must also concede that, given the problems in excavating, reporting, and preserving the material remains, we cannot in many cases distinguish with certainty a tavern from other types of shops.[86] By the same token, it is impos-

---

82. See chap. 8.

83. For recent discussions of the place of the phallus in Roman erotic art, see the notes to chap. 7.

84. For inns, see 6.1.1, 6.2.4, 7.1.44–45, 7.11.11, 14, with Jashemski, "Copa" (1963/4), 6.7.15, with Packer, "Middle and Lower Class Housing" (1975) 136; 1.1.6–9, 1.2.24, 7.12.34–35, 1.11.16, 5.2.13, 6.9.1, 14, 6.14.35–36, with Packer, "Inns at Pompeii" (1978). Still more examples in Ruddell, *Business* (1964). For rental housing at Pompeii, see now Pirson, "Rented Accommodation" (1997); Pirson, *Mietwohnungen* (1999). I am not certain that rental housing can be effectively distinguished from inns, and so forth. Pirson ("Rented Accommodation," 166 n. 7) excludes from consideration "the letting-out of single rooms on a short-term basis." How can we be certain that subletting did not occur on the premises he does examine?

85. Ulp. D. 23.2.43 pr.; cf. 9; also Ulp. D. 3.2.4.2; Alex. Sev. C. 4.56.3 (a. 225). See the discussion in chaps. 1 and 7.

86. For Pompeii, see Gassner, *Kauflāden* (1986) 21, 37, 80 (and 2–7, 10, for ambiguous terminology); Jongman, *Economy* (1988) 169; for Ostia, see Girri, *Taberna* (1956) 3, 44.

sible to know how many brothels are missing from the list given above.[87] Even so, it is disappointing how little attention archaeologists have paid to the brothel, especially given the general interest in ancient sexuality that classicists have shown since the 1970s. We still must rely on Matteo Della Corte, whose identifications of Pompeian buildings are widely mistrusted, for the most extensive analysis—as brothels—of the physical remains for too many of these places.

It is not simply a matter of a careful, scientific reexamination of the physical remains and/or their (re)publication according to the more exacting standards that now prevail. The re-excavation of sites is unlikely to turn up much new sexual graffiti or erotic art, though finds of this kind are not utterly impossible. What is more likely to bear fruit and so what is urgently needed is the careful evaluation of the use of space in venues where prostitution has been suspected, always with the understanding that the absence of masonry beds proves little in itself. Disagreement over the identification of individual brothels is inevitable, but such dissension should be regarded as salutary in an environment where absolute certainty is usually impossible. The challenge to archaeologists, in particular to Pompeianists, is simply to raise the issue, presenting the evidence in a manner that allows nonspecialists, such as social historians interested in Roman sexuality, to decide for themselves how convincing they find a conclusion, whether negative or positive, about the presence of a brothel on a given site. It is regrettable to see how often, even in excellent publications of very recent vintage, the question is never raised or, if it is raised, it is summarily dismissed.[88]

For that reason, it is risky to attempt to go further. All the same, a tentative list, set forth pending direct inspection of the material remains and correction by my betters, may be useful. I consider the following candidates to be "more likely" as brothels: cat. nos. 1, 2, 5, 6, 8, 10, 11, 12, 14, 18, 19, 20, 22, 23, 24, 25, 26, 27, 29, 30, 31, 32, 36, 37, 38, 40.[89] The total is twenty-six

---

87. These may include entire subtypes that have in part or largely vanished, such as the *caupona* with upstairs brothel. See, for example, 7.12.15–16, with Franklin, "Games and a *Lupanar*" (1985/6) 320. Pirson's work on rental accommodation at Pompeii, *Mietwohnungen* (1999) contains a wealth of information, no small part of which may be of service in the identification of brothels.

88. The superbly documented Pugliese Carratelli, *Pompei* (1990–1999) is, apart from scattered exceptions, disappointingly reticent on the subject of brothel-identification in regard to the buildings that fall within its scope. The very few close reexaminations of already excavated sites that have been conducted in recent years at Pompeii, though in most respects exemplary, are also disappointing in this one respect. See nos. 4, 5, 6 in the catalog. For less recent and somewhat better treatment of this type, though it still leaves something to be desired, see cat. nos. 29, 30.

89. For the application of the criteria, one should consult the individual entries. I note here only that I tend to weigh the graffiti containing prices as heavily as Wallace-Hadrill does the "hic

brothels, though some of these should perhaps be combined, that is 19/20, 22/23, 26/27, reducing the total to twenty-three. I would rate 13 and 21 as "less likely."

A minimum of three subtypes of brothel emerges from my survey.[90] There is the lone example of the Purpose-Built brothel: 26/27. Next there is the tavern or *caupona/popina* with rooms in back and/or upstairs: cat. nos. 1, 2, 3, 8, 9, 10, 11, 12, 15, 17, 18, 19, 20 (or 19/20), 22, 23 (or 22/23), 24, 25, 30, 31, 33, 35, 39, 40. Other possible examples of this type include cat. nos. 4, 7, 13, 14, 16, 41. The third subtype cannot be differentiated any further at this time, beyond the observation that it appears to fit under the classification of lower-class lodgings.

If the list is more or less correct in its identification of brothels, it is interesting to see the second type, the tavern-brothel, emerge as the dominant subtype.[91] Though generally smaller than our one purpose-built example, these brothels seem to have been far more numerous and would therefore have harbored many more prostitutes overall. If the hypothesis about the numbers of purpose-built brothels in the Regionary Catalogs representing purpose-built brothels is correct (chapter 6), a similar ratio of tavern-type to purpose-built brothel may have held true for Rome and elsewhere in the Roman world.

---

futui" type. As seen in chaps. 2 and 7, graffiti—of whatever kind—are not an absolutely reliable indicator of the presence of a brothel. A particular instance where this principle holds for price-graffiti can be seen in the case of the House of the Vettii, discussed at the beginning of this appendix. Their absence is of course hardly conclusive either. I should also call attention to the peculiar cases of cat. nos. 29 and 30, where *none* of the criteria are significant, but where the presence of cribs—three in all—speaks very loudly, in my opinion, in favor of the identification of two brothels.

90. Cf. the categorization of modern Nevada brothels into bar houses, parlor houses, and mixed, that Shaner *Madam* (2001) 39 offers. See also Albert, *Brothel* (2001) 20.

91. It may be useful to compare the description of saloons with attached prostitution-quarters in nineteenth-century New York City that Hill, *Their Sisters' Keepers* (1993) 187, 190 provides. Cf. the wine shops operated by brothel-keepers in nineteenth-century Paris: Corbin, *Women for Hire* (1990) 56–57.

Appendix 2

A CATALOG OF POSSIBLE
CRIBS AT POMPEII

The same abbreviations for the specialist literature on brothel-identification set forth in appendix 1 are used here. I give no explicit indication for these authors when they identify a location as a *cella meretricia*, that is, as a crib. Cantarella 87, accepts nine *cellae* for Pompeii without discussion of specifics; I assume these are the same ones that are given by Eschebach 175. As in the case of brothels, I exclude what I take to be an improbable identification. Here there is but one example: 6.14.28, which Della Corte identifies as a *cella meretricia* in the index to his second (though it does not appear as such in his third) edition of *Case* and which is more likely to be part of a brothel, though to my knowledge no one has yet identified it as such.[92]

   1. 7.2.28. YFE: 1844.[93] Masonry bed; flower stands. *Pompei* 145 (public

---

92. Della Corte, *Case²* (1954) 72–76, 429.

93. The "year of first excavation" is taken from Eschebach and Müller-Trollius, *Gebäude-verzeichnis* (1993). In some cases this is the only date of excavation. When no date is given for the crib itself, I take the date available from the nearest building, which is perhaps not always a reliable indicator, to be sure.

latrine); Eschebach and Müller-Trollius 260, 492. *PPM* 6.718–19 (= 7.2.27–29 at 28: public latrine).[94]

Context. Next door: 7.2.27 (workshop with private house); 7.2.29 (the same). Across: 7.4.34 (shop).

2. 7.4.42. YFE: 1833. Masonry bed; flower stand; vaulted ceiling; niche for latrine; erotic wall painting. Eschebach 175; *CTP* 2.280; La Torre 93 n. 29; *Pompei* 148; Eschebach and Müller-Trollius 281, 492; Wallace-Hadrill 53 with n. 70; Savunen 113. *PPM* 7.1–3.[95]

Context. Next door: 7.4.41 (latrine [part of wool works]); 7.4.43 (back door to private house). Across: 7.3.33–35 (workshop/dwelling).

3. 7.6.14. YFE: 1868. Three *dolia* embedded in the floor. *CTP* 2.282 (shop of Edivius or Elpidius Sabinus; dwelling of *pornoboskoi* [pimps]);[96] *Pompei* 151 (*caupona* or *taberna*); Eschebach and Müller-Trollius 294: Large shop room.

Context. Next door: 7.6.13 (stairway to upper floor of *caupona*); 7.6.15 (possible crib). Across: 6.6.1, 8, 12–13 (private house). See also no. 4.

4. 7.6.15. YFE: 1868. Masonry bed; small hearth. *Pompei* 151 (*caupona* or *taberna*); Eschebach and Müller-Trollius 294: *cella vinaria* (?). See also no. 3.

Context. Next door: 7.6.14 (possible crib); 7.6.16 (shop with business/commercial establishment—*caupona* [hotel?]). Across: 7.5.2, 7–8, 10, 12, 24 (Forum Baths).

5. 7.11.12. YFE: 1862. See figure 3. Masonry bed; vaulted ceiling (under staircase); tufa phallus over the entrance. Della Corte 204–5, 491; Eschebach 175; *CTP* 2.290; La Torre 93 n. 29; *Pompei* 157; Eschebach and Müller-Trollius 324, 492; Wallace-Hadrill 53 with n. 70; Savunen 113; DeFelice 278. *PPM* 7.463–77 (= 7.11.11–14, at 7.11.12).[97]

---

94. 7.2.28 was identified as a latrine as far back as Fiorelli, *Scavi* (1873) 35; Fiorelli, *Descrizione* (1875) 194–95.

95. See Fiorelli, *Descrizione* (1875) 461: "small brothel" ("lupanare piccolo")/public latrine (cf. 222–23, where the identification is that of a public latrine); *CIL* 4 p. 787: *cella meretricia*/"small brothel" ("lupanare piccolo").

96. This identification was made by Schulz, "Scavi" (1841) 118.

97. Identified as a *cella meretricia* as far back as Fiorelli, *Scavi* (1873) 25; Fiorelli, *Descrizione* (1875) 279.

Context. Next door: 7.11.11 (*caupona*/hotel); 7.11.13 (*caupona*). Across: 7.1.44–45a (hotel); 7.1.46–47 (back doors to private house).

6. 7.12.33. YFE: 1863. Masonry bed (under staircase). Eschebach 175; La Torre 93 n. 29; *Pompeii* 158; Eschebach and Müller-Trollius 332, 492; Wallace-Hadrill 53 with n. 70; Savunen 113; DeFelice 281.[98]

Context. Next door: 7.12.32 (small business/commercial establishment with wool works); 7.12.34 (*popina* with hotel and accommodations for draft animals [*stabulum*] [?]). Across: 7.10.5, 8, 13 (business/commercial establishment with wool works).

7. 7.13.15. YFE: 1863. Masonry bed; narrow entrance; phallic amulet found; erotic graffito shared with nos. 8 and 9: *CIL* 4.2028. Eschebach 175; La Torre 93 n. 29; *Pompei* 158; Eschebach and Müller-Trollius 335, 492; Wallace-Hadrill 53 with n. 70; Savunen 113; DeFelice 282. *PPM* 7.652–54.[99]

Context. Next door: 7.13.14 (back door to private house); 7.13.16 (possible crib). Across: 7.10.3, 14 (private house).

8. 7.13.16. YFE: 1863. Masonry bed; wall painting of a quadruped whose two front feet are phalluses; erotic graffito shared with nos. 7 and 9: *CIL* 4.2028. Eschebach 175; La Torre 93 n. 29; *Pompei* 158; Eschebach and Müller-Trollius 335, 492; Wallace-Hadrill 53 with n. 70; Savunen 113; DeFelice 282. *PPM* 7.652–54.[100]

Context. Next door: 7.13.15 (possible crib); 7.13.17 (private house). Across: 7.10.3, 14 (private house).

9. 7.13.19. YFE: 1820. Masonry bed, painted red; erotic graffito shared with nos. 7 and 8: *CIL* 4.2028. Eschebach 175; La Torre 93 n. 29; *Pompei* 158; Eschebach and Müller-Trollius 336, 492; Wallace-Hadrill 53 with n. 70; DeFelice 282. *PPM* 7.652–54.[101]

---

98. Breton, *Pompeia*³ (1870) 441–42 (evidently); Packer, "Inns" (1978) 51 n. 113.

99. Identified as a *cella meretricia* as far back as Breton, *Pompeia*³ (1870) 452; Fiorelli, *Descrizione* (1875) 298.

100. Identified as a *cella meretricia* as far back as Breton, *Pompeia*³ (1870) 452; Fiorelli, *Descrizione* (1875) 298.

101. Identified as a *cella meretricia* as far back as Breton, *Pompeia*³ (1870) 452; Fiorelli, *Descrizione* (1875) 298.

Context. Next door: 7.13.18 (possible brothel [cat. no. 29]); 7.13.20 (possible brothel [cat. no. 30]). Across: 7.10.1–2, 15 (business/commercial establishment).

10. 7.16.8. YFE: 1846. No masonry bed (under a staircase). *Pompei* 159 (storeroom/"*thermopolium*"); Eschebach and Müller-Trollius 347 (?), 492.

Context. Next door: 7.16.7 (*popina*); 7.16.9 (small bakery). Across: 7.7.10, 13 (private house).

11. 9.6.2. YFE: 1878 (?). Masonry bed (?) (under a staircase); three erotic graffiti around the corner: *CIL* 4.5203, 5204, 5206. Eschebach 175; La Torre 93 n. 29; *Pompei* 175; Eschebach and Müller-Trollius 426, 492; Wallace-Hadrill 53 with n. 70; Savunen 113.

Context. Next door: 9.6.1 (back door to shop/dwelling); 9.6.3 (private house). Across: 9.3.19–20 (bakery).

12. 9.7.15. YFE: 1880 (?). Masonry bed (?) (under a staircase); four erotic graffiti nearby: *CIL* 4.2413h (with p. 222), 2413m, 5345, 5372. Eschebach 175; La Torre 93 n. 29; *Pompei* 175; Eschebach and Müller-Trollius 433, 492; Wallace-Hadrill 53 with n. 70; DeFelice 298.

Context. Next door: 9.7.14 (possible brothel [cat. no. 38]); 9.7.16 (private house). Across: 9.1.22, 29 (private house).

13. 9.7.17. YFE: 1867 (?). Masonry bed (?) (under a staircase). Eschebach 175; La Torre 93 n. 29; *Pompei* 175; Eschebach and Müller-Trollius 433 (latrine?) 492; Wallace-Hadrill 53 with n. 70; DeFelice 298.

Context. Next door: 9.7.16 (private house); 9.7.18 (shop with private house). Across: 9.1.22, 29 (private house).

Appendix 3

A CATALOG OF POSSIBLE
PROSTITUTES AT POMPEII

The names given below are not exhaustive regarding all known, or know-able, Pompeian female prostitutes, though at minimum the list includes all prostitutes whose names are found in this book. I also include males who are said to charge a price for sex and note their gender after their names. I would appreciate learning of missing names.

A word of caution is in order here. Of all the elements of this book, this one comes closest simply to replicating Roman misogyny. In fact, that is very nearly the point. My intent is to list the women whom the Romans identify, or appear to identify, as prostitutes. I cannot be absolutely certain that any of these identifications is correct.[102] Allegations of promiscuity, or the willingness to perform a sexual act, are just that. So I do not, for example, write "allegedly offers fellatio." Most if not all of this evidence, inscriptions in the form of casual graffiti, involves mere allegation.

My aim then is to be as cautious as possible. When a woman's name is simply found, as it often is at Pompeii, on the wall of an establishment that can be identified as a brothel and/or a tavern, I note that the name is "identified from context." When the rationale is more tenuous, I indicate this explicitly, as in "identified from context: next door to a tavern."[103] Given the uncertainty that

---

102. For those readers without Latin, please note that "Incerta" refers to a prostitute whose name is unknown.

103. I acknowledge my debt to a preliminary list of Pompeian prostitutes collected by Evans, *War* (1991) 218. Savunen, *Women* (1997) 102–18, is also a good source of information about Pompeian prostitutes.

lingers over the identification of brothels, I refrain from explicit attempts at linking possible prostitutes with possible brothels, at least for now. This list is intended merely as a convenience and not as a tool to be deployed in a circular process of identification of both prostitutes and brothels.[104]

The Pompeian evidence offers several women as possible prostitutes with the same or a similar name. Rarely if ever can we be certain that these are the same person, though individuals with a penchant for statistical analysis should be warned that this uncertainty cuts both ways. It is possible that more than one woman named Fortunata worked at the same brothel, just as it is possible that the same Fortunata worked in more than one brothel. I have tried to eliminate obvious duplicates but have not pressed too hard.

Another uncertainty militating against resort to such analysis is that surrounding the chronology of the inscriptions. Not all of these women, if they were indeed prostitutes, need have worked at the same time. We might assume that nearly all of the inscriptions date close to the destruction of the city in A.D. 79, but we should note the case of Tyche, whose inscription, a very rare dated example, derives from 3 B.C.

Once again, to be clear, there is no guarantee that even women explicitly identified as prostitutes by the ancient sources were so in actual fact.[105] My ultimate purpose in providing this list is to facilitate further research on Roman prostitution and misogyny.

The meaning of the term *verna* in the Pompeian epigraphs is uncertain; scholars are unable to choose between "native Pompeian" or "home-born slave."[106] No discussion of prostitutes' names is possible in this place, but it is worth noting that the Pompeian evidence for names suggests that most prostitutes were slaves, ex-slaves, or at minimum lived in social conditions close to slavery.[107]

Acria. Price: 4 *asses. CIL* 4.4259.
Aegle. (identified from context). *CIL* 4.7862.

---

104. There is a long tradition of more or less creative reconstruction of the "love life" of the people of Pompeii: Della Valle, "Amore" (1937); Della Corte, *Amori e amanti* (1958); D'Avino, *Women of Pompeii* (c. 1964); Gigante, *Civiltà* (1979) 203–21.

105. See the cautious approach taken by Savunen, *Women* (1997) 103, 107–8 (cf. her position on the women whose names are found at the Pompeian address 9.14.4); Cantarella, *Pompei* (1998) 75.

106. Treggiari, "Lower Class Women" (1979) 84 n. 36; Eichenauer, *Arbeitswelt* (1988) 121; Herrmann-Otto, *Ex Ancilla Natus* (1994) 344–46.

107. The arguments of Allison, "Placing Individuals" (2001) that Greek names are evidence of the survival of an ethnic community, whatever their merits, find no place here.

Afillia. Price: 2 ½ *asses*. *CIL* 4.7764.[108]

Afra (Helpis). (identified from context). *CIL* 4.2993zg.

Afrodite. (identified from context). *CIL* 4.1382, 1384.

Amaryllis. Offers fellatio. *CIL* 4.1510 (cf. 1507 [weaver]): possibly mere insult).

Amunus (male). Price: 4 *asses*. *CIL* 4.3964.

Anedia (?). (identified from context). *CIL* 4.2269.

Anthis. (Identified from context: next door to a tavern). *CIL* 4.8218a–b; cf. f–g.

Aplonia. (identified from context). *CIL* 4.2197.

Apronia Secundina. (identified from context). *CIL* 4.7062–63.[109]

Arbuscula. Price: 2 *asses*. *CIL* 4.7068.

Arria. (identified from context). *CIL* 4.8911.[110]

Asellina. (identified from context). *CIL* 4.7863, 7873.

Aspasia. Offers fellatio (?). *CIL* 4.10129.

Athenais. Price: 2 *asses*. *CIL* 4.4150.

Attica. Price: 16 *asses*. *CIL* 4.1751.

Attica. (identified from context). *CIL* 4.2172.

Attine. Offers sex. *CIL* 4.2258.

Beronice. (identified from context). *CIL* 4.2198, 2256.

Callidrome. (identified from context). *CIL* 4.2206.

Camudia. Offers fellatio. *CIL* 4.8449.

Capella Bacchis. (identified from context). *CIL* 4.8238, 8246.

Cestilia. (identified from context). *CIL* 4.2413h.

Chloe. (identified from context). *CIL* 4.1646.[111]

Cicada. (identified from context). *CIL* 4.2993db.

Cosconia. Offers fellatio. *CIL* 4.8124.[112]

Cresimus (male). Price: 4 *asses*. *Verna*. *CIL* 4.3964.

Cressa. (identified from context). *CIL* 4.2215.

Culibonia. Nickname for a prostitute? *CIL* 4.8473.

Dafne. (identified from context: near a crib). *CIL* 4.680.

---

108. Savunen, *Women* (1997) 106, is skeptical of the identification as a prostitute (she also treats Afillia and Ianuaria as one person).

109. Savunen, *Women* (1997) 107, is skeptical.

110. Savunen, *Women* (1997) 107, is skeptical.

111. See the discussion in Savunen, *Women* (1997) 104.

112. See Solin, "Pompeiana" (1968) 108–11, whose reading of "lena" is unpersuasive, however.

Dionusia (or Itonusia, the preferred reading). Offers fellatio. CIL 4.1425.

Drauca. Price: 1 denarius (= 16 asses). CIL 4.2193.

Egidia. Offers fellatio. CIL 4.4192.

Epafra. Price: 10 asses. CIL 4.4259.

Euche. Price: 2 asses. Verna. CIL 4.5345; 5372?

Euplia. CIL 4.2310b; 5048 (filia or fellatio? Price of 5 asses?); cf. 10004.

Eutychis Graeca. Price: 2 asses. "Moribus bellis." CIL 4.4592, 4593(?).

Fabia. (identified from context). CIL 4.2239.

Fabia. (identified from context). CIL 4.2413m + p. 222.

Faustia. (identified from context). CIL 4.1636.

Faustilla. Offers sex. CIL 4.2288.

Felic(u)la. Offers sex. CIL 4.2199–2200.

Felic(u)la. Price: 2 asses. Verna. CIL 4.4023; 4066; cf. 8917, 9051a.[113]

Felicula. Offers fellatio. CIL 4.8711a.

Felix (male). Price: 1 as (for fellatio). CIL 4.5408.

Firma. Price: 3 asses. CIL 4.4259.

Firma. Price: 2 asses. CIL 4.8454.

Fortunata. Offers fellatio. CIL 4.2224, 2259, 2275.[114]

Fortunata. Offers fellatio. CIL 4.2310e, 10005.

Fortunata. Price: 23 asses. CIL 4.8034.

Fortunata. Price: 2 asses. CIL 4.8185.[115]

Fortunata. (identified from context). CIL 4.8984.

Fyllis. Offers fellatio. CIL 4.7057.

Glycera. (identified from context). CIL 4.5120.

Glyco. Offers cunnilingus; halicaria. 2 asses. CIL 4.3999, 4001.[116]

Helpis. (identified from context). CIL 4.2189.

Ianuaria. (identified from context). CIL 4.2201a, 2227a, 2233, 2236.

Ianuaria. Price: 2 ½ asses. CIL 4.7764.[117]

Ianuaria. Offers fellatio. CIL 4.8361.

Ianuaria. Offers fellatio (?) CIL 4.8465b.

Ias. (identified from context). CIL 4.1379, 2174.

---

113. Savunen, Women (1997) 106, is skeptical.

114. On Fortunata, see also CIL 4.111: Marcellum Fortunata cupit.

115. Savunen, Women (1997) 106, is skeptical.

116. Halicaria is perhaps not relevant to her prostitution, but instead suggests she may have been a part-timer: see chap. 2.

117. Savunen, Women (1997) 106, is skeptical; also identifies Ianuaria and Afillia as the same person.

Incerta. Price: 2 ½ *asses*. *CIL* 4.4150.

Incerta. Price: uncertain. *Verna*. *CIL* 4.4593.

Incerta (Al . . . re?). Price: 5 *asses*. *Verna*. *CIL* 4.5204.

Incerta. Price: 2 (?) *asses*. *Verna*. *CIL* 4.5206.

Incerta. Price: 2 *asses*. *CIL* 4.5372.

Incerta. Offers fellatio. Price: 3 *asses*. *CIL* 4.8160.

Incerta. Price: 8 *asses*. *CIL* 4.8187.

Incerta. Price: 10 *asses*. *CIL* 4.8357b.

Incerta. Price: 4 *asses*. *CIL* 4.10078a.

Ionas (or Ionis). Offers fellatio. *CIL* 4.2402, 2403, 2404, 2406.

Isidorus (male). Price: 2 *asses*. *CIL* 4.4441, 4699 (cunnilingus; *verna*), 4700.

Itonusia (or Dionusia). Offers fellatio. *CIL* 4.1425.

Iucunda. (identified from context). *CIL* 4.1376, 1379, 1380, 1385.

Iucunda. (identified from context). *CIL* 4.1633, 1643.

Lais. Offers cunnilingus. *CIL* 4.1578.

La(h)is. Price: 2 *asses* (for fellatio). *CIL* 4.1969.

Libanis. Price 2 *asses* (for fellatio). *CIL* 4.2028 + p. 704.

Logas. Price: 8 *asses*. *Verna*. *CIL* 4.5203.

Lucilla. Offers sex. *CIL* 4.1948.

Macula. (identified from context). *CIL* 4.2993db.

Mandata (?). (identified from context). *CIL* 4.3922.[118]

Maria (?). Offers fellatio. *CIL* 4.1840.

Maria. (identified from context). *CIL* 4.7866.

Maria. Price: 2 ½ *asses*. *CIL* 4.8224.

Maritimus (male). Price: 4 *asses* (for cunnilingus). *CIL* 4.8939, 8940.

Menander (male). Price 2 *asses*. "Bellis moribus." *CIL* 4.4024.

Methe. Offers fellatio. *CIL* 4.4434.

Midusa. Offers sex. *CIL* 4.4196.

Mula. Offers sex. *CIL* 4.2203, 2204.

Mula (or Mummia). Price (?): 2 *asses* (for fellatio). *CIL* 4.8185.[119]

Myrine. (identified from context; price of 7 *asses*?). *CIL* 4.1402, 10033b, c.

Myrtale. Offers fellatio. *CIL* 4.2268, 2271.

Myrtis. Offers fellatio. *CIL* 4.2273, 2292, 2293.

Mystis. (identified from context). *CIL* 4.1639.

---

118. Savunen, *Women* (1997) 109, is skeptical.

119. Savunen, *Women* (1997) 106, is skeptical.

Naereia or Nereia.[120] Price: 2 *asses*. *CIL* 4.8394.

Nebris (or Naebris). (identified from context). *CIL* 4.5118, 5145, 5146.

Nica Glaphyrine. (identified from context). *CIL* 4.1664.

Nice. Offers fellatio. *CIL* 4.2178a, 2278.

Nicepor (male). Price: 2 (?) *asses*.[121] *CIL* 4.3964.

Nicopolis. (identified from context: next door to a tavern). *CIL* 4.8218a, d–e (cf. 8171).[122]

Nymphe. Offers fellatio. *CIL* 4.1389.

Optata. Price: 2 *asses*. *Verna*. *CIL* 4.5105.

Palmyra (?). (identified from context). *CIL* 4.8475.

Panta. (identified from context). *CIL* 4.2178b.

Parte. Price: "sescentaria" (i.e., "astronomical"). *CIL* 4.4398.

Parthenope. (identified from context). *CIL* 4.5108.

Phoebe. (identified from context). *CIL* 4.5125.

Pieris. Price: 2 *asses*. *CIL* 4.5338.

Pitane. Price: 3 *asses*. *CIL* 4.4439.

Prima. Price: 1 *as*. *CIL* 4.8241, 8248, 8270.

Primigenia. (identified from context). *CIL* 4.3916 (cf. 3957).[123]

Primigenia. (identified from context). *CIL* 4.8988.

Primilla. (identified from context). *CIL* 4.8360.

Pyramis. (identified from context). *CIL* 4.1382a.

Pyris. Offers fellatio. *CIL* 4.4158.

Quartilla. (identified from context: next door to a tavern). *CIL* 4.8212a–b, 8218k–l.[124]

Quinta. (identified from context). *CIL* 4.10038d.

Quintilia. (identified from context). *CIL* 4.1634.

Restituta. Price: 2 *asses*. *CIL* 4.1374 (reading uncertain).

Restituta. Offers fellatio. *CIL* 4.1631, 1665.[125]

Restituta. (identified from context; "Bellis moribus"). *CIL* 4.2202.

---

120. I owe these versions of the name to Dr. Antonio Varone, p.c.

121. See the editorial note on *CIL* 4.3964.

122. Savunen, *Women* (1997) 107, is skeptical.

123. Savunen, *Women* (1997) 107, 109, is skeptical.

124. Savunen, *Women* (1997) 107, is skeptical.

125. These two inscriptions lie across the street from each other at 7.6.34–36 and 7.15. Savunen, *Women* (1997) 111–12, with n. 156, persuasively links them to the same woman. For another example, see n. 129.

Restituta. (identified from context). CIL 4.3951.

Rufa. (identified from context). CIL 4.1629a.

Rufa. Offers fellatio. CIL 4.2421.

Rufilla. Offers fellatio. CIL 4.1651.

Rupinus (male). Price: 2 (?) asses. Verna. CIL 4.5205, 5206.

Rusatia. (identified from context). CIL 4.2262.

Rustica. Offers cunnilingus. CIL 4.4264.

Sabina. Price: 2 asses. Offers fellatio. CIL 4.4150, 4185.

Salvia. Offers fellatio. CIL 4.1427.

Satria. (identified from context). CIL 4.8294.

Secunda. (identified from context). CIL 4.1376, 1377, 1381.

Serena. (identified from context). CIL 4.3928, 3929, 3930.

Serena. (identified from context). CIL 4.8978.

Sergia Compse. (identified from context). CIL 4.10171.[126]

Setia. (identified from context). CIL 4.1580.[127]

Somene. (identified from context). CIL 4.5122, 5123.

Sop(h)e. Offers fellatio. CIL 4.5095.

Spendusa. (identified from context). CIL 4.1403.

Spes. Price: 9 asses. "Moribus bellis." CIL 4.5127.

Spes. Price: 2 asses. CIL 4.8511.[128]

Successa. Price: 5 asses. Verna. "Bellis moribus." CIL 4.4025.

Successa. (identified from context). CIL 4.5104, 5131, 5137, 5150, 5153.

Successa. (identified from context: next door to a tavern). CIL 4.8211.

Successus (male). Price: 3 asses. CIL 4.3964.

Synoris. (identified from context). CIL 4.1397, 1398(?), 1408.

Terna. Offers sex. CIL 4.4816.

Timele. Offers fellatio. CIL 4.1378, 1387–1388a.

Tyche. Price: 5 asses. CIL 4.2450. (3 B.C.).

Tyndaris. (identified from context). CIL 4.5190.

Valeria. Offers fellatio. CIL 4.10033a.

Veneria. Offers fellatio or masturbation. CIL 4.1391.

126. Savunen, Women (1997) 107, is skeptical.

127. Savunen, Women (1997) 107, is skeptical.

128. Savunen, Women (1997) 107, is skeptical.

Veneria. (identified from context). *CIL* 4.1642, 4836.[129]
Veneria. Price: 2 *asses*. *CIL* 4.8465a.
Victoria. (identified from context). *CIL* 4.2221, 2225–28.
Vibia Iucunda. (identified from context). *CIL* 4.5113.
Vitalio (male). Price: 4 *asses*. *CIL* 4.4277.
Zmyrina. (identified from context). *CIL* 4.7863–64, cf. 7221.

129. These two inscriptions lie across the street from each other at 7.6.34–36 and 7.15. Savunen, *Women* (1997) 111–12, with n. 156, persuasively links them to the same woman. For another example, see n. 125.

BIBLIOGRAPHY

Abbreviations of periodicals generally follow those given in *L'année Philologique*.

Adams, C., and R. Laurence, eds. *Travel and Geography in the Roman Empire*. London, 2001.

Adams, J .N. *The Latin Sexual Vocabulary*. Baltimore, 1982.

———. "Words for 'Prostitute' in Latin." *RhM* 126 (1983): 321–58.

Albert, A. *Brothel: Mustang Ranch and Its Women*. New York, 2001.

Alföldy, G. *The Social History of Rome*. Rev. ed. Baltimore, 1988.

Allison, P. M. "Placing Individuals: Pompeian Epigraphy in Context." *JMA* 14, no. 1 (2001): 53–74.

Alston, R. *The City in Roman and Byzantine Egypt*. London, 2002.

Alston, R., and R. D. Alston. "Urbanism and the Urban Community in Roman Egypt." *JEA* 83 (1997): 199–216.

Amery, C., and B. Curran Jr. *The Lost World of Pompeii*. Los Angeles, 2002.

Anderson, W. S. Review of *Looking at Lovemaking*, by J. R. Clarke. *BMCR* 98.8.12 (1998).

Ando, C. *Imperial Ideology and Provincial Loyalty in the Roman Empire*. Berkeley, 2000.

André, J.-M. "L'espace urbain dans l'expression poétique." In *Rome: L'espace urbain et ses representations*, edited by F. Hinard and M. Royo, 82–95. Paris, 1991.

———. "Sénèque et les problèmes de la ville." *Ktema* 19 (1994): 145–54.

André, J.-M., and M.-F. Baslez. *Voyager dans l'Antiquité*. s.l., 1993.

Andreau, J. "Histoire des séismes et histoire économique: Le tremblement de terre de Pompéi (62 ap. J.-C.)." In J. Andreau, *Patrimoines, échanges et prêts d'argent: L'économie romaine*, 271–310. Rome, 1997. Originally published as *Annales ESC* 28, no. 2 (1973): 369–95.

———. "Il terremoto del 62." In *Pompei 79*, edited by F. Zevi, 40–44. Naples, 1984.

————."Deux études sur les prix à Rome: Les 'mercuriales' et le taux de l'intérêt." In *Économie antique: Prix et formation des prix dans les économies antiques*, 105–20. Saint-Bertrand-de-Comminges, Fr., 1997.

————. "Rome capitale de l'Empire, la vie économique." *Pallas* 55 (2001): 303–17.

————. "Sull'economia di Pompei." In *Pompei*, edited by P. G. Guzzo, 109–10. Milan, 2001.

Andreau, J. and Maucourant. "À propos de la 'rationalité économique' dans l'antiquité gréco-romaine: Une interprétation des thèses de D. Rathbone [1991]." *Topoi* 9 (1999): 47–102.

Andrés Santos, F. J. "Función jurisdiccional de los ediles en las ciudades hispano-romanas según las leyes municipales." *HAnt*. 22 (1998): 157–74.

Annequin, J. "Entre signifiant et signifié, femmes et femmes esclaves dans le corpus des interprétations de la 'Clé des Songes' d'Artémidore." In *Femmes-esclaves: Modèles d'interprétation anthropologique, économique, juridique*, edited by F. Reduzzi Merola and A. Storchi Marino, 251–66. Naples, 1999.

Arce, J. "El inventario de Roma: *Curiosum y Notitia*." In *The Transformations of VRBS ROMA in Late Antiquity* (= *JRA* Suppl. 33), edited by W. V. Harris, 15–22. Portsmouth, R.I. 1999.

Archäologie und Seismologie: La regione vesuviana dal 62 al 79 d.C., Problemi archeologici e sismologici. Munich, 1995.

Athanassiadi-Fowden, P. *Julian and Hellenism: An Intellectual Biography*. Oxford, 1981.

Aubert, J.-J. *Business Managers in Ancient Rome: A Social and Economic Study of Institores, 200 B.C.–A.D. 250*. Leiden, Neth., 1994.

Axer, J. "I prezzi degli schiavi e le paghe degli attori nell'orazione di Cicerone pro Q. Roscio Comoedo." In *Actes du 1975 Colloque sur l'esclavage*, edited by I. Biezunska-Malowist and J. Kolendo, 217–25. Paris, 1979.

Babcock, W. S., ed. *Paul and the Legacies of Paul*. Dallas, 1990.

Bagnall, R. *Egypt in Late Antiquity*. Princeton, N.J., 1993.

Balsdon, J. P. V. D. *Roman Women: Their History and Habits*. New York, 1963.

Bammel, C. P. "Pauline Exegesis, Manichaeism and Philosophy in the Early Augustine." In C. P. Bammel, *Tradition and Exegesis in Early Christian Writers*, edited by C. P. Bammel, XVI Aldershot, Eng., 1995. Originally published in L. R. Wickham and C. P. Bammel, *Christian Faith and Greek Philosophy in Late Antiquity* (Leiden, Neth., 1993).

Barattolo, A., and F. Romaldi. "Impianti igienici a Pompei: Rapporto preliminare." *RSP* 11 (2000): 263–70.

Barrett, A. A. *Livia: First Lady of Imperial Rome*. New Haven, 2002.

Barry, K. *Female Sexual Slavery*. Englewood Cliffs, N.J., 1979.

————. *The Prostitution of Sexuality*.² New York, 1995.

Bateson, J. D. "Roman *Spintriae* in the Hunter Coin Cabinet." In *Ermanno A. Arslan Studia Dicata* 2, edited by R. Martini and N. Vismara, 385–94. Milan, 1991.

Bauman, R. A. *Impietas in Principem: A Study of Treason Against the Roman Emperor with Special Reference to the First Century A.D.* Munich, 1974.

————. *Women and Politics in Ancient Rome*. London, 1992.

Beaucamp, J. *Le statut de la femme à Byzance (4ᵉ–7ᵉ siècle)*. Vol. 1, *Le droit impérial*. Paris, 1990.

————. *Le statut de la femme à Byzance (4ᵉ–7ᵉ siècle)*. Vol. 2, *Les pratiques sociales*. Paris, 1992.

Bernheimer, C. *Figures of Ill Repute: Representing Prostitution in Nineteenth-Century France*. Cambridge, 1989.

Bernstein, L. *Sonia's Daughters: Prostitutes and Their Regulation in Imperial Russia*. Berkeley, 1995.

Berry, J. "The Conditions of Domestic Life in Pompeii in A.D. 79: A Case-Study of Houses 11 and 12, Insula 9, Region I." *PBSR* 65 (1997): 103–25.

————, ed. *Unpeeling Pompeii: Studies in Region I of Pompeii*. Milan, 1998.

Best, J. *Controlling Vice: Regulating Brothel Prostitution in St. Paul, 1865–1883*. Columbus, Ohio, 1998.

Bickerman, E. *Chronology of the Ancient World*.² Ithaca, N.Y., 1980.

"Blackfriars." *St Thomas Aquinas, Summa Theologiae: Latin Text and English Translation, Introductions, Notes, Appendices, and Glossaries*. Vol. 32. London, 1975.

Bloomer, W. M. *Valerius Maximus and the Rhetoric of the New Nobility*. Chapel Hill, N.C., 1992.

Bodel, J. "Dealing with the Dead: Undertakers, Executioners and Potter's Fields in Ancient Rome." In *Death and Disease in the Ancient City*, edited by V. M. Hope and E. Marshall, 128–51. London, 2000.

Boghossian, P. A. "What Is Social Construction?: Flaws and Contradictions in the Claim That Scientific Beliefs Are 'Merely Locally Accepted.'" *TLS* 5108 (February 23, 2001): 6–8.

Bonucci, C. "Scavi: Pompei." *BdI* (1829): 145–50.

Boswell, J. *The Kindness of Strangers: The Abandonment of Children in Western Europe from Late Antiquity to the Renaissance*. New York, 1988.

Bosworth, A. B. "Vespasian and the Slave Trade." *CQ* 52.1 (2002): 350–7.

Bouffartigue, J. *L'Empereur Julien et la culture de son temps*. Paris, 1992.

Bowersock, G. W. *Julian the Apostate*. London, 1978.

————. *Fiction as History: Nero to Julian*. Berkeley, 1994.

Bradley, K. R. "Social Aspects of the Slave Trade in the Roman World." *MBAH* 5 (1986): 48–59.

————. *Slaves and Masters in the Roman Empire: A Study in Social Control*. Rev. ed. Oxford, 1987.

————. *Discovering the Roman Family: Studies in Roman Social History*. Oxford, 1991.

————. *Slavery and Society at Rome*. Cambridge, 1994.

————. "Prostitution, the Law of Rome, and Social Policy." *JRA* 13, no. 2 (2000): 468–75.

Braund, D. "Piracy under the Principate and the Ideology of Imperial Eradication." In *War and Society in the Roman World*, edited by J. Rich and G. Shipley, 195–212. London, 1993.

Braund, S. H. "City and Country in Roman Satire." In *Satire and Society in Ancient Rome*, edited by S. H. Braund, 23–47, 128–32. Exeter, 1989.

Brendel, O. J. "The Scope and Temperament of Erotic Art in the Greco-Roman World." In *Studies in Erotic Art*, edited by T. Bowie and C. V. Christenson, 3–69, figs. 1–48. New York, 1970.

Breton, E. *Pompeia décrite et dessinée*.²· Paris, 1855.

———. *Pompeia décrite et dessinée.*[3] Paris, 1870.

Brock, S. P., and S. A. Harvey. *Holy Women of the Syrian Orient.* Berkeley, 1987.

Brown, F. E. "Houses and Shops of the Final Period." In *The Excavations at Dura-Europos: Preliminary Report of the Ninth Season of Work, 1935–1936.* Pt. 1, *The Agora and Bazaar*, edited by M. I. Rostovtzeff, 69–158. New Haven, 1944.

———. "Sculpture and Painting." In *The Excavations at Dura-Europos: Preliminary Report of the Ninth Season of Work, 1935–1936.* Pt. 1, *The Agora and Bazaar*, edited by M. I. Rostovtzeff, 159–67. New Haven, 1944.

Brown, P. "Late Antiquity." In *A History of Private Life*, vol. I, *From Pagan Rome to Byzantium*, edited by P. Veyne, 235–312. Cambridge, 1987.

———. *The Body and Society: Men, Women, and Sexual Renunciation in Early Christianity.* New York, 1988.

———. *Augustine of Hippo: A Biography.* Rev. ed. Berkeley, 2000.

———. *Poverty and Leadership in the Later Roman Empire.* Hanover, NH, 2002.

Brown, S. "Death as Decoration: Scenes from the Arena on Roman Domestic Mosaics." In *Pornography and Representation in Greece and Rome*, edited by A. Richlin, 180–212. Oxford, 1992.

Bruhns, H. "Armut und Gesellschaft in Rom." In *Vom Elend der Handarbeit: Probleme historischer Unterschichtenforschung*, edited by H. Mommsen and W. Schulze, 27–49. Stuttgart, 1981.

Brundage, J. A. "Prostitution in the Medieval Canon Law." *Signs* 1 (1975/6): 825–45.

———. *Law, Sex, and Christian Society in Medieval Europe.* Chicago, 1987.

Brunt, P. A. *Italian Manpower, 225 B.C.–A.D. 14.* Rev. ed. Oxford, 1987.

Bruun, C. "Water for Roman Brothels: Cicero *Cael.* 34." *Phoenix* 51 (1997): 364–73.

Buckland, W. W. *The Roman Law of Slavery: The Condition of the Slave in Private Law from Augustus to Justinian.* Cambridge, 1908. Reprint, New York, 1969.

Bustany, C., and N. Géroudet, *Rome: Maîtrise de l'espace, maîtrise du pouvoir, de César aux Antonins.* Paris, 2001.

Butler, A. M. *Daughters of Joy, Sisters of Misery: Prostitutes in the American West, 1865–90.* Urbana, Ill., 1985.

Butrica, J. L. "Using Water 'Unchastely': Cicero *Pro Caelio* 34 Again." *Phoenix* 53, nos. 1–2 (1999): 136–39.

Butrica, J. L. "Using Water 'Unchastely': Cicero *Pro Caelio* 34 Again—Addendum." *Phoenix* 53, nos. 3–4 (1999): 336.

Buttrey, T. V. "The *Spintriae* as a Historical Source." *NC* 13 (1973): 52–63.

Calza, G. "Gli scavi recenti nell'abitato di Ostia." *MonAnt.* 26 (1920): 321–430, 3 plates.

Calza, R., and E. Nash. *Ostia.* Florence, 1959.

Cancelo, J. L. "Anotaciones al problema del Mal en San Augustín." *Cuadernos de pensamiento* 9 (1994): 111–28.

Cantarella, E. *Bisexuality in the Ancient World.* Rev. ed. New Haven, 2002.

———. *Pompei: I volti dell'amore.* Milan, 1998.

Cantilena, R. "Vizi privati e pubbliche virtù: Il 'Gabinetto degli oggetti riservati' del Museo di Napoli." In *L'amore: dall'Olimpo all'alcova*, edited by G. Macchi, 51–60. Milan, 1992.

Carandini, A. "Columella's Vineyard and the Rationality of the Roman Economy." *Opus* 3 (1983): 177–204.

———. *Schiavi in Italia: Gli strumenti pensanti dei Romani fra tarda Repubblica e medio Impero*. Rome, 1988.

Carson, D. A. *Showing the Spirit: A Theological Exposition of 1 Corinthians 12–14*. Grand Rapids, Mich., 1987.

Casson, L., *Travel in the Ancient World*. Rev. ed. Baltimore, 1994.

Cavallo, G. "Segni e voci di una cultura urbana." In *Roma antica*, edited by A. Giardina, 247–79. Rome, 2000.

Cèbe, J.-P. *Varron: Satires Ménippées: Édition, traduction et commentaire*. 13 vols. Rome, 1972–99.

Champlin, E. "The Suburbium of Ancient Rome." *AJAH* 7, no. 2 (1982): 97–117.

Chapkis, W. *Live Sex Acts: Women Performing Erotic Labor*. New York, 1997.

Chauvin, C. *Les chrétiens et la prostitution*. Paris, 1983.

Chevallier, R. *Voyages et déplacements dans l'empire romain*. Paris, 1988.

Cilliers, L. "Public Health in Roman Legislation." *Acta Classica* 36 (1993): 1–10.

Cipriani, G., and N. Milano. "'Atti osceni' nella Roma antica: I termini della legge." *Aufidus* 10, no. 30 (1996): 105–24.

Ciprotti, P. *Conoscere Pompei*. Rome, 1959.

Citroni Marchetti, S. *Plinio il Vecchio e la tradizione del moralismo romano*. Pisa, 1991.

Clark, G. *Women in Late Antiquity: Pagan and Christian Lifestyles*. Oxford, 1993.

Clarke, J. R. "New Light on the Iconography of Jupiter, Ganymede, and Leda in the Painting of the House of Jupiter and Ganymede in Ostia Antica." *Kölner Jahrbuch für Vor- und Frühgeschichte* 24 (1991): 171–75.

———. "The Decor of the House of Jupiter and Ganymede at Ostia Antica: Private Residence Turned Gay Hotel?" In *Roman Art in the Private Sphere: New Perspectives on the Architecture and Decor of the Domus, Villa, and Insula*, edited by E. K. Gazda, 89–104, figs. 4.1–15. Ann Arbor, Mich., 1994.

———. *Looking at Lovemaking: Constructions of Sexuality in Roman Art, 100 B.C.–A.D. 250*. Berkeley, 1998.

———. "Look Who's Laughing at Sex: Men and Women Viewers in the *Apodyterium* of the Suburban Baths at Pompeii," In *The Roman Gaze: Vision, Power, and the Body*, edited by D. Fredrick, 149–81. Baltimore, 2002.

———. *Art in the Lives of Ordinary Romans: Visual Representation and Non-Elite Viewers in Italy, 100 B.C.– A.D. 315*. Forthcoming.

Clarke, S. "The Pre-Industrial City in Roman Britain." In *Theoretical Roman Archaeology: First Conference Proceedings*, edited by E. Scott, 49–66. Aldershot, Eng., 1993.

Clayson, H. *Painted Love: Prostitution in French Art of the Impressionist Era*. New Haven, 1991.

Coarelli, F. "La consistenza della città nel periodo imperiale: *Pomerium, vici, insulae*. In *La Rome impériale: Démographie et logistique* (= Coll. Éc. Franç. Rome 230), 89–109. Rome, 1997.

———. "Roma, la città come cosmo." In *Mégapoles méditerranéennes: Géographie urbaine rétrospective*, edited by C. Nicolet et al., 288–310. Paris, 2000.

Cohen, B. *Deviant Street Networks: Prostitution in New York City*. Lexington, Mass., 1980.

Cohen, E. E. "An Economic Analysis of Athenian Prostitution." In *Prostitutes and Courtesans in the Ancient World*, edited by C. A. Faraone and L. K. McClure. Forthcoming.

Cohen, E. S. "'Courtesans' and 'Whores': Words and Behavior in Roman Streets." *Women's Studies* 19 (1991): 201–8.

Cohen, S. *Visions of Social Control: Crime, Punishment and Classification*. Cambridge, 1985.

Colin, X. "Commerçants itinerants et marchands sedentaires dans l'Occident romain." In *Mercati permanenti e mercati periodici nel mondo romano*, edited by E. Lo Cascio, 149–60. Bari, 2000.

Collin, F. *Social Reality*. London, 1997.

Collins, R. F. *First Corinthians*. Sacra Pagina Series, vol. 7. Collegeville, Pa. 1999.

Connelly, M. T. *The Response to Prostitution in the Progressive Era*. Chapel Hill, N.C., 1980.

Conticello, B. "Lavori in concessione." In *Progetto Pompei I: Un bilancio*. Naples, 1988.

Corbin, A. *Women for Hire: Prostitution and Sexuality in France After 1850* (Translated by A. Sheridan).

Cornell, T. J., and K. Lomas, eds. *Urban Society in Roman Italy*. New York, 1995.

Costello, J. G. *"Red Light Voices:* An Archaeological Drama of Late Nineteenth-Century Prostitution." In *Archaeologies of Sexuality*, edited by R. A. Schmidt and B. L. Voss, 160–75. London, 2000.

Courtney, E. A *Commentary on the Satires of Juvenal*. London, 1980.

Crawford, M. H., ed. *Roman Statutes* (= BICS Supplement 64). 2 vols. London, 1996.

Cursi, M. F. *La struttura del "postliminium" nella Repubblica e nel Principato*. Naples, 1996.

Dalby, A. *Empire of Pleasures: Luxury and Indulgence in the Roman World*. London, 2000.

Dalla, D. *Ubi Venus Mutatur: Omosesssualità e diritto nel mondo romano*. Milan, 1987.

D'Aloe, S. *Les ruines de Pompéi jusqu'en 1861*. Naples, 1861.

D'Ambra, E. "The Calculus of Venus: Nude Portraits of Roman Matrons." In *Sexuality in Ancient Art*, edited by N. B. Kampen, 219–32. Cambridge, 1996.

D'Ambrosio, A. "I monili dallo scavo di Moregine," *MEFRA* 113.2 (2001): 967–80.

D'Arms, J. H. *Commerce and Social Standing in Ancient Rome*. Cambridge, 1981.

———. "Performing Culture: Roman Spectacle and the Banquets of the Powerful." In *The Art of Ancient Spectacle*, edited by B. Bergmann and C. Kondoleon, 301–19. New Haven, 1999.

Dauphin, C. "Brothels, Baths and Babes: Prostitution in the Byzantine Holy Land." *Classics Ireland* 3 (1996): 47–72.

Dauphin, C. "Bordels et filles de joie: La prostitution en Palestine byzantine." In *Eupsychia: Mélanges offerts à Hélène Ahrweiler*, edited by M. Balard et al. 1: 177–94. Paris, 1998.

Davidson, J. *Courtesans and Fishcakes: The Consuming Passions of Classical Athens*. New York, 1998.

D'Avino, M. *The Women of Pompeii*. Translated by M. H. Jones and L. Nusco. Naples, n.d. [c. 1964].

De Caro, S. *Il gabinetto segreto del museo archeologico nazionale di Napoli*. Naples, 2000.

Decker, J. F. *Prostitution: Regulation and Control.* Littleton, Colo., 1979.

DeFelice, J. F. *The Women of Pompeian Inns: A Study of Law, Occupation, and Status.* Ph.D. diss., Miami University, Ohio, 1998.

————. *Roman Hospitality: The Professional Women of Pompeii.* Warren Center, Pa., 2001.

De Jorio, A. *Plan de Pompéi et remarques sur les édifices.* Naples, 1828.

De Kleijn, G. *The Water Supply of Ancient Rome: City Area, Water, and Population.* Amsterdam, 2001.

Delacoste, F., and P. Alexander. *Sex Work: Writings by Women in the Sex Industry.*² San Francisco, 1998.

Delcourt, M. "Le prix des esclaves dans les comédies Latines." *AC* 17 (1948): 123–32.

De Ligt, L. "Demand, Supply, Distribution: The Roman Peasantry between Town and Countryside. I. Rural Monetization and Peasant Demand." *MBAH* 9 (1990): 24–56.

————. "Demand, Supply, Distribution: The Roman Peasantry between Town and Countryside. II. Supply, Distribution and a Comparative Perspective." *MBAH* 10 (1991): 33–77.

————. *Fairs and Markets in the Roman Empire: Economic and Social Aspects of Periodic Trade in a Pre-Industrial Society.* Amsterdam, 1993.

Della Corte, M. *Case e abitanti a Pompei.*¹ Pompei, 1926.

————. *Pompeii: The New Excavations (Houses and Inhabitants).*² Valle di Pompei, 1927.

————. *Piccola guida di Pompei.* Pompeii, 1932.

————. *Case ed abitanti di Pompei.*² Rome, 1954.

————. *Amori e amanti di Pompei antica.* Pompeii, 1958.

————. "Le iscrizioni di Ercolano." *Rend. Acc. Arch. Lett.*, n.s. 33 (1958): 239–308.

————. "Pompei: Iscrizioni scoperte nel quinquennio 1951–1956." *NSA*, 8th ser., no. 12 (1958): 77–184.

————. *Case ed abitanti di Pompei,*³ edited by P. Soprano. Naples, 1965.

Della Valle, G. "L'amore in Pompei e nel poema di Lucrezio." *A&R*, 3d ser., no. 5 (1937): 139–75.

De Martino, F. "Per una storia del 'genere' pornografico." In *La letteratura di consumo nel mondo greco-latino: Atti del convegno internazionale, Cassino, 14–17 settembre 1994,* edited by O. Pecere and A. Stramaglia, 295–341. Cassino, It., 1996.

De Simone, A., et al., *Pompei: L'informatica al servizio di una città antica.* 2 vols. Rome, 1988.

De Simone, A., and S. C. Nappo, eds. . . . *Mitis Sarni Opes.* Naples, 2000.

De Souza, P. *Piracy in the Greco-Roman World.* Cambridge, 1999.

De Ste. Croix, G. E. M. *The Class Struggle in the Ancient Greek World.* Ithaca, N.Y., 1981.

De Vos, A., and M. De Vos. *Pompei Ercolano Stabia.* Rome, 1982.

D'Hautcourt, A. "'Quand je serai grand, je serai banquier': Une idée du jeune M. Aemilius Scaurus." *RBPh* 79 (2001): 203–11.

Dierichs, A. *Erotik in der römischen Kunst.* Mainz, Ger., 1997.

Di Porto, A. *Impresa collettiva e schiavo 'manager' in Roma antica (II sec. a.C.–II sec. d.C.).* Milan, 1984.

Di Vita, A. "L'urbanistica nelle città punico-romane della Tripolitania." *L'Africa romana* 10, no. 2 (1994): 685–87.

Dixon, S. *Reading Roman Women*. London, 2001.

———. *The Roman Mother*. Norman, Okla., 1988.

Doignon, J. *Oeuvres de Saint Augustin 4.2: Dialogues philosophiques, De Ordine—L'ordre*. Paris, 1997.

Drexhage, H.-J. *Preise, Mieten/Pachten, Kosten und Löhne im römischen Ägypten bis zum Regierungsantritt Diokletians* (= *Vorarbeiten zu einer Wirtschaftsgeschichte des römischen Ägypten* 1). St. Katharinen, Ger., 1991.

———. "Einige Bemerkungen zu den *empora* und *kapēla* im römischen Ägypten (1.–3. Jh.n. Chr.)." *MBAH* 10, no. 2 (1991): 28–46.

———. "Preise im römischen Britannien (1.–3. Jh. n. Chr.)." In *Miscellanea oeconomica: Studien zur antiken Wirtschaftsgeschichte*, edited by K. Ruffing and B. Tenger, 13–25. St. Katharinen, Ger., 1997.

Dunbabin, K. M. D. "*Baiarum grata voluptas*: Pleasures and Dangers of the Baths." *PBSR* 57 (1989): 6–46, plates III–XV.

Duncan-Jones, R. *The Economy of the Roman Empire: Quantitative Studies.*[2] Cambridge, 1982.

———. *Structure and Scale in the Roman Economy*. Cambridge, 1990.

———. *Money and Government in the Roman Empire*. Cambridge, 1994.

Dupré Raventós, X., and J. A. Remolà, eds. *Sordes Urbis: La eliminación de residuos en la ciudad romana, Actas de la reunión de Roma (15–16 de Noviembre de 1996)*. Rome, 2000.

Dyck, A. R. *A Commentary on Cicero, De Officiis*. Ann Arbor, Mich., 1996.

Dyer, T. H. *Pompeii: History, Buildings, and Antiquities*. Rev. ed. London, 1875.

Dyroff, A. "Über Form und Begriffsgehalt der augustinischen Schrift De Ordine." In *Aurelius Augustinus: Die Festschrift der Görres-Gesellschaft zum. 1500 Todestage des Heiligen Augustinus*, edited by M. Grabmann and J. Mausbach, 15–62. Cologne, 1930.

Dyson, S. L. *Community and Society in Roman Italy*. Baltimore, 1992.

Dyson, S. L., and R. E. Prior. "Horace, Martial, and Rome: Two Outsiders Read the Ancient City." *Arethusa* 28 (1995): 245–63.

Eck, W. "Cum Dignitate Otium: Senatorial Domus in Imperial Rome." *SCI* 16 (1997): 162–90.

Edlund, L., and E. Korn. "A Theory of Prostitution." *Journal of Political Economy* 110, no. 1 (2002): 181–214.

Edwards, C. *The Politics of Immorality in Ancient Rome*. Cambridge, 1993.

———. *Writing Rome: Textual Approaches to the City*. Cambridge, 1996.

———. "Unspeakable Professions: Public Performance and Prostitution in Ancient Rome." In *Roman Sexualities*, edited by J. P. Hallett and M. P. Skinner, 66–95. Princeton, 1997.

Eichenauer, M. *Untersuchungen zur Arbeitswelt der Frau in der römischen Antike* (=*Europ. Hochschulschr.* 3.360). Frankfurt am Main, Ger., 1988.

Ellingworth, P., and H. A. Hatton. *A Translator's Handbook on Paul's First Letter to the Corinthians.*[2] New York, 1994.

Elsner, J., "Inventing Imperium: Texts and the Propaganda of Monuments in Augustan

Rome." In *Art and Text in Roman Culture*, edited by J. Elsner, 32–53, 284–87. Cambridge, 1996.

Erdkamp, P. "Agriculture, Underemployment, and the Cost of Rural Labour in the Roman World." *CQ* 49, no. 2 (1999): 556–72.

———. "Beyond the Limits of the 'Consumer City': A Model of the Urban and Rural Economy in the Roman World." *Historia* 50, no. 3 (2001): 332–56.

Ericsson, L. O. "Charges against Prostitution: An Attempt at a Philosophical Assessment." *Ethics* 90 (1980): 335–66.

Eschebach, H. *Die städtbauliche Entwicklung des antiken Pompeji* (= *MDAI[R]* Suppl. 17). Heidelberg, 1970.

———. *Pompeji: Erlebte antike Welt*. Leipzig, Ger., 1978.

———. "Die Casa di Ganimede in Pompeji VII 13, 4: Ausgrabung und Baugeschichte." *MDAI(R)* 89 (1982): 229–313.

Eschebach, L., and J. Müller-Trollius. *Gebäudeverzeichnis und Stadtplan der antiken Stadt Pompeji*. Cologne, 1993.

Evans, J. K. *War, Women and Children in Ancient Rome*. London, 1991.

Evans, R. J. "Prostitution, State and Society in Imperial Germany." *P & P* 70 (1976): 106–29.

Evans Grubbs, J. "Virgins and Widows, Show-Girls and Whores: Late Roman Legislation on Women and Christianity." In *Law, Society and Authority in Late Antiquity*, edited by R. W. Mathisen, 220–41. Oxford, 2001.

Eyben, E. *Restless Youth in Ancient Rome*. London, 1993.

Fabre, G. *Libertus: Recherches sur les rapports patron-affranchi à la fin de la République romaine* (= *Coll. Éc. Franç. Rome* 50). Rome, 1981.

Fagan, G. G. "Interpreting the Evidence: Did Slaves Bathe at the Baths?" In *Roman Baths and Bathing: Proceedings of the First International Conference on Roman Baths Held at Bath, England, 30 March–4 April 1992*. Pt. 1, *Bathing and Society* (= *JRA* Suppl. 37), edited by J. De Laine and D. E. Johnson, 25–34. Portsmouth, R.I., 1999.

———. *Bathing in Public in the Roman World*. Ann Arbor, Mich., 1999.

Falck, U. *VEB Bordell: Geschichte der Prostitution in der DDR*. Berlin, 1998.

Farmer, S. "Down and Out and Female in Thirteenth-Century Paris." *AHR* 103, no. 2 (1998): 345–72.

Felletti Maj, B. M. "Ostia—La Casa delle Volte Dipinte: Contributo all'edilizia privata imperiale." *Bollettino d'Arte* 45 (1960): 45–65.

———. *Ostia: Le pitture della Casa delle Volte Dipinte e della Casa delle Pareti Gialle* (*Monumenti della pittura antica scoperta in Italia* 3, nos. 1–2). Rome, 1961.

Finnegan, F. *Poverty and Prostitution: A Study of Victorian Prostitutes in York*. Cambridge, 1979.

Fiorelli, G. *Pompeianarum Antiquitatum Historia*. 3 vols. Naples, 1860–1864.

———. *Gli scavi di Pompei dal 1861 al 1872*. Naples, 1873.

———. *Descrizione di Pompei*. Naples, 1875.

Fisher, N. R. E. "Roman Associations, Dinner Parties, and Clubs." In *Civilization of the Ancient Mediterranean: Greece and Rome*, edited by M. Grant and R. Kitzinger, 2: 1199–1225. New York, 1988.

Flemming, R., "*Quae Corpore Quaestum Facit:* The Sexual Economy of Female Prostitution in the Roman Empire." *JRS* 89 (1999): 38–61.

Flexner, A. *Prostitution in Europe.* New York, 1914.

Flory, M. R. "Family and *Familia:* Kinship and Community in Slavery." *AJAH* 3 (1978): 78–95.

Fogel, R. W., and S. L. Engerman. *Time on the Cross: The Economics of American Negro Slavery.* Rev. ed. New York, 1989.

Földi, A. "*Caupones* e *stabularii* nelle fonti del diritto romano." In *Mélanges Fritz Sturm,* edited by J.-F. Gerkens et al., 1: 119–37 Liège, Belg., 1999.

Foley, M. P. "Cicero, Augustine, and the Philosophical Roots of the Cassiciacum Dialogues." *REA* 45 (1999): 51–77.

Forbes, S. R. *Rambles in Naples: An Archaeological and Historical Guide.*4 London, 1893.

Fortin, E. L. "Augustine's City of God and the Modern Historical Consciousness." *The Review of Politics* 41, no. 3 (1979): 323–43.

———. "Introduction." In *Augustine: Political Writings,* edited by E. L. Fortin and D. Kries, vii–xxix. Indianapolis, 1994.

Foucault, M. *The History of Sexuality I: An Introduction.* Translated by R. Hurley. New York, 1978.

Franklin, J. L. "Games and a *Lupanar:* Prosopography of a Neighborhood in Ancient Pompeii." *CJ* 81, no. 4 (1985/6): 319–28.

———. *Pompeis Difficile Est: Studies in the Political Life of Imperial Pompeii.* Ann Arbor, Mich., 2001.

Franzoi, A. *Copa: L'ostessa, poemetto pseudovergiliano.* Padua, It., 1988.

Frasca, R. *Mestieri e professioni a Rome: Una storia dell'educazione.* Florence, 1994.

Fraser, P. M. "A Syriac *Notitia Urbis Alexandrinae.*" *JEA* 37 (1951): 103–8.

Frayn, J. M. *Markets and Fairs in Roman Italy.* Oxford, 1993.

Frézouls, E. "Rome ville ouverte: Réflexions sur les problèmes de l'expansion urbaine d'Auguste à Aurélien." *L'Urbs: Espace urbain et histoire* (= *Coll. Éc. Franç. Rome* 98), 373–92. Rome, 1987.

Friedländer, L. *Darstellungen aus der Sittengeschichte Roms in der Zeit von Augustus bis zum Ausgang der Antonine* 1.10 edited by G. Wissowa Leipzig, Ger., 1922.

Frier, B. W. "The Rental Market in Early Imperial Rome." *JRS* 67 (1977): 27–37.

———. "Cicero's Management of His Urban Properties." *CJ* 74 (1978/9): 1–6.

———. "Pompeii's Economy and Society." *JRA* 4 (1991): 243–47.

———. "Subsistence Annuities and Per Capita Income in the Early Roman Empire." *CP* 88 (1993): 222–30.

———. *Landlords and Tenants in Imperial Rome.* Princeton, 1980.

———. Review of *Roman Homosexuality,* by C. A. Williams, *BMCR* 99.11.05 (1999).

Frost, F. "Solon *Pornoboskos* and Aphrodite Pandemos." *Syllecta Classica* 13 (2002): 34–46.

Fulford, M. "Economic Interdependence among Urban Communities of the Roman Mediterranean." *World Archaeology* 19, no. 1 (1987): 58–75.

Fulford, M., and A. Wallace-Hadrill. "The House of *Amarantus* at Pompeii (I.9,11–12): An Interim Report on Survey and Excavations in 1995–96." *RSP* 7 (1995–96): 77–113.

———. "Unpeeling Pompeii." *Antiquity* 72 (1998): 128–45.

———. "Towards a History of Pre-Roman Pompeii: Excavations beneath the House of Amarantus (I.9.11–12), 1995–8." *PBSR* 67 (1999): 37–144.

Funari, P. P., and A. Zarankin. "Algunas consideraciones arqueológicas sobre la vivienda doméstica en Pompeya." *Gerión* 19 (2001): 493–511.

Gabba, E. *Del buon uso della ricchezza: Saggi di storia economica e sociale del mondo antico.* Milan, 1988.

Gallo, I. "Eros nell'antica Pompei." *Rassegna storica salernitana* 22 (1994): 203–10.

Gardner, J. F. *Being a Roman Citizen.* London, 1993.

———. "Women in Business Life: Some Evidence from Puteoli." In *Female Networks and the Public Sphere in Roman Society* (= *Acta Inst. Rom. Finl.* 22), edited by P. Setälä and L. Savunen, 11–27. Rome, 1999.

Garnsey, P. "Urban Property Investment." In *Studies in Roman Property*, edited by M. I. Finley, 123–36. Cambridge, 1976.

———. "Independent Freedmen and the Economy of Roman Italy under the Principate." *Klio* 63, no. 2 (1981): 359–71.

———. *Famine and Food Supply in the Graeco-Roman World: Responses to Risk and Crisis.* Cambridge, 1988.

Garnsey, P., and R. Saller. *The Roman Empire: Economy, Society and Culture.* Berkeley, 1987.

Garon, S., *Molding Japanese Minds: The State in Everyday Life.* Princeton, 1997.

Garrido-Hory, M. "Femmes, femmes-esclaves et processus de feminisation dans les oeuvres de Martial et de Juvénal." In *Femmes- esclaves: Modèles d'interprétation anthropologique, économique, juridique*, edited by F. Reduzzi Merola and A. Storchi Marino, 303–13. Naples, 1999.

Gassner, V. *Die Kaufläden in Pompeii.* Ph.D diss., University of Vienna, 1986.

Gell, W. *Pompeiana: The Topography, Edifices and Ornaments of Pompeii, The Results of Excavations since 1819.³* 2 vols. London, 1832.

Geremek, B. *The Margins of Society in Late Medieval Paris.* Cambridge, 1987.

Gering, A. "Habiter á Ostie: La fonction et l'histoire de l'espace 'privé.'" In *Ostia: Port et porte de la Rome antique*, edited by J.-P. Descœudres, 199–211. Geneva, 2001.

Gibson, M. *Prostitution and the State in Italy, 1860–1915.²* Columbus, Ohio, 1999.

Gigante, M. *Civiltà delle forme letterarie nell'antica Pompei.* Naples, 1979.

Gilfoyle, T. J. *City of Eros: New York City, Prostitution, and the Commercialization of Sex, 1790–1920*, New York, 1992.

———. "Prostitutes in History: From Parables of Pornography to Metaphors of Modernity." *AHR* 104, no. 1 (1999): 117–41.

Ginouvès, R. *Dictionnaire méthodique de l'architecture grecque et romaine.* Vol. 3. Rome, 1998.

Giovannini, M. J. "The Dialectics of Women's Factory Work in a Sicilian Town." *Anthropology* 9 (1985): 45–64.

———. "Female Chastity Codes in the Circum-Mediterranean: Comparative Perspectives." In *Honor and Shame and the Unity of the Mediterranean*, edited by D. D. Gilmore, 61–74. Washington, D.C., 1987.

Girri, G. *La taberna nel quadro urbanistico e sociale di Ostia.* Rome, 1956.

Gold, B. K. "The Perception of Urban Life in Juvenal's Satires." In *The Shapes of City Life in Rome and Pompeii: Essays in Honor of Lawrence Richardson Jr. on the Occasion of His Retirement,* edited by M. T. Boatwright and H. B. Evans, 53–69. New Rochelle, N.Y., 1998.

Goldman, M. S. *Gold Diggers and Silver Miners: Prostitution and Social Life on the Comstock Lode.* Ann Arbor, Mich., 1981.

Goldsmith, R. W. "An Estimate of the Size and Structure of the National Product of the Early Roman Empire." *Review of Income and Wealth* 30, no. 3 (1984): 263–88.

———. *Premodern Financial Systems: A Historical Comparative Study.* Cambridge, 1987.

Goodall, R. *The Comfort of Sin: Prostitutes and Prostitution in the 1990s.* Folkestone, Eng., 1995.

Goodyear, F. R. D. "The *Copa*: A Text and Commentary." *BICS* 24 (1977): 117–31.

Goold, G. P. *Propertius: Elegies.* Rev. ed. Cambridge, 1999.

Gorjanicyn, K. "Sexuality and Work: Contrasting Prostitution Policies in Victoria and Queensland." In *Politics of Sexuality: Identity, Gender, Citizenship,* edited by T. Carver and V. Mottier, 180–89. London, 1998.

Goro von Agyagfalva, L. *Wanderungen durch Pompeii.* Vienna, 1825.

Gourevitch, D., and M.-T. Raepsaet-Charlier. *La femme dans la Rome antique.* Saint-Amand-Montrond, Fr., 2001.

Gowers, E. *The Loaded Table: Representations of Food in Roman Literature.* Oxford, 1993.

———. "The Anatomy of Rome from Capitol to Cloaca." *JRS* 85 (1995): 23–32.

Grahame, M. "Material Culture and Roman Identity: The Spatial Layout of Pompeian Houses and the Problem of Ethnicity." In *Cultural Identity in the Roman Empire,* edited by R. Laurence and J. Berry, 156–78. London, 1998.

———. "Recent Developments in Pompeian Archaeology." *JRA* 12 (1999): 567–75.

———. *Reading Space: Social Interaction and Identity in the Houses of Roman Pompeii (A Syntactical Approach to the Analysis and Interpretation of Built Space).* Oxford, 2000.

Greene, K. *The Archaeology of the Roman Economy.* Berkeley, 1986.

Gros, P., and M. Torelli. *Storia dell'urbanistica: Il mondo romano.*³ Rome, 1994.

Guidobaldi, F. "Le *domus* tardoantiche di Roma come 'sensori' delle trasformazioni culturali e sociali." In *The Transformations of VRBS ROMA in Late Antiquity* (= *JRA* Suppl. 33), edited by W. V. Harris, 53–68. Portsmouth, R.I. 1999.

———. "Le abitazioni private e l'urbanistica." In *Roma antica,* edited by A. Giardina, 133–61. Rome, 2000.

Guilhembet, J.-P. "La densité des *domus* et des *insulae* dans les XIV Régions de Rome selon les *Régionnaires*: Représentations cartographiques." *MEFRA* 108 (1996): 7–26.

———. "Présentation bibliographique: Pour un bilan des recherches récentes." *Pallas* 55 (2001): 9–20.

Gulino, R. M. *Implications of the Spatial Arrangement of Tabernae at Pompeii, Region One.* Ph.D. diss., University of Minnesota, 1987.

Gunermann, H. H. "Literarische und philosophische Tradition im ersten Tagesgespräch von Augustinus' *De Ordine*." *Recherches augustiniennes* 9 (1974): 183–226.

Günther, R. *Frauenarbeit-Frauenbindung: Untersuchungen zu unfreien und freigelassenen Frauen in den stadtrömischen Inschriften.* Munich, 1987.

———. "Matrona, *vilica* und *ornatrix*: Frauenarbeit in Rom zwischen Topos und Allt-agswirklichkeit." In *Frauenwelten in der Antike: Geschlechterordnung und weibliche Lebenspraxis*, edited by T. Späth and B. Wagner-Hasel, 350–76. Stuttgart, 2000.

Gusman, P. *Pompei: La ville, les moeurs, les arts.*² Paris, 1906.

Guy, D. J. *Sex and Danger in Buenos Aires: Prostitution, Family, and Nation in Argentina.* Lincoln, Nebr., 991.

Guzzo, P. G. "Per un'interpretazione dei quadretti erotici di Pompei." In *Il gabinetto segreto del museo archeologico nazionale di Napoli*, edited by S. De Caro, 40–47. Naples, 2000.

Guzzo, P. G., and A. D'Ambrosio. *Pompeii.* Naples, 1998.

Guzzo, P. G., and V. Scarano Ussani. *Veneris figurae: Immagini di prostituzione e sfruttamento a Pompei.* Naples, 2000.

———. "La schiava di Moregine." *MEFRA* 113, no. 2 (2001): 981–97.

Hacking, I. *The Social Construction of What?* Cambridge, 1999.

Hanawalt, B. A. *'Of Good and Ill Repute': Gender and Social Control in Medieval England.* Oxford, 1998.

Harris, W. V. "Towards a Study of the Roman Slave-Trade." In *The Seaborne Commerce of Ancient Rome: Studies in Archaeology and History* (= MAAR 36), edited by J. H. D'Arms and E. C. Kopff, 117–40. Rome, 1980.

———. "Between Archaic and Modern: Some Current Problems in the History of the Roman Economy." In *The Inscribed Economy: Production and Distribution in the Roman Empire in the Light of the Instrumentum Domesticum* (= JRA Suppl. 6), edited by W. V. Harris, 11–29. Ann Arbor, Mich., 1993.

———. "Child-Exposure in the Roman Empire." *JRS* 84 (1994): 1–22

———. "Demography, Geography and the Sources of Roman Slaves." *JRS* 89 (1999): 62–75.

Harsin, J. *Policing Prostitution in Nineteenth-Century Paris.* Princeton, 1985.

Hart, A. *Buying and Selling Power: Anthropological Reflections on Prostitution in Spain.* Boulder, Colo., 1998.

Harvey, R. A. *A Commentary on Persius.* Leiden, Neth., 1981.

Hays, R. B. *First Corinthians: Interpretation, A Bible Commentary for Teaching and Preaching.* Louisville, Ky., 1997.

Helbig, W. *Wandgemälde der vom Vesuv verschütteten Städte Campaniens.* Leipzig, Ger., 1868.

Henry, M. M. "The Edible Woman: Athenaeus's Concept of the Pornographic." In *Pornography and Representation in Greece and Rome*, edited by A. Richlin, 250–68. Oxford, 1992.

Heres, T. L. "Cherche: Logement à Ostie." In *Ostia: Port et porte de la rome antique*, edited by J.-P. Descœudres, 221–29. Geneva, 2001.

Hermansen, G. "The Population of Imperial Rome: The Regionaries." *Historia* 27, no. 1 (1978): 129–68.

———. *Ostia: Aspects of Roman City Life.* Edmonton, 1981.

Herrmann-Otto, E. *Ex Ancilla Natus: Untersuchungen zu den "hausgeborenen" Sklaven und Sklavinnen im Westen des römischen Kaiserreiches* (= Forsch. ant. Sklav. 24). Stuttgart, 1994.

Hershatter, G. *Dangerous Pleasures: Prostitution and Modernity in Twentieth-Century Shanghai*. Berkeley, 1997.

Herter, H. s.v. Dirne. *RAC* 3 (1957): 1149–1213.

———. "Die Soziologie der antiken Prostitution im Lichte des heidnischen und christlichen Schrifttums." *JbAC* 3 (1960): 70–111.

Herzig, H. E. "Frauen in Ostia: Ein Beitrag zur Sozialgeschichte der Hafenstadt Roms." *Historia* 32, no. 1 (1983): 77–92.

Heyl, B. S. *The Madam as Entrepreneur: Career Management in Brothel Prostitution*. New Brunswick, N.J. 1979.

Hicks, G. *The Comfort Women: Japan's Brutal Regime of Enforced Prostitution in the Second World War*. New York, 1997.

Hill, M. W. *Their Sisters' Keepers: Prostitution in New York City, 1830–1870*. Berkeley, 1993.

Himmelfarb, E. J. "Capitol Sex." *Archaeology* 52, no. 4 (1999): 18.

Hinard, F. "Rome dans Rome: La Ville définie par les procédures administratives et les pratiques sociales." In *Rome: L'espace urbain et ses représentations*, edited by F. Hinard and M. Royo, 31-—54. Paris, 1991.

Hobson, B. M. *Uneasy Virtue: The Politics of Prostitution and the American Reform Tradition*. Rev. ed. Chicago, 1990.

Høigård, C., and L. Finstad. *Backstreets: Prostitution, Money and Love*. Translated by K. Hanson et al. University Park, Pa., 1992.

Honoré, T. *Sex Law*. London, 1978.

Hope, V. M. "Contempt and Respect: The Treatment of the Corpse in Ancient Rome." In *Death and Disease in the Ancient City*, edited by V. M. Hope and E. Marshall, 104–127. London, 2000.

Hopkins, K. "Economic Growth and Towns in Classical Antiquity." In *Towns in Societies: Essays in Economic History and Historical Sociology*, edited by P. Abrams and E. A. Wrigley, 35–77. Cambridge, 1972.

———. "Models, Ships and Staples." In *Trade and Famine in Classical Antiquity*, edited by P. Garnsey and C. R. Whittaker, 84–109. Cambridge, 1983.

———. "Looking at Lovemaking." *JRA* 12, no. 2 (1999): 559–60.

———. "Rome, Taxes, Rents and Trade." *Kodai* 6/7 (1995/1996): 41–75. Reprint in W. Scheidel and S. von Reden, eds., *The Ancient Economy*, 190–230. Edinburgh, 2002.

———. "Rents, Taxes, Trade and City of Rome." In *Mercati permanenti e mercati periodici nel mondo romano*, edited by E. Lo Cascio, 253–67. Bari, 2000.

Horden, P., and N. Purcell. *The Corrupting Sea: A Study of Mediterranean History*. Oxford, 2000.

Horsfall, N. *The Culture of the Roman Plebs*. London, 2003.

Horsley, R. A. *1 Corinthians: Abingdon New Testament Commentaries*. Nashville, 1998.

Hoskins Walbank, M. E. Review of *Urban Society in Roman Italy*, edited by T. J. Cornell and K. Lomas. *BMCR* 96.2.8 (1996).

Immerwahr, H. "Dipinti from G5, C2." In *The Excavations at Dura-Europos: Preliminary Report of the Ninth Season of Work, 1935–1936*. Pt. 1, *The Agora and Bazaar*, edited by M. I. Rostovtzeff, 203–65. New Haven: 1944.

Ioppolo, G. *Le Terme del Sarno a Pompei: Iter di un'analisi per la conoscenza, il restauro e la protezione sismica del monumento*. Rome, 1992.

Isager, J. *Pliny on Art and Society: The Elder Pliny's Chapters on the History of Art*. London, 1991.

Jacobelli, L. *Le pitture erotiche nelle Terme Suburbane di Pompei*. Rome, 1995.

———. *Spintriae e ritratti Giulio-Claudii: signifacto e funzione delle tessere bronzee numerali imperiali*. vol. 1. Milan, 2000.

———. "Pompeii: Città di Venere." In *Louis Barre: Museo seg reto*, edited by L. Carcia y garcia and L. Jacobelli, 35–122. Pompeii, 2001.

Jacoby, D. "The Migration of Merchants and Craftsmen: A Mediterranean Perspective (12th–15th Century)." In *Trade, Commodities and Shipping in the Medieval Mediterranean*, edited by D. Jacoby. Aldershot, Eng., 1997. I Originally published in *Le migrazioni in Europa, sec. XIII–XVIII*, edited by S. Cavaciocchi, 533–60. Florence, 1994.

Jahn, O. A. *Persii Flacci, D. Iunii Iuvenalis, Sulpiciae Saturae*.4 Edited by F. Buecheler and F. Leo. Berlin, 1910.

Jashemski, W. F. "A Pompeian Copa." *CJ* 59, no. 8 (1963/4): 337–49.

———. "Pompeii and Mount Vesuvius, A.D. 79." In *Volcanic Activity and Human Ecology*, edited by P. D. Sheets and D. K. Grayson, 587–622. New York, 1979.

———. *The Gardens of Pompeii, Herculaneum, and the Villas Destroyed by Vesuvius*. Vol. 1. New York, 1979. Vol. 2. New Rochelle, N.Y., 1993.

Jeffreys, S. *The Idea of Prostitution*. North Melbourne, 1997.

Jenkinson, J. R. *Persius: The Satires*. Warminster, 1980.

Jobst, W. "Das 'öffentliche Freudenhaus' in Ephesos." *JÖAI* 51 (1976/7): 61–84.

Johns, C. *Sex or Symbol: Erotic Images of Greece and Rome*. Austin, Texas, 1982.

Johnson, A. C. *An Economic Survey of Ancient Rome*. Vol. 2, *Roman Egypt to the Reign of Diocletian*. Baltimore, 1936.

Johnston, D. *Roman Law in Context*. Cambridge, 1999.

Jongman, W. *The Economy and Society of Pompeii*. Amsterdam, 1988.

Joshel, S. R. *Work, Identity, and Legal Status at Rome: A Study of the Occupational Inscriptions*. Norman, Okla., 1992.

Kajanto, I. "Balnea, Vina, Venus." In *Hommages à Marcel Renard* (= *Collection Latomus* 102), edited by J. Bibauw, 2: 357–67. Brussels, 1969.

Kampen, N. *Image and Status: Roman Working Women in Ostia*. Berlin, 1981.

Kappeler, S. *The Pornography of Representation*. Minneapolis, 1986.

Kardos, M.-J. *Topographie de Rome: Les sources littéraires latines*. Paris, 2000.

———. "L'*Vrbs* dans les *Épigrammes* de Martial: Poésie et réalité." *RÉL* 79 (2001): 201–14.

———. "L'*Vrbs* de Martial: Recherches topographiques et littéraires autour des *Épigrammes* V,20 et V,22." *Latomus* 60, no. 2 (2001): 387–413.

———. "Quartiers et lieux de Rome dans les *Épigrammes* de Martial." *BAGB* (2002): 119–35.

Karras, R. M. *Common Women: Prostitution and Sexuality in Medieval England*. Oxford, 1996.

————. "Review Essay: Active/Passive, Acts/Passions: Greek and Roman Sexualities." *AHR* 105, no. 4 (2000): 1250–65.

Kaser, M. *Das römische Privatrecht.* Vol. 1.² Munich, 1971.

Kazhdan, A. s.v. Patria of Constantinople. *Oxford Dictionary of Byzantium.* Vol. 3, 1598. Oxford, 1991.

Kehoe, D. P. "Economic Rationalism in Roman Agriculture." *JRA* 6 (1993): 476–84.

————. "Investment in Estates by Upper-Class Landowners in Early Imperial Italy: The Case of Pliny the Younger." In *De Agricultura: In Memoriam Pieter Willem de Neeve (1945–1990)*, edited by H. Sancisi-Weerdenberg et al, 214–37. Amsterdam, 1993.

————. *Investment, Profit, and Tenancy: The Jurists and the Roman Agrarian Economy.* Ann Arbor, Mich., 1997.

Kellum, B. "The Spectacle of the Street." In *The Art of Ancient Spectacle*, edited by B. Bergmann and C. Kondoleon, 283–99. New Haven, 1999.

Kelly, H. A. "Bishop, Prioress, and Bawd in the Stews of Southwark." *Speculum* 75 (2000): 342–88.

Kirbihler, F. "Les femmes magistrats et liturges en Asie Mineure (IIᵉ s. av. J.-C. - IIIᵉ s. ap. J.-C.)." *Ktema* 19 (1994): 51–75.

Kirchhoff, R. *Die Sünde gegen den eigenen Leib.* Göttingen, Ger., 1994.

Kirschenbaum, A. *Sons, Slaves and Freedmen in Roman Commerce.* Jerusalem, 1987.

Kißel, W. *Aules Persius Flaccus: Satiren.* Heidelberg, 1990.

Kleberg, T. *Hôtels, restaurants et cabarets dans l'antiquité romaine: Études historiques et philologiques.* Uppsala, Sw., 1957.

Kleijwegt, M. *Ancient Youth: The Ambiguity of Youth and the Absence of Adolescence in Greco-Roman Society.* Amsterdam, 1991.

————. "*Iuvenes* and Roman Imperial Society." *Acta Classica* 37 (1994): 79–102.

Kneißl, P. "Mercator-negotiator: Römische Geschäftsleute und die Terminologie ihrer Berufe." *MBAH* 2 (1983): 73–90.

Kolowski Ostrow, A. *The Sarno Bath Complex.* Rome, 1990.

Kondoleon, C. "Timing Spectacles: Roman Domestic Art and Performance." In *The Art of Ancient Spectacle*, edited by B. Bergmann and C. Kondoleon, 321–42. New Haven, 1999.

Körner, C. *Philippus Arabs: Ein Soldatenkaiser in der Tradition des antoninisch-severischen Prinzipats.* Berlin, 2002.

Krause, J.-U. *Witwen und Waisen im römischen Reich.* 4 vols. Stuttgart, 1994–95.

Krenkel, W. A., "Skopophilie in der Antike." *WZ Rostock* 26 (1977): 619–31.

————. "Männliche Prostitution in der Antike." *Das Altertum* 24, no. 1 (1978): 49–55.

————. "Fellatio und Irrumatio." *WZ Rostock* 29 (1980): 77–88.

Kromer, K. *Römische Weinstuben in Sayala (Unternubien)* (= *Österr. Ak. Wiss. phil.-hist. Kl. Denkschr.* 95). Vienna, 1967.

Kudlien, F. "Der antike Makler—ein verleugneter Beruf." *MBAH* 16, no. 1 (1997): 67–84.

Kunst, C. "Ein Dach für Viele: Das römische Privathaus zwischen Repräsentation und Ökonomie." *ZRGG* 52, no. 4 (2000): 289–308.

Kurke, L. *Coins, Bodies, Games, and Gold: The Politics of Meaning in Archaic Greece.* Princeton, 1999.

Kurylowicz, M. "Das Glücksspiel im römischen Recht." *SZ* 102 (1985): 185–219.

Landolfi, L. *Banchetto e società romana dalle origini al I secolo a.C.* Rome, 1990.

La Rocca, E., M. De Vos, and A. De Vos. *Guida archeologica di Pompei.* Verona, 1976.

———. *Pompei.²* Milan, 1994.

Larsson Lovén, L. "*Lanam fecit*—Woolworking and Female Virtue." In *Aspects of Women in Antiquity: Proceedings of the First Nordic Symposium on Women's Lives in Antiquity, Göteborg 12–15 June 1997,* edited by L. Larsson Lovén and A. Strömberg, 85–95. Jonsered, Swe., 1998.

La Torre, G. F. "Gli impianti commerciali ed artigianali nel tessuto urbano di Pompei." In *Pompei: L'informatica al servizio di una città antica,* A. De Simone et al., 1: 75–102. Rome, 1988.

Laurence, R. "Emperors, Nature and the City: Rome's Ritual Landscape." *Accordia Research Papers* 4 (1993): 79–87.

———. "Modern Ideology and the Creation of Ancient Town Planning." *European Review of History* 1 (1994): 9–18.

———. *Roman Pompeii: Space and Society.* London, 1994.

———. "The Organization of Space in Pompeii." In *Urban Society in Roman Italy,* edited by T. J. Cornell and K. Lomas, 63–78. New York, 1995.

———. "Writing the Roman Metropolis." In *Roman Urbanism: Beyond the Consumer City,* edited by H. M. Parkins, 1–20. London, 1997.

Le Gall, J. "Métiers de femmes au Corpus Inscriptionum Latinarum" *RÉL* 47 (bis) (1969): 123–130. (= *Mélanges M. Durry*).

Lee, G. *The Satires of Persius.* With an introduction and commentary by W. Barr. Liverpool, 1987.

Legras, B. "Droit et violence: La jeunesse d'Alexandrie sous les Sévères (à propos du P.Oxy. LXIV 4435)." In *Atti del XXII congresso internazionale di papirologia.* Edited by I. Andorlini et al. 2: 777–86. Florence, 2001.

Lenel, O. *Das Edictum Perpetuum: Ein Versuch zu seiner Wiederherstellung.³* Leipzig, 1927. Reprint, Aalen, Ger., 1974.

Leontsini, S. *Die Prostitution im frühen Byzanz.* Ph.D. diss., University of Vienna, 1989.

Leppin, H. *Histrionen: Untersuchungen zur sozialen Stellung von Bühnenkünstlern im Westen des römischen Reiches zur Zeit der Republik und des Principats* (= *Antiquitas* 1, no. 41). Bonn, 1992.

Lind, H. "Ein Hetärenhaus am Heiligen Tor?: Der Athener Bau Z und die bei Isaios (6, 20f.) erwähnte Synoikia Euktemons." *MH* 45, no. 3 (1988): 158–69.

Lindsay, H. "Death-Pollution and Funerals in the City of Rome." In *Death and Disease in the Ancient City,* edited by V. M. Hope and E. Marshall, 152–73. London, 2000.

Ling, R. *The Insula of the Menander at Pompeii I: The Structures.* Oxford, 1997.

Lo Cascio, E. "Crisi demografica e storia socioeconomica tra principato e basso impero: Dagli 'aspetti sociali del quarto secolo' a 'la fine del mondo antico.'" *Quaderni Catanesi* 2 (1990): 67–92.

———. "Le procedure di recensus dalla tarda repubblica al tardo antico e il calcolo della popolazione di Roma." In *La Rome impériale: Démographie et logistique* (= *Coll. Éc. Franç. Rome* 108), 3–76. Rome, 1997.

———. "Introduzione." In *Mercati permanenti e mercati periodici nel mondo romano*, edited by E. Lo Cascio, 5–11. Bari, 2000.

———. "La population." *Pallas* 55 (2001): 179–98.

Loomis, W. T. *Wages, Welfare Costs and Inflation in Classical Athens*. Ann Arbor, Mich., 1998.

Lugli, G. *Monumenti minori del Foro Romano*. Rome, 1947.

Lyapustin, B. "Women in the Textile Industry: Production and Morality" (in Russian; English summary). *VDI* 3 (1985): 36–46.

Macfarlane, A. "History and Anthropology." *Rural History* 5, no. 1 (1994): 103–8.

Mackey, T. C. *Red Lights Out: A Legal History of Prostitution, Disorderly Houses, and Vice Districts, 1870–1917*. New York, 1987.

Magoulias, H. J. "Bathhouse, Inn, Tavern, Prostitution and the Stage as Seen in the Lives of the Saints of the Sixth and Seventh Centuries." *EHBS* 38 (1971): 233–52.

Mahood, L. *The Magdalenes: Prostitution in the Nineteenth Century*. London, 1990.

Maiuri, A. *L'ultima fase edilizia di Pompei*. Spoleto, It., 1942.

———. "Gli scavi di Pompei dal 1879 al 1948." In *Pompeiana: Raccolta di studi per il secondo centenario degli scavi di Pompei*, 9–40. Naples, 1950.

Manganaro, G. "Graffiti e iscrizioni funerarie della Sicilia orientale." *Helikon* 2, nos. 3–4 (1962): 485–96.

Marcus, S. *The Other Victorians: A Study of Sexuality and Pornography in Mid-Nineteenth-Century England*. New York, 1966.

Marinucci, A. "La maison de Diane (I iii 3–4)." In *Ostia: Port et porte de la rome antique*, edited by J.-P. Descœudres, 230–44. Geneva, 2001.

Markus, R. A. "The Roman Empire in Early Christian Historiography." *The Downside Review* 81 (1963): 340–54.

Marquardt, J. *Das Privatleben der Römer*. 2 vols. Leipzig, 1886. Reprint, Darmstadt, 1990.

Martin, D. *The Corinthian Body*. New Haven, 1995.

Martin, R. P. *The Spirit and the Congregation: Studies in 1 Corinthians 12–15*. Grand Rapids Mich., 1984.

Marx, G. "Ironies of Social Control: Authorities as Contributors to Deviance through Escalation, Nonenforcement and Covert Facilitation." *Social Problems* 28, no. 3 (1981): 221–46.

Mastroroberto, M. "Pompei e la riva destra del Sarno." In . . . *Mitis Sarni Opes*, edited by A. De Simone and S. C. Nappo, 25–48. Naples, 2000.

———. "Il quartiere sul Sarno e i ricenti rinvenimenti a Moregine." *MEFRA* 113, no. 2 (2001): 953–66.

Mau, A. "Scavi." *BdI* 10 (1879): 193–210.

———. *Führer durch Pompeji*.² Leipzig, Ger., 1896.

———. *Pompeii: Its Life and Art*. Translated by F. W. Kelsey. New York, 1899.

———. s.v. comissatio, *RE* 4 (1901): 610–19.

———. *Pompeji in Leben und Kunst*.² Leipzig, 1908.

———. *Pompeji in Leben und Kunst: Anhang zur zweiten Auflage*. Leipzig, 1913.

———. *Führer durch Pompeji*⁵ edited by W. Barthel. Leipzig, 1910.

———. *Führer durch Pompeji*[6] edited by A. Ippel. Leipzig, 1928.

Maurin, J. "*Labor matronalis*: Aspects du travail féminin à Rome." In *La femme dans les sociétés antiques: Actes du colloque de Strasbourg (mai 1980 et mars 1981)*, edited by E. Levy, 139–55. Strasbourg, 1983.

Mayer-Maly, T. "Das Notverkaufsrecht des Hausvaters." *SZ* 75 (1958): 116–55.

Mazois, F. *Les ruines de Pompéi*. 4 vols. Paris, 1824–1828.

McDonald, W. A. "Villa or Pandokeion?" In *Studies Presented to David Moore Robinson on His Seventieth Birthday*, edited by G. E. Mylonas, 1: 365–73. Saint Louis, 1951.

McGinn, T. A. J. *Prostitution and Julio-Claudian Legislation: The Formation of Social Policy in Early Imperial Rome*. Ph.D. diss., University of Michigan, 1986.

———. "The SC from Larinum and the Repression of Adultery at Rome." *ZPE* 93 (1992): 273–95.

———. s.v. Prostitution. *Encyclopedia of Social History*. New York, 1994. 588–91.

———. "The Legal Definition of Prostitute in Late Antiquity." *MAAR* 42 (1997 [1998]): 73–116.

———. "Caligula's Brothel on the Palatine." *ECM/CV*, n.s. 17 (1998): 95–107.

———. *Prostitution, Sexuality, and the Law in Ancient Rome*. Oxford, 1998.

———. "The Social Policy of Emperor Constantine in *Codex Theodosianus* 4.6.3." *TR* 67 (1999): 57–73.

———. "Satire and the Law: The Case of Horace." *PCPS* 47 (2001): 81–102.

———. "The Augustan Marriage Legislation and Social Practice: Elite Endogamy versus Male "Marrying Down." In *Speculum Iuris: Roman Law as a Reflection of Social and Economic Life in Antiquity*, edited by J.-J. Aubert and B. Sirks, 46–93. Ann Arbor, Mich., 2002.

———. "Pompeian Brothels and Social History,." In *Pompeian Brothels, Pompeii's Ancient History, Mirrors and Mysteries, Art and Nature at Oplontis and the Herculaneum 'Basilica'* (= *JRA* Suppl. 47), edited by C. Stein and J. H. Humphrey, 7–46. Portsmouth, R. I. 2002.

———. *Roman Prostitution*. Forthcoming.

McIntosh, M. "Who Needs Prostitutes?: The Ideology of Male Sexual Needs." In *Women, Sexuality and Social Control*, edited by C. Smart and B. Smart, 53–64. London, 1978.

McKeown, J. C. "Augustan Elegy and Mime." *PCPS*, n.s. 25 (1979): 71–84.

Meiggs, R., *Roman Ostia*.[2] Oxford, 1973.

Memmer, M. "*Ad Servitutem aut ad Lupanar*: Ein Beitrag zur Rechtsstellung von Findelkindern nach römischem Recht." *SZ* 108 (1991): 21–93.

Meneghini, A. "Trasformazione di una residenza domestica in impianto commerciale a Pompei: L'esempio della bottega 1–11–1,2." *RSP* 10 (1999): 11–22.

Merten, E. W. *Bäder und Badegepflogenheiten in der Darstellung der Historia Augusta* (= *Antiquitas* 4: *Beiträge zur Historia-Augusta-Forschung* 16). Bonn, 1983.

Meyer-Zwiffelhoffer, E. *Im Zeichen des Phallus: Die Ordnung des Geschlechtslebens im antiken Rom*. Frankfurt, 1995.

Millar, F. "The World of the *Golden Ass*." *JRS* 71 (1981): 63–75.

Mitterauer, M. *Historisch-anthropologische Familienforschung: Fragestellungen und Zugangsweisen*. Vienna, 1990.

Moine, N. "Augustin et Apulée sur la magie des femmes d'auberge." *Latomus* 34, no. 2 (1975): 350–61.

Mols, S. T. A. M., and J. A. K. E. De Waele. "Rapporto preliminare degli scavi eseguiti dall'Università Cattolica di Nimega nell'Insula VI,14,43 a Pompei (7–25 Luglio 1997)." *RSP* 9 (1998): 208–9.

Mommsen, T. *Römisches Staatsrecht.*³ 3 vols. Leipzig, 1887. Reprint, Graz, 1969.

Montserrat, D. *Sex and Society in Graeco-Roman Egypt.* London, 1996.

Morel, J.-P. "La topographie de l'artisanat et du commerce dans la Rome antique." In *L'Urbs: Espace urbain et histoire (Ier siècle av. J.-C.—IIe siècle ap. J.-C.)* (= *Coll. Éc. Franç. Rome* 98), 127–55. Rome, 1987.

———. "Métiers, rues et sociabilité dans le monde romain." In *La rue, lieu de sociabilité?: Recontres de la rue, Colloque Rouen 1994,* edited by A. Leménorel, 149–59. Rouen, 1997.

———. "Artisanat et manufacture á Rome (1er s. av. n.è.–IIe s. de n.è.)." *Pallas* 55 (2001): 243–63.

———. "Rome capitale: les productions et le commerce de César à Commode." In *Rome, ville et capitale de César à la fin des Antonins,* edited by Y. Le Bohec, 141–62. Paris, 2001.

Morley, N. "Cities in Context: Urban Systems in Roman Italy." In *Roman Urbanism: Beyond the Consumer City,* edited by H. M. Parkins, 42–58. London, 1997.

———. "Markets, Marketing and the Roman Élite." In *Mercati permanenti e mercati periodici nel mondo romano,* edited by E. Lo Cascio, 211–21. Bari, 2000.

Mouritsen, H. *Elections, Magistrates and Municipal Élite: Studies in Pompeian Epigraphy.* Rome, 1988.

———. "Order and Disorder in Late Pompeian Politics." In *Les élites municipales de l'Italie péninsulaire des Gracques à Néron* (= *Coll. Éc. Franç. Rome* 215), edited by M. Cébeillac-Gervasoni, 139–144. Rome, 1996.

———. "Mobility and Social Change in Italian Towns During the Principate." In *Roman Urbanism: Beyond the Consumer City,* edited by H. M. Parkins, 59–82. London, 1997.

———. "Electoral Campaigning in Pompeii: A Reconsideration." *Athenaeum* 87, no. 2 (1999): 515–23.

———. "Roman Freedmen and the Urban Economy: Pompeii in the First Century A.D." In *Pompei tra Sorrento e Sarno: Atti del terzo e quarto ciclo di conferenze di geologia, storia e archeologia, Pompei, gennaio 1999–maggio 2000,* edited by F. Senatore, 1–27. Rome, 2001.

Mratschek-Halfmann S. *Divites et Praepotentes: Reichtum und soziale Stellung in der Literatur der Prinzipatszeit* (= *Historia Einzelschr.* 70). Stuttgart, 1993.

Mrozek, S. *Lohnarbeit im klassischen Altertum: Ein Beitrag zur Sozial- und Wirtschaftsgeschichte.* Bonn, 1989.

Murphy, E. *Great Bordellos of the World: An Illustrated History.* London, 1983.

Myerowitz, M. "The Domestication of Desire: Ovid's *Parva Tabella* and the Theater of Love." In *Pornography and Representation in Greece and Rome,* edited by A. Richlin, 131–57. Oxford, 1992.

Myers, K. S. "The Poet and the Procuress: The *Lena* in Latin Love Elegy." *JRS* 86 (1996): 1–21.

Nappo, S. *Pompeii: Guide to the Lost City*. London, 1998.

Nathan, G. *The Family in Late Antiquity: The Rise of Christianity and the Endurance of Tradition*. London, 2000.

Navarre, O. s.v. meretrices. *DS* 3 (1918): 1823–39.

Neri, V. *I marginali nell'occidente tardoantico: Poveri, 'infames', e criminali nella nascente società cristiana*. Bari, It., 1998.

Neudecker, R. *Die Pracht der Latrine: Zum Wandel öffentlicher Bedürfnisanstalten in der kaiserzeitlichen Stadt* (= *Studien zur antiken Stadt* 1). Munich, 1994.

Niccolini, F., and F. Niccolini. *Le case ed i monumenti di Pompei designati e descritti*. 4 vols. Naples, 1854–96.

Nicolet, C., *Space, Geography, and Politics in the Early Roman Empire*. Ann Arbor, Mich., 1991.

Nielsen, I. *Thermae et Balnea: The Architecture and Cultural History of Roman Public Baths*. 2 vols. Aarhus, Denmark 1990.

Nieves, E. "Anxious Days in Bordello Country: Resort Plan Brings What Nevada Brothels Hate Most: Attention." *The New York Times*, 19 August 2001, A16.

Nippel, W. *Public Order in Ancient Rome*. Cambridge, 1995.

Niquet, H., "The Ideal of the Senatorial Agriculturalist and Reality during the Roman Republic and Empire." In *Double Standards in the Ancient and Medieval World*, edited by K. Pollmann, 121–33. Göttingen, Ger., 2000.

Nivola, P. S. *Laws of the Landscape: How Policies Shape Cities in Europe and America*. Washington, D.C., 1999.

Nordh, A. *Libellus de Regionibus Urbis Romae*. Lund, Swe. 1949.

Noy, D. *Foreigners at Rome: Citizens and Strangers*. London, 2000.

Nussbaum, M. C., and J. Sihvola. "Introduction." In *The Sleep of Reason: Erotic Experience and Sexual Ethics in Ancient Greece and Rome*, edited by M. C. Nussbaum and J. Sihvola, 1–20. Chicago, 2002.

Nutton, V. "Medical Thoughts on Urban Pollution." In *Death and Disease in the Ancient City*, edited by V. M. Hope and E. Marshall, 65–73. London, 2000.

O'Connor, E. "Martial the Moral Jester: Priapic Motifs and the Restoration of Order in the Epigrams." In *Toto Notus in Orbe: Perspektiven der Martial-Interpretationen*, edited by F. Grewing, 187–204. Stuttgart, 1998.

Ogilvie, R. M. *A Commentary on Livy, Books 1–5*. Rev. ed. Oxford, 1970.

Orlin, E. "Why a Second Temple for Venus Erycina?" In *Studies in Latin Literature and Roman History*, edited by C. Deroux, 10: 70–90. Brussels, 2000.

Orsi, P. "Catania: Scoperte varie di antichità negli anni 1916 e 1917." *NSA* (1918): 53–71.

Otis, L. L. *Prostitution in Medieval Society: The History of an Urban Institution in Languedoc*. Chicago, 1985.

Overbeck, J. *Pompeji in seinen Gebäuden, Alterthümern und Kunstwerken*.[1] Leipzig, Ger., 1856.

———. *Pompeji in seinen Gebäuden, Alterthümern und Kunstwerken*.[4] Edited by A. Mau. Leipzig, Ger., 1884.

Owens, E. J. "Residential Districts." In *Roman Domestic Buildings*, edited by I. M. Barton, 7–32. Exeter, 1996.

Pacioni, V. *L'unità teoretica del De Ordine di S. Agostino*. Rome, 1996.

Packer, J. "La casa di Via Giulio Romano." *Bull. Comm.* 81 (1968/1969): 127–48.

———. *The Insulae of Imperial Ostia* (= MAAR 31). Rome, 1971.

———. "Middle and Lower Class Housing in Pompeii and Herculaneum: A Preliminary Survey." In *Neue Forschungen in Pompeji,* edited by B. Andreae and H. Kyrieleis, 133–46. Recklingshausen, Ger., 1975.

———. "Inns at Pompeii: A Short Survey." *CrPomp* 4 (1978): 5–53.

Palombi, D. s.v. Lupanarii. *LTUR* 3 (1996): 198.

Papi, E. s.v. Domus: M. Aemilius Scaurus. *LTUR* 2 (1995): 26, 392.

———. "*Ad delenimenta vitiorum* (Tac. *Agr.* 21): Il *balneum* nelle dimore di Roma dall'età repubblicana al I secolo d.C." *MEFRA* 111.2 (1999): 695–728.

———. La *turba inpia*: Artigiani e commercianti del Foro Romano e dintorni (I sec. a.C.–64 d.C.)." *JRA* 15.1 (2002): 45–62.

Parkins, H. M., and C. Smith, eds. *Trade, Traders and the Ancient City.* London, 1998.

Parkins, H. M. "The 'Consumer City' Domesticated?: The Roman City in Élite Economic Strategies." In *Roman Urbanism: Beyond the Consumer City,* edited by H. M. Parkins, 83–111. London, 1997.

Parrish, D. "Introduction: The Urban Plan and Its Constituent Elements." In *Urbanism in Western Asia Minor: New Studies on Aphrodisias, Ephesos, Hierapolis, Pergamon, Perge and Xanthos* (= JRA Suppl. 45), edited by D. Parrish. Portsmouth, R.I., 2001.

Parslow, C. "Beyond Domestic Architecture at Pompeii." *AJA* 103, no. 2 (1999): 340–43.

Paterson, J. "Trade and Traders in the Roman World: Scale, Structure and Organisation." In *Trade, Traders and the Ancient City,* edited by H. M. Parkins and C. Smith, 149–67. London, 1998.

Patterson, J. R. "On the Margins of the City of Rome." In *Death and Disease in the Ancient City,* edited by V. M. Hope and E. Marshall, 85–105. London, 2000.

Paul, C. *Zwangsprostitution: Staatliche errichtete Bordelle im Nationalsozialismus.* Berlin, 1994.

Pavan, E. "Police des mœurs, société et politique à Venise à la fin du Moyen Age." *RH* 536 (1980): 241–88.

Pavolini, C., *Ostia.*³ Rome, 1989.

———. *La vita quotidiana a Ostia.* Rome, 1991.

Peachin, M. Review of *Rome and the Enemy* by S. Mattern *BMCR* 00.06.03 (2000).

Perring, D. "Spatial Organisation and Social Change in Roman Towns." In *City and Country in the Ancient World,* edited by J. Rich and A. Wallace-Hadrill, 273–93. London, 1991.

Perry, M. E. "'Lost Women' in Early Modern Seville: The Politics of Prostitution," *Feminist Studies* 4 (1978): 195–214.

———. "Deviant Insiders: Legalized Prostitutes and a Consciousness of Women in Early Modern Seville." *Comparative Studies in Society and History* 27 (1985): 138–58.

———. *Gender and Disorder in Early Modern Seville.* Princeton, 1990.

Petermandl, W. "Kinderarbeit im Italien der Prinzipatszeit: Ein Beitrag zur Sozialgeschichte des Kindes." *Laverna* 8 (1997): 113–36.

Peterse, K. et al. "Secondo rapporto preliminare degli scavi esiguiti dall'Università Cattolica di Nimega nella Casa degli Scienzati, VI.14.43 e nell'Insula VI.14 a Pompei (9–30 luglio 2000)." *RSP* 11 (2000): 249–52.

von Petrikovits, H. "*Lixae.*" In H. von Petrikovits, *Beiträge zur römischen Geschichte und Archäologie,* 2.75–79. Cologne, 1991. Originally published in *Roman Frontier Studies 1979,* edited by W. S. Hanson and L. J. F. Keppie, 3: 1027–35. Oxford, 1980.

Pevsner, N. *A History of Building Types.* Princeton, 1976.

Phang, S. E. *The Marriage of Roman Soldiers (13 B.C.–A.D. 235): Law and Family in the Imperial Army.* Leiden, Neth., 2001.

Pirson, F. "Rented Accommodation at Pompeii: The Evidence of the *Insula Arriana Polliana* VI 6." In *Domestic Space in the Roman World: Pompeii and Beyond,* edited by R. Laurence and A. Wallace-Hadrill, 165–81. Portsmouth, R.I. 1997.

———. *Mietwohnungen in Pompeji und Herkulaneum: Untersuchungen zur Architektur, zum Wohnen und zur Sozial- und Wirtschaftsgeschichte der Vesuvstädte.* Munich, 1999.

Platner, S. B., and T. Ashby. *A Topographical Dictionary of Ancient Rome.* Oxford, 1929.

Pleket, H. W. "Urban Elites and the Economy in the Greek Cities of the Roman Empire," *MBAH* 3 (1984): 3–36.

———. "Agriculture in the Roman Empire in Comparative Perspective." In *De Agricultura: In Memoriam Pieter Willem De Neeve (1945–1990),* edited by H. Sancisi-Weerdenberg et al, 317–42. Amsterdam, 1993.

Pollard, N. "The Roman Army as 'Total Institution' in the Near East?: Dura-Europos as a Case Study." In *The Roman Army in the Near East* (= *JRA* Suppl. 18), edited by D. L. Kennedy, 211–17. Ann Arbor, Mich., 1996.

Pompei: L'informatica al servizio di una città antica. 2 vols. Rome, 1988.

Prato, C., and D. Micalella, eds. *Giuliano imperatore contro i cinici ignoranti.* Lecce, 1988.

Prell, M. *Sozialökonomische Untersuchungen zur Armut im antiken Rom: Von den Gracchen bis Kaiser Diokletian.* Stuttgart, 1997.

Presuhn, E. *Pompeji: Die neuesten Ausgrabungen von 1874–1881.*[2] Leipzig, Ger., 1882.

Prus, R., and S. Irini. *Hookers, Rounders, and Desk Clerks: The Social Organization of the Hotel Community.* Toronto, 1980.

Pugliese Carratelli, G., et al. *Pompei: Pitture e Mosaici.* 10 vols. Rome, 1990–1999.

Purcell, N. "The *Apparitores:* A Study in Social Mobility." *PBSR* 51 (1983): 125–73.

———. "Livia and the Womanhood of Rome." *PCPS,* n.s. 32 (1986): 78–105.

———. "Town in Country and Country in Town." In *Ancient Roman Villa Gardens,* edited by E. B. MacDougall, 185–203. Washington, D.C., 1987.

———. "The City of Rome." In *The Legacy of Rome: A New Appraisal,* edited by R. Jenkyns, 421–53. Oxford, 1992.

———. "The City of Rome and the *Plebs Urbana* in the Late Republic." *CAH*[2] 9 (1994): 644–88.

———. "The Roman *Villa* and the Landscape of Production." In *Urban Society in Roman Italy,* edited by T. J. Cornell and K. Lomas, 151–79. New York, 1995.

———. "Rome and Its Development under Augustus and His Successors." *CAH*[2] 10 (1996): 782–811.

———. "The Populace of Rome in Late Antiquity: Problems of Classification and Historical Description." In *The Transformations of VRBS ROMA in Late Antiquity* (= *JRA* Suppl. 33), edited by W. V. Harris, 135–61. Portsmouth, R.I. 1999.

———. "Rome and Italy." *CAH²* 11 (2000): 405–43.

Raeder, H. "Kaiser Julian als Philosoph und religiöser Reformator." In *Julian Apostata* Originally published in Darmstadt, Ger., 1978. (= *C&M* 6 [1944]: 179–93), edited by R. Klein, 206–21.

Rainer, J. M. *Bau- und nachbarrechtliche Bestimmungen im klassischen römischen Recht.* Graz, Austria 1987.

Ramage, E. S. "Urban Problems in Ancient Rome." In *Aspects of Greco-Roman Urbanism: Essays on the Classical City*, edited by R. T. Marchese, 61–92. Oxford, 1983.

Ramirez Sabada, J. "La prostitución: Un medio de vida bien retribuido?" In *La mujer en el mundo antiguo*, 225–35. Madrid, 1985.

Randazzo, S. "*Collegia Iuvenum:* Osservazioni in margine a D. 48.19.28.3." *SDHI* 66 (2000): 201–22.

Raper, R. A. "The Analysis of the Urban Structure of Pompeii: A Sociological Examination of Land Use (Semi-Micro)." In *Spatial Archaeology*, edited by D. L. Clarke, 189–221. London, 1977.

———. "Pompeii: Planning and Social Implications." In *Space, Hierarchy and Society: Interdisciplinary Studies in Social Area Analysis* (= *BAR Intl. Series* 59), edited by B. C. Burnham and J. Kingsbury, 137–48. Oxford, 1979.

Rathbone, D. *Economic Rationalism and Rural Society in Third-Century* A.D. *Egypt: The Heroninos Archive and the Appianus Estate.* Cambridge, 1991.

———. "More (or Less?) Economic Rationalism in Roman Agriculture." *JRA* 7 (1994): 432–36.

———. "Prices and Price Formation in Roman Egypt." In *Économie antique: Prix et formation des prix dans les économies antiques*, 183–244. Saint-Bertrand-de-Comminges, Fr., 1997.

Reduzzi Merola, F. *Servo Parere: Studi sulla condizione giuridica dei schiavi vicari e degli sottoposti a schiavi nelle esperienze greca e romana.* Camerino, It., 1990.

Reinsberg, C. *Ehe, Hetärentum und Knabenliebe im antiken Griechenland.* Munich, 1989.

Renucci, P. *Les idées politiques et le gouvernement de l'empereur Julien* (= *Collection Latomus* 259). Brussels, 2000.

Reynolds, H. *The Economics of Prostitution.* Springfield, Ill., 1986.

Richardson, L. *A New Topographical Dictionary of Ancient Rome.* Baltimore, 1992.

Richlin, A. *The Garden of Priapus: Sexuality and Aggression in Roman Humor.* Rev. ed. Oxford, 1992.

Riggsby, A. M. "'Public' and 'Private' in Roman Culture: The Case of the *Cubiculum.*" *JRA* 10 (1997): 36–56.

Robinson, D. J. "The Social Texture of Pompeii." In *Sequence and Space in Pompeii*, edited by S. E. Bon and R. Jones, 135–44. Oxford, 1997.

Rodgers, R. H. "Frontinus *Aq.* 76.2: An Unnoticed Fragment of Caelius Rufus?" *AJP* 103, no. 3 (1982): 333–37.

Rodríguez Neila, J. F. "El trabajo en las ciudades de la Hispania romana." In *El trabajo en la Hispania romana*, edited by J. F. Rodríguez Neila et al., 9–118. Madrid, 1999.

Rolfe, E. N. *Pompeii: Popular and Practical.* Naples, 1888.

Roper, L. "Discipline and Respectability: Prostitution and the Reformation in Augsburg." *History Workshop* 19 (1985): 3–28.

———. *The Holy Household: Women and Morals in Reformation Augsburg.* Oxford, 1989.

Rosen, R. *The Lost Sisterhood: Prostitution in America, 1900–1918.* Baltimore, 1982.

Rosenfeld, B.-Z. "Innkeeping in Jewish Society in Roman Palestine." *Journal of the Economic and Social History of the Orient* 41, no. 2 (1998): 133–58.

Rosivach, V. J. "Solon's Brothels." *LCM* 20, nos. 1–2 (1995): 2–3.

———. "The Sociology of the *Copa.*" *Latomus* 55, no. 3 (1996): 605–14.

Rossiaud, J. "Prostitution, Youth, and Society in the Towns of Southeastern France in the Fifteenth Century." In *Deviants and the Abandoned in French Society* (= *Annales ESC* 31 [1976]: 289–325), edited by R. Forster and O. Ranum, 4: 1–46. Baltimore, 1978.

———. *Medieval Prostitution.* Translated by L. G. Cochrane. Oxford, 1988.

Rostovtzeff, M. I., et al., eds. *The Excavations at Dura-Europos: Preliminary Report of the Ninth Season of Work, 1935–1936.* Pt. 1, *The Agora and Bazaar.* New Haven, 1944.

Rowe, G. "Trimalchio's World." *SCI* 20 (2001): 225–45.

Rowell, H. T. "*Satyricon* 95–96." *CP* 52, no. 4 (1957): 217–27.

Rubin, G. "The Traffic in Women: Notes on the 'Political Economy' of Sex." In *Toward an Anthropology of Women,* edited by R. Reiter, 157–210. New York, 1975.

Ruddell, S. M. *The Inn, Restaurant and Tavern Business in Ancient Pompeii.* Master's Thesis, University of Maryland, 1964.

Ryan, F. X. "Zum Majestätsverbrechen in den Bedürfnisanstalten unter Tiberius." *Gerión* 20.1 (2002): 413–5.

Rybczynski, W. "City Lights." *The New York Review of Books* 48, no. 10 (2001): 68–70.

de Ste. Croix, G. E. M. *The Class Struggle in the Ancient World.* Ithaca, 1981.

Saliou, C. *Les lois des bâtiments: Voisinage et habitat urbain dans l'empire romain.* Beirut, 1994.

Saller, R. P. *Personal Patronage under the Early Empire.* Cambridge, 1982.

———. *Patriarchy, Property and Death in the Roman Family.* Cambridge, 1994.

Sandnes, K. O. *Belly and Body in the Pauline Epistles.* Cambridge, 2000.

Savunen, L. *Women in the Urban Texture of Pompeii.* Pukkila, Fin., 1997.

Scarano Ussani, V. Review of *Les lois des bâtiments* by C. Saliou. *Ostraka* 7 (1998): 217–20.

———. "Il *lenocinium* del *balneator.*" *Ostraka* 9 (2000): 255–63.

———. "Alle terme, fra mnemotecnica e umorismo . . ." *RSP* 12/13 (2001/2002): 11–14.

Schaps, D. M. "What Was Free about a Free Athenian Woman?" *TAPA* 128 (1998): 161–88.

Scheidel, W. "The Most Silent Women of Greece and Rome: Rural Labour and Women's Life in the Ancient World (I)." *Greece & Rome* 42, no. 2 (1995): 202–17.

———. "Finances, Figures and Fiction." *CQ* 46, no. 1 (1996): 222–38.

———. "Reflections on the Differential Valuation of Slaves in Diocletian's Price Edict and in the United States." *MBAH* 15 (1996): 67–79.

———. "The Most Silent Women of Greece and Rome: Rural Labour and Women's Life in the Ancient World (II)." *Greece & Rome* 43, no. 1 (1996): 1–10.

———. "Quantifying the Sources of Slaves in the Early Roman Empire." *JRS* 87 (1997): 156–69.

———. "Progress and Problems in Roman Demography." In *Debating Roman Demography*, edited by W. Scheidel, 1–81. Leiden, Neth., 2001.

Schneider, K. s.v. "meretrix," *RE* 15 (1931) 1018–27.

Schoonhoven, A. V. "Residences for the Rich?: Some Observations on the Alleged Residential and Elitist Character of *Regio VI* of Pompeii." *BABESCH* 74 (1994): 219–46.

Schrage, W. *Der Erste Brief an die Korinther 3 (1Kor 11.17–14.40): Evangelisch-Katholischer Kommentar zum Neuen Testament 7.3.* Zurich, 1999.

Schulz, H. W. "Scavi: Rapporto intorno gli scavi pompeiani negli ultimi quattro anni." *BdI* (1838): 148–201.

———. "Scavi: Rapporto sugli scavi pompejani negli ultimi due anni, 1839–1841." *BdI* (1841): 113–124.

Schuster, B. *Die freien Frauen: Dirnen und Frauenhäuser im 15. und 16. Jahrhundert.* Frankfurt am Main, Ger., 1995.

Schuster, P. *Das Frauenhaus: Städtische Bordelle in Deutschland, 1350 bis 1600.* Paderborn, Ger., 1992.

Scobie, A. "Slums, Sanitation, and Mortality in the Roman World." *Klio* 68, no. 2 (1986): 399–433.

Searle, J. *The Construction of Social Reality.* New York, 1995.

Seifert, D. J., E. B. O'Brien and J. Balicki. "Mary Ann Hall's First-Class House: The Archaeology of a Capital Brothel." In *Archaeologies of Sexuality,* edited by R. A. Schmidt and B. L. Voss, 117–28. London, 2000.

Seigle, C. S. *Yoshiwara: The Glittering World of the Japanese Courtesan.* Honolulu, 1993.

Shackleton Bailey, D. R., ed. *Valerius Maximus: Memorable Deeds and Sayings.* 2 vols. Cambridge, 2000.

Shaner, L. *Madam: Inside a Nevada Brothel.* Rev. ed. s.l., 2001.

Shaw, B. D. "The Bandit." In *The Romans,* edited by A. Giardina and translated by L. G. Cochrane, 300–41. Chicago, 1993.

Sigismund Nielsen, H. "Ditis Examen Domus?: On the Use of the Term *Verna* in the Roman Epigraphical and Literary Sources." *C&M* 42 (1991): 221–40.

Signorelli, A. "La legittimazione della subordinazione femminile nelle società agrarie." In *Femmes-esclaves: Modèles d'interprétation anthropologique, économique, juridique,* edited by F. Reduzzi Merola and A. Storchi Marino, 1–11. Naples, 1999.

Simonetta, B., and R. Riva. *Le tessere erotiche romane (spintriae): Quando ed a che scopo sono state coniate.* Lugano, Switzerland, 1981.

Skidmore, C. *Practical Ethics for Roman Gentlemen: The Work of Valerius Maximus.* Exeter, 1996.

Skinner, M. "Rescuing Creusa: New Methodological Approaches to Women in Antiquity." *Helios* 13, no. 2 (1986): 1–8.

———. "Zeus and Leda: The Sexuality Wars in Contemporary Classical Scholarship." *Thamyris* 3.1 (1996): 103–23.

Sleightholme, C., and I. Sinha. *Guilty without Trial: Women in the Sex Trade in Calcutta.* New Brunswick, N.J. 1996.

Smadja, E. "L'affranchissement des femmes esclaves à Rome." In *Femmes-Esclaves:*

Modèles d'interprétation anthropologique, économique, juridique, edited by F. Reduzzi Merola and A. Storchi Marino, 355–68. Naples, 1999.

Smallwood, E. M. *The Jews under Roman Rule from Pompey to Diocletian: A Study in Political Relations.*² Boston, 2001.

Soards, M. L. *New International Biblical Commentary: 1 Corinthians.* New Testament Series. Peabody, Mass., 1999.

Solin, H. "Pompeiana." *Epigraphica* 30 (1968): 105–25.

Soricelli, G. "Appendice II: Il piano superiore delle Terme Suburbane." In L. Jacobelli, *Le pitture erotiche delle Terme Suburbane di Pompei,* 107–17. Rome, 1995.

Spano, G. "La illuminazione delle vie di Pompei." *Atti della reale accademia di archeologia, lettere, e belle arti di Napoli* 7 (1920): 3–128.

Sperber, D., *The City in Roman Palestine.* Oxford, 1998.

Stager, L. E. "Eroticism and Infanticide at Ashkelon." *BAR* 17 (1991): 34–53, 72.

Stansell, C. *City of Women: Sex and Class in New York, 1789–1860.* Urbana, Ill., 1987.

Stavrakakis, Y. N. "Thessaloniki Brothel." *Archaeology* 51, no. 3 (1998): 23.

Storey, G. R. "The Population of Ancient Rome." *Antiquity* 71 (1997): 966–78.

———. "Regionaries-Type Insulae 1: Architectural/Residential Units at Ostia." AJA 105, no. 3 (2001): 389–401.

———. "Regionaries-Type Insulae 2: Architectural/Residential Units at Rome." AJA 106, no. 3 (2002): 411–34.

Stumpp, B. E. *Prostitution in der römischen Antike.* Berlin, 1998.

Sturdevant, S. P., and B. Stoltzfus. *Let the Good Times Roll: Prostitution and the U.S. Military in Asia.* New York, 1992.

Suerbaum, W. "Sex und Crime im alten Rom: Von den humanistischen Zensur zu Cato dem Censor." *WJ* 19 (1993): 85–109.

Sullivan, B. *The Politics of Sex: Prostitution and Pornography in Australia since 1945.* Cambridge, 1997.

Sutton, R. F. "Pornography and Persuasion on Attic Pottery." In *Pornography and Representation in Greece and Rome,* edited by A. Richlin, 3–35. Oxford, 1992.

Symanski, R. "Prostitution in Nevada." *Annals of the Association of American Geographers* 64, no. 2 (1974): 357–77.

Tantillo, I. "Gli uomini, le risorse" In *Roma antica,* edited by A. Giardina, 85–111. Rome, 2000.

Taylor, Q. P. "St. Augustine and Political Thought: A Revisionist View." *Augustiniana* 48, nos. 3–4 (1998): 287–303.

Temin, P. "A Market Economy in the Early Roman Empire." *JRS* 91 (2001): 169–81.

Thédenat, H. *Pompéi: Vie publique.*² Paris, 1910.

Thurmond, D. L. "Some Roman Slave Collars." *Athenaeum* 82, no. 2 (1994): 459–93.

Tomei, M. A. "*Domus* oppure *Lupanar?*: I materiali dallo scavo Boni della 'Casa Republicana' a ovest dell'arco di Tito." *MEFRA* 107, no. 2 (1995): 549–619.

Toner, J. P. *Leisure and Ancient Rome.* Oxford, 1998.

Tong, B. *Unsubmissive Women: Chinese Prostitutes in Nineteenth-Century San Francisco.* Norman, Okla., 1994.

Traina, G. "I mestieri" In *Roma antica,* edited by A. Giardina, 113–31. Rome, 2000.

Traub, J. "The Land of the Naked Cowboy." *New York Review of Books* 49, no. 2 (February 14, 2002): 29–31.

Treggiari, S. *Roman Freedmen during the Late Republic.* Oxford, 1969.

———. "Libertine Ladies." *CW* 64 (1970/1971): 196–98.

———. "Domestic Staff at Rome in the Julio-Claudian Period, 27 B.C to A.D. 68." *Histoire Sociale* 6 (1973): 241–55.

———. "Family Life among the Staff of the Volusii." *TAPA* 105 (1975): 393–401.

———. "Jobs in the Household of Livia." *PBSR* 43 (1975): 48–77.

———. "Jobs for Women." *AJAH* 1, no. 2 (1976): 76–104.

———. "Lower Class Women in the Roman Economy." *Florilegium* 1 (1979): 65–86.

———. "Questions on Women Domestics in the Roman West." In *Schiavitù, manomissione e classi dipendenti nel mondo antico,* 185–201. Rome, 1979.

———. "Urban Labour in Rome: *Mercenarii* and *Tabernarii.*" In *Non-Slave Labour in the Greco-Roman World,* edited by P. Garnsey, 48–64. Cambridge, 1980.

———. *Roman Marriage: Iusti Coniuges from the Time of Cicero to the Time of Ulpian.* Oxford, 1991.

———. "The Upper-Class House as Symbol and Focus of Emotion in Cicero." *JRA* 12 (1999): 33–56.

Trexler, R. C. "La prostitution florentine au XVᵉ siècle." Translated by J.-P. Desaive. *Annales ESC* 36 (1981): 983–1015.

Trillmich, W. "Die Charitengruppe als Grabrelief und Kneipenschild." *JDAI* 98 (1983): 311–49.

Trousset, P. "Organisation de l'espace urbain de Bararus (Rougga)." *L'Africa romana* 10, no. 2 (1994): 603–613, 2 plates.

Tsujimura, S. "Ruts in Pompeii: The Traffic System in the Roman City." *Opuscula Pompeiana* 1 (1990): 58–86.

Turner, B. S. *The Body and Society.*² London, 1996.

Unger, F. W. *Quellen der byzantinischen Kunstgeschichte.* Vienna, 1878. Reprint, Osnabrück, Ger., 1970.

Van Andringa, W. "Autels de carrefour, organisation vicinale et rapports de voisinage à Pompéi." *RSP* 11 (2000): 47–86.

van Minnen, P. "Did Ancient Women Learn a Trade Outside the Home?: A Note on SB XVIII 13305." *ZPE* 123 (1998): 201–3.

van Nuffeln, P. "Deux fausses lettres de Julien l'Apostat (La lettre aux Juifs, *Ep.* 51 [Wright], et la lettre à Arsacius *Ep.* 84 [Bidez])." *VChr.* 55 (2001): 131–50.

Varone, A. *Erotica Pompeiana: Iscrizioni d'amore sui muri di Pompei.* Rome, 1994.

———. "Più terremoti a Pompei?: I nuovi dati degli scavi di Via dell'Abbondanza." In *Archäologie und Seismologie: La regione Vesuviana dal 62 al 79 d.C., Problemi archeologici e sismologici,* 29–35. Munich, 1995.

———. *L'erotismo a Pompei.* Rome, 2000.

———. "Un nuovo programma decorativo a soggetto erotico." In *Veneris figurae: Immagini di prostituzione e sfruttamento a Pompei,* edited by P. G. Guzzo and V. Scarano Ussani, 61–65. Naples, 2000.

———. "Il lupanare." In *Pompeii: La vita ritrovata,* edited by F. Coarelli, 194–201. Udine, Italy, 2002.

Verstraete, B. C. Reviews of *Rethinking Sexuality,* edited by D. H. J. Larmour et al. and *Roman Sexualities,* edited by J. P. Hallett and M. B. Skinner. *Phoenix* 52, nos. 1–2 (1998): 149–53.

Veyne, P. "La 'plèbe moyenne' sous le Haut-Empire romain." *Annales HSS* 55.6 (2000): 1169–99.

Vismara, C. "*Civitas:* L'organizzazione dello spazio urbano nelle province del Nord Africa e nella Sardegna." *L'Africa romana* 10, no. 1 (1994): 45–52.

Viti, A. "Ad Calidium: L'insegna del piacere di Lucio Calidio Erotico (Saggio epigrafico con note critico-bibliografiche)." *Almanacco del Molise* 2 (1989): 115–35.

Wagner, H., "Zur wirtschaftlichen und rechtlichen Bedeutung der Tabernen." In *Studi in onore di Arnaldo Biscardi,* edited by F. Pastori, 3: 391–422. Milan, 1982.

Walde, C. *Antike Traumdeutung und moderne Traumforschung.* Dusseldorf, 2001.

Walkowitz, J. R. *Prostitution and Victorian Society: Women, Class, and the State.* Cambridge, 1980.

————. *City of Dreadful Delight: Narratives of Sexual Danger in Late-Victorian London.* Chicago, 1992.

Wallace-Hadrill, A. "Pliny the Elder and Man's Unnatural History." *Greece & Rome* 37, no. 1 (1990): 80–96.

————. "Roman Arches and Greek Honours: The Language of Power at Rome." *PCPS,* n.s. 36 (1990): 143–81.

————. "Elites and Trade in the Roman Town." In *City and Country in the Roman World,* edited by J. Rich and A. Wallace-Hadrill, 241–72. London, 1991.

————. "Houses and Households: Sampling Pompeii and Herculaneum." In *Marriage, Divorce and Children in Ancient Rome,* edited by B. Rawson, 191–227. Oxford, 1991.

————. *Houses and Society in Pompeii and Herculaneum.* Princeton, 1994.

————. "Public Honour and Private Shame: The Urban Texture of Pompeii." In *Urban Society in Roman Italy,* edited by T. J. Cornell and K. Lomas, 39–62. New York, 1995.

————. "Case e abitani a Roma." In *Roma imperiale: Una metropoli antica,* edited by E. Lo Cascio, 173–200. Rome, 2000.

————. "Case e Società." In *Pompei,* edited by P. G. Guzzo, 113–17. Milan, 2001.

————. "Emperors and Houses in Rome." In *Childhood, Class and Kin in the Roman World,* edited by S. Dixon, 128–43. London, 2001.

Ward, R. B. "Women in Roman Baths." *HTR* 85, no. 2 (1992): 125–47.

Warscher, T. *Pompeji: Ein Führer durch die Ruinen.* Berlin, 1925.

Watson, N., *The First Epistle to the Corinthians: Epworth Commentaries.* London, 1992.

Welch, K., s.v. "Subura" *LTUR* 4 (1999): 379–83.

Wesch-Klein, G. *Soziale Aspekte des römischen Heerwesens in der Kaiserzeit.* Stuttgart, 1998.

White, L. *The Comforts of Home: Prostitution in Colonial Nairobi.* Chicago, 1990.

Williams, S., and G. Friell. *Theodosius: The Empire at Bay.* New Haven, 1994.

Winkler, J. J. *The Constraints of Desire: The Anthropology of Sex and Gender in Ancient Greece.* New York, 1990.

Wiseman, T. P. "A Stroll on the Rampart." In *Horti romani: Atti del convegno internazionale, Roma 4–6 maggio 1995* (= BCAR Suppl. 6), edited by M. Cima and E. La Rocca, 13–22. Rome, 1998.

————. "The Games of Flora." In *The Art of Ancient Spectacle,* edited by B. Bergmann and C. Kondoleon, 195–203. New Haven, 1999.

Wissemann, M. "Das Personal des antiken römischen Bades." *Glotta* 62 (1984): 80–89.

Witherington III, B. *Conflict and Community in Corinth: A Socio-Rhetorical Commentary on 1 and 2 Corinthians.* Grand Rapids, Mich., 1995.

Wyke, M. *The Roman Mistress.* Oxford, 2002.

Yegül, F. *Baths and Bathing in Classical Antiquity.* New York, 1992.

Young, G. K. *Rome's Eastern Trade: International Commerce and Imperial Policy, 31 B.C.– A.D. 305.* London, 2001.

Youtie, H. C. "Records of a Roman Bath in Upper Egypt." In *Scriptiunculae* Vol. 2, 990–93. Amsterdam, 1973. (= [with added notes] *AJA* 53 [1949]: 268–70).

Zaccaria Ruggiu, A. *Spazio privato e spazio pubblico nella città romana* (= *Coll. Éc. Franç. Rome* 210). Rome, 1995.

Zajac, N. "The *Thermae:* A Policy of Public Health or Personal Legitimation?" In *Roman Baths and Roman Bathing: Proceedings of the First International Conference on Roman Baths Held at Bath, England, 30 March–4 April 1992.* Pt. 1, *Bathing and Society* (= *JRA* Suppl. 37), edited by J. DeLaine and D. E. Johnson, 99–105. Portsmouth, R.I. 1999.

Zanker, P. "Veränderungen im öffentlichen Raum der italischen Städte der Kaiserzeit." In *L'Italie d'Auguste à Dioclétien* (= *Coll. Éc. Franç. Rome* 198), 259–84. Rome, 1994.

———. *Pompeii: Public and Private Life.* Cambridge, 1998.

Zevi, F. "La storia degli scavi e della documentazione." In *Pompei 1748–1980: I tempi della documentazione,* 11–21. Rome, 1981.

———. "L'arte 'popolare'." In *La pittura di Pompei,* 267–73. Milan, 1991.

Zimmer, G. *Römische Berufsdarstellungen.* Berlin, 1982.

INDEX OF SOURCES

Tab. Lar.
  14–15: 141

INDEX OF PERSONS

For more on possible prostitutes from Pompeii, see appendix 3.

INDEX OF SUBJECTS